THIRD EDITION

Counseling and Psychotherapy

Theories and Interventions

David Capuzzi
Portland State University

Douglas R. Gross
Professor Emeritus, Arizona State University

Merrill
Prentice Hall

Upper Saddle River, New Jersey
Columbus, Ohio

Library of Congress Cataloging-in-Publication Data
Counseling and psychotherapy : theories and interventions / [edited by] David Capuzzi
with Douglas R. Gross.—3rd ed.
    p. cm.
  Includes bibliographical references and indexes.
  ISBN 0-13-094754-7 (casebound)
   1. Counseling. 2. Psychotherapy. 3. Counseling—Case studies. 4. Psychotherapy—Case
studies. I. Capuzzi, Dave. II. Gross, Douglas R.

BF637.C6 C634 2003
158'.3—dc21

                                                    2002070860

Vice President and Publisher: Jeffery W. Johnston
Executive Editor: Kevin M. Davis
Editorial Assistant: Autumn Crisp
Production Editor: Mary Harlan
Production Coordination: Tiffany Kuehn, Carlisle Publishers Services
Design Coordinator: Diane C. Lorenzo
Cover Design: Jeff Vanik
Cover Image: SuperStock
Text Design: Carlisle Publishers Services
Production Manager: Laura Messerly
Director of Marketing: Ann Castel Davis
Marketing Manager: Amy June
Marketing Coordinator: Tyra Cooper

This book was set in Garamond by Carlisle Communications, Ltd. It was printed and bound by Maple-Vail Book
Manufacturing Group. The cover was printed by Phoenix Color Corp.

Pearson Education Ltd.
Pearson Education Australia Pty. Limited
Pearson Education Singapore Pte. Ltd.
Pearson Education North Asia Ltd.
Pearson Education Canada, Ltd.
Pearson Educación de Mexico, S.A. de C.V.
Pearson Education—Japan
Pearson Education Malaysia Pte. Ltd.
Pearson Education, *Upper Saddle River, New Jersey*

Merrill
Prentice Hall

10 9 8 7 6 5 4 3 2 1
ISBN: 0-13-094754-7

Meet the Authors

Meet the Editors

David Capuzzi, Ph.D., N.C.C., L.P.C., is a past president of the American Counseling Association (formerly the American Association for Counseling and Development) and is professor of Counselor Education in the Graduate School of Education at Portland State University in Portland, Oregon.

From 1980 to 1984, Dr. Capuzzi was editor of *The School Counselor* for the American School Counselor Association. He has authored a number of textbook chapters and monographs on the topic of preventing adolescent suicide and is co-editor and author, with Dr. Larry Golden, of *Helping Families Help Children: Family Interventions with School Related Problems* (1986) and *Preventing Adolescent Suicide* (1981). He co-authored and edited *Youth at Risk: A Prevention Resource for Counselors, Teachers, and Parents* in 1989, 1996, and 2000; *Introduction to the Counseling Profession* in 1991, 1997, and 2001; and *Introduction to Group Counseling,* with Douglas R. Gross in 1992, 1998, and 2002. He has also authored or co-authored articles in a number of ACA and related journals.

A frequent speaker and keynoter at professional conferences and institutes, Dr. Capuzzi has also consulted with a variety of school districts and community agencies interested in initiating counseling and intervention strategies for adolescents at risk for suicide. He has facilitated the development of suicide prevention, crisis management, and postvention programs in communities throughout the United States; provides training on the topic of "youth at risk"; and serves as an adjunct faculty member at other universities. He is the first recipient of the ACA's Kitty Cole Human Rights Award.

Douglas R. Gross, Ph.D., N.C.C., is a professor emeritus of Arizona State University in Tempe, where he was a faculty member in the counseling program for 29 years. His professional work history includes public school teaching, counseling, and administration. He has been president of the Arizona Counselors Association, president of the Western Association for Counselor Education and Supervision, chairperson of the Western Regional Branch Assembly of the American Counseling Association (formerly the American Association for Counseling and Development), president of the Association for Humanistic Education and Development, and treasurer and parliamentarian of the ACA.

In addition to his work on this textbook, Dr. Gross has contributed chapters to 13 other texts: three editions of *Youth at Risk: A Prevention Resource for Counselors, Teachers, and Parents* (1989, 1996, 2000); three editions of *Introduction to the Counseling Profession* (1991, 1996, 2001); three editions of *Introduction to Group Counseling* (1992, 1998, 2002); two editions of *Foundations of Mental Health Counseling* (1986, 1996); *Counseling: Theory, Process and Practice* (1977); and *The Counselor's Handbook* (1974). His research has appeared in *The Journal of Counseling Psychology; The Journal of Counseling and De-*

velopment; The Association for Counselor Education and Supervision Journal; The Journal of Educational Research; Counseling, and Human Development; The Arizona Counselors Journal; The Texas Counseling Journal; and *The AMCHA Journal.*

Dr. Gross currently serves as consultant to Corondolet Management Institute and conducts training in the areas of bereavement, grief, and loss.

Meet the Contributors

Valerie Appleton, Ed.D., M.F.C.C., A.T.R., N.C.C., is a professor in the Department of Counseling, Developmental, and Educational Psychology at Eastern Washington University, Spokane, Washington. She is the director of the Counselor Education Program and two CACREP accredited emphases: Mental Health and School Counseling. Dr. Appleton has been a licensed marriage, family, and child counselor and registered art therapist since 1981. She serves as executive director of the editorial board for *Art Therapy,* the journal of the American Art Therapy Association. Her research includes the use of art in trauma intervention and the broader area of counselor education.

G. Miguel Arciniega, Ph.D., is an associate professor in the Division of Psychology in Education at Arizona State University in Tempe. Dr. Arciniega has been director of minority counseling projects and institutes, teacher corps, and centers for bilingual and bicultural education. He has consulted extensively with federal, state, and local agencies about counseling minorities and has also consulted with Aid for International Development (AID) in Central and South America. He has published several articles concerning multicultural counseling.

Larry D. Burlew, Ed.D., is a professor of counseling at the University of Bridgeport. His teaching experience has been primarily with urban universities, while his counseling experience has been with employee assistance programs, college students, midlife adults, AIDS clients, and gay men. He developed an appreciation for alternative forms to Western therapy through work and study on spiritual development, shamanism, past-life therapy, and Eastern philosophies. He has published extensively in counseling and related professional journals and is co-editing a text on sexuality counseling.

Cass Dykeman, Ph.D., is an associate professor of counselor education at Oregon State University. He is a National Certified Counselor, Master Addictions Counselor, and National Certified School Counselor. Dr. Dykeman received a master's degree in counseling from the University of Washington and a doctorate in counselor education from the University of Virginia. He served as principal investigator for a $1.5 million federal school-to-work research project. In addition, he is the author of numerous books, book chapters, and scholarly journal articles. Dr. Dykeman is past president of both the Washington State Association for Counselor Education and Supervision and the Western Association for Counselor Education and Supervision. He is also past chairperson of the School Counseling Interest Network of the Association for Counselor Education and Supervision. His current research interests include school violence, addiction, counseling, and brief counseling techniques.

Tim Evans, Ph.D., is a clinical faculty member of the Department of Rehabilitation and Mental Health Counseling at the University of South Florida. He is the coordinator of the Graduate Certificate Program in marriage and family therapy. Dr. Evans received his doctorate from the University of Georgia and completed an APA counseling psychology internship at the University of Delaware. Dr. Evans served on the board of directors for the

International Committee for Adlerian Summer Schools and Institutes (ICASSI), where he has taught Adlerian psychology throughout Europe and North America. He serves on the editorial boards for *The International Journal of Action Methods: Psychodrama, Skills Training and Role Playing* and *The Journal of Individual Psychology*.

Mary Lou Bryant Frank, Ph.D., received her training as a family therapist and a counseling psychologist at Colorado State University. At Arizona State University in Tempe, she coordinated the eating disorders program, co-coordinated the master's and doctoral practicum training program, and concurrently taught in the counseling department. She established and taught in the master's program in community counseling at North Georgia College & State University. She has contributed a chapter to Capuzzi and Gross's *Introduction to Group Counseling* and has published in the *Journal of Counseling and Development*. Dr. Frank received a Distinguished Service Provider Award in counseling for 1989-1990. She has been a consultant and speaker at eating disorders conferences, private hospitals, and universities. She has served as assistant academic dean and associate professor of psychology at Cinch Valley College of the University of Virginia. She was a professor and head of the Department of Psychology, Sociology, Philosophy, and Community Counseling at North Georgia College & State University. Currently, she serves as Dean of Undergraduate Studies and General Education at Kennesaw State University.

Melinda Haley, B.S., an Oregon Laurels Scholarship recipient for the past 2 years, is currently pursuing a master's degree in community mental health counseling and plans to enroll in a doctoral program in either counselor education or counseling psychology after graduation. Ms. Haley has been employed as a research assistant at Portland State University for the past 2 years and currently works as an intern in the psychiatric dorm of Inverness Jail, in Portland, Oregon. Her supervised responsibilities at the jail include assessment, diagnosis, treatment planning, and the provision of psychotherapeutic treatment to inmates.

Ms. Haley's current research interests include, but are not limited to, personality disorders and personality development over the life span; criminology and the psychology of repeat offenders; multicultural issues, including racial bigotry and the psychology of ethnic cleansing; and posttraumatic stress disorder and the efficacious factors in trauma counseling.

Ms. Haley is a co-author of "Psychotherapy Groups" in *Introduction to Group Counseling* (2002), and is author of "Transitioning Into Single Parenthood," in *Approaches to Group Work: A Handbook for Practitioners* (2003). In addition, Ms. Haley is at work on two novels, *Yanqui* and *American Holocaust*.

Richard J. Hazler, Ph.D., is a professor of counselor education at Ohio University. He earned his Ph.D. at the University of Idaho. Previous professional work includes positions as an elementary school teacher and counselor in schools, prisons, the military, and private practice. Dr. Hazler is editor of the "Student Focus" column for the American Counselor Association's *Counseling Today,* is on the editorial board of the *Counselor Education and Supervision Journal,* and is widely published on a variety of counseling and human development issues. His books include *The Therapeutic Environment: Core Conditions for Facilitating Therapy* (2001) with Nick Barwick, *Helping in the Hallways: Advanced Strategies for Enhancing School Relationships* (1998), and *Breaking the Cycle of Violence: Interventions for Bullying and Victimization* (1996).

Barbara Herlihy, Ph.D., N.C.C., L.P.C., is a professor in the counselor education program at the University of New Orleans. Her scholarly work has focused primarily on ethics in counseling and reflects her additional interests in counseling theory, supervision, and multicultural counseling. Dr. Herlihy has worked as a professional counselor in schools, community agencies, and private practice. Her work as a teacher, scholar, and counselor is grounded in feminist philosophy and practices.

Cynthia R. Kalodner, Ph.D., is associate professor and director of training of the counseling psychology doctoral program in the Department of Counseling, Rehabilitative Counseling, and Counseling Psychology at West Virginia University. She received her doctorate in counseling psychology from Pennsylvania State University in 1988. Previously, she was an assistant professor in the counseling psychology program at the University of Akron. Dr. Kalodner also completed a postdoctoral fellowship studying public health at Johns Hopkins University. Her present research focuses primarily on eating disorders, including cognitive behavioral approaches to understanding and treating women with eating disorders, media influence on eating disorders, and prevention issues.

Rolla E. Lewis, Ed.D., is an associate professor of counselor education at Portland State University, where he serves as coordinator for the school counseling specialization in the counselor education master's program. He has taught and counseled students in alternative and public school settings. He was accorded the 2001 Civic Engagement Award at Portland State University for creating a university-community collaboration with a local school district. In addition, the Oregon Counseling Association presented Dr. Lewis with the Leona Tyler Award for outstanding contributions to the profession of counseling in 2001.

Mary Finn Maples, Ph.D., N.C.C, is a professor of counseling and educational psychology at the University of Nevada, in Reno. Since 1985, Dr. Maples has also served as faculty for the National Judicial College and the National College of Juvenile and Family Law, the Council of Chief Justices, as well as several state judicial education agencies. Her consulting specialties include attitudes and values in judicial decision-making; enhancement of judicial administrative competence; judicial leadership for the third millennium; collegiality and gracious confrontation; organizational dynamics; active listening for the judiciary; and team-building and workplace motivation. Many of these programs have been nationally recognized.

Dr. Maples has over 100 publications, and has presented programs or workshops to over 200 organizations in the last 20 years.

She has held the presidencies of the international American Counseling Association and the National Association for Spiritual, Ethical, and Religious Values in Counseling. She has received numerous national awards for her leadership activities.

Vivian J. Carroll McCollum, Ph.D., is a professor of counseling at the University of New Orleans and holds a Ph.D. in marriage and family therapy from St. Louis University. Her professional specialty is multicultural issues in counseling and the effects of client/counselor interaction in school counseling, career counseling, and family therapy. Dr. McCollum has over 20 years of experience as a college counselor, school counselor, private practitioner, and counselor educator.

Al Milliren, Ed.D., is an associate professor of counseling education in the School of Education at the University of Texas of the Permian Basin. Dr. Milliren earned his bachelor's degree from Bradley University, where he also earned a master's degree in counseling and guidance. He received his doctorate in educational psychology from the University of Illinois, Urbana-Champaign, in 1971, specializing in elementary school counseling. Dr. Milliren has over 35 years experience working with Adlerian psychology as a professional school counselor, as a counselor in private practice, and as a university professor. He has numerous publications and presentations to his credit in the areas of both counseling and education.

John F. Newbauer, Ed.D., is a health service provider in psychology and holds diplomates in the American Board of Psychological Specialties (Psychological Testing) and the Professional Academy of Custody Evaluators. He is also a member and fellow of the American College of Forensic Examiners. He is co-founder and president of Phoenix Associates, Inc. He sees child, adolescent, and adult outpatients, and performs forensic evaluations related to child custody and civil and criminal competency. He is a member of the core faculty at the Adler School of Professional Psychology, and has taught at the University of St. Francis, Southern Illinois University, and Ball State University. He is the president-elect of the North American Society of Adlerian Psychology.

Betty J. Newlon, Ed.D., is professor emeritus of the University of Arizona, Tucson, Arizona, where she served as a faculty member in the counseling program for 25 years. During this time, she served as president of the Arizona Counselors Association and was an editorial board member of the *Journal of Individual Psychology* and the *Vocational Guidance Quarterly.* She has authored numerous book chapters, monographs, and research articles. Dr. Newlon's current research interests include the life planning process of older adults, particularly grandmothers.

Gregory J. Novie, Ph.D., has been in private practice as a psychologist since 1985. His areas of research interest include countertransference with borderline and narcissistic patients and the therapeutic action of psychotherapy. Dr. Novie received his master's degree in rehabilitation counseling from Southern Illinois University and his doctorate in educational psychology from Arizona State University in Tempe. He received his psychoanalytic training from, and is a member of, the Southwest Center for Psychoanalytic Studies. He is also a member of the division of psychoanalysis of the American Psychological Association.

Catherine B. Roland, Ed.D., is a counselor educator at the University of Arkansas, Fayetteville. She received her Ed.D. in 1977 from the University of Cincinnati and has lived in New York, Philadelphia, and New Orleans, where she had a full-time private practice for many years. She has been active in the American Counseling Association as a former board member and committee chair. Her interests include gender and diversity issues in counseling, counseling and spirituality, and research on women and nontraditional, non-talk counseling approaches. She is advisor to Chi Sigma Iota at the University of Arkansas and fully enjoys working with and mentoring her students.

Donna M. Roy, B.A., received her Bachelor of Arts in German from the University of Maine at Orono and her M.I.A. (Master of International Administration) from the School of International Training in Brattleboro, Vermont. She has 20 years' experience in teaching, training, and mentoring adolescents and adults. In her private counseling practice, she draws from advanced professional training in Hakomi body-centered psychotherapy as well as experiential study of dream states, ritual, and ceremony. She is currently a student in Portland State University's master's program in counselor education, specializing in community counseling.

Susan E. Schwartz, Ph.D., is a Jungian analyst trained at the C. G. Jung Institute in Zurich, Switzerland, with a doctorate in clinical psychology. She is a senior analyst, teacher, and secretary at the C. G. Jung Institute in Santa Fe, New Mexico. She gives lectures and workshops worldwide on various aspects of Jungian analytical psychology and has a private practice in Scottsdale, Arizona.

Conrad Sieber, Ph.D., completed a postdoctoral fellowship in the counselor education program at Portland State University, where he taught courses on program evaluation in educational and social service agencies and supervised counseling practicum students and interns. He also pursued interests in treating post-traumatic stress disorder, in person-centered psychology, and in developing educational/counseling programs for disadvantaged youth. Dr. Sieber received his doctoral degree from Colorado State University and completed an internship at Ohio State University. He has 5 years of professional experience in university counseling centers, where he coordinated and developed group therapy programs, evaluated clinical services, and was actively involved in training graduate students. Currently, he maintains a private practice in Portland, Oregon, evaluates educational and counseling programs, and consults with public schools and institutions of higher education. Dr. Sieber has authored counseling book chapters and articles for professional publications.

Ann Vernon, Ph.D., is professor and coordinator of counseling at the University of Northern Iowa in Cedar Falls. In addition, she is a therapist in private practice, specializing in working with children and adolescents and their parents. Dr. Vernon is considered one of the nation's leading experts on applications of REBT to school-age clients. She has written numerous books, chapters, and articles on this topic, including: *Thinking, Feeling, Behaving, and the Passport Program,* an emotional education curriculum based on REBT. Dr. Vernon regularly presents REBT workshops throughout the United States, Canada, and abroad. She is on the Albert Ellis board of trustees and is the director of the Midwest Center for REBT.

Robert E. Wubbolding, Ph.D., clinical counselor and psychologist, is the director of the Center for Reality Therapy in Cincinnati, the director of training for the William Glasser Institute in Chatsworth, California, and professor emeritus of counseling at Xavier University. Author of 10 books on reality therapy, including *Reality Therapy for the 21st Century,* he has taught reality therapy in North America, Asia, Europe, Australia, and the Middle East. His work has focused on making reality therapy a cross-cultural approach with other applications to management, addictions, and corrections. He has extended the central procedure of self-evaluation to include 22 applications based on choice theory. His current interest is reviewing research studies validating the use of reality therapy.

He has been an elementary and high school counselor, a high school teacher, an administrator of adult basic education, and a correctional counselor.

Preface

Counseling and Psychotherapy: Theories and Interventions presents a variety of theories and conceptual frameworks for understanding the parameters of the helping relationship. These parameters can include models for viewing personality development; explaining past behavior; predicting future behavior; understanding the current behavior of the client; diagnosing and treatment planning; assessing client motivations, needs, and unresolved issues; and identifying strategies and interventions for use during the counseling and psychotherapy process.

Theories help organize data and provide guidelines for the prevention and intervention efforts of counselors and therapists. They direct a professional helper's attention and observations and offer constructs, terminology, and viewpoints that can be understood by colleagues and used during supervision and consultation sessions. Theory directly influences the interventions used by counselors and therapists to promote a client's new insight, new behavior, and new approaches to relationships and problem solving. The greater a counselor's or therapist's awareness of the strengths and possibilities inherent in numerous theoretical frames of reference, the greater the potential for understanding the uniqueness of a particular client and for developing the most effective treatment plan.

This book is unique in both format and content. All the contributing authors are experts who provide state-of-the-art information about theories of counseling and psychotherapy. (See the "Meet the Authors" section for their backgrounds.) In addition, each chapter discusses applications of the theory presented as it relates to one particular case study—a hypothetical client named Jonathan whom we are introduced to on page 48. This book also includes information that is sometimes not addressed in other counseling and psychotherapy textbooks: a chapter that focuses on the importance of achieving a personal and professional identity before beginning work with clients, a chapter on feminist theory, a chapter on Eastern approaches, and a chapter on body-centered counseling and psychotherapy. The book's unique approach enhances its readability and should engage reader interest in the material.

Features of the Text

This book is designed for students who are beginning their study of individual counseling and psychotherapy. It presents a comprehensive overview of each of the following theories: psychoanalytic, Jungian, Adlerian, existential, person-centered, Gestalt, cognitive-behavioral, rational emotive behavior theory, reality, family, brief, feminist, Eastern, and body-centered. Each theory is addressed from the perspective of background, human nature, major constructs, applications (which includes a discussion of the goals of counseling and psychotherapy, the process of change, and intervention strategies), evaluation (which evaluates both the supporting research and the limitations of the theory), clients with mental disorders, a summary chart, and a case study consistent with the theoretical model under discussion.

We know that one text cannot adequately address all the factors connected with a given theory; entire texts have been written discussing each of the theories in this book. We have, however, attempted to provide readers with a consistent approach to analyzing and studying each theory and have included examples of how to apply the theory to a case study.

The format for this text is based on the contributions of the co-editors, who conceptualized the content and wrote the first two chapters, as well as the contributions of 23 authors selected for their expertise in various theories. Each chapter contains theoretical and applied content. The text is divided into the following four parts: "Foundations for Individual Counseling and Psychotherapy," "Theories of Counseling and Psychotherapy," "Eastern and Nontraditional Approaches," and "Multicultural Considerations."

Part I, "Foundations for Individual Counseling and Psychotherapy" (Chapters 1 and 2), begins by offering general information about the helping relationship and individual counseling. This introductory information is followed by a chapter titled "Achieving a Personal and Professional Identity," as it is not possible for the counselor or therapist to make use of a theory or conceptual framework unless he or she is self-assured and clear about personal boundaries.

Part II, "Theories of Counseling and Psychotherapy" (Chapters 3 through 14), presents information on the 12 theories selected for inclusion in this portion of the text. Each of these chapters—"Psychoanalytic Theory," "Jungian Analytical Theory," "Adlerian Counseling and Psychotherapy," "Existential Counseling and Psychotherapy," "Person-Centered Theory," "Gestalt Theory," "Cognitive-Behavioral Theories," "Rational Emotive Behavior Therapy," "Reality Therapy Theory," "Family Theory," "Brief Theories," and "Feminist Theories"—presents the theory and then applies the theory to the case study of Jonathan.

Part III, "Eastern and Nontraditional Approaches" (Chapters 15 and 16), involves discussion of theoretical approaches that stem from Eastern philosophy ("Eastern Theories") and nontraditional approaches ("Body-Centered Counseling and Psychotherapy").

Part IV, "Multicultural Considerations" (Chapter 17), is focused solely on counseling considerations with diverse populations ("Counseling and Psychotherapy: Multicultural Considerations").

New to This Edition

This edition of our text includes some additional features that we think will be of high interest to the readership. The updated chapter on feminist theory presents an excellent overview of the evolution of feminist theory and addresses human nature, major constructs, applications, clients with mental disorders, evaluation, and the case of Jonathan. This chapter emphasizes the work of Nancy Chodorow, Carol Gilligan, Jean Baker Miller, Judith Jordan and Janet Surrey, Sandra Bem, and Ellyn Kaschak.

The chapter on family theory is included to sensitize the reader to the fact that counselors and therapists engaging clients in individual work must keep in mind the systemic variables influencing clients and the fact that some clients may need family counseling and psychotherapy as part of a comprehensive treatment plan. The chapter on brief theories is included because of the influence of managed care on the provision of mental health services in almost all settings. This chapter provides information on solution-focused brief therapy, narrative therapy, and health realization.

In response to the increasing interest in alternative approaches to counseling and psychotherapy, this edition includes a revised chapter on Eastern theories. Few textbooks of this nature address conceptual frameworks that are nontraditional or external to the mainstream models usually adopted by practitioners and academicians in Western culture. A new chapter on body-centered counseling and psychotherapy is also included. Finally, in response to the continued interest in Rational Emotive Behavior Theory, a new chapter, separate from the one on cognitive-behavioral theories, has been developed to present the contributions of Albert Ellis and his colleagues.

Readers of the third edition will find the Web-assisted site (located at *http://www.prenhall.com/capuzzi*) helpful in the process of mastering the content of the text. This site is designed to assist the reader in a variety of ways. For each chapter, the following information is provided: a chapter pretest, a chapter overview, lists of key terms and key people, suggested classroom exercises designed to enhance instruction as well as to provide experiential components to the learning experience, individual exercises that can be completed, questions for study and discussion, links to websites, and a chapter posttest. Professors adopting this text are invited to tie some of the course assignments and requirements to the content of this Web-assisted site.

We, the co-editors and the 23 other contributors, have made every effort to give the reader current information and content focused on both theory and application. It is our hope that the third edition of *Counseling and Psychotherapy: Theories and Interventions* will provide the foundation that students need to make decisions about follow-up study or specific theories as well as the development of their own personal theory of counseling and psychotherapy.

Acknowledgments

We would like to thank the 23 professionals who contributed their time and expertise to the development of this textbook for students interested in individual counseling and psychotherapy. We also thank our families, who supported and encouraged our writing and editing efforts, as well as the counselor education faculty at Portland State University. Thanks go out to our editors and the other staff members at Prentice Hall for their collaborative and thorough approach to the editing and production of this textbook. We would like to give special recognition to Melinda Haley, graduate assistant and student in the community counseling specialization of the counselor education program at Portland State University, for her assistance in meeting publication deadlines. Without the dedicated efforts of this group of colleagues, we know this book could not have been published.

We are also grateful to the reviewers of this edition for their comments and suggestions: Mary H. Guindon, Johns Hopkins University; Carol Hightower Parker, Texas Southern University; and William J. Weikel, Moorehead State University.

Discover the Companion Website Accompanying This Book

The Prentice Hall Companion Website: A Virtual Learning Environment

Technology is a constantly growing and changing aspect of our field that is creating a need for content and resources. To address this emerging need, Prentice Hall has developed an online learning environment for students and professors alike—Companion Websites—to support our textbooks.

In creating a Companion Website, our goal is to build on and enhance what the textbook already offers. For this reason, the content for each user-friendly website is organized by chapter and provides the professor and student with a variety of meaningful resources.

For the Professor—

Every Companion Website integrates **Syllabus Manager**™, an online syllabus creation and management utility.

- **Syllabus Manager**™ provides you, the instructor, with an easy, step-by-step process to create and revise syllabi, with direct links into Companion Website and other online content without having to learn HTML.
- Students may logon to your syllabus during any study session. All they need to know is the web address for the Companion Website and the password you've assigned to your syllabus.
- After you have created a syllabus using **Syllabus Manager**™, students may enter the syllabus for their course section from any point in the Companion Website.
- Clicking on a date, the student is shown the list of activities for the assignment. The activities for each assignment are linked directly to actual content, saving time for students.
- Adding assignments consists of clicking on the desired due date, then filling in the details of the assignment—name of the assignment, instructions, and whether it is a one-time or repeating assignment.

- In addition, links to other activities can be created easily. If the activity is on-line, a URL can be entered in the space provided, and it will be linked automatically in the final syllabus.
- Your completed syllabus is hosted on our servers, allowing convenient updates from any computer on the Internet. Changes you make to your syllabus are immediately available to your students at their next logon.

For the Student—

Common Companion Website features for students include:

- **Chapter Objectives**—outline key concepts from the text.
- **Interactive Self-quizzes**—complete with hints and automatic grading that provide immediate feedback for students. After students submit their answers for the interactive self-quizzes, the Companion Website **Results Reporter** computes a percentage grade, provides a graphic representation of how many questions were answered correctly and incorrectly, and gives a question-by-question analysis of the quiz. Students are given the option to send their quiz to up to four email addresses (professor, teaching assistant, study partner, etc.).
- **Web Destinations**—links to www sites that relate to chapter content.
- **Learning Network**—the Pearson Learning Network offers a wealth of additional resources to aid in their understanding and application of content.
- **Message Board**—serves as a virtual bulletin board to post—or respond to—questions or comments to/from a national audience.
- **Chat**—real-time chat with anyone who is using the text anywhere in the country—ideal for discussion and study groups, class projects, etc.

To take advantage of the many available resources, please visit the *Counseling and Psychotherapy: Theories and Interventions,* Third Edition, Companion Website at

www.prenhall.com/capuzzi

Brief Contents

Contents

II   Theories of Counseling and Psychotherapy   41

16 Body-Centered Counseling and Psychotherapy   387
Donna M. Roy

Foundations for Individual Counseling and Psychotherapy

Counseling and psychotherapy encompass a number of relationship and personal and professional modalities in which the counselor or therapist needs to be proficient. These modalities include not only the creation of essential core conditions that are both foundational to the establishment of a helping relationship and prerequisite to change on the part of the client, but also the achievement of a personal and professional identity that will enable the counselor or therapist to facilitate the process of counseling and psychotherapy.

The helping relationship is the foundation on which the process of counseling and psychotherapy is based. It is not possible to use the concepts and associated interventions of a specific theory unless such applications are made in the context of a relationship that promotes trust, insight, and behavior change. Chapter 1, "Helping Relationships in Counseling and Psychotherapy," is designed to aid students in the development and delivery of the helping relationship. To achieve this purpose, the helping relationship is presented in terms of definitions, descriptions, stages, core conditions, personal characteristics, and helping strategies, particularly in terms of their application to diverse populations.

Chapter 2, "Achieving a Personal and Professional Identity," discusses why the personal and professional identity of the helping professional must be addressed before and during the process of studying and applying individual approaches to counseling and psychotherapy. The chapter addresses the importance of health and wellness for the helping professional, recognition of values and cultural bias in theory and practice, awareness of the daily world of the practitioner, and achieving perspective and balance between the individual as a person and the individual as a professional. A model for the development of a personal theory is also provided.

As these chapters indicate, practitioners must achieve high levels of competence, effectiveness, and expertise to create a helping relationship beneficial to clients. They must also develop the ability to know themselves from both personal and professional perspectives. We have made every attempt to introduce readers to these topics in the chapters included in this section of the text. Readers are encouraged to do additional reading and follow-up course work and to commit to personal counseling or therapy to achieve the purposes we have outlined in these chapters.

Helping Relationships in Counseling and Psychotherapy

Douglas R. Gross
Professor Emeritus
Arizona State University

David Capuzzi
Portland State University

T he following scenario depicts a student, much like you, who is in the early stages of a preparatory program leading to a degree in counseling, psychology, or clinical social work. George is currently enrolled in a course dealing with personality theory and its application to counseling and/or therapy. Courses such as this, combined with both George's personal dynamics and life experiences, serve as the foundation on which the professions of counseling and psychotherapy rest—a foundation defined for our purposes as the **helping relationship.** The information contained in the scenario serves as an introduction to our discussion of this relationship.

George maneuvered his car through the heavy traffic at the entrance to the university parking area. He was annoyed that it was taking him so long to park this morning. He had left home early so that he would have plenty of time, prior to class, to meet with the other four members of his study group. Already 10 minutes behind his timeline and concerned that he would not have enough time to review all the material before his group's presentation, he parked his car and caught the tram into the main part of the campus. He was oblivious to the various classroom buildings he passed and to the other people on the tram. His thoughts centered on the fact that his group was presenting first this morning and he wanted the presentation to go well.

George's instructor had divided the class into seven groups and assigned each group a different theoretical system. His group had been assigned Rational Emotive Behavioral Theory (REBT), and had been instructed to present the major constructs of the theory as well as a demonstration of its use in counseling and/or psychotherapy. His part of the presentation centered on serving as a counselor to a role-played client who was having problems maintaining relationships. George was very familiar with both the concepts behind REBT and their application in the counseling/therapeutic process, and he and the group member role playing the client had spent a good deal of time practicing their interaction. He was frightened because he knew that people would be watching and he was acutely aware that a major portion of his group's evaluation would be based on how well he was able to demonstrate the application of the theoretical system assigned.

When the tram reached the stop closest to his building, George disembarked and raced to the fourth floor, where he joined the other four members of his group. He soon found out that he was not the only member of the group anxious about the presentation. Each member of the group took a few minutes to outline what he or she would be doing during the presentation. The group spent the rest of the time setting up the room, getting materials ready, and assuring each other that things would go well. George realized that much of his anxiety stemmed from the fact that this was the first time he had been called upon to demonstrate both knowledge and skill other than through tests and papers. He believed that the counseling/therapy demonstration came much closer to what would be expected of him in the "real" setting. He felt ready for the most exciting yet frightening experience of his educational program.

This scenario occurs each semester when students are confronted with having to demonstrate their ability to translate textbook knowledge into therapeutic application. All of the classes you have taken to this point have been preparing you for this encounter. It is often the first time you are called upon to integrate learned knowledge and skills into a counseling or therapeutic relationship—a helping relationship. The fact that you must demonstrate this untried relationship for both peers and instructors adds both excitement and anxiety. The excitement stems from being able to put your knowledge and skills to a practical test. The anxiety stems both from a lack of experience in establishing this relationship and knowing that its success depends not only on your knowledge and skill, but also on your ability to integrate into this relationship your personal dynamics.

This chapter will aid you in understanding the various factors that affect the helping relationship: definitions and descriptions, stages, core dimensions, strategies, and issues of diversity. We hope the information presented in this chapter will help you realize that your excitement and anxiety can be natural and productive. We also hope you will be able to incorporate this information into effective models of the helping relationship.

Helping Relationships: Definitions and Descriptions

The helping relationship appears to be a cornerstone on which all effective helping rests (Combs & Gonzales, 1994; Miars, Burden, & Pedersen, 1997; Miars & Halverson, 2001; Purkey & Schmidt, 1987; Seligman, 2001; Terry, Burden, & Pedersen, 1991). Words such as *integral, necessary,* and *mandatory* are used to describe this relationship and its importance in the ultimate effectiveness of the **helping process.** Even though different theoretical systems use different words to describe this relationship (See Chapters 3 through 15), each addresses the significance of the helping relationship in facilitating client change. Kottler and Brown (1992), in their *Introduction to Therapeutic Counseling,* made the following comments regarding the significance of this relationship:

Regardless of the setting in which you practice counseling, whether in a school, agency, hospital, or private practice, the relationships you develop with your clients are crucial to any progress you might make together. For without a high degree of intimacy and trust between two people, very little can be accomplished. (p. 64)

In further support of the significance of the helping relationship, Brammer and Mac-Donald (1996) said:

The helping relationship is dynamic, meaning that it is constantly changing at verbal and nonverbal levels. The relationship is the principal process vehicle for both helper and helpee to express and fulfill their needs, as well as to mesh helpee problems with helper expertise. Relationship emphasizes the affective mode, because relationship is commonly defined as the inferred emotional quality of the interaction. (p. 52)

The ideas expressed in these two statements describe the essential value of the helping relationship in the process of counseling or psychotherapy and the significant role that the counselor or therapist plays in developing this relationship. Through this relationship, client change occurs. Although the creation of this relationship is not the end goal of the process, it certainly is the means by which other goals are met. It serves as the framework within which effective helping takes place.

Although universally accepted definitions and descriptions of the helping relationship should be easy to find, such is not the case. Despite the importance of this relationship in the overall helping process, a perusal of textbooks and articles dealing with counseling and psychotherapy discloses the lack of a common definition. Rogers (1961), for example, defined a helping relationship as one "in which at least one of the parties has the intent of promoting the growth, development, maturity, improved functioning and improved coping with life of the other" (p. 39). Okun (1992) stated that "the development of a warm, trustful relationship between the helper and helpee underlies any strategy or approach to the helping process and, therefore, is a basic condition for the success of any helping process" (p. 14). According to Miars and Halverson (2001), "The ultimate goal of a professional helping relationship should be to promote the development of more effective and adaptive behavior in the client" (p. 51).

It is easy to see the difficulty in categorically stating an accepted definition or description of the helping relationship, regardless of which of these statements you choose to embrace. Yet despite the differences, each carries with it directions and directives aimed at a single goal: the enhancement and encouragement of client change. The following definitive characteristics of the helping relationship embrace this goal and describe our conceptualization of this relationship.

- The relationship is initially structured by the counselor or therapist, but is open to cooperative restructuring based upon the needs of the client.
- The relationship begins with the initial meeting and continues through termination.
- The persons involved in the relationship perceive the existence of trust, caring, concern, and commitment and act accordingly.
- The needs of the client are given priority over the needs of the counselor or therapist.
- The relationship provides for the personal growth of all persons involved.

- The relationship provides the safety needed for self-exploration by all persons involved.
- The relationship promotes the potential of all persons involved.

The major responsibility in creating this relationship rests initially with the counselor or therapist, with increasing demands for client involvement and commitment over time. It is a shared process, and only through shared effort will this relationship develop and flourish. This development evolves in stages that take the relationship from initiation to closure. The stages in this evolving process are the subject of the following section.

Helping Relationships: Stages

The helping relationship is a constant throughout the counseling or psychotherapeutic process. The definitive characteristics we have already presented indicate that the relationship must be present from the initial meeting between the client and the counselor or therapist and continue through closure. Viewing the helping relationship as a constant throughout the helping process leads to visualizing this process from a developmental perspective. This development can best be viewed in terms of a narrow path whose limits are established by the client's fear, anxiety, and resistance. Such client reactions should not be seen as lack of commitment to change; rather, they need to be understood in terms of the unknown nature of this developing alliance and the fact that this may be the first time the client has experienced this type of interaction. These reactions are often shared by the counselor or therapist, based upon his or her level of experience. The path broadens through the development of trust, safety, and understanding as this relationship develops. The once narrow path becomes a boulevard along which two persons move courageously toward their final destination: change. The movement along this broadening path is described by various authors in terms of stages or phases. Osipow, Walsh, and Tosi (1980), in discussing the stages of the helping relationship, stated:

> Persons who experience the process of personal counseling seem to progress through several stages. First, there is an increased awareness of self and others. Second, there is an expanded exploration of self and environment (positive and negative behavioral tendencies). Third, there is increased commitment to self-enhancing behavior and its implementation. Fourth, there is an internalization of new and more productive thoughts and actions. Fifth, there is a stabilization of new behavior. (p. 73)

Brammer (1985) divided this developmental process into two phases, each with four distinctive stages. Phase one is titled "Building Relationships" and includes preparing the client and opening the relationship, clarifying the problem or concern of the client, structuring the process, and building a relationship. Phase two is titled "Facilitating Positive Action" and involves exploration, consolidation, planning, and termination.

Purkey and Schmidt (1987) set forth three stages in building the helping relationship, each containing four steps. Stage one, "Preparation," includes having the desire for a relationship, expecting good things, preparing the setting, and reading the situation. Stage two is "Initiating Responding," and includes choosing caringly, acting appropriately, honoring the client, and ensuring reception. The third and final stage, "Follow-up," includes interpreting responses, negotiating positions, evaluating the process, and developing trust.

Egan (1998) stated that the helping relationship minimally can be broken down into three phases: that of relationship building, that of challenging the client to find ways to change, and that of facilitating positive client action. The goal of the first phase is to build a foundation of mutual trust and client understanding. In the second phase, the counselor challenges the client to "try on" new ways of thinking, feeling, and behaving. In the third phase, the counselor aids the client in facilitating actions that lead toward change and growth in the client's life outside the counseling relationship.

Authors such as Corey and Corey (1993), Gladding (2000), Hackney and Cormier (1996), and Miars and Halverson (2001) provide other models of the developmental nature of the stages of the helping relationship. Although the terms used to describe these stages may differ, there seems to be a consistency across these models: The reader moves from initiation of the relationship through a clinically based working stage to a termination stage. The following developmental stages show our conceptualization of this relationship-building process and are based on the consistency found in our research and our clinical experience.

- *Stage 1: Relationship Development.* This stage includes the initial meeting of client and counselor or therapist, rapport building, information gathering, goal determination, and informing the client about the conditions under which counseling will take place (e.g., confidentiality, taping, counselor/therapist/ client roles).
- *Stage 2: Extended Exploration.* This stage builds on the foundation established in the first stage. Through selected techniques, theoretical approaches, and strategies, the counselor or therapist explores in depth the emotional and cognitive dynamics of the person of the client, problem parameters, previously tried solutions, decision-making capabilities, and a reevaluation of the goals determined in Stage 1.
- *Stage 3: Problem Resolution.* This stage, which depends on information gained during the previous two stages, is characterized by increased activity for all parties involved. The counselor or therapist's activities include facilitating, demonstrating, instructing, and providing a safe environment for the development of change. The client's activities focus on reevaluation, emotional and cognitive dynamics, trying out new behaviors (both inside and outside of the sessions), and discarding those that do not meet goals.
- *Stage 4: Termination and Follow-up.* This stage is the closing stage of the helping relationship and is cooperatively determined by all persons involved. Methods and procedures for follow-up are determined prior to the last meeting.

It is important to keep in mind that people do not automatically move through these identified stages in a lockstep manner. The relationship may end at any one of these stages based upon decisions made by the client, the counselor or therapist, or both. Nor is it possible to identify the amount of time that "should" be devoted to any particular stage. With certain clients, much more time will need to be devoted to specific stages. Brown and Sre-balus (1988), in addresing the tentative nature of these relationship stages, caution their readers:

> Before we describe a common sequence of events in counseling, it is important to note that many clients, for one reason or another, will not complete all the stages of counseling. The process will be abandoned prematurely, not because something went wrong, but because of factors external to the counselor-client relationship. For example, the school year may end for a student client, or a client or counselor may move away to accept a new job. When counseling is in process and must abruptly end, the participants will feel the incompleteness and loss. (p. 69)

Viewing the helping relationship as an ongoing process that is composed of devel-opmental stages provides counselors and therapists with a structural framework within which they can function effectively. Inside this framework fit the core conditions and strategies that serve the goals of movement through the relationship process and en-hancement and encouragement of client change. We discuss these core conditions and strategies in the following two sections.

Helping Relationships: Core Conditions

The concept of basic or **core condition** related to the helping relationship has its basis in the early work of Rogers (1957) and the continued work of such authors as Carkhuff and Barenson (1967), Combs (1986), Egan (1994), Ivey (1988), Patterson (1974), and Truax and Carkhuff (1967). The concept incorporates a set of conditions that, when present, en-hance the effectiveness of the helping relationship. These conditions vary in terminology from author to author, but generally include the following: **empathic understanding, respect and positive regard, genuineness and congruence, concreteness, warmth,** and **immediacy.**

It should be obvious in reviewing this listing that the concept of core or basic con-ditions relates directly to various personal characteristics or behaviors that the counselor or therapist brings to and incorporates into the helping relationship. It is difficult to pin-point with any exactness how such characteristics or behaviors develop. Are they the re-sult of life experiences, classroom instruction, or some combination of both? Our experience in education favors the last explanation. Core conditions or behaviors must already be present to some degree in our students for our instruction to enhance or ex-pand them.

The remainder of this section deals with core conditions and relates these directly to personal characteristics or behaviors of counselors or therapists that should enhance their ability to effectively utilize these conditions in the process of helping. Although definitions, emphases, and applications of these conditions differ across theoretical systems, there ap-pears to be agreement about their effectiveness in facilitating change in the overall help-ing relationship (Brammer, Abrego, & Shostrom, 1993; Brems, 2000; Gladding, 2000, 2001; Sexton & Whiston, 1994; Thompson, 1996).

Empathic Understanding

Empathic understanding is the ability to feel *with* clients as opposed to feeling *for* clients. It is the ability to understand feelings, thoughts, ideas, and experiences by viewing them from the client's frame of reference. The counselor or therapist must be able to enter the client's world, understand the myriad of aspects that make up that world, and communicate this understanding so that the client perceives that he or she has been heard accurately.

Egan (1998) identified both primary and advanced levels of empathic understanding. At the primary level, it is the ability to understand, identify, and communicate feelings and meanings that are at the surface level of the client's disclosures. At the advanced level, it is the ability to understand, identify, and communicate feelings and meanings that are buried, hidden, or beyond the immediate reach of a client. Such feelings and meanings are more often covert rather than overt client expressions.

Personal characteristics or behaviors that enhance a counselor's or therapist's ability to provide empathic understanding include, but are not limited to, the following.

- The therapist has knowledge and awareness of his or her own values, attitudes, and beliefs and the emotional and behavioral impact they have on his or her own life.
- The therapist has knowledge and awareness of his or her own feelings and emotional response patterns and how they manifest themselves in interactive patterns.
- The therapist has knowledge and awareness of his or her own life experiences and his or her personal reactions to those experiences.
- The therapist possesses the capacity and willingness to communicate these personal reactions to his or her clients.

Respect and Positive Regard

Respect and positive regard are defined as the belief in each client's innate worth and potential and the ability to communicate this belief in the helping relationship. This belief, once communicated, provides clients with positive reinforcement relative to their innate ability to take responsibility for their own growth, change, goal determination, decision making, and eventual problem solving. It is an empowering process that delivers the message to clients that they are able to take control of their lives and, with facilitative assistance from the counselor or therapist, foster change. Communicating and demonstrating this respect for clients takes many forms. According to Baruth and Robinson (1987), it "is often communicated by what the counselor does not do or say. In other words, by not offering to intervene for someone, one is communicating a belief in the individual's ability to 'do' for himself or herself." (p. 85)

Personal characteristics or behaviors that enhance a counselor's or therapist's ability to provide respect and positive regard include, but are not limited to, the following.

- The therapist respects himself or herself.
- The therapist views himself or herself as having worth and potential.
- The therapist can model and communicate this positive self-image to clients.
- The therapist can recognize his or her own control needs, and has the ability to use this recognition in a manner that allows clients to direct their own lives.

Genuineness and Congruence

Genuineness and congruence describe the ability to be **authentic** in the helping relationship. The ability to be real as opposed to artificial, to behave as one feels as opposed to playing the role of the helper, and to be congruent in terms of actions and words are further descriptors of this core condition. According to Boy and Pine (1982),

> The counselor's genuineness is imperative if the client is to achieve genuineness. If the counselor is truly genuine, he or she engages in counseling attitudes and behaviors that influence clients to be genuine. The authentic counselor feels compelled to be involved in facilitative behaviors that have meaning and relevance for clients rather than to adopt superficial and mechanical behaviors that have little or no value. (p. 8)

Implicit in this statement is the idea of the counselor's ability to communicate and demonstrate this genuineness, not only for relationship enhancement but also to model this core condition so that clients can develop greater authenticity in their interactions with others.

Personal characteristics or behaviors that enhance a counselor's or therapist's ability to prove genuineness and congruence include, but are not limited to, the following.

- The therapist is self-aware and has the ability to demonstrate this awareness through words and actions.
- The therapist understands his or her own motivational patterns and has the ability to use them productively in the helping relationship.
- The therapist is able to present his or her thoughts, feelings, and actions in a consistent, unified, and honest manner.
- The therapist is self-confident and has the ability to communicate this capacity in a facilitative way in the helping relationship.

Concreteness

Concreteness is the ability not only to see the incomplete picture that clients paint with their words, but also to communicate to clients the figures, images, and structures that will complete the picture. In the process of exploring problems or issues, clients often present a somewhat distorted view of the actual situation. Concreteness enables the counselor or therapist to help clients identify such distortions and fit them together in such a way that clients are able to view the situation in a more realistic fashion. Concreteness helps clients clarify vague issues, focus on specific topics, reduce degrees of ambiguity, and channel their energies into more productive avenues of problem solution.

Personal characteristics and behaviors that enhance a counselor's or therapist's ability to provide degrees of concreteness include, but are not limited to, the following.

- The therapist has the capacity for abstract thinking and is able to "read between the lines."
- The therapist is willing to risk being incorrect as he or she attempts to fill in the empty spaces.
- The therapist believes in his or her own competence in analyzing and sorting through the truths and partial truths in clients' statements.
- The therapist can be objective while working with clients in arriving at the reality of clients' situations.

Warmth

Warmth is the ability to communicate and demonstrate genuine caring and concern for clients. Using this ability, counselors and therapists convey their acceptance of clients, their desire for clients' well-being, and their sincere interest in finding workable solutions to the problems that clients present. The demeanor of the counselor or therapist is often the main avenue for communicating and demonstrating warmth, for it is often through nonverbal behaviors—a smile, a touch, tone of voice, a facial expression—that genuine caring and concern are communicated. The counselor's or therapist's capacity for transmitting concern and caring to clients, either verbally or nonverbally, enables clients to experience, often for the first time, a truly accepting relationship.

Personal characteristics or behaviors that enhance a counselor's or therapist's ability to demonstrate warmth include, but are not limited to, the following.

- The therapist possesses the capacity for self-care and the ability to demonstrate this capacity in both actions and words.
- The therapist possesses the capacity for self-acceptance, basing this acceptance on his or her assets and liabilities.
- The therapist desires his or her own well-being and has the ability to demonstrate this desire through both words and actions.
- The therapist possesses the desire to find, and has successful personal experience in finding, workable solutions to his or her own problems, and has the ability to communicate this desire through words and actions.

Immediacy

Immediacy is the ability to deal with the here-and-now factors that operate within the helping relationship. These factors are described as overt and covert interactions that take place between the client and the counselor or therapist. A client's anger at a counselor or therapist, the latter's frustration with a client, and the feelings of the client and counselor or therapist for each other are all examples of factors that need to be addressed as they occur and develop. Addressing such issues in the safety of the helping relationship should help participants in two ways: they will gain insight into personal behavioral patterns that may be conducive and not conducive to growth, and they will use this insight in relationships outside the helping relationship.

Dealing with these factors can be threatening; it is often easier to deal with relationships in the abstract and avoid personal encounters. A counselor or therapist needs to be able to use this factor of immediacy to show clients the benefits that can be gained by dealing with issues as they arise. According to Egan (1998), immediacy not only "clears the air," but also is a valuable learning experience.

Personal characteristics or behaviors that enhance a counselor's or therapist's ability to use immediacy effectively include, but are not limited to, the following.

- The therapist has perceptive accuracy in interpreting his or her own feelings for, thoughts about, and behaviors toward clients.
- The therapist has perceptive accuracy in interpreting clients' feelings for, thoughts about, and behaviors toward him or her.

- The therapist has the capacity for and willingness to deal with his or her own issues related to clients on a personal as opposed to an abstract level.
- The therapist is willing to confront both himself or herself and clients with what he or she observes to be happening in the helping relationship.

Helping Relationships: Strategies

The previous section identified the core conditions that need to be present for the effective development of the helping relationship. The difference between these core conditions and **strategies** are the subject of this section.

Core conditions relate to specific dynamics present in the personality and behavioral makeup of counselors or therapists so that they are able to communicate to clients. The term *strategies* refers to skills gained through education and experience that define and direct what counselors or therapists do within the relationship to attain specific results and to move the helping relationship from problem identification to problem resolution.

Varying terms have been used to address this aspect of the helping relationship. Some authors prefer the term *strategies* (Combs & Avila, 1985; Cormier & Cormier, 1991; Gilliland, James, & Bowman, 1989; Hackney & Cormier, 1994); others prefer *skills* (Hansen, Rossberg, & Cramer, 1994; Ivey, 1988; Miars & Halverson, 2001); still others prefer the term *techniques* (Belkin, 1980; Brown & Pate, 1983; Osipow et al., 1980). The terms, however, are interchangeable.

We decided to use the term *strategies,* which denotes not only deliberative planning, but also action processes that make the planning operational. We believe that both factors are necessary. For the purpose of the following discussion, we have grouped the strategies in the following categories.

- strategies that build rapport and encourage client dialogue
- strategies that aid in data gathering
- strategies that add depth and enhance the relationship

Note that specific strategies, such as those stemming from various theoretical systems, are not included in this section. They will be presented in Chapters 3 through 15, which deal with specific theories. It is also important for you to understand that there is much overlap between these arbitrary divisions. Strategies designed to build rapport and encourage client dialogue may also gather data and enhance relationships. With this caveat in mind, we present the following strategies.

Strategies That Build Rapport and Encourage Client Dialogue

This group of strategies includes active listening strategies that enhance the listening capabilities of counselors and therapists. When used effectively, these strategies should provide an environment in which clients have the opportunity to talk and to share their feelings and thoughts with the assurance that they will be heard. By using such strategies, counselors and therapists enhance their chances of providing such an environment.

This set of strategies includes **attending** and **encouraging, restating, paraphrasing, reflecting content and perception checking,** and **summarizing.** The following paragraphs present explanations and examples of these strategies.

Attending and Encouraging   These strategies use the counselor's or therapist's posture, visual contact, gestures, facial expressions, and words to indicate to clients not only that they are being heard but also that the counselor or therapist wishes them to continue sharing information.

Example

Encouraging	COUNSELOR/THERAPIST: (*smiling*) Please tell me what brought you in today.
	CLIENT: I'm having a hard time trying to put my life in order. I'm very lonely and bored, and I can't seem to maintain a lasting relationship.
Attending/ Encouraging	COUNSELOR/THERAPIST: (*leaning forward*) Please tell me more.
	CLIENT: Every time I think I have a chance of developing a relationship, I screw it up by saying or doing something dumb.
Encouraging	COUNSELOR/THERAPIST: (*nodding*) This is helpful; please go on.

Restating and Paraphrasing   These strategies enable a counselor or therapist to serve as a sounding board for the client by feeding back thoughts and feelings that the client verbalizes. Restating involves repeating the exact words used by the client. Paraphrasing repeats the thoughts and feelings of the client, but the words are those of the counselor or therapist.

Example

	CLIENT: I don't know why I do these dumb things. It's almost as if I did not want a relationship.
Restating	COUNSELOR/THERAPIST: You don't know why you do dumb things. It may be that you don't want a relationship.
	CLIENT: I do want a relationship, but each time I get close I seem to do everything in my power to destroy it.
Paraphrasing	COUNSELOR/THERAPIST: You are very sure that you want a relationship, but each time you have the opportunity you sabotage your chances.

Reflecting Content and Reflecting Feeling   These strategies enable the counselor or therapist to provide feedback to the client regarding both the ideas (content) and the emotions (feelings) that the client is expressing. By reflecting content, the counselor or therapist shares his or her perceptions of the thoughts that the client is expressing. This can be done either by using the client's words or by changing the words to better reflect the counselor or therapist's perceptions. By reflecting feelings, a counselor or therapist goes beyond the ideas and thoughts expressed by the client and responds to the feelings or emotions behind those words.

Example

	CLIENT: *Sabotage* is a good word. It's like I see what I want, but instead of moving toward it, I take a different path that leads nowhere.
Reflecting Content	COUNSELOR/THERAPIST: You have a good idea of what you want, but when you see it developing, you turn and walk the other way.
	CLIENT: I am not sure *walk* is the right word. *Run* is more descriptive of what I do, and all the time I'm looking back to see if anyone is following.
Reflecting Feeling	COUNSELOR/THERAPIST: You're afraid of getting close to someone, so you put as much distance between the other person and yourself as possible. I also hear that you're hoping that someone cares enough about you to run after you and stop you from running away.

Clarifying and Perception Checking   These strategies enable a counselor or therapist either to ask the client to define or explain words, thoughts, or feelings (clarifying), or to request confirmation or correction of perceptions he or she has drawn regarding these words, thoughts, or feelings (perception checking).

Example

	CLIENT: If what you say is true, I'm a real jerk. What chance do I have to be happy if I run away every time I get close to someone else?
Clarifying	COUNSELOR/THERAPIST: You say you want to be happy. What does *happy* mean to you?
	CLIENT: (*long pause*) I would be happy if I could let someone care for me, get to know me, want to spend time with me, and allow me to just be me and stop pretending.
Perception Checking	COUNSELOR/THERAPIST: Let me see if I'm understanding you. Your view of happiness is having someone who cares enough about you to spend time with you and to allow you to be your self. Am I correct?

Summarizing   This strategy enables the counselor or therapist to do several things: (1) to verbally review various types of information that have been presented to this point in the session; (2) to highlight what the counselor or therapist sees as significant information based on everything that has been discussed; and (3) to provide the client with an opportunity to hear the various issues that he or she has presented. Therefore, summarizing provides both the client and the counselor or therapist with the opportunity not only to review and determine the significance of information presented but also to use this review to establish priorities.

Example

	CLIENT: Yes, I think that's what I'd like to have happen. That would make me happy. I would be in a relationship, feel cared about, and yet be able to be myself without having either to run or pretend.
Summarizing	COUNSELOR/THERAPIST: We've talked about many things today. I'd like to review some of this and make plans for our next meeting. The parts that stick out in my mind are your loneliness, boredom, and desire to have a lasting relationship, your behaviors that drive you away from building such a relationship, and your need for caring and the freedom to be yourself. Am I missing anything?
	CLIENT: Only that I want someone who wants to spend time with me. I think that's important.
Summarizing	COUNSELOR/THERAPIST: So now we have a more complete picture that includes loneliness, boredom, desire for a relationship, desire for someone to spend time with, desire for someone who cares, and the need to be yourself. On the other side of the picture, we have your behaviors that keep this from happening. Where do you think we should begin next week?

Strategies That Aid in Data Gathering

This group of strategies includes all of the active listening strategies plus three strategies designed to extract specific information and gain greater depth of information in areas that are significant in the client's statements. As with active listening strategies, a counselor or therapist who uses the following strategies enhances his or her chances of gaining significant information. This set of strategies includes **questioning, probing,** and **leading.** The following paragraphs present explanations and examples of these strategies.

Questioning   This strategy, when done in an open manner, enables the counselor or therapist to gain important information and allows the client to remain in control of the information presented. Using open questioning, the counselor or therapist designs questions that encourage the broadest client responses. Open questions, as opposed to closed questions, generally cannot be completely answered by either yes or no, nor can they be answered nonverbally by shaking of the head. This type of questioning places responsibility on clients and allows them a degree of control over what information will be shared.

Example

Open Questioning	CLIENT: I've thought a lot about what we talked about last week, and I feel I have to work on changing my behavior. COUNSELOR/THERAPIST: Would you tell me what you think needs to be done to change your behavior? CLIENT: (*short pause*) I need to stop screwing up my chances for a relationship. I need to face what it is that makes me run away.
Open Questioning	COUNSELOR/THERAPIST: Would you please talk more about the "it" that makes you run away? CLIENT: I can't tell you what it is. All I know is that I hear this voice saying, "Run! Run!"

Probing and Leading   These strategies enable a counselor or therapist to gather information in a specific area related to the client's presented concerns (probing), or to encourage the client to respond to specific topic areas (leading). Each of these enables the counselor or therapist to explore at greater depth areas that are seen as important to progress within the session.

Example

Probing	COUNSELOR/THERAPIST: I want you to be more specific about this "voice." Whose voice is it? What does it say to you? CLIENT: (*very long pause*) I guess it's my voice. It sounds like something I would do. I'm such a jerk.
Leading	COUNSELOR/THERAPIST: You told me whose voice it is, but you didn't tell me what the voice says. Would you talk about this? CLIENT: (*raising his voice*) It says, "Get out or you're going to get hurt. She doesn't like you and she'll use you and drop you just like the rest."

Strategies That Add Depth and Enhance the Relationship

This group of strategies is used to enhance and expand the communicative and relationship patterns that are established early in the counseling or therapeutic process. When used effectively, these strategies should open up deeper levels of communication and strengthen the relationship patterns that have already been established. Counselors or therapists using these strategies model types of behaviors that they wish their clients to emulate. Such behaviors include, but are not limited to, **risk taking, sharing of self, demonstrating trust,** and **honest interaction.** This set of strategies includes **self-disclosure, confrontation,** and **response to nonverbal behaviors.** The following paragraphs present explanations and examples of these strategies.

Self-Disclosure   This strategy has implications for both clients and counselors or therapists. In self-disclosing, the counselor or therapist shares with the client his or her feelings, thoughts, and experiences that are relevant to the situation presented by the client. The counselor or therapist draws upon situations from his or her own life experiences and selectively shares these personal reactions with the client. It is important to note that self-disclosure can have both a positive and negative impact on the helping relationship, and care must be taken in measuring the impact it may have. From a positive perspective, it carries with it the possibility of modeling self-disclosure for the client or helping the client gain a different perspective on the presenting problems. From a negative perspective, self-disclosure might place the focus on the counselor's or therapist's issues rather than on those of the client. When used appropriately, gains are made by all persons involved, and the relationship moves to deeper levels of understanding and sharing.

Example

Self-Disclosure	COUNSELOR/THERAPIST: (*aware of the client's agitation*) The anger I hear in your voice and words triggers anger in me as I think of my own lost relationships.
	CLIENT: (*smiling*) I am angry. I'm also glad you said that. Sometimes I feel like I'm the only one who ever felt this way.
Self-Disclosure	COUNSELOR/THERAPIST: (*smiling*) I am very pleased with what you just said. At this moment, I also do not feel alone with my anger.

Confrontation   This strategy enables the counselor or therapist to provide the client with feedback in which discrepancies are presented in an honest and matter-of-fact manner. A counselor or therapist uses this strategy to indicate his or her reaction to the client, to identify differences between the client's words and behaviors, and to challenge the client to put words and ideas into action. This type of direct and honest feedback should provide the client with insight as to how he or she is perceived, as well as indicate the degree of counselor or therapist caring.

Example

	CLIENT: (*smiling*) I feel angry at myself a great deal. I want so much to find a person and develop a relationship that lasts.
Confrontation	COUNSELOR/THERAPIST: You've said this several times in our sessions, but I'm not sure I believe you, based on what you do to keep it from happening. Make me believe you really want this to happen.
	CLIENT: What do you mean, you don't believe me? I just told you, didn't I? What more do you want?
Confrontation	COUNSELOR/THERAPIST: Yes, I've heard your words, but you haven't convinced me. I don't think you've convinced yourself, either. Say something that will convince both of us.

Responding to Nonverbal Cues   This strategy enables a counselor or therapist to go beyond a client's words and respond to the messages that are being communicated by the client's physical actions. Care must be taken not to overgeneralize regarding every subtle body movement. The counselor or therapist is looking for patterns that either confirm or deny the truth of the words the client uses to express himself or herself. When such patterns become apparent, it is the responsibility of the counselor or therapist to share these patterns with the client. It becomes the client's responsibility to confirm or deny the credibility of the perception.

Example

Nonverbal Responding

CLIENT: (*turning away*) Yes, you're right. I'm not convinced this is what I want. (*smiling*) Maybe I was never meant to be happy.

COUNSELOR/THERAPIST: What I said made you angry and, I would suspect, hurt a little. Did you notice you turned away before you began to speak? What were you telling me when you turned away?

CLIENT: (*smiling*) What you said did hurt me. I was angry, but I'm also embarrassed not to be able to handle this part of my life. I don't like your seeing me this way.

Nonverbal Responding

COUNSELOR/THERAPIST: I've noticed that on several occasions when you talk about your feelings such as anger, embarrassment, or hopelessness, you smile. What does the smile mean?

CLIENT: (*long pause*) I guess I want you to believe that it isn't as bad as it sounds, or that I'm not as hopeless as I think I am.

COUNSELOR/THERAPIST: It is bad, or you wouldn't be here, and *hopeless* is your word, not mine. Our time is up for today. Between now and next week, I want you to think about what we've discussed. See you next week?

The strategies we have outlined in this section enable a counselor or therapist to achieve more effectively both the process and outcome goals related to counseling or therapy. Choosing which strategy to use, when to use it, and its impact on the helping relationship is based upon the education, experience, and personal dynamics that a counselor or therapist brings to the helping relationship.

Issues of Cultural Diversity

A final factor that impacts the helping relationship is that of cultural diversity. Awareness of cultural diversity addresses the counselor's or therapist's openness and motivation to understand more about his or her own diversity as well as the cultural differences that clients bring to the helping relationship (Arciniega & Newlon, 1999; Mathews & Atkinson, 1997; Sue & Sue, 1999). Such understanding is often characterized as the cornerstone on which the helping relationship rests. This understanding, based upon both education and life experience, should enable counselors or therapists to increase their sensitivity to the issues that confront clients, should enable them to develop insight into the many variables that affect clients, and should enable them to place clients' issues, problems, and concerns in their proper perspective. The key word in these last three statements is *should*. Experience indicates that the key factor in the development of cultural awareness is the individual's receptiveness, openness, and motivation to gain such awareness. Without these characteristics, education and experience will have little value. The combination of these characteristics with both education and experience enhances the chances of changing the *should* to *will*.

According to Weinrach and Thomas (1998), the emphasis on issues of diversity goes by several names: *cross-cultural counseling, multicultural counseling, counseling for diversity,* and *diversity-sensitive counseling.* Included under these titles is not only racial diversity, but also diversity in areas such as age, culture, disability, education level, ethnicity, gender, language, physique, religion, residential location, sexual orientation, socioeconomic situation, trauma, and multiple and overlapping characteristics of all of these. It should be obvious that the portrait titled "Diversity" is painted with a very broad brush.

If one considers the "racial diversity" set forth in Chapter 17 of this text, "Counseling and Psychotherapy: Multicultural Considerations," and realizes that within each of these four racial groups exist areas of diversity such as age, disability, sexual orientation, gender, religion, and so forth, then one is able to grasp the true complexity that surrounds the subject of diversity. Patterson (1996) points out that "Because every client belongs to numerous groups, it does not take much imagination to recognize that the number of combinations and permutations of these groups is staggering. Attempting to develop different theories, methods and techniques for each of these groups would be an insurmountable task" (pp. 227-228).

This "insurmountability" could leave the counselor or therapist believing that there is very little he or she can do to individualize the helping process via theories, methods, and techniques to better meet the needs of such a diverse client population. However, it may not be the theories, methods, and techniques that need to be changed, but the counselor's or therapist's knowledge, attitudes, values, and behaviors as these relate to diversity. If counselors or therapists enter into helping relationships aware of the degree of diversity that exists within each client, have taken the time and effort to better understand the factors surrounding these diversities, have come to accept and appreciate their own diversity and the value they place on diversity in others, and are able to communicate understanding, acceptance, and appreciation of this diversity to clients, then perhaps the insurmountable becomes surmountable.

For example, counselors or therapists who work primarily with the elderly must become aware that this population (65 years and older) brings to counseling or therapy diversity in race, gender, culture, and language, and must also understand the diversity specific to this population's life stage: increased disability, increased health problems, increased trauma due to loss of significant others, lowered socioeconomic status due to retirement and living on a fixed income, and decreased self-importance stemming from living in and with a society that places a more positive emphasis on youth.

Awareness and understanding are the first steps. Counselors or therapists must also accept and appreciate their own diversity and the part it plays in their evaluation of others, as well as learn to accept and appreciate this diversity in others. As this relates to the elderly, counselors or therapists are not free from **ageism** (society's negative evaluation of the elderly) and its attitudes and values that impede both acceptance and appreciation. Confronting and changing these negative attitudes and values in self and being able to demonstrate to clients, through both words and behaviors, that such negative attitudes and values have no place in the helping relationship, provide counselors and therapists with the tools to accomplish the final step in this process, **communication** (McAuliffe et al., 2000).

How does one communicate understanding, acceptance, and appreciation in the helping relationship? A look back at the core conditions presented earlier in this chapter should be a good starting point. Empathic understanding, respect and positive regard, genuineness and congruence, concreteness, warmth, and immediacy all address ways of communicating understanding, acceptance, and appreciation and are foundational to the helping relationship. According to Patterson (1996), the nature of this relationship, as prescribed by the core conditions, has been known for a long time and has applicability across groups regardless of diversity. Therefore, a helping relationship based on the identified core conditions would be applicable not only to the elderly but also to clients presenting with other issues of diversity such as sexual orientation, disability, religion, and so forth. According to Weinrach and Thomas (1998), "The core conditions are nondiscriminatory. . ." (p. 117).

Patterson (1996, 2000) further contends that the counselor's or therapist's competence in providing this type of therapeutic relationship rests in the personal qualities he or she brings to the relationship. The development of these personal qualities and gaining the awareness, understanding, acceptance, appreciation, and competence to communicate these can only be achieved through education, life experiences, work experiences, self-evaluation, and the counselor's or therapist's willingness to be open to the learning inherent in these experiences.

According to McFadden (1996), counselors and therapists must strive to be "culturally competent." The culturally competent counselor or therapist "not only implies recognition of and respect for members of diverse populations but also fosters an outcome that enables clients to function effectively in their own culture and with the majority population while promoting biculturality" (p. 234).

Pedersen (1996) uses the term *culture-centered approach* to describe counseling or therapy that ". . .recognizes that the person herself or himself has internalized patterns of behavior that are themselves culturally learned. If the emphasis is placed—as it should be—on accuracy of assessment, appropriateness of understanding, and competence of practice, then the counselor will need sensitivity to the cultural context" (p. 237).

Cultural diversity addresses the counselor's or therapist's openness and motivation to gain awareness, understanding, acceptance, and appreciation of client diversity and to develop the skills necessary to communicate this to the client in the helping relationship. Personal characteristics or behaviors that enhance a counselor's or therapist's ability to become culturally aware include, but are not limited to, the following.

- The therapist has the need and the personal motivation to understand his or her own cultural diversity as well as that of others.
- The therapist seeks out education, work experiences, and life experiences that will afford him or her the opportunity to gain greater awareness of cultural diversity.

- The therapist is open to new ideas and differing frames of reference as they relate to cultural diversity.
- The therapist has the self-assurance needed to admit what he or she does not know about the diversity of clients and possesses the willingness to learn from clients.
- The therapist is aware of his or her own cultural stereotypes and biases and is open to changing them through education and experience.

Conclusions

The helping relationship is the foundation on which the process of counseling or psychotherapy rests. It is best viewed in terms of developmental stages, the first of which begins with the initial meeting of the client and the counselor or therapist, and is characterized by rapport building, information gathering, goal determination, and information sharing. Building on the foundation established in the first stage, later stages address extended exploration and problem resolution, then lead to the final stage in this process: termination and follow-up.

The helping relationship, when viewed from this developmental perspective, progresses from stage to stage because of the presence of certain components that the counselor or therapist brings to the relationship. The first of these are the core conditions of empathic understanding, respect and positive regard, genuineness and congruence, concreteness, warmth, and immediacy. These conditions are personality characteristics of a counselor or therapist that he or she is able to incorporate into the helping relationship.

The second component is a set of strategies aimed at building rapport and encouraging client dialogue, data gathering, and relationship enhancement. These conditions are skills and techniques that a counselor or therapist gains through education and experience and is able to use effectively within the helping relationship.

The third component centers on issues of cultural diversity and the counselor's or therapist's motivation and willingness to develop awareness, understanding, acceptance, and appreciation of client diversity. These factors, when communicated effectively, often are viewed as the cornerstone on which the helping relationship is based.

In combination, the developmental nature of the helping relationship, the presence of the core conditions, the implementation of the various strategies, and attention paid to issues of diversity create a facilitative environment in which both the client and the counselor or therapist have the strong potential for positive growth. The potential exists; guarantees do not. Achieving the true potential of the helping relationship depends upon what the client and counselor or therapist bring to the relationship and what each takes from it.

In closing, we return to George as he prepares for his group demonstration. He appears to be gaining the knowledge and skill that is necessary and demonstrates the desire to be effective in the counselor-client relationship. These qualities should aid him as he attempts to provide the core conditions. His education is providing him with both a theoretical foundation and some practice in the helping process. This background should aid him as he begins to apply the helping strategies. We are unable to evaluate George's comprehension of cultural diversity. It would be our hope that his educational program would provide him with formal instruction in this area as well as supervised experiences that would increase his desire to better understand this complex area. His classroom experiences should help reduce his anxiety and fear by enhancing his awareness of cultural diversity and the ability to apply the core conditions and strategies in a theoretical system of his choosing. His excitement should increase as he enters the complex and challenging arena of the helping relationship.

Achieving a Personal
and Professional Identity

David Capuzzi
Portland State University

Douglas R. Gross
Professor Emeritus
Arizona State University

How well do I really know myself, and how effective will I be with clients? Do I really understand my chosen profession and the stressors involved? These are just two of the questions we believe each of you should continually ask yourself as you progress through your graduate education and clinical supervision experience. Some careers can be pursued without a high level of self-awareness, but the profession of counseling or psychology is not one of them. Knowledge of theory and research and expertise in translating that knowledge into strategies and interventions can be delivered only through the being and personhood of the provider. Each member of the helping professions is given an enormous amount of responsibility every time client interactions occur. This responsibility can be upheld only if each counselor or therapist maintains a sense of health and wellness to ensure that the understanding and support, assessment, and treatment planning that a client receives are the best they can possibly be. The more a counselor or therapist has developed, integrated, and accepted an identity as a person and as a professional, the better that individual is at giving the incredible gift of helping another human being develop a unique sense of self.

Personal and professional identity must be addressed before and during the process of studying and applying individual approaches to counseling and psychotherapy. It is not easy, for example, for the beginning graduate student to be receptive to peer and supervisor feedback as it relates to individual work with clients. The student must have enough self-awareness and a great enough sense of well-being to be receptive to suggestions for changes that are needed to maximize therapeutic effectiveness. As we noted in Chapter 1, on-site observations of individual sessions and required videotaping and playback for supervisory purposes escalate the stress level of any graduate student. If students can develop high levels of self-acceptance and self-understanding, they will receive more benefit from the supervision process and have greater potential for developing clinical skills.

Many students are enrolled in graduate programs that require participation as a client in either individual or group counseling for the purpose of facilitating their continued personal growth. This requirement helps students avoid the confusion that arises when client issues are similar to unresolved personal issues. Such personal issues often surface during the practicum or internship experiences required of students. For this reason, many graduate programs expect enrollees to complete requirements for counseling or therapy (Meier & Davis, 2001) prior to initiating practicum and internship courses and placements. At times, supervisors may recommend that students seek additional counseling or therapy at the same time they are enrolled in their practicum or internship.

Because of the stresses and complexities of the helping professions, faculties in counseling and psychology departments are becoming more definitive and assertive about expectations for the wellness and functionality of potential counselors and therapists. Many educators and clinical supervisors are stressing the need for counselors and therapists to involve themselves in consultation and counseling or psychotherapy after graduation in order to maintain personal growth, wellness, and treatment-planning ability. Many experienced professionals stress the importance of involving significant others in ongoing couples or family counseling so that, as the counselor or therapist grows and changes, friends and family members can participate in and understand that process of change.

This chapter addresses the importance of health and wellness for the counselor or therapist, as well as the importance of recognizing values and cultural bias in theory and practice, becoming aware of the daily world of the practitioner, and achieving perspective and balance between personal and professional roles. It also includes some brief comments about developing a personal theory.

The Importance of Health and Wellness

The personal qualities, traits, and characteristics of the counselor or therapist have long been recognized as an extremely important component of the helping relationship (Brems, 2000; Carkhuff & Berenson, 1977; Egan, 1975; Evans, 1997; Rogers, 1961). As noted by Okun (1987), a continually increasing database supports the concept that counselors and therapists are effective only if they are self-aware and able to use themselves as the instruments through which change occurs. One way of conceptualizing this role in the relationship is to compare the contribution the counselor or therapist makes to a client's growth and maturation to that of a painter working on a canvas, an architect designing a building, or a sculptor chiseling a statue. The client presents possibilities and options, which are much like the raw materials of canvas and paint, building site and construction materials, or chisels and stone. The artist approaches the task with a database of information and the expertise to translate a concept or mental image into something beautiful or functional. Whether the database and expertise of the artist can be fully accessed most often depends on the mental, emotional, physical, and spiritual sensitivities with which the artist approaches the work. Creativity can be compromised or never actualized if the being of the creator is impaired, tired, or dysfunctional because everything the artist has to contribute is conveyed through the person of the artist.

The counselor or therapist is the conveyer of possibilities and potentials to the client. If the being or personhood of the counselor or therapist is impaired at the time of an encounter with a client, it may be difficult to see the client's potential and use those possibilities for engaging in a mutually rewarding relationship to achieve desirable outcomes. The health and wellness of the counselor or therapist have much to do with the art form inherent in the helping relationship.

Approaches to Health and Wellness

There are a number of approaches to health and wellness that are described, researched, and prescribed by those wishing to sensitize counselors and therapists to the importance of self-care as a prerequisite to caregiving. We have identified three commonly discussed models for presentation: the **personal characteristics model,** the **psychological health model,** and the **multidimensional health and wellness model.** Each model provides counselors and therapists with concepts that are helpful and applicable to the maintenance of their own sense of well-being and the ability to cope successfully with both personal and professional responsibilities.

The Personal Characteristics Model   Person-centered counseling theory offers a well-researched analysis of how counselors and therapists might work with clients. The person-centered school identifies accurate **empathy,** nonpossessive **warmth, positive regard,** and **genuineness** as the "necessary and sufficient conditions" for therapeutic change (Rogers, 1957; Truax & Carkhuff, 1967). *Empathy*—often defined as the capacity to view and understand the world through another person's frame of reference (Egan, 1975)—is one of the most extensively studied personal characteristics or variables in process-outcome research. Most reviews of studies that analyze the relationships between empathy and outcome show positive relationships in one-half to two-thirds of the research under scrutiny (Orlinsky & Howard, 1978, 1986). *Genuineness*—defined as consistency in values, attitudes, and behaviors on the part of the counselor or therapist—is also the focus of therapeutic process research and is generally related positively to therapeutic outcomes (Orlinsky & Howard, 1986).

Counselor or therapist **affirmation**—the ability to communicate positive regard, warmth, and acceptance to the client—is also significantly associated with positive therapeutic outcomes (Orlinsky & Howard, 1978). In addition, Carkhuff and his associates have stressed the importance of concreteness or specificity of expression (Carkhuff & Berenson, 1977). As we noted in Chapter 1, concreteness means that the practitioner's response serves to clarify the meaning the client is communicating so that the client's self-understanding is actually enhanced.

The personal characteristics model for addressing the health and wellness of the counselor or therapist has been discussed from perspectives other than that of Carl Rogers. A number of writers and researchers focus on the importance of the personal characteristics of the counselor or therapist on the outcome of counseling or psychotherapy (Goldfried, Greenberg, & Maramar, 1990; Hanna & Bemak, 1997; Hanna & Ottens, 1995; Seligman, 2001; Whiston & Sexton, 1993). Combs and his colleagues (1969) conducted a series of studies resulting in the conclusion that the personal beliefs and traits of the counselor or therapist differentiated between effective and ineffective helping. Effective helpers seem to perceive others as able, rather than unable, to solve their own problems and manage their own lives. Effective helpers also perceive others as dependable, friendly, worthy, able to cope, and able to be communicative and self-disclosing. In general, effective helpers maintain a positive view of human nature and approach family, friends, colleagues, and clients in a trusting, affirming way. A **composite model of human effectiveness** was suggested by George and Cristiani (1990) as a means of analyzing the personal characteristics of effective helpers. The elements of this composite model included openness to and acceptance of experiencing, awareness of values and beliefs, ability to develop warm and deep relationships with others, willingness to be seen by others as one actually is, willingness to accept personal responsibility for one's own behaviors, and development of realistic levels of aspiration. Meier and Davis (2001) suggest that helpers who are the most effective strive to apply the four following principles to assess characteristics and traits that impact their own ability to assist others and may reflect their own level of health and wellness: (1) become aware of your personal issues, (2) be open to supervision, (3) avoid hiding behind the use of too many tests, and (4) consult when presented with an ethical dilemma.

The literature related to the personal characteristics model that is available to counselors or therapists is voluminous (Schmidt, 2002; Seligman, 2001). Characteristics such as assertiveness, flexibility, tolerance of ambiguity, honesty, emotional presence, goal-directedness, and self-respect have all been addressed to the point that the beginning counselor or therapist may find the suggested profile somewhat overwhelming and threatening. The important thing to remember is that it is not possible to achieve the perfection that such idealized models suggest. All of us have flaws and imperfections that can obstruct our ability as helpers, just as all of us have unique strengths and capabilities that enable us to influence others positively. We believe that effective counselors and therapists are able to maintain a sense of personal well-being and happiness despite flaws or inadequacies, and we stress the importance of a perspective that ensures that personal issues do not diminish the capacity to engender personal growth on the part of clients.

The Psychological Health Model   The following provocative scenario (Kinnier, 1997) can be used to introduce some of the dilemmas inherent in suggesting criteria for psychological health.

Imagine a psychological health contest between the John Wayne persona of the 1950s silver screen and the Leo Buscaglia persona of the 1990s lecture circuit. Which "persona" would win? Among John Wayne's celluloid traits were his stoicism and his readiness to fight. He rarely displayed any weaknesses or "shared his feelings" with anyone. In contrast, Leo Buscaglia's most salient public traits have been his readiness to cry and "share his feelings" with everyone. Is "strong and silent" healthier than "vulnerable and expressive"? For males? For females? Does the answer depend entirely upon the biases of the judges and the context of a specific time and place (p. 48)?

To cope with dilemmas such as the one posed by Kinnier, the majority of mental health practitioners have focused upon identifying symptoms of psychopathology instead of criteria for mental health. It has been easier to identify undesirable behaviors and emotions than it has been to identify and agree upon behavior and emotions indicative of mental health. Cross-cultural differences have further complicated attempts to delineate the traits of a psychologically healthy client. It is difficult to establish acceptable criteria for psychological health because such criteria are intricately woven into a particular cultural and temporal background. Nevertheless, a number of theoreticians and practitioners have emphasized psychological health models as approaches to promoting the health and wellness of clients.

More than four decades ago, Jahoda (1958) proposed six criteria for mental health: a positive attitude toward self, continual movement toward self-actualization, purpose or meaning in life, the ability to function independently and autonomously, an accurate perception of reality, and mastery of the environment. Basic self-esteem was viewed as essential by luminaries such as Allport (1961), Erikson (1968), Jung (1954), Maslow (1970), Rogers (1961), and Sullivan (1953). Personal autonomy and competence were emphasized by Fromm (1955), Horney (1950), Maslow (1970), and Rogers (1961). The capacity to give and receive love as a criterion for psychological health has also been endorsed by Adler (1978), Allport (1961), Erikson (1968), Freud (1930), Fromm (1955), Maslow (1970), and Sullivan (1953). More recent discussions of a variety of criteria for the psychological health of the practicing counselor or therapist can be found in Brems (2000), Campbell (2000), Schmidt (2002), and Skovholt (2001).

Following a survey of psychological literature to determine what criteria for psychological health had been identified by theoreticians and researchers, Kinnier (1997) proposed nine criteria for psychological health. We believe these criteria apply to counselors and therapists as well as to their clients.

1. *Self-acceptance.* Self-esteem seems to be a prerequisite for developing other important components of psychological health. Psychologically healthy individuals experience strong feelings of self-acceptance and self-love. Individuals who love and respect themselves have the capacity to love and respect others and possess the foundation for becoming self-actualized.

2. *Self-knowledge.* The importance of self-exploration and self-knowledge cannot be overemphasized. Psychologically healthy individuals know themselves well and stay aware of their feelings, motivations, and needs. They are introspective and committed to understanding themselves.

3. *Self-confidence and self-control.* Individuals who are psychologically healthy have confidence in themselves and can function independently of others. They have appropriate skills for assertive behavior, but do not unnecessarily impose their views or will on others. Such individuals have an internal locus of control, believe that they can exert reasonable control over their lives, and feel capable of achieving their goals.

4. *A clear (though slightly optimistic) perception of reality.* Perceptions of the people, events, and objects around us are always subjective, but there is usually enough societal consensus about the nature of reality to provide beneficial comparisons with our own point of view. Psychologically healthy individuals have a clear perception of reality and an optimistic view of life. They view themselves, their present circumstances, and their futures accurately and positively, which enhances possibilities and potentials.

5. *Courage and resilience.* Danger and risk surround the daily lives and decision-making opportunities of most individuals; therefore, failures, crises, and setbacks are inevitable. Psychologically healthy individuals are aware of this reality, adapt well to challenges and changed circumstances, and can bounce back from disappointments and

setbacks. As Kinnier notes, "Psychologically healthy individuals bravely confront their fears and accept their responsibility. They are prepared to take risks when appropriate. They accept setbacks and failures as part of life, and as the popular song says, after a fall they 'pick themselves up, dust themselves off, and start all over again'" (1997, p. 55).

6. *Balance and moderation.* The theme of balance and moderation is one that recurs in psychological literature. Psychologically healthy individuals work and play, laugh and cry, enjoy planned and spontaneous time with family and friends, and are not afraid to be both logical and intuitive. They are rarely extremists or fanatics, and usually they do not do anything in excess.

7. *Love of others.* The capacity to care deeply about the welfare of another person or the condition of humanity in general is another characteristic of the psychologically healthy person. Mental health professionals from a number of theoretical orientations believe that the ability to give and receive love, the desire to develop close ties to another person or persons, and the need to belong to another person, family, or group are fundamental to mental health. Psychologically healthy individuals are not reticent about loving and caring for others. They need to experience close interpersonal relationships and are intimate with at least one other person.

8. *Love of life.* The psychological benefits of humor, spontaneity, and openness have been touted by numerous professionals. People who are active, curious, spontaneous, venturesome, and relaxed have traits that promote their capacity to partake of and enjoy life. Psychologically healthy people embrace the opportunities that life presents, do not take themselves too seriously, and look forward to the unexpected with the vitality to cope, solve problems, and move on to the future with a positive perspective.

9. *Purpose in life.* Individuals vary in their choice of the most meaningful aspects of life. Work, love, family, intellectual or physical accomplishment, or spirituality may become the primary focus for one individual or another. While variation among individuals is bound to exist, the important achievement for each person is to develop a purpose—an investment—that creates a sense of meaning and satisfaction. The joy and sense of exhilaration and accomplishment that result from finding meaning and purpose in life are prime factors in the maintenance of psychological health.

The Multidimensional Health and Wellness Model   As noted by Myers (1991), several different wellness models have been proposed for use by counselors and therapists. One of the most common models defines wellness holistically by considering it from spiritual, mental, and physical aspects of functionality. Other models describe dimensions such as spirituality, physical fitness, job satisfaction, relationships, family life, nutrition, leisure time, and stress management (Ardell, 1988; Brems, 2000). Quite often, physical wellness is given more attention than other dimensions of wellness because physical illness cannot be as easily ignored (Evans, 1997). Most systemic models of wellness, however, suggest that all the identified dimensions of wellness interact and that they must all be evaluated in the process of assessing a person's state of wellness (Skovholt, 2001). In 1984, Hettler proposed six dimensions of wellness—intellectual, emotional, physical, social, occupational, and spiritual—as components of a lifelong paradigm to promote health and wellness. Health has been defined as the absence of illness; wellness goes far beyond the absence of illness and incorporates a zest and enthusiasm for life that results when the dimensions of wellness (intellectual, emotional, physical, social, occupational, spiritual) have been addressed, developed, and integrated. "With a holistic focus, wellness incorporates not just the whole person, but the whole person throughout the totality of the life span" (Myers, 1991, p. 185). A person can be "well" even when undergoing treatment for physical illness because the physical dimension is just one dimension of the wellness model. One of the best recent discussions of holistic models was published in the *Journal of Counseling and Development* (Myers, Sweeney, & Witmer, 2000). This discussion extends and modifies the original model presented by Sweeney and Witmer in 1991 and Witmer and Sweeney in 1992. This discussion describes the revisions of the original model, reviews research that supports each component of the revised model, and describes the use of the Wheel of Wellness as a basis for working holistically with clients. The five major life tasks discussed in conjunction with the revised model are (1) spirituality, (2) self-direction, (3) work and leisure, (4) friendship, and (5) love.

The importance of this brief discussion of the multidimensional health and wellness model should be understood by all those undertaking the study of theories of counseling and psychotherapy. The counselor's or therapist's role in facilitating the wellness of clients creates a natural link between counseling and psychotherapy and wellness; however, the emphasis in the link is on counselors or therapists helping clients. Little emphasis has been placed on the importance of counselors or therapists helping themselves, and even less attention is given to counselors' or therapists' wellness behaviors (Evans, 1997). In addition to the fact that counselors or therapists need to address wellness with respect to both their clients and themselves, it is important that counselors and therapists assess what the various theories of counseling and psychotherapy offer with respect to the dimensions of health and wellness. Some of the theories and approaches included in Part II of this book do not encourage the counselor or therapist to approach clients from a multidimensional health and wellness perspective, nor do they encourage the practitioner to engage in personal care from a holistic frame of reference. One of the tasks of a beginning counselor or therapist is to think about developing a theory or approach to the helping relationship. This may entail the adoption of one of the theories presented in this textbook, the development of an integrated model, or the conceptualization of a personalized theory or approach based on the study of theory and research as well as experience with clients. We encourage you to consider a number of perspectives before conceptualizing a personal theory of counseling and psychotherapy, for no single theory provides a perspective that could be described as multidimensional.

Values and Cultural Bias in Theory and Practice

As you read the theory chapters in Part II of this book, you should think about the way the values and cultural biases of the chief proponents of each theory may have influenced the development of the theory. In addition, you should assess personal values and understandings of cultural differences. In this section of the chapter, we introduce you to a discussion of values and cultural bias in theory and practice. After presenting Chapters 3 through 16, we reintroduce the topic of cultural differences and further refine the subject in Chapter 17.

Values in Theory and Practice

Everyone has a set of beliefs that guides decisions, determines one's ability to appreciate the people and things in the environment, governs conscience, and influences perceptions of others (Belkin, 1984; Pederson, 2000; Schmidt, 2002). Because the **values** of a counselor or therapist are an integral part of what is brought to a relationship with a client, we think it is important to consider the role values play in theory and practice and in achieving a personal and professional identity.

One of the key issues to consider is whether, during the process of counseling or psychotherapy, counselors or therapists can avoid conveying their values to their clients (Corey, 2001; George & Cristiani, 1990). Some (especially professionals associated with the orthodox **psychoanalytic** point of view) maintain that a counselor or therapist must remain neutral with clients and avoid communicating value orientations. In such circumstances, a counselor or therapist would strive to appear nonmoralizing, ethically neutral, and focused on the client's values. If topics such as pro-choice versus pro-life, religion, euthanasia, or gay, lesbian, and bisexual orientation were to arise during the counseling or psychotherapy process, the counselor or therapist would not take a position. The reason for such neutrality is the belief that it is important for clients to move from an external to an internal locus of control during the counseling or psychotherapy process. Values introduced by the counselor or therapist would be detrimental to such an objective.

As early as 1958, however, Williamson voiced an opposing position and promoted the idea that counselors and therapists cannot avoid letting clients know about their values and should be open and explicit about the nature of those values. Williamson reasoned that counselor or therapist neutrality may be interpreted by clients to mean that the professional is supporting client behavior that is not acceptable by social, moral, or legal standards. Samler (1960) went further and encouraged counselors and therapists to develop an awareness of their own values and how these values relate to and influence the development of client values. He further believed that assisting clients to change their values is a legitimate goal and a necessary component of the helping relationship. As early as 1958 and as recently as 1989, Patterson pointed out that the values of the counselor or therapist influence the ethics of the helping relationship and the goals, techniques, and interventions employed in the context of helping. Eugene Kelly's (1995) study focused upon the value orientations of counselors in the domains of universal values, mental health values, individualism-collectivism values, and religious-spiritual values to identify values that characterize counselors or therapists and may represent values taught to clients during the counseling or psychotherapy process.

We believe it is imperative for counselors and therapists to be aware of their own values and to consider the influence that these values have upon clients. The following questions may prove useful to the helper in the process of examining values issues.

- Am I completely cognizant of my own values?
- Do my values influence my preference for particular theoretical frameworks (such as rational-emotive behavior theory or Jungian concepts) and associated techniques and interventions?
- How will I resolve dilemmas that arise when my values and those of my client are opposed?

- What is my belief about whether a counselor or therapist can remain neutral and avoid communicating value orientations to clients?
- What is my role in helping clients delineate their values more clearly?

Cultural Bias in Theory and Practice

In 1962, C. Gilbert Wrenn was one of the first to suggest that practitioners were providing counseling and psychotherapy from a narrow cultural perspective. He encouraged counselors and therapists to broaden their **monocultural** perspectives and be more responsive to clients from different cultural backgrounds. By the mid-1970s, more emphasis on the issue of **cultural bias** in theory and practice began to appear in the literature. For example, Sue (1997), Katz (1985), and Pedersen (1987) pointed out that traditional counseling or psychotherapy is based exclusively on white culture and fails to meet the needs of culturally diverse client populations. Today, it is widely acknowledged that current theories are derivatives of Western culture and are not universally applicable to cross-cultural counseling and psychotherapy situations (Corey, 2001; McFadden, 1988; Richardson & Molinaro, 1996; Schmidt, 2002; Vontress, 1988).

Because the United States is becoming increasingly diversified, recognition of the cultural bias that exists in theories and techniques of counseling and psychotherapy becomes even more important in the process of achieving a personal and professional identity. Christopher (1996) addresses diversity issues through the concept of **moral visions.** He notes that moral visions are constellations of cultural values and assumptions that shape our experience of life and the stances we take toward life. He points out that different cultures provide different moral visions. The ideal person in traditional Confucian China was first and foremost characterized by filial loyalty and being a dutiful son or daughter. In contrast, in the American culture, attributes such as authenticity and autonomy are reinforced. Moral visions both prescribe and describe what a person should be or become, and they influence the development of theories of counseling and psychotherapy. Most Western counseling or psychotherapy theories are moral visions that presuppose the importance of individualism. For example, **behaviorist, cognitive-behavioral,** and **reality** theories emphasize utilitarian individualism. They stress rationality, control over emotions, enhanced human liberty, the importance of achieving self-defined goals, and opposition to irrational authority. **Humanistic** theories, such as **person-centered** and **Gestalt** theories, promote the importance of turning inward, of making contact with inner experiencing, and of identifying and expressing feelings. Such emphases may not be congruent with the moral visions of clients from other cultures.

Usher (1989) provided some helpful guidelines for assessing the cultural bias inherent in theories of counseling and psychotherapy. We include those guidelines here to extend the discussion of cultural awareness and diversity that we began in Chapter 1, and to alert the reader to some of the pitfalls associated with attempts to apply Western frames of reference to all clients irrespective of their cultural identity and experience. We do not intend to discourage counselors and therapists from making appropriate use of current theory; rather, we want to sensitize practitioners to the importance of cultural differences as determiners of approach selection and the development of a personal theory of counseling and psychotherapy.

Assumptions About Normal Behavior   A very real source of cultural bias is the assumption that *normal* means the same thing to members of various social, political, economic, and cultural backgrounds. Although some clients may believe that being reasonably assertive or responsibly individualistic is a normal goal, such traits may be considered inappropriate in other cultures. Pedersen (1987) argued that "what is considered normal behavior will change according to the situation, the cultural background of a person or persons being judged, and the time during which a behavior is being displayed or observed" (p. 16). He pointed out the danger of diagnostic errors when using definitions of normalcy grounded in the perspective of the culture in which a particular theory or conceptual frame of reference was developed.

Emphasis on Individualism   A number of theories (e.g., person-centered and **rational-emotive behavior theory**) emphasize the welfare and centrality of the individual and deemphasize the importance of obligation and duty to family, organizations, and society. Because such themes are central to some cultures' value systems, it would be a mistake for the counselor or therapist to promote individualism on the part of a client for whom such a focus would be contrary to cultural or ethnic identity. For example, an Asian-American client might not return to a counselor or therapist who did not respect what the client communicated about deference to the wishes of parents or other older members of the extended family.

Fragmentation by Academic Disciplines   Many theories of counseling and psychotherapy have been developed without considering the potential contributions of other academic disciplines such as sociology, anthropology, theology, and medicine. A counselor or therapist who uses a theory that has been developed from a narrow perspective may be handicapped in attempts to facilitate the helping relationship with a client who is culturally different. It is important for all counselors and therapists to take courses or participate in training experiences offered by other disciplines or by those who maintain a different cultural perspective.

Dependence on Abstract Words   Counselors and therapists with a Western frame of reference live in a low-context (i.e., less emphasis on how the meaning of a statement is affected by the context) culture, and they may depend on abstract words associated with theory and practice and assume that these abstractions will be understood by others—including clients—in the same way they are understood by the professional. Such abstractions may have little meaning, or take on different meanings, when used outside the cultural context in which they were initially developed. For example, would all clients understand the concepts of self-actualization or fictional finalism? Many clients are not receptive to abstractions or conceptualizations that, in a culture not based on Western values, worldviews, or protocols, may seem removed from the reality of life.

Overemphasis on Independence   Usher (1989) cited Pedersen (1987), who criticized theories and practices that devalue necessary dependencies inculcated by certain cultures. Because most counselors and therapists in this country view the independence of the client as desirable and neglect the function of healthy dependencies in some cultures, many of the theories used by counselors and therapists do a disservice to clients who have grown up and continue to function in a different cultural context. There are many cultural groups that value a person's capacity to subjugate individual desire to the overall welfare of the family, community, or organization. It is important for counselors and therapists to be both sensitive to and respectful of such a perspective.

Neglect of Client Support Systems   Many theoretical orientations do not recognize the role that family and peers play in providing support for a troubled client to the same extent that they recognize the role of the professionally prepared counselor or therapist. (Neither do the proponents of many approaches to counseling and psychotherapy.) It may be necessary for counselors and therapists to incorporate the client's natural support system into a treatment plan. In some cultures, talking with family members or friends may be more acceptable than talking with a trained professional who is usually a total stranger.

Dependence on Linear Thinking   Most theories make the assumption that clients relate to linear thinking. Linear thinking emphasizes cause-and-effect relationships, whereas the nonlinear or circular thinking characteristic of some cultures does not separate cause and effect, does not follow a singular stream of thought, and invites free association. It is important for counselors and therapists to realize that for some clients, conversation about topics seemingly unrelated to counseling or psychotherapy may be an essential element of a productive helping relationship.

Focus on Changing the Individual Rather than the System   Quite often, counselors and therapists who use Western theory as the sole basis for practice assume that their role is to make the client more congruent with the system. Such a role can be quite problematic when Western culture-bound paradigms, such as the DSM, are used to assess the behavior of clients who are culturally different (Lewis-Fernandez & Kleinman, 1995). If counselors or therapists do not question whether the "system" is in the best interests of a culturally different client, are they simply serving as agents of the status quo?

Neglect of History   Some counselors and therapists minimize the relevance of a client's personal and cultural history, focusing more intensively on present behavior, the current problem, and immediate events. Clients from some cultures, such as Native American cultures, see themselves as closely connected to their ancestors. Their current problems cannot be fully understood without consideration of their history. Such clients might not return to a counselor or therapist who did not provide opportunities to explore the present in terms of past experience as well as present needs.

Cultural Encapsulation   It is important for counselors and therapists to guard against the possibility of becoming **culturally encapsulated** by the mainstream group with which they are associated. When such encapsulation occurs, assumptions and beliefs may not be questioned, and clients from diverse cultural backgrounds may not be treated effectively because of the operation of certain biases on the part of the professional. The more counselors and therapists can experience and learn about other cultural groups, the less likely they will be to approach clients with biases that prevent effective helping. Both the American Counseling Association and the American Psychological Association have endorsed the importance for all counselors and therapists to develop multicultural awareness, knowledge, and skills so they can be more effective and avoid making wrong or culturally inappropriate assumptions about working with clients. We encourage the readers of our text to begin reading in this area (Abreu, Gim Chung, & Atkinson, 2000; Ariel, 1999; Locke, Myers, & Herr, 2001; Pederson, 2000) and to evaluate the theories described and discussed in Part II of this text in the context of working with clients whose history and experience are different from that of the reader.

The Daily World of the Practitioner

There is no doubt that there is a complex relationship between elements of the therapeutic process and the demands experienced by the counselor or therapist on a daily basis (Moursund & Kenny, 2002). The clients with whom one works, the setting, the expectations of colleagues and supervisors, one's personal life, and significant others are constantly interacting and, at times, reciprocally influencing outcomes. We believe that an important part of developing a personal and professional identity is becoming as aware as possible of the daily world of the practitioner and the stresses that sometimes impede the counselor's or therapist's well-being and the services provided to clients.

The demands inherent in just about any work environment (school, college, university, mental health center, hospital, private practice, rehabilitation clinic, etc.) are tremendous. Concerns about having enough clients, students, supervisees, research funds, publications, involvements in professional and community organizations, collected fees, malpractice, and liability insurance are just a few examples of the kinds of demands that converge on counselors and therapists. As Freudenberger (1983) notes, the very nature of the therapeutic personality often makes it difficult to say no, and many people engaged in counseling and psychotherapy find themselves overextended, tired, and overly involved with work. For some professionals, the drive to develop a reputation for excellence, coupled with the need for success, must be monitored carefully to avoid chronic discontent and eventual **burnout** (Skovholt, 2001).

The demands that clients place upon counselors and therapists are a significant factor in a practitioner's daily world. In the span of just a few days, many counselors and therapists find themselves confronted with the problems of the chronically mentally ill, the terminally ill, the physically or sexually abused, the suicidal, the eating disordered, the substance abuser, and clients with a host of other concerns and issues. Most research to date (e.g., Finch & Krantz, 1991; Hellman & Morrison, 1987; Pines & Maslach, 1978) indicates that counselors and therapists in settings that serve large numbers of seriously disturbed clients experience higher rates of personal depletion, less career satisfaction, and more impaired working relationships with colleagues. This information is quite pertinent for those planning to place themselves in settings in which there is a high probability of working with challenging clients.

The ominous shadow of malpractice hovers all too often over the daily world of the practitioner. Rates for liability insurance have risen as clients have become more litigious and counselors and therapists have become fair game. Because many clients enter the counseling or psychotherapy process with expectations about becoming better, perhaps in an unrealistically short period of time, counselors and therapists are vulnerable to having client disappointments or frustrations worked out in court rather than in a therapeutic environment. More and more lawyers have chosen to specialize in personal injury and malpractice cases and actively seek clients who are discontented with the results of counseling and psychotherapy (Kaslow & Schulman, 1987). Even when the counselor or therapist is innocent, the insurance carrier or one's own legal counsel may suggest an out-of-court settlement in order to avoid the trauma of a trial, the possibility of a guilty verdict, the accompanying censure by professional organizations, and the possibility of losing required state licensing. To the beginning—and even to the experienced— counselor or therapist, such a settlement can seem like an admission of guilt, yet preparing for and going through a trial can pose an even greater ordeal and create a high level of stress. In addition, such trials may attract a great deal of unwelcome media attention. Because counselors and therapists believe in the sanctity and privacy of the therapeutic encounter, such public exposure can be a bitter experience, with negative impacts on personal well-being as well as on the lives of family members.

More than any other professional, the counselor or therapist must continually deal with the reality of terminations. Whether the treatment process has been successful or not, the ending of a helping relationship may be experienced as another separation and, quite often, as a permanent loss. Despite the fact that counselors and therapists are prepared during their educational and supervisory experiences for the inevitability of terminating with clients, endings may be difficult and force the counselor or therapist to deal with unresolved personal losses (departure of adult children, death of significant others, divorce).

Terminations can also become transformations when clients appear in different roles in the life of the counselor or therapist. Examples of these roles include former clients who may later reenter as trained mental health professionals or, as is often the case in small communities, become part of the social milieu of the counselor or therapist. The reality of termination or transformation can be a source of satisfaction or stress depending upon how the counselor or therapist views the nature of the posttreatment void or the posttreatment relationship.

In many ways, the daily world of the counselor or therapist may threaten relationships outside the workplace. For example, in the process of striving to improve working relationships with co-therapists, colleagues, and supervisors, counselors or therapists may share much of their inner selves and, in so doing, develop satisfying relationships built on trust, respect, and mutual understanding. These relationships may supplant or replace other significant relationships outside the workplace. As a result, a marriage or long-term relationship may begin to seem less interesting and rewarding unless some steps are taken to prevent this from happening.

In addition to the impact that relationships with colleagues may have on the personal life of a counselor or therapist, the expression of admiration by clients, trainees, and colleagues may also result in some unexpected fallout. Significant others outside the workplace may begin to resent the attention that the counselor or therapist receives from clients and colleagues, or the counselor or therapist may begin to expect the same level of admiration from significant others. In either situation, resentment, frustration, and anger may result. Again, counselors and therapists need to take steps to prevent this from occurring.

Finally, the basic principle of confidentiality may create problems for the counselor or therapist in relationships outside the workplace. Counselors and therapists cannot talk about their clients except in the context of receiving supervision or consultation or in situations when the best interests of the client or society are at stake. Significant others may feel shut out, especially when they know that others have access to information unavailable to them.

Achieving Perspective and Balance

Our previous discussion of the daily world of the counselor or therapist is necessarily limited in scope, yet we believe the discussion does convey the fact that counselors and therapists deal with demands and stresses that can place them at risk for burnout (Schulz, Greenley, & Brown, 1995; Skovholt, 2001) and personal depletion. Because it is important to maintain a high level of personal health and wellness, we think the following guidelines may prove useful to individuals in training as well as to other members of the profession.

Know the Warning Signs for Burnout

How do graduate students or practicing counselors or therapists know they are heading for difficulty when striving to develop and maintain a high level of professional competence? Kaslow (1986) lists some of the signs of burnout.

- not wanting to go to work
- constantly complaining about disliking one's practice or feeling overwhelmed by it
- experiencing a sense of foreboding or imminent doom
- viewing life as dull, heavy, and tedious
- experiencing an increasing number of negative countertransference reactions to patients or students
- being extremely irritable, withdrawn, depressed, or intolerant at home
- suffering frequent illnesses of inexplicable origin
- wanting to run away from it all or having periodic suicidal ideation

Kaslow (1986) notes that when two or more of these indicators appear periodically and with gradually increasing frequency, intensity, and duration, a counselor or therapist has entered a warning zone and should seek personal counseling and psychotherapy, take a vacation, cut back on obligations, and so on until he or she re-experiences perspective and balance. There are a variety of additional sources that beginning counselors or therapists should read that either describe or discuss the topic of burnout (Corey, 2001; Moursund & Kenny, 2002; Skovholt, 2001). One of the most interesting and thought-provoking treatments of the topic appears in Christiane Brems' text, *Dealing with Challenges in Psychotherapy and Counseling* (2000).

Consider Networking Options

It is not always necessary to enter a counseling or psychotherapy relationship to achieve balance and perspective. Counselors and therapists have a number of beneficial protections that they can use to renew and revitalize their ability to function in a positive way. They can establish a network of professional contacts to provide different options for support and continued professional development. For example, working with a cotherapist, asking a colleague to view a client session through a one-way mirror and then offer feedback, or seeking clarification and assistance from a supervisor can provide invaluable support and ideas for treatment options when working with a difficult client.

Any one of these networking options can help a counselor or therapist to share the burden of providing counseling or psychotherapy or to break through an impasse in a client/practitioner relationship (Kaslow & Schulman, 1987).

Most communities provide opportunities for professionals to join a support group to share personal or professional concerns. Often there are local opportunities to attend workshops and training sessions to enhance expertise or develop new skills. Such workshops also allow practitioners to meet and talk with other counselors and therapists who share similar interests. It is always important to participate in some combination of local, state, regional, or national professional organizations such as the American Counseling Association, the American Psychological Association, or the American Association of Marriage and Family Therapists. Professional organizations provide a myriad of opportunities for continued learning and networking with other members of the helping professions (Brems, 2000; Skovholt, 2001). An excellent source for graduate students is involvement with a local chapter of Chi Sigma Iota, an international honor society for students, alumni, and supporters of counselor education programs and departments.

Refer Clients When Appropriate

Another way to maintain perspective and balance is to be amenable to the possibility of referring clients who are difficult or chronic or whose issues fall outside your ability to provide adequate care. A referral can be done in a positive way from the vantage point of a client, and colleagues will view it as a sign of professional integrity and wisdom. Sometimes, when a client is struggling with issues too close to those of the counselor or therapist, referral of the client is preferable to undertaking or prolonging work in which one becomes overly involved.

Disengage from the Professional Role

The experienced counselor or therapist knows how to disengage from the role of being a professional so that time with friends and family members, social engagements, vacations, and avocational interests can be enjoyed. Disengaging provides opportunities for rest, relaxation, and rejuvenation while relieving the practitioner from obligations. It is important for counselors and therapists to experience nurturing interpersonal relationships, just as it is important for clients to spend time with significant others. At times, counselors and therapists can become so enmeshed in the demands of the profession that it becomes difficult to enjoy opportunities for fun and relaxation.

Consider Possible Options for Renewal

We began our careers in the 1960s as members of the profession of counseling and human development. At that time, the daily world of the practitioner was quite different from the way it is today. Standards for credentialing, education, and supervision, although reasonably demanding, were not as specific, time-consuming, and exacting as they are currently. As the profession has matured, the expectations for graduate work, **credentialing,** practice, and **continuing education** have become decidedly more demanding and stress-producing. Because of these demands, many professionals develop a pattern of overload that can be traced back to graduate education and, quite often, to some inherent needs and predispositions that make overload seem acceptable as a way of life.

We do not believe that it is possible to continue indefinitely as an effective counselor or therapist unless options for renewal are considered and pursued. These options are unique for each counselor or therapist and can only be identified on an individual basis. Exercise, time with friends, participation in a choral group, leaves of absence or sabbaticals, travel, gardening, white-water rafting, massages, time with significant others, and time alone are examples of the hundreds of options—and combinations of options—that may have appeal as well as potential for practitioner renewal.

In a very interesting study, Richard and Eileen Mackey (1994) analyzed the impact of personal therapy on the outlook of the practicing professional. Results indicated that counselors and therapists emerged from the experience with new ideas for therapeutic techniques, enhanced empathy, better understanding of the therapeutic process, higher levels of self-awareness, and greater ability to set limits, establish boundaries, and maintain an appropriate balance between closeness and distance in professional relationships. All of these outcomes are pertinent to "renewal" and to the avoidance or overcoming of burnout.

It is not possible to nurture others unless we provide the self-nurturance and renewal that maintains and restores our capacity as helpers. As we have already mentioned, the health and wellness of the helper has much to do with the art form inherent in the helping relationship. Readers are referred to Coster and Schwebel (1997), Dupree and Day (1995), and Skovholt (2001) for additional information about avoiding burnout.

The Importance of a Personal Theory

After you finish reading this chapter, you will begin a fascinating exploration of theories of counseling and psychotherapy. Some theories will have more personal appeal than others; all of them will present some stimulating perspectives about human nature and about providing help to those seeking assistance. In addition, each will suggest a variety of theory-congruent strategies or applications designed to help clients achieve desired changes in behavior, outlook, motivation, and so on. We want the contents of this book to help you think about a personal theory of counseling and psychotherapy. We also want you to give considerable thought to how the formulation of a personal theory of counseling and psychotherapy could be helpful to you as you work with clients.

From time to time, the topic of developing a personal theory of counseling and psychotherapy is addressed in the professional literature. Three of the earliest discussions of this topic were put forth by Lister (1964), Shoben (1962), and Passons (1975). More recently, developing a personal theory of counseling and psychotherapy has been addressed briefly by Corey (2001) and Seligman (2001). We think it is important for counselors or therapists to understand how a personal theory can be helpful in the process of working with clients.

A counselor or therapist can use a personal theory to provide a framework for understanding the meaning of a client's behavior. This statement will have added meaning as you begin reading Chapters 3 through 16 and notice that each theory is discussed from the perspective of the same six-point paradigm. One aspect of the paradigm is focused on how clients develop personalities across the life span; the associated information directs the observations of the counselor or therapist and helps the counselor or therapist assess the client's behavior in relation to how the theory suggests that behavior has developed. This observation process also helps the counselor or therapist discriminate between relevant and irrelevant aspects of client behavior as well as connect what, at first, may seem like disjointed pieces of information about client behavior.

Developing a personal theory should also assist the counselor or therapist with understanding how change in client behavior might be precipitated. If a counselor or therapist uses a framework that addresses how personality and behavior has developed, then he or she should also have ideas about how to modify that behavior during the counseling and psychotherapy process. Readers will note that the change process is addressed in conjunction with discussing and evaluating each of the theories in this text and that suggestions for interventions that can be used to modify behavior are connected to the assumptions the theory makes about human development across the life span and the change process as described. In a similar vein, the goals of counseling and psychotherapy are derivatives of the conceptual framework provided by the theory and used by the counselor or therapist to guide the counseling and psychotherapy process.

A personal theory should provide reasonable guidelines for the clinician as observations and assessments are made and treatment plans are developed. A personal theory, however, should never be rigidly adhered to and should always be modified as the expertise and experience of the counselor or therapist accumulates over time. We think the following suggestions for circumventing problems in the development and application of a personal theory are worth noting.

1. Stay cognizant of your own feelings, values, beliefs, expectations, and personality traits that influenced, and continue to influence, your personal theory.
2. Study existing theories of counseling and stay updated on new developments, including research data that can be applied to existing theories as well as your personal theory.
3. Be open to the use of alternative and Eastern approaches to counseling and psychotherapy.
4. Do not incorporate elements of existing theory into your personal theory if they are incongruent with your belief system and personality traits.
5. Assess your personal theory in the context of using it with diverse populations and make modifications to meet the needs of clients whose life experiences and values are different than yours.
6. Modify your personal theory as time and experience accrue.
7. Use the six-point paradigm, as presented in Chapters 3 through 16 of this text, as the organizational structure around which to develop the conceptual framework you plan to use with clients.

The personal theory you decide to develop will gradually be identified as you accumulate knowledge about theory, research, and practice and build experiences with clients through practicum, internships, and volunteer and paid positions. We encourage you to begin thinking about the conceptual frame of reference with which you plan to approach clients, but we discourage you from adopting a position until you carefully explore possibilities and participate in a variety of clinical opportunities with associated one-to-one and group supervision experience.

As you read the introduction to Part II of this text, notice the six-point paradigm that is used to present each theory addressed in our text: background, human nature, major constructs, applications, evaluation, and a case study based on the description of "The Case of Jonathan." These six dimensions can be used as the basis for beginning to formulate your own personal theory of counseling. We suggest that you use the six-point paradigm to write down the elements of your personal theory. At first, you may just want to outline your thoughts and you will probably want to make revisions as you reflect upon the content of our text and begin to counsel clients. We believe that it is important for every professional counselor or therapist to think through his or her belief system related to how clients develop the behavior patterns that are observed and how behavioral change can be facilitated. In addition and as previously noted, we believe that interventions used by the counselor or therapist to facilitate change must always be tied to what the counselor or therapist believes about the inherent nature of the clients being served and any associated constructs that inform the theoretical set the counselor or therapist uses to guide "practice." Theory, research, and practice should always be closely aligned and each of us has an obligation to think through our way of working with clients. We must be willing to revise and modify our preferred way of doing our work as we, as individual professionals, grow and mature and as new theory and research is made available for our use.

Conclusions

This chapter has stressed the importance of achieving a personal and professional identity as you begin to study theories of counseling and psychotherapy and gain experience in translating theory into practice. We believe that personal identity and professional identity are interrelated and fundamental to being able to understand, evaluate, and apply the theories presented in this text. Because the health and wellness of the counselor or therapist is a prerequisite to effectiveness, we addressed this topic through descriptions of personal characteristics, psychological health, and multidimensional health and wellness models.

The values and cultural biases of each counselor or therapist do have an impact on the use and application of theory as well as the structuring of the helping relationship. We hope you will make personal assessments of your values and sensitivity to culturally diverse client populations as well as evaluate the values and cultural biases upon which the theories presented in subsequent chapters are based.

At times, students enroll in college and university programs for preparing counselors and therapists without being totally aware of the demands they will encounter. By describing the daily world of the counselor or therapist and the importance of achieving perspective and balance, this chapter provides an initial overview of the stresses and expectations as well as the importance of learning how to cope with professional demands. We believe each person needs to develop a realistic understanding of the profession and understand that this knowledge is an essential component for the development of personal and professional identity.

Finally, this chapter stressed the importance of thinking about the conceptual frame of reference with which clients are approached. Although some practitioners may adopt an existing theory, many will develop a personal theory to inform and guide their practices with clients. We want you not only to obtain the benefits provided by the information in this book, but also to develop the analytic and evaluative skills that will enable you to apply this information effectively to client populations. Effective application will result when a practitioner is able to find a compatible balance between theoretical tenets and the personal and cultural characteristics that serve as a basis for his or her uniqueness. At that point, you will have answers to the two questions that began this chapter.

Theories of Counseling and Psychotherapy

In Part I of this text, we examined two basic areas that are significant to the individual counseling process and to the person of the counselor or therapist. We discussed the helping relationship and the issues surrounding the counselor or therapist's personal and professional identity. We believe that this foundation was necessary before introducing you to the theories of counseling and psychotherapy that are the subject of Part II.

Part II contains 12 chapters, each of which addresses a selected theoretical system that has direct application to the counseling or therapy process. We selected the theoretical systems based upon their current use in the field of counseling and therapy, and we chose the chapter authors based upon their expertise and their current application of the theoretical system in their work with clients. To provide the reader with a consistent format, each chapter contains information dealing with the following areas.

- *Background.* Historical information related to the development of the theoretical system and the individual(s) responsible for its development.
- *Human nature.* A developmental perspective. The process of individual development over time, as defined by the theoretical system.
- *Major constructs.* The structural components that comprise the theoretical system.
- *Applications.* This section of each chapter is comprised of the following subsections.

  Overview. An introduction to the three areas that follow.

  Goals of counseling and psychotherapy. A description of desired client outcomes based upon the tenets of the theory.

  The process of change. The factors within the theory that address what brings about change in the individual.

  Intervention strategies. Techniques for implementing the process of change.

- *Clients with mental disorders.* Discusses how each theory can be used with clients with mental disorders.
- *Evaluation.* This section of each chapter is comprised of the following subsections.

  Overview. An introduction to the three areas that follow.

  Supporting research. Current research studies that form the bases for continued use of the theoretical system.

  Limitations. A description of the factors that limit the use of this theoretical system with clients and types of presenting problems.

  Summary chart. A chart that summarizes the information in the chapter.

- *Case study.* The application of the theoretical system to the development of a treatment or counseling plan for a client. The same case study information was used by all authors in Parts II and III of the text.

The first three chapters in Part II deal with the theoretical systems, often classified as *analytical,* that were developed by Sigmund Freud, Carl Jung, and Alfred Adler. Chapter 3, "Psychoanalytic Theory," provides background information relative to counseling and therapy within a psychoanalytic framework and emphasizes current use of this framework for individual counseling and therapy. Chapter 4, "Jungian Analytical Theory," takes the reader from the development and definition of the major constructs of Jungian psychology to their application in the case of Jonathan, the subject of our hypothetical case study. We think readers will find this journey both intriguing and enlightening. Chapter 5, "Adlerian Counseling and Psychotherapy," highlights the contributions of Alfred Adler and demonstrates the application of his major constructs in current approaches to counseling and psychotherapy.

Chapter 6, "Existential Theory," sets forth the philosophical underpinnings of existential counseling and psychotherapy and demonstrates how this philosophy translates into approaches that can be used by the counselor or therapist in working with clients. Chapter 7, "Person-Centered Theory," deals specifically with the work of Carl Rogers and highlights the continual development of this theoretical system from Rogers' work in the early 1940s to the last years of his life, when he traveled to the most troubled places in the world and used his person-centered approach to promote peace among warring groups. Chapter 8, "Gestalt Theory," emphasizes the pioneering work of Frederick Perls and his development of Gestalt counseling and psychotherapy. Major concepts and interventions are presented in combination with their current use in counseling and therapy

The next three chapters in Part II deal with the theoretical systems, often classified as *behavioral, cognitive behavioral,* or *rational emotive,* that were developed by Beck, Meichenbaum, Glasser, and Ellis. Chapter 9, "Cognitive-Behavioral Theories," provides the reader with a general background about both the behavioral and cognitive-behavioral theoretical views and discusses how the cognitive-behavioral approach developed from the behavioral point of view. Emphasis is given to the work of Aaron Beck and Donald Meichenbaum. Chapter 10, "Rational Emotive Behavioral Theory," emphasizes the work of Albert Ellis with special attention directed to the ABCDE model for understanding how thoughts and behaviors are related. Contributions to counseling and therapy made by Ellis and his colleagues are stressed. Chapter 11, "Reality Therapy Theory," highlights the work of William Glasser and places special emphasis on a system he developed to provide a delivery system for reality therapy in helping others remediate deficiencies, make better choices, and become more fully self-actualized.

Chapter 12, "Family Theory," provides the reader with ideas for working with families, as it is important to understand that individual approaches do not adequately address the patterns of communicating and relating that connect individuals to each other in families. The purpose of the chapter is to help the reader find ways to add systems-level interventions to the individualistic approaches studied in previous chapters. We think readers will find this chapter both interesting and informative.

Chapter 13, "Brief Theories," provides the reader with information about brief, solution-focused counseling and psychotherapy, narrative counseling and therapy, and health realization. We think readers will find this information pertinent to their future roles as practitioners.

Chapter 14, "Feminist Theories," which has evolved gradually over time as a response to women's rejection of traditional psychotherapies, addresses some of the sexist, oppressive aspects of many of the currently used theories of counseling and psychotherapy and encourages counselors and therapists not to apply theories based on male developmental models to women.

We think that the theoretical systems included in Part II provide the reader with a comprehensive and current review of major counseling and psychotherapy approaches to working with individuals. Our conviction is strengthened by our selection of authors, who not only have expertise in the specific theoretical systems, but also practice these approaches in working with clients.

We asked each author or set of authors, in Parts II and III of this text, to address the following case study information in the development of a treatment or counseling plan that is consistent with the specific theoretical system presented. This approach gives readers the opportunity to view the theoretical systems from a comparative perspective as they search for the theoretical system that is most appropriate for their future work as counselors or therapists.

The Case of Jonathan

Client Demographics

The client, Jonathan, is a 36-year-old Native American male. He is the youngest of six children, raised on the Navajo reservation in New Mexico. He attended the Bureau of Indian Affairs School on the reservation, dropping out when he was 16. He returned the following year and earned his high school diploma. He attended the University of New Mexico for 2 years, pursuing a degree in nursing. At the age of 20, he dropped out of the nursing program and returned to the reservation. He secured a job at the Bureau of Indian Affairs Hospital and worked in several positions during his tenure at the hospital. He has been married twice and is currently separated from his second wife. He has four children, three from his first marriage, two boys and a girl, and one from his second marriage, a girl. The four children range in age from 6 to 15. He has been separated from his second wife for approximately 7 months, and at the time of the separation left the reservation. He is currently living in Phoenix, Arizona, and works in a residential treatment facility that specializes in providing alcohol and drug treatment for adolescents.

Presenting Problem

Jonathan arrived 10 minutes late for his initial appointment. He was apologetic, explaining his difficulty in finding the mental health agency. He appeared uncomfortable and somewhat apprehensive as he explained that his supervisor had suggested that he talk with someone at the agency regarding some of the difficulties he was having at work. During the intake process, he explained that he was having difficulties getting along with both his co-workers and his supervisor. He stated that he couldn't seem to relate to the people with whom he worked. They always seem to expect more that he can deliver. They are always on his back. His work is never good enough to suit his supervisor. He describes the supervisor as a perfectionist who wants everyone else to be the same.

Jonathan explained that the situation at work is making him very depressed. He is having difficulty sleeping, and his sleep is often interrupted with very disturbing dreams. He is very lonely, misses seeing his children and his family, but feels that he had no future on the reservation. He is having financial difficulties due to the cost of living in Phoenix and his need to pay child support to his first wife and provide financial support to his second wife and daughter. He is drinking more than he should and is having a difficult time controlling his anger and frustration. He has had several arguments with both co-workers and his supervisor, the last of these resulting in his being suspended for 3 days without pay. He has tried to find other employment, but nothing seems to work out. He believes this is due to the fact that he is a Native American and most employers are prejudiced. This has only added to his anger. It scares him when he thinks of what he might do if something does not change. He refused to elaborate on that statement, but feels that he is trapped. In his words, "He is not wanted in the 'White Mans' world and has no future in his own."

Family Background

Jonathan describes his family of origin as close knit, held together by both cultural and tribal values. He was raised to be proud of his Native American background, his language, and tribal traditions. He had three older brothers and two older sisters. One brother was killed in a traffic accident and one sister died during childbirth. His remaining siblings and his parents continue to live on the reservation. His two older brothers manage a trading post on the reservation and his sister is a full-time mother to her three children. His parents continue to farm although, due to declining health, they are requiring much more assistance from their children. His parents and siblings were very upset when he left the reservation and have put a lot of pressure on him to return. This has become more urgent because of the declining health of his parents.

Early Adult Years

Jonathan's decision to quit school at the age of 16 was precipitated by the death of his brother. Jonathan had been driving the car and always felt that there was something that he could have done to avoid the accident. The car had been struck by a drunk driver who crossed the median and hit them head on. If only he had been able to swerve, he believes, his brother might still be alive. Jonathan had been thrown from the car and sustained only a broken shoulder. His guilt and grief over his brother's death and the reaction of his family had all added up to Jonathan's leaving school and spending the year trying to figure out what he was going to do about all of this. His parents and siblings were very upset by his leaving school, but were also dealing with their own grief and tolerated his not returning to school. Jonathan did not seem to be very sure about whether his family blamed him for the accident. He went back to school the following year and earned his high school diploma.

His 2 years at the University of New Mexico were difficult ones in terms of relationships and finances. He had received a scholarship, but he was away from the reservation and away from his girlfriend. During his second year at the University, his girlfriend announced that she was pregnant. Jonathan left school at the end of the year, returned to the reservation, got a job at the local hospital, and they were married 1 month after his return. The marriage resulted in three children and lasted 6 years. During the last year of the marriage, Jonathan began drinking heavily and seeing another woman. He and his first wife were divorced 6 years ago.

Post-Divorce Years

Six months after the divorce, Jonathan married again and within 4 months he and his new wife had a daughter. Things went well during the first few years of the marriage, but earlier patterns returned. Jonathan began to drink again, and his wife began to suspect that he was seeing another woman. Six months ago, they agreed to a trial two-month separation that has been continued three times. From Jonathan's perspective, the chances of reconciliation do not look good. He states that he loves his wife but does not know how to live in this type of relationship. He believes that this is the same thing that happened in his first marriage, and that no matter what he tries to do to make the relationship work, it is never good enough. His reaction is often to get very angry and walk away. He often turns to drink and other women for solace. He feels that if he and his wife cannot salvage their marriage, he will never again place himself in this type of relationship. He feels guilty for being an absent father to his children and thinking that there is something that he should do or could do to make all of this better. He decided to leave the reservation at this time, hoping that he could find answers to his problems. He also believed that the reservation could not provide him with the professional or financial opportunities he needed. It was shortly after his move to Phoenix that he began to have disturbing dreams. According to Jonathan, these dreams generally entail the following.

> I am on a long bus filled with very noisy people. We all seem to be going to different places. When I talk with other people on the bus, I get the impression that some think that the bus is going to California, while others think that it is going to New York. I bought a ticket to Albuquerque. As the bus moves along, the passengers get more irritated and begin to argue as to where the bus is going and when it will reach its destination. The more the passengers argue, the faster the bus goes. We pass signs indicating California, New York, and Albuquerque, but the bus never stops long enough for anyone to get off. At each stop, the bus seems to get much longer and no one can reach the exit prior to the bus starting again. I do my best to explain the problem to the bus driver, but she doesn't seem to hear me or ignores me. I end up shouting at the driver and she ends up laughing at me. I pick up a piece of pipe and start pounding the steering wheel to stop her from laughing. I also realize, as I look back from the front of the bus, that all of the other passengers have disappeared. I am all alone with the laughing driver. It is about this time that I wake up and find that I am not able to get back to sleep. I have had this same type of dream about four times in the past six weeks.

These dreams, coupled with the situation at work and the marital separation, seem to leave Jonathan very depressed, angry, lonely, and without direction. In his words, "I have little to live for. I have ruined the lives of three families plus my own life, and who knows what I am doing to my children."

Psychoanalytic Theory

Gregory J. Novie
Southwest Center for Psychoanalytic Studies
Phoenix, Arizona

This chapter provides a brief outline of psychoanalytic theory and technique. It has been written for the beginning clinician and is intended as an introduction to a complex psychotherapeutic process. Its goal is to interest the student in further exploring psychoanalysis as a treatment option. A suggested reading list has been provided for those who wish to go beyond the basic information of this chapter.

Beginning with the work of Sigmund Freud, the chapter reviews a history of psychoanalysis and then divides and presents the psychoanalytic movement from the perspective of three historical periods. The first period is dominated by Freud and covers his early work through the end of World War I. The second period, which follows the end of World War I, is dominated by the establishment of training institutions and the emergence of the American Psychoanalytic Association. The third period begins with the end of World War II, continues into the present, and deals with the expansion of psychoanalysis worldwide.

Building on this historical background, the chapter presents a developmental perspective of human nature that emphasizes unconscious dynamics and the processes involved in change. These dynamics include psychic determinism or causality, consciousness as an exceptional rather than a regular attribute of the psychic process, displacement, condensation, psychosexual stages, and defense mechanisms. The developmental theory espoused by Freud is used to explain not only the etiology of human behavior but also the etiology of human neuroses and psychoses. This developmental perspective both explains client dynamics and provides a framework for the intervention strategies used by the counselor or therapist.

Background

The history of psychoanalysis begins with Sigmund Freud (1856–1939). Freud had collaborated with his mentor, Josef Breuer, to write the first psychoanalytic paper, *Studies in Hysteria,* in 1895. This paper was about the "founding case" (Gay, 1988, p. 63) of psychoanalysis, a patient referred to as "Anna O." Before Freud, the field of psychology was considered a speculative philosophy on one hand and an empirical study of psychophysiological processes on the other, and the study of the human mind was limited to religious and magical thought. With psychoanalysis, psychology took a definite first step in the direction of scientific thinking about human motivation. As Fenichel (1945) observed, "An understanding of the multiplicity of everyday human mental life, based on natural science, really began only with psychoanalysis" (p. 4).

Fine (1979) divides the history of psychoanalysis into three periods. The first period is dominated by Freud and covers his early work through the end of World War I. During this period, Freud drew adherents to his cause, many of whom became the early pioneers of the psychoanalytic movement. The context of Western European and Viennese society during this period involved strict social norms and mores regarding sexuality. In such a Victorian setting, sexuality—and particularly female sexuality—was permitted very limited expression. It was the blocking or **repression** of such sexuality that led to Freud's (and Breuer's) conception of **hysteria.** Repression is a **defense mechanism,** a mental process that "defends" our conscious mind from unwanted and painful thoughts and feelings. In hysteria, patients presented vague complaints of paralysis and pain without organic causes—the present-day psychosomatic disorders. What Freud discovered was that such patients transferred feelings and thoughts about important people in their life onto the therapist. It was this discovery of **transference** that continues as a fundamental concept in psychoanalytic thought.

The first psychoanalytic society was formed in Vienna after the turn of the century; a few years later, as psychoanalysis gained recognition, the International Psychoanalytical Association was founded. This period led to the emergence of psychoanalysis, which has since evolved into a dynamic psychology and a philosophy of cultural importance.

The second period, which dates from 1918 to 1939, was dominated by the establishment of training institutions and the emergence of the American Psychoanalytic Association. With the organization of many new psychoanalytic societies in democratic countries, specific regulations were adopted for the training of psychoanalysts. The training system that is now almost universally standard involves a tripartite model, the foundation of which includes the candidate's personal analysis. "It may be assumed that since about 1930 every practicing analyst has been through a training analysis" (Fine, 1979, p. 3). The training also includes theoretical instruction that lasts about 4 years and control analyses in which the candidate in training is supervised in the conduct of several analyses. Candidates are typically drawn from the mental health professions, especially in the United States, which has the largest membership of psychoanalysts belonging to the International Psychoanalytical Association. The significance of this second historical period is marked by not only the proliferation of psychoanalytic education worldwide, but also by the expansion of psychoanalytic thought through the creation of a sizable body of scientific literature. Such literature typically utilizes the case study method of one or a few patients.

The third period begins with the end of World War II and continues into the present. This period is marked by the further expansion of psychoanalysis worldwide. The 1992–93 roster of the International Psychoanalytical Association, the latest one available, lists 8,197 members, 45 component and provisional societies, and one regional society (the American Psychoanalytic Association). The roster includes 18 societies in Europe, 16 in

Latin America, 3 in the Middle and Far East, 1 in Australia, and 8 in North America. This third historical period is also marked by the expansion of psychoanalytic theory beyond classical Freudian metapsychology. Pine (1985) enumerates four distinct psychoanalytic psychologies that have developed within psychoanalytic metapsychology: Freud's drive theory, and the newer theories of **ego, object relations,** and **self-psychology.**

Recent developments in American health care are also affecting the perception of modern psychoanalysis. The contemporary psychotherapeutic scene has been greatly influenced by modern health care marketing. Rising health care costs have engendered the development and promotion of a variety of abbreviated psychotherapeutic strategies. Managed-care programs such as health maintenance organizations, preferred provider agreements, and employee assistance programs typically rely on interventions designed to keep costs to a minimum. Accordingly, the field of psychotherapy has become a veritable "convenience market" in which reducing the total number of contacts between the counselor or therapist and the client is a priority. Similarly, the choices available to persons who decide to get help are limited by the health care option to which they subscribe. It is not surprising, therefore, that a precise definition of psychotherapy has been further obscured by rapidly expanding methods designed to limit costs. Wolberg (1977) lists no fewer than 36 definitions that "generally do not agree on the techniques employed, the process included, the goals approximated or the personnel involved" (p. 14).

Amidst these "innovations," psychoanalysis has lost favor as a treatment option, except perhaps in a few urban areas. Because it is recognized as a depth psychology, and because the analytic method involves multiple weekly sessions over an extended period of time, it has little short-term economic advantage in the contemporary marketplace of managed health care. Nevertheless, despite the predicted demise of psychoanalysis, new training institutes continue to form in major metropolitan areas, indicating a continued interest in psychoanalysis on the part of professional counselors and therapists. In part, this may be the result of dedication to a dynamic theory and method that seeks to understand and change psychopathology as well as the forces operative in the therapeutic process. It may also reflect counselors' and therapists' dissatisfaction with technique-oriented strategies and their wish to increase the use of self as a tool in the therapeutic process. (Personal analysis is a requirement for psychoanalytic training.)

What distinguishes psychoanalysis as a psychotherapeutic theory and method? Wolberg (1977) divides the varieties of psychotherapy into three main groups: **supportive therapy, reeducative therapy,** and **reconstructive therapy.** His schema depicts a gradation from lesser to greater complexity in the perceived objectives of each therapeutic strategy. For example, whereas in supportive therapy the object "is to bring the patient to an emotional equilibrium as rapidly as possible" (p. 68), reeducative therapy attempts to achieve more extensive goals through an "actual remodeling of the patient's attitudes and behavior in line with more adaptive life integration" (p. 101). The difference is in the specific therapeutic technique employed. In supportive strategies, reassurance, suggestion, relaxation, and persuasion may be used. In contrast, reeducative approaches rely more on reconditioning. The counselor or therapist introduces behavioral reinforcers or the therapeutic relationship (approval/disapproval) to modify, liberate, or promote self-growth.

The objectives of reconstructive therapies offer the greatest complexity. The goal of reconstructive psychotherapy is to bring the client to an awareness of crucial unconscious conflicts, their derivatives, and how these limit his or her daily life. In contrast, supportive efforts toward this kind of insight are minimal, and the reeducative emphasis is less on searching for unconscious causes than on promoting new and better forms of conscious behavior through conscious action. Counselors or therapists who direct their efforts toward reconstructive changes within the client have typically turned toward psychoanalytic methods and theories because of their emphasis on bringing unconscious conflicts to awareness.

Human Nature: A Developmental Perspective

(**Authors' note:** In order to give examples of major constructs in the next two sections of this chapter, the following brief case history was created.)

Case History: Juanita

The client is a 43-year-old Latino female. She is the eldest of five children and was raised in a large metropolitan area in the Southwest. Religion plays a very significant role in her life. She is a college graduate, has taught math and science in a middle school for the past 4 years, and tends to pour all of her energy into her students, which often causes a strained relationship with her own children. She is divorced from her husband of 5 years; the divorce was very much opposed by her parents and family. She was referred by her physician, with complaints of insomnia, not eating properly, frequent unexplained crying spells, depression, the inability to maintain meaningful relationships with various males, and lack of concentration. She has sought help from her priest, co-workers, and her mother. Other significant information includes the fact that Juanita took care of her brothers and sisters growing up because of the demands of her mother's and father's business. Juanita also describes a dream that she has had on several occasions.

> I am always running, and there are shadowy figures behind me. I am in a large warehouse-type structure with lots of boxes and crates. The boxes and crates are all marked with arrows reading "Exit." The arrows are all going in different directions, therefore, I never find my way out and the figures keep getting closer. I wake up in a cold sweat, breathing rapidly, heart pounding, and a scream stuck in my throat. As I can't sleep, I usually go to the kitchen and drink coffee.

The Freudian Unconscious

In the late 19th century, medically oriented approaches assumed that neuroses were caused by some unknown organic factor, and therapeutic measures were limited to electric shock and hypnotism (Fine, 1979). Freud isolated himself from this mainstream position, as Fine observes, and in the process made his first major discovery: "The key to neuroses lies in psychology, and all neuroses involve a defense against unbearable ideas" (1979, pp. 21–25). In an attempt to understand clinical data, Freud arrived at two fundamental hypotheses concerning mental development and functioning, hypotheses that can apply to normal as well as pathological activity. According to Brenner (1974), these two hypotheses, "which have been abundantly confirmed, are the principle of psychic determinism or causality, and the proposition that consciousness is an exceptional rather than a regular attribute of psychic processes" (p. 2).

According to the first principle, **psychic determinism,** mental activity is not meaningless or accidental; nothing in the mind happens by chance or in a random way, and all mental phenomena have a causal connection to the psychic events that precede them. An example of this principle can be drawn from the case study of Juanita. The presenting information and the client's childhood history are organized in such a way as to develop a context of continuity between early psychic experiences and the symptoms we assume to be a consequence of these experiences. We ask ourselves, "What caused this?" and we organize our data around this question because we are confident that a coherent answer exists that is connected to the rest of the client's psychic life. We assume that each neurotic symptom is caused by other mental processes. For example, Juanita complains of insomnia and difficulty concentrating and perhaps feels that these are signs of some spiritual problem; hence, her first effort at seeking help is with her priest. As counselors or therapists, however, we presume that there are psychological causes outside of the client's conscious awareness.

Freud first noted the principle of psychic determinism in relation to dreams. He discovered that "each dream, indeed each image in each dream, is the consequence of other psychic events, and each stands in coherent and meaningful relationship to the rest of the dreamer's psychic life" (Brenner, 1974, p. 3). This principle contrasts with the notion that dreams are products of random brain activity during sleep, an idea popularly held by neurologists and psychiatrists 70 years ago and by some organic theorists today.

The second principle, that of **unconscious mental processes,** is closely linked to the first. This principle accounts for the apparent discontinuities in the client's perception of symptom and cause, for the causal connection has become part of the unconscious process. In the case study, Juanita has repressed her mental conflicts into the unconscious, thereby causing her symptoms. It follows, then, that if the unconscious cause or causes can be discovered through the therapeutic process, the causal sequence becomes clear and the client's insight leads to cure. It should be noted that this brief explanation is a rather simplified version of what in actuality is a long and complex treatment process in which the client examines through free association a variety of unconscious mental processes. This simplified explanation also ignores the role of interpersonal influence— that of the client-therapist relationship—as a mutative factor in psychoanalysis.

Freud (1938/1940) argued that "the governing rules of logic carry no weight in the unconscious; it might be called the Realm of the illogical" (pp. 168–169). He also declared: "We have found that processes in the unconscious or in the Id obey different laws from those in the preconscious ego. We name these laws in their totality the primary process, in contrast to the secondary process, which governs the course of events in the preconscious ego" (p. 164). In other words, Freud called attention to the fact that a portion of the mind, which is particularly active in our dreams, our emotional life, and our childhood, works within a framework of timelessness, spacelessness, and the coexistence of opposites. For example, timelessness is implied in our clinical work when we take for granted the simultaneous presence of an adult client and his or her expressions of infancy. Freud's notions of **displacement** (an idea's emotional emphasis becomes detached from it and is superimposed on some other ideas) and **condensation** (several ideas are expressed through a single idea) exemplify spacelessness. We recognize in clinical work that feelings expressed toward an uncaring employer may be an unconscious replication of childhood feelings felt toward a parent in the past or toward the counselor or therapist in the present. These feelings are displaced onto the employer as a defense against a painful memory or onto the counselor or therapist against the threat of awareness. Displacement is essentially a disconnecting of some feeling toward someone and a reconnecting of it to someone else (who had nothing to do with the original feeling), without being aware of it. Usually we displace such affect onto people who bear some resemblance to the original person. For example, if a man goes through a bitter divorce, he may displace onto the next woman he dates the resentment he feels toward his ex-wife.

Condensation is a more difficult and abstract concept. Think of it as a mosaic in which many parts are put together in a disorganized way, so that the end product becomes an amalgam of images, shapes, and colors. The mechanism of condensation is the mind's way of unconsciously keeping from awareness disturbing affects and thoughts by rendering them confusing and distorted. It is perhaps similar to an abstract artwork in which the themes depicted by the artist are blended together in a strange and logic-defying way. Freud and his followers identified a number of defensive strategies, or **defense mechanisms,** unconsciously employed by the mind; these defy normal logic but act to protect the subject from awareness of unwanted feelings.

In *The Ego and the Mechanisms of Defense* (1966), Anna Freud specified such defense mechanisms as **regression, repression, reaction formation, isolation, undoing, projection, introjection,** and **displacement.** Repression and projection, commonly seen in clinical practice, are unconscious defensive processes. Repression refers to "an operation whereby the subject attempts to repel, or to confine to the unconscious, representations (thoughts, images, memories) which are bound to an instinct" (Laplanche & Pontalis, 1973, p. 390). Projection is an "operation whereby qualities, feelings, wishes or even 'objects,' which the subject refuses to recognize or rejects in himself, are expelled from the self and located in another person or thing" (p. 349). The other mechanisms operate similarly by unconsciously protecting the subject from awareness of repressed conflict and subsequent anxiety. For the reader's information, Table 3.1 presents a discussion of the more commonly referred to defense mechanisms.

Prejudice, for example, represents a culturally defined projection of one group's disavowed aspects of itself onto another (usually subordinate) group. For example, in American culture, blacks were seen as overly sexual, dishonest, and lazy, projections of unwanted traits of the dominant cultural group. Groups of young men attacking male homosexuals would also be a refusal of these young men to accept loving or tender feelings toward other men—finding it too threatening to consider such feelings and hence needing to defend by projecting them onto others and then attacking. Reaction formation is a process whereby an individual will take the opposite stance (unconsciously) to protect from awareness one's gratification in the abhorred position. For example, a man may become a preacher and rail against "sins of the flesh" as a way to defend against his own sexual impulses. What is often a sign of a reaction formation is the zeal with which someone embraces a position and simultaneously attacks the opposite—expressed in Shakespeare's words "he doth protest too much."

Table 3.1
Defense Mechanisms

Regression
This is a process whereby a client will decompensate and become less rational, literally "moving backward" in terms of reasoning, judgment, and thinking. For example, an adult client had been severely depressed and suicidal for a number of weeks. One session she began to refer to herself by another name, that of a 9-year-old girl. She spoke in a little girl's voice and language. Typically, regression is not so extreme, but usually there is some form of a loss of reasoning and judgment.

Repression
Repression is the first and foremost defense mechanism. Repression seals off and pushes down into the unconscious and out of our awareness unwanted thoughts and feelings. For example, a therapist, after working a year with a client, remarked that he had said nothing about his mother. The client told her, with anger and surprise, "We don't talk about her in here!" The client was demonstrating that he had repressed or sealed off or pushed beneath awareness any negative thoughts or feelings about his mother.

Reaction Formation
Reaction formation involves the denial of faulty impulses by going to the opposite extreme. For example, an evangelist, who has a history of sexual acting out, rails against immorality. The evangelist finds defense against his own sexual desires by taking the offensive and condemning such desires and behaviors in others.

Isolation (Isolation of Affect)
Isolation involves avoiding painful feelings by detachment from the source of such feelings. For example, a person may avoid feelings of guilt, centering on some act or behavior, through lengthy cognitive speculations regarding the differences between good and bad.

Undoing
Undoing involves taking back, softening, or restructuring statements or admissions as a result of the anxiety produced by the original statement or admission. For example, a client may express affection for the counselor or therapist but, because of the anxiety this produces for the client, he/she states that he/she has feelings such as these for a lot of people.

Projection
Projection involves the shifting of blame or the assigning of one's faults to others. Think of a movie projector inside one's head. It projects onto a screen (another person or group) one's own fears, fantasies, and conflicts. For example, a highly prejudiced person often denies his prejudice by stating that, "I do not hate them; they hate me."

Introjection
Introjection involves the adoption of other people's attitudes or behaviors as if they were one's own. Introjection is best viewed as partial identification as the individual only adopts that which lowers anxiety. For example, a child may incorporate his parents' values and standards into his personality not because they are correct, but because they protect him from the negative outcomes possible in opposing these same standards and values.

Displacement
Displacement involves the transferring of emotional reactions from one person or situation to another. For example, the person who has had a difficult day at work based upon demands of his/her supervisor arrives home and yells at his/her spouse or children. The home situation produces less anxiety than the work situation.

Freud's Developmental Theory

"In psychoanalytic treatment, the client regresses and recapitulates, in a modified form, early developmental phases. Both neuroses and psychoses are based on a series of fixations on and regressions to these past ego stages and orientations" (Giovacchini, 1987, p. 87). Freud postulated the **psychosexual stages** of infantile sexuality as oral, anal, and phallic, which linked developmental theory with sexual impulses. This meant that Freud believed sexual expression went beyond what is ordinarily considered sexual, for he postulated infantile activities as erotic.

In essence, psychosexual stages refer to a sequential acquisition of progressively sophisticated modes of gratification from various bodily zones that are necessary for growth and development. The term **libido** describes instinctual energy that belongs to the sexual drive. The discharge of this energy leads to pleasure, and the part of the body that leads to such pleasure is referred to as an **erogenous zone.** Erikson (1963) elaborated on these erogenous zones: "oral-sensory, which includes the facial apertures and the upper nutritional organs; anal, or the excretory organs; and the genitalia" (pp. 73–74). He posited modes of functioning within each zone. These included modes of incorporation, retention, elimination, and intrusion. The following examples show how modes may interplay with each zone.

Orality represents a method of relating to the external world. The infant's smiling is an indication of ability to recognize objects in the external world as separate from the self. The first mode of approach in the oral zone is incorporation, that is, to "take in" in a dependent fashion what is offered by the mother. Modes of incorporation dominate this stage, yet other modes are also expressed. According to Erikson (1963), "There is in the first incorporative stage a clamping down with jaws and gums; there is spitting up and out (eliminative mode); and there is a closing up of the lips (retentive mode). In vigorous babies even a general intrusive tendency of the whole head and neck can be noticed, a tendency to fasten itself upon the nipple and, as it were, into the breast (oral intrusive)" (p. 73).

In clinical work, one might refer to orally dependent clients. This indicates that extreme dependence is the result of a predominance of oral elements in adult functioning. This functions as a metaphor to describe a fixation at the oral stage of development, wherein the overly dependent adult client tends to relate to the world in terms of a need to be nurtured. While the child actually requires this nurturing to survive, the adult client is seen as wanting to be taken care of, to be soothed and nurtured in a psychological sense. A client described as an oral character may use any or all of the modes described previously: spitting out what the counselor or therapist offers, or intrusively penetrating into the counselor or therapist's space, demanding to be "fed." Erikson (1963) saw the primary conflict at this level as one of developing the sense of basic trust versus the sense of mistrust.

To Freud, control of the anal sphincter initiates the anal stage of development and is seen as an important contributor to adult structure. Control of the sphincter, which is part of the total muscle system activated at this stage, places an emphasis on the duality of rigidity and relaxation, flexion and extension. As noted by Erikson (1963), "The development of the muscle system gives the child a much greater power over the environment in the ability to reach out and hold on, to throw and to push away, to appropriate things and to keep them at a distance. This whole stage, then, which the Germans called the stage of stubbornness, becomes a battle for autonomy. For as he gets ready to stand more firmly on his feet the infant delineates his world as 'I' and 'you,' 'me' and 'mine.' Every mother knows how astonishingly pliable a child may be at this stage, if and when he has made the decision that he wants to do what he is supposed to do" (p. 82). Accordingly, the conflict at this stage involves the antithesis of letting go and holding on, of autonomy versus shame and doubt.

The **Oedipus complex,** which is one of the most controversial and best known of Freud's theories, dominates the phallic stage. At this stage, the child has moved away from a two-person system of mother-child interaction to a triangular relationship with both mother and father. The Oedipus legend, from Greek mythology, assumes the child's wish to possess the parent of the opposite sex, which creates a conflict with the parent of the same sex. In more graphic terms, and truer to the original legend, incestuous feelings are combined with patricidal impulses. In the case of the boy who wishes to possess his mother, he fears retaliation by the father and fantasizes the father's revenge of castration (i.e., the father's retaliation will be directed at the boy's penis), which is termed *castration anxiety*. This complex is necessary for later development because the threat of castration leads the child to internalize, as a permanent part of his psychic structure, a prohibiting, controlling superego that is the foundation of morality. In the case of a girl, the unconscious wish is to marry the father and to take care of him in a much better way than she imagines the mother is capable of doing. While these theories remain controversial today and are seriously questioned by modern developmental theorists, they continue to be used as important metaphors in understanding clinical material.

Post-Freudian Psychoanalytic Theory

According to Pine (1990), it was Fairbairn (1941) who coined the term *object relations theory* and focused attention not on the pleasure-seeking motivation (Freud's drive theory) but on the object-seeking nature of motivation. Pine went on to describe how it was a new method of clinical work—infant and child observation—that added momentum to this shift in emphasis from an internal drive based on instinct to seeking an object (person). Others contributing to this shift and expansion of knowledge and theory included Melanie Klein, Donald Winnicott, and Heinz Kohut. Kohut (1977) developed a theory and technique that came to be known as **self psychology,** which emphasized the concept of self as the organizing construct of experience, rather than innate drives and instincts.

These post-Freudian theorists, taken together, can be seen as expanding psychoanalytic theory from Freud's one-person system to a two-person system. Rather than seeing the individual as a closed and separate system attempting to negotiate a balance between inner needs striving for gratification on the one hand and the constraints of society (the reality principle) on the other, the scope has widened to include another person (the analyst). Freud's metaphor for psychoanalytic treatment was the surgeon removing a tumor (repressed memory). In addition, Freud conceived the analyst as a mirror (non-reactive, non-contributory) reflecting back only those unconscious desires and fears emanating from the client. Winnicott (1958), who was a pediatrician before becoming a psychoanalyst, saw therapy as more like the relationship between a mother and an infant, where there is a highly attuned emotional sensitivity, first on the mother's part and then, as the infant develops, of a more reciprocal nature. To underscore how important the object relation is in development and in psychotherapy, Winnicott would say there is no such thing as an infant. These object relations theorists did not discard Freud's drive theory but tended to add to it the significance of interaction with important others in the formation of personality and pathology.

Rabin (1995) described a recent paradigm shift in psychoanalysis that can be characterized by a number of different terms such as *intersubjectivity theory* (Stolorow, Brandshaft, & Atwood, 1987), *relational theorizing* (Mitchell, 1988), and *social constructivism* (Hoffman, 1991). Rabin argued that this shift is "from the positivistic belief that there are ultimate truths to be found within the intrapsychic structure of the patient, with the analyst as the arbiter of reality, to the 'postmodern' perspective, where all knowledge is perspectival, contextual and nonuniversal. *The analyst and the patient together create or construct* what is clinically useful" (p. 467) (emphasis added). This paradigm shift is away from Freud's metaphor of analyst as archeologist, sifting through strange symbols (dreams, slips of the tongue, symptoms) to decipher these meanings and present them to the client via an interpretation. This shift has also entailed a greater awareness of and use of the therapist's feelings and thoughts during a therapy session, data referred to as **countertransference.** Freud viewed such reactions as contaminating therapy and saw them as a function of unrecognized neurotic conflicts within the analyst. However, recent trends are toward the recognition and use of countertransference as a tool to facilitate therapy (Lecours, Bouchard, & Normandin, 1995). Table 3.2 compares the drive, ego, object relations, and self theories we have discussed.

Major Constructs and Processes of Change

The assumptions upon which the system of psychoanalytic theory rests are referred to as **metapsychology** (Rapaport & Gill, 1959). As noted by Greenson (1967), "The clinical implications of metapsychology intimate that in order to comprehend a psychic event thoroughly, it is necessary to analyze it from six different points of view—the topographic, dynamic, economic, genetic, structural and adaptive" (p. 21).

The **topographic** point of view is the first major construct. It contrasts unconscious versus conscious mental processes. The deeper layer of the mind, the unconscious, has only the aim of discharging impulses. Both conscious and unconscious expressions are present in clinical material and can be described as manifest and latent. In order to illustrate this construct, we will use the dream material noted in Juanita's clinical study. The client reports recent occurrences of dreams such as the following:

> I am always running, and there are shadowy figures behind me. I am in a large warehouse-type structure with lots of boxes and crates. The boxes and crates are all marked with arrows reading "Exit." The problem is that the arrows are all going in different directions. Therefore, I never find the exit, and the figures keep getting closer and closer. I wake up in a cold sweat, breathing rapidly, heart pounding, and a scream stuck in my throat. I lie there trying to calm down, knowing that I am too afraid to go back to sleep. In a little while I get up and spend the rest of the long night sitting at the kitchen table drinking coffee.

In psychoanalytic clinical work, it is essential to have the client's association to a dream in order to verify our assumptions about the latent, or unconscious, meaning of a

Table 3.2
Comparison of Theoretical Approaches

	Drive	Ego	Object Relations	Self
Motivating Force	Instincts	Instincts and growth	Seeking object to satisfy instincts	Feelings of inadequacy
Goal of Therapy	Uncovering unconscious conflicts	Uncovering methods of defending against conflicts, developing inherent potential	Uncovering the way one relates to others in getting needs met	To enable clients to better meet their needs for feeling worthwhile
Role of Counselor	Mirror	Mirror	Participant observer	Participant observer
Central Agent of Change	Interpretation	Interpretation	Experience of therapeutic relationship	Experience of therapeutic relationship

symbol or the dream itself. To interpret the meaning of a dream without these associations would be to impose our own thoughts onto the client, a process derogatorily called **wild analysis.** Because we do not have Juanita's associations in this case, we will guess at some possible associations in order to illustrate the metapsychological points of view. We might assume, for example, that the **manifest symbol** of the warehouse would unconsciously represent (i.e., have a latent meaning of) a place that holds things, as could the boxes and crates. A large warehouse gives the feeling of much open space, perhaps emptiness. The structures that could hold things (comfort as in being held) are all marked in different directions. She has turned to numerous people for support and has found no way out of the emptiness/depression (warehouse). While the conscious representation of a warehouse with labeled boxes and crates represents order and control, the unconscious representation stands for chaos without exit. Both stand in topographical relation to the other: one conscious, the other unconscious. A further elaboration, and much more presumptive one, is that the warehouse is not only symbolic of her depression and emptiness but also at a deeper level of intestine and bowel. We might assume that at this level Juanita's not eating is about control versus chaos, a desperate attempt to deny her need to put something into her, be it need for food or for relationships and sexual intimacy.

Dynamic and economic points of view are the second and third major constructs of psychoanalytic metapsychology. In order to understand these two points of view, it is necessary to explore Freud's idea of the **psychoeconomic hypothesis.** This hypothesis requires a construct of **psychic energy,** much like physical energy, with principles of pleasure-pain and constancy. An explanation of the idea of psychic energy is necessary prior to defining the dynamic and economic points of view.

For Freud, the development of instincts necessitated conflict. For example, when the two primary instincts of sexual and aggressive drives strive toward expression, they clash with the reality principle, leading to states of pent-up tension. As noted by Giovacchini (1987):

> Psychoanalysis requires a concept of psychic energy to explain the various movements of the psychic apparatus, those involved in action, problem solving, reestablishment of emotional equilibrium, and growth. A hypothesis of psychic energy must be based on certain general principles that dictate the distribution and production of energy and how it is to be used. (p. 62)

Giovacchini further noted:

> Freud relied on two principles on which he built his concepts of psychic energy, the principle of constancy and the pleasure principle, more specifically, the pleasure-pain principle. The constancy principle is based on the hypothesis that the function of the nervous system and the psychic apparatus is to keep the level of excitation at its lowest point. The pleasure principle is related to the constancy principle in that it asserts that lowering the level of excitation, which connotes release and relief, leads to pleasure, whereas increased excitation creates tension and disruption and is experienced as pain. (p. 63)

This **tension-discharge hypothesis** supports the dynamic point of view, which assumes that mental phenomena are the result of the interaction of psychic forces seeking discharge. This was based in part on the theories of hydraulic systems in physics during Freud's time. Greenson (1967) tells us that "this assumption is the basis for all hypotheses concerning instinctual drives, defenses, ego interests, and conflicts. Symptom formation, ambivalence, and over-determination are examples of dynamics" (p. 23).

The way in which psychic energy is distributed, transformed, or expended defines the economic point of view. To illustrate these points of view, assume that Juanita was in a state of dammed-up instinctual tension before the recent outbreak of her depressive symptoms. However, her ego was beginning to lose the ability (in the dream the shadowy figures are getting closer and closer) to carry out defensive operations so that she could function without such obvious debilitating symptoms. These operations seemed to be consistent with a compulsion for activity such as was exemplified by her pouring all of her energy into her students. It would be expected that her need for activity and control was bolstered by a variety of stereotypical rituals and repetitions, not only as they concerned herself (i.e., her thoughts and her body, as in not eating) but also as they involved her interpersonal interactions (not letting men get close). This coping style would be necessary to contain instinctual forces—such as intense rage and fear of abandonment—from explosive expression. The client's strained relationship with her children precipitated the most recent outbreak of symptoms such as nightmares and insomnia.

Juanita's ego has lost the ability to cope with this influx of affect seeking discharge, and she did not think she could have waited much longer for an appointment. The impulse to rage is frozen in its attempt for expression as in her dream "a scream is stuck in my throat." This reflects the conflict around intentionally holding onto and involuntarily letting go of something from within. In this instance, the something within happens to be a scream, which unconsciously could be equated with her sense of self, a self she struggled to find in the midst of family and cultural pressures to be what was expected of her.

This brings us to the fourth major construct of psychoanalytic metapsychology, the **genetic point of view,** which concerns an understanding of the origin and development of psychic phenomena. It explains how the past is being brought to the present and why a certain compromise solution has been adopted. To return again to the case example, Juanita's history and associations in analytic sessions would no doubt highlight the importance her mother played in her adopting a particular defensive style as well as those psychic conflicts already noted.

The fifth major metapsychological construct is the **structural point of view,** which assumes that the psychic apparatus can be divided into several persisting functional units. "The concept of the psychic apparatus as consisting of an ego, id, and superego is derived from the structural hypothesis" (Greenson, 1967, p. 25). The id is the agency from which all instincts derive, while the ego is the agency that mediates these drives with the external environment. Based on a signal of anxiety, the ego brings a number of defensive operations into play. It works as an agency of adaptation with functions such as control over perception, voluntary motility, and the setting up of affective memory traces, to name just a few. The superego is the agency of the personality within which develops a framework of conscience, self-observation, and the formation of ideals. It acts as a judge or censor for the ego.

To illustrate the structural point of view as it applies to Juanita, assume that the ego's defensive functions have weakened under the pressure of her divorce and her family's criticism and shunning of her. Her pouring herself into her students to the neglect of her children has mobilized the conflict she likely experienced as a child when her parents "poured" themselves into the family business to the neglect of Juanita (as she became mother to her younger siblings). This conflict centers in part around the expression of anger (the trapped scream, the depressive shutting down). Further assume that as she progresses in analysis she will no longer regress in this way when confronted with similar situations, for her ego functions will have replaced inadequate defenses with new insight and greater freedom of choice in responding.

Thus far, all the examples used from the case study reflect attempts at **adaptation,** the last major metapsychological construct. A person's relationship to his or her environment, objects of love and hate, and society are based on the adaptive point of view.

Applications

Overview

The following sections present information dealing with the goals and intervention strategies that have application to psychoanalytic theory. The goals of psychoanalytic theory stress changing the personality and character structure of the individual through resolving unconscious conflicts and developing more effective ways of dealing with problems, particularly in relationships. The intervention strategies that are part of psychoanalytic theory place special emphasis on free association, dream analysis, analysis of transference, analysis of resistance, interpretation, and the interactions that take place between the client and the counselor or therapist. The goals and intervention strategies that follow are designed to enhance the change process for the individual.

Goals of Counseling and Psychotherapy

The goals of psychoanalysis place emphasis on the resolution of clients' problems to enhance the clients' ability to cope with life changes (to make their way of relating to self and important others more meaningful and enriching), their working through unresolved developmental stages, and their ability to cope more effectively with the demands of the society within which they live. Although these goals vary with the client and with the psychoanalytic approach (drive theory, ego psychology, object relations, self psychology), each approach seeks the attainment of its goals through the exploration of unconscious material, particularly as it relates to the client-analyst relationship.

Intervention Strategies

Freud's technique for uncovering hidden psychic processes evolved over a period of several years, and despite some relatively minor variations, it is still in use today. The classical technique entails a process of **free association** (letting thoughts drift over events of daily life, past history, and dreams) on the part of the client, who is typically in a recumbent position with the counselor or therapist sitting behind and out of sight. The practitioner maintains a position of neutrality, referred to as the **rule of abstinence,** based on denying the client's wish for gratification of instinctual demands, such as wanting to have a more personal relationship with the analyst by asking about his or her personal life, or for the analyst to agree with the client. These techniques minimize the actual presence of the counselor or therapist and allow the client to focus more freely on intrapsychic matters such as fantasies, dream analysis, childhood-based conflicts, and defensive or resistive operations that block awareness of unconscious processes. More important, they facilitate the development of the **transference,** defined by Laplanche and Pontalis (1973) as "infantile prototypes that re-emerge and are experienced with a strong sensation of immediacy and are directed toward the analyst within the analytic situation. This is the terrain on which all the basic problems of a given analysis play themselves out: the establishment, modalities, interpretation and resolution of the transference are in fact what define the cure" (p. 455).

In other words, transference involves the client's reliving—in the presence of the counselor or therapist—the repetitious and rigid defenses of the past. It is the analysis and the eventual understanding of these defenses within the transference that make change possible. For example, if a client says something and the analyst is silent, the client might feel that the analyst is critical of what was said, and not only feel but also be convinced that this is what the analyst thinks. We would likely find that one or both parents often reacted with indifference to the client and that this pattern was being reactivated as a "here and now" experience for the client. The early pattern of experience with the parent was being "transferred" onto the analytic relationship. It is strategic on the part of the analyst to maintain enough of a neutral and anonymous presence—sort of like a blank screen—onto which the client can project these transferences. The analyst would then help the client become aware of such patterns (expecting criticism or needing approval) and how these cause problems in living.

The aim of the analytic technique, primarily through the analysis of transference, is to increase clients' insight into themselves. The analysis also seeks to strengthen ego functions, such as being able to look at oneself realistically, that are required for gaining understanding. The most important analytic procedure is **interpretation**—making unconscious phenomena conscious. Strachey (1934) stated in a classic paper that interpretation modifies existing psychic structure, where structure is conceived as stable and enduring ways of relating to oneself and others. Greenberg (1996), however, wrote that the client-therapist interaction is mutative "because structure itself consists of internalized interactions represented in a particular way" (p. 36).

Empathy, intuition, and the counselor or therapist's own unconscious and theoretical knowledge all contribute to the construction of an interpretation. Other analytic procedures include confrontation, clarification, and working through. This latter procedure is of great significance because it involves the continued analysis of resistances brought about after an insight has been achieved. It refers to the broadening and deepening of insight that leads to permanent change. An example of a resistance would be a client who takes great pains in coming to sessions exactly on time, not a minute before or after. This would be thought of as a resistance to whatever experience the client might fear in being late or early. Being late could represent aggression toward the therapist (making him or her wait), and being early a feeling of need of the therapist and fear the therapist will be disapproving. Working through in this case would involve confronting the client with this behavior and helping him or her sort through feelings, thoughts, and fears about the behavior. As such resistance often continues for some time, this process takes several weeks or months to work through to the point where the client does not act (or freezes oneself from acting in this case), but can put his or her feelings into words and perhaps fantasies (images or daydreams) and arrive at an understanding that would then obviate the necessity of that particular resistance.

Gill (1996) described what he believes to be a major shift in conceptualizing therapeutic action or change. This shift is away from the emphasis on interpretations to an emphasis on what he calls the "experiential factor." What he means is that the experience between the client and the counselor or therapist is what is mutative. This shift has meant a greater awareness of and appreciation for how the therapist experiences the therapeutic interaction and how this experience (which includes countertransference) influences the course of change (or lack thereof). In training analysts, this shift is seen in a drifting away from supervising analysts' trying to help the analyst trainee find the "right" interpretation to trying to understand what is happening in the experience of a therapy session, not only with the client but also within the analyst trainee. Interpretations would then be less about the "there and then" and more about the "here and now."

Clients with Mental Disorders

Up until the 1950s, it was believed that psychoanalysis could only be applied to intelligent, motivated, and fairly high functioning clients. It was believed that the process of psychoanalysis induced a regression in the client and that such instability and turmoil could not be weathered by more disturbed clients. Many papers were written on the subject of **analyzability,** which is essentially deciding whether a client can benefit (and will not be harmed by) a psychoanalytic approach. Since the 1950s, there has been increasing applications to more disturbed clients. Indeed, if psychoanalysis is the therapy that attempts the most fundamental and profound change, should it not be applied to those clients who are in the greatest despair of mental disorders? Put another way, if a loved one had a serious condition, would you not want to consider all available treatments to aid recovery? Especially those that might be regarded as the most powerful in producing change?

Many, if not most, psychoanalytically oriented counselors or therapists would say that you do not begin psychotherapy as a psychoanalysis. As with any other approach, you begin by taking a history, making comments to indicate you understand and perhaps have empathy for the client's suffering, and work to establish goals the client wants to accomplish. It is only after a period of months of psychotherapy that a psychoanalyst would begin to think about shifting the therapy to a psychoanalysis. Hence, there has been much literature in the past 10–20 years on the subject of such shifting.

There are no hard and fast rules that state which mental disorders are most successfully treated by a psychoanalytic approach. To illustrate, a client who has been in once-a-week psychotherapy for over a year is considering increasing to two sessions a week. Her goal at the start of treatment was to find out if she had a drinking problem. Over the course of the year, this presenting problem changed to the issue of her fear of being in a relationship. She fears she will become emotionally vulnerable and then be devastated by the person leaving her "because they always do," she says. One of her first associations to the idea of a second session was that one day, out of the blue, I would decide not to see her any more and she would be greatly hurt. The unconscious conflicts underlying this expectation would be explored in a psychoanalytic approach. It is evident that transference reactions are strong and provide the client an opportunity to work through (put into words, understand) what these conflicts are about and why. More frequent sessions intensify these transference reactions.

Evaluation

Overview

This section of the chapter presents information dealing with research supporting psychoanalytic theory and its application to counseling and therapy and also the limitations that surround the use of this theoretical approach. Thousands of research studies have been conducted on the scientific status of psychoanalysis, and this research is ongoing. Limitations exist in terms of both cost of treatment and geographical setting.

Supporting Research

Psychoanalysis shares with other fields of study in the social sciences the problem of demonstrating itself as scientific. In addition, because it is a method of therapy, research limitations are imposed upon it that do not exist in other fields. For example, a simple research design of treating one person analytically while using a similar person as a control would be unethical. Therefore, the empirical value of psychoanalysis has to be founded on clinical investigations—that is, the empirical testability of psychoanalytic theory must be demonstrated in the treatment situation. As Grunbaum (1984) notes, "The naturalistic setting or 'psychoanalytic situation' is purported to be the arena of experiments in situ, in marked contrast to the contrived environment of the psychological laboratory with its superficial, transitory interaction between the experimental psychologist and his subject"

(p. 100). The following information is a cursory review of research findings from studies of the psychoanalytic theory and method.

In *The Scientific Credibility of Freud's Theories and Therapy,* Fisher and Greenberg (1977) compiled a synthesis of almost 2,000 individual studies on the scientific status of psychoanalysis. They concluded that Freudian theory had been subjected to more scientific appraisal than any other theory in psychology and that results had borne out Freud's expectations. Similarly, Luborsky and Spence (1978) emphasize that the psychoanalytic session has epistemic superiority over validity obtained from the more artificially controlled conditions of an experiment and supports Freud's general theory of unconscious motivation.

Despite these affirmations, particularly as they relate to the clinical observation of the major motivational forces of mental life, current criticism of psychoanalysis focuses on its use of multiple sessions and overall length of treatment. Opponents of psychoanalysis point to the efficacy of briefer models of treatment, especially in contemporary health care settings where cost of care is a major concern. They argue that brief, technique-oriented psychotherapy may be just as effective in alleviating a specific symptom without uncovering unconscious dynamics. This debate is not so much about the empirical testability or value of psychoanalysis as it is about the economics of treatment.

Limitations

Psychoanalysis in the United States has traditionally been limited to educated middle- to upper-class clients who are able to afford the cost of treatment. Likewise, counselors or therapists using psychoanalysis have tended to practice mainly in areas of large urban populations. Therefore, the urban and rural poor, as well as the rural middle and upper class, have not had access to psychoanalytic services. Even if this limitation were alleviated by a national health care plan, the overall cost of educating a counselor or therapist, as well as the personal sacrifices involved in analytic training, automatically tend to limit the availability of practitioners certified in psychoanalysis. It is a rigorous training method that severely taxes interested candidates both financially and emotionally. The unfortunate outcome of this last limitation is that it restricts the pool of psychotherapists, whose training includes—in fact, mandates—personal therapy of considerable duration.

It is not surprising that counselors and therapists, on occasion, harbor disturbing feelings toward their clients. These strong passions of both love and hate can skew how well the therapy is conducted. Sometimes a practitioner is aware of these strong emotions, but sometimes they are buried in the unconscious, making an understanding of the source and usefulness of these feelings unavailable as a means of improving the therapeutic process. In this regard, psychoanalytic training provides an advantage that could be offered to any counselor or therapist who wishes to go beyond a method of brief or technique-limited therapy. Those who do not have an understanding of the source and rationale for emotions experienced in therapeutic situations may be shortchanging themselves and their clients.

The limitations of psychoanalytic methods, as applied to large populations of both rural and urban poor, may never be alleviated. Yet, greater strides may be made toward offering counselors and therapists, through psychoanalytic training, a sound procedure for better understanding themselves and their clients, thereby improving their overall therapeutic skill.

Summary Chart—Psychoanalytic Theory

Human Nature

Human nature is dynamic, based upon the flow and exchange of energy within the personality. This view is based on two fundamental hypotheses concerning mental development and functioning: psychic determinism, or causality (nothing happens by chance or in a random way, and all mental phenomena have a causal connection to the psychic events that precede them); and unconscious mental processes (a portion of the mind works within a framework of timelessness, spacelessness, and the coexistence of opposites).

Major Constructs

- The topographic hypothesis means that there exists a conscious and unconscious mind.
- The dynamic hypothesis sees the mind as a closed energy system where every effect has a cause.
- The economic hypothesis entails the pleasure-pain and constancy principles.
- The structural hypothesis divides the mind into id, ego, and superego.
- The adaptive hypothesis describes how the individual attempts to cope with societal demands.

Goals

The goals of psychoanalysis place emphasis on the resolution of clients' problems so as to enhance clients' personal adjustment, their working through unresolved developmental stages, and their ability to cope more effectively with the demands of the society within which they live.

Change Process

The changing of the personality and character structure of the individual involves resolving unconscious conflicts, working through unresolved developmental issues, and developing skills to cope with particular societal relationship demands.

Interventions

- Free association involves encouraging the client to say whatever comes to mind.
- Analysis of dreams is important because dreams reflect the status of the analytic relationship.
- Analysis of transference is an attempt to state what is happening between client and analyst.
- Analysis of resistance involves putting into words what is blocking the patient's awareness.
- Interpretation refers to the analyst's formulation of what is taking place in the analysis.

Limitations

- More than any other treatment, psychoanalysis requires the client's commitment in terms of time, money, and personal effort.
- Psychoanalysis is a long-term treatment.
- Psychoanalysis is generally available only in urban areas as a result of the availability of trained analysts.
- A rigorous training program requiring time, money, and emotional commitment of practitioners is a formidable obstacle.

The Case of Jonathan: A Psychoanalytic Approach

In order to continue to illustrate the psychoanalytic method and theory outlined in the preceding pages, it is necessary to invent a session as we might imagine it unfolding. As already noted, the research material of psychoanalysis is drawn from the productions of clients in therapeutic settings—that is, free association, dream analysis, and so on. This material is used to substantiate psychoanalytic theories regarding mental functions. Accordingly, this section provides clinical material as it might unfold in order to serve as an example as well as to explain ideas about unconscious processes.

With this client, it may be hard to distinguish a psychoanalytic approach from other positions. The client is experiencing severe symptoms of depression, alcohol abuse, severe guilt, and suicidal ideation. Indeed, he says he has little to live for and feels responsible for "ruining" the lives of almost everyone he has gotten close to. He is in jeopardy at his job after having been recently suspended for angry arguments. It seems clear that turmoil is reaching the boiling point and that to encourage him to explore unconscious conflicts and dynamics at this point is ill-timed. Similar to most other approaches, the first step in treatment with Jonathan would be problem-solving in nature, including a possible psychiatric referral for medication to lessen the severity of his anger and depression.

What would distinguish a psychoanalytic approach at this beginning phase of treatment is not so much what could be directly observed in a session. It is more in the mind of the psychoanalytically-oriented therapist. It is the hypotheses and questions generated in the therapist's mind about what is happening inside the client's mind. In engaging in such internal theorizing, the therapist can guide his or her interventions. For example, with Jonathan there seems a great risk that he will leave therapy abruptly. His solution attempt for his problems on the reservation was to leave. He seeks the immediate amelioration of depressed feelings with alcohol, and this speaks to his limited frustration tolerance. Therapy is not likely to afford him the immediate gratification of alcohol, and he will likely become easily disenchanted. Add to this that he believes non-Native Americans are prejudiced against him and assuming the therapist is not Native-American, basic issues of trust are immediately present. The therapist might ask Jonathan if he could work with a non-Native American or if he would prefer to be referred out. At this early stage and with this type of client, analyzing the client's feelings about prejudice are certainly premature. The classically Freudian technique is one of such analyzing, but in this day and age, that would be a caricature more befitting a Hollywood movie. An analytic approach would recognize that the first and most pressing need therapeutically is to build trust. Asking about Jonathan's desire on the ethnicity of the therapist is an intervention toward that goal. It recognizes Jonathan's belief and concern without interpreting it as some expression of neurotic conflict.

A second strategy to develop trust would be to attempt to establish a working alliance. For example, the therapist could engage Jonathan as an ally in trying to figure out what he could do to minimize the tension on his job. This would lead to the therapist's asking many questions about the job and, in particular, Jonathan's thoughts and feelings about co-workers and his supervisor. At every opportunity, the therapist would make comments to indicate an empathic understanding of Jonathan's perspective—to see it and feel it through his eyes. With a client as guarded and angry and depressed as Jonathan, this is the greatest challenge to the therapist. What makes this so challenging is that clients such as Jonathan elicit emotional reactions from others, including the therapist. Jonathan is likely to express anger early on to the therapist; perhaps being 10 minutes late the first session is such an expression. Perhaps as a sign of his conflict around anger he was apologetic. He was also coerced into coming to the appointment, so he is perhaps even more guarded and perhaps resentful.

How do therapists develop skill in empathic attunement? One defining feature of therapists with psychoanalytic training is that undergoing one's own analysis is required. Such therapists have been in Jonathan's position as client. Such therapists have not only talked the talk, they've walked the walk. They are aware—not only intellectually but at a gut level—of what it feels like to be vulnerable, to not know, to seek help from another, to admit failure. As therapy progresses with Jonathan, more defining features of a psychoanalytic position will emerge. Perhaps chief among these are transference-related comments. For example, if Jonathan came late to a session and apologized profusely, the therapist might say something like, "You know, I had the feeling that you were apologizing for more than just being late, that you seemed to feel very bad about it, more so than what one would expect. Any thoughts about that?"

As therapy progresses, more observations and interpretations about Jonathan's feelings toward the therapist (his transference reactions) will be commented on and explored. The purpose is to help Jonathan see and understand, in the here-and-now immediate relationship with the therapist, how and why he relates to people the way he does. This opportunity would seem crucial for a client like Jonathan, as so much of his history and reported problems have to do with a fundamental breakdown in relating to other people.

No psychoanalytic approach would be complete without a discussion about a client's dream. Dreams and slips of the tongue in everday speech were seen by Freud as windows into the unconscious. In psychoanalytic therapy, dreams are most important for what they communicate about a client's hidden (unconscious) thoughts and feelings about the therapist. In time, the therapist becomes the object of the client's thoughts and feelings, and long-standing fears and hopes from important others (mainly parents) get transferred onto the therapist. A dream in the course of therapy can only be understood and useful if one sees the context in which the dream originated. In other words, what has been going on in the session or sessions prior to the dream? In the case of Jonathan, there is a recurring dream at the beginning of treatment that would not involve the therapist. This would be of interest in that this recurring dream might change over the course of treatment to reflect the conflicts that would arise, in particular, conflicting feelings toward the therapist. Nevertheless, an attempt at analyzing Jonathan's dream can be made.

My first reaction to this dream is that he's trapped and that there is movement. This speaks to the urgency Jonathan feels: things are hurtling along and he is losing control. I would be concerned about suicide more so with this dream, given that Jonathan has already said he has little to live for. Another striking feature of the dream is that the bus driver is a woman: a woman is in control of his fate. She laughs at him, sadistically, as he acts out his impotence by banging with a pipe on the steering wheel. At the end of the dream, he is with the laughing driver, and yet he feels alone.

The usefulness of such a dream lies in what associations the client and the therapist make while discussing it. Such associations are a continuation of the dream and help to flush out some of its meanings. Of particular significance would be meanings regarding the client's feelings and thoughts about the therapist. If this dream occurred months into treatment, it might be speculated that the laughing bus driver is the therapist, taking the client places he does not want to go (painful feelings and memories) and never stopping long enough to allow the client to disembark (three or four sessions a week).

Suggested Readings

Bollas, C. (1999). *The mystery of things*. New York: Routledge.

Caspi, A. (2000). The child is father to the man: Personality continuities from childhood to adulthood. *Journal of Personality and Social Psychology, 78,* 158–172.

Eagle, M. N. (1999). A critical evaluation of current conceptions of transference and countertransference. *Psychoanalytic Psychology, 17,* 24–37.

Galatzer-Levy, R. M., & Barach, H. (2000). *Does psychoanalysis work?* New Haven: Yale University Press.

Jones, E. E. (2000). *Therapeutic action: A guide to psychoanalytic therapy*. Northvale, NJ: Jason Aronson.

Kaley, H., Eagle, M., & Wolitzky, D. (Eds.). (1999). *Psychoanalytic therapy as health care: Effectiveness and economics*. Hillsdale, NJ: Analytic Press.

Kirshner, L. (1999). Toward a postmodern realism for psychoanalysis. *Journal of the American Psychoanalytic Association, 47,* 445–463.

Meissner, W. W. (2000). On analytic listening. *Psychoanalytic Quarterly, 69,* 317–367.

Mitchell, S. (2000). *Relationality: From attachment to intersubjectivity*. Hillsdale, NJ: Analytic Press.

Teicholz, J. G. (1999). *Kohut, Loewald, and the postmoderns*. Hillsdale, NJ: Analytic Press.

Jungian Analytical Theory

Susan E. Schwartz
C. G. Jung Institute of Santa Fe, New Mexico

Everything good is costly, and the development of personality is one of the most costly of all things. It is a matter of saying yea to oneself, of taking oneself as the most serious of tasks, of being conscious of everything one does, and keeping it constantly before one's eyes in all its dubious aspects—truly a task that taxes us to the utmost. (Jung, 1967, p. 24)

Background

Jungian analytical psychology originated with the Swiss psychiatrist Carl Gustav Jung. An early member of Freud's psychoanalytic circle, Jung had at one point been designated by Freud to head the psychoanalytic movement. However, through a series of events, dreams, and interactions with Freud, it became clear to Jung that he could not agree with Freud concerning the primacy of the sexual trauma theory and Freud's approach to psychological phenomena. Their differences were accentuated in Jung's book *Symbols of Transformation*. The ideas Jung articulated in this book were pivotal to his being ostracized by Freud and the psychoanalytic organization, as he made different interpretations of psychological processes.

After resigning from teaching psychiatry at the University of Zurich and leaving his position at the Burkholzi Psychiatric Clinic in Zurich, Jung spent 6 years with no outer production but his private analytical practice. All his energy was absorbed in a psychological crisis, a personal and professional journey precipitated by the break with Freud. Through deepening psychological work involving journaling and dialoguing with dreams, constructing figures and cities in sand, drawing, chiseling in stone, researching myth, Eastern religions, and ancient cultures, Jung developed the concepts later appearing in his writings and methodology of personality transformation, which he called the **process of individuation.**

Jung's work at the Burkholzi Clinic, under Eugen Bleuler (famous for his studies in schizophrenia), included his development of the word association test. This psychological test revealed the complexes with their archetypal core and confirmed the influence of the unconscious on conscious life. The research brought Jung and Freud together because both were unearthing evidence about the existence and effects of the unconscious. Jung also discovered what he later termed the *collective unconscious* from working with schizophrenic patients. The dreams and actions of these patients reflected the images and symbols found in ancient religions, alchemy, myths, and tales of the world. Jung says,

> At a time when all available energy is spent in the investigation of nature, very little attention is paid to the essence of man, which is his psyche, although many researches are made into its conscious functions … yet deciphering these communications seems to be such an odious task that very few people in the whole civilized world can be bothered with it. Man's greatest instrument, his psyche, is little thought of, if not actually mistrusted and despised. "It's only psychological" too often means: "it is nothing." (1964, p. 102)

Jung's basic premise resonated with his belief in the reality of the **psyche.**

Jung, born in 1875, descended from a heritage of clergymen. His father was a minister in a small town outside of Basel, Switzerland. During preparation for his confirmation in the Protestant church, Jung was dismayed by his father's lack of faith and inability to convey his spirituality. This lacuna led to Jung's lifelong search for spiritual components within the psyche. (*Spiritual* refers to a connection to the meaning of one's life and also to whatever is beyond one's life.) This and other disappointing experiences with his father contributed to Jung's projection of the father image onto Freud, 20 years his senior. On their trip to America to lecture at Clark University in 1907, Freud refused to share his dreams and interpreted Jung's dreams in personalistic modes. From the disappointment in this experience, Jung began the eventual severance of their friendship, propelling him on a different path. The psychological struggles in their relationship portray aspects of the initiation process when a son separates from his father.

Jung was significantly influenced by observing the two personalities of his mother. He perceived her outward compliance with social rubrics, while under her breath she expressed contrasting individual opinions. Jung later used this concept in his theoretical distinction between the **personal unconscious** and collective unconscious and the **ego** and **Self.** His mother and father, whose relationship was emotionally distant, represented the dichotomies of **spirit** and **matter, anima** and **animus, persona** and **shadow.**

Jungian analytical psychology derived from Jung's life, and its theories and substantiations came from his clinical work. He said, "My life is what I have done, my scientific work; the one is inseparable from the other. The work is the expression of inner development" (1963, p. 211). Jung found parallels to his psychological explorations in the various religions and symbols of the world, the medieval science of alchemy, and in myths and fairy tales. They all delineated the classic psychological patterns evident in his clinical practice and supported two of Jung's contributions to psychology: the collective unconscious and the process of individuation.

Prior to a discussion of the various tenets of Jungian analytical theory, Figure 4.1 "Jungian Vocabulary" is presented to aid the reader in better understanding the special terminology used by Jung in explaining various aspects of his theory.

The author of this chapter used only Jung's original writings as references for the chapter. A listing of current publications is provided for the reader in the "Suggested Readings" section at the end of the chapter.

Anima: The constellation of feminine qualities in a man

Animus: The masculine side of a woman

Archetype: All typical, universal human manifestations of life—whether biological, psychological, or spiritual. They reflect instinctive reactions that have an inherited mode of psychic functioning and arise from the collective unconscious.

Complex: An energic constellation composed of a cluster of images with a similar feeling tone, presenting as more or less well-organized and autonomous parts of the personality.

Ego: The center of the field of consciousness. Its role is to maintain relation with other psychological contents. It establishes boundaries between a person and others.

Persona: The person's presentation put forth to the world. It is structured from parental introjects, social role expectations, and peer expectations.

Psyche: The essence of a person; the totality of all psychic processes. It is composed of the conscious and unconscious.

Self: The Self provides the blueprint of life and is the center and guide to the personality. It expresses the unity of the personality and encompasses the experienced as well as the not yet known. The Self contains the uniqueness of each person entwined with the entirety of life—human, plant, animal, inorganic matter, and the cosmos.

Shadow: The "not I" subpersonality. It symbolizes the other or dark side that is an invisible but inseparable part of the psychic totality. It has both positive and negative forms and can be manifest in both personal and collective figures.

Figure 4.1
Jungian Vocabulary

Human Nature: A Developmental Perspective

The psyche, the essence of a person, is composed of the conscious and unconscious, and is the matrix from which consciousness arises. The personal unconscious is composed of the forgotten, repressed, and subliminally perceived events and reactions in one's life. The collective unconscious includes symbols, images, and **archetypes** common to all peoples. The foundation of every individual contains these deposits of human reactions to universal situations occurring since primordial times. The personality is composed of the ego, persona, shadow, anima, animus, and Self.

Ego

The ego is the center of the field of consciousness, and its role is to maintain relation with other psychological contents. It is personally oriented with the task of developing subjective identity and self-worth, and establishes boundaries between a person and others. The ego must be functional for the inner gifts to be actualized.

The ego's archetypal core is the Self, the director of the whole personality. The first half of life involves the ego separation from the Self. In the second half of life, ego and self reunite and assimilate alienated aspects of the personality. The process of individuation requires giving up the will of the ego for a resilient relationship with the Self.

Persona

In Jungian psychology, the word *persona* (from the Greek, meaning "sounding through a mask") denotes the presentation put forth to the world. The persona is structured from parental introjects, social role responsibilities, and peer expectations. Although the genuine nature of a person comes through the public face, the persona can be a cover for personality weaknesses and conjoin with the need for protection and acceptance. The persona either prevents the inner conflicts and insecurities from attaining visibility, or its creative aspects lead to growth.

The persona is like a skin mediating the inside and outside and functioning in dynamic and compensatory relation to the ego, shadow, anima and animus, and Self. The persona bridges the gap between the ego and the outside world, while the animus and anima, the inner masculine and feminine images, mediate between the ego and the core of the Self. The persona corresponds and is compensatory to the habitual outer attitude, and the animus or anima reflects the habitual inner attitude. If rigid, the persona severs a person from the natural instincts, and the anima and animus remain undifferentiated and the shadow repressed. In this situation, the ego lacks flexibility and adaptation.

There are problems when the individuality of a person is suppressed or neglected to fit **collective ideals**—outer expectations substitute for one's individual standpoint. If external values are artificially adapted, a person acts in false and mechanistic conduct to himself or herself and others. Inordinate dependence on the persona denotes self-distrust and inauthenticity.

Shadow

The shadow, or "not-I" subpersonality, and its differentiation from the ego are part of the movement into personality awareness. Jung says,

> The shadow ... usually presents a fundamental contrast to the conscious personality. This contrast is the prerequisite for the difference of potential from which psychic energy arises. Without it, the necessary tension would be lacking.... One is flat and boring when too unsullied and there is too much effort expended in the secret life away from the eyes of the others. Without its counterpart virtue would be pale, ineffective, and unreal. Their impact on consciousness finally produces the uniting symbols. (1963, p. 707)

The shadow confronts a person with dilemmas arising from being a part of the collective consciousness. Jungian psychology warns of the danger of blind obedience to the collective, resulting in neglect of the individual. Jung brought attention to the shadow because he lived through two world wars where the **collective shadow** brutally ruled. Facing the shadow promotes reflection on human nature and reveals individual values. Living the shadow consciously implies taking responsibility for oneself and others, owning talents and problems, and taking back projections. The moral obligation to live one's potential appears in dream figures that signify repressed personality aspects.

We are often ambivalent about the shadow, which contains the worst and best in the personality. The dark side gains strength when potential is denied. Although it is bitter to accept the shadow—the black, the chaos, the melancholia—doing so can be the start of psychological work. Jung thought of the shadow as the first complex to personalize in analysis. It also contains material with the potential for healing.

The shadow is difficult to confront and assimilate because of the ease of unconsciously projecting it onto others. We prefer to entertain idealized images of ourselves rather than acknowledge weaknesses or shame. Recognizing the shadow means giving up the ideal or perfect. The shadow gives dimensionality to life, makes one real, and allows the ego to use its strength. Owning one's shadow makes it easier to solve relationship and family problems rather than projecting the unwanted or rejected contents. By taking back projections, the personality attains definition, style, and inner unity.

Integration of the personal shadow provides a bridge from the ego to the **contra-sexual** part of the personality. Jung says that a person "will have every opportunity to discover the dark side of his personality, his inferior wishes and motives, childish fantasies and resentments, etc.: in short, all those traits he habitually hides from himself. He will be confronted with his shadow, but more rarely with the good qualities, of which he is accustomed to make a show anyway. He will learn to know his soul, his anima" (1963, p. 673). (Please note Jung's use of the masculine pronoun reflects the bias of his era.)

Anima

In Jungian psychology, the anima (from the Greek, meaning "soul") connotes the constellation of feminine qualities in a man. It personifies his relation to these aspects, the image of woman inside himself, and his projections onto females. In each era the feminine image changes. The anima initially is experienced from a male's psychological life with his mother or the primary female figure in his life and is influenced by his personal and archetypal experience of the feminine. Becoming conscious of this sexual polarity is essential for personality completeness and psychological union of the masculine and feminine aspects. This concept applies to all people, regardless of sexual orientation.

The anima is an archetype, and, like all archetypes, is never wholly comprehended. It is discovered with inner work. If separate from his feminine nature, a man can become uneasy, uncommitted, avoid conflict, and drift. Disconnected from the feminine and his emotions, he pays sparse attention to his psyche, and this constricts inner and outer freedom. Flat and monotonous moods signify anima neglect and cause various reactions such as depression, impotence, and even suicide. When out of touch with this aspect of his personality, a man might use drivenness, accomplishment, or physical performance to avoid inner reflection. Fearing the feminine, he becomes distant from inner and outer relationships, and the anima cannot sufficiently function as the bridge to the ego and the self.

The inner feminine becomes known through images from the unconscious, which are associated with the instinctual part of life, the flow of emotion, the rhythm of nature, and the physicality of pleasure. The anima can take the forms of the creative muse, lover, caregiver, and so on. Jung defines the anima as implying the "recognition of the existence of a semiconscious psychic complex, having partial autonomy of function" (1953a, p. 302). He describes the anima as expressing spiritual values and being close to nature. As the anima becomes increasingly differentiated, a man assumes an active rather than a passive role in relation to the feminine. In reference to this, Jung describes consciousness arising from the anima: "It lives of itself, makes one live, and cannot be fully part of consciousness" (1959, par. 57). This statement refers to the transcendent and archetypal aspects that extend the personality beyond ego consciousness.

Animus

The animus (from the Greek, meaning "spirit" or "breath") refers to the masculine side of a woman. It is influenced by the collective image of man that woman inherits, her experience of masculinity from contact with her father or other primary male figures, and the masculine principle in the culture. If the animus is undeveloped, without sufficient room for expression or growth, it hinders the feminine through internal castigations and sufferings, undermining her participation in life. Classically interpreted, the animus signifies woman's feeling relationship to man, culture, and spiritual life, reflecting the predominance of the masculine deity in Western culture.

Feminine nature is pushed into the background by the negative animus. Unassimilated, unacknowledged, or projected, the negative animus causes chronic self esteem problems, power struggles, and self alienation. The negative animus manifests in a voice of critical commentary or issues excessive commands and prohibitions. Drawn to a destructive fascination with the animus, a person may sever contact with the world, give up her or his soul, be dreamy and without focus, or be driven to accomplishment.

There are problems if a father has no limits and is either all giving or a rigid disciplinarian. If he is encased in a distant and foreboding authority structure, a daughter is not personally affected in a positive way. If his emotion is absent or he is physically unavailable, a negative father complex forms. Activating the masculine principle brings courage, determination, force, and authority. These qualities from a positive father complex enable a person to be effective and competent in the world.

The anima and animus together form a **heiros gamos,** or an internal union of opposites in the personality, appearing in dreams, ancient symbols like yin and yang, and relationships. In current Jungian thought, the anima and animus characteristics are found in both males and females to different degrees depending on the person.

Self

Behind all psychological patterns lies the Self, the blueprint of life and the unfolding center and guide for the personality. The Self contains the uniqueness of each person entwined with the entirety of life—human, plant, animal, inorganic matter, and the cosmos. The Self is a synthesis for personality emergence, a cohesive force establishing balance and well-being and guiding the whole personality. It causes us to be what we are and is based on the innate drive toward self-realization.

The Self is personal, yet its striving nature affects the progress of humanity. The empirical symbols of the Self are identified with an aura of numinosity, and its images have strong emotional value. They appear in dreams in many forms such as animals, hermaphroditic figures, jewels, flowers, and geometric concentrically arranged figures known as **mandalas.** *Mandala* is a Sanskrit word meaning "magic circle," and is one of the oldest religious symbols. Jung discovered the mandala in the dreams of his patients, where it functioned as a creator and preserver of development and pushed the personality through chaos toward potential wholeness.

The question is not how the Self is created during the course of life, but the extent of its attaining consciousness. The Self is a **temenos,** a center for the source and ultimate foundation of our being, transcending personal vision. It is a metapsychological concept referring to the entirety of the psyche and containing the whole range of psychic phenomena.

The Self, composed of archetypes and instincts, is supraordinate to the conscious ego. This center of the personality, the midpoint that embraces the conscious and the unconscious psyche, is also the whole circumference. "The beginnings of our whole psychic life seem to be inextricably rooted in this point and all our highs and ultimate purposes seem to be striving toward it" (Jung, 1967, p. 67). The Self is without bounds, an illimitable and indeterminable unconscious where one is simultaneously oneself and connected beyond the personal.

We are born with the Self as the matrix of potential faculties waiting to be actualized. "In the last analysis," Jung says, "every life is the realization of a whole, that is, of a self, for which reason this realization can also be called individuation" (1953b, p. 330). The Self is paradoxical, containing both positive and negative polarities for the organizing of experiences, operating through the ego, and having continuity throughout time.

Major Constructs

When psychic energy, or libido, is lost from consciousness, it passes into the unconscious and activates the contents of the archetypes and complexes. Jung's concept of **enantio-dromia**, a term he borrowed from the Greek philosopher Heraclitus, means "flowing into the opposite." The psyche is a dynamic, self-regulating system governed by opposition, based on complementary or compensatory factors pulsing through all psychological constructs. The point is not to radically convert from one side to the other, but to integrate personality aspects.

Jungian psychology is teleologically oriented, based on a philosophy of human development proceeding from childhood though adulthood. Each stage of life requires new attitudes, renewed orientation, and reanchoring to different contexts. The major constructs that undergird this development are psychological types, complexes, archetypes, symbols, and the personal and collective unconscious.

Psychological Types

Jung's notion of typology orients itself toward conscious life. The terms *extravert* and *introvert* originated with Jung. They represent the two attitudes for perceiving the world and one's relationship to it. An extravert looks at the world and then to himself or herself, whereas an introvert uses the perspective of the inner world and then perceives the outer. The extravert is influenced by collective norms, the introvert by subjective factors. Jungian analysts are predominantly introverts, as are often those who come for this kind of counseling or psychotherapeutic treatment. The work emphasizes the mix of conscious and unconscious and appeals to people searching the psychological depths to find their way.

In addition to the two attitudes, there are four functions that determine a person's psychological perception of the conscious world: *sensation,* perceiving through the senses; *thinking,* giving order and understanding; *feeling,* which weighs and values; and *intuition,* the leap to future possibilities. In each person, one function, called the *superior function,* predominates and takes its particular form according to social and cultural influences. Another function, called the *inferior function,* remains mostly unconscious and is connected to the shadow. The functions are limited to four, a number regarded throughout cultural history as designating wholeness and totality.

The main or superior function becomes the most developed and the two accessory functions reasonably so, leaving the fourth or inferior function undifferentiated, primitive, impulsive, and out of conscious control. Because human nature is not simple, we rarely find an absolutely pure type. The functions change in dominance depending on the activities at different life stages. The attitudes do not change but are realized as a person progresses through life. For example, a child may appear to be an introvert in a quiet and withdrawn family, but later in life he or she may uncover this adaptation and release the pent-up extraversion.

Each attitude can be paired with each function, making eight psychological combinations in all. For example, a person may be introverted sensation thinking, extraverted sensation feeling, and so on. The complementary or compensatory relation between the opposite functions is a structural law of the psyche. In the second half of life, the inferior function gains attention as the psychological situation naturally alters to round out the personality.

A sensation type person takes life as it comes, focusing on the conscious daily perception of physical stimuli. Intuition and sensation are called *irrational functions*—the *rational functions* are logical and associated with thinking and feeling. Intuition is the opposite function to sensation, and the person of this type is imbued with creative capacities and inspirations. Intuitive types perceive possibilities, but can be so removed from the present and the senses that they forget the physical world. Thinking is apparent in persons ruled by intellectual motives; their life actions are based on objective data. Such people prefer logic and order, and emotion and feeling are repressed. A thinking person tends to be cold and has difficulty understanding human relationships. In contrast to this, a feeling type is especially concerned with human relationships, but feeling is not to be confused with emotion. Any function can lead to emotional reactions. A feeling person weighs, accepts, or refuses by evaluating what something is worth.

The Myers-Briggs Type Indicator is a popularized adaptation of Jung's principles of **typology.** It is not taught in Jungian institutes because it is solely oriented to conscious functioning, and is not Jung's original conception.

Complex

A complex is an energic **constellation** with varying degrees of autonomy, ranging from hardly disturbing ego functioning to attaining predominance over the personality. It is composed of a cluster of images or ideas with a similar feeling tone, presenting as a well-organized and autonomous part of the personality. The psyche's inherent tendency to split into complexes brings dissociation, multiplicity, and the possibility of change and differentiation.

Jungian counseling or psychotherapy aims to separate the complexes from the unconscious into conscious awareness. Jung says we all have complexes and the real issue is whether or not they are controlling us. Complexes either repress or promote consciousness, inhibit or inspire, hinder development or provide the seeds for new life. Complexes are like magnets, drawing psychological and archetypal experience into a person's life. They occur where energy is repressed or blocked, point to unresolved problems and weaknesses, and develop from emotional wounds. When a complex is touched, it is accompanied by exaggerated emotional reactions and may also be experienced physically.

A complex does not completely disappear, but the arrangement of energy changes with awareness. The psychic energy caught in the complex is accessed for personality development. No complex should entirely control the personality, but the ego complex dominates during waking life. The particular makeup of a complex is apparent through images pertaining to the unconscious psychological situation occurring in dreams and the synchronous events of waking life. One's destiny can be adversely affected by a complex, and psychological issues can remain unresolved for generations. For example, a woman with a negative father complex can transfer a limited purview onto everything male and operate from negatively biased perceptions.

Archetype

The personal unconscious consists of complexes, and the collective unconscious is composed of archetypes. The word *archetype* originated with Plato, and means "ideal form" or "first imprint." The archetype is at the core of the complex. It is imbued with the tendency to form images rich in emotional content with infinite possibilities for analysis. The repetitions and clustering of archetypes are called **motifs.**

The archetype is a formless structure with infinite varieties, enmeshed in history, and more or less pertinent to a time or place in the evolution of the psyche. The archetype is expressed and comprehended through mythological and sacred images in cultural and personal life. Jung comments on this when he says that "it is only possible to come to a right understanding and appreciation of a contemporary psychological problem when we reach a point outside our own time from which to observe it. This point can only be some past epoch that was concerned with the same problems, although under different conditions and in other forms" (1954, p. viii).

We inherit a tendency to structure experiences of psyche and **soma** in typical and predictable ways called archetypes. These archetypes have a basic form, express the human psyche, and define a pattern of development. Yet Jung states, "No archetype can be reduced to a simple formula. It is a vessel which can never empty and never fill. It has a potential existence only, and when it takes shape in matter it is no longer what it was. It persists throughout the ages and requires interpreting anew. The archetypes are imperishable elements of the unconscious, but they change their shape continually" (1959, p. 301).

These building blocks of the psyche operate in basic psychological instinctual patterns that are counterparts to the biological instincts. Instincts are impulses of action without conscious motivation. Like a snake appearing in a dream, instincts are collective, universal, and regularly occurring phenomena, without individuality yet having personal significance. Jung describes the archetype as composed of two poles. The "psychic infra-red," or the biological psyche of one end, gradually passes into the "psychic ultra-violet" on the psychic end. The archetype describes a field both psychic and physical. The essence of the archetype forms a bridge where spirit and matter meet.

Jung says that the archetype "represents or personifies certain instinctive data on the dark, primitive psyche, the real but invisible roots of consciousness" (1959, p. 271). An archetype cannot be described but is circumscribed by the opposites of its spectrum. Archetypes are impersonal personifications of human potential encompassing the deeper currents of life. Their images in dreams, mythology, religions, and fairy tales gain relevance with personal application. The remembrance of a favorite fairy tale or myth and its archetypal journey help a person glean meaning from life's sorrows and joys. Archetypes inform everyday life. They are at work in relationships, organizations, family systems, and the way life is experienced and interpreted.

Symbol

The Jungian definition of *symbols* includes the personal and collective, conscious and unconscious. A symbol is felt, often viscerally, as in an important dream. Jung describes this feeling as "numinous," giving significance and depth to life, and connecting with the transcendent.

Each symbol has two sides, one related to the conscious ego and one turned toward the archetypal contents of the collective unconscious. The unconscious produces answers to psychological problems through its symbolic images, which are compensatory to the conscious mind. A symbol takes energy from the unconscious and transforms it to resolve conflicts and channel self-expression. It unfolds as a working metaphor throughout life. Symbols are spontaneous psychic manifestations pertinent for individual and societal change.

It seems understandable that if people are biologically related, they are psychologically related, especially on collective and archetypal levels. Jung studied myths, the fundamental symbolic expressions of human nature, as representing typical psychic phenomena. The mythological patterns reflect the distinctive psyche of a given culture or religion and contain universal symbolic relevance. Myths and their symbols help bring order out of psychological chaos.

The word *symbol* derives from the Greek *symbolon,* which means "coming together." A symbol arises from conflict or disorientation, joins two separate elements, and mobilizes energy. Symbols spontaneously arise from the unconscious psyche, transform it into conscious experience, and energize the ego. Signals in the form of symbols are received through dreams every night.

Psychic contents not yet conscious express themselves in symbolic ways. Because the unconscious contains the germs of future psychological situations and ideas, Jung calls the transmutation of libido or energy through symbols the **transcendent function.** Conscious and unconscious confront each other, and the symbol provides a bridge to a third possibility which is transcendent. It is activated after an experience of disintegration, when the personality is jarred by psychological threats to the status quo.

Because the psyche is as real as the body and encompasses the spiritual and biological realms, the unconscious is the matrix of psychogenic symptoms signaling disharmony with conscious life. To the extent that we are unaware of the symbolic dimension of existence, the problems of life are experienced as symptoms. The ability to recognize the symbolic images behind the symptoms transforms the experience.

Personal Unconscious

The unconscious is continually engaged in the grouping of unconscious contents and coordinates with conscious life by presenting a compensatory relationship to it. The personal unconscious is composed of the memories originating from childhood including past and present events; fantasies, wishes, and desires acquired through life. The personal part of the unconscious holds those qualities that, as a result of trauma, phase of life, and outer situations, reside just below the surface of consciousness and are accessible through dreams, counseling or therapy, and synchronous events of daily life. The personal unconscious is part of what defines us as uniquely ourselves, but it is limited in scope and content. Jung describes it as the subjective psyche and demarcates this from what he calls the collective unconscious or the objective psyche, which extends beyond the personal sphere

CONSCIOUS COMPONENTS—COLLECTIVE AND PERSONAL
PERSONA
EGO—center of the field of consciousness
    TYPOLOGY—
        ATTITUDES:
            Introvert, Extravert
        FUNCTIONS:
            Thinking, Feeling, Sensation, Intuition
SHADOW

UNCONSCIOUS COMPONENTS
COLLECTIVE COMPONENTS   PERSONAL COMPONENTS
    ARCHETYPES   COMPLEXES
        Images, myths, symbols   PERSONAL MEMORIES
                                                Repressed, forgotten,
                                                Traumas

SHADOW
ANIMUS/ANIMA

Figure 4.2
A Jungian Picture of the Psyche—Body, Mind, and Soul

and is unlimited. The point of Jungian psychological treatment is to become conscious of the unconscious contents, both personally and collectively, and the many ways their combination facilitates getting to the roots of the personality for growth and development.

Collective Unconscious

The collective unconscious encompasses all previous aspects of the psyche. This concept distinguishes Jungian analytical psychology from other approaches. The unconscious is not only personal, but also collective and impersonal. The collective unconscious consists of the sum of the instincts and their correlates, the archetypes. This storehouse of potentially energizing, enriching, and also abhorrent material brings the understanding and knowledge that furthers development of each human being. The complexity of the psyche means that our comprehension of it is, at the most, partial because there is no finite knowledge of its boundaries or complete nature.

The collective unconscious goes beyond the individual ego, and its nature is revealed through cultural myths, religious images and symbols, dreams, drawings, active imagination, dance, or any creative work. The collective unconscious contains the deposit of human reactions to universal situations, initiations, and rites of passage through the stages of life operating since primordial time.

Figure 4.2 provides an overview of the major constructs that explain the developmental process inherent in Jungian analytical psychology.

Applications

Overview

The following sections present information dealing with the goals, process of change, and intervention strategies that apply to Jungian analytical psychology. The goals of Jungian psychology stress the processes of individuation, personality unity, and transcendence. The transformation of personality depends on the potential for growth inherent in each person. The intervention strategies that follow are designed to both meet the goals and enhance the change process for an individual, with concurrent ramifications for society.

Goals of Counseling and Psychotherapy

Individuation and personality unification are central to Jungian psychology. Individuation, the differentiation of the various components of the psyche, addresses the development of the unique elements of an individual. As a person gains knowledge of the various personality aspects, these aspects synthesize into what Jung termed the *transcendent function*. Transcendence involves a constant striving for wholeness, integration of the personality, and realization of the self.

The Process of Change

Jungian psychology is conceptually broad and attempts to address the isolation and confusion of modern times. The uneasy ambience and aimlessness of our age impels the search for fulfillment. The illnesses of society—the boredom, joylessness, and inability to love—adversely affect interpersonal and intrapersonal relationships.

The transformation of character follows the potential for growth inherent in the human psyche. When the conscious attitude is at an impasse, psychic energy is drawn into the unconscious and emerges in dreams, images, and synchronous events. Jung's concept of **synchronicity** involves the acausal and meaningful coincidences that impart order in the world, opening the way toward experiencing the Self. For example, the *I Ching*, the ancient book of Chinese wisdom, is based on synchronicity. Asking a question and throwing yarrow sticks or coins provides a symbolic answer to the presenting problem.

Over a lifetime, psychic energy transforms. The individuation process, or the way a person comes into his or her uniqueness, requires the differentiation and reintegration of the unconscious. The process reflects the archetypal, spiritual, and religious activities of the psyche. Jungian counseling or psychotherapy is a method encompassing the phases of education, catharsis, rebirth, and transformation. The process recaptures developmental difficulties where growth is stopped. Renewal comes with initiatory experiences reactivating the psyche.

Jung found the individuation process repeated in history, religious rituals, tribal ceremonials, and initiatory practices. He studied Eastern religions and mystical wisdom literature, the spiritual disciplines of the Kaballah, gnosticism, Kundalini yoga, and so on, as analogous methods to the individuation process. He extensively researched alchemy, a medieval science and precursor to modern day chemistry. The symbols and goals of alchemical work, or symbolically turning lead into gold, parallel the individuation process, the stages of psychological development, dream symbols, and issues of the transference and countertransference.

A person can proceed, often until midlife, functioning reasonably well, but part of the personality remains undeveloped and dormant. A crisis comes, relationships alter, and life becomes tumultuous. Beliefs become challenged, a terminus is reached, and change must occur, with some new direction taken. The energy stored in the unconscious pushes to be known. The prospective, or forward-moving, function of the psyche leads to further development and finding a sense of purpose in life. Jung is noted for recognizing the significance of the second half of life as a time for deepening the personality.

Jungian analysts use the chair and/or couch. People are seen weekly, and preferably two or more times a week. A higher frequency of sessions encourages depth, concentration, and activation of the unconscious influence upon conscious functioning. Because the process of individuation plays out differently for each person, there are no prescribed techniques, no formal treatment goals set by the Jungian counselor or therapist, nor reliance on the traditional pathological categorizing.

Problems develop due to an ossified approach to life and disunity with oneself. The disorder is not only painful, but also becomes an impetus for personality growth. The issue is not whether one has difficulties, but the way they are handled. The psychological illness is simultaneously a warning and a natural attempt at healing. The process of change is not quick or easy. Consciously suffering the psychic pain of the past allows it to transform so that the person gains a more satisfying present and future life. This approach is applicable to people of all ages, including children.

Intervention Strategies

Dreams   Dreams are a natural way to discover and unravel the mysterious workings of the personality. More than just bizarre images that come with sleep, they are as real as waking life. Dreams address core issues, and throughout history they have been recognized as a source of inspiration.

The belief that dreams are a means of divine communication or an occult way of discerning the future was pervasive in the ancient Near East. In biblical times, dreams were considered the agents of God's word, announcing his will to the dreamer. Dream interpretation was an important part of the spiritual life of the ancient Greeks and Egyptians, whose word for *dream* was derived from the verb "to awaken." In all races and at all times, dreams were regarded as truth-telling oracles.

Attending to dreams is a way to obtain information about unknown and untapped psychological areas. Dream information enhances the day world and shines a light on the repressed qualities and contents robbing the individual of actualizing potential. Big dreams occur at significant life markers or crisis times, with dream messages providing inroads to the psyche. Dream books do not suffice as ready-made guides for interpretation because the dream and its symbols cannot be separated from the dreamer. Following dreams leads to recovery of oneself as dreams weave together current experiences with those from the past and future.

Dreams keep us from straying from the truths of the body. Their images are symbolic portrayals of an actual unconscious situation, bringing its potency to life and triggering emotional reactions. Physical disorders in dreams express psychological issues and may serve as an early warning system for illness. Dreams often suggest treatment, contain methods and tools for psychological and physical healing, and crystallize a problem into something workable and understandable.

The Jungian form of counseling or psychotherapy involves not only the treatment of a symptom, but also the reconstruction of an individual and the restoration of human dignity. As Jung writes, "One should never forget that one dreams in the first place, and almost to the exclusion of all else, of oneself" (1964, p. 312). What the dream has to say is always seen in light of the attitude of the conscious mind of the dreamer. When inner potential is negated or ignored, pathology appears; when the gold of the personality becomes stuck and repressed into the unconscious, things go badly.

Recurring dreams, nightmares, and childhood dreams are all crucial expressions of the unconscious and relate to factors primary in the life of the individual and his or her culture. Through personal associations, the dreamer is led deeper into the psyche and finds similar motifs repeated in religions, legends, myths, and fairy tales. Although we have lost the formal rites of initiation, all people have a psychological need to access the spirit which cultural lore imparts. These initiatory processes are stored in the unconscious and emerge through dreams and fantasy material to replenish the personality.

The dream is not merely the ego reflecting on itself, but a communication from the unconscious—beyond, yet in relation to, the ego. To concern oneself with dreams is a way of accessing one's true nature and gaining knowledge to free the complexes. Children are easily in touch with their dreams because they are psychologically closer to the unconscious. For adults, work is needed to get back to this state. Too often the rational world takes over and the inner life is negated.

The dream is like a play with an opening scene, statement of the problem, action, climax, and resolution. The dream characters represent compensatory expressions of the personality. Awareness of the projection of one's qualities onto dream figures is a way to reclaim them. On the subjective level, the figures in dreams are personified features of the dreamer's personality. On the objective level, they represent an actual person or someone in close relation, such as a partner, child, or parent. It is worth noting in the dream where the dreamer stands, the position and action of the dreaming ego, and whether one is an observer, a participant, or not present. There is meaning in the sequential order of events, the people who appear, and those named or unnamed. The latter represent qualities remote from consciousness and, therefore, less identifiable. A dream placed in a foreign or familiar country or not on earth reveals the distance of the psychological information from conscious awareness. Holding the living relationship between the conscious and unconscious, called by Jung the "tension of the opposites," helps sustain and organize a person while he or she pursues the psychological "treasure hard to attain" in the unconscious.

The dream is an important means of facilitating inner work and addressing the blind spots of one's personality. Dream images arise from involuntary psychological processes not controlled by the ego or will. In working with the dream, one stays consonant with the facts and does not distort or change the information. By sticking to the dream images, the reasons for psychological blocking and resistance gradually emerge. The Jungian counselor or therapist uses theory to create a flow of information without distorting the dream into an intellectual venture.

In dreams, nothing is absolute; not everything is analyzable at the time of the dream, and clarification may emerge with later dream material. Personality definition develops through its aspects being named, while the dream retains a mystery by keeping some things hidden. Dreams are self-regulating and depict the psyche's forward and regressive movements. Dreams are more or less synchronous with daily life, and they parallel or anticipate actual occurrences. Dreaming is growth-producing by synthesizing psychological aspects. When understood, this natural process reinforces reliance on the psyche and its wisdom. Concentration and value placed on the dream world fosters personality integration and individuation.

Transference and Countertransference   Jungian analytical psychology reweaves the personality through the container, or temenos, of the counseling or psychotherapeutic relationship. The transference relates to past personal dramas as well as the archetypal struggle of each person on the path toward self-realization.

During a Jungian session, a client discusses dreams, active imagination, personal relationships, current problems, childhood development, transference, synchronous occurrences, and so forth. All of these are worked on additionally outside of the sessions through journaling feelings, emotions, and thoughts and by engaging in creative endeavors that make the unconscious conscious. Presenting problems vary, and treatment usually goes beyond the initial symptoms. People naturally become intrigued with themselves as they awaken to the meaning of their existence.

Addressing transference and countertransference is part of the art of Jungian counseling or psychotherapy. "The unrelated human being lacks wholeness, for he can achieve wholeness only through the soul, and the soul cannot exist without its other side, which is always found in a 'you'" (Jung, 1966, p. 454). Through the attention and reflection of the Jungian counselor or therapist, clients learn to regard themselves psychologically and to comprehend and honor the reality of the psyche. The discourse between two individuals is actually a discourse among four. Present are the Jungian counselor or therapist and his or her anima or animus, as well as the client and his or her anima or animus. Treatment involves exploring how all the characters interact within the therapeutic vessel as the archetypal process of individuation unfolds.

Transference portrays the inner situation, expectations, complexes, fantasies, and feelings of the client. Part of the psyche looks for a bridge from the past into present reality. Transference is defined by its phenomenon of **projection,** or seeing oneself in another, and occurs in all relationships. Split off or unintegrated parts of the client are projected onto the counselor or therapist, who embodies the family, the unused aspects of the personality, and the potential of the client—until the client begins to take back the projections. The relationship enacts the unconscious drama holding the client through exploring current and past issues, discovering what archetype colors the person, and finding the hints at solutions present in dreams and fantasies. The counselor or therapist needs emotional clarity to differentiate the client's projections from his or her own. The treatment relies on the totality of the psyche of both participants.

In order to be aware of his or her complexes and psychological composition, a Jungian counselor or therapist has intensive personal analysis prior to and during formal training at a Jung Institute. One must engage in his or her own psychological work to facilitate psychological transformation with others. Countertransference reflects the counselor or therapist's reacting to the client and gives useful information. The nonverbal communication, timing, and sensitivity of the counselor or therapist relies on the psychological and physical signals received from the client. The counselor or therapist's personality corresponds to the unconscious of the client in this shared interactive space. Each counselor or therapist must ask whether feelings about the client stem from his or her unconscious and unintegrated conflicts, or whether the reaction is to the unconscious drama of the client. The mutual transformation occurring through this process demands honesty and perseverance of both participants. Jung says, "The doctor is therefore faced with the same task which he wants the patient to face" (1954, p. 167).

Jung comments about the transformative process, "I have no ready made philosophy of life to hand out...I only know one thing: when my conscious mind no longer sees any possible road ahead and consequently gets stuck, my unconscious psyche will react to the unbearable standstill" (1954, p. 84). Jung describes the counselor or therapist as a wounded healer, reminiscent of the shaman or medicine man in various cultures who can activate the healing powers of the sick.

Active Imagination   In a state of "abaissement du niveau mental" (a lowering of consciousness), the ego loses energy and a person receives information from the unconscious. One approaches active imagination with the intent to accept whatever arises from the psyche, and without the ego assuming control. From this state people create or make sense of the unknown material that floats up from the unconscious by writing, drawing, dancing, and so forth. A person takes the symbols and images and communes with them without the pressure of producing something rational.

Clients with Mental Disorders

Practitioners of Jungian analytical psychology examine the psyche in depth with their clients, using the presenting symptoms as a springboard into discovering the totality of the personality. Those people with more severe problems like personality disorders, borderline disorders, or narcissistic and schizoid diagnoses are well suited to this approach. Also, those who have been abused in various ways benefit from this form of psychological treatment because the severe and usually early wounding typical of these diagnoses sets up a need for intense self-discovery. Due to the severity, it often takes longer for these psychological situations to resolve and the process involves making a connection between the inner and outer life on many levels—both conscious and unconscious. Often people with these diagnoses tend to be creative and have enough anguish as well as strength to persevere in the process of reaching into the wounds to attain healing.

Evaluation

Overview

The following section presents information dealing with research supporting Jungian analytical psychology, as well as the limitations that surround the use of this approach. It is important for the reader to understand that, based upon the nature of Jungian analytical psychology, little traditional research has been done with this approach to counseling and psychotherapy. However, clinical results, gleaned from a heuristic perspective, provide support for the continued use of Jungian analytical psychology. The limitations addressed in this section occur according to choice of the client who seeks to embark on this journey of self-discovery.

There is a misconception that people who use Jungian treatment are already fairly healthy. This is not necessarily the case. In fact, Jung used many creative approaches to heal the psyche and it is fallacious to assume that Jungian therapy and counseling treatment are not crisis oriented or for people with urgent problems just because there are no outlined steps or procedures to specifically follow. Many people seek Jungian counseling and psychotherapy for urgent problems and emotional disturbances, severe or otherwise. Once these clients regain some personality balance, the original disturbance becomes the impetus leading them on the path into their deeper selves. Jung was an early proponent of the mind, body, and soul connection and has influenced a variety of body workers and theorists in all these areas. It is the significance he gave to the symbolic meanings in physical symptoms that allows for understanding and using the body and mind conjunction in this mode of treatment.

Supporting Research

There is little statistical research about Jungian analytical psychology. The process is non-replicable, confidential, and based on individual and archetypal processes. Tests are not usually administered in this depth approach to the psyche. The heuristic approach from personal and archetypal research validates this transformative process. Jung claimed the scientific proof resided in his empirical researches into myth themes, world tales, primitive cultures, and religious ceremonies and rituals. The growing popularity of Jungian psychology correlates with the cultural need to compensate emptiness and loss of meaning by reconnecting with unconscious realms.

Jung made significant contributions to the fields of sand play therapy, art therapy, and psychology. He advocated analysts coming from a wide background, the crucial point being that they have a personal analysis. His interest in Eastern philosophy, mystical religions, and mythology brought him in contact with many of the great thinkers of the 20th century. Jungian counselors and therapists lecture and write on topics ranging from classical Jungian thought to music, mathematics, philosophy, Eastern and Western religion, and modern psychological developments.

As in all fields of counseling and psychology, outcome studies are conducted worldwide to assess the effect of this psychological approach. Jungian journals carry articles referring to the results supporting the value of this intense approach for gaining psychological knowledge and solving the problems of life.

Limitations

Jungian analytical psychology has limitations in the sense that most people who embark on this path are often of an intellectual bent, have reached a certain level of accomplishment, and are looking not only for crisis intervention but also to enhance the meaning of their lives. Their outer functioning may look sufficient to others, but they know they are living below their level of satisfaction and must plumb psychological depths to stretch their personality. This is not an elitist approach, but some people have an impetus for deeper psychological development, as well as more time, money, and personal effort to expend.

It requires more than a cursory look at oneself, and the psyche is rigorous in its demand for attention once it is discovered. So although the approach is useful for all ages and backgrounds, the internal desire and the ability for strenuous work are requirements and set the limitations. Often people do not know at the beginning what is entailed in this process, yet some part of their psychological makeup agrees to take a long and arduous internal look. Sometimes it is surprising to discover who remains in the work and who finds it inappropriate.

Essentially, this approach is useful for those who want to invest in themselves over time and not for the short term, and for those who wish to go beyond the symptoms and proceed into the psyche. These people have wonder, fear, and a need to work out their underlying malaise, depression, anxiety, or other presenting problem through discovering what lies in the unconscious. Those who fit this approach will naturally find this way.

Summary Chart—Jungian Analytical Theory

Human Nature
The foundation of every individual contains deposits of human reactions to universal situations occurring since primordial times. This foundation is reflected in the concepts of the ego, persona, shadow, anima, animus, and self.

Major Constructs
The complex is a cluster of impressions with similar feeling tones having an autonomous functioning. The archetype, or inherited mode of psychic functioning, is at the core of the complex. It becomes known through symbols arising from the collective unconscious. The symbols contain answers to psychological problems. The collective unconscious contains the deposits of the human psyche from the beginning of time. The psychological types are oriented to conscious life. People are introverted, taking the world from a subjective standpoint, or extraverted, which means they look outward before registering their inner reactions. The four functions are the ways libido, or psychic energy, manifests: *sensation,* what is happening now; *intuition,* future leap of ideas; *thinking, intellect* and *logic;* and *feeling,* the valuing of a person or thing.

Goals
Individuation is the unification of the personality by incorporating the conscious and unconscious realms.

Change Process
The transformation of character follows the potential for growth inherent in the human psyche. When the current conscious attitude is at an impasse, psychic energy is drawn into the unconscious and emerges in dreams, images, and synchronous events. The individual process, or the way a person comes into his or her uniqueness, requires the differentiation and reintegration of unconscious psychological complexes.

Interventions
Dream analysis provides an important way to understand the unconscious and its impact on conscious life. Transference and countertransference are part of the dynamic process occurring in the therapeutic relationship. Active imagination and other creative productions support the movement of the psyche from problems to solutions.

Limitations

This approach requires the client's serious and usually long-term commitment in terms of time, money, and personal effort. Clients, based on personality makeup, are self-selecting of this theoretical approach.

■ The Case of Jonathan: An Analytical Approach

Psychological problems call attention to one-sided attitudes and create possibilities for movement. A crisis brings change because the resulting personality disunity activates the unconscious and spurs on the need to examine oneself. Conflict in personal and collective values and the arousal of basic needs are touchstones for growth and the ingredients for developing authentic self-definition. Being involved in Jungian work equips people to become their own interpreters of life and to decipher meaning from their experiences.

The beginning paragraph of the case study informs us about Jonathan's cultural background, influencing his personality development, his emotional and spiritual life, and family relationships, all of which are in turmoil. Family and tribal values seemed to have meaning for him in the past, and he is experiencing a tension of opposites between the predominant white urban culture and the Native American reservation culture. This creates emotional suffering both within himself and in relationships with others and also is pulling him into psychological exploration.

Childhood issues, unresolved grief around separation, as well as his current situation of loneliness contribute to Jonathan's use of ineffective behaviors exhibited by the complexes operating autonomously and taking over his ego functioning. His current work with adolescents seems a good situation for him as he is developmentally stuck at this age and is acting out in similar ways to them. The work can provide a mirror for him and might be a place to gain the self awareness Jonathan needs to function more effectively with himself and others. The initial information about Jonathan reveals his ego lacking sufficient connection to the self, or core of his being, as he is easily distracted by fighting with others and is unable to find direction professionally, relationally, or internally. These reactions signal a damaged ego-self connection that negatively affects his confidence, as well as his ability to fuction or access enough internal support.

Because we develop an image of our Self as a child, Jonathan's treatment will explore childhood history, adolescence, and the grief and mourning from a series of incomplete connections and unresolved separations. The death of his brother and the subsequent guilt and grief may be part of why Jonathan does not complete things or commit to his life. There is a repeat of the number 6 through his history that is curious and may be a clue for him. He quit school at 16 when his brother died, divorced 6 years ago, was married for 6 years, and 6 months ago separated from his second wife, whom he married 6 months after the divorce. There were 6 children in his family. It could be interesting and helpful for him to follow this thread into his life.

Jonathan has not learned that he is good enough and keeps on reinforcing that he cannot do it. He is not using his heritage or its myths and legends that could sustain him. Rather, an internal rift has formed a disconnection from his spiritual heritage, leaving him bereft of his moorings. Jonathan's alcoholism shows he is drinking the wrong kind of spirit and it is downing him. He seems also to be using alcohol to disconnect from his physical self, to deny consciousness, and also as a call for help. Current conflicts are heightened as is his drinking so he will start to pay attention to the issues of relationships, commitment to himself, and learn to handle the cultural conflict. Jung says,

> But if we can reconcile ourselves with the mysterious truth that the spirit is the life of the body seen from within, and the body an outer manifestation of the life of the spirit—the two being really one—then we can understand why the striving to transcend the present level of consciousness through acceptance of the unconscious must give the body its due, and why recognition of the body cannot tolerate a philosophy that denies it in the name of the spirit. (1968, Par. 2142)

Part of Jungian counseling or psychotherapy involves exploring childhood, recurrent, and present dreams. The dream emanates from the unconscious and is compensatory to consciousness for personality adjustment and rectification. Taken alone, a dream is ambiguous and contains a multiplicity of meanings. A series of dreams, however, shows an arrangement around a particular problem, a circumambulation (or "walking around") to gain different perspectives. Few or no associations demonstrate repression and difficulty accessing the material because of resistance. The initial dream presented by a client depicts the prognosis for the course of the counseling or psychotherapy. The dream is a useful instrument for opening dialogue with the inner dimensions of the psyche. It expresses psychological truths about the dreamer—often differently than the dreamer can comprehend or acknowledge consciously.

Rather than the counselor or therapist supplying brilliant associations, a correct dream interpretation is what fits for the dreamer. Later on, as a therapeutic relationship is established, Jonathan will benefit from dialoguing with the dream figures, drawing them, and/or writing his reactions and amplifications. The first session is a time to establish rapport and build a place where he can begin to share his material. His efforts, along with those of the Jungian counselor or therapist, aim to translate the conflicts in his life into means for developing consciousness and different approaches to his issues.

In this instance, Jonathan's repetitive dream gives us some clues about his major issues, and at the same time presents no definitive answer about whether he will get through his dilemmas. The dream shows Jonathan swamped by unconscious contents—mostly associated with the feminine side—that call for a deepened relationship to them. Its recurrence demonstrates that the problem is not solved. Jonathan does not give an emotional reaction after the dream except to say he is unable to go to sleep. The unconscious obviously is disturbing him and wants him to pay attention, but part of Jonathan's personality does not listen, and he seems powerless against it. As his ego position has weakened, he is depleted and his self-esteem decreases. Substituting the unhealed wounds with a persona adaptation, such as blending into the white culture, is not possible.

The dream portrays shadow aspects erupting from repression, and the other people on the bus represent Jonathan's unknown psychological parts. They, too, are held hostage by the bus driver and cannot find a way out. Having no exit denotes an existential crisis. Jonathan is in the midst of a cultural and personal identity crisis demonstrated by the turmoil in the dream. The dream bus represents a collective way of travel and here is driven by the feminine. However, the masculine should be running a man's personality, not the feminine. The dream shows Jonathan has to get in contact with the driver so he can take charge. The complex related to Jonathan's self-worth is activated and the ego's networking capacity with other parts of the personality is disjointed, has neither direction nor focus, and his destructive impulses are taking over. Unable to listen to the interior parts of himself creates the violence and rage portrayed in the dream. Unrecognized personality elements turn against his personality, become destructive, and negatively affect his urge for life. The feminine side can lead to transformation and renewal, but when obfuscated and laden with repressed guilt and shame, conflict results. The spirit darkens and the unconscious assumes a devouring nature, forcing attention inwards. Jonathan's external and current situation replicate earlier experiences, just like the dream itself recurs. Depressive illnesses are often caused by painful losses inadequately mourned and summarily repressed. In many mythologies, dealing with death and dismemberment represent the transitory stages leading to rebirth and new growth.

At the moment and for a long time, Jonathan has been disabled by his depression—which can be a force stopping him or initiating him toward individuation. It corresponds to the nigredo, or the dark beginnings of the alchemical process, and can help him progress through various stages for regaining the treasure in his personality. Taken, these steps are part of Jonathan's overcoming his psychological inertia and facing reality rather than being crushed by it.

The Jungian counselor or therapist sits with a client to cultivate the therapeutic alliance, develop rapport, and mutually explore messages from the dreams and his reactions. Every rent in a client's psychic life adds to his burdens and also can illuminate the path to be taken. The dream stimulates encountering these problems, yet Jonathan has not developed a means for internal communication. The affirmative feeling to his Self is absent and his emotional needs unmet. The intensity of his suffering raises questions of timing and technical ability of the Jungian counselor or therapist based on the careful observation and evaluation of his capacity to comprehend.

According to the DSM-IV, we can say the problem is a depressive disorder with alcoholism. Inner emptiness, undifferentiated feelings, and being run by the anima denote internal estrangement. Jonathan's dark feelings overtake the ego and disturb his ability to function. He gets drunk, fights, leaves relationships and retreats—all signifying grief, avoidance and confusion in his life. Jung states, "Over against the polymorphism of the...instinctual nature there stands the regulating principle of individuation. . . . Together they form a pair of opposites...often spoken of as nature and spirit. . . . This opposition is the expression and perhaps also the basis of the tension from which psychic energy flows" (1960, p.58).

What mixture of emotions does Jonathan carry about his family and the pressures he internalized from childhood? An authentic sense of self is rooted in a well-developed identity based on identification with the parent of the same sex; hence, the important influence in a son's early years of his father's presence. Is there some discord between the inborn archetype of father that Jonathan acts out by leaving his role as a father? The child perceiving his parents tends to repeat the pattern in himself and with subsequent partners. Jonathan lives at a distance from his children who symbolize the future, potential, and new life and he has problems with love and intimacy. Therapy would explore what he experienced with his parents and their relation to him, especially during traumatic times and when he was the same age as his children are now.

Leaving home represents separation from the "participation mystique" binding Jonathan to his family and Native American culture. This is a phase Jung used to denote the interpersonal and unconscious melding between people. It is necessary to be close enough to gain rootedness and become internalized. Although seemingly identified with his background, Jonathan radically broke from it by leaving the reservation and entering the white culture. If he is not yet released from the parental complex, Jonathan cannot access his own position. If father, mother, family, or culture is insufficiently attached to, a hole in the psyche of a son forms and fills with splits and confusions that destructively affect work, relationships, and self-regard.

Jonathan is not consciously aware of any of the archetypal energies flowing through him, nor does he access his natural powers. Jonathan's story can be likened to the Native American vision quest a boy takes as part of his initiation into manhood—but this one has gone awry. He is not using his cultural wisdom or its rituals that could solidify his sense of identity as a man. Most likely his behavior reflects an internal situation of the shadow in union with the anima, his inner feminine side, which is blinding his perception of his world. In many fairy tales the hero must be able to fight his battles to gain strength, not to just rebel. If he accomplishes the necessary tasks, he can have the princess. Jonathan also must learn this lesson or else he is in danger of losing his courage, resolution, and will not develop his Eros, or sense of relatedness.

The development of Jonathan's feeling side arises from an innate need for balance to his thinking. Jonathan does not know how to be intimate and keeps on repeating the same relationship problems. These factors evidence the characteristics of an introverted attitude in a man who is a thinking sensation type. Adaptation to the environment fails with an overdeveloped superior function, in this case, thinking. The blocked libido causes his inferior feeling function to be activated. The immaturity of the psyche makes itself apparent in crisis situations. As the problem becomes acute, the lack of internal solidity is increasingly perceptible. The opposite sides of Jonathan's nature are embattled and unable to be contained within himself. Jonathan needs to learn to access the fundamental inner structures and be able to handle his anxiety if he is to gain psychological growth. Jung referred to this as the "canalization of libido," or the energy transformation of psychic intensities or values from one psychological aspect to another. This is a process of progression and regression and creates internal adaptation so the personality flow recommences.

As stated earlier, Jungian treatment includes using transference and countertransference. His psychological work will be affected by conscious and unconscious impressions, input, and reactions of the counselor or therapist. For Jonathan, the therapy or counseling relationship will no doubt be affected by the conflict he exhibits with men and women and within himself—the difficulties with trust and intimacy. As with dreams, the Jungian counselor or therapist does not direct, but listens to the way Jonathan's psyche leads them both. Jung says, "No one can overlook either the dynamism or the imagery of the instincts without the gravest injury to himself. Violation or neglect of instinct has painful consequences of a physiological and psychological nature for whose treatment medical help is required" (1959, p.57).

No capacity is more terrible and difficult to break than the one an individual imposes on himself or herself. As Jonathan's dream warns, the captivity by the anima is what he must confront. The situation may be released through developing a conscious and responsible attitude to the anima and the shadow, making the contents knowable and the energy usable. Jonathan's situation of distress, blackness of feeling, and intimations from the unconscious signal he needs a reconciliation of the warring elements and a conscious differentiation within his psyche.

Collective answers cannot satisfy the individual, as each person has a unique psychological complexity. The path involves turning to the unconscious and gleaning its resources for creativity and knowledge in a process of differentiating and integrating unconscious contents. Emergence of the personality is fraught with the struggle to separate the chaos beginning any psychological endeavor. Relationships with oneself and others rests on the dynamism inherent in the psychological quest for individual identity. Through suffering, we discover the meaning of our personal destiny, which entails taking the total self seriously.

Suggested Readings

Edinger, E. (1999). *Archetype of the apocalypse: A Jungian study of the Book of Revelation.* Chicago: Open Court Publishing Co.

Fordham, M. (2000). *Technique in Jungian analysis.* London: Karmac Books.

Hannah, B. (1999). *The inner journey: Lectures and essays on Jungian psychology.* Saratoga: Bookwood Services.

Hawker, C., & Samuels, A. (2000). *The interpretation of realities: Jung and the postmodern.* London: Routledge.

Hillman, J. (1997). *Soul's code: In search of character and calling.* New York: Warner Books.

Jacob, M. (2000). *Jungian psychotherapy and contemporary infant research: Basic patterns of emotional exchange.* London: Routledge.

Kalshed, D. (1997). *The world of trauma: Archetypal defenses of the personal spirit.* London: Routledge.

Perry, J. (1998). *The trials of the visionary mind: Spiritual emergency and the renewal process.* New York: State University of New York Press.

Schwartz-Salant, N. (1998). *The mystery of human relationship: Alchemy and the transformation of the self.* London: Routledge.

Shorr, A. (1999). *The essential Jung.* Princeton: Princeton University Press.

Stevens, A. (2001). *Jung: A very short introduction.* Oxford: Oxford University Press.

Ulanov, A. (2000). *Religion and the spiritual in Carl Jung.* New Jersey: Paulist Press.

Von Franz, M. L. (1999). *Archetypal dimensions of the psyche.* Boston: Shambhala Publications.

Adlerian Counseling and Psychotherapy

Alan P. Milliren
Associate Professor of Counseling Education
The University of Texas of the Permian Basin

Timothy D. Evans
Clinical Faculty
University of South Florida

John F. Newbauer
Core Faculty
Adler School of Professional Psychology

Introduction

Individual Psychology was founded by **Alfred Adler.** It is a cognitive, goal-oriented, social psychology interested in a person's beliefs and perceptions, as well as the effects that person's behavior has on others. It is one of the few psychologies interested in democratic processes in the home, school, and work place. Individual Psychology promotes social equality, which means granting each other mutual respect and dignity regardless of our inherent differences. It is not a set of techniques, but rather a comprehensive philosophy of living. The three most fundamental principles are: (1) behavior is goal oriented; (2) humans are fundamentally social, with a desire to belong and have a place of value as an equal human being; and (3) the individual is indivisible and functions with unity of personality (Ferguson, 1984). These principles, which make Individual Psychology unique from other approaches, are described in Adlerian psychology as **purposiveness, social interest,** and **holism.** Together, these principles describe the person as moving in unity toward self-chosen goals that reflect a human value for belonging and social contribution.

The term *Individual Psychology* (Adler, 1932) is often misunderstood. Adler stressed the unity or indivisibility of the person; thus, he named his theory Individual Psychology.

The term *individual* was used to focus on the whole individual at a time when others, like Freud, were focusing on a divided and, therefore, conflictual personality. In other words, the word *individual* differed significantly from Freud's concept of duality where everything is in conflict, such as the id, ego, and superego or the conscious, subconscious, and preconscious. Instead, Adler developed a holistic theory of psychology that emphasized the unity of the individual working toward a goal (Ferguson, 2000a). This holistic approach, along with other fundamental components, characterizes contemporary Adlerian psychology.

Background

Alfred Adler was born on February 7, 1870, in a small suburb of Vienna (Ellenberger, 1970). He was Hungarian by birth and later became a citizen of Vienna, Austria. Adler was the second son in a family of six children, not counting two who died in early infancy. Interestingly enough, his older brother's name was Sigmund. Adler seemed to view Sigmund as someone who was always ahead of him, a true "first born" with whom he felt he could never catch up. Later in his life, another Sigmund (Freud) would also seem to serve as a rival. Despite the rivalry in childhood between Alfred and his brother, they seemed to remain friendly toward each other as adults.

Adler was a sickly child and suffered from rickets and fits of breathlessness. His illness as well as the death of his younger brother Rudolf seemed to strengthen his goal of becoming a physician. In 1895, he graduated from the Medical School of the University of Vienna and established his medical practice. In December of 1897, Adler married Raissa Epstein, a woman who had come from Russia to study in Vienna. According to Carl Furtmueller (1946), Adler met Raissa at a socialist political meeting and was very impressed with her. Later, she continued to be active in the socialist party and the Adlers frequently entertained the Trotskys, who lived in Vienna from 1907 to 1914. Perhaps because of his association with socialism and also his wife's influence, Adler was very much in favor of women having the same rights and privileges as men. Alfred and Raissa had four children: Valentine, Alexandra, Kurt, and Cornelia (Nelly).

In 1898, Adler published the *Health Book for the Tailor Trade,* a forerunner of health psychology, which was consistent with a stress/diathesis model of disturbance. This publication associated the health problems of tailors with the unhygienic conditions under which they worked. Hoffman (1994) avers that "Adler's purpose in *Health Book for the Tailor Trade* was clearly not to provide a dispassionate, scholarly tome. Rather, in a pattern that was to become characteristic of Adler throughout his career, he explicitly linked his writing to the need for definite action" (p. 36). It is interesting to note that within this 31-page monograph many of the roots of Adler's later psychological theory can be found, especially regarding the "role of physician as social activist and reformer" (p. 37).

In 1902, Adler served for a brief period in the Hungarian army as a general physician. Later that year, he received a postcard from Sigmund Freud inviting him to join a Wednesday evening study circle, which eventually became the Viennese Psychoanalytic Society. Adler was one of the first four physicians to be invited by Freud to attend this group, although "how Adler and Freud first came to know each other has never been satisfactorily determined" (Hoffman, 1994, p. 41). It is probably accurate that Adler was never a pupil of Freud's. This one point, alone, became a significant element in the Adler-Freud relationship, which eventually terminated with considerable bitterness. From 1902 until 1911, Adler was a central part of the Viennese Psychoanalytic Society, becoming its president in 1910. Adler published his famous paper on organ inferiority in 1907.

Adler disagreed with Freud over the role that sexuality and social factors played in motivation and development. Adler had developed a social theory that emphasized personal beliefs or "fictional finalism," a concept that is similar to subjective perception. This differed from Freud's view of behavior as being biologically or physiologically determined. Freud branded Adler's emerging social theory of Individual Psychology as "radically false" and insisted that it failed to contribute a "single new observation" to science (Hoffman, 1994, p. 90). Eventually, his differences with Freud became so intense that Adler and several members of the Society left in 1911. They founded their own group, known as the Society for Free Psychoanalysis, which ultimately became the Society for Individual Psychology.

In 1911, Adler became a Viennese citizen. He also read Hans Vaihinger's book, *The Philosophy of the 'As If'*, which seemed to have a strong impact on his developing theory. In 1912, he produced his second book, *The Nervous Character*, which was followed 2 years later by the introduction of the *Journal of Individual Psychology*. During WWI, Adler served in a neuropsychiatric unit of the Austro-Hungarian army. His experience in the war seemed to significantly shape his ideas about human nature.

Following the war, Vienna was in great turmoil. What once had been a proud city was now full of orphans and in need of order. Adler worked as a consultant in the schools of Vienna, holding clinics with teachers, parents, and students in what has become known as the **open forum** model of counseling (Evans & Milliren, 1999). In this model, Adler would meet in an open, public forum with teachers and parents and ask them about the child being considered. He would then interview the child and eventually make recommendations for the teachers, the parents, and sometimes the child. "By involving the audience in the counseling session, Adler emphasized helping the family through education" (Evans & Milliren, 1999, p. 135). These "public counseling demonstrations challenged the then-traditional practices of individual therapy" (p. 135), and can be viewed as a milestone in the development of community mental health programs. Adler "believed that therapy was not for an elite but should be made available to everyone. His public demonstrations reflected this desire to make psychology available to what Adler considered the 'common man.'" (p. 135).

In the late 1920s, Adler began to travel to the United States to lecture in public and academic settings. He was very well received in the United States and had considerable coverage in the popular press. In fact, he was considered one of the most prominent psychiatrists of his day. In 1927, Adler published *Understanding Human Behavior* and discussed the important concept of **social interest,** which was only suggested in his early writings. His ideas of the inferiority complex, birth order, community feeling, and social interest became popular psychological concepts.

The Nazis came to power in Germany in the 1930s and soon became a powerful force in Austria as well. Adler envisioned the upcoming conflict and made plans to leave his homeland. He began to spend more and more time in the United States and planned to move there after his lecture tour in the summer of 1937. Adler had a very ambitious tour planned, with lectures in The Hague, England, and Scotland. He was to be accompanied on this tour by his daughter, Alexandra, who was also a psychiatrist. Alfred Adler died during the first part of that tour in Aberdeen, Scotland, on May 28, 1937 (Hoffman, 1994).

Rudolf Dreikurs was influenced by Adler's teaching and practice in Vienna (Terner & Pew, 1978). Dreikurs, in his early days of practicing psychiatry in Vienna, became involved with Adler and his child guidance centers. Both Adler and Dreikurs were convinced that Individual Psychology should focus on the education of children in the home and school, which would increase the level of the child's functioning, develop his or her citizenship, and be preventive instead of remedial. In 1937, Dreikurs moved to the United States, where he helped to promote and further develop Adlerian psychology.

As much as the popularity of Adler's psychology grew in the United States in the early to mid-1930s, it was Rudolf Dreikurs who "popularized" the approach and contributed significantly to the further development of the theory. In the late 1930s and early 1940s, Dreikurs worked in Chicago to initiate child guidance centers. Open-forum family counseling or therapy was practiced, and the concept of democratic family relationships was stressed in these centers. "Dreikurs' dream was to establish child guidance centers all over the world and his understanding of children was of unique importance" (Hooper & Holford, 1998, p. 142). It was the setting of the child guidance centers that "helped inspire one of Dreikurs' most important contributions in psychology, the **four goals of misbehavior** in children" (Terner & Pew, 1978, p. 155).

In 1962, Dreikurs established the first International Summer School for the study of Adlerian psychology. This is now known as the International Committee for Adlerian Summer Schools and Institutes (ICASSI). After a long career promoting and teaching Adler's psychology and philosophy of life, Rudolf Dreikurs died in 1972.

Human Nature: A Developmental Perspective

Adlerian psychology is interested in understanding the **lifestyle** or the law of psychological movement of the individual. Each person comes into this world dependent on others for food, clothing, shelter, and nurturance. Our survival as a species depends on our ability to cooperate and be our brothers' and sisters' keeper. Beecher and Beecher (1966) describe how baby turtles are capable of surviving from the moment they are hatched. A turtle never sees its father, only briefly encounters its mother, and is not affected by this lack of contact. Most animals are able to provide for themselves as adults within 2 years. Homo sapiens require at least 12 years before achieving the minimum capability for meeting the challenges of living. Unlike the turtle, the human infant cannot survive on his or her own. Thus, human beings must develop the skills of cooperation and will always find it necessary to live in a group. In order to develop properly, the human infant must be protected, fed, educated, and have human relationships for about a fourth of his or her life span. As the growing child learns to become more competent, he or she begins to gain a sense of mastery over the environment.

The pattern or style that characterizes how the individual "goes about going about" becomes useful in assessing why that individual behaves as he or she does. Understanding the client's lifestyle gives the counselor/therapist a better understanding of behavior and serves as a useful guide as counseling or therapy progresses. Although the emphasis in this process is on understanding the individual's behavior, it is always done from the client's subjective viewpoint. The counselor's role is not to establish the facts of the client's experience, but to investigate the client's perception of it.

> Early experiences, no matter how dramatic or potentially traumatic, are not specifically causative of personality traits because each child will determine for himself or herself the significance of the experience. The power of subjective interpretation of reality is apparent, for example, if one interviews adult identical twins about some incident that occurred quite early in their lives and that they shared. It is clear from their recollections that the twins do remember the same incident. But when they are asked to pinpoint which was the most vivid moment in the incident and how they felt at that moment, their answers are likely to indicate that they experienced the incident in totally different manners. (Dinkmeyer, Pew, & Dinkmeyer, 1979, p. 26)

Successful counseling will help the individual understand his or her "subjective psychological movement" or "private logic."

Early Development

From the moment of birth, each child acts "as if" he or she is attempting to answer the question, "How do I fit in?" The family is the first social group to which the child belongs. Thus the child begins to make numerous assumptions about who he or she is, how others are, how the world should be, and how the world will treat him or her. The child's ordinal position in the family plays a role in developing this view of self and the world and has a significant impact on the child's developing pattern of living or lifestyle. Because no two human beings have exactly the same reaction to the same situation, each child will interact with and interpret experience in the family differently. No two children, born into the same family, grow up in exactly the same situation. Interestingly enough, this is true even for twins.

The perception of the family environment differs from one child to another and can change over time for a variety of reasons. For example, the family structure changes considerably with the birth of each child. Not only is each new child born into an increasingly larger family, but also the age differences and gender of each of the children can significantly affect the position of every other child. This is even more pronounced in families where a certain child may be accorded a more important position, such as an eldest son or daughter. Ernesto, a sixth grader from a fairly large family, describing himself as the eldest, proceeded to list three or four younger brothers and sisters. Later, when the family was observed while attending a parent meeting, it appeared that Ernesto also had two older sisters. When asked about it, the boy remarked, "Oh yeah, but they don't count!" This "fortunate" young man was the eldest son in a family where such a position was highly valued. It was "as if" no one else counted. The older sisters became "invisible."

Many factors significantly impact the family environment. Parents are older and more experienced as each child enters the family. Family finances may shift and change, and the family may relocate. Extended family members or other significant individuals may move in and out of the family group. Death or divorce of the parents becomes an important factor influencing the family environment. Remarriage of one or both of the parents adds the presence of a stepparent and possibly stepbrothers or stepsisters. Specific family values and the general psychological atmosphere of the family are extremely influential, such as in families where all the children are involved in athletics, are all musical, or all have advanced educational degrees. In each case, these specific activities were highly valued by the parents, and it was "as if" one couldn't "belong" without pursuing and developing competence in these areas.

The counselor/therapist should pay attention to health and development issues that exist for different family members. It is not uncommon for the eldest daughter in a family to assume the "mothering" role when the real mother is sickly, out of the home, working full time, or otherwise unable to function in that capacity. A child with developmental disabilities may overshadow brothers and sisters because the family devotes more time to this particular child. The death of a child may create a "phantom" sibling that the other children must live up to in terms of accomplishments because of parental expectations. While there are a number of typical characteristics that seem to be more or less "universal," interpreting birth order is not a cut-and-dried process.

Birth Order/Family Constellation

Although Adler is known for emphasizing birth order, his views are often misunderstood. The position of the child in the birth order is not deterministic. It only provides probabilities that a child will have particular types of experiences (Shulman & Mosak, 1977). Adlerian psychology considers not only individual development, but also the social context in which it occurs. The social field of the child includes the parents, the siblings, and other significant individuals that create the multitude of relationships influencing the child. Although there are numerous factors that would indicate exceptions, there are some general characteristics of various birth order positions. Counselors and therapists are cautioned, however, to use this information in the context of what they know about the individual and the individual's family of origin.

Only Children   Only children are unique; they grow up in a world that is heavily populated with adults. Because there are no other children with whom to compete, they may work extremely hard to achieve an adult level of competence. When the parents are extremely capable, the child sometimes finds it far too difficult to compete with any measure of success, may become discouraged, and either give up or look for alternative pursuits where he or she might be outstanding. Where the child cannot be "good enough" in positive and constructive ways, he or she may become "good" at misbehaving. These children have given up hope of ever being responsible and capable. In contrast, only children sometimes receive so much attention and service from the adults in their world that they attempt to remain helpless and irresponsible. These children have not given up; they just never got started!

It is not unusual for only children to become quite egocentric. After all, they never had to contend with sharing anything. Ed and Sally, a young married couple, constantly squabbled about whose things belonged to whom. She complained that he was far too stingy, while he complained that she was always taking his things without permission. Sally, having grown up in a large family where the general attitude was "What is yours is ours" saw no need to ask to use things that, to her, were community property. Ed, however, had grown up in an atmosphere of "What is mine is mine." He related that his mother had a cabinet where he could lock up the toys he wanted to keep away from others. As they grew to understand the attitudes each developed as a result of growing up in their respective families, the squabbling ceased and Ed and Sally attempted to be more respectful of each other's attitude.

Another fairly typical characteristic of only children is that they often grow up enjoying being the center of attention. This is particularly true when the child is the first or only grandchild and, therefore, is valued just for existing. In many instances, the only child has developed a talent of one sort or another and expects to be able to take center stage as the star. When only children have been catered to or often been given their own way, they may refuse to be cooperative when others do not give in to them. Barbara, an only child, commented that she would often call her mother to pick her up if, when playing at a friend's house, the other child wouldn't play or do what Barbara wanted. Only children often develop skills for relating only to adults, especially if that is their primary social environment, and not to their peers. As a result, they become content being loners and feel no need to develop relationships with other children.

Oldest Children   Oldest children have had the "good fortune" of being only children for some period of time, whether one or several years. If a gap of approximately 5 years exists between two children in one family, then each of the children would appear to be more like an only child. Unfortunately, when the birth of the second child occurs, an elder child often feels "dethroned." Sometimes, this generates feelings of being unloved or neglected, and the child tries to compensate. Often, he or she may try to regain a position of superiority through good deeds (e.g., becoming overly responsible, serving as the caretaker of the rest of the children, taking on extra chores or activities, or excelling at academics). If this doesn't work, eldest children may achieve superiority through being the best of the worst! It is not unusual to find that gender issues become quite significant. For example, when a firstborn male is followed closely by the birth of a female sibling, this can easily lead to a more or less permanent dethronement of the male child.

Richard, the oldest child in his family, developed into the "responsible" child, almost to the point of excess. He took it upon himself to look after everybody and everything, becoming especially involved in this activity after his father divorced his mother when he was 9. Richard then took over the "chores" that had previously been his father's. Richard was already mature beyond his years, and this further defined his role as the man of the house, a role that his mother regularly reinforced because she was so grateful for having such a good son. Unfortunately, Richard devoted so much of his time and effort to taking care of things at home that he refused to participate in athletics and other social activities at school. As a consequence, he ignored his age-mates and did not develop the necessary skills for relating to them. As he got older, he complained of lack of friends and closeness in relationships, but justified this by asserting that he had to take care of his family.

Juanita was the eldest child in her family. Because her mother was working two jobs in order to support the family, Juanita's stance in the world was to become "a better mother than her mother." From the young age of 5, she recalls numerous occasions where she told the younger children that they had to mind her because she was "the mother in this house!" When she was 12, her mother remarried, quit working, and stayed home to take care of the children. Juanita was not prepared for this change of events, and because she had not developed social skills for participation in activities outside the home, she didn't know what to do. At 14 she resolved to quit school as soon as she could and have a family of her own.

She became promiscuous, and by the time she was 16, had given birth to a son and was pregnant with her second child.

Second Born   Second-born children often find themselves in an uncomfortable position, and many will adopt the "Avis Attitude," where being second only makes them try harder. Unfortunately, during the early years, the second born always has someone in front who is more advanced. This might be mitigated if the oldest is a boy and a second-born girl shows up within a year or so. However, if the eldest child is successful, second borns are easily discouraged and give up hope of achieving a place in any area or activity occupied by the eldest. As a result, the second-born child usually develops characteristics opposite of the first born. If a third child is born, the second born may feel "squeezed."

Ruth, a second-born child in a family with five children, indicated that she always felt that she was in the shadow of her sister. When she was interviewed about her family constellation, Ruth said Emily was 27 months older. The interviewer asked Ruth why it was important to her to be so specific about the age difference. Ruth commented, "Because she really *is* more than 2 years older than I am." She indicated that those extra months gave Emily an unfair advantage, which was why Emily was so much better!

Raul, also a second born, had an older brother, Juan, who was developmentally delayed. Raul excelled academically and became the valedictorian of his high school class, but he never felt as though he was given full attention or acknowledgement by his parents for his achievements. Meeting the needs of Juan's learning differences required considerable time and attention from his parents. Though it would have been quite easy for Raul to revert to the "useless side" and achieve recognition through misbehavior, he found academics to be a means for expressing his capabilities and receiving encouragement outside the family.

Middle Children   Like second borns, middle children have a sibling who is in the lead, but they also have a sibling who is close on their heels. Not only do they have to keep up, but also they feel that they have to run as fast as they can to stay ahead. Depending on the capabilities of the other siblings, middle children may often feel like Nathan, who indicated that he was never sure of his abilities or himself. His major strength was being social, with numerous friends and contacts, a characteristic possessed by neither his older brother nor his younger sister. However, this led to academic difficulties in high school, which in turn limited his college choice. Consequently, he believes that his undergraduate degree is not of the same quality as those held by his siblings. For the most part, he is extremely unsure of how he stacks up, and this plays out in his career, where he has been unable to stay in any one job for more than 2 years. He has never been fired, but he is always dissatisfied with not being given enough recognition for the things he achieves. Of the three children, however, Nathan has the most empathy for others.

Youngest Child   Youngest children often find themselves in an enviable position in the family because they may be pampered and spoiled by parents and older siblings. They often have too many things done for them; others may assume their decision-making and other responsibilities. Because of this unique position, youngest children may easily become discouraged and develop feelings of inferiority. The youngest child, perhaps because there are limited expectations for his or her success, often becomes the most successful child in the family. Gary conveyed an easy-going, laid-back style and seemed never to get caught up in struggles for superiority or accomplishment. The youngest of three boys, he never had a chance to be first at anything, but he maintained a strong, positive attitude about his childhood and the fact that his brothers always seemed to be competing to be first. When asked why this didn't bother him, he explained that he was always the first to vote that he would "go last!"

Youngest children, no matter how capable they are, tend not to be taken seriously by others. Sondra, at age 46, was the youngest child in a family of six children. She regularly complained that no one in the family would consult her or listen to her ideas, even though she was the primary caregiver for her aging parents. Her older siblings would question all of her decisions regarding the care of the parents, and when major health issues were to be decided, her input was always, according to Sondra, discounted. This meant that Sondra, an extremely capable woman, was easily discouraged and harbored considerable feelings of inferiority.

Early Recollections

In addition to collecting the client's birth order/family constellation information, it is important to take note of the memories or recollections that the client holds regarding early experiences. Recollections must be distinguished from reports of experiences; the most significant memories have an "as if" component to them. The individual recalls the experience *as if* it were occurring at the moment. Again, the counselor or therapist is not interested in the exact nature of the individual's experience, but in that individual's perception of it. Out of a myriad of experiences, the client chooses to select only certain ones that support or influence current functioning. These memories exist for the individual as little "life lessons" kept available as guides for decision-making about the challenges of living. It is the interpretation of these selected events that the individual carries with him or her as reminders of the goals and limits for participation in life.

Alfred Adler (1931) noted that:

Among all psychic expressions, some of the most revealing are the individual's memories. Her memories are the reminders she carries about with her of her limitations and of the meaning of events. There are no "chance" memories. Out of the incalculable number of impressions that an individual receives, she chooses to remember only those which she considers, however dimly, to have a bearing on her problems. These memories represent the story of her life, a story she repeats to herself for warmth or comfort, to keep her concentrated on her goal, or to prepare her, by means of past experiences, to meet the future with a tried and tested approach. (p. 58–59)

Powers and Griffith (1987) state that early recollections tend to be quite consistent with the individual's current world view regarding life, self, and others.

To understand this process requires that we recognize it as dynamic, seeing it as an active recollecting in the present moment of recall. Of all our movements, the activity of remembering is the most characteristic. It is in this activity that we reveal the style of our movement in purest form. If hyphenation could make our meaning clearer we would say that in our early re-collections we are re-constituting our world from its beginnings; re-membering the elements of our lives into the one body of our identity; re-calling assertions of meaning out of ourselves against the threats of confusion or despair; re-viewing ourselves in our situations in our practiced way of looking at things. (p. 185)

As one's world view changes, so will the nature of the various recalled memories. Early recollections have embedded in them beliefs about self, others, and the world, as well as ethical convictions and plans of action.

From early recollections it is possible to identify the goal toward which the person is directed. In addition to early recollections, recurrent dreams and even favorite fairy tales and childhood stories are considered as part of the database for understanding the lifestyle. When working with parents, Walton (1996a, Evans & Milliren, 1999) explores their "most memorable observation" or MMO. The MMOs provide clues to the dynamics of the family and are decisions that the parent made in adolescence about how family life was *going to be* when he or she had the opportunity to have his or her own family. "Use of this technique can allow the counselor to help a parent see how he or she: (1) overemphasizes the likelihood of occurrence of a situation the parent guards against; (2) overemphasizes the negative influence of such a situation if it should occur; and (3) underestimates his or her ability to deal with the situation in an effective problem-solving way if it should occur" (Walton, 1996b, p. 4).

Wingett (personal communication, 11/26/2001) suggests that counselors and therapists listen for key words as the client describes the problem. Often, clients will use the words "lost" or "stuck" to describe the situation that brought them into counseling, (i.e., "I am stuck in this mess and don't see any way out," or "I'm just lost in this and don't know where to turn"). Counselors often follow up by asking the client about his or her experiences with being lost: "Tell me about a time in your life when you were lost or stuck. Maybe you were lost while traveling or at the mall, or separated from others in an unfamiliar setting." Or the therapist might invite the client to tell about a time in his or her life when he or she was stuck in the snow or sand or mud. By getting the details of these experiences in terms of what the client was thinking and feeling, and how the client proceeded to handle the situation, the counselor or therapist will be able to ascertain the nature of the client's problem-solving approach to life.

Major Constructs

One of the difficulties encountered when attempting to study Adler's theory is the unsystematic manner that characterized his writing. On only rare occasions did Adler present his mature theory in an organized or concise form; most of his writings focused on topics or sub-topics related to his theory. However, in one paper that appeared in the first volume of the *International Journal of Individual Psychology* (Adler, 1935), Adler presented a short overview of the basic principles of Individual Psychology.

Basic to an understanding of Individual Psychology is the concept that the individual has the **creative power** to interpret experiences, both internal and external, influenced by both heredity and environment, in an individualistic, subjective manner. From these interpretations, the individual develops an "attitude toward life," or **life style,** which is expressed in relationship to oneself, others, and the world. Adler discussed the belief that the individual "relates himself always according to his own interpretation of himself and his present problems" (Adler, 1935, p. 5). "Man does not merely react. He adopts an individual attitude" (Dreikurs, 1950, p.4).

Though each individual is uniquely different from others with an approach to life that is entirely his or her own creation, no one can escape the necessity of solving a great number of problems. It is here that we begin to see the complications arising from one's inability to solve these problems adequately. Three general types of problems arise:— work, friends, and family. Dreikurs (1950) describes these as the **three life tasks:**

> The human community sets three tasks for every individual. They are: work, which means contributing to the welfare of others; friendship, which embraces social relationships with comrades and relatives; and love, which is the most intimate union with someone of the other sex and represents the strongest and closest emotional relationship which can exist between two human beings. (pp. 4–5)

In the context of meeting these challenges of living, there is also a consideration of the **social embeddedness** of the individual: "The individual cannot be considered apart from society. He is inextricably embedded in it. His very thinking, using language as the main tool, is socially determined, since language is a social product and is socially acquired" (Ansbacher, 1965, p. 341). Adler often spoke of the **iron-clad logic of social living,** in essence indicating that all human problems were social problems. To be successful, the individual could not operate in terms of **private logic,** but had to function in keeping with the **common sense.**

As a social evolutionist, Adler believed progress could be made only through the conscious efforts of the individual. If people were not willing to contribute, or if they functioned in a manner contrary to the concept of evolution, then "the psychological decline and fall of the individual" (Ansbacher & Ansbacher, 1964, p. 39) would surely occur. Thus, one's efforts at cooperation and contribution were essential elements of a mentally healthy life style.

Adler believed that the whole individual could not be understood by only looking at parts or individual characteristics. Life, for him, was characterized by movement: the **psychological movement** of the individual in pursuit of a goal. In this movement, the whole of the personality is expressed—the individual's mind, body, emotions, perceptions, and all functions move toward this chosen goal. Without recognizing this goal-directed nature of the individual, one cannot see the individual as a whole (Dreikurs, 1950). In Adler's view, the individual functions *as if* he or she were striving to compensate for a **felt minus** situation by attempting to achieve a plus.

Thus, the Adlerian view of the person is that of an indivisible, social being whose behavior occurs as an interaction within the social setting. However, the individual, from an Adlerian perspective, is not just reactive but is proactive—acting on the environment *in order to* make things happen or to achieve a desired outcome. There is freedom of choice and **goal-directedness** of behavior. In effect, the individual is perceived as being able to *choose* those behaviors that will move him or her toward a desired objective. Motivation is viewed as more of a pull than a push, with the individual moving toward those immediate and long-range outcomes or objectives that are important in the frame of reference of the individual.

There are as many variations of personally acceptable goals of success as there are individuals. "In my experience I have found that each individual has a different meaning of, and attitude toward, what constitutes success" (Adler, 1935, p. 6). As long as the individual has a feeling of belonging and is prepared to meet the tasks of life, he or she will have a positive or healthy view of life and behaviors will be directed toward the useful side of life. It is only when the individual is ill-prepared to meet the challenges of living that he or she switches to the useless side. In these latter instances, the individual will have a negative view of life and will behave in a manner in opposition to the logic of social living. What better argument is there for early involvement with children and parent education programs?

Adler was not one to present *typologies* of human beings, for he believed that each individual had to be described according to his or her own unique pattern. Although Adler did develop some general principles describing the nature of the individual, "his main interest was in the description, understanding, and modification of the unique individual" (Ansbacher & Ansbacher, 1964, p. 660). Therefore, the focus of Individual Psychology is predominantly on the ideographic description of behavior—on the specific psychological movement involved in the individual's personal orientation to life. However, there were several occasions when Adler did indicate four different general types, although he did so only for purposes of teaching in order to show "the attitude and behavior of individuals toward outside problems" (Adler, 1935, p. 6).

> Thus, we find individuals whose approach to reality shows, from early childhood through their entire lives, a more or less dominant or 'ruling' attitude. This attitude appears in all their relationships. A second type—surely the most frequent one—expects everything from others and leans on others. I might call it the 'getting' type. A third type is inclined to feel successful by avoiding the solution of problems. Instead of struggling with a problem, a person of this type merely tries to 'side-step' it, in an effort thereby to avoid defeat. The fourth type struggles, to a greater or lesser degree, for a solution to these problems in a way which is useful to others. (Adler, 1935, p. 6)

Each individual, with his unique orientation to life, retains and maintains this approach "from childhood to the end of his life, unless he is convinced of the mistake in his creation of his attitude toward reality" (Adler, 1935, p. 6). This process is similarly described by Combs and Snygg (1959) in that the individual strives to maintain and enhance the phenomenal self—a self that is a product of the individual's own creation. Thus, Adler not only considered the human being as a totality, but also he viewed the individual as a **unity.** This unity, or what Adler termed the *life style,* is comparable to what is often noted as the *ego* and is expressed in the individual's "thinking, feeling, acting; in his so-called conscious and unconscious—in every expression of his personality" (Adler, 1935, p. 7).

Of the four types presented by Adler, the first three—"the 'ruling' type, the 'getting' type, and the 'avoiding' type—are not apt, and are not prepared to solve the problems of life. These problems are always social problems. Individuals of these three types are lacking in the ability for cooperation and contribution" (Adler, 1935, p. 7). Those who lack in the ability to cooperate and contribute, when meeting up with the external problems of living, are confronted with a form of inadequacy or *shock.* "This shock leads up to the individual's failures—which we know as neurosis, psychosis, etc. Significantly, the failure shows the same style as the individual" (Adler, 1935, p. 7). Thus, these first three types are inadequately prepared for life. Although they may be able to function somewhat effectively as long as they are not faced with a critical situation, they will eventually encounter a problem demanding more cooperation and contribution, or **social interest,** than they are prepared to offer.

"In the fourth type (the socially useful type), prepared for cooperation and contribution, we can always find a certain amount of *activity* which is used for the benefit of others. This activity is in agreement with the needs of others; it is useful, normal, rightly embedded in the stream of evolution of mankind" (Adler, 1935, p. 7). It was Adler's belief that the individual was firmly embedded in society. It was only within the social milieu that the individual could be understood; the extent or quality of this relationship, as characterized by social interest, was the measure of mental health. Adler wrote in terms of the iron-clad logic of social living, and only those who were able to cooperate with and contribute to the general welfare were capable of achieving *significance* or, in terms of contemporary writers, *self-actualization*.

For Adler, life was movement and it was the nature of this movement on the part of the individual that was of interest to the Individual Psychologist. For some, this movement might be described as *active* in form; for others, this may be more *passive*. Such movement is quite easy to observe in children. For example, one child may tend to be more energetic in his or her behavior or activity level, while another may be content to sit by and observe what is going on. For the most part, this degree of activity remains constant throughout one's life, but may only become apparent when the individual experiences favorable or, particularly, unfavorable situations. "But it is the individual shade of interpretation that matters in the end. And when reconstructing the unity of a personality in his relationships to the outer world, Individual Psychology fundamentally undertakes to delineate the individual form of creative activity—which is the life style" (Adler, 1935, p. 8).

The Evolution of Adler's Concept of Belonging and Fundamental Human Striving

Adler's theory of Individual Psychology might best be described as a "work in progress," as the development of his theory took place in three separate, though not mutually exclusive, phases (Dreikurs, 1967). The first phase covered the period from 1907 to about 1912 (Shulman, 1951). During this time, Adler placed his emphasis on the role of *organ inferiority*. A review of Adler's writings from these earlier years indicates that three basic elements of his mature theory were developed. First, Adler postulated the concept of the unity of the individual, although, at this early time, the context was physiological. He talked about the confluence of drives—that every drive is connected with one or more other drives—though, more directly, he was still concerned with these as physiological processes (Ansbacher & Ansbacher, 1956).

Adler also began to postulate his motivational principle. Originally, in 1908, Adler wrote about the *aggression drive,* which served as the superordinate force that provided the direction for the confluence of drives. Here we see the dynamic nature of his early theoretical development wherein the individual strives for a level of success or satisfaction. In 1910, the aggression drive was replaced by the concept of *masculine protest,* the difference being that the physiological, objective psychology of Adler was shifting to a psychological, subjective one. Adler viewed the masculine protest as "the striving to be strong and powerful in compensation for feeling unmanly, for a feeling of inferiority" (Ansbacher & Ansbacher, 1956, p. 45).

The third element of Adler's early theory, proposed in 1908, was the need for affection—the goal toward which the confluence of drives is struggling. The need for affection was Adler's idea that an *inner disposition* of the individual required other people and social relationships to be satisfied. This described the nature of the striving of the individual; however, Adler cautioned that the satisfaction or blocking of the gratification of this need should only be done for culturally useful purposes. Thus, we see the beginnings of Adler's emphasis on community and the beginnings of his approach to working with children. However, Adler's psychological theory basically reflected a strong biological orientation, which lasted until around 1912, when his theory began to shift "toward a socially oriented, subjectivistic, holistic psychology of attitudes" (Ansbacher & Ansbacher, 1956, p. 76).

The Second Phase of Individual Psychology's Belonging and Human Striving

This next phase of development for Adler and his theory lasted about 4 years, from 1912 to 1916, when an increased emphasis was placed on the feeling of inferiority. By now, Adler had established his own psychological "school," having withdrawn from Freud's psychoanalytic circle the previous year (1911). The break with Freud coincided with the appearance of Vaihinger's *The Philosophy of 'As If,'* which served as a major impetus to the direction of Adler's theoretical development (Ansbacher & Ansbacher, 1956). With the introduction of *The Neurotic Character* in 1912, it was obvious that Adler was considerably influenced by Vaihinger and, as a result, a major modification in the theory of neurosis had taken place.

Vaihinger's greatest influence on Adler's Individual Psychology was in respect to the concept of the **fictional goal.** This fiction is a subjective creation of the individual that offers a basis for action *as if* such were a true and logical assessment of reality. The fictional structure, when combined with a teleological orientation, resulted in Adler's concept of the fictional goal (or fictional final goal, or guiding fiction). This fictional goal is an ever-present creative product of the individual and serves as the end state to be achieved by his or her strivings. The concept of the fictional goal also "became the principle of unity and self-consistency of the personality structure" (Ansbacher & Ansbacher, 1956, p. 90) and was a means by which the individual could compensate for feelings of inferiority.

Having established the principle of the unity of the personality in terms of a *fictional finalism,* the striving for this goal became the dynamic force in Adler's theory. The general description of this force, from 1916 on, remained predominantly the same in that the psychological movement of the individual took place in terms of a striving for perfection, from below to above, from a felt minus to a plus, from inferiority to superiority. It was in these early days, though, that Adler wrote from the frame of reference of "the neurotic patient; it was the neurotic whom Adler showed as striving for enhancement of his self-esteem or for the safeguarding of it. When he generalized from the neurotic, he described the normal individual as behaving in the same way, only less clearly so and to a lesser degree" (Ansbacher & Ansbacher, 1956, p. 101).

Adler, during this second phase in theory development, called the striving for superiority the **will to power,** a will that increased proportionately in strength with the extent of the strength of the feeling of inferiority. "In effect, the pleasure of *feeling* powerful was directly related to the displeasure of feeling powerless" (Ansbacher & Ansbacher, 1956,

p. 111). At this time in Adler's theory development, we find the neurotic serving as the frame of reference for describing the normal individual. However, this orientation was to change as Adler's theory continued to mature.

The Third and Final Phase of a Developing Individual Psychology

Upon Adler's return to Vienna in 1916, after serving in the war as a doctor at the front, he presented the concept of **Gemeinschaftsgefühl,** or *social interest,* to his old group. Although this was not a totally new idea for Adler, the weight he attached to it was, "for he knew *now* that it was the one question at issue between man and his fate" (Bottome, 1957, p. 122). The period from 1916 until Adler's death in 1937 marks the last major modification to be introduced into the theory of Individual Psychology. During these later years, Adler's efforts were spent, in part, in an attempt to develop the simple theme of social interest. "What Adler was in search of was a reconciliation between individual and society, a means of effecting a reintegration of the maladjusted neurotic with his environment through a simple and rational code of conduct that would satisfy the demands of both" (Way, 1962, p. 186).

By the 1930s, Adler recognized that feelings of inferiority were not a fundamental condition of human nature, but a mistaken approach to life. Adler shifted his notion of the individual's striving for superiority to a fundamental desire to belong, to feel worthwhile as a human being, and be part of the human community (Ferguson, 1989). Not only had Adler found the concept describing the ideal state of the individual's relationship to his environment, but also he had changed his frame of reference from the neurotic to humankind in general. He had developed a criterion for normalcy—social interest—and could now rewrite his theory in terms of the normal individual.

Neurosis was now defined as the extent to which the individual possessed a discouraged attitude toward life. The "normal" individual functions courageously, cooperating and contributing to the extent of his or her social interest. Thus, the process of curing the neurosis as well as the process of educating children toward "normal adjustment" requires a program of help that is aimed at expanding and strengthening the individual's social interest. In this final phase, Adler established the most important and major element in his theory: the concept of social interest became the sole criterion of mental health and the increase of social interest was the major therapeutic goal.

Social Interest

For Adler, the criterion for "success" in life, in essence the healthy personality, is inherent in the extent to which the individual embodies social interest (Gemeinschaftsgefühl) in his or her characteristic approach to life and life problems. It is this conceptualization that describes the ideal state of the individual's mental health. Adler's term, *Gemeinschaftsgefühl,* presents considerable difficulty in terms of translation into English and, much like the terms *Gestalt* or *Vorstellung,* there is no available English equivalent that conveys the same meaning. A number of terms—"social feeling, community feeling, fellow feeling, sense of solidarity, communal intuition, community interest, social sense, and social interest" (Ansbacher & Ansbacher, 1956, p. 134)—have been used. Adler seemed to prefer the latter term, *social interest,* which he used in most of his later writing (Ansbacher & Ansbacher, 1956; Dreikurs, 1950).

Not only does the term *Gemeinschaftsgefühl* present translation problems, but also, as Ansbacher (1966) points out, these are minor difficulties in contrast to the problem of understanding what the concept really means. In Adler's own words, "it becomes clear that the difficulty with this term is not one of the translation from German into English, but one of the definition, no matter which language or which particular term one might choose" (Ansbacher, 1966, p. 14). To advocate the sole use of the term *Gemeinschaftsgefühl* does not solve the problem since it would still convey little or no meaning, particularly to those with few or no German language skills.

Referring to the original German term for a moment, Gemeinschaftsgefühl is a composite of *Gemeinschaft* which is "a community, an aspect of the cosmos" and *Gefühl* which is "subjective state, an attitude, a state of the organism preparatory to action" (Buchheimer, 1959, p. 242), two words conveying a two-part or two-dimensional whole. In this view, Gemeinschaftsgefühl becomes a mediating factor providing for the reconciliation of the individual's internal, personal, subjective environment or frame of reference with the demands of the person's external, common, objective environment or surroundings. Ansbacher (1968) indicates that these can be considered as the psychological *process* dimension and the *object* (outside world) dimension at which the process is directed.

A review of Adler's writings reveals that he utilized and described Gefühl or "interest" in "social interest" in terms of three different aspects: of its being an aptitude or innate potentiality; of its being a set of abilities; and of its being a generalized attitude. Ansbacher (1968) describes these as three developmental steps.

> In Step 1 social interest is an assumed *aptitude* for cooperation and social living that can be developed through training. In Step 2 this aptitude has been developed into the objective *abilities* of cooperating and contributing, as well as understanding others and empathizing with them. In Step 3 social interest is a subjective *evaluative attitude* determining choices and thus influencing the dynamics of the individual. When not backed up by the skills represented in Step 2, such an attitude of social interest may not be sufficient to meet all contingencies. (p. 132)

Assuming that social interest, then, is an aptitude or innate potentiality, it must be consciously developed until, as Bottome (1957) quotes Adler as saying, it becomes "as natural as breathing or the upright gait" (p. 168). The next step—the function of education and training—is the development of this potential, converting the aptitude into an ability or skill. Just as one must train a potential for music or numbers or artistic productions, so must the social interest be trained. The development of this capability for social interest makes an excellent argument for implementing character education training and other comparable programs. With this training in social interest comes the development of the capacities for cooperation and contribution. In brief, these could be described, in total, as the ability to accept *what is* (the implication here being one of cooperation) with a view of *what could be* (the implication being the element of contribution).

Emphasizing the abilities of cooperation and contribution as basic elements of the "interest" in social interest, Dreikurs (1950) indicates "each individual has to make an adjustment to two social levels which oppose each other. Fulfilling the social tasks which confront us means meeting not only the acute obligations presented to us by the needs of the groups around us, but also the needs for improvement and social development" (p. 9). Social interest requires that the individual have enough contact with the present to make his or her move toward the future meaningful and enough vision of the future to go beyond mere conformity. "The ideal expression of social interest is the ability to play the game with existing demands for cooperation and to help the group to which one belongs in its evolution closer toward a perfect form of social living" (Dreikurs, 1950, p. 8).

The social interest dimension described by cooperation is best exemplified by the ability of the individual to give and take. He or she must not only feel a part of life as a whole, but also must be willing to accept the good and the bad aspects of living. The person might be described as being neither optimist nor pessimist, but as one who functions effectively within the realities of the situation. He or she operates as a part of life, in conjunction with others. One of the measures, then, of the degree of social *interest* developed by the individual is expressed by the extent to which the individual is willing to cooperate. Though many individuals may have only a limited capacity to cooperate, life does not always present to them such demanding problems that their cooperation is found to be in short supply. Often, they are never called upon to cooperate to such an extent that they will be found lacking in their ability. It is only under difficult situations and stress that we can truly assess the cooperative ability of the individual.

Not only must the individual develop his or her capacity for cooperation, but he or she must also develop a capacity for contribution—a willingness to consider in his or her own personal striving for overcoming and perfection the welfare of others. Humans do not live an isolated existence; every action and feeling has some effect and impact on others. Adler considered it to be a major function of each individual that he become his "brother's keeper" (Bottome, 1957). A major aspect of this dimension is the idea that there is no one-to-one correspondence between contribution and reward, and the individual must be able to give far more than he or she receives. This willingness to contribute must take place in a context of primary concern for others and the general welfare. Concern for personal benefit can only be secondary and must follow solely as "spill out" from the primary concern (Dreikurs, 1950).

In summary, the individual must be able to function on two planes: a horizontal and a vertical. The horizontal plane consists of the day-to-day demands of social living and is part of the here and now. This includes the individual's immediate relationships to all elements of this environment incorporating all things and all persons with which he or she comes in contact, either directly or indirectly. Thus, the horizontal plane is not restricted solely to social relationships, as may be implied by the term *social interest,* but is viewed as the totality of the person's environment. This plane might be adequately described as a *continuum of cooperation*—the extremes of which can be characterized in terms of the cooperative movement displayed by the individual—whether it be *with,* in a synergistic relationship, or *against,* in a hostile, fighting relationship toward the total spectrum of environmental elements.

The second plane, which is vertical in nature, consists of a type of evolutionary movement that is continuous and upward in direction. This plane can be designated as a *continuum of contribution* and refers to a general striving for improvement and social development. At the extremes, we would find the individual either moving *toward* improvement in a constructive manner inclusive of the welfare of others or moving *away* from social development in a destructive manner and ignoring the social good. To remain solely on the horizontal plane would constitute a type of conformity in the individual that would have no element of a futuristic or evolutionary orientation. Devoting sole attention to the vertical would constitute a striving for superiority without a concomitant interest in the immediate environment. A balance or equilibrium must be maintained between the two directions of these planes if the social interest is to exist to any high degree in the individual.

The third developmental step results in the individual's moving closer to achieving a subjective evaluative attitude toward life. However, without the development of the previously mentioned capacities for cooperation and contribution, the arrival at such an attitude on the part of the individual would be inadequate in the face of meeting all the challenges of living. The development of freedom, for example, without the concomitant attitudes of commitment and responsibility is as disastrous for the individual as it is for him or her to have feelings of insecurity or inferiority. Thus, a mentally healthy attitude toward life not only allows for a feeling of value and self-worth, but also influences the nature and direction—a direction of moving ever closer to a more adequate form of social living—of the activities the individual proposes to undertake.

Life, as viewed by Adler, presented the individual with two often contradictory demands. On the one hand, the individual had to be capable of meeting the acute demands of the existing environment; he or she had to have the capacity to cooperate. On the other hand, the demands for the need for social improvement and development required the individual to possess the capacity to make a contribution. The resolution of this dilemma necessitates that the individual find that balance between present needs and the demands of evolution (Dreikurs, 1950). Fortunately, there seems to exist in all human beings a recognition of the "necessity of being human, of contributing and cooperating in human society" (Wolfe, 1930, p. 26). Even the neurotic exemplifies this awareness by spending her life continually justifying the reasons for avoiding humanity and humanism. The social interest cannot be avoided and, in its ultimate form, establishes an ideal and a direction for the strivings of the individual and the group as a whole.

The meaning of *Gemeinschaft,* or the "social" in "social interest," is too often viewed from the limited perspective of social relations. The German term, in fact, has a much broader meaning than that implied in the word *social* (Ansbacher, 1968). Dreikurs (1950), while describing the difficulty that *Gemeinschaftsgefühl* creates for translation, indicated that the main difficulty lies in the term *Gemeinschaft.* "It is not identical with any of the many English words which are used for it . . . although all the various terms, 'community,' 'society,' 'group,' have some of the connotations implied in 'Gemeinschaft.' It is perhaps closest to the term commonweal which contains some of the significant aspects" (p. 4). "Even Adler extended the meaning of *Gemeinschaft,* the social in social interest, to a variety of 'objects' one would not necessarily assume under this term. In fact nearly all objects in the world are potentially included" (Ansbacher, 1968, p. 133).

> Social interest remains throughout life. It becomes differentiated, limited, or expanded and, in favorable cases, extends not only to family members but also to the larger group, to the nation, to all of mankind. It can even go further, extending itself to animals, plants, and inanimate objects and finally even to the cosmos. (Ansbacher & Ansbacher, 1956, p. 138)

Thus, *Gemeinschaft,* as Adler used the term, is not restricted solely to the social community but describes a holistic relationship between man and the cosmos. Way (1962) describes this relationship: "The feeling for the *Gemeinschaft* is wider that the term 'society' suggests. It embraces a sense of relatedness, not only to the human community, but to the whole of life..." (p. 201). As one's horizons expand, relationships begin to include more and more of life, and ultimately, there is a feeling of connectedness with the whole of the universe, society, and nature.

Social interest is a blending of the Gemeinschaft with the Gefühl; it describes a picture of what *can be* rather than what *is*. Social interest establishes an ideal rather than a norm or median as the direction for the strivings of humankind. It is more than a concept of adjustment, as it implies courage, initiative, and creativity. It places the whole of our existence upon a dynamic foundation of movement and improvement, belonging and cooperation. Social interest represents an *ideal norm* and, therefore, can be used as a standard against which the functioning of the individual can be compared. It serves as a relative index of the individual's mental health status.

Role of Emotions and Feelings

Adlerians view emotions as an element of motivation. "Without strong emotions, no strong acts are possible" (Dreikurs, 1967b, p. 213). The psychological movement of the individual is goal-directed and, in addition to a life style goal, the individual has immediate goals. Emotions are the fuel that helps one attain those goals. Emotion comes from two Latin words, *ex* or *e* which means "out of," and *movere,* which means "to move." Hence, emotions help one "move out" of a situation in a way that is consistent with the life style and one's immediate goals. As Adler explains:

> They depend on his goal and his consequent style of life. The feelings are never in contradiction to the style of life. We are no longer, therefore, in the realm of physiology or biology. The rise of feelings cannot be explained by chemical theory and cannot be predicted by chemical examination. In Individual Psychology, while we presuppose the physiological processes, we are most interested in the psychological goal. (Ansbacher & Ansbacher, 1956, p. 226)

Adler divided emotions into conjunctive and disjunctive emotions. Conjunctive emotions, such as joy, love, excitement, and caring, serve the purpose of bringing people closer together. Disjunctive emotions such as anger, jealousy, bitterness, hatred, and loathing are emotions that distance us from each other. The Ansbachers (1956) provide us with an excellent example of this movement from Adler's writings:

> The emotion of joy, for example, cannot stand isolation. In its expressions of seeking company and embracing another, it shows the inclination to play the game, to communicate, and to share the enjoyment. The entire attitude is engaging. It is extending the hand, so to speak, a warmth which radiates toward the other person and intended to elevate him as well. All the elements of union are present in this emotion. (p. 227)

Depending on the life style goal and the immediate goals of the individual, the person chooses the type of emotion that will serve his or her purpose. Joe was angry a lot.

He reported that he had been abused by his mother and father and was determined not to be abused by others. The question to be asked here is, "What use does Joe's anger serve?" He admitted that he thought others would try to hurt him eventually, so he created a shield of anger in order to minimize that potential hurt and to keep people at a distance from him. The anger also served the purpose of intimidating others and getting them to acquiesce when there was a quarrel because most people backed down when they saw how upset Joe became. Typically, anger is chosen on those occasions when the individual believes himself or herself to be powerless. Although there is no guarantee that anger will make another person cooperate, it is self-reinforcing because it creates the illusion of being in power. Emotions are purposive and serve the goals of the life style and of the immediate situation.

Amy is described by school personnel as "being out of control." Amy, a 17-year-old, has learned to use her emotions to suit her goal of power (e.g., "I am equal to you by being more powerful"). Whenever Amy does not like something that others are doing or when she does not want to give in to the demands of the school, she has fits of temper. On one occasion, when Amy was in the school library, her teacher asked her to put up her book and get ready to leave. Amy didn't respond and the teacher continued to tell her to put up the book. As the teacher began to get frustrated and demand that Amy comply, the school director stepped in to force the issue. Amy "blew up," yelling for them to leave her alone and proceeding to sweep the books off the shelves that were nearest to her.

Of interest here is the fact that, as Amy was clearing off the book shelves, she completely missed a full cup of coffee the director had set down on the top of one of the bookcases. Amy had emptied everything else off that bookcase; what would explain the fact that the coffee cup was missed? From an Adlerian perspective, the answer was clear. Amy was not driven by anger, but was using it; she was able to decide what she would destroy and what she wouldn't. In this case, she seemed to know that the director's coffee was off limits. As a rule, when Amy responded by "being out of control," the faculty and staff in the school would back off and leave her alone to do whatever she wanted. Amy was not *out of control,* but was using her anger to be *in control.*

Emily might be best described as "thin-skinned" and oversensitive. Her friends are very careful around her in terms of what they say or might suggest. They all comment that being with Emily is like walking on eggs. They avoid discussion of subjects that have a tendency to upset her and constantly check in with her to make sure she is "okay" with the activities they are engaged in. Although Emily does not have the awareness, it is clear that she uses her "sensitivity" to control her environment and her friends. As a consequence, Emily has a difficult time keeping friends and is unable to understand why. Fred, however, is easy-going, enjoys life, and always has something positive to say to and about others. He is inquisitive and curious about his world and seems to be a "people magnet." Others seem to be naturally drawn to him and he is never at a loss for being with friends.

After describing a person without emotion, Dreikurs (1967b) commented:

> We can see now why we need emotions. They provide the fuel, the steam, so to speak, for our actions, the driving force without which we would be impotent. They come into play whenever we decide to do something forcefully. They make it possible for us to carry out our decisions. They permit us to take a stand, to develop definite attitudes, to form convictions. They are the only basis for strong personal relationships to others, for

developing interests and for building alliances of interests with others. They make us appreciate and devaluate, accept and reject. They make it possible for us to enjoy and dislike. In short, they make us human beings instead of machines. (p. 207–208)

Depending on the life style goal and the immediate goals of the individual, the person chooses the type of emotion that will serve his or her purpose(s). Emotions are not something that control the individual; rather, the individual learns to use emotions to pursue goals. As a way of preserving one's self-esteem, it sometimes seems as if the emotion dominates the person; however, with closer analysis, one finds the reverse to be true.

Applications

Overview

Adler identified three phases of the counseling/therapy process: *understanding* the client, *explaining* the client's behavior to him or her in a way that makes sense, and *strengthening social interest,* the "working through" part of counseling or therapy (Ansbacher & Ansbacher, 1956). Dreikurs (1956) expanded the three phases to four with the addition of *building relationships* as an initial step. This was consistent with the research on counseling and psychotherapy that was current in his time. It might be interesting to note here that Adler never discussed the relationship element of the counseling/therapy process other than to say it was similar to talking with a good friend. Dreikurs referred to the four phases as building a *relationship* of mutual trust and respect; psychological *investigation* to understand the client's life style and the present area of operation; *interpretation* to help the client learn about his or her unique motivations, intentions and goals, which are often unconscious or unaware; and *reorientation* or re-education, which has encouragement as a central ingredient. Dreikurs emphasized that these phases often overlap.

Mozdzierz, Lisiecki, Bitter, & Williams (1986) expand on the roles and functions of an Adlerian counselor or therapist and emphasize that these are not stages or phases of counseling and therapy in any chronological sense of the term. Rather, they are processes or elements that the counselor or therapist needs to attend to with different degrees of emphasis at different times. Rapport is usually one of the first processes or elements requiring attention by the counselor/therapist, but understanding the client is also an important step in the initial part of treatment and may actually enhance the rapport building by helping clients feel that someone actually understands them. A more important emphasis for the Adlerian counselor or psychotherapist is that the patterns of living that the client has adopted be disclosed to the client in a way that makes sense. At various times during counseling or therapy (e.g., after a particularly discouraging week or difficult confrontation), the role of rapport building may again be emphasized while the other three processes take a temporary back seat. Similarly, at some point it may be useful to explore additional early recollections or solicit other information typically thought of as part of understanding the client or patient in an effort to help the client learn about himself or herself.

Goals of Counseling and Psychotherapy

Dreikurs (1967c) distinguished counseling and psychotherapy from each other based on the idea that each of these has different objectives. Counseling was described as focusing on an acute situation aimed at the solution of immediate problems. It was viewed as a process of learning to adapt to the challenges presented by the tasks of life. The goal was not to change the life style as much as to help the client understand how his or her life style may interfere with completing the tasks of life. Therapy, however, had a goal of changing the life style and was designed to affect the whole personality and lead to the re-organization of the client's life. Both counseling and psychotherapy, however, are accomplished in light of the over-arching goal of enhancing the client's social interest.

Contemporary Adlerians tend to see counseling and psychotherapy as more similar, as do clinicians and counselors in general. The goal of counseling and psychotherapy for Adlerians is to assist clients to understand their unique life styles and help them learn to think about self, others, and the world, and to act in such a way as to meet the tasks of life with courage and social interest. While Adlerian counseling and therapy may vary from short term to rather long term, it is generally considered to be one of the forms of brief therapy primarily because of its emphasis on interpretation, confrontation, and working with the client to understand and explain the client to himself or herself. The re-orientation phase of psychotherapy emphasizes the development of social interest and involves a great deal of encouragement with a variety of strategically planned learning experiences over an extended period of time, particularly for those clients who have severe deficits (Stein & Edwards, 1998).

The Process of Change

Change seems to occur in Adlerian psychotherapy and counseling because of a variety of mechanisms. Dreikurs (1956) posited that insight was an important part of change, although it was not the only therapeutic agent. He believed that change occurred as the client began to recognize his or her goals and intentions. He spoke of a process Adler called "spitting in the patient's soup" as a way of helping the client become aware of his or her motivation. Once the client becomes aware of his or her motivation for the behavior, the behavior becomes less desirable. One can continue to eat soup that has been spat in, but it may not be as appetizing. Dreikurs believed that it was not only making the person aware of goals and motivation that helped the person to change, but also making the person aware of his or her own power, of the ability to make decisions, of freedom to choose directions. Encouragement is an essential element in counseling and therapy. Encouragement begins in therapy with the relationship based on mutual respect and trust. It is the process of restoring the patient's faith in self and the realization of strength and ability as well as dignity and worth. According to Dreikurs, "Without encouragement neither insight nor change is possible" (Dreikurs, 1956, p. 118).

Shulman (1973) has written about the process of confrontation in counseling or therapy and credits it as an important ingredient in change and success of Adlerian strategies. He sees confrontation as a way of provoking therapeutic movement. Because a major goal of Adlerian counseling or psychotherapy is to recognize and change mistaken goals and beliefs and their associated moods and actions, confrontation is frequently used as a way of holding the mistaken goals and beliefs up in front of the client, as with a mirror. Confrontation presents an opportunity to the client to make an immediate change in beliefs, behaviors, or mood. Because confrontation is an active method, the counselor/therapist has to make the client aware of his or her private logic and goals, the ownership of these, and the ability to change them.

Adler's emphasis on understanding the interpersonal nature of behavior and the facilitating of change processes rather than on analyzing intrapsychic processes contributed to the eventual split between him and Freud. The focus became one of empowering discouraged individuals to resolve problems by recognizing their strengths and assets rather than by focusing on their weaknesses. For Dreikurs, all psychotherapy involved the correction of faulty social values and attitudes. He saw psychotherapy as a way of teaching cooperation.

> We find four attitudes essential for cooperation, with their counterparts disrupting it. These are: (1) social interest—hostility; (2) confidence in others—distrust and suspicion; (3) self-confidence—inferiority; (4) courage—fear. Social interest is an expression of a sense of belonging; lack of social interest limits or impedes cooperation and makes an opponent appear as an enemy. Fear seems to be the chief obstacle to adequate social functioning in a democratic atmosphere; it can be regarded as the sin of free man. (Dreikurs, 1967a, p. 152)

Intervention Strategies

Life Style Analysis   Life Style Analysis is the process of learning to understand the goals and motivations of the client. This is a mutual process in which both the client and counselor or therapist learn more about the beliefs and patterns of behavior that the client has developed in a creative attempt to address life's challenges. The life style is a cognitive blueprint one has developed that includes ideas about self, others, and the world. It also includes ethical convictions (e.g., what I should be, what life should be, and so on.) and a unifying function or goal toward which all movement is directed. The life style is an ongoing process. It is similar to personality, but slightly different in that it includes one's patterns of behaviors as well as one's beliefs and perceptual schema. One's life style not only affects what one does but also how one sees the world, other people, and the self. If a person has a life style that includes the belief that other people are hostile, that person will find validation on a daily basis of other people's hostility through the apperception of reality. **Apperception** is the process of experiencing or perceiving things mediated by attribution of meaning and significance to those experiences or perceptions.

There are many methods of life style analysis ranging from a more formal or structured approach to the less formal and structured. Shulman and Mosak (1988) have developed a standardized way of collecting life style data and suggest ways of interpreting that data. Powers and Griffith (1987) have another standardized method of data collection and emphasize slightly different aspects in interpreting the data. Other Adlerians see life style analysis unfolding as therapy or counseling continues and do not gather the data in quite so systematic a manner as do these authors.

In brief counseling and therapy, often only those data regarding relevant lifestyle elements are obtained. Walton (1996c) suggests five questions for brief life style analysis.

1. Complete the following statement: "I was the kid who always. . . ."
2. Which sibling did you think was most different from you when you were a child? How? (If the client is an only child, ask, "How were you different from the other kids?"

3. When you were a child, what did you think was most positive about your mother? Father? Was there anything you rejected about Mom and Dad?
4. Unforgettable or most memorable observations: "When you were growing up, can you recall any conclusions you made about life such as—*when I get to be an adult, I certainly will always …,* or *I will never let this happen in my family (or in my life)?*"
5. Finally, obtain two early memories (recollections): "What was the earliest specific incident you can recall?" (Record these in the present tense in the precise words of the client.) "What moment was most vivid? What feeling is connected with the incident?"

Other than in brief counseling or therapy, data for life style analysis usually involves the collection of information in some or all of the following areas.

Family Constellation.   The family constellation includes the ordinal and psychological position in the family of reference along with an understanding of the relationships between the siblings, the parents, and the parents and children as the client perceives them. These evaluations on the part of the client form a part of the basic convictions upon which his or her anticipation of life, self, and others are based.

Family Atmosphere.   The family atmosphere is set by the relationship between the parents. The client's evaluation of this atmosphere as a child becomes important to the decisions he or she makes about how life and relationships should be and is retained and used in later life. To explore the general climate of the household, climate-related terms may be used (i.e., "sunny," "partly cloudy," "tornadic," "icy"). The participation of each parent in the creation of the family atmosphere is a significant aspect of the child's **gender guiding lines.**

Family Values.   Family values represent what both parents want for the children. These are the values that are shared by both the mother and father and, typically, are indicated by the ways in which all children in the family are alike. Each child in the family must take a position with respect to these values that operate as "family imperatives." Although most children are likely to support the family standard, it is not unusual for one child to ignore it, defy it, or take a contrary position. Exploration of family values can be accomplished by asking a child, "What is important to mother? To father?" With an adult, one might say, "Growing up as a child, what was important to mother? To father?" Asking for mottoes is another means of ascertaining family values: "If mother had a motto, something she might put on a plaque or a poster, what would it be? If your father had a motto, what would it be?"

Gender Guiding Lines.   The values not shared by the parents but held by only one take on a different significance. The child experiences these as elements of the gender guiding lines—what it means to be a "real" man or a "real" woman. These unshared values form the rules and patterns for a person's expectations regarding gender and are often perceived by the person as if it is destiny.

Family Role Played by Each Child.   Reed (1995), when discussing family roles assumed by children of alcoholics, identifies the following four roles: the Hero, the Scapegoat, the Lost Child, and the Mascot. Milliren (1995) discusses the need for educators (and counselors/therapists) to "recognize the almost driven nature of the 'hero,' to understand the purposes of the behaviors of the 'scapegoat,' to have insight into the aloneness of the 'lost child,' and to know the need for affiliation on the part of the 'mascot' " (p. xvii). Other role descriptors have also been provided by Typpo and Hastings (1984): the Responsible One, the Caretaker, the Family Pet, the Forgotten Child, the Problem Child, the Acting-Out Child, and the Adjuster. All of these are life style patterns adopted by children to cope with the family situation. These roles become so ingrained that they continue on through life even after the need for the coping style is no longer required.

Early Developmental Experiences.   It is sometimes useful to explore the nature of early development experiences (i.e., early experiences with peers, adults, school, and sex) in order to obtain an additional dimension of the conclusions the client drew about how life should be. Sometimes these will take the form of early recollections.

After these data are collected, a report is usually prepared. The discussion and modification of the report becomes a collaborative activity between the counselor/therapist and the client. This process takes the form of a dialogue that allows the counselor/therapist and client to begin to examine the beliefs he or she holds about life and living. The purpose for life style assessment is to help clients understand who they are, how they became who they are, and to bring their unconscious goals into a level of greater awareness. It is important to note here that Adlerians use the term *unconscious* only as an adjective. There is no such thing for them as "the unconscious," and it may be more accurate to use the concept "out of awareness" when describing unconscious processes. Because the life style is the set of rules that the individual lives by, it is important for him or her to come to understand his or her movement through life. Once these rules are clarified, the person is in a better position to change disliked or unproductive elements.

Encouragement   Encouragement is the key in promoting and activating social interest and psychological "muscle" or hardiness. Social interest and psychological hardiness are required to take life in stride without becoming discouraged and to create meaning and purpose in life (Evans, 1997a). Encouragement is a fundamental Adlerian concept for helping parents (Meredith & Evans, 1990) and teachers (Evans, 1995, 1996) improve relationships with children and create an atmosphere of cooperation and democracy in the family and school. Encouragement is probably the universal therapeutic intervention for Adlerian counselors and therapists. Encouragement is not a technique; rather, it is a fundamental attitude or "spirit."

Although the concept of encouragement is simple to understand, it is difficult to define. Simply stated, encouragement is the process of giving courage to another. Encouragement is not a special language used to gain compliance or cooperation. Rather, it is a fundamental attitude regarding human nature. Encouragement is a spirit, conveyed through interactions with others. Human beings are worthwhile merely because they exist. It is their birthright to belong. Belonging is not something you have to achieve through your accomplishments. Thus, encouragement is Mr. Rogers telling our children, "I like you just the way you are," not "I like you when you do it well enough, fast enough, and get it all correct." The most fundamental encouragement an adult can give a child is the sense that he or she has significance, even when things go poorly. The most fundamental encouragement a spouse can convey to his or her partner is that the partner counts by the mere fact of his or her existence. Communicating this spirit will develop an individual's capacity to withstand adversity and the willingness to function when things go poorly. Involving oneself in living life, especially in times of adversity, is an act of courage.

Courage is the willingness to move forward, one step at a time, in the face of adversity and in spite of how one feels. It is produced through encouragement and comes from a feeling of belonging and contribution. A major source of courage comes from acceptance and recognition of competence rather than a focus on failure. To instill courage, the therapist or counselor must stimulate a sense of belonging on the part of the client and impart an appreciation for the ironclad logic of social living. Instilling courage involves recognizing the strengths and abilities of the client, assisting the client in setting goals that are attainable in a reasonable amount of time, and helping the client identify the steps and methods by which these goals may be attained. Some clients need more help with the process of identifying steps and methods for goal attainment, while others may need more assistance with identifying the goals. Still others have been so discouraged that they feel like they do not belong to the human race.

Encouragement is the single most important quality in getting along with others. It is so important that the lack of it could be considered the basic factor in misbehavior, divorce, job loss, suicide, and other human problems. Encouragement is the key ingredient in all positive professional and personal relationships. The ability to function in today's world balances on one's ability to nurture and convey concern for others. Encouragement is desperately needed today; fear, power, and the threat of punishment are not effective in developing responsible, capable, and fully functioning individuals. Dreikurs (Terner & Pew, 1978) said that human beings need encouragement like plants need water. Yet so few of us know how to encourage ourselves and others. An encouraging person infuses life into the world. Encouragers are so comfortable with human nature that they convey faith in a person just because he or she exists.

Fear, worry, and obsession are all forms of negative thinking that create discouragement. Conjuring up fears taints our present opportunities. Fear puts a stranglehold on our ability to function. Some individuals worry so much that they develop a negative attitude and go around reacting, obsessing, and pointing out all the dangers of life in an attempt to control the world. None of this activity solves the problem; it just makes people difficult to be around. After a while, others either avoid or minimize their contact with the negative thinker. The discouragement that flows from their tongues poisons the well. They send admonitions of doom and gloom that extract the joy from life. Fear and excessive worry convey a vote of "no confidence." In this way, we treat ourselves as inferior and reflect doubt in our ability to handle life. Fear is diminished by developing a more adequate and trusting view of self.

Half of the job of encouragement lies in avoiding being discouraging. All criticism and/or external control, like rewards and punishments, are viewed as discouraging. Criticism is the poison that sours a marriage and destroys adult-child relationships. According to Evans (1997a), there are five general ways to discourage.

1. setting high expectations or unrealistic standards
2. focusing on mistakes in a misguided attempt to motivate
3. making comparison among people

4. making pessimistic interpretations
5. dominating by being overly responsible

No corrective effort of a person's behavior is possible without encouragement. The worse the behavior, the more encouragement is needed. Yet individuals who misbehave are most likely to receive the least amount of encouragement. Instead of building on a discouraged person's strengths, we tear him down; instead of recognizing the person's efforts and improvement, we point out her mistakes; instead of allowing the person to feel like he belongs and can become responsible through shared decision-making, we control and punish.

To become encouraging, we need to get out of our feeling of the need for external control (Glasser, 1999) and stop being mistake centered. We need to first make the relationship a priority and develop a friendly and respectful atmosphere. Encouragement is often mistaken as praise, yet praise is external control. Praise focuses on outcomes, doing well, uses superlatives, and is conditional. Encouragement will focus on effort or improvement rather than results. It focuses on strengths and assets, rather than identifying weaknesses, limitations, deficits, or disorders. Encouragement can be given at any time, no matter how poorly things are going; praise, rewards, and punishment can only be given with good or bad results. Encouragement separates the deed from the doer. A particular behavior can be disturbing, but the individual is not labeled as "bad." Encouragement will point out specific behaviors that contribute, improve, or display strength. Finally, encouragement is focused on intrinsic motivation so that encouraging someone is also a means for helping him or her develop self-control (Evans & Milliren, 1999).

Every person with whom we come in contact feels better or worse by how we behave toward him or her. Our attitude toward others either brings out their very best or very worst. Encouragers contribute, cooperate, and help out in life. They have discovered that the meaning in life is to help, not burden. Inappropriate behavior is the result of discouragement and derives from feeling alienated, different, or as if one does not belong. "All symptoms of neuroses and psychoses are forms of expression of discouragement. Every improvement comes about solely from encouraging the sufferer. Every physician and every school of neurology is effective only to the extent that they succeed in giving encouragement. Occasionally, a layman can succeed in this also. It is practiced deliberately only by Individual Psychology" (Adler, 1926).

Clients with Mental Disorders

At first, Adler attributed all psychopathological behavior to exaggerated feelings of inferiority. Later, both Adler and Dreikurs believed that mental disorders reflected a tremendous sense of inadequacy and an inability to develop a quality human relationship along with a lack of social interest. The greater the social interest, the greater the level of functioning. To feel equal and adequate to the task at hand results in one's being able to participate in a constructive and useful manner. This willingness to cooperate is social interest. When it is lacking, one feels less than others and, instead of moving toward others as a member of the human community, one moves toward self-elevation. The movement away from others may be toward personal glory, which can be a useful compensation, or, if the inadequacy is too great, it will move toward the useless side of life. All mental disorders can be reduced to this analogy (Dreikurs, 1961).

Adlerians view behavior as occurring on a continuum rather than as a dichotomy; they do not believe it is "either/or" but rather "degree of" that differentiates one person from another. While some theories of counseling/psychotherapy propose a categorical difference between those who are "mentally ill" and those who are "normal," Adlerians believe that people act in ways that are consistent with their life style goals. Adlerians believe that the only reliable diagnosis of symptoms—particularly psychosomatic symptoms—is to ascertain their function or use. Dreikurs (Terner & Pew, 1978) suggests the use of "**the Question,** a quick technique for differentially diagnosing whether a symptom is psychogenic or organic" (p. 185). Because behavior is purposive, there is usually some payoff or outcome toward which the behavior is directed, even though the individual may be unaware of it. If the symptom has no function, or particular gain, the Adlerian counselor/therapist would then conclude that the problem had organic origins and would need to be treated by a physician (Dreikurs, 1956).

One of the most important things an Adlerian counselor can do is to continually ask, "What's the use for this behavior?" Richard, a therapist in private practice, had asked to consult about a case he was working on because he couldn't understand one of his clients. Martha, a fourth grader, had been referred for having difficulty at home and at school. As Richard discussed the case, he related two incidents that occurred while he was interviewing this little girl. First, Richard had asked about an incident involving Martha and her younger brother where Martha had refused to share her drawing materials. When asked to explain, Martha immediately began to cry, and Richard said that he thought she was expressing remorse about not sharing with her brother. A while later in the interview, when Richard was discussing what she might do differently in these situations with her brother, Martha began to cry again. He asked why she was crying, and Martha said she felt like she was such a bad person for not sharing with her brother.

What Richard forgot to do was ask, "What's the use?" He failed to look for the purpose of the behavior and, as a result, was led to believe that his client was a sweet little girl who felt extremely sorry for the fact that she had not shared her things. However, after initiating a discussion of what the possible purpose might be, Richard happened to mention that Martha's mother was extremely demanding in her expectations for Martha's behavior. "After all, Martha is the eldest and needs to set the example!" With this background information, it was suddenly clear as to the purpose of Martha's crying. Martha was acting as if she believed that crying would allow her to avoid being punished for misbehaving. Richard mentioned that when Martha cried, he dropped the subject and went on to talk with her about other things. Richard further shared that the mother had told him that her response, whenever Martha would burst into tears, was to just tell her to not do it again. The mother was afraid of Martha's extreme sensitivity about everything and did not want to do anything to upset her further. Rather than being extra sensitive, however, Martha was using her sensitivity as "water power" to manipulate the situation.

Shulman (1962) talks of persons with schizophrenia or bipolar disorder as sharing three characteristics: (1) extremely low self-esteem; (2) extremely high-flown goals in life; and (3) drastic measures for narrowing the gap between the self-image and the self-ideal (p. 151). There are, of course, some genetic or organic factors that are often involved in what is commonly called *major mental illness* (e.g., schizophrenia, bipolar disorders, major depression). However, these are viewed as dispositions or propensities that increase the potential for developing these types of behavior patterns rather than determining factors.

The environment and learning history need to be taken into consideration. Persons with schizophrenia are not all alike. Neither are all persons with bipolar disorder alike. Some lead lives that are more productive than others, while some have totally given up and feel isolated, totally different from other human beings. Again, the purpose of counseling and therapy, whether it is individual, group, or milieu treatment, is to foster the sense of belonging, of competence, and of courage to participate in life.

For Adlerians, a major mental illness such as schizophrenia or bipolar disorder is a part of life that must be dealt with through education, medication, socialization, and encouragement rather than through stigmatization and isolation. Community support programs such as Fountain House in New York, Thresholds in Chicago, and other community-based programs around the world exhibit a philosophy that is very similar to Adler's: "We are not alone." This was the emphasis of the first members at Fountain House who bonded together to assist each other in their re-entry into society after years of hospitalization and isolation from others. From this movement, it is clear that the principles of belonging, helping each other, useful contribution, and support are essential elements in the intervention process (Beard, Propst, & Malamud, 1982).

A person with a major mental illness still has to decide what to do about the mental illness and about the tasks of life. Like a physical illness, mental illness of organic etiology may need medical intervention. If medication is necessary to allow one to function better, then its importance needs to be addressed as part of treatment. For many who have a major mental illness, learning to recognize the onset of stress and alternatives to cope with stress are important aspects of treatment. For Adlerians, social treatment and involvement in community activities is frequently the focus of interventions. Group therapy and community drop-in centers, in which a sense of belonging, membership, and useful contribution are encouraged, help the person with major mental illness to develop social interest and to learn to address the tasks of life in a constructive manner.

Evaluation

Overview

Of all of the personality and counseling theories, Alfred Adler's Individual Psychology is probably among the least well-known. However, it has had the greatest influence on current approaches to counseling and psychotherapy (Corey, 1996). Willingham (1986), writing about the current status of Adlerian Psychology, indicates that Adler had an influence on various theories and methodologies in counseling, psychotherapy, and education. He quotes Wilder (1959) as stating: "Most observations and ideas of Alfred Adler have subtly and quietly permeated modern psychological thinking to such a degree that the proper question is not whether one is Adlerian, but how much of an Adlerian one is (p. xv)" (Willingham, 1986, p. 165). "Modern applied psychology is increasingly congruent with Individual Psychology in that many applications in organizational psychology and counseling with families and school utilize concepts and methods that strongly resemble Adlerian ideas and practices" (Ferguson, 2000a, p. 14).

In many respects, Adler developed a personality theory and approach to counseling and psychotherapy that was far ahead of his time. Watts (2000) indicates that "many contemporary approaches have 'discovered' many of Adler's fundamental conclusions, often without recognition of his vision and influence" (p. 11). Watts also believes that, as much as Adlerian counseling may be viewed as antiquated by students, educators, and practitioners, it "solidly resonates with postmodern approaches to counseling" (p. 16). In fact, "Adlerian theory addressed social equality and emphasized the social embeddedness of human knowledge long before multiculturalism became chic in the counseling profession" (p. 16).

Unfortunately, the simplicity of Adlerian psychology is often used as its major criticism, of which Adler was apparently aware. The simplicity and common sense approach of Adlerian theory is illustrated by a story told about Adler when he was scheduled for a series of lectures in Aberdeen, Scotland:

> His host was psychology professor Rex Knight, who came to greet Adler at the Caledonia Hotel. After exchanging mutual greetings in the lobby, the two men sat down briefly to chat on a sofa. Suddenly, a handsome young man swaggered over. "I hear that you two gentlemen are psychologists. I bet there's nothing that either of you can tell me about myself."
>
> Knight looked quizzically to Adler for an answer, who raised his eyes and gazed deliberately at the young man. "Yes, I think there's something that I can tell you about yourself." As the stranger smiled expectantly, Adler continued, "You're very vain."
>
> "Vain!" was the startled reply. "Why should you think that I'm vain?"
>
> "Isn't it vain," Adler said simply, "to come up to two unknown gentlemen sitting on a sofa and ask them what they think of you?"
>
> As the young man left baffled, Adler turned to Knight and commented, "I've always tried to make my psychology simple. I would perhaps say that all neurosis is vanity, but that might be too simple to be understood." (Hoffman, 1994, p. 322)

Simple solutions such as recommending that a teacher and parent encourage a student who is doing poorly in school or removing the parent from sibling fights in order to reduce the conflict are strategies that work. Many times, results are what validate the theory for the practitioner and the client.

Supporting Research

Adler developed his theory for the common man, offering common solutions for dealing with the day-to-day problems of living. It was a therapeutic, educational, and rehabilitative model that was a part of the pioneering work taking place in modern psychiatry. By the 1930s, it was being applied to everyday real-life problems in parenting, schools, marriage, and the workplace. Empirical evidence for the theory came from case results rather than experimental designs (Ferguson, 2001). In the 1950s and 1960s, most cited studies involving Adlerian psychology were conducted by non-Adlerians (Mosak & Dreikurs, 1973). Until the last 30 years or so, however, very little research emerged on the effectiveness of Adlerian psychology. Watkins (1982) writes:

> Admittedly, as theoretical and practical interests grow, so must the body of research which supports and extends one's theoretical and practical understanding. The decade of the seventies saw more research studies being done to test the usefulness of Adlerian constructs and concepts than had been done in many preceding years. (p. 90)

Watkins (1983) reports that during the years from 1970 through 1981, there were 75 research studies in the *Journal of Individual Psychology*. Birth order "and its effects on personality development and functioning" (p. 100) was the most researched area with 24 studies. "Social interest is examined in 19 studies (25 percent), early recollections in 6

(8 percent), and lifestyle in 4 (5 percent)" (p. 100). Watkins concludes his survey by indicating that "research on Individual Psychology has flourished during the period examined (and, as a side note, has been quite confirmatory)" (p. 103). He cautions, though, that the study of clinical populations is extremely limited and "there is a definite need for further Adlerian-oriented research on inpatients and outpatients alike" (p. 104).

In a follow-up study, Watkins (1992) examined the research activity with Adlerian theory appearing in the *Journal of Individual Psychology* during the years 1982 to 1990. He notes that 103 studies appeared during this 9-year period. This was a marked increase over the previous 12 years that he had reported on earlier (Watkins, 1983). Although he did not attempt to evaluate the quality of the studies reported, Watkins (1992) does conclude "that research into Adler's theory is still on the increase (at least in *IP*) and suggests it is a vital theory that lends itself to empirical inquiry" (p. 108). Since 1990, the reported research has continued to grow, with the *Journal of Individual Psychology* publishing additional studies on marriage, children, substance abuse, classroom management, behavioral problems in children and youth, and offenders. A number of other professional journals have included research articles on Adlerian theory as well.

A number of university faculty (i.e., Dr. John Dagley of the University of Georgia, Dr. Roy Kern of Georgia State University, and Dr. Eva Dreikurs Ferguson of Southern Illinois University, Edwardsville) have guided their doctoral students toward researching and refining Adlerian concepts. A leading figure in the development and validation of Adlerian research on life style is Dr. Roy Kern, who has set out to validate Adler's psychology and develop a number of instruments based on Adlerian principles. For the past 25 years, Dr. Kern has been developing objective instruments for the assessment of life style that are designed to be used in clinical and educational consultation as well as research. This has led to the publication of 50 or more research articles and over 40 dissertations. As a result, Dr. Kern has provided a means to validate many of the Adlerian constructs. Some of the instruments now available include the Life Style Questionnaire Inventory, the Kern Life Style Scale, Life Style Personality Inventory, and the Basic Adlerian Scales for Interpersonal Success—Adult Form (BASIS-A) (Kern, Snow, & Ritter, in press).

Perhaps one of the best validations of Adlerian theory has been the results experienced by clients and practitioners and how the theory and writings have become international and cross-cultural. Dreikurs started the International Committee for Adlerian Summer Schools and Institutes (ICASSI) in 1962, with the first school being in Denmark. ICASSI has developed into a rich international social experience wherein long-term relationships have emerged between people from many nations. ICASSI is held in a different country each year, and has at least 24 different nationalities represented at each summer institute.

Limitations

One of the issues regarding Adlerian theory and practice is the lack of research demonstrating its specific effectiveness in counseling and therapy. Although this could be addressed as a major limitation, the problem plagues not just Adlerians, but all approaches to counseling and therapy. An early problem with experimental research was that the European Adlerians were, at times, unduly suspicious of research based upon statistical methods. To further complicate matters, the idiographic (case method) approach upon which Adlerians relied did not lend itself to conventional research methodology. Statistical methods tend to be more appropriate for group research and were not considered particularly applicable. Adlerian psychology also rejects the notion of causality and focuses on intent and the social field in which behavior takes place. These are hard concepts to measure with statistics.

Much of the research derived from many studies was not designed to examine Adlerian counseling or psychotherapy, but are clearly applicable to it. Eva Dreikurs Ferguson's book, *Motivation: A Biosocial and Cognitive Integration of Motivation and Emotion,* does a thorough job of examining significant research and how it applies to Adlerian theory.

> The book integrates Adlerian principles and methods with contemporary scientific psychology, especially in the areas of motivation and emotion. The book presents a vast amount of studies in scientific psychology that support Adlerian theory. The book provides evidence, in support of Adlerian psychology, that scientific psychology increasingly shows the validity of Adlerian concepts, of holism, psychic/mental determinants influencing neurochemical and physiological processes, and the impact of social processes on psychological well-being. The book integrates Adlerian ideas in line with research in modern scientific psychology. (E. D. Ferguson, personal communication, November 28, 2001)

Both Adler and Dreikurs have been criticized personally as well as professionally for their theoretical formulations. Both individuals were extremely forceful personalities whose "conceptualizations and ideas were rich in insights. These insights contrasted with beliefs then currently espoused, and rejection of these ideas often became confounded with rejection of the person as well as his ideas" (Ferguson, 2001, p. 325). Part of this criticism came from the sphere of the depth psychologists who argued that the methods of Adler and Dreikurs were too superficial; the other part came from the cognitive behavioral theorists who viewed them "as too dynamic, too concerned with inner motivation" (Ferguson, 2001, p. 325). So, on the one hand, to some, Adlerian theory appears to lack the depth that the more analytic approaches offer and, on the other hand, Adlerian theory is not as scientific as the more behavioral approaches might prefer. "The cognitive-social personality theory and methods of Adler and Dreikurs are very different from behavioristic approaches and, by criteria of broad and long-term health-providing effects, the theory and methods are indeed deep" (Ferguson, 2001, p. 337).

Another possible limitation in the application of Adlerian theory is the emphasis on social connectedness and individual responsibility. Mentally healthy or fully functioning individuals possess high levels of cooperation and contribution and are perceived as being in charge of the decisions they make about life. There is no room for blaming others or society for one's situation in life. However, these beliefs run contrary to the general cultural thinking regarding human behavior and human relationships.

> Thus, Individual Psychologists find themselves becoming agents of change for the community and the culture. As community values change, Adlerian methods become easy to apply. Until such changes in community beliefs occur, however, *Adlerian methods and Individual Psychology will be ahead of their time.* (Ferguson, 2000a, p. 19)

Summary Chart—Adlerian Theory

Human Nature

Adlerian psychology is interested in understanding the life style or the law of psychological movement of the individual. Early experiences and one's birth order and family constellation play a major role in the development of the life style or personality, although these factors are solely formative and not deterministic. As the individual pursues the need to belong and find a place of significance, he or she draws conclusions about the world and his or her personal worth. These conclusions combine to form a system of beliefs that guides all of the person's future interactions.

Major Constructs

The most fundamental principles of Adlerian Psychology include the following.

1. *Purposiveness*—All behavior is goal-directed or purposive. Although not always aware of the purpose, each individual moves through the world in such a way as to make things happen or to achieve a desired outcome. The person is not pushed by causes, but rather is pulled by his or her goals and dynamic striving.
2. *Social Interest*—People are social beings who want to belong; they want to be able to find a place in the group. Because participation in a group requires a high level of co-operation and contribution, the development of social interest or *Gemeinschaftsgefühl* is a necessity for success in life. All of life's problems are basically problems of inter-actions with others and require a high level of social interest for their resolution.
3. *Holism*—The person is seen as a dynamic, unified organism moving through life in definite patterns toward a goal. The person cannot be understood in part, but must be viewed in totality. In combination, these principles describe the person as moving in unity toward self-chosen goals that reflect a human value for belonging and social contribution.

Goals

Three general types of problems arise: work, friendship, and family. The primary goal of counseling or therapy is to assist the client in the development of social interest, for this is required for the effective resolution of life's problems.

Change Process

The life style of the individual serves as a road map that governs one's journey through life. If the person holds a number of mistaken beliefs about self, others, and the world, then the process of change involves helping the individual to reassess and reorient his or her belief system. The counseling/therapy process emphasizes four elements: (1) relationship and rapport building; (2) information gathering; (3) interpretation and goal setting; and (4) re-education/re-orientation. The counselor/therapist works in an atmosphere of encouragement wherein the client is empowered to utilize his or her strengths to make new decisions about how to achieve significance.

Interventions

The primary interventions in Adlerian counseling and therapy include life style analysis and encouragement. Life style analysis is the process of discovering the goals and motivation of the client. Because the life style contains the person's beliefs and perceptual schema about self, others, and the world, the aim of life style analysis is to help the client identify those elements that are working well and those that are not. Encouragement is viewed as the universal therapeutic intervention designed to assist the client in developing the courage to face life's problems. Adlerians may use a variety of additional techniques and methods as long as they are philosophically consistent with the basic theoretical premises of the approach.

Limitations

Many of the beliefs in Adlerian theory tend to run counter to the prevailing general thinking in the culture regarding human behavior and relationships. Adlerian theory is neither analytic/dynamic nor behavioral/scientific. It is a cognitive, goal-oriented social psychology; it is a simplistic and common-sense approach. Nonetheless, a growing body of research seems to indicate that Adlerian theoretical concepts are consistent with contemporary scientific psychology. Studies of outcome effectiveness with this approach will help to expand the acceptance of Adler's and Dreikurs' ideas. Adlerian theory continues to be ahead of its time.

▪▪▪ The Case of Jonathan—An Adlerian Approach

General Considerations

There are probably as many different styles of Adlerian counseling/therapy as there are individual Adlerians. However, certain principles will always be in evidence. As mentioned in the introduction to this chapter, three basic principles are critical to understanding and implementing Adlerian theory: purposiveness, social interest, and holism. These principles will be explored within four elements of the counseling/therapy process: relationship and rapport building, information gathering, interpretation and goal setting, and re-education/re-orientation.

Relationship and Rapport Building

It is essential that the counselor/therapist develop rapport with Jonathan and take the time, both initially and throughout counseling/therapy, to understand the world from Jonathan's perspective. All of the basic attending and listening skills are important to this element of the counseling/therapy process. By using the skills of reflection, empathic listening, clarification, and questioning, the counselor/therapist builds rapport, which is the foundation for a successful therapeutic relationship. The counselor/therapist listens not only to what the client is saying, but also to how it is presented, looking for patterns. Instead of getting caught up in the specific content, the counselor/therapist works to see how one piece of information can fit into the totality of the client's view of life and living. As the session progresses, the use of all of these skills opens the door to understanding the logic and limits with which the client operates.

In addition, the counselor/therapist listens for **gold mines** in the client's story and must be mindful of the **recognition reflex** when interacting with the client. Gold mines are those elements that the client mentions that are clues to major areas for exploration. For example, Jonathan mentions that he was raised to be proud of his Native American heritage, but never clarifies whether or not he is proud of it. Because he later explains that he is not wanted in the "white man's world," one might suspect that he actually rejects his background and upbringing. This is a gold mine that should be explored—some nuggets of truth about Jonathan's view of the world might be uncovered.

The recognition reflex is one of Dreikurs' major contributions to Adlerian counseling/therapy and describes the person's spontaneous reaction to information that is discovered about oneself (Terner & Pew, 1978). This reaction carries with it a physical response of a smile, a nod, or other behavioral acknowledgement when the client realizes that the information just received is accurate. It is an internal "Me" or "Not Me" feeling, as if looking in a mirror, that responds to feedback a person receives from the external world. As the counselor/therapist explores Jonathan's story, he or she may resort to the use of the stochastic method of guessing, (i.e., a form of educated guessing or jumping to conclusions). This allows the counselor/therapist to see what happens when the client tries on the information provided. Often the person will say "No," but the analog or external behavior will say "Yes." Even if the guess is wrong, the feedback gained from the client will serve to help clarify what is really going on for him/her. It is not possible to tell from the case material if any feedback was given to Jonathan in this first interview. However, in order to gain an accurate picture of Jonathan's functioning, some stochastic guessing and interpretive feedback will have to be provided during the counseling/therapy session.

Maybe the most important point in this discussion of the relationship is that each session should be viewed as a process of shared exploration. Care should be taken in interpreting the information received, and when feedback is provided, the skills of reflection and clarification become extremely useful. Feedback should always be tentative, (i.e., "Is it possible that ...?" or "Could it be...?") rather than dogmatic. This allows the client to work with the information in his or her own way. It was suggested to a mother who was attending parent counseling sessions that it might be possible that her problems with her children were the result of her wanting to be a good mother. She became quite indignant and, with tears in her eyes, informed the counselor that that was ridiculous. "I just don't want to be a bad one!" she said. Often, what seems to be a logical explanation for the purpose of behavior is not at all workable in terms of the client's private logic or view of the world.

Information Gathering

Although it is essential that the counselor/therapist build rapport and create a therapeutic relationship through the use of listening and reflecting skills, during the information gathering phase it is important to ask questions of or elicit statements from the client that generate meaningful responses. Effective questions help to define the goals of counseling or therapy and are necessary for obtaining the information needed to facilitate the change desired on the part of the client. Most Adlerian counselors/therapists are quite active in directing the counseling/therapy process; however, the content of therapy or the client's story is left to the client. The counselor/therapist should not be afraid of interrupting the client, although this should be accomplished in a respectful and empathic manner. It is the counselor/therapist's role to facilitate the process by keeping the session focused.

During this phase, the counselor/therapist would be seeking to gain a picture of Jonathan's world view. The counselor/therapist will direct the process of discovering how Jonathan sees himself, how he believes others should treat him, and how he views his place in the world. The nature of the questions/statements asked would be open-ended in an effort to seek expanded information rather than being closed-ended, leading to only a "yes" or a "no." A good place to begin would be by exploring his family constellation and birth order. A sample question/statement on the part of the counselor/therapist might be: "Tell me about your childhood. What was it like growing up in your family? Did you have brothers and sisters and what was your relationship to each of them?"

Jonathan is the youngest of six children, and it would be useful to know how he dealt with being youngest. This could be found out easily enough by exploring in more detail the family of origin in regard to relationships among the siblings, the family atmosphere, and his early recollections. Because his self-statement regarding his referral problem had to do with getting along with others, it may be that he was a youngest child who developed a sense of entitlement. He may have developed a life position where he expects others to do for him and treat him in special ways. As a result, he may have developed a very discouraged life style and ended up feeling that he was not as competent as others, that he could only do things if others were very supportive. Although complete information is not available, this conclusion is quite consistent with other elements of the story Jonathan presents.

The dream represents a similar situation. He is on a bus, being carried along by someone else. A passive approach to life is involved. Everyone on the bus (everyone in the world, in his way of thinking, perhaps) is heading for a place of promise: New York, California. He is going to Albuquerque. In thinking of his dream within the cultural context of a Native American, the driver is the image of the trickster, a part of life that is represented frequently by the coyote or, among some peoples, as the raven. This bus driver has led Jonathan on a journey in search of big adventure and pay off. But, as is always true of life, there is no payoff when one lets someone else drive the bus. All that is left is irritation and disappointment when the vehicle of life does not take the individual where he or she wants to go. His response is the typical spoiled child's response: using force to keep her from laughing at him. Notice he doesn't seem to be concerned any longer about where his journey is taking him, only that someone is laughing at him. The trickster, by leading him on with promises of the big city, has left him alone, lonely and now unable to sleep. The trickster tries to teach a lesson. What might the lesson be?

The case does not provide any data regarding Jonathan's early recollections (ERs), and this would be one aspect that the Adlerian counselor/therapist would want to pursue. A recollection is a specific memory ("I remember one night when …") as opposed to a report, which is a general memory ("Every night my mother would …"). The counselor/therapist might want to ask Jonathan: "Think back as far as you can and tell me the first thing you remember." The events of the recollections should be written down exactly as the client presents them. This will become extremely important during the interpretation phase of the session and will allow the counselor/therapist to be more accurate. It is important to follow up each recollection with a query about the affective component by asking the client how he or she felt about the experience at the time it was occurring.

> One helpful method of obtaining significant information is to consider the memory as a newspaper story. Your job is then to compose the 'newspaper headline' to present the story in the paper. In other words, read the story, then summarize the key points in a sample newspaper bold-print heading. (Eckstein, Baruth, & Mahrer, 1982 p. 30)

The counselor/therapist should not be afraid to guess at the meaning of the recollections and be cognizant of the client's recognition reflex. Encourage the client to share as many early recollections as possible with two or three as a minimum and six to eight as a maximum.

The counselor/therapist is cautioned against getting caught up in **factophilia.** This term was coined by Dreikurs (Terner & Pew, 1978) and refers to the empty talk and endless fact-gathering that often occurs in counseling/therapy. For example, a person might ask someone what he or she had for dinner and, instead of just getting the simple answer, "Meatloaf," he or she receives a running account of the recipe and preparation activities. Too often, counselors/therapists get caught up in thinking that detail is important. As a rule, it only tends to keep the focus on superficial content rather than on the discovery of the essence of the client's psychological movement. Again, it is important to realize that the responsibility for counseling/therapy rests with the counselor/therapist; the goal is to help the client learn why he or she functions in a particular manner.

A summary of the information gathered from Jonathan could be organized according to Adler's three life tasks: work, friendship, and love. In the area of work, Jonathan is discouraged. He believes his employers expect too much of him, and he has trouble relating to his coworkers. His failures seem to extend to other employment opportunities as well. In terms of friendship, Jonathan discusses family and coworkers but never mentions friends. He says he feels lonely and drinks, and one would assume that he is doing the latter activity alone. Love seems to elude Jonathan. He does not seem to be able to develop an intimate relationship with his wife and turns to other women for comfort and solace. He misses his children, but does nothing to bring himself closer to them. In these three tasks of life, it would appear that Jonathan does not want to recognize his responsibility for being a major part in his own problems. As soon as he begins to understand the purposes for the behaviors behind his complaints, Jonathan may be freed to work toward improvement of his life situation.

Interpretation and Goal Setting

The notes indicate that "others seem to expect more than he can deliver," a sad commentary as far as Jonathan's own feeling of self-efficacy is concerned. Jonathan perceives himself as inferior to others and also seems to perceive others as excessively critical. He reports that his work is "never good enough" and that others are "always on his back." He describes his boss as a "perfectionist." These are all symptoms of his discouragement. His marriages have gone the same way, and he has the same complaint. He reports that things went well "during the first few years of marriage," but he alleges that no matter what he tries to do to make the relationship work, his effort is never good enough. The question becomes "Good enough for whom?" More than likely the answer is *for him*. He struggles with his own uncertainty, although it is clear that Jonathan votes with his feet. In his head, he seems to think that he is torn between staying in the relationship and leaving, but when the chips are down, Jonathan elects to leave.

Guilt seems to be one theme that runs through this man's journey. He seems to use guilt to make himself feel better. While it appears that outwardly he is suffering from guilt, in fact, his guilt does not lead to constructive action but only passive acceptance of his ruined life. He complains that he feels guilty for being an absentee father and yet has moved away. To feel guilty that one is not living close to one's children does not change the behavior. It does serve the purpose of making one feel better, however. He can say to himself, "At least I feel badly about not being with my children. Look how I suffer from my guilt." "Dreikurs pointed out that although guilt feelings purport to show a high moral sense, they are in fact a substitute for responsible actions. The good intentions are a smoke screen for avoiding what the person knows to be responsible behavior" (Ferguson, 1984, p. 26).

Guilt is a way of artificially making himself feel better. Jonathan is able to feel more noble than his actions would indicate that he might be. This represents a neurotic solution to the life task of intimacy or sex. Rather than actually remaining in a marriage that may be difficult and remaining close to his children, he moves away. By creating guilt in himself, Jonathan makes it seem like he is suffering because it is impossible to be with them. In reality, he left his wife and children and moved to a big city for the "needed professional or financial opportunities." One must ask the question, "Needed for what?" This may be just another way in which Jonathan flaunts or disregards the family and tribal value of being close knit as a family. If he wants to be a father to his children, he needs to be near them, not hundreds of miles away. He should be able to find similar jobs on the reservation. His parents' health is declining and requires more of his time and assistance. More than likely he feels put upon by these demands upon him. One guess would be that Jonathan feels resentful of all these demands, having been the youngest in the family with older siblings and parents who took care of all his needs. He feels entitled to a better life. He wants someone who will comfort him like the other women he runs to when the challenge of marriage becomes more than he feels capable of handling.

Resolving the guilt over his brother's death is an issue with which Jonathan needs to deal. Exploration of the event and the responses of those who were close to him may help clarify the meanings that he attributes to this life experience. Adler was fond of paraphrasing Epictetus by saying that what happens to us is not as important as the meaning we make of what happens to us. Exploring what did happen by remembering his thoughts and feelings about the event is an important way of approaching the issue of the sense he makes of this accident. An extremely important part of this is how he remembers his parents and siblings reacting to the accident. At the present time, it would appear that he has conveniently forgotten. How did those he loved and whose judgment he valued react? How did this change his opinion of himself, of others, or life? Most importantly, how did this impact his sense of belonging? Twenty years after the fact, Jonathan still suffers over his brother's death. One must realize he has chosen to suffer and he has become extremely practiced at being a better mourner than anyone else in the family! Because it was an accident, Jonathan has to look at the purpose of continuing to feel guilty about his brother's death.

Jonathan's drinking is a problem for him, as is his seeking the comfort of other women. Attendance at Alcoholics Anonymous may be an important part of his treatment. Many tribal groups do not approve of the use of alcohol by their members. Again, this is an area that should be explored with Jonathan as it is possible that this is his way of rebelling against his heritage and displaying his lack of acceptance of the cultural and tribal values. In addition, Jonathan may be also passively rebelling against other important family values such as family relationships, earning a living, providing for one's family, and getting an education. Instead of openly opposing these values, Jonathan has taken the stance of becoming a failure. Thus, he justifies his inability to meet these standards by blaming his indecision and incompetence, as well as other people. He was even late to his first counseling/therapy appointment because, as Jonathan stated, he "had difficulty finding the mental health agency." Jonathan is quite consistent in his approach to life and provides an excellent example of the concept of unity of the personality.

What the counselor/therapist wishes to identify at this point is the private logic of the client—the conclusions drawn about one's self, others, and the world. These conclusions are considered to be the **basic mistakes** of the client because they are not aligned with what Adler called "the common sense of social living" (Manaster & Corsini, 1982). Mosak (1979) has developed a system of categorization of the basic mistakes that can be used by the counselor/therapist to summarize Jonathan's current beliefs. A few of Jonathan's faulty beliefs appear in the following list.

1. *Overgeneralizations (use of all, never, always)* "No matter what I do to make my marriage work, it's never good enough." "The people I work with are always on my back."
2. *False or impossible goals of "security"* "I am not wanted in the 'white man's world.'" "I have no future of my own." "I am trapped in my situation." "Other women can solve all my problems."
3. *Misperceptions about life and life's demands* "People always expect more than I can deliver." "I don't know what I will do if things don't change."
4. *Minimization or denial of one's worth* "I have ruined the lives of three families plus my own life." "My work is never good enough."
5. *Faulty values.* "People are prejudiced against Native Americans." "I am responsible for my brother's death." "Leaving is the answer to solving life's problems."

It is important for the counselor/therapist to establish mutually acceptable goals for counseling/therapy. "Therapeutic cooperation requires an alignment of goals. When the goals and interests of the patient and therapist clash, no satisfactory relationship can be established" (Dreikurs, 1967, p. 65). A common mistake among many counselors/therapists is to not spend enough time engaging in goal alignment. If counseling/therapy is to satisfactorily progress, both parties have to be reading from the same sheet of music. The lack of goal alignment frequently happens in agency and school settings where clients are referred or ordered to participate in counseling/therapy. In these instances, a third party, for example, a judge, teacher, parent, or other agency, often dictates the goals of counseling/therapy. Feeling pressured to proceed and succeed, the counselor/therapist attempts to impose the goals on the client. Failure is likely to occur when these circumstances exist.

When a client approaches counseling or therapy, there is an expectation that some sort of change will occur. However, clients want to believe that the change will occur in others and that this external change will make it easier for them to do what they have always done. They want to lose the problem without changing the attitudes or beliefs upon which they operate. Counselors/therapists, however, approach the process of counseling/therapy with the expectation that the client will change. Without some level of agreement and cooperation in terms of working toward mutually established goals, clients and counselors/therapists will be working at odds with each other.

> Winning the patient's cooperation for the common task is a prerequisite for any therapy; maintaining it requires constant vigilance. What appears as 'resistance' constitutes a discrepancy between the goals of the therapist and those of the patient. In each case, the proper relationship has to be re-established, differences solved, and agreement reached. (Dreikurs, 1967, p. 65)

Evans (1997b) suggests that counselors/therapists work with clients to determine a starting point by asking in which areas they would like to get better or improve. At a minimum, the counselor/therapist can ask about the life tasks and have the clients rate themselves on a scale of 1 to 10 as to how they feel about how well these are being accomplished.

Work:	1 — 2 — 3 — 4 — 5 — 6 — 7 — 8 — 9 — 10
Love and Marriage:	1 — 2 — 3 — 4 — 5 — 6 — 7 — 8 — 9 — 10
Friendships (Male):	1 — 2 — 3 — 4 — 5 — 6 — 7 — 8 — 9 — 10
Friendships (Female):	1 — 2 — 3 — 4 — 5 — 6 — 7 — 8 — 9 — 10

Other areas appropriate for Jonathan might include the following.

Leisure:	1 — 2 — 3 — 4 — 5 — 6 — 7 — 8 — 9 — 10
Finances:	1 — 2 — 3 — 4 — 5 — 6 — 7 — 8 — 9 — 10
Parenting:	1 — 2 — 3 — 4 — 5 — 6 — 7 — 8 — 9 — 10
Getting Along with Self:	1 — 2 — 3 — 4 — 5 — 6 — 7 — 8 — 9 — 10
Finding a Meaning in Life:	1 — 2 — 3 — 4 — 5 — 6 — 7 — 8 — 9 — 10
Relationships (Spouse):	1 — 2 — 3 — 4 — 5 — 6 — 7 — 8 — 9 — 10
Relationships (Children):	1 — 2 — 3 — 4 — 5 — 6 — 7 — 8 — 9 — 10
Relationships (Boss):	1 — 2 — 3 — 4 — 5 — 6 — 7 — 8 — 9 — 10
Relationships (Coworkers):	1 — 2 — 3 — 4 — 5 — 6 — 7 — 8 — 9 — 10

When the ratings are complete, the counselor/therapist asks the client which of these areas were the most satisfying at the present time and which he or she might want to work to improve. Once the client selects an area for improvement, the development of a goal can proceed. For example, if the client selects an area that was rated as a 6, the counselor/therapist might ask what it would take to move that to a 7 or 8. In this process, it is useful to explore with the client what he or she has already done, what stops him or her from improving at the present time, and what personal resources he or she might have that will contribute to improving the situation. In Jonathan's situation, there are a lot of options for places to begin.

Re-Education and Re-Orientation

Therapy or counseling with Jonathan will involve encouragement and confrontation. The Adlerian counselor or therapist will actively attempt to hold up a mirror to Jonathan so that he can see himself, his behavior, and his strengths. Recognizing who he is and what decisions he actually has power over will be an important part of counseling or therapy. "Spitting in the soup" of his guilt and the other feelings that he uses to enable him to escape responsibility will allow him to rely on his own sense of strength and empower him to make different decisions. It should be pointed out to him that many of his current problems (loneliness, being away from his children, and a collapsing marriage) are the result of his present attempts to solve his problems.

One's problems are often a result of the solutions attempted in the past that have failed. Instead of looking for new solutions, the individual continues to behave in a way that adds to the problem rather than becoming the solution. Instead of doing what he has always done, Jonathan will be encouraged to try something new. Jonathan needs to be aware of the decisions he has made about life and the purposes of the choices he has pursued in his behavior. When he has come to an understanding of his current life plan, he can then be empowered to make different choices. Encouragement will be very important with Jonathan, as he seems to be convinced that he has no power. Holding up the mirror of his life will help him see that he has power, but that it was misdirected. Mistakes can be corrected, new directions can be chosen, and his situation can become more hopeful.

Existential Theory

Mary Lou Bryant Frank
Kennesaw State University

Introduction

The primary confrontation with death, being, and personal responsibility was addressed by the existential philosophers and has found life and significance in the existential therapies. **Existentialism** embodies the understanding of the individual in the cultural context and time as well as the nature, meaning, and feelings of that existence (Epp, 1998). While deriving from the term *ex-sistere,* meaning "to stand out" or "to emerge" (May, 1961), existentialism also embodies the concepts of "being" and "becoming" (Bauman & Waldo, 1998) and as such implies a process. Similarly, existential theory is an emergent, vital part of the third force of psychology, attempting to look at the experiences, transitions, and meanings of our lives in the framework of development, culture, and time.

Existential counseling and psychotherapy address issues of death (our mortality), freedom (the ability to choose), responsibility (accountability for our actions), anxiety (**angst,** the tension we have in being alive), **phenomenology** (uniqueness and intentionality of our awareness), isolation (aloneness), **guilt** (regret over our choices), and meaninglessness (realizing any meaning we ascribe to life is a personal construction) (Abroms, 1993; Gould, 1993; Loy, 1996; May, 1953; Yalom, 1980). Despite the universal nature of these core struggles of life, existentialism is not a prevailing force in psychology. The theory is seen as difficult to understand and therefore apply (Epp, 1998). The emphasis of most counseling theories is on the rational, objective, and scientific techniques of behavioral, cognitive, and cognitive-behavioral counseling. In essence, this emphasis has relegated existentialism to being combined with interpersonal theories such as humanism. But this is nothing new. Existentialists were the "homeless waifs who were not permitted into the better academic neighborhoods" (Yalom, 1980, p. 21).

However, contemporary thought is leading many to an awakened need for existential answers. Current trends reflect an emphasis on health and wellness (Evans, 1997; Jones & Meredith, 2000; Waldrop, Owen, Lightsey, Ethington, Woemmel, & Coke, 2001), loss and death (Bower, Kemeny, Taylor, & Fahey, 1998; Coward, 2000; Kraus & Shaw, 2000), contextual and family of origin concerns (Mandara & Murray, 2000; Nichols & Schwartz, 1998), religiosity and spirituality (McCullough, Worthington, Maxey, & Rachal, 1997; Miller, 2001), culture (Axelson, 1999; Chodorow, 1999; Fine, Weis, Powell, & Wong, 1997; Ibrahim, 1985; Kraut & Lundmark, 1998; Vontress, Johnson, & Epp, 1999), gender (Skowronski & Lawrence, 2001; Worden & Worden, 1998), and process issues in counseling (Corey, 2001; Hepner, Multon, Gysbers, Ellis, & Zook, 1998). An existential perspective uniquely and directly addresses the core struggles in each of these growing areas.

Psychological theories are an intimate reflection of the values and biases of the real people creating the theories, and existential theory is no exception. A behavioral approach reflects a theorist to whom science and logic are the organizing factors for existence. An existentialist is a theorist to whom science is complementary to **meaning,** for whom relationships are as important as the scientific advancement of a theory, for whom the **subjective** individual experience is as important as the objective factual report, and who is involved as much in the **process** as in the product (May, 1983; Willis, 1994). For an existentialist, the journey is as important as the destination (Bugental, 1978; Weisman, 1993), and the existential journey is not superficial (Yalom, 1980):

> To explore deeply from an existential perspective does not mean that one explores the past; rather it means that one brushes away everyday concerns and thinks deeply about one's existential situation. It means to think outside of time, to think about the relationship between one's feet and the ground beneath one, between one's consciousness and the space around one; it means to think not about the way one came to be the way one is, but that one is. . . . The future-becoming-present is the primary tense of existential therapy. (p. 11)

Unlike traditional psychoanalytic and psychodynamic counselors and therapists, existentialists are not deficiency-focused. Instead, they concentrate on potentialities. Existentialists hope to aid individuals in developing schemata to understand and cope with their lives. Likewise, existentialists represent a diverse population. In as many ways that meaning can be gleaned from life, there are avenues to describe the process of finding meaning. Just as some existentialists are more psychodynamic in their orientation (Abroms, 1993; Yalom, 1980), others are more humanistic (Bugental, 1978; Maslow, 1968; Owen, 1994). Another circle of existentialists seems to be a part of the newest wave in psychology—transpersonal theory (Wilber, 1997)—while other approaches address existential issues through spirituality (Hinterkopf, 1998; Miller, 1999).

For some individuals, meaning emerges from the struggle with life and death, destiny and freedom, isolation and connection. Anticipated by Maslow (1971), **transpersonal psychology** offers a haven for those individuals finding meaning in the spiritual realm. The existential philosophers **Buber** (1970) and **Tillich** (1987), as well as the psychological theorists Maslow (1968) and Wilber (2000), were explicit that, from an existential quest, a spiritual awakening could unfold. For some people, hope emerges from despair. However, not all existentialists find meaning through spirituality. Some find that the quest for meaning is always filled with the anxiety of ultimate death (Cannon, 1991; Yalom, 1980; Yalom, 1999). However, transpersonal psychology and the approaches emphasizing spirituality are frameworks for examining the process of spiritual development that may surface after scratching the existential veneer.

The purpose of this chapter is to outline the background of existentialism, explore the developmental nature of the quest for meaning, examine the major constructs of existential thought, describe applications of the theory, summarize the evaluation of the theory, and explore the theory's limitations. The theory is summarized by an applied case analysis. In the process of understanding a theory about existence, it is my hope that the reader will gain a deeper sense of self, an appreciation for what it means to be alive, and a heightened respect for the human struggle.

Background

Arising from the philosophic roots of **Kierkegaard, Nietzsche,** and **Sartre,** existentialism gained an audience within the post-World War II European community where it found form and voice. Emerging from the atrocities of war, vanquished idealism, and fragmented family life, the philosophers of this period developed a perspective reflecting the realities of their harsh existence. In the midst of the destruction, people reverberated to the philosophical writings of Nietzsche (1889) almost 50 years earlier: God must also be dead. People saw death as the core event permeating their existence. These experiences with mortality reflected a new perspective that, although not always optimistic, was full of realism.

Kierkegaard was a primary influence on other existentialists such as **Heidegger,** Buber, and Nietzsche. Kierkegaard (1944) pursued scientific truth from the landscape of the human perspective. Our greater problems were not a result of lack of knowledge or technology, he believed, but lack of passion and commitment (May, 1983). Kierkegaard was convinced that the goal of pure objectivity was not only unattainable, but was also undesirable and immoral; these beliefs foreshadow recent findings in physics (Bohm, 1973; Evans, 1996; Miller, 1997) and gender studies (Belenky, Clinchy, Goldberger, & Tarule, 1997). They also were reflected in the anti-reductionistic concept of *consilience* proposed by biologist E. O. Wilson (1998). Kierkegaard had the revelation that, unless science is examined in a relational context, truth is not possible (Bretall, 1951). Objective, detached understanding is an illusion; a subject can never be truly separated from the process of being observed and the context of that observation. It is no small wonder that Kierkegaard was not favored among the more objective, cognitive, and behavioral theorists who were influenced by Descartes.

According to Descartes, an objective, rational examination was crucial to the development of empirical science. Consistent with this viewpoint was the prevailing thought of Copernicus who provided the scientific model of a detached observer that we see embodied in current scientific research methodology. From Descartes emerged a mechanistic theory of mind and body only causally interacting. In the midst of a Cartesian mindset, Heidegger (1949) developed an alternate paradigm. Building on Kierkegaard, Heidegger continued to develop existential thought. Heidegger's concept was antimechanistic and antitheoretic in a Cartesian sense. To Heidegger (1962), theories and humans were imperfect, and an objective reality was not reality at all. Existence is only understood in terms of being in the world through subjective participation. Heidegger noted that in striving for exactness, the Cartesian system was missing reality.

Heidegger's (1962) notions of choice also influenced the existential psychologists. Heidegger reasoned that each choice one makes represents the loss of an alternative. The past becomes important in terms of lost opportunities. Future choices are limited because of past choices and the time remaining to fulfill them. We have the freedom to choose, but must balance this with the responsibility for our choices. By encountering these limitations, we may experience **nothingness,** guilt, and anxiety. These core concerns reverberated among authors around the world. The field of literature was ripe for existential development (e.g., Dostoyevsky, Tolstoy, Kafka, Sartre, Camus, Hemingway, Eliot, Fitzgerald, Stein, Ellison, Faulkner, Wolfe, Pound, Blake, Angelou, Rand, Doctorow, Walker, and Frost). Both in the United States and Europe, the best literary minds echoed existential rumblings.

North American psychologists initially reflected the focus on universal concerns through **humanism.** The third force arose as an answer to the limitations of the Freudian and behaviorist approaches. The positive aspects of humanness (e.g., love, freedom with responsibility, self-actualization, potential, transcendence, uniqueness, choice, creativity) were missing from Freudian and behavioral theories. The development of the Association for Humanistic Psychology spawned a positive arena for collaboration. The humanistic element focused on human capacities and potentialities (Craig, 1995; Milton, 1993). Demonstrating the natural evolution from humanistic to existential, many humanistic theorists (e.g., Maslow, Bugental, Frankl, and May) moved into an existential position. Although humanism was the initial paradigm, existentialism built on the respect for the individual and added the dimensions of **ontology,** experiential awareness, and responsibility.

May's many works (1953, 1969, 1979, 1983, 1992) are noteworthy because of his major contributions to the emergence of existential counseling or psychotherapy from the humanistic perspective. The subtle differences between humanism and existentialism are evident in his description of the goal of counseling or psychotherapy (May, 1961):

> In my judgment, the existential approach is the achieving of individuality (including subjective individuality) not by passing or avoiding the conflictual realities of the world in which we immediately find ourselves—for us the Western world—but by confronting these concerns directly and through the meeting of them, achieving one's individuality. (p. 51)

Through his honest, direct confrontation with anxiety, will, freedom, meaning, and myth, he forged the basis of the development of existential counseling and therapy in this past century. Existentialism also has roots in contemporary religious thought. Religion's differing perspectives kindle a conflict. The disagreement is one between **essence** (representing scientific, objectivity, and facts) and **existence** (representing what is real for each individual). In Western culture, essence has triumphed over existence (May, 1983). However, this battle takes place on holy ground, as indicated by Tillich: "The story of Genesis, chapters 1–3, if taken as myth, can guide our description of the transition from essential to existential being. It is the profoundest and richest expression of man's awareness of his existential estrangement and provides the scheme in which the transition from essence to existence can be treated" (1987, p. 190). The quest for knowledge and understanding is what eventually separates humanity from the safety of objectivity. Descartes may have won the battle, but Tillich would contend that the war is not resolved.

Existential questions themselves have a religious flavor. Some existentialists would say that religion is a superficial defense against the ultimate reality of death (Yalom, 1980), because it has nothing to do with the worldly questions of **meaninglessness,** anxiety, and existence (Tillich, 1987). However, the dichotomy may be more one of semantics than substance. As Tillich (1987) wrote:

> Whenever existentialists give answers, they do so in terms of religious or quasi-religious traditions which are not derived from their existential analysis, [but] from hidden religious sources. They are matters of ultimate concern or faith, although garbed in a secular gown. Existentialism is an analysis of the human predicament. And the answers to the questions implied in man's predicament are religious, whether open or hidden. (pp. 187–188)

Tillich contends that the existential dilemmas are religious questions in secular terms. Buber (1970) similarly emphasizes the religious lineage within existential ancestry through the reverence implicit in some relationships. When "a man addresses with his whole being the You of his life that cannot be restricted by any other, he addresses God" (p. 124). When an individual no longer relates to another as an object, as an extension of himself or herself, or as a means to an end, he or she enters a relationship expressed by "I to Thou" (p. 124). The essence of the ideal existential encounter embodies respect, honor, and divinity.

The religiosity that develops from the existential quest is developmental. From an individual's struggle with consciousness and responsibility, and from unconscious existential choices, the third stage of development emerges as a "**spiritual unconscious**" (Frankl, 1975). Unconscious religiosity is intrinsic to our ability to transcend our situation and transform our perspective and emotional reaction. Whether the spiritual dimension is labeled, inherently perceived, or ignored, it is an element of an existential development.

Beginning from a philosophical approach to the world, existentialism has evolved to an approach to helping people cope with the uncertainty and complex pressures of their lives. Recognizing the individual nature of experience in the context of an objective, scientifically oriented society, existential counselors and therapists validate the anxiety people experience. The importance of choice and responsibility in coping with these pressures has led existentialists today to honor the individual's experience and realize the religiosity embedded in existential questions. Central to the development of this approach and working through the existential concerns is the importance of the human encounter. Following the path of early existential theorists, existentialism is grounded in realism, attempting to acknowledge the authentically human experience, the importance of meaning, and the reality of change.

Human Nature: A Developmental Perspective

The universality of existential concerns is evident in children as well as adults. May (1992) was the first to propose an existential developmental model moving from a naïve stage of innocence, to adolescent rebellion and struggle, to conventional ascribing to tradition, and then finally moving beyond the ego and self-actualizing. Neither discrete nor linear, these "stages" are evident in many of May's myths (1992). For instance, May used them to exemplify the stages of female development through myths such as "Briar Rose" (p. 194). In defining strategies for helping troubled adolescents, Hanna, Hanna, and Keys (1999) perceived existential approaches as valuable in establishing and maintaining the therapeutic relationship as well as in addressing issues of freedom and responsibility, core developmental issues and central components of existential counseling or psychotherapy. Kerr, Cohn, Webb, and Anderson (2001) validate these stages in their exploration of the reasons why boys do not achieve their potential and often become depressed. They also discuss the reasons bright men go into midlife crises and believe they are failures. In both instances, these authors suggest that it is important for these and others in our culture to find meaning, especially at critical points in our lives. Although existentialism does not have discrete stages, the importance of finding meaning has developmental implications.

Addressing core existential concerns helps to promote health and further development. Existential counseling focuses on the possibilities that are available and presses the client and counselor to become more alive, aware, and sensitive while coming to terms with the realities of mortality and aloneness (Bauman & Waldo, 1998). Pramling and Johansson (1995) and Yalom (1980) have examined the development of existential concerns with death. Their findings indicate that such concerns, first expressed as **death anxiety,** are found in preschool children. The anxiety produced by awareness of nonexistence is overwhelming, even to a young child. Most children cope with death by denying it. Parents and adults foster denial in the first phase of life by avoidance and hesitant confrontation.

By the time of adolescence, however, denial becomes ineffective, and the initiation into adulthood reintroduces the reality of death and isolation and necessitates a search for new meaning. Adults find the development of age the ultimate loss. By the time individuals are older, death has increased complexity and is in danger of being minimized by health care professionals (Emanuel & Emanuel, 1998). Through each developmental stage, it is easy to encounter denial and avoidance of death. Rather than avoiding the realities of mortality, existentialists see death and aging as the ultimate opportunity to grow. Ram Dass (2000) found the loss of ability he experienced after a stroke and coming to terms with his own aging providing him with an increased awareness and appreciation of life:

> This culture sees life as collecting experiences. But, aging is an emptying out and beginning to experience the moment, what's happening right now. In our culture, we value old people who act young. We don't value old people for acting old, for their wisdom. For them to hear their own wisdom, they have to experience their own silence. That's one of the ways the stroke was a blessing—it increased my silence. (Gross, 2000, p. 12)

By facing our mortality in the various stages of our existence, we can live more fully.

Despite the contemporary focus on superficial, commercial fulfillment, many people still search for existential meaning as they reach critical points developmentally. By studying older adults, Kraus and Shaw (2000) discovered that perceived control over the most important life-role was the main factor reducing the odds of death. Finding personal meaning, an existential concept, from that life-role was the key element. Stressful health problems also were the focus of a study by Bower et al. (1998). In a study of bereaved HIV-seropositive men, individuals who found meaning in their losses were healthier, regardless of their preexisting health status. The results suggest that finding meaning seems to be associated with improved immune system response and overall health.

Additionally, in a survey of mental health workers in Hong Kong (Yiu-kee & Tang, 1995), existential variables (e.g., death, freedom, responsibility, anxiety, isolation, meaninglessness) were found to be correlates of burnout, emotional exhaustion, and depersonalization. For individual development to be complete, there must be a sense that we have found meaning and therefore peace in our lives.

Gaining understanding about the meaning of life and taking responsibility for one's life serve to influence and inspire our development. The process of development, whether spiritual or secular, is characterized by anxiety, for which death is the primary cause (Bolen, 1996; Deurzen-Smith, 1991; Loy, 1996). Existential concerns permeate human existence.

Although beginning in childhood, most existential concerns become salient in adulthood (Reker & Chamberlain, 2000). The developmental necessity of examining the issues of death may be coming to terms with nonbeing (Heidegger, 1949), **ontological anxiety** (Tillich, 1987), loss of the world (Bretall, 1951; Nietzsche, 1967), or realizing the fear of loss of self (Hillman, 1989). "To venture causes anxiety, but not to venture is to lose one's self" (May, 1979, p. 55). Facing death is critical in coming to terms with life (Howe, 1997; Leifer, 1996). Kubler-Ross (1975) indicates that "it is the denial of death that is partially responsible for people living empty, purposeless lives" (p. 164).

Hillman (1996) also indicates that it is our denial and fear of death that lead us to devise theories focusing on development, parents, social conditions, genetic predispositions, and other concerns arising out of our perceptions. As Krueger and Hanna (1997) write, "Death has a paradoxical quality in that the fear of it is paralyzing to the individual who avoids it, while at the same time acceptance of its inevitability can free the individual from the trivial life that results from that avoidance" (p. 197). Whether one transcends (Willis, 1994), develops heightened awareness (Loy, 1996), or is shaken by the struggle (May, 1983), individuals are forever changed by their confrontation with or their denial of death.

A Worldview

Unique among theorists, existentialists have conceptualized their philosophy in context. They suggest that all theories have usefulness, but for different individuals and issues. As indicated by Bugental (1996), in a discipline that is at odds with itself, it is unique in being able to identify the utility of other approaches:

> Psychology, or at least American psychology, is a second rate discipline. The main reason is that it does not stand in awe of its subject matter. Psychologists have too little respect for psychology. In the future, I hope that there would be more appreciation of the great range of human potential, and that attempts to be only objective or only subjective would seem as ludicrous as they really are. (p. 135)

As professionals, we seldom see value in approaches that do not fit personal or prevailing preferences. Bugental (1978) was the first to see the theories in perspective. According to Bugental, there are six levels of helping goals, extending from behavioral change to spiritual development. Corresponding to the six goals are six different types of helping, from behavioral to transpersonal.

Others have also seen the value of a broader perspective. Vontress, Johnson, and Epp (1999) indicate that existential counselors or therapists need to be flexible, integrating other counseling approaches as appropriate for the given client. Wilber (1993, 1997) also offers a broader viewpoint, incorporating other theoretical orientations into a developmental schema. Wilber's theoretical model is transpersonal and more reflective of Eastern religion than Tillich's (1987) focus on the Western perspective. For Wilber (1997), an individual's pathology is seen as a matter of degree, beginning with psychotic symptoms and advancing to spiritual struggles. Like Bugental, Wilber sees each theory as subtly answering the questions raised at various levels of dysfunction. The physiological and biochemical interventions (psychiatry) are more effective for psychotic symptoms. Psychodynamic and existential therapies are the bridge to transpersonal techniques. Each theory is seen as having a contribution, but none has the answer for all people or all issues. Besides viewing itself in the context of other counseling or psychotherapy theories, existential theory also perceives the individual in an ever-changing environment. Within a family, a gender, a language, a culture, a time period, and a system, individuals struggle to find identity and meaning.

Existentialism strives to help honor the pain that occurs at many levels of experience. As described by Van Kaam (1966), "Existential psychology sees man as living in a human world; therefore when my counselee enters my room, he is not alone, but rather brings with him a whole world . . . nothing exists for any human being that does not have a certain meaning for him" (p. 61). Unique among theories (Torres-Rivera, Phan, Maddux, Wilbur, & Garret, 2001), existentialism directly addresses the contextual elements shaping the individual's reality.

Major Constructs

Approaches to Existentialism

Existentialism embodies differing perspectives and approaches. It would be possible for an individual to see three forces within the existential perspective: **dynamic existentialism, humanistic existentialism,** and **transpersonal existentialism.** Common to all approaches is the nature and quality of the existential relationship. However, dynamic existentialists (Abroms, 1993; Cannon, 1991; Yalom, 1980), like their Freudian predecessors, focus attention on the resolution of inner conflict and anxiety. Humanistic existentialists emphasize unconditional acceptance, awareness of personal experience, and authenticity rather than resolving existential conflicts. The transpersonal existential approach perceives death as an opportunity for the individual to rise above the given circumstances. According to this approach, most people experience tragedy, but in equal proportion, they experience joy (Maslow, 1968). Health is the ability to transcend the environment, drawing from the joyful aspects of existence.

Death

Death is the ultimate truth. Both in myth and in reality, it is ever present. In *The Cry for Myth,* Rollo May tells us that "We are able to love passionately because we die" (1992, p. 294). How we have accepted this mortal condition—or found ways to ignore it—determines our psychological well-being. Death is encountered in all counseling or psychotherapeutic experiences. Presenting concerns such as grief need to be addressed, but also most existential healing involves letting go of the unhealthy or dysfunctional parts of self, relationships, or ideals.

Well-being involves becoming more honest and authentic. In working through resistance to authenticity, clients watch as part of themselves die. Suicidal and homicidal feelings are common during this period. Drawing from Horney's notion of idealized and despised images of self, Bugental (1978) asserts that both images are false and must die for the real person to emerge: "But there is a fearful wrenching involved in that relinquishment. The nakedness seems, and indeed is, so terribly vulnerable and so truly mortal. Usually the 'killing' of the old self occurs in some kind of break out experience" (p. 79). A confrontation with death signals the rebirth of a more aware and more authentic being.

Freedom

Freedom comes after our confrontation with our inaccurate representation of ourselves. It emerges only after we realize that the world is an arbitrary construction of our awareness. Hence, we can make each moment the way we wish, and make our future different from any moments in our past. Although we can choose each thought we have, there are costs and benefits for each decision. Bolen (1996) draws a parallel between the concentration camp situation described by Frankl (1984), where he outlined his existential approach, which he called **logotherapy,** and the situation facing individuals with AIDS and cancer. In both cases, we have the freedom to choose our reaction to these deplorable situations. Survivors of victimization have the power to choose their reaction to the injustice, just as those individuals hurt by society, others, or themselves can regain their dignity by honoring their pain and choosing not to be dominated by it (Walker, 1994). Kelly (1955) proposed that our choosing was ultimately a cognitive process built from our own constructions of reality. The emotional readiness to make decisions and the choice of reactions to them are keys to the meaning gleaned from the encounter. Freedom is silhouetted by responsibility.

Isolation

Isolation is a separation from oneself as much as from others. The isolation from our true self keeps us from connecting and contributing to the larger social order in more productive ways. We are isolated and defended by our own false identities. Out of our own fears, we erect walls to prohibit the connections we most desire. As Bugental (1978) states, "When I begin to realize that my truest identity is as process and not as fixed substance, I am on the verge of a terrible emptiness and a miraculous freedom" (p. 133). However, our sense of self is mediated because our inner nature is not strong, overpowering, and unmistakable like the instincts of animals. It is weak and delicate and can be easily overcome by habit, cultural pressure, and wrong attitudes (Maslow, 1968). Even though our creativity never disappears, it may struggle to surface. Because of external pressures and our own restraints, we may not be totally free to actualize.

Culture

Sartre defined culture as the "objective mind" (Cannon, 1991). It is the context of the world that concurrently shapes individuals as they construct it. Existential counseling or psychotherapy, by definition, addresses the cultural, contextual dynamics of counseling or psychotherapy. Solomon, Greenberg, and Pyszczynski (1991) indicate that our culture gives our world meaning and protects us from anxiety regarding death. In several studies (Greenberg, Pyszczynski, Solomon, Rosenblatt, Veeder, Kirkland, & Lyon, 1990; Rosenblatt, Greenberg, Solomon, Pyszczynski, & Lyon, 1989), existentialists have shown that when individuals are asked to think about death or are faced with death anxiety, they tend to adhere more to their cultural values and biases. Culture can become a means of escape when one is faced with fear of demise.

Other existentialists believe that connecting with others individually and within our culture helps individuals to heal from their isolation (Maslow, 1954). Torres-Rivera et al. (2001) also describe existential counseling or psychotherapy as uniquely able to address the cultural dynamics in relationships. However, the more we force a connection, the further we are pushed apart. The more we struggle to understand our feelings, the more they elude our realization. When we begin acknowledging and accepting who we are in our cultural context, we can start to connect with others and then, again, with ourselves.

Meaninglessness/Meaningfulness

Out of our will to love and live, we arrive at meaning in our lives (May, 1969). In gaining a deeper awareness of ourselves, we also gain a deeper sense of others. Our efforts to gain understanding involve confronting aspects of ourselves before we develop the heightened sense of the world that gives our lives meaning. Yalom (1980) and Bugental (1978) describe the despair of the reality of meaninglessness in the world. Bugental (1978) believes we can attain meaningfulness once we become more open to life experience. Maslow's (1971) writings impress us with the notion that through awareness and actualization, people can transcend their present situation. We transcend—that is, find meaning in our world—by fully being aware of ourselves. Truly being oneself involves being more integrated within and without. Paradoxically, as people become more open to their true feelings, they are better able to join with others and be one with the world. The person is more able to love. Through transcendence, the person also becomes more capable. When people are most truly themselves, they are also more creative, aware, and productive. Life is not as painful a struggle. People are more aware of the potentialities in their lives and within themselves. Meaning is implicit in discovering ourselves and in our awareness of others.

Authenticity and Vulnerability: Two Sides of the Existential Self

Becoming a more authentic person means that an individual lives grounded (Loy, 1996) with honesty, compassion (Dass & Bush, 1992), and awareness (Weisman, 1993). The **vulnerable** person, the authentic person's counterpart, is always in conflict, lacking self-honesty and honesty with others (Weisman, 1993). Bradshaw (1993) indicates that in our culture we may feel that a false, vulnerable self is needed to be loved. Needing courage and hope, the vulnerable individual passively lacks the confidence and support to sustain coping in an unpredictable and unsympathetic world. The virtue of authenticity is achieved with sustained effort, while vulnerability passively summons pain. Bound to autonomy, the authentic individual doesn't need people but is able to benefit from relationships, whereas through relationships, the vulnerable, false-self struggles to find comfort by escaping being genuinely known.

Existential Relationships

Outcome research indicates that the helping relationship is the most important aspect of the counseling or psychotherapy process (Mahoney, 1991). Across all of the applications of existential thought, the form and quality of the relationship are consistent. There is a sense of relational truth embedded in the encounter (May, 1983; Willis, 1994). Bugental (1978) describes the relationship as professional, dedicated to healing and growth, and sensitive. Reiter (1995) indicates that it is imperative that the counselor or therapist be emotionally authentic—otherwise the power imbalance is counter-therapeutic as well as unresponsive to the emotional influence the client has on the counselor or therapist. Although skilled, the counselor or therapist is present with the client in a very real and immediate existence. But these only describe the functions, not the substance of the encounter.

The diversity and substance of relationships were probably best described by Buber (1970). According to Buber, relationships may be experienced at several levels or at a combination of different levels. Some individuals relate to the world and to others as "I to I." Because other people are not seen as objects or individuals, these relationships are characterized by indirectness. People speak at or about others, but seldom to them. These individuals take and never give.

"I to it" relationships depict an individual relating to another as an object. These relationships do not persist. The individual generally moves to another level of relating, whether it is more intimate or more detached.

Another level of relationship is among people who relate to others and the world as "it to it." For these individuals, "I" has little meaning, for they do not have much sense of self. People relating to others at the "it to it" level have no room for any "I"-ness.

The next relationship level is called "we to we." These people also have no sense of "I." This relationship is generally seen in young children. No one has any individuality or objectivity.

"Us to them" describes a relationship between the chosen few and the damned. Some people will triumph, and others will fail. The lesser individuals are not even heard by the chosen "us" because they represent "them." All the good attributes are wrapped up in "us"; all the negative ones are represented by "them."

The "I to you" relationship implies treating the other individual as a person. The encounter involves two rather than one to an object or one to a despised part. There are more possibilities for understanding within an "I to you" relationship.

The profound meeting, the core of the existential connection, is the "I to Thou" relationship. As discussed earlier, this relationship involves an encounter with God and a deeper respect for the individual. The notion of transcendence is a part of the connection at this level. The most potent form of help involves being present in a respectful, honoring encounter (Dass & Gorman, 1985). In the final analysis, "I to Thou" relationships provide hope for genuine understanding.

In the "I to Thou" relationship, the counselor or therapist is merely a guide on a journey (Bugental, 1978). Offering respect for the client, the counselor or therapist is also a traveler on the same road. In the "I to Thou" level, the whole person is considered and honored. "Existential healing occurs in this mode of existence and is accomplished by the action of the reality between a person and the other in dialogue" (Heard, 1996, p. 239). The counseling or psychotherapeutic relationship may reflect several levels of encounter at a given time for the client and the counselor or therapist. Whatever the level, the counselor or therapist affects and is affected by the helping process.

Hazards on the Journey

The journey through the "dark night of the soul" can be difficult for counselors and therapists (Bugental, 1978, p. 77). They must protect themselves, their time, and their private lives. Making several such painful journeys with clients is bound to affect practitioners at a very personal level. Kopp writes: "Doing counseling is like remembering all the time that you are going to die. Because the counseling hour has a definite beginning and ending, we are kept aware of its being temporary. There is only me, and you, and here, and now. We know in advance that it will not last, and we agree to this" (1972, p. 42). Being an existential counselor or therapist means being open to continued learning and awareness because existential helping operates at an intense level of involvement.

If we are to listen to Freud's warning, truly being with clients may be harmful to the helping process. The counselor or therapist may be ineffective by engaging in an authentic encounter. Yalom (1980, 1992) argues that the helping relationship needs to achieve a balance, but the counselor or therapist should not be afraid of contact with another person or of being known. It requires a delicate harmony on a journey that is uncharted and unlike other counseling or psychotherapeutic approaches.

Additionally, May (1979) suggests that there is a potential for losing the scientific focus when working with people at an existential level. In rebelling against the rationalistic tradition of contemporary psychology, existential counselors and therapists might be detached from philosophical or technical realities. The trend toward transpersonal theory only underscores the danger. Ignoring the need to delineate therapeutic interventions, the existential counselor or therapist may be professionally vulnerable.

Despite all the concerns and warnings, there is value in taking the risk to encounter another person at the existential level. For the field, existentialism is an alternative and the only viewpoint solidly grounded in theory (May, 1983) and philosophy (Corey, 2001). Most significantly, clients find this approach very helpful (Yalom, 1980).

Applications

Overview

Existential counseling and psychotherapy have found application among diverse settings, individuals, and groups. The field of family counseling (Charny, 1992; Goldenberg & Goldenberg, 2000; Lantz, 1993; Lantz & Alford, 1995; Mandara & Murray, 2000; Nichols & Schwartz, 1998) has embraced existentialism as providing a contextual approach based on choice, responsibility, and growth. Group counseling also has been an arena for applications of the existential model. The interpersonal relationships of a group are directly addressed by an existential approach (Brabender & Fallon, 1993; Corey, 2000; Meir, 1996; Yalom, 1995) because these struggles are easily addressed in the context of others. An existential model has also been applied to the following: individuals and families struggling with AIDS (Bower, Kemeny, Taylor, & Fahey, 1998; Nord, 1996; Vaughan & Kinnier, 1996), children (Pramling & Johansson, 1995), developmental concerns (Chessick, 1996; Jones & Meredith, 2000; Lantz & Gomia, 1995; Sheikh & Yalom, 1996; Steen, 1996), minorities (Corey, 2000; Lantz & Alford, 1995), clients with deep seated concerns (Malson, 1997; Rosenbluth & Yalom, 1996; Van Deurzen, 1998; Warah, 1993), those with chronic illness (Kraus & Shaw, 2000; Leifer, 1996; Somerfield, Curbow, Wingard, & Baker, 1996), and individuals in supervision (Torres-Rivera, Phan, Maddux, Wilbur, & Garrett, 2001; Worthen & McNeill, 1996). Although existentialism is not the primary theory adopted by counselors and therapists, it is having a considerable impact.

Goals of Counseling and Psychotherapy

The existential goals of counseling or psychotherapy and change are "tragically optimistic" (Frankl, 1984, p. 161). Existential counseling or psychotherapy has the following core principles (Frankl, 1984): suffering is a human achievement and accomplishment, guilt provides the opportunity to change oneself for the better, vulnerability motivates us to become authentic, and life's unpredictability provides an individual incentive to take responsible action. Although steeped in philosophy, these principles hardly provide a working primer for the budding existential counselor or therapist. The goals for existential counseling and psychotherapy are simple. Existential change is a process whereby meaning is gleaned from common, worldly endeavors. Clients are transformed through courageous and subtle encounters with aspects of their humanness.

The Process of Change

Change evolves from a client's willingness to participate in the interpersonal encounter by confronting loneliness, experiencing individuality, encountering true connection, and developing the inner strength to transcend the life situation (Brabender & Fallon, 1993; May, 1953; Weisman, 1993). By discussing and "working through" these issues, research by Kennedy-Moore and Watson (2001) has shown that individuals achieve resolution, increased insight, and improved relationships. But the process of change begins much earlier. By reaching out to be with another person authentically, the client begins the process of transformation. Anxiety loses its power, and clients change as their fears melt into vital energy. Tillich (1980) indicates that courage to be oneself evolves out of personal anxiety.

The process of existential change involves coming to terms with anxiety through awareness of responsibility and choice. As Yalom writes in *When Nietzsche Wept* (1992), "Don't underestimate the value of friendship, of my knowing I'm capable of touching and being touched. . . . I realize I have a choice. I shall always remain alone, but what a difference, what a wonderful difference, to choose what I do—choose your fate, love your fate" (p. 301). Through increased awareness of self and experience of the world, combined with their awareness of choice and responsibility, clients can experience their potential. Instead of a veiled existence, they are living consciously and responsibly; they are connecting with others as well as with aspects of themselves. The actual process of change may move very rapidly: clients may bloom into creative, energized individuals able to self-actualize. The process may also unfold more gradually. Regardless, the catalyst for change is the relationship facilitating the development of awareness, acceptance, responsibility, vulnerability, and authenticity in the individual.

The change process discussed thus far has been in the context of individual counseling or psychotherapy. But as indicated by the numerous citations in a recent text for group counseling (Capuzzi & Gross, 1998), many people have found the existential model useful for understanding and implementing the group process. The multiple relationships provided by the group can promote a change toward greater awareness and genuineness through an awareness provided by the relationships. The existential treatment perspective, directly addressing the meaning found in relationships, is a central focus of group development (Brabender & Fallon, 1993).

Corey (2000) also indicated that existential approaches to group therapy are useful for a variety of populations. Multicultural populations especially benefit from this approach because of the focus on understanding individuals' realities in a social context as well as providing choices and hope. Beyond group counseling to working with group meetings and organizations, Owen (1997) based the "new" approach of "open space technology" on two constructs: personal freedom and responsibility, prominent existential themes. Existentialism remains embedded in the process of individual and group growth and development.

Intervention Strategies

Although supported by a fully developed theory and philosophy, existentialism offers no set of techniques (May, 1983). As you read about the interventions, you will notice that traditional techniques do not exist in this approach. In most theories, understanding follows technique, but the existential counselor or therapist allows the approach to flow from the clients and the theory rather than from a generic intervention. Existential theory is steeped in phenomenological awareness. Therefore, the following intervention strategies flow from a respectful understanding of the individual clients.

Telling the Story: Finding the Meaning of Myth   In his last work, May (1992) viewed myths as central to gaining existential meaning: "Each one of us is forced to do deliberately for oneself what in previous ages was done by family, custom, church, and state, namely, form the myths in terms of what we can make some sense of experience" (p. 29). In his book, he discussed the ways in which myths provide insight and meaning. In the counseling or psychotherapy session, stories may be facilitative in helping clients understand events in their lives. Clients also create their story as they detail their past and future.

Binswanger and Boss (1983) articulate the intervention of canvassing a client's experience. The client's history is gathered, but is not explained or categorized. Instead, the existential intervention "understands this life history as modifications of the total structure of the patient's being in the world" (p. 284). The practitioner is viewing the client's history through the client's being and awareness rather than focusing on pathological development. As the story unfolds, the client can see the patterns from a larger perspective. "Healing through narration and opening up involve an existential act of self-transcendence of an embodied person who organizes his or her experience in time" (Mishara, 1995, p. 180). Life myths literally order and focus the world, giving life meaning and value.

Sharing Existence in the Moment   The existential relationship is the primary therapeutic intervention, and the client is an existential partner. Viewed with compassion, the client is not met with pity or sympathy (Dass, 2000; Dass & Bush, 1992; Dass & Gorman, 1985). The counselor or therapist must be genuinely present on the "sharp edge of existence in the world" (Binswanger & Boss, 1983, p. 285). As Bugental (1978) asserts, "Presence is the quality of being in a situation in which one intends to be as aware and as participative as one is able to be at that time and in those circumstances. Presence is carried into effect through mobilization of one's inner (toward subjective experience) and outer (toward the situation and any other person in it) sensitivities. . . . Presence is being there in the body, in emotions, in relating, in thoughts in every way" (pp. 36–37). Emerging from the intervention is a deep sense of relatedness, which Heuscher (1987) calls *love*.

Included in the relatedness, and therapeutically significant, the counselor or therapist must be able to use himself or herself as an indicator of what is occurring within the client. "It is not possible to have a feeling without the other having it to some degree also. . . . The use of one's self as an instrument requires a tremendous self-discipline on the part of the therapist" (May, 1979, p. 122). Being not only implies presence, but also restrains the counselor's or therapist's own distortions, thoughts, and feelings as he or she participates in the client's world.

Centered Awareness of Being   The existential counselor or therapist helps the client become more centered, more aware. The key is becoming consistently aware. "Analysis and confrontation of one's various inauthentic modes . . . particularly extrinsically oriented, non-autonomous, or death denying . . . seems to be the key therapeutic technique on this level" (Wilber, 1986, p. 137). By eliminating the extrinsically focused aspects of themselves, clients become more aware of themselves in the environment. The subjectivity gained in centering (Bugental, 1978) can lead to other levels of understanding or transcendence (Kopp, 1972; Maslow, 1968; Wilber, 1993). Only by looking inward does the client develop insight and a keener awareness of personal problems (May, 1983). The most important first step is becoming more conscious of reality and authentically examining the various aspects called Self.

Self-Responsibility   Taking responsibility for growth is important, but taking responsibility for self-destructive actions is not easy. This intervention involves helping clients take ownership of their lives. First, they must be accountable for their choices. Equally important is letting go of the responsibility that others own in the process of relating (Gould, 1993; Wilber, 1986). Being responsible acknowledges that obligation can be assumed, shared, and owned by others.

Dream Work   Counselors and therapists working in a variety of approaches have seen dreams as the window to the unconscious. In existential counseling and therapy, dreams have an additional usefulness. The focus is on the client's "dynamic, immediately real and present" (May, 1983, p. 152) existence viewed through the dream rather than the set of dynamic mechanisms at work. "In the dream we see the whole man, the entirety of his problems, in a different existential modality than in waking, but against the background and with the structure of the a priori articulation of existence, and therefore the dream is also of paramount therapeutic importance for the existential analyst" (Binswanger & Boss, 1983, p. 285).

Through dream work, the counselor or therapist is better able to help the client see the pattern of being in the world and know the possibilities of existence through the dream (Binswanger & Boss, 1983). Though unsettling, the existential experience of dreams moves the individual closer to authenticity. Existential dreams "deepen self-perception" (Kuiken, 1995, p. 129). Dreams are like insight. They provide a reflection of inner vision, and the dreamer is compelled to discover their meaning.

Disclosing and Working Through Resistances   Addressing resistances to awareness requires a sensitive intervention, and the counselor or therapist is most effective when addressing issues supportively. This intervention creates both anxiety and joy for the client (May, 1983). Bugental (1978) suggests that counselors and therapists use comments such as "You can feel how much that way of being has cost you all of your life" and "You have wanted so much to be loved that you have often forgotten to take care of your own needs" (p. 90). The client owns the responsibility and the power to address the issues blocking awareness and authenticity. The counselor or therapist serves as the midwife in the birth of a more authentic being.

Confronting Existential Anxiety   Probably the most important intervention is being aware of the client's existential issues. The complex societal and individual reaction to death stirs complex emotions in most individuals (Kubler-Ross, 1975). It takes courage to discuss the forbidden subject of death. As Yalom (1980) says, "If we are to alter therapeutic practice, to harness the clinical leverage that the concept of death provides, it will be necessary to demonstrate the role of death in the genesis of anxiety" (p. 59). Sometimes this may be accomplished by a review of one's life (Vaughan & Kinnier, 1996). In such interventions, individuals are encouraged to examine and resolve issues by focusing on their life stories. By confronting the ultimate losses (e.g., relationships, life, and self) and by being present through the resultant anxiety, counselors and therapists have a powerful tool to help individuals work through fear.

Sustaining Changes in Being   When clients relinquish their old selves by stepping into the unknown, they place an inordinate amount of faith in their counselor or therapist guide. The guide needs to answer with faith in the client. Bugental (1978) offers guidance to the counselor or therapist for this most critical period, suggesting that the practitioner provide support by transferring power back to the client. Counselors or psychotherapists may constantly be attuned to unresolved issues in therapy. As part of supporting the new ways of being, they must also address the paradigm shift from the objective to the subjective and then to the integrated reality. Life is not experienced by total detachment through immersion, but rather by a combination of those perspectives. By mourning the disillusionment and years of unnecessary struggle, the client maintains growth.

Closure   Facing the end of the helping relationship is the final confrontation with reality. It is expected that additional issues will arise to delay the inevitable ending. The intervention of termination requires continued authenticity and willingness to be present. The counselor or therapist and the client may never meet again. Paralleling every other loss in the lives of both the client and the counselor or therapist, termination represents a very real death to both people. It is critical that the practitioner help the client by processing the ending of counseling or therapy, by creating a good parting. The difficulty with this intervention is that it exposes the reality of ending that is present in all relationships.

Clients with Mental Disorders

Existential counseling has been used with a wide variety of presenting problems. A mental disorder is always a potential consequence of feeling alone in an isolating culture and context, living without meaning, suffering with loss and death, confronting anxiety, and struggling with responsibility and freedom. Whatever the reason, mental disorders represent the loss of an individual's potential. In the confrontation with life and death, many people develop a desperate sense of isolation (Cannon, 1991; Krueger & Hanna, 1997).

Within a culture that is increasingly electronically distancing, it is a normal reaction for people to feel alone and disconnected. Isolation can also suggest the separation of self from the inner experience. Cultural overvaluing of individualization creates detached, unaffected people who often cover up problems by living cognitively and intellectualizing the human experience. Instead of being in the world, individuals feel alienated and forsaken. Until they have come to terms with their struggle, these individuals have literally lost their world and their community. Similarly, problems arise when people experience world changes and then have to readjust and find new meaning for their lives. Equally difficult is the loss of relationships, jobs, and potential. In every case, individuals can experience hopelessness and despair.

The full spectrum of anxiety disorders are a direct result of existential struggles and can be addressed through existential counseling. Existentialists have varying approaches to **angst,** or existential anxiety, but they all would concur with Tillich (1980) that "The basic anxiety, the anxiety of a finite being about the threat of nonbeing, cannot be eliminated. It belongs to existence itself" (p. 38). Anxiety is a universal experience of being "thrown" into existence (Heidegger, 1962), of being alive in a threatening time and being aware of the predicament. Viewing the center of the panic as something to be explored and understood rather than escaped serves to disempower the anxiety. Without recognition and understanding, it may serve as the focus of existence and also create other, more serious psychopathologies (e.g., major depression, psychotic disorders, and somatic disorders).

Hansen (1999) specifically noted the usefulness of existential counseling in working with individuals with borderline personality disorder, schizophrenia, depression, and mania. Resistance to addressing struggles with relatedness and tension is natural and has been used to help facilitate understanding existential possibilities (Craig, 1995). Existentialists believe that relationships can be transformed through counseling to allow a person to live more authentically (Loy, 1996). Still, relationships and the resulting anguish and stress are always present in struggling to understand our purpose in life.

The existential crisis and confrontation of it also produces depression and dysthymia. Often, depression is a last attempt to hold on to the defenses against anxiety (Bugental, 1978) as well as being a natural reaction to a lack of meaning in life (May, 1992). **Anomic depression** (Frankl, 1984) is the term used to describe the affective reaction to meaninglessness. Lantz (1993) indicates that "feelings of emptiness and defeat, lowered self esteem, discouragement, and moral disorientation" (p. 60) characterize the anomic struggles that research has shown to be different from other forms of depression. Working through existential issues can be a struggle. Through this journey, the client gains insight, understanding, and responsibility, which allows him or her to be more resilient in the face of new life pressures.

Likewise, the more individuals are satisfied with life, the more at peace they are with death. Critically ill patients with meaningless lives (Yalom, 1980) were more anxious and subsequently more depressed than those whose lives were satisfying. Existential counseling or psychotherapy has been seen as the critical variable in working with suicidal clients (Rogers,

2001). By understanding the ways clients construct meaning, counselors or psychotherapists have a theoretical basis for understanding the dynamics of the desire to die. Although depressed, the person is not really prepared for the emotional confrontation with death. The fear of approaching the universal questions is as strong as the fear of not approaching them. The individual is estranged in a chasm of existential depression.

Individuals with bipolar disorders represent the combined struggle with both anxiety and depression. Combining the fear and anxiety of being and non-being with the conflict over meaninglessness can produce the dually conflicted individual diagnosed as bipolar. Existential counseling addresses the pain experienced at both extremes in a manner allowing the individual an increased sense of self awareness and the ability to impact this dualistic struggle.

A wide variety of disorders result in problems in being false with one's self. These problems can span the gamut of personality disorders to substance abuse disorders and eating disorders. In discussing the problems arising from inauthenticity, Heidegger (1962) described the genuine person as one who has a profound awareness of existence. The lack of *Dasein,* of "being there," implies that the person is unauthentic, avoiding presence, accessibility, responsibility, and expression. The individual adopting a "false self" is disconnected and wooden (Weisman, 1993). But living an inauthentic existence does not happen in isolation.

We all live in relationships, in a culture, and in a time period. Finding our authentic self is accomplished by "being there" and by "being with" others (Willis, 1994). Likewise, the inauthentic existence is characterized by difficulty with interpersonal relationship as well as with oneself. By increasing our awareness, we become more authentic and more present, and we allow ourselves to learn to be comfortable with ourselves and with others. For instance, the counselor or therapist who views clients as individuals within a cultural system, not just as individuals defined solely by psychological diagnoses and treatment plans, is beginning to live authentically. Conversely, the inauthentic person pathologically resists being known. It is impossible to experience a veiled life. Everything that makes the person alive and allows the individual freedom remains imprisoned behind the mask of inauthenticity.

Maslow's (1954) seminal work with self-actualized people provided additional insight into the psyches of creative individuals who were unable to fulfill their true potential. Not everyone with capability becomes self-actualized. Maslow (1968) cites three reasons why people do not achieve their potential: lower instinctive pressure to self-actualize, cultural institutions that control or inhibit creativity, and tendencies toward fear and regression. Without these constraints, Maslow suggests, actualization is a natural process. But individuals who do not actualize experience shame, anxiety, and defeat. Remorse may be a guide back to actualization; but if the warning is not taken, individuals live knowing they did not reach their potential. In our culture, women and members of minority groups represent repressed individuals; these groups have often been discouraged to self-actualize and encouraged to self-doubt (Belenky et al., 1997; Bepko, 1989; Gerardi, 1990; Horner, 1972; Parham & Helms, 1985; Sue, Ivey, & Pedersen, 1996). Although taking responsibility is ultimately the solution (Weisman, 1993; Yalom, 1992), often it is not deemed worthy of effort. Once self-actualization is aborted, individuals see their lives as meaningless.

Before the final stage of transcendence that seems to characterize most existential breakthroughs (Maslow, 1968; May, 1979; Tillich, 1987), some people get bogged down with existential guilt and despair, often producing suicide attempts. As indicated by Tillich (1987):

> Life is marked by ambiguity, and one of the ambiguities is that of greatness and tragedy. This raises the question of how the bearer of the New Being is involved in the tragic element of life. What is his relation to the ambiguity of tragic guilt? What is his relation to the tragic consequences of his being, including his actions and decisions, for those who are with him or who are against him and for those who are neither one nor the other? (p. 228)

For one who is on the verge of understanding meaning in one's life, guilt may prove the ultimate undoing. Heidegger (1949) described the guilt flowing from heightened awareness and questioned the right of anyone to let himself or herself be killed for the truth. "He who does so," writes Tillich, "must know that he becomes tragically responsible for the guilt of those who kill him" (1987, p. 229). Existential guilt is not irrational; rather it is grounded in responsibility. Guilt is the "worm in the heart of the human condition, an inescapable consequence of self-consciousness" (Loy, 1996, p. 9). Still, it prohibits the individual from joining and participating in the awareness of reality. When unable to work through this existential crisis, the individual is left with the consequences of unremitting shame and responsibility.

Of all the mental disorders discussed thus far, possibly the most unsettling is a loss of self in the world, or **existential isolation.** (This can be seen in avoidant, dependent, obsessive compulsive personality disorders as well as major depression.) When individuals fail to develop inner strength, worth, and identity, they move beyond being isolated to feeling a profound sense of loneliness. Existential isolation occurs when an individual fails to develop an authentic sense of self in the world (Weisman, 1993). The person instead internalizes anxiety and searches for any available sanctuary.

Willis (1994) and Yalom (1980) describe two basic means of escape for the existentially isolated individual: existing through others, and suffocating or fusing with them. For some people, safety lasts only as long as their existence is perceived. Being alone means being abandoned and forgotten. The other defense that individuals use to seek protection from existential isolation is fusion. By living through and for others, they lose their boundaries and, in essence, their personhood. Under the popular label of codependence, women have been stereotypically described as suffocating others to regain their symbiotic attachment (Hogg & Frank, 1992). Csikszentmihalyi's (1992) research indicates that the answer lies in becoming a part of life. However, in the despair of existential isolation and loneliness, many individuals have lost hope of finding a place in the world.

Evaluation

Overview

Trying to evaluate the efficacy of existential counseling runs against its very assumptions. May (1961) indicated:

> Methodology always suffers from a cultural lag. Our problem is to open our vision to more of human experience, to develop and free our methods so that they will as far as possible do justice to the richness and breadth of man's experience. (p. 35)

Malterud (2001) also describes how traditional quantitative methods only measure what can be controlled and counted. The counselor's or psychotherapist's intuitive abilities and knowledge, although subjective, will help us better understand the process. Unfortunately, existentialists tend to be congruent. The theory that focuses on existence over essence is more centered on theory, counseling or psychotherapy, and people than on generating testable hypotheses, research design, and advancing the theory through scientific analysis (Binswanger & Boss, 1983; Funder, 1997).

Supporting Research

Counseling or psychotherapy outcome research has led to some interesting developments. It is becoming clearer that one theoretical approach to counseling or psychotherapy is not measurably more effective than any other. Ahn & Wampold (2001) conclude from multiple studies that it is better to study the counseling or psychotherapeutic process and the factors promoting growth and healing because studies comparing techniques are essentially non-productive. The process variables common to humanistic and existential psychodynamic studies tend to be the areas in which research needs to focus.

Concurrently, others have found the same phenomenon. In *The Heart and Soul of Change: What Works in Therapy,* Hubble, Duncan, and Miller (1999) bring together research that shows that 85% of client change is due to non-specific counseling or psychotherapeutic factors. Issues such as spiritual faith and community membership account for 40% of client change, relationship factors account for 30%, and 15% is accounted for by hope and expectancy. These variables are addressed in existential counseling or psychotherapy. By addressing the personal encounter, validating the process as much as the content, existential counseling or psychotherapy offers the framework that counselors or psychotherapists and clients are most seeking.

Efforts to apply existentialism to specific populations have been significant, but the research is beginning to increase. Corey (2000) indicates that existentialism is easily applied to not only multicultural but also international clients because the counselor or psychotherapist focuses on the subjective experience of the client's perspective and background. Research done by Torres-Rivera and others (2001) noted the importance of personal awareness and realistic training in developing multiculturally aware counselors or psychotherapists. They found that the existential counseling or psychotherapy model is vital to training multiculturally sensitive counselors or psychotherapists.

Jagers and Smith (1996) examined spirituality from an "Afrocultural" perspective with respect to several variables, including existential well-being. Attinasi (1992) and Vontress (Epp, 1998) suggest that existentialism is uniquely suited to address cross-cultural issues. Maples, Dupey, Torres-Rivera, Phan, Vereen, & Garrett (2001) found that an existential approach to counseling or psychotherapy with ethnically diverse clients using humor could be very helpful in working with clients with different cultural backgrounds. In another study, Greenberg and colleagues found that confronting existential issues elicits more tenacious cultural values (1990). A study by Baldwin and Wesley (1996) examined the impact of existential anxiety on students who were given scenarios measuring cultural polarization. In that study, even those individuals with higher self-esteem, when exposed to existential anxiety, showed more cultural bias. Existential variables are vital to cultural awareness and solid counseling or psychotherapeutic skills.

Single or group case studies have proved helpful in examining existential concerns. A schizophrenic was studied and found to have core existential concerns (Schmolling, 1984). Lantz and Pegram (1989) studied several clients and cited the importance of the "will to meaning" across all cases. A discussion of anorexia and existential issues is reflected in a book by Malson (1997). She describes the human existential dilemma and its connection with women struggling with finding themselves amid diverse societal demands. All studies indicate the need for further investigation. Among the studies surveyed, some lack the ability to be generalized (Hazell, 1989), and others reflect analysis that is correlational (Blyski & Westman, 1991; Hazell, 1984). Much work needs to be done to fully understand and apply existential theory.

Wong (1997) indicated a need for increased research on the healthy aspects of existentialism and the search for meaning. It was his contention that better understanding of the anti-reductionistic, subjective, existential approach would lead to the advancement of this theory. Outlining meaning seeking as a construct and developing a "Personal Meaning Profile," Wong (1997) attempts to find a path toward validation of this counseling or psychotherapy utilizing Frankl's (1984) terminology for existential counseling, *logotherapy*. At this point, assessing existential counseling or psychotherapy is like trying to measure the counseling or psychotherapy progress with a yardstick, knowing that the progress is neither linear nor unidimensional.

Limitations

Existentialism is not for everyone. It proposes a world view in which each theoretical approach has a place with optimal effectiveness. Systemic concerns, by their nature, deserve a family approach. Likewise, individuals with serious ego deficits will benefit from the psychoanalytic model. Each theoretical model reflects different levels of goals and needs of the client. Although existentialism may be used with a wide spectrum of concerns, it requires that individuals be ready to look at their fears, anxieties, and responsibilities. An existential approach also focuses on the interpersonal nature of counseling and psychotherapy and provides the client insight into other relationships. Nevertheless, not providing clients with specific direction and solutions to their problems may be unsettling to those who want a more prescriptive, objective approach.

Existentialism faces the world acknowledging the subjective experience. Because subjectivity runs counter to much of today's thought, it is understandable that existentialism may not answer the client's perceived needs. For example, upon encountering existentialism, Szasz (1987) was struck by the fantasy of this relative world. Understandably, some clients may also be skeptical because of the lack of clearly defined steps involved in treatment. Existentialism is not for the client who wants to avoid pain or experience immediate relief from struggle. Whether or not existential counseling or psychotherapy is brief, the existential search tends to go beyond four or five sessions.

Existential counseling or psychotherapy relies heavily on the verbal encounter. The underlying assumption of healing for existentialists is rooted in the helping relationship. Individuals who avoid contact with others will find this approach intrusive. Silence has its uses in existentialist counseling or psychotherapy (Dass & Gorman, 1985), but most existential counselors and therapists rely on the verbal exchange.

Because existential counseling or psychotherapy is based on existential theory, the criticism that existentialism lacks a guiding theory (Sue, Sue, & Sue, 2000) seems unfounded. A closer examination provides insight into the reason. By definition and historical development, existentialism is not based on the Cartesian, objectively oriented theory. As such, it lacks the common theoretical premise of problem-focused counseling or psychotherapy that guides the cognitive, behavioral, and psychoanalytic approaches. Although not sharing the theoretical assumptions of some predominant theories, it is not without a theoretical basis.

Probably the most evident challenge for existentialism is the lack of scientific exploration specifically focused solely on existential interventions. While cognitive behaviorists are generating incremental, specific research to validate their own theory, existential research is being evidenced in different forms. In medicine, counseling or psychotherapy, and related health care fields, existential concerns are being discussed and studied in outcome research, in developmental studies, and in studies of supervision and training. There is not a lack of research, but a lack of focus on the term *existentialism* specifically. Existentialists would seem to be defenseless in a battle of science, but in actuality are becoming woven into the fabric of the healing process.

However, the studies mentioned in this chapter begin to show that the struggle over theoretical validation has not yet been resolved. Not only is the lack of proof of the specific theoretical approach problematic, but also individuals without a solid sense of integrity are attracted to a model lacking a sequence of techniques and guidelines. Encounter groups are only one example of an early experiential existential model lacking the scrutiny of statistical substantiation. Existential counselors or psychotherapists need to continue to find palatable ways in which to study their unique approach (albeit inconsistent with their subjective model). If they do not, existentialism will be a haven for critical scientific scrutiny and unusual and fanciful approaches with no substance.

Because most strengths also embody weaknesses, the underlying faith in a client's potential for growth may appear shallow and unprofound. Met at a concrete level, the question of "Who am I?" appears inconsequential. Existentialism's strength in honoring the person may be comprehended as a cursory gesture.

Summary Chart—Existential Theory

Human Nature
Existential theory is realistically optimistic about human nature. People exist in a culture and context, and all struggle with the universal concerns of death, freedom, isolation, and meaninglessness.

Major Constructs
Existentialism addresses the following constructs: confronting universal fears of death, understanding our ultimate isolation, finding purpose in a predominantly meaningless existence, coming to terms with anxiety, accepting the burden of freedom of choice, realizing the responsibility we have for our lives, and living authentically.

Goals
The goal of existential counseling and psychotherapy is to confront anxieties about the givens of existence. Existentialism involves learning to live more authentically and gaining meaning from common, everyday endeavors and pain. Clients transform through courageous and subtle encounters with aspects of their humanness and through the interpersonal relationship with the counselor or therapist.

Change Process

Change evolves from a client's willingness to participate in the interpersonal encounter by confronting loneliness, experiencing individuality, encountering true connection, and developing the inner strength to transcend the life situation.

Interventions

Interventions in existential counseling and psychotherapy include understanding the client's world, sharing existence in the moment, fostering a centered awareness of being, encouraging self-responsibility, working with dreams, confronting existential anxiety, and learning to put closure on relationships.

Limitations

Existential theory utilizes a subjective approach to understand a world that is currently most popularly understood within an objective system. Existentialism relies on verbal exchange and authenticity. The theory does not rely on scientific testing to validate itself. Because most strengths also embody weaknesses, the underlying faith in a client's potential for growth may appear shallow and unprofound.

■ The Case of Jonathan: An Existential Approach

Jonathan's presenting concerns reflect an existential struggle with death, isolation, freedom, and meaninglessness. The death of his brother caused an early trauma that he has not been able to fully address. He has not been able to find himself in a satisfying relationship and has battled depression and loneliness. No one has validated his pain or acknowledged his loss of self in the world. Jonathan challenged cultural traditions by leaving the reservation. He seems torn between two worlds that are incompatible. Cultural and family expectations have impacted his work and his recent pressure to return home to the reservation and care for his aging parents. Confronting this loss of self, of identity, Jonathan experiences existential isolation and despair. To find meaning—or to escape from finding it—he has become depressed, developed problems at work, moved from relationship to relationship, disconnected from his family, and abused alcohol. Still, his anger, fear, and frustration are clearly a result of a crisis of selfhood.

The life Jonathan has constructed is fragile and he realizes the exigency of the situation. His nightmares reflect his lack of purpose and direction in life and his angry and helpless reaction to it. He has difficulty in maintaining a job or relationships. In the past, Jonathan has been able to cope by finding meaning in and through others (new relationships). Ultimately, his choices have never filled the void left by the death of his brother.

The potential loss of his freedom by needing to return to the reservation seems to have intensified the nightmares, as well as his deteriorating relationships at work, financial problems, drinking, and likely permanent separation from his current wife. However, his flight through others has never been fulfilling and now he is alone with building responsibilities he feels unable to handle. The problems in being able to find other meaningful work are compounded by encountering prejudice.

Although he attempts to distance himself from his culture, he continues to be faced by it. In trying once more to escape his problems, he is having increased difficulty and is "alone with the laughing driver" on a bus going nowhere he wants to go. For Jonathan, alcohol has also proven ineffective in helping him to find respite. In facing his life without culture and with increased pressures to create a new meaning out of his painful past, Jonathan has no way to turn to escape. He is left alone and afraid.

Treatment/Intervention Plan

Jonathan's desire to work on these issues is paramount. His current depression and hopelessness could be paralyzing. A medication consult may be necessary if his depression does not abate and alcohol abuse needs to be assessed. Because his current defense of withdrawal and escape are not working, he was asked to come to counseling by his supervisor. His lateness to the session indicates he is reticent and careful, but the amount of information he provided shows openness to the process. His current pain may also be a positive in motivating him to change.

The goal of counseling will be to help gain an understanding of Jonathan's current condition. (In this process, Jonathan will also gain perspective on his situation.) First, it will be important to discuss his cultural background and any feelings he has about the counseling or psychotherapy experience as well as any cultural differences or similarities that may exist between Jonathan and the counselor or psychotherapist. Also, it will be important to discuss the gender of the counselor or psychotherapist with Jonathan. If he has any concerns about this, a referral will need to be made immediately. Next it will be important to hear his story. In telling his struggle and pain, Jonathan needs to be heard and validated. He will be facing his fears while he focuses on the issues prompting the depression: the death (and his responsibility for it) of his brother, the separation from his family, separation from his current wife (and any feelings he has about the problems in these relationships), the difficulty living in a predominantly white culture, the relationships with his children, the use of alcohol to escape, and his career identity (currently working in a residential drug and alcohol treatment program for adolescents).

In all areas, Jonathan experienced loss and meaninglessness, leading to hopelessness. It is important to note that, in spite of everything, he has persisted. Ultimately, he will gain freedom and understanding by acknowledging his struggle and being heard and respected by the counselor or psychotherapist. He will also have his counselor or psychotherapist with him as he confronts his anxiety about having to decide what to do next and whether to return to the reservation. Jonathan has made choices that were unpopular with his spouses, family, and culture. In seeking to establish himself in the world, Jonathan has found others in his life to be like a group of 'angry faces' wanting to take him different places and the person in charge laughing at his lack of ability to impact his own direction.

His withdrawal has occurred over several years and relationships and has been in reaction to external pressures, which are now increasing as a result of the pressure from his family, his problems at work, financial issues, relationship problems, increased drinking, and his general affect. Jonathan has not been able to move beyond his feelings of responsibility over his brother's death when he was 16. He has developed a pattern of detaching from relationships, which was difficult in view of the pressures from his culture to be intricately connected. Jonathan has not been true to himself or others, and that has left him isolated in a world without meaning or direction.

Case Analysis

The first phase of treatment will be developing a therapeutic relationship. Because Jonathan has been victimized by his culture and the majority culture, developing trust and groundwork for the "I to Thou" relationship is important for counseling or psychotherapy to begin. A concurrent component is helping to assess the extent of alcohol use/abuse. Counseling or psychotherapy will not be effective if Jonathan is under the influence of alcohol. In the past, he has sought to detach in relationships; now Jonathan will need to be committed to working through these issues that continue to follow him from relationship to relationship, and job to job. By addressing this core aspect of self, he can gain power over his life and his choices.

The dream seems to be a revealing of his sense of powerlessness, frustration, and lack of direction. Understanding that the ideal and final interpretation will be made by Jonathan, the following discussion emerges from an existential interpretation. Jonathan's real self is confronting his sense of lack of direction and ultimate aloneness in a situation where he feels powerless (alone with a bus driver who does not listen and laughs at him).

The culture (bus that the people feel is going everywhere) seems to really be going nowhere in particular, although he had a ticket to Albuquerque (home). He feels trapped (no one has time to get off at the bus stops). His anger (pounding on steering wheel) only serves to make everyone else disappear. He is left alone and unable to have any power over where he is going on a bus with a driver who laughs at his desire for help. It could be that he is the bus driver, detached from his own desire to find his way home. He cannot figure out how to escape from his situation and is afraid and angry. This shows that Jonathan is focused and motivated to confront these aspects of himself and his world. He would welcome someone to help him to deal with his helpless feelings. Escape no longer is providing solace. He has not been able to find "home." There is a sense he may be ready to change.

The counselor or psychotherapist will need to help Jonathan confront the anxiety of death. By meeting his fears of loss and engulfment and encountering the aspects of himself that are painful and angry, he will sense all that he has encountered and survived. Jonathan will also develop a stronger sense of himself and his responsibility for making his own choices. He can find a place in the world that is not bound by the bus, the driver, or the people without direction. By continuing to flee from relationships, work, and life, Jonathan avoids being and living. He is trapped in his fears by his substance abuse, depression, and isolation.

Counseling or psychotherapy will involve helping Jonathan on his journey as he encounters the fears embodied by the individuals on the bus and the frustration of not having control over his life. It will be important for the counselor or psychotherapist not to fall into the easy pattern of offering him insight or direction (giving another voice to where the bus is destined). Instead, it will be important for Jonathan to integrate his own voice and sense of self. This will occur through the process of validating his losses, his pain, understanding cultural pressures, and helping him to find meaning in himself and his existence. Unfortunately, the path (bus) he has taken thus far has not gotten him where he wants to go or provided any relationships or understanding. He has felt alone, out of control, angry, and afraid.

The counselor or psychotherapist is providing a context of relating that will help Jonathan to learn that his escape from others through drinking, his not staying committed in relationships, and his not knowing how he wanted to deal with his family only keep him mired in anxiety and depression. By facing his insecurities and losses, he will gain a sense of inner strength, awareness, and self. By taking responsibility (getting behind the wheel), he can realize the freedom he has to be himself and choose. It also will cause him to be responsible for his choices. Once he has recognized his power and responsibility, he can be himself in relation to others. He will no longer be alone.

Group counseling and support for alcohol use/abuse, especially with others struggling with cultural issues, might be helpful when Jonathan has developed a better sense of himself. The group would allow Jonathan to connect with others with similar struggles, to validate his pain and his struggles to make peace with himself, and to develop healthier ways of relating to others and making choices.

Person-Centered Theory

Richard J. Hazler
Ohio University

Introduction

The person-centered theory of **Carl R. Rogers** is one of the most popular in the fields of psychology, counseling, and education. Rogers' perceptions of people and of how a supportive environment can assist in their development have had an immense impact on a wide variety of professions and on parenting. This approach to people was a major deviation from the psychoanalytic and behavioral models for working with people that were predominant in the early part of the 20th century.

Person-centered theory offered a new way to look at individuals, their development, and how they can be helped to change. From this frame of reference, people were viewed as fully in charge of their lives and inherently motivated to improve themselves. The responsibility for personal behaviors and the ability to choose to change them was also seen as belonging fully to the individual. Here was a way to view and deal with human beings that did not rely on other people (counselors, psychologists, parents, teachers, and so on.) as the primary directors of change. People could now control their own change if the right conditions were offered.

Rogers saw all individuals as having inherent qualities that made nurturing possible; attempting to change basic personality characteristics or behaviors was not necessary. He believed people saw the world from their own unique perspective, which is referred to as a **phenomenological** perspective. No matter what that phenomenological view of the world was, it was further assumed that all people are continually attempting to actualize their best and most productive selves. This positive and optimistic view of human beings is often challenged by those who call attention to the unlimited opportunities for observing people as they think and act in ways that are harmful to themselves and others. But Rogers believed these thoughts and actions were primarily reflections of a distorted view of oneself and the world, distortions caused by trying to meet the expectations of others rather than trying to actualize one's own self.

The origins of Rogers' beliefs, their development into a major helping process, and an examination of the essential ingredients of that process will serve as a foundation for this chapter. Information on the counselor's or therapist's role in providing interventions and the methods used to carry out that role will then provide the practical base for beginning to implement the process.

Background

Carl R. Rogers

Person-centered theory began to make an impact on psychology in the 1940s. Carl R. Rogers was the individual behind the theory, and his influence was so great that it is commonly referred to as **Rogerian theory.** The major concepts of the autonomous self, reliance on one's unique experiences, the desire and ability to make positive personal changes, and movement toward the actualization of potentials are all observable in Rogers' personal development.

Rogers was born in 1902 into a morally and religiously conservative family that was strictly religious, devoted to its children, and committed to the concept of hard work. Dancing, watching movies, smoking, drinking, and anything that vaguely suggested sexual interest were clearly forbidden, although little was said about them. The family was able to convey its directions in subtle ways that were generally unspoken but nevertheless very clear to everyone.

The family was largely self-contained, and the young Rogers had few friends. He became a loner of sorts, spending most of his time working, thinking, and reading. His early lifestyle caused him to pay close attention to his personalized experience of the world. In later years, this concept would become better known as a phenomenological approach to counseling or psychotherapy.

Rogers' family moved to a farm 30 miles west of Chicago when he was 12. It was here that his work ethic was reemphasized; he also developed an interest in science and experimentation. He spent much of his time studying the insects and animals that were now available to him. His father emphasized a scientific approach to all issues, insisting that all farming should be as scientific and modern as possible. These concepts of hard work, scientific study, experimentation, and evaluation would later set Rogers apart from other theorists: he was the first to intentionally and creatively subject experientially recognized human development and therapeutic processes to rigorous scientific study. This aspect of his work is often overlooked by those interested in his theories, but it is a major contribution to the development of professionalism in counseling and psychotherapy.

Rogers left home to study agriculture in college, but later turned to religious studies and eventually to clinical psychology as he became more interested in people, beliefs, and values. His religious beliefs, like those of his parents, were strong. However, the more he studied and discussed the issues, the more his views diverged from his parents'. A 6-month trip to China as part of the World Student Christian Federation Conference encouraged his change to a more liberal viewpoint.

Explaining these changes to his parents was extremely difficult and often disappointing for all concerned. However, Rogers reported great growth in his intellectual and emotional independence from these open confrontations. The experience left him much more confident in himself, his beliefs, and his ability to deal with difficult situations. This idea that individuals can and must rely on themselves for direction and strength was to become another major emphasis in his theory, as well as in his own life.

Rogers graduated from the University of Wisconsin, married, and in 1924 began to study for the ministry at Union Theological Seminary in New York City. His focus of attention changed during his 2 years at Union as he became more and more interested in psychology and education. Consequently, he transferred to Columbia University to study psychology, and eventually earned his Ph.D. there in 1931.

Following graduation from Columbia, Rogers worked with children in Rochester, New York, for 12 years; later he was on the faculty at Ohio State University, the University of Chicago, and the University of Wisconsin. His final stop was at the Center for Studies of the Person at La Jolla, California, beginning in 1963. This period of time until his death in 1987 was extremely productive. It included work in education and in individual and group counseling and psychotherapy. The last years of his life were spent traveling in the most troubled places in the world, using his person-centered approach to promote peace among warring groups.

Theory Background

The field of counseling or psychotherapy in the 1920s and 1930s relied on techniques that were highly diagnostic, probing, and analytic, but unsupported by scientific research. Rogers' first major work, *Counseling and Psychotherapy* (1942), was a clear reaction to this situation and to his work with children. "So vast is our ignorance on this whole subject [counseling and psychotherapy]," he wrote, "that it is evident that we are by no means professionally ready to develop a definitive or final account of any aspect of psychotherapy" (p. 16). He presented **nondirective** counseling and psychotherapy in this work along with a clear call for a more scientific approach to research on both his nondirective and other, more directive techniques.

Client-Centered Therapy (1951) was a culmination of a decade of practice and research in which Rogers expanded his concepts and renamed his approach. This new emphasis changed the role of the counselor or therapist from an individual who only reflected the content of client statements to one who identified the client's underlying emotions in client words and through the helping relationship. The effect of this new work was to expand the dimensions of accurate empathy with the client and to force the counselor or therapist to go beyond simple reflection of client words.

In 1957, Rogers moved to the University of Wisconsin, where his efforts at research on his theory increased and broadened. Here he tested his ideas on hospitalized schizophrenics rather than on the primarily normal population he had been working with at the University of Chicago. His research confirmed the view that the conditions present in the helping relationship did have a significant effect on both the progress of counseling or psychotherapy and the outcomes for clients (Rogers, 1967). Rogers' work with client populations ranging from normal to extremely disturbed encouraged him to broaden the use of his ideas to include all people.

Person-Centered is the term currently used to emphasize the personal nature of counseling or psychotherapy and other relationships in education, business, and government agencies. The therapeutic or helping relationship is now envisioned as one of person to person rather than healthy counselor or therapist to unhealthy client.

Person-centered theory developed out of a close examination of individual helping relationships, but during the 1970s and 1980s, Rogers began focusing more on groups than on individuals. He was a major promoter of personal-growth groups, where individuals worked together for the purpose of self-actualizing growth rather than toward a more limited goal of overcoming psychological illnesses (Rogers, 1970). Another group adaptation saw Rogers using person-centered concepts in a group-process format to deal with critical world conflicts. He traveled to areas with major social conflicts, such as Central America (Thayer, 1987), South Africa (Rogers & Sanford, 1987), Northern Ireland (Rogers, 1987b), and even the Soviet Union (Rogers, 1987a), to facilitate growth groups with leaders and nonleaders who had fought, but never tried to understand each other. His accounts of these encounters make it clear that a person-centered orientation can be promoted in groups as well as in individual relationships.

The enduring nature of Rogers' work can be seen in every current article or book that examines person-centered theory. Their discussions of the theory, practice, and research aspects all emphasize his work over any other, even though that work is now decades old. Rogers' contributions continue to be the core of the theory although many professionals have expanded it. Researchers and educators such as Truax and Carkhuff (1967), Carkhuff (1969), and Barrett-Lennard (1998) have emphasized the measurement and instruction of Rogers' core conditions in efforts to improve evaluation of counselor effectiveness and to develop more successful counselor training models. Today, virtually all counselor or therapist education programs emphasize early on these conditions and related techniques.

Modern-day issues such as managed care and medical treatment models have greatly increased the emphasis on diagnosis, symptom elimination, problem behavior reduction, and time-limited treatment that are not conducive to a person-centered approach. Their primary focus on techniques rather than the relationship Rogers advocated have made full compatibility difficult. At the same time, all these approaches still begin with relationship and each of these areas is increasingly giving greater recognition to the importance of Rogers' core conditions. Even such technique-driven counseling or therapy models as family counseling (O'Leary, 1999), applied behavioral analysis (Holburn & Vietze, 2000), and brief therapy (Presbury, Echterling, & McKee, 2002) are emphasizing the essential nature of these conditions for counseling success. Modern counselors or therapists may not find many books with *person-centered counseling* in the title, but they will see the ideas deeply ingrained in virtually every modern approach to counseling.

Human Nature: A Developmental Perspective

The person-centered approach to counseling or psychotherapy implies great confidence in each client. This confidence arises out of a belief that all people have innate motivation to grow in positive ways and the ability to carry out such a growth process. This highly positive view of human nature varies widely from other theories that view human nature as evil, negative, or a nonissue. Such a positive view of human nature is essential for the person-centered practitioner because of the major responsibilities clients are given in the direction, style, and content of the helping relationship. The person-centered perception of people is based on four key beliefs: (1) people are **trustworthy,** (2) people innately move toward **self-actualization** and health, (3) people have the **inner resources** to move themselves in positive directions, and (4) people respond to their **uniquely perceived world** (phenomenological world). The interaction of these characteristics with a person's external environment brings about the most desirable aspects of development.

People Are Trustworthy

Person-centered counselors or therapists must treat their clients as trustworthy, or there will be no reason to allow them to take a leadership role in the helping relationship. From this point of view, words such as *good, constructive,* and *trustworthy* describe natural characteristics of human beings, although people also appear to take actions that demonstrate the opposite. These inappropriate actions are taken when the individual's ideal view of self does not match the real **self.** Individuals use defensive thoughts and actions to protect themselves from the recognition that they are not living the lives they believe they should. Such actions are not deceitful; rather, they are direct actions based on conflicting perceptions of a person's world. All individuals are trying to improve and to act in the world as they see it in as honorable a manner as possible.

Consider the teenage girl who skips school and has been arrested for the fourth time for shoplifting. Many in society will judge her to be a bad person or one who cannot be trusted, and the girl knows this. The person-centered counselor or therapist must believe that the young woman will be trustworthy in their relationship if and when she is convinced that she has a meaningful relationship with a counselor or therapist who is genuine and trusting. A major part of that relationship will be the counselor's or therapist's conveying genuine trust through words and actions. Anything less than this trusting relationship will serve to convince the girl that this is just another person who will not trust her. The result is that she will have little motivation to work on her own potential for trustworthiness in the therapeutic relationship.

Movement toward Actualization

Human beings are viewed by the person-centered theorist as always striving to obtain the maximum amount from themselves. They seek any means to develop all their abilities "in ways that maintain or enhance the organism" (Rogers, 1959, p. 196). This is the driving force in the positive development of the individual. It clearly moves the individual away from control by others and toward **autonomy** and self-control. The movement toward actualization provides individuals rather than outside persons (parents, counselors, therapists, teachers) with the primary motivational strength behind development. This energy source is also seen as potentially more influential than environmental factors such as socioeconomic status, hunger, or danger, even though these often affect how the individual perceives or seeks self-actualization.

The problem teenage girl discussed previously would likely be seen by many to have inadequate self-control and little desire to overcome her problems. The result is that individuals and society as a whole will probably seek to control her and force her to grow in ways deemed appropriate by others. The person-centered view, however, emphasizes the concept that the girl is actually working toward making the most out of herself and that she will continue to do so regardless of what others do. What others can do is provide a safe environment where the girl can lower her defenses and explore her antisocial behaviors without fear of failure and nonacceptance. When this occurs, she can be expected to continue to pursue self-actualization, but now in ways that are more appropriate and socially acceptable.

Inner Resources

The actualizing tendency provides the motive for positive development in people. But do individuals have the capacity to carry out this motivation? Person-centered theory presumes that individuals do have that capacity (Rogers, 1961). Holding the belief that people have the motivation to grow in positive directions does not mean that counselors or therapists will also have confidence in their ability to follow through on that motivation. The person-centered approach emphasizes a belief that this ability to grow in positive directions is available to them. Certainly some of the most heartwarming stories told throughout the ages have demonstrated how people can overcome tremendous odds to become successful. These same stories also cause people to question why success occurs for some and not others.

Person-centered theory emphasizes that these potential differences in degree of ability to overcome are not as important as persons' beliefs that they can accomplish what they set out to do. In many ways, it presumes a fairly well-accepted principle of human dynamics, which states that people always have much more potential than they use most of the time. Person-centered counselors or therapists must believe in this principle if they are to help clients recognize and accept their own abilities.

The person-centered counselor or therapist must have confidence that the troubled girl we have been discussing has the inner resources as well as the motivation to grow. The demonstration of this confidence-building belief allows for the emergence of the creative ideas and actions that can expand potential options and encourage growth in new directions. When this confidence is not conveyed, both counselor or therapist and client are likely to aim for goals that are far short of her potential.

Individually Perceived World

The person-centered view recognizes that events will be perceived differently by different people (Rogers, 1961). Two armies fight, two adults argue, and relationships often break down because each side perceives what is "right" to be different from the other side's perception. The person-centered view of these examples is that individuals or groups relate to the world and their own actions from a unique context or **phenomenological perspective.** Therefore, words, behaviors, feelings, and beliefs are selected to match the specialized view of the world held by each individual.

The idea that no two people perceive the world in exactly the same way explains much of the variation we see in the previous three concepts. Our troubled girl surely does not perceive the world as the safe and kind place that another person who is successful in school and has a comfortable family life does. Neither will she perceive it as the rational world that the counselor or therapist is likely to see. It is quite possible that the girl is stealing, in part, because of a different perception of the world. She sees this behavior as the only one available for her to help feed herself, her mother, and her infant sister. Person-centered counselors or therapists must recognize these differently perceived worlds, work unendingly to understand them, and seek to help clients grow through their personally perceived world rather than through the world as it is perceived by the counselor, therapist, or others.

Interaction with External Factors

A person-centered view of human development gives attention to external factors that affect psychological development in addition to critical internal forces. Even as infants, people make choices that induce growth and actualize potential. They reject experiences that are perceived as contrary to their well-being. However, these naturalistic ways of making choices become confused as the developing person recognizes that other individuals may provide or withhold love based on how well the person assimilates values and behaviors set by others. This recognition can move individuals away from using their own best judgment to make personal choices and promote an alternate method that requires taking actions based on the presumed desires of others. The two theoretical concepts used to explain this aspect of development are **unconditional positive regard** and **conditions of worth** (Rogers, 1959).

Individuals who are given unconditional positive regard by significant people in their lives receive recognition of their positive nature, including their motivation and ability to become increasingly effective human beings. The worth and value of the individual are not questioned in this case, although specific behaviors or beliefs can be rejected as inappropriate. A parent might say to the young woman we have been following, "You are a good person and I know you want the best for us, but the stealing was just wrong and was punished."

Individuals who are given and can recognize unconditional positive regard being provided to them feel permitted to continue trusting themselves as positive human beings. The belief is conveyed that they will make errors of judgment and behavior, but that as positive individuals they will also strive to examine themselves continually and be able to take actions for their own improvement. Being provided with unconditional positive regard helps individuals to continue seeking their own development with the confidence that they will become increasingly effective human beings.

Many times, the regard and love offered by others have strings attached as would be the case if the girl who stole had been told by her parent, "You're just a common criminal and no daughter of mine!" Children faced with this type of love that is conditioned on doing only those things that a parent wants and where differences or mistakes are unacceptable can come to believe that they are only good, loved, cared for, fed, or valued if they do just as others believe they should. These conditions of worth pressure developing persons to devalue their inherent potential for choice making and growth. They begin looking for directions and decisions that originate from external sources instead of trusting their more natural internal ones. This process moves developing individuals away from confidence in their ability to run their own lives and pushes them to seek validation based on the lives of others who appear to be more positive than they are.

Major Constructs

The core of person-centered theory is a set of beliefs about people and relationships rather than a series of programmable verbal and behavioral techniques. Counselors or therapists interested in implementing this theory must look first to themselves and their perceptions of others rather than to what specific behaviors ought to be performed. This is a challenging task, particularly for new practitioners who are seeking to find out what they should "do" and to what extent they "do things well." The following constructs are essential beliefs involved in person-centered theory. Practitioners must have a clear perception of them before they can implement a person-centered approach effectively.

No Two People See the World Exactly Alike

According to the phenomenological approach, no two people can be expected to see things as happening in exactly the same way. Practitioners must recognize that whatever they personally believe reality to be will be different from the client's perspective and that each client will have a unique perspective. Therefore, asking the client to believe or act in a way that "everyone knows is right" becomes the counselor's or therapist's opinion, based on his or her own phenomenological view rather than some ultimate "fact." Because helping someone from a person-centered approach emphasizes this concept, it is imperative to understand the client's perspective as thoroughly as possible.

Consider the case of a physically abusive husband who was court ordered into counseling. One part of his reasoning for why he hit his wife hard and so often that she needed to be hospitalized was, "I come home from work, there is no food on the table, there are dishes in the sink, and then she back talks me. Of course I hit. Anybody would!"

No counseling degree is needed to realize that, "No, anyone wouldn't hit her and certainly not like you did." Our perceived world makes it clear that this is not appropriate thinking or behaving. It is, however, an obvious sign that the client has a very different view of the world than the counselor or therapist and almost everyone else. Person-centered counselors know that arguing with this person will not change his mind. What will help is to first gain an accurate picture of his perceived world in order to gain a better understanding of why he thinks this way and what will impede or assist change.

Empathic Understanding

Empathic understanding is critically important to the person-centered approach; it is the counselor's or therapist's perception of the client's phenomenological world. *Empathy* refers to the understanding of the client's world from the client's point of view. This is no easy task because it is hard for counselors or therapists to set aside their own biased views of the world in an attempt to see things through the client's eyes. All other actions they take will be inappropriate without empathy because those actions will be based upon inaccurate perceptions of the client. This construct allows practitioners to respond effectively and assures clients that their confidence in the counselor or therapist is justified.

Knowing the content of what a client says as well as the feelings behind it are the two essential elements of empathic understanding. The words and reasoning for the abuser striking his wife are important information that we can get from his words. The feelings, however, may come out in words like *anger, hate,* or *frustrated,* or in other ways like reddening of the face, facial expressions, posture, laughter, or tears. Empathic understanding uses all of these verbal and nonverbal clues to understand clients.

Empathic understanding has two important tasks that practitioners must accomplish to make it a useful construct: understanding, and accurately conveying that understanding. The most obvious of these is that counselors or therapists must set aside their own beliefs and enter the client's world so that they can understand. Setting aside one's disdain for the abusive spouse above is no easy task, but not doing so will taint any understanding of the person with the counselor's or therapist's own biases.

Understanding, by itself, has only minimal counseling empathic value. The client must also be aware of exactly what the practitioner understands. This second dimension is crucial in order for empathic understanding to be useful. Empathic understanding only improves the helping relationship when the client clearly recognizes what it is the counselor or therapist understands, so the counselor or therapist must be able to effectively communicate that understanding back to the client.

People Make Simple Mistakes in Judgment

People make simple mistakes in judgment all the time. They also make choices that appear to be right to them, but that are ineffective because they are made to match the perceived world of others' rather than an individual's own best judgment. People are attempting to act as they believe others would have them act (conditions of worth) rather than trusting their own positive, growth-oriented nature, their **tendency to actualize.**

Counselors or therapists who demonstrate faith in the whole person rather than denigrating clients for mistakes of behavior allow their clients the freedom to explore their inner world without fear of rejection. Lacking such unconditional positive regard, clients may try to do what they believe the counselor or therapist wants in order to achieve a better life. Unfortunately, these actions will only increase client beliefs that they cannot personally make effective choices. They may find some more socially acceptable ways of behaving, but they will not have gained confidence in their own ability to seek more changes as the need arises.

Confidence in the Client

In comparison to other theories, person-centered theory places tremendous confidence in clients even knowing that they will make mistakes in judgment along the way. This confidence is based on the belief that people are innately good and continually seeking a fully functioning experience in the world even as they make mistakes. People's tendency to actualize personal potential in positive ways is the force that the person-centered practitioner recognizes and seeks to free from self-induced constraints.

The repeat history of the abusive spouse example makes trusting so difficult that often the courts need to step in to protect others. That, however, is the work of the courts and not the counselor whose person-centered task is to believe in this person's desire to do the right thing even though he is currently unable to perceive what that is or how to do it. This contrasts with other views of human nature that do not allow the practitioner to trust because client difficulties are seen as weaknesses or deficiencies that will stand in the way of personal progress unless the counselor or therapist corrects them. Person-centered clients are treated as effective human beings who will succeed regardless of the nature of their difficulties.

Perceived World of the Client May Not Approximate the World Sought

Individuals come to counseling or psychotherapy for help because of difficulties evolving from the fact that the world they perceive is not in close proximity to the world they would naturally seek for themselves. The natural, growth-oriented, self-trusting nature of these people has been pushed into conflict with their chosen world, where they continually look outside their true selves for decisions. They act based on perceptions of what others think is right, and the results of their actions are not personally fulfilling or effective. This conflict is termed **incongruence.**

It is a common occurrence, for example, to find that abusive persons have also experienced an abusive environment. They have often struggled inside themselves—verbally and even physically—to reject the unnatural, hurtful, and untrusting aspects of the environment, but at some point they come to believe that this is "just the way things are" because others do it. They take actions based on the acceptance of this direction from others, only to find it comes into conflict with the receiving and giving of love, caring, and self-trust they naturally desire. The result is increasing levels of incongruence both within themselves and between them and others.

Congruent Individuals Trust Their Worldview

Congruent persons are the individuals who trust their view of the world and their ability to act on their basic positive nature. They feel confident about reacting in the present moment because of a belief in their organism's ability to discriminate between appropriate and inappropriate behaviors. This self-trust is then generally verified by those around them because their actions tend to be beneficial both personally and socially. Where human fallibility causes errors in reactions, congruent individuals also have a view of the world that allows the reactions of others to be evaluated and appropriate adaptive responses taken for the immediate and distant future. More congruent people are not infallible, but they do have the ability to recognize and use mistakes to grow without devaluing themselves.

The congruence-versus-incongruence construct helps explain the concept of **anxiety** in person-centered theory. Low personal anxiety occurs when the perceived self is in line with actual experiences (congruence). Alternatively, the degree to which individuals' perceptions of themselves do not match the way they actually are (incongruence) is directly related to higher levels of anxiety. It is significant for the practitioner to recognize that in person-centered theory, efforts are made to increase congruence in the client rather than directly reduce anxiety.

Applications

Overview

The person-centered concept of a growth-oriented and competent individual in need of counseling or psychotherapy presumes a scenario analogous to the growth of a simple garden bean. The bean seed has all the potential to grow, but must be provided with the proper climate in order for it to achieve its full potential. It will develop as expected if placed in fertile ground where adequate warmth, sun, and water are available. Human hands do not need to touch it under the ground, nor should those hands help pull it out of properly prepared ground. In fact, such human attempts to directly manipulate will almost surely threaten the bean's development! The effective gardener knows that arranging correct conditions and leaving the actual plant alone as much as possible is the best way to allow it to reach its greatest potential.

Fostering the natural growth of the bean is analogous to how one applies person-centered theory to counseling and psychotherapy. The client has all the necessary but as yet unfulfilled potential for attaining greater self-understanding, self-acceptance, self-growth, self-satisfaction, and self-actualization. The practitioner's task is to provide the essential growth conditions of a genuine human relationship where acceptance, caring, and a deep understanding of the client are developed and communicated effectively to the client. The application of these conditions involves the intervention strategies that allow persons to make changes in the direction of their greatest potential.

Goals of Counseling and Psychotherapy

Movement from incongruence to congruence identifies the cornerstone person-centered goal for people who are having psychological or sociological difficulties. They are attempting to perceive more accurately their own positive nature and learn to use it more effectively in their everyday lives. As this occurs, they will better accept both their strengths and weaknesses as legitimate and evolving parts of their positive nature. This acceptance reduces distortions in their view of the world and leads to greater accuracy in the match between how they see themselves and their interactions with people, ideas, and things.

Reduced distortions and a greater trust in one's evolving positive nature lead to other specific outcomes that practitioners often identify as goals of counseling or psychotherapy. People finding success in counseling or psychotherapy generally become more flexible and creative in their thoughts and actions as they free themselves from stereotypes and inappropriately imposed conditions of worth. They begin to see a wider range of feelings in themselves, gain more confidence in the expression of those feelings, and feel enthusiasm about the new aspects of their lives that are opened up by these experiences. These newfound levels of freedom to trust the accuracy of their feelings and thoughts allow them to take the actions necessary to overcome feelings of helplessness, powerlessness, and the inability to make decisions about the present and future. This new level of self-empowerment is perhaps the most noticeable outcome for everyone around an individual who has benefited from person-centered counseling or psychotherapy.

The Process of Change

The process of change through the helping relationship is guided by the presence of three basic conditions: genuineness, acceptance and caring, and empathic understanding. As Rogers writes, "Studies with a variety of clients show that when these three conditions occur in the therapist, and when they are to some degree perceived by the client, therapeutic movement ensues, the client finds himself painfully but definitely learning and growing, and both he and his counselor regard the outcome as successful." He continues, "It seems from our studies that it is attitudes such as these rather than the therapist's technical knowledge and skill, which are primarily responsible for therapeutic change" (1961, p. 63). Over the past 40 years this perspective on the significance of the relationship to the process of change has been integrated within virtually all schools of counseling and psychotherapy (Farber, Brink, & Raskin, 1996; Hazler & Barwick, 2001).

The first of these three conditions is the **genuineness** of the counselor or therapist. Clients must perceive that this individual is a real person who has feelings, thoughts, and beliefs that are not hidden behind facades. This genuine nature allows clients to trust that whatever specifics of the relationship emerge, they can be recognized as both personal and honest. It also allows the client to see that being open and genuine, which includes revealing one's fallibility, is not a condition from which competent human beings must shrink. Most of our daily relationships are not highly genuine, but are instead controlled by facades and roles that cause us to doubt the information we receive from people.

The second condition is **acceptance and caring** provided by the counselor or therapist, which allows clients to be less anxious about their perceived weaknesses and the prospect of taking risks. The weaknesses we perceive in ourselves generally become those things we least want others to see, so we try to hide our weaknesses whenever possible. Limitations often result in some degree of embarrassment, with an accompanying tendency to work even harder at hiding them. Persons needing assistance are working hard to hide their perceived weaknesses both from others and from themselves. Often they will even identify a less-threatening weakness as the problem in order to avoid examining a more personally threatening one. Acceptance and caring, if consistently felt by the client as unconditional positive regard, offer the opportunity to reduce the degree of stress caused by these fears in the relationship. This, in turn, will increase the chance that the client can recognize, discuss, and work on these problem areas rather than hide from them.

The third condition for change is the practitioner's **empathic understanding** of the client. This deep recognition of the client's internal frame of reference must be successfully communicated to the client in order to be effective. Neither the practitioner nor the client can ever fully understand the client. However, the degree to which they effectively explore the client's world together to arrive at a common understanding will improve the client's abilities to understand and, therefore, take action in his or her life.

These three basic conditions provide the necessary environment that allows individuals to implement their **actualizing** tendencies. They arrive in counseling or psychotherapy questioning their abilities and ideas, afraid of the weaknesses they recognize, and even more afraid of those that they expect are unknown to them. They have been seeking answers from other people, whom clients believe must clearly have better answers. All of these conditions make them fearful of letting their true selves be seen by others or even themselves, so they wear a variety of masks to present a "better" picture than what they fear is there. Providing the basic therapeutic conditions allows clients to explore themselves and their fears, and to experiment with new ways of thinking and behaving within a safe and growth-oriented environment.

Receiving attention and support from a genuine individual who can be trusted allows clients to explore themselves in areas and ways they cannot in less-therapeutic situations. Having another person closely and consistently listen helps clients begin observing and listening to themselves better: "You're right, I am angry. And now that I say it out loud, I realize I've been angry for a long time." They begin to drop masks as they recognize aspects of themselves to be not quite as bad as they thought: "I do have the right to be angry even when someone else doesn't want me to be that way. I'm not comfortable with that idea, but it is there for now." Self-recognition and self-acceptance are key first steps in the growth process.

As individuals become open to their true experiences and more trusting of their own **organism,** they begin to see the blocks to growth that have burdened them. They also gain the confidence needed both to recognize and deal with their problems on their own. These new levels of self-confidence allow for the dropping of protective masks and for accepting strengths and weaknesses as aspects that are both real and changeable over time. An internal **locus of control** develops as clients take control of their lives rather than following the direction of others who have been running their lives.

A major part of the development process in clients is a recognition that they are fallible human beings who are always in a growth process. This is very different from the belief that one must be perfect in order to be good or loved. Acceptance of this position allows people to view themselves as continuing to learn and grow throughout their lives and to see success as regular improvement rather than perfection.

Clients' confidence in their own ability to evaluate themselves, decide how to change, actually change, and accept their errors reduces anxiety and the dependence on others for directing their lives. An accurate perception of the real world and their part in it will continue to give importance to the reactions and beliefs of others, but this information will now be seen as more equal in significance to their own views. Consequently, clients will take more responsibility for their own existence and need less external intervention.

Intervention Strategies

The counselor or therapist looking for a specific list of things to say, actions to take, or diagnoses to make will not find them in this theory. Person-centered theory is much more related to who counselors or therapists *are* rather than what they *do*. A practitioner's actions are focused around providing the conditions of genuineness, unconditional positive regard, and empathy in the relationship. No book can say how all individuals should be genuine because each of us is different. Likewise, how a practitioner genuinely shows unconditional positive regard or empathy is also dictated to some degree by the type of person he or she is. This section suggests two general concepts regarding therapeutic intervention techniques: some thoughts on how to be genuine, and some specific behaviors that have consistently been identified with communication of the core conditions.

Being Genuine   To be genuine, counselors or therapists need to look closely at themselves before deciding how to be or what to do. Obviously, one cannot be genuine by thinking, saying, or doing what someone else does. Knowing oneself, then, becomes critical: it allows actions and words to be congruent with the way one really is while at the same time helping the practitioner match the client's needs. Person-centered counselors or therapists need to be knowledgeable about themselves and reasonably comfortable with this information. They must be more congruent than their clients, or the likelihood is that more will be taken from the client than is given. One clear way to deal with these issues is for practitioners to seek quality helpful relationships, including counseling or psychotherapy, for themselves and to work as hard on their own continued growth as they ask their clients to work.

Being genuine does not mean sharing every thought or feeling with the client. Such a tactic would simply take the focus off the client and put it on the practitioner, which is not a part of person-centered helping or any other type of helping. What is appropriate is being a helpful, attentive, caring person who is truly interested in the client and able to demonstrate that interest. We have all experienced the type of situation in which an acquaintance says, "I know how you feel," and we know very well the words coming from this near stranger are nothing more than words. Not only do we reject the words, but also we lose faith in the person's honesty. The same person might have said, "I hardly know you, but if it's anything like my own loss, it must hurt a great deal." The second statement recognizes the reality of the two people rather than trying to indicate more understanding than is reasonable to believe. There are as many genuine statements or nonstatements as there are people and situations. The right one matches the person the counselor is with his or her unique situation with the client at a given time.

Active Listening   The first technique emphasized in person-centered theory is **active listening** and its reflection of content and feelings. Demonstrating empathy for the client requires highly attentive and interactive listening skills. Counselors or therapists must first show that they are paying attention. The physical steps most common to this are facing clients, leaning toward them, and making good eye contact. This position and the use of facial and body expressions that relate to the clients' comments will at least initially put practitioners and clients in physical contact. After putting themselves in the best possible position to listen, practitioners must then hear and see what is communicated. Both the words and the actions of the client are used to develop an understanding of the content and feelings being presented.

Taking in information is only the first part of active listening. Practitioners must then reflect the content and feelings of clients back to them. "I hear you saying . . .": "So you are feeling . . ."; and "You seem to be feeling . . . because of . . ." are samples of the ways counselors or therapists explore with the client how accurate their empathy truly is.

It is to be expected that the genuine counselor or therapist will not always have a full understanding of the client's world and will make varying degrees of mistakes trying to reflect it. The process of active listening helps both parties clarify the content and feelings of a situation and is a learning process for each participant. Practitioners who can treat their own mistakes and growth during this learning process in a genuine manner as a natural part of life also help clients accept their uncertainties and weaknesses.

Reflection of Content and Feelings   The first steps in the empathy exploration process tend to be the recognition and reflection of the actual words stated and the feelings that are most obvious. As client and counselor or therapist get to know each other better, an effective practitioner becomes better able to see behind these surface interactions and begins to see and convey feelings clients do not even recognize they are expressing. For example, a client may be distracted or become more quiet periodically during the session. Initially, these reactions may appear related to the specific topic at hand. However, over time, the counselor or therapist may be able to tie those reactions to some general concept that pulls the different discussion topics together. Describing to the client what has been recognized can be very valuable even when it is as little as extended listening, observing, and reflecting of the person's world. At its most powerful, reflection can also bring together complex elements of the client's world that draw a much more accurate picture of the client as a whole than the individual elements provide separately.

Immediacy   Many of the most powerful interactions are those in which the content and feelings involved relate directly to the immediate situation between the client and the counselor or therapist; in other words, they depend on **immediacy.** Recognition, understanding, and use of feelings are seen as major problems for clients from the person-centered perspective. Immediacy provides a here-and-now approach to the relationship in general and to feelings in particular. The relationship between client and practitioner is seen as the most important therapeutic factor in part because it is available for immediate examination. Therefore, the feelings that both client and counselor or therapist are currently experiencing are often the most therapeutic ones available. Statements that receive primary emphasis are ones like "How are you feeling now?" and "Your statements make me feel . . ."

However, statements seen as less-therapeutically useful might be, "Why did you feel that way?" "What did the other person think?" or "What did you believe then?"

A major reason for person-centered theory's emphasis on the here and now is that reactions between client and counselor or therapist can be verified, checked, and explored immediately by both participants. Statements or feelings from the past make use of only the client's perspective, thus giving the practitioner a reduced opportunity to be a vibrant part of the client's experience.

Appropriate Self-Disclosure   A truly genuine relationship lets the client see relevant parts of the counselor or therapist's phenomenological world as well as the client's world. Appropriate **self-disclosure** allows clients to compare their views of the world with the view of another individual whom they have come to trust and value as a significant human being. Under nonthreatening circumstances, these comparisons give clients the chance to review and revise their views based on information they might otherwise not have had available or which has been too threatening to accept. A supportive relationship allows client forward movement to try out new thoughts and behaviors based on the comparative information. Much like the growth of the bean mentioned earlier, clients are allowed to use the supportive atmosphere and comparative information to develop at the rate and in a manner most appropriate for them.

Personalized Counselor or Therapist's Actions   One of the great misconceptions among new practitioners is that listening and reflecting is all the person-centered counselor or therapist does. This rigid reaction to his concept of an evolving and personalized theory was a major frustration to Rogers throughout his professional life. After one demonstration counseling session, Rogers was confronted by a workshop participant who said, "I noticed that you asked questions of the client. But just last night a lecturer told us that we must never do that." Rogers responded, "Well, I'm in the fortunate position of not having to be a Rogerian" (Farber et al., 1996, p. 11). Rogers used his own thoughts and personality in many creative ways, just as all quality person-centered counselors or therapists do. These are the aspects of therapy that appear as metaphor, humor, confrontation, and at times even interpretation or directiveness.

Many counselors or therapists now use Rogers' relationship development model as the foundation on which to build other cognitive, behavioral, or emotional approaches. Boy and Pine (1999), for example, see additional stages in which person-centered counselors or therapists use their own creative methods to help clients recognize and deal with problems after the essential relationship elements have been established. They also argue that because each client is different, person-centered counselors or therapists must adjust their methods as much as possible to fit the specific preferred mode of the client. Their view is that a true person-centered approach will have a consistent foundation, but that the full range of the relationship must build upon the unique aspects of the counselor or therapist, the client, and their personalized relationship together.

Much of Rogers' work has been so well integrated into other theories and practices that the person-centered labels have been dropped. However, there are others who give more attention to the person-centered element of their work. They reflect a wide variety of diverse approaches, just a sample of which would include person-centered expressive therapy

(Rogers, 2001), person-centered family therapy (O'Leary, 2001), multimedia approaches to person-centered counseling, client-centered psychodrama (Brazier, 1993), psychological testing (Watkins, 1993), and person-centered applied behavioral analysis (Holburn & Vietze, 2000). Person-centered theory may not get the name recognition that it did 30 years ago, but the impact of its core concepts continues to be seen throughout the field.

Non-Client-Centered Interventions   It is important to note the kind of techniques that will *not* be used as true parts of person-centered counseling. One key example is diagnosis and detailed treatment planning, which have become significant parts of the mental health field today. Increasingly, insurance companies and government agencies require clear-cut statements of the client's so-called illness, its severity, and the estimated length of time it will take to be corrected. Because person-centered counselors and therapists do not view clients in an ill versus well context, they can have a great deal of trouble working with these issues. Person-centered theory is much better suited to helping people progress than it is for getting them over some designated condition. Person-centered practitioners who find themselves in situations where they need to design extensive diagnosis and treatment models must give close attention to how and to what degree they can integrate these relatively divergent processes.

Many new counselors or therapists identify with a person-centered approach because it fits what they want to do and what has helped them grow in other positive relationships. However, when they attempt to use this approach, they often get caught up in many non-person-centered techniques, mostly for their own comfort. For example, there is little need for extensive **questioning** in the person-centered approach, for the task is to follow the client rather than to continually suggest what issues need to be explored. New practitioners in particular tend to question clients more than necessary. They are likely to begin seeking extensive information in clients' pasts rather than talking about current perceptions and interactions. Finally, they tend to find themselves overanalyzing client comments and reactions in order to develop elaborate rationales for why clients do what they do. These reactions may come in part from the fact that student trainees have completed many years of education where such tactics are highly effective methods for succeeding in academia. Now they are faced with doubts about their own ability to use the skills they have been taught with real clients who can be hurt. This lack of confidence and experience often causes them to fall back on the questioning and directing tactics of the traditional academic community rather than the responding and following tactics of the person-centered approach. Just as clients need time and proper conditions to learn to trust in their organism, it also takes time for new person-centered counselors or therapists to trust in their developing organisms.

Clients with Mental Disorders

The discussion of clients with mental disorders can be problematic for person-centered counselors or therapists who generally find that traditional assessment and assignment of mental disorder categories are not useful to treatment. These conceptualizations encourage those outside of the client to identify the problems and the direction of treatment. The person-centered approach, however, places therapeutic attention on the client's perceptions of difficulties, goals, and treatment directions. These differences are significant considering that the current state of the mental health field maintains assessment and diagnosis as expected elements. The result is that person-centered counselors who want employment in most mental health agencies or desire insurance payments for their private practice need to deal with this form of labeling at least for communication purposes.

A meta-analysis of studies on experiential therapies, the bulk of which were person-centered, showed positive effects across a wide range of disorders (Greenberg, Elliott, & Lietaer, 1994). For example, adaptations of person-centered counseling have been found to be useful with diagnoses that varied from the more common depressive disorders (Elliott, Clark, Wexler, Kemeny, Brinkerhoff, & Mack, 1990) to those such as borderline personality disorder (Bohart, 1990), schizophrenia (Prouty, 1998), and dementia (Zeman, 1999).

Although person-centered counseling has been found to have value throughout diagnostic categories, there are treatment issues that are likely to make it less effective as the primary technique. Disorders that require clients to learn specific skills such as those in sex therapy require much more counselor directness and behavioral methods. Also, the client-directed nature of person-centered theory requires a significant degree of client motivation so that those who do not have such motivation to grow through counseling or therapy become less viable candidates for person-centered counseling or therapy as the sole model for treatment.

Evaluation

Overview

The person-centered movement brought about innovations in research and training as well as a new approach to counseling and psychotherapy. Emphasizing objectivity in the examination of client/practitioner relationships moved the profession forward in the evaluation of specific interaction variables in the process of counseling or therapy. This solid research background has not erased all problems from this approach, however, as it still has limitations. These include being considered a simplistic theory when it is actually quite complex; requiring greater trust in the client than people often are able to offer; and having few of the specific tactics for new counselors or therapists to fall back on that other theories provide. An overview of these factors and others critical to understanding person-centered theory are summarized at the end of this section.

Supporting Research

Carl Rogers' perception of people, counseling, and psychotherapy as highly personal and individualized often gives newcomers to the field a sense that he and his theory deemphasize research in favor of personal interaction. This perception could not be further from the truth. In fact, his early research has been recognized by some as "the birth of psychotherapy research" (Barrett-Lennard, 1998, p. 261). Rogers was a major innovator in the development of research techniques for counseling, psychotherapy, and person-centered theory. He recognized that for any theory or technique to remain credible and become more effective, solid research is essential (Rogers, 1986).

Rogers pioneered the use of taped transcripts (Cain, 1987) and other clinical measures of interacting to broaden the scope of psychological research (Hjelle & Ziegler, 1992).

These techniques, along with the use of the Q-sort method, helped bring the more subjective aspects of people, counseling, and psychotherapy into respectability. Among his earliest significant publications were books on extensive research studies with standard mental health center populations (Rogers & Dymond, 1954) and more cases of people with schizophrenia (Rogers, 1967). All this work demonstrated his commitment to research on his theory and established his basic concepts as valid and reliable sources of client progress.

Rogers' research and teaching tool that gets the most use today is the tape recording and transcribing of sessions with clients. Note taking from memory was not satisfactory. He wanted to hear and see as much of the interaction as possible to judge both the client's reactions and his own work. This taping and evaluating of sessions has become common practice today, and many of Rogers' tapes and transcripts of counseling sessions continue to be reviewed and analyzed in detail (Farber, Brink, & Raskin, 1996).

The **Q-sort** method of data collection became a major influence in the acceptance of Rogers' theory. Developed by William Stephenson (1953), a colleague of Rogers at the University of Chicago, the Q-sort method employs many different formats for people to sort attributes of themselves into various categories and levels. Generally, when the method is used in person-centered research, subjects are asked to perform the task once for self-description and another time for ideal self-description. These two sortings are then compared to see how well their perceived and real selves match. The theory suggests that the closer the match of the real and perceived selves in a person, the more congruent the person is. Because congruence is theorized to improve during effective person-centered interaction, researchers can look for increasingly closer matches between these two measures as counseling or psychotherapy continues. This procedure enabled Rogers to validate many of his theoretical constructs and procedures.

Most research on the person-centered approach has continued the focus on necessary and sufficient conditions for successful counseling or psychotherapy (Cain, 1987). It motivated many studies in its early years, but recently the momentum for such research has declined significantly (Combs, 1988). This may be due in part to the general acceptance of Rogers' basic concepts as necessary, if not sufficient, and the extensive research done on them in the 1950s and 1960s. This acceptance is so widespread throughout the thinking and practice of the profession that we no longer consider many of his concepts "Rogerian" (Goodyear, 1987). They are more often now referred to as basic essentials to the helping relationship.

These basic relationship essentials have continued to get attention in more current research efforts. Studies continue to show that these relationship variables constitute a major portion of the success variance across counseling theories (Duncan & Moynihan, 1994; Hubble, Duncan, & Miller, 1999).

Potential weaknesses in person-centered research have not been ignored by the profession. The methodological aspects of some studies have been questioned by some researchers. Concerns about sophistication and rigor have been raised (Prochaska & Norcross, 1999), and similar comments have led others to ask whether these problems raise doubts about the validity of the theory (Watson, 1984). These concerns may deserve particular attention when considered alongside the fact that less person-centered research is now being conducted at the same time that the core conditions are widely accepted.

Person-centered theory has remained relatively unchanged over the last 30 years, according to some authorities (Cain, 1986). Combs (1988) suggested that this lack of development of the basic theory is the reason for a lessening of research in the area. Whether or not a lack of theory development has brought about less research in this area, it is clear that for the theory to grow, both new ideas and additional research will be necessary in the future.

Limitations

Person-centered theory may suffer most from the fact that it appears so simple to learn. The concepts are relatively few, there is not a long list of details to remember, and one does not need to recall a specific tactic for each diagnostic problem a client might have. The counselor or therapist can be lulled into a feeling of security by this apparent simplicity. For example, simple listening and reflecting of words and surface feelings are usually beneficial at the very beginning of a session. However, continued surface-level interactions that do not attend to the many dimensions of both the client and practitioner quickly become seen as repetitive, nondirectional, and trite.

The reality is that the few basic concepts in person-centered theory have a virtually unlimited complexity because counselors or therapists must be fully aware of both their clients' and their own changing phenomenological worlds. They must respond to the interactions between these worlds in ways that best fit the genuine natures of the client and the practitioner. This is a difficult task that requires an excellent understanding and continuing awareness of oneself and the client. New counselors or therapists in particular have a difficult time with this complexity. Persons who are working hard and feeling under pressure to remember and do a "new thing" or a "right thing" will naturally find it very difficult to be genuine and aware of all that is happening around and within themselves and others. Acting on what they recognize adds yet another level of difficulty to the task at hand.

The supportive nature of person-centered theory is often misinterpreted to mean that one should not be confrontational with clients. Counselors or therapists often need to do more than listen and reflect. Effectively functioning people confront themselves all the time, and counselors or therapists must recognize that appropriate confrontation is a natural part of an effective helping relationship. Person-centered theory makes room for such confrontation, but it gives few specific guidelines as to where, when, and how it should occur.

A great deal of trust in the positive motivation and abilities of oneself and one's clients is required of the person-centered counselor or therapist. Without this trust, many of the other person-centered concepts lose their true value, and a therapeutic interaction can become little more than polite conversation. Such trust in people and a process is not easy to provide in all circumstances. Human beings have difficulty suspending their mistrust because fears, previous experiences, and preconceived notions are a natural part of the human condition that affect everyone. The more extreme one's negative experiences and reactions are, the more difficult it is to act fully on the person-centered belief system. The result is that most practitioners can place confidence in a bright, college-educated, law-abiding, depressed client, but have more difficulty maintaining a similar confidence in a depressed rapist or murderer.

Person-centered practice requires a great deal of personal knowledge, understanding, and awareness, as well as a willingness to act on this information. There are few techniques or activities to fall back on if the counselor or therapist does not have or cannot act on this information about the helping relationship. Many other theories provide more activities or tactics that allow the practitioner to give the process a boost when the relationship is not all it could be.

Summary Chart—Person-Centered Theory

Human Nature
This theory emphasizes a highly positive view of human nature in which people can be trusted to be continually seeking productive directions toward maximum self-actualization. Perceiving unconditional positive regard from their environment supports this development, while conditions of worth inhibit it and produce non-self-actualizing thoughts and behaviors.

Major Constructs
Clients have psychological and sociological difficulties to the degree that their phenomenological worlds do not match their true positive nature (incongruent) and its use in their everyday lives. Empathic understanding of the client's world is essential in helping clients find a more congruent match between their phenomenological world and their actions, feelings, thoughts, and responses from others.

Goals
Counselors or therapists provide a safe, caring environment where clients get in closer touch with essential positive elements of themselves that have been hidden or distorted. Less distortion and more congruence lead to greater trust that their organisms can be relied on for effective reactions to people and situations. This added trust results in reduced feelings of helplessness and powerlessness, fewer behaviors driven by stereotypes, and more productive, creative, and flexible decision making.

Change Process
The change process is stimulated when counselors or therapists provide the core conditions of genuineness, acceptance and caring, and empathic understanding. Change takes place as clients perceive these conditions and begin exploring and testing new thoughts and behaviors that are more in line with their positive, growth-oriented nature. This exploration, testing, and learning leads to increasing trust in their organisms' ability to think and act in a wider variety of circumstances.

Interventions
This theory is marked by a minimum of specific intervention techniques, as counselors or therapists are asked "to be genuine in a relationship" rather than to perform a rigid set of actions. Interacting in the immediacy of the situation and then evaluating the results with the use of active listening, reflection of content and feelings, appropriate self-disclosure, and other personally, professionally, and situationally responsive interactions are essential.

Limitations
Success is dependent on counselors or therapists maintaining high trust in the feelings and actions of the client and themselves. Lack of trust often causes practitioners to fall back on safe, passive reflection responses. These are necessary early on, but become increasingly inadequate as the need for a more comprehensive therapeutic relationship develops, one that includes directness that comes with additional culturally, situationally, and personally relevant feelings and interactions.

■ ■ ■ The Case of Jonathan: A Person-Centered Approach

The use of a client case study to view person-centered theory raises several problems. To begin with, the standard case-study concept suggests that a collection of historical factors will be used to describe and diagnose an illness. However, person-centered theory places more emphasis on clients' perceptions of and feelings about their world as opposed to the facts as seen by others. It disdains looking at work with clients as illness-focused. Additionally, the relationship with the counselor or therapist is much more critical to the success of therapy than the client's specific historical case development. Many person-centered practitioners might, therefore, choose to ignore the concept of a clinical case history.

The problem with this approach is that it may convey the idea that person-centered counselors do not seek understanding of clients' perceived experiences or expect to observe specific progress outside the therapeutic relationship. The fact is that the reason person-centered practitioners attend so closely is precisely because they want to understand the clients' perceived experiences as well as possible. They then use that understanding within a therapeutic relationship that is unique to the particular phenomenological worlds of the client and the counselor or therapist. Finally, like all good counselors or therapists, person-centered practitioners also must evaluate the progress of clients both inside the therapeutic relationship and in the outside world. The modified case study that follows attempts to take each of these factors into account by examining potential phenomenological aspects of the client's situation as though the information had been acquired within the therapeutic relationship. Assumptions will be added that might reflect other information the counselor or therapist acquires about feelings and emotions not included in the more content-oriented case description. It will further emphasize Jonathan's relationship with the counselor or therapist, and suggest potential directions that Jonathan's growth might take as a result of a positive therapeutic relationship.

Jonathan's Phenomenological World

As would be expected with clients entering counseling or therapy, Jonathan has a phenomenological view of the world that is incongruent with his true feelings, abilities, and potential. He has incorporated unattainable conditions of worth that come from a mixture of culture, conflicts in cultures, family, and personal relationships. In his currently perceived world, he will never be able to be a good enough son, father, Native American, employee, colleague, or partner to satisfy those whose approval he desires. The harder he tries to please others, the further he gets away from personal feelings of self-worth and the less pleasing he does of anyone, including himself. He has lost trust in his own organism's ability to feel, think, decide, and act in productive ways, and consequently he is trying to act in a world as others see it—a strategy that will not bring him the growth or success he is naturally seeking.

The fact that Jonathan's phenomenological world is frequently out of line with the world that actually affects him causes Jonathan great anxiety. He looks outside himself for ways to act, only to find that what others point to as the "right" way does not satisfy anyone—least of all himself. He knows that who he is and what he does are not working, but he cannot identify other ways to view the situation and no longer trusts himself to provide that direction.

Actualizing Tendencies

It is clear that Jonathan has never fully given in to the conditions of worth that direct him in non-actualizing ways. He keeps experimenting with new challenges and finding success for periods of time in spite of the disapproval of his actions by others. Decisions to take time away from high school to better understand himself, going back and graduating, trying life outside the reservation, returning to the reservation and recognizing its importance to him, making different attempts at responsibility in marriages, and seeking better ways to deal with work all demonstrate an actualizing tendency that keeps Jonathan moving forward even in the face of mounting conditions of worth placed on him by others. He was referred to counseling by his employer, but his openness to talking about his experiences, weaknesses, anxieties, and desires for growth speak positively for his motivation to get more out of himself and to take the necessary actions.

Jonathan has been seeking a variety of ways to actualize his most appropriate self and has demonstrated that he has the tools to succeed. This is a person who has seen his brother die in a car he was driving, struggled with the clash of his involvement in two very different cultures, and still found times of success at school, work, and in relationships. His abilities seem clear even as his success is frustrated because of distorted views and the absence of caring relationships where he could be accepted for who he truly is and will work to be. This situation distracts him from recognizing alternative views of himself and potential actions that could lead to much greater self-actualization. The growth Jonathan seeks will be found to the degree he gains the confidence in himself that will allow him to maintain involvement during difficult times rather than attempting to escape as he has by physically and emotionally leaving situations and by abusing alcohol.

The Counselor's or Therapist's Role

A counselor or therapist valuable to Jonathan will empathically work with his situation, see his inner strength, trust in his willingness and ability to move in positive directions, and provide the core therapeutic conditions that will allow his actualizing tendencies to flower. These conditions will help Jonathan clarify the intricacies of his own feelings and see the value in sharing his views accurately with another person. Jonathan also needs a close relationship with a counselor or therapist who is not burdened by false fronts so that he can trust the legitimacy of the human interaction (genuineness).

Providing unconditional positive regard for Jonathan can be conveyed in part by showing confidence in him as a competent person who can think and act effectively. The counselor or therapist will not lead Jonathan to specific topics, suggest ways for him to act, identify his problems for him, or direct, reward, or punish him. Showing both attention and active listening without placing judgments on the information will help demonstrate this condition.

The counselor or therapist will listen and observe closely in order to grasp all of Jonathan's verbal and nonverbal thoughts and emotions. To achieve this, the counselor will convey back to Jonathan what she or he sees, hears, and feels, so that together they can check on the accuracy of their communications. Mistakes, underestimations, and overestimations are common in this process of developing accurate empathic understanding. It should be viewed as a learning process for both parties involved rather than a set of correct statements made by the counselor or therapist. Jonathan presents ideas, the counselor or therapist tries to reflect them and possibly tie them into other previously recognized concepts, and both parties negotiate to reach mutual understandings. It is only from such struggle that accurate understanding arises.

Unconditional positive regard and accurate empathic understanding begin to look false and misleading to the client unless genuineness is also conveyed. Jonathan needs to see himself in a relationship that is open and honest. It must be made clear that what the counselor or therapist thinks, does, and says are consistent, and that taking on the role of counselor does not mean one cannot be a real person at the same time. Such consistency will allow Jonathan to trust the reality of the relationship, as well as the ideas, skills, and behaviors that develop from it. He will learn to use the counselor or therapist as a model for the idea that he, too, can develop such congruence. As progress continues, Jonathan will recognize that because this is a positive human relationship with a genuine person, the ideas and actions can be transferred to his life outside counseling or therapy. The relationship, therefore, will be viewed as an immediate, natural, real, and dependable experience that can be duplicated in many respects beyond the helping relationship.

The person-centered practitioner is often considered to be caring and kindly, but it must also be recognized that the core conditions offer a great deal of challenge to the client. Jonathan will not always want to hear how the counselor or therapist is reacting to him, as this may require that he confront aspects of himself that are difficult to accept. Only the truly empathic counselor or therapist, who is also genuine, can successfully overcome such difficult issues. The many challenging times and confrontations in a person-centered approach are those that would be expected in any genuine human relationship. The added benefit in this particular relationship is that the counselor or therapist is a professionally trained as well as caring individual.

Expectations for Progress

The person-centered counselor or therapist who adequately and consistently provides the necessary therapeutic conditions can expect Jonathan to progress in some general ways. It should be made clear, however, that Jonathan may not change in the ways that others deem to be best. Jonathan is seeking himself. Although that self is affected by certain other people, progress in counseling or therapy will likely reduce the impact these others have on Jonathan. This influence by the thoughts and actions of others will be replaced by increasing trust in his organism so that Jonathan will begin to see his personal ability to control his own life while still considering the needs of others.

As Jonathan starts to trust his relationship with the counselor or therapist, he becomes more free to talk of difficult issues and recognizes that this person will still think well of him, no matter how inappropriate certain aspects of his feelings, thoughts, and actions appear to be. These issues begin appearing in a light that is different from what Jonathan had envisioned previously. Generally, the new view offers problems in a manageable form that is not nearly as terrible or insurmountable as Jonathan had perceived. Excitement about finding new ways to see the world will likely be followed by struggles to understand his new perceptions and how he will need to relate to them differently.

Jonathan will soon find a need to explore his new ways of viewing, feeling, and acting in the world outside of counseling or therapy. He will want to know how his children, family, boss, and others will respond if he chooses to act differently. Such issues will be explored in the therapeutic relationship before trying them on others. Jonathan will want to examine both the good and bad results after they have been tried in real life. The new ideas, observations, and attempted behaviors in each situation will expand Jonathan's view of the world and likely bring him back to the counselor or therapist for help in integrating the newfound information.

There will be pleasures, fears, successes, and disappointments in Jonathan's development, just as in everyone's. But he will come to recognize that there are important lessons in each experience and that everything learned increases his confidence in his ability to direct himself and correct mistakes. Eventually, he may learn to have enough confidence in his own immediate reactions to use a productive combination of his own ideas and those of others to develop positive outcomes. He will also recognize that, even when things do not work out as planned, he is effective enough as a human being to overcome mistakes.

Gestalt Theory

Melinda Haley
Portland State University

Conrad Sieber
Forest Grove School District

Mary Finn Maples
University of Nevada, Reno

Background

Although Fritz Perls is credited with being the foremost practitioner of Gestalt counseling and psychotherapy, his method was influenced by the Gestalt psychologists who preceded him. Max Wertheimer, Wolfgang Kohler, and Kurt Koffka of the "Berlin school" initiated the Gestalt movement in the United States when they fled the rise of Nazism in Germany (Litt, 2000; Murray & Farahmand, 1998; Rock & Palmer, 1990). Perls' biographer, Martin Shephard (1975), wrote that "the traditional Gestalt psychologists claim [Perls]" (p.198), but Perls stated that "the academic Gestaltists, of course, never accepted me . . . I certainly was not a pure Gestaltist" (1969a, p. 62). The Austrian philosopher Christian von Ehrenfels may be credited with the initial use of the term *gestalt,* which appeared in his essay "On Gestalt Qualities" in 1890. This publication ignited a current of thought that created a strong position in both philosophy and psychology during the first half of the 20th century. Yet it was the psychologists of the Berlin school who laid the psychological groundwork for Perls' application of Gestaltism in counseling and psychotherapy.

Perls himself first used the term **Gestalt therapy** in his 1947 text *Ego, Hunger, and Aggression.* Readers of this early work had mixed reactions. Yontef (1981) stated that while the roots for Gestalt therapy were established in Gestalt psychology, there were doubts as to whether "the Gestalt therapy system has much to do with Gestalt psychology" (p. 1). Henle (1978) concluded that "the two approaches, Gestalt psychology and Gestalt therapy," have "nothing in common" (p. 26), and Cadwallader (1984) stated that Gestalt therapy has "rather little to do with Gestalt psychology" (p. 192).

Contemporary readers have also made the observation that it is often difficult to separate Gestalt therapy from its best known advocate, Fritz Perls. Shane (1999b) states it bluntly: "Perls's application of Gestalt therapy revolved around his own personal style and interpretation of Gestalt therapy, which emphasized his own personal prejudices, technical preferences, and intellectual hobbyhorses" (p. 49). Yet Emerson and Smith (1974) wrote that "no one can understand Gestalt therapy well without an adequate background in Gestalt psychology" (p. 8). Emerson and Smith (1974), Kogan (1976), and Yontef (1981) believe that Perls moved from psychoanalysis to Gestalt therapy in 1947, and Perls confirmed this in *Ego, Hunger, and Aggression.*

Frederick (Fritz) Perls

Friedrich Saloman Perls was born in 1893, the middle child and only son of middle-class Jewish parents in Berlin. He later anglicized his name, becoming *Frederick,* although most people called him "Fritz" (Thompson & Rudolph, 2000). His childhood experiences were much like those of most American children who became adults in the middle of the 20th century. He recalled that his childhood was fairly happy, although he related more positively to his younger sister than his older, and at times his relationship with his father was tempestuous (Shane, 1999a; Thompson & Rudolph, 2000). He did well in primary school, but by the seventh grade his spirit of rebellion began to assert itself and ultimately he got himself expelled from grade school (Corey, 2001; Shane, 1999a; Thompson & Rudolph, 2000). Nevertheless, he persevered and tolerated the mediocrity of those years, ultimately receiving a medical degree in 1920 after a brief stint as a medical corpsman during World War I—He found his war experience brutal in military Authoritarianism and racial prejudice. These experiences influenced his humanitarianism but also left him with a deep cynicism about human nature (Seligman, 2001; Shepard, 1975).

His early training in psychoanalysis took place in Austria and Germany, and he became associated with neurologist Kurt Goldstein. While working as Goldstein's assistant at Frankfurt am Main's Institute for Brain Injured Soldiers in 1926, Perls became interested in the transforming of Gestalt psychology into Gestalt therapy (McBride, 1998; Perls, 1969b; Shane, 1999b). Goldstein's work significantly affected Perls' later counseling and psychotherapy interventions (Wheeler, 1991). However, Perls' early works reveal that he had disagreements with principles of psychoanalytic, behavioral, and structural theories.

Perls' ability to think for himself and create his own theories may have been rooted in his nature: he was always a free spirit (Perls, 1969b). Henle (1978) believes that Perls viewed most of his differences with Gestalt psychology as insurmountable because he regarded himself as an organismic psychologist, or a viewer of humankind in its holistic sense. According to Henle (1978), the difference between Gestalt psychology and Gestalt therapy is that the former is concerned with perception and cognition while the latter focuses on personality, psychopathology, and psychotherapy. Perls particularly admired the work of Kurt Lewin because of his holistic approach to human nature (Perls, 1969b).

When Hitler came to power, Perls and his new wife, Lore, relocated to Johannesburg, South Africa, and he shed the Freudian psychoanalytic influence. They were, in fact, the first psychologists in South Africa (Segal, 1997; Shane 1999a). In 1946, he immigrated to the United States, where he published *Gestalt Therapy: Excitement and Growth in the Human Personality* in 1951. Following the favorable reception of this text, he established several Gestalt Institutes throughout the country, the first in New York in 1952. His work at the Esalen Institute in California established him as a prominent practitioner of Gestalt counseling and psychotherapy.

It is important to consider the historical period in which a particular theorist lived and worked in order to better understand and appreciate that person's theory or model of counseling and psychotherapy. The language of the time and the way people lived and loved, worked and played are crucial to understanding theorists and practitioners decades later. Consider Perls' statement in *Gestalt Therapy Verbatim* (1969a): "It took us a long time to debunk the whole Freudian crap. We are entering the phase of the quacks and the con-men who think if you get some breakthrough, you are cured" (1969a, p. 1). In fact, Perls had a negative experience with Freud in 1936 when the two engaged in a brief conversation at a convention in Vienna. Perls felt humiliated by Freud, which may have triggered a sensitivity to the humiliating experiences he had with his father during childhood. Thus, this interchange may have contributed to Perls' desire to prove Freud's theories obsolete (Perls, 1969a). Therefore, Perls' recognized the need to change from the historical-archeological Freudian viewpoint to the existential-experiential form of counseling and therapy currently seen in Gestalt therapy (Litt, 2000).

Having been influenced by the works of Wertheimer, Koffka, and Kohler, Perls made his most memorable representations, translations, extensions, and practice during a time of unrest, questioning authority, the rejection of traditional customs, and the opening of the free spirit during the decade of the 1960s. Perls felt that those years when he was still strengthening his theory helped him make this discovery: "The meaning of life is that it is to be lived; and it is not to be traded and conceptualized and squeezed into a pattern of systems. We realize that manipulation and control are not the ultimate joy of life" (1969a, p. 3). But we are left to ponder whether he was merely reflecting the growing freedom of the human spirit at that time, or advancing it.

Laura Perls

Fritz Perls' work was carried on after his death in 1970 by his wife, Laura Perls. It has become increasingly clear since her own death in 1990 that Lore (Laura) Posner Perls (b. 1905) contributed significantly to Gestalt counseling and psychotherapy, having studied with Max Wertheimer and gaining recognition as a Gestalt psychologist in her own right (McBride, 1998; Rosenblatt, 1991; Serlin & Shane, 1999). She continued her work long after her husband's death, becoming an influential force in Gestalt therapy and the training of Gestalt therapists until her own death.

Laura Perls has always maintained that she contributed two chapters to Perls' book, *Ego, Hunger and Aggression* (Shane, 1999b). In a 1977 interview, published in *The Gestalt Journal*, Laura stated explicitly that she had written "the chapter on the dummy complex and the one on insomnia" (Rosenfeld, 1978/1982, p. 13). She also stated that she and Fritz recognized the existential nature of Gestalt therapy, but the depreciatory connotations of the time linked existentialism with Sartre and the nihilistic approach, so this connection was downplayed by Perls (Ford, & Urban, 1998; Rosenfeld, 1978/1982).

Paul Goodman

Another person whose participation in the development of Gestalt therapy has recently come to the fore is Paul Goodman. Goodman, upon meeting Perls in 1949, was already an accomplished classical scholar, wrote fiction and political criticism, and had been deeply influenced by his studies of Freud, Rank, and Reich (Shane, 1999a). It was a fortuitous meeting, as Fritz Perls was looking for a man learned in these areas to help him edit what came to be known as *Gestalt Therapy: Excitement and Growth in the Human Personality.*

While Perls received recognition initially for this work, many scholars have since come to credit Goodman with writing at least half of the manuscript, specifically the half dealing with the theory of Gestalt therapy (Serlin & Shane, 1999; Shane, 1999b). His role is now seen as one of collaboration with Fritz and Laura Perls and his own contribution to development of the theory is acknowledged. While Fritz Perls is still credited as Gestalt therapy's most boisterous and ardent promoter, there are those who now consider Paul Goodman its chief theoretician (Meier & Davis, 2001; Serlin & Shane, 1999; Shane, 1999a; Shane 1999b).

Phenomenology, Existentialism, Field Theory, Dialogue, and Gestalt Therapy

Gestalt therapy was not the only influence that inspired Gestalt psychology. While the roots of Gestalt therapy can most certainly be found in phenomenology and field theory, there exists within it the influential existentialist writings of Soren Kierkegaard, Friedrich Nietzsche, Martin Buber, Paul Tillich, Martin Heidegger, the writings of Aristotle, William James, John Dewey, and Immanuel Kant, the philosophies of Zen Buddhism and Taoism, as well as some basic principles from psychoanalytic theory, humanistic theories, and Reichian body therapy (Oaklander, 1999; Portnoy, 1999; Shane, 1999b; Taylor, 1999; Thompson, 2000). The coagulation of all these perspectives placed the focus on improving clients' awareness of their subjective experience, facilitating their ability to become authentic and make choices that lead to a meaningful life, and setting in motion the natural process of growth that moves toward integration within self, and between self and the environment (Corey, 2001).

Phenomenology   Phenomenology is the study of human experience through attending to the subjective observations of individuals (Hazler, 2001; Warwar & Greenberg, 2000). Inquiry into experience, or observing one's own experience, is inherently a subjective undertaking. The focus of inquiry may be internal (on the self), or external (on the environment), but the observations of the individual are considered to be relevant and meaningful. Phenomenology suggests a conscious awareness of the subject's own experience through self-observation. This contrasts with the empirical objectivist perspective, which views individual subjective experience with suspicion and assumes that it obscures rather than reveals "reality." In Gestalt therapy, what the client subjectively experiences in the present is seen as relevant and important information for improving accurate awareness. Thus, insight is developed through focused awareness and experimentation (O'Leary, Purcell, McSweeney, O'Flyn, O'Sullivan, Keane, & Barry, 1998; Yontef & Simkin, 1989).

Existentialism   Existential thought came to the fore during the 19th century when philosophers in Europe began contemplating the absolutism of such prior concepts as: What is truth and what is fact? And was the "whole" person (Gestalt) more than the sum of the parts? (Hazler, 2001). These ideas challenged the behavioral school of thought that existed in the 19th and early 20th centuries and gave way to an entire new approach in looking at the individual.

Existentialism is concerned with human existence as directly experienced. People seek to find meaning in their experience. They often discover in this process that they live in a context, within a society, that molds and shapes experience based on shared assumptions about "reality"—what is, how the world is, what people should be and do. These constructions of reality may distort one's understanding and experience of self, others, and the larger world. Yontef and Simkin (1989) note that the basis for inauthenticity is self-deception, which is often based on an uncritical acceptance of societal values and norms that construct reality. When one becomes a false self, living in ways that do not have their basis in truth, one feels dread, guilt, and anxiety. Gestalt therapy helps clients become authentic by increasing self-awareness, thereby enabling them to make choices about how they organize their experience to be more truly genuine and meaningful.

Field Theory   The Gestalt therapy perspective relies heavily on **field theory,** which is explored at more length later in this chapter (Corey, 2001; Shane, 1999b; Yontef & Simkin, 1989). Kurt Lewin developed field theory out of the ashes of his experiences in World War I (Shane, 1999b). In contrast to a reductionistic, unilinear, cause-and-effect model, field theory focuses on the whole, in which all the elements found within the field are in relationship to and influence one another. Thus, no individual part operates in isolation from any of the other parts in the field. For example, individuals have a body and a mind that interact to create the whole person. They do not exist in isolation from one another. This approach is descriptive rather than interpretive. The emphasis taken by Gestalt therapy from field theory is in observing, describing, and defining the structure of the field.

Dialogue   The importance of **dialogue** in the counselor or psychotherapist/client relationship has been recognized, and this enhanced recognition is thought to be the most important advance in Gestalt therapy in recent years (Corey, 2001; Warwar & Greenberg, 2000; Yontif, 1998). The main objective to the dialogue component of Gestalt therapy is to facilitate rapport and relationship building with the client. From a phenomenological perspective, the counselor or psychotherapist makes contact with the client and views the client empathically. Empathic exploration of the individual is essential; its purpose is not to collect data, but is instead to learn about the client from his or her unique point of view. In other words, as psychotherapists and counselors, we learn to walk in the client's shoes.

The fundamental theory behind the dialogic approach is that, as individuals, we develop in relationship to other people. When a person is supported through a genuine and trusting relationship, that person can grow in a positive direction and gains a positive sense of self. In contrast, when a person is not supported, he or she often experiences shame and this can thwart the growth of a positive concept of self (Hazler, 2001; Warwar

& Greenberg, 2000). Therefore, empathic understanding through dialogue is seen as an important part of the change process.

Human Nature: A Developmental Perspective

Perhaps one of the most attractive features of Gestalt theory is its attention to the holistic nature of humankind. As in existentialism and phenomenology, genuine knowledge is the expected outcome of what is apparent and evident in the experience of the perceiver (Ford & Urban, 1998). While the traditional Gestalt psychologists remained focused on cognition, perception, and motivation, Gestalt counselors and psychotherapists engage the whole organism (person) and operate from the perspective that human beings have the capacity and strength to grow, to develop, and to become the persons they are meant to be (Hazler, 2001). A basic assumption is that individuals can cope with their life problems, especially if fully aware of what is happening in and around them.

Centered in the present (Kempler, 1973), the person in Gestalt counseling or psychotherapy is always in the process of being what he or she is in the here and now, in the process of becoming the person that he or she *can* be. Further, Perls believed in the ability of persons to change and to be responsible for both their behavior and, inevitably, the directions they take in their lives. A valuable aspect of the Gestaltist's view of human nature is that persons gain more from experiences and involvement in activities than from talk. That is, sharing direct experience of feelings, thoughts, or sensations is more valuable than talking about these experiences.

Perls was seen by his contemporaries as a consummate actor (Shephard, 1975). That is, they viewed him as successful in eliciting behaviors from clients that traditional psychoanalysts, behaviorists, and structuralists may not have been able to elicit. Perls, Hefferline, and Goodman (1951) commented on the psychoanalytic belief that the ego confines itself to perceiving and is otherwise inactive. In contrast, in Gestalt counseling and psychotherapy, they suggest, the client is active, dynamic, and involved in the counseling and psychotherapy process, not just a passive observer (p. 71). Furthermore, Perls (1969a) described his view of human nature by noting that the person or organism always works as a whole: "We *have* not a liver or a heart. We *are* liver and heart and brain and yet, even this is wrong—we are *not* a summation of parts but a *coordination* of the whole. We do not have a body, we are a body, we are somebody" (p. 6).

Major Constructs

Field Theory: Organism and Environment

The scientific paradigm forming the basis of the Gestalt therapy perspective is field theory with a view to the organism-environment as a field of activity (Shane, 1999b; Yontef & Simkin, 1989). In contrast to a reductionistic, unilinear, cause-and-effect model, field theory focuses on the whole, in which all the elements found within the field are in relationship to and influence one another (Thompson & Rudolph, 2000). Field theory is based on the principle of interdependence.

The metaphor of a baseball game helps illuminate this construct. In a baseball game, there is a field defined by boundary lines demarcating the field of play from that which is outside the field of play. All the elements central to play are on the field: players, bats, ball, and bases. All these elements interact to create the game. Just as a pitcher and batter must interact for the game to occur, there must also be a first baseman, shortstop, and outfielders. Even the bases themselves are needed. All are necessary for the whole called a baseball game. For instance, a ball without a bat is meaningless when it comes to having a game. Thus, no individual part operates in isolation from any of the other parts in the field.

Phenomenological Field   The **phenomenological field** is one kind of field, the one that is the focus of Gestalt therapy. This field changes according to the individual's focused awareness. At one moment, the focus may be entirely internal, attending to self and its interrelated parts. During the next moment, the phenomenological field may shift to a focus on the person in relationship to his or her external environment, which is made up of its own constituent and interacting parts. When the focus is internal, the field is represented by parts of the self, which may be broadly defined as mind and body. This includes thoughts, feelings, senses, and actions, all of which are inseparable, just as the person's relationship to the external environment forms a set of interacting elements (Hazler, 2001). For instance, one's family or school/workplace environment involves many other people with whom one relates and whom one influences. Thus, interacting parts of self—such as thought, feeling, and sensing—influence one another and cannot be understood in isolation, just as the person is influenced by and influences his or her environment.

The phenomenological field—that is, the subjective focused experience of the person—is defined by individuals, as they are observers of their own experience both internally and/or externally (Hazler, 2001). For instance, an internal focus on the phenomenological field of the individual reveals the interrelated parts of self—mind, body, thoughts, feelings, and senses. They are interdependent. If the phenomenological field is external—focused, for example, on the person in relationship to the family environment, each family member is recognized as a part of a larger whole. In this field, family members are a part of the whole that is family, and for the family to exist, each part or family member has a relationship to all other family members. It is the interdependence and reciprocal influences of family members on one another that creates the whole family. The family cannot be known by focusing only on one member; the interrelationship of family members to one another must be explored while allowing for the fact that individuals within the family also have differences from one another. Knowing isolated parts of a whole, independent from their influence on one another, does not fully describe the dynamic nature of that whole, whether that is the whole person or the family.

These examples help illustrate another key concept of Gestalt therapy: **holism.** Gestalt therapy is holistic rather than reductionistic; it is concerned with the differentiation of and interrelationship of the parts that make up the whole, rather than focusing on parts in isolation from one another (Shane, 1999b). As the old saying goes, "The whole is greater than the sum of its parts" (McBride, 1998).

Differentiation and Contact   In Gestalt therapy, a healthy individual is one who can differentiate self while also making contact with others. Contact involves the ability to be fully present, in the moment, and available (Corey, 2001; Oaklander, 2000). In fact, life is described as a constant process of contact and separation between the person and those one is in relationship to, such as family members and loved ones, colleagues, and employers. Contact and differentiation, connection and separation define a goal of Gestalt therapy: to help clients become more integrated within themselves and in relationship to others—in other words, helping to create **differentiated unity.**

Differentiated unity for the client as a whole person means awareness of thoughts, feelings, and senses (i.e., taste, smell, hearing, touch, sight)—an integration of mind and body. In the organism/environment field, this means integration of the person into his/her environment. When any of these avenues are blocked, we cannot make contact with others (Oaklander, 2000). Thus, concepts of mind-body integration are not new to Gestalt therapy, which through its foundation in field theory critiques the prevailing medical model paradigm that dichotomizes mind and body as separate entities. When people cannot become differentiated, often what happens is **confluence.** This is the process whereby a person loses sight of himself or herself by incorporating too much of the environment or others into the self (Thompson & Rudolph, 2000).

Boundaries   For survival, the organism—that is, the individual—must make contact with the environment. The function of the individual's boundaries is to simultaneously be firm enough to differentiate self from others, yet open or permeable enough to make contact with others. In this process, the individual assimilates nourishment from the environment and rejects or keeps out that which is not nourishing. For instance, within a family a teenager may have boundaries firm enough to understand that he is unique in certain ways from an admired older brother and, therefore, accept pursuing his own interests, yet flexible enough to accept his brother's love and support. Thus, differentiated contact naturally leads to health and development (Shane, 1999b; Wolfert & Cook, 1999; Yontef & Simkin, 1989).

Boundary disturbances occur when boundaries between self and others are overly rigid, creating isolation, or overly permeable, creating a merger in which differentiation of self is lost to confluence with the other. An example of a boundary disturbance is **retroflection,** an internal split within the self in which elements of the self are rejected as not-self. In this situation, the individual does to self what is normally done to the environment (Corey, 2001; Yontef & Simkin, 1989)—that is, differentiating between nourishing and toxic elements in the environment, assimilating the former and rejecting the latter. The individual in this case disowns parts of self. This undermines health and functioning.

Introjection occurs when material from the environment is taken in without discrimination concerning its nourishing or toxic qualities (Corey, 2001). For instance, children usually introject parental and societal values, not having the maturity to differentiate between beliefs that are and are not congruent with their growth and health. It is often in young adulthood that people begin to recognize the difference between values congruent with their well-being and those introjected from parents and society that create difficulties.

Projection involves taking parts of self and directing them outwards onto others (Corey, 2001). Some people are unaware of disowned parts of themselves and routinely project them onto others. This interferes with self-awareness, coming to terms with these disowned elements of the person, and accepting them. **Deflection** is the avoidance of contact through diversion (Corey, 2001). That is, instead of being direct and genuine in a relationship, the individual may present a disingenuous, false image of himself or herself to others as a way of avoiding contact. However, deflection also occurs when the individual fails to receive from, attend to, or be aware of information coming from the environment. An example would be a situation where an individual pretends to listen to a colleague while his or her thoughts are actually elsewhere. The information from other to self is deflected (Yontef & Simkin, 1989).

Dichotomies and Polarities   In field theory, there is a distinction made between dichotomies and polarities. **Dichotomies** are unnatural splits in which a field is made up of separate, competing, either/or parts instead of integrated elements in relationship to one another that form a whole. For instance, dichotomizing the self into good and bad parts and then attempting to ignore or repress the bad parts is detrimental to growth and health. However, **polarities** are a natural part of fields. Fields are differentiated into polarities—opposite parts that work in tandem or contrast one another to help clarify meaning. Here we are describing a process based on electrical fields, that is, their complementary differentiation into positive and negative poles (Yontef & Simkin, 1989). Health and energy are found through integration, not dichotomization of polarities.

Another way to think of this is to consider the difference between continua and categories. A continuum represents a domain that is connected along a line where differences reside at opposite ends or poles, yet the poles are connected along the continuum. Categories split a domain—for example, separating caring for self and caring for others into dichotomous categories with no connection to one another. The individual develops integration by, for instance, discovering both easily accepted and disowned parts of self. The caring, kind, and nurturing mother comes to recognize and also identify with the more aggressive, assertive side of herself that seeks to get her own needs met. Meeting her own needs can complement her capacity to nurture. Here, caring for others and caring for self lie at two ends of a continuum, with each pole representing the greatest distinction between the two.

When **integration** fails, splits occur. The parts of the person—those elements of mind and body that make him or her what he or she is—are experienced as separate, not integrated. Thus, a mother may dichotomize her capacity to be a caretaker from her ability to care for herself. Yet health is found in integration, where difference is accepted and various parts of the self work together. Thus, the process of healing dichotomies requires increased awareness of the way the client dichotomizes experience, whether the focus of awareness is internal or external dichotomies. Yontef and Simkin (1989) describe this process of healing as integrating into a whole that which is differentiated into natural polarities that complement and/or help define one another.

Foreground and Background   Another principle of Gestalt therapy is that of the **foreground** and **background** in a phenomenological field. The goal, if it can be called this, is a well-formed figure standing in contrast to a broader, less-well-defined background (Seligman, 2001). The figure is in the forefront of the individual's awareness of the phenomenological field at any one time. Thus, for example, the phenomenological field could be defined as the family as background, and the specific relationship between two family members, such as mother and daughter, in the foreground. Problems occur when foreground and background are not well formed and clearly distinct from one another. Continuing the foregoing example, with the mother-daughter relationship in an ambiguous foreground, it is difficult to distinguish that relationship from the background of the family as a whole. In this instance, it is easy to see that attempts to become more aware of and work with this relationship are obscured by the lack of clarity between foreground (the mother-daughter relationship) and the background of the family.

For instance, some families have members so enmeshed with one another that it is difficult to distinguish between each in terms of their thoughts, feelings, beliefs, attitudes, or the nature of member-to-member relationships. The members appear like carbon copies of one another even in terms of maintaining the same feelings and attitudes, and exist in an undifferentiated enmeshed family relationship where, for instance, the marital relationship is difficult to distinguish from parent-child relationships. However, health is found when the foreground is clear enough to be differentiated from background so that the most important current needs and concerns within the field can be properly attended to. Thus, in a healthy person or person-environment field, the figure changes as needed to meet new and ever-changing circumstances. The most important needs/concerns come into the foreground and are distinguishable from the background. For instance, in the preceding family example, once the mother-daughter relationship has been in the foreground and is appropriately defined and tended to, it can recede into the background as another element of the family comes to the foreground, possibly the relationship between the parents themselves. Or, if the phenomenological field is the individual client, awareness of feelings in the present may be in the foreground at one moment, while awareness of current thoughts about betrayal by a loved one may move to the foreground in the next. Here, ill-defined foreground and background would lead to thoughts and feelings that are amorphous and cannot be differentiated from one another. Clients with this difficulty often need the therapist's help in distinguishing between thoughts and feelings so that each may be better understood and the relationship between thought and feeling can be clarified—in other words, how one affects the other.

Yontef and Simkin (1989) state that health defines a situation where awareness accurately represents and brings to the foreground the dominant need of the whole field. Gestalt therapy also abides by the law of **homeostasis**—that is, the organism's tendency to seek balance within itself and between itself and its environment. Thus, if the person needs food for energy, he or she becomes hungry, the need for food comes to the foreground, and the person eats. This returns the body to a state of homeostasis where there is enough food to provide the energy needed for proper functioning.

The Gestalt psychology principle of **pragnanz** is instructive in concluding the examination of the foreground-background dynamic. It states that the field will form itself into the best Gestalt that global conditions will allow. That is, interacting elements in a field, and their structure in relationship to one another, tend to form themselves, creating foreground and background in the best possible way. Thus, there is an innate drive toward health and growth found in nature, of which humans are a part.

Awareness

Awareness is the key to Gestalt therapy. In fact, a major goal of Gestalt therapy is awareness itself (Corey, 2001; McBride, 1998; Oaklander, 1999; Seligman, 2001). Through awareness, the organism/person naturally proceeds toward growth, integration, and differentiated unity, in which the parts of the field are separate from and in contact with one another. Awareness is consciousness of what is, whether that is being in touch with the various parts of self—mind, body, thoughts, feelings, and senses—or consciousness of self in relationship to other elements in the environment, both those that are potentially nourishing as well as those that are toxic. The premise is that the person has the capacity to be aware of his or her own needs and priorities. Persons can accurately know themselves and the environments of which they are a part and make decisions that are congruent with their growth. Awareness, knowing the environment, and being in touch with one's self means that the individual is responsible for self-knowledge, self-acceptance, the ability to make contact, and ultimately to make choices (Hazler, 2001).

Yontef and Simkin (1989) note that some people do not know their own behavior, others live in the present as if there were no past, and "most" live in the future as if it were now. They are commenting on the lack of awareness and consciousness of many people for what is, right now, in the present moment. Awareness sounds like a simple thing, but in Western societies, with all their rush and distraction, awareness can be rare. Awareness requires individuals to make "vigilant" contact with the most important aspects of the organism/environment field using the full support of their sensorimotor, emotional, cognitive, and energy processes (Yontef & Simkin, 1989).

In Gestalt therapy, clients are directed to move from talking about experience to directly experiencing what they are focusing on at any given moment in counseling and therapy. For instance, experiencing and expressing feelings is different as a process from talking about those very same feelings. Thus, Perls differentiated between intellectualizing and/or a tendency of people to talk about their feelings and experiences versus the direct experience and, thus, increased awareness of thoughts, feelings, and senses. Yontef and Simkin (1989) state that aware persons know what they do, how they do it, that alternatives exist, and that they choose to be as they are. This does not mean that the environment, or genetics, or previous learning do not create some constraints on the individual. However, it highlights the importance of differentiating between what is chosen and what is given (Yontef & Simkin, 1989). Often people have more choices and/or are unconsciously making choices that constrict their lives and growth potential. For instance, children do not choose the family they are born into, but once they begin to mature, they do have choices about familial values they do or do not accept as congruent with their emerging sense of self. Similarly, parents do not choose the specific child they give birth to, but they do choose how to parent.

Gestalt counselors and therapists focus in the here and now. Thus, the process of becoming aware is taking place here and now. The process of awareness—owning, choice, responsibility, and contact—leads to natural and spontaneous change. Therefore, clients do not need to be manipulated by the counselor or therapist to make growth-enhancing changes. Instead, the counselor or therapist engages the client in a process of increasing awareness of self, others, and the environment. Through counseling and therapy, clients come to master their own process of awareness, setting in motion their natural tendency to heal and grow (Yontef & Simkin, 1989). Through constructivism, Gestalt psychotherapists and counselors also recognize that the individual is in charge of his or her own reality. The Gestalt therapist tries to help clients recognize if their reality is perceived in organized "wholes" or "gestalts" (Shane, 1999b).

Clearly, if the natural process of growth were going well, a client would be unlikely to come to therapy. Thus, it is helpful to understand the meaning of **impasse.** Typically, clients reach an impasse—that is, become stuck—when they doubt their ability to be self-supporting and have relied too heavily on external support, which is no longer available. According to Yontef and Simkin (1989), clients become stuck when they replace the normal need for internal self-support with overdependence on external support. That is, they get their needs met, not through healthy self-support, but by manipulating others to do what needs to be done for themselves. Clients usually bring this dynamic to the therapy process. They enter therapy with the wish that the counselor or therapist do their work for them. In Gestalt therapy, the counselor or therapist facilitates client awareness, while declining to do the client's work. For instance, Gestalt therapists eschew therapist interpretation of client material—a replacement of client awareness with therapist awareness—in favor of facilitating clients' coming to their own understanding through a process focused in the here and now on the "what and how" of the clients and their concerns. That is, what the client is doing and how the client does it is the focus. In Gestalt therapy, *why* clients do what they do is not important. In fact, focusing on why tends to lead to client rationalizations and defensiveness that distract from, rather than contribute to, the process of growth.

Responsibility

Clients are seen as responsible or response-able. While it can be important to distinguish between true limitations and real alternatives, ultimately the client has the responsibility to choose and value, to create a healthy balance between self and surroundings (Hazler, 2001; Seligman, 2001). On a personal level, the choice is often between organismic and arbitrary regulation—that is, self-determination through awareness and acceptance of one's own values and beliefs versus an arbitrary regulation created by the introjection of another's, often one's parents' and society's—worldview. Therefore, clients need to sort out which values and beliefs are theirs and which have been imposed by others, and whether or not these imposed values are consistent with their own health and growth. For instance, in a society that views women as less capable than men, a female client will need to identify these introjected societal values and choose her own. Her values will hopefully reflect a healthier view of the competence of the members of her gender.

In this process of taking responsibility, the aim of the counselor or therapist is to help the client become more self-regulating instead of acquiescing to arbitrary regulation, and to become more appropriately self-supporting instead of being overly dependent on external support (Ford & Urban, 1998). To accomplish this, the client must address **unfinished business**—those important needs, concerns, and issues that require the client's attention. Through increased conscious awareness, clients also discover disowned parts of self. These disowned parts of self are raised into awareness, considered, and assimilated if congruent with the core of the client's true self, or rejected if alien to the client's deepest sense of self. This process of re-owning and taking responsibility facilitates integration. In this therapy model, both client and counselor or therapist are self-responsible. Counselors and therapists are responsible for the nature of their presence with the client, having both self-knowledge and knowledge of the client. They maintain nondefensiveness, while keeping their awareness and contact processes clear and in tune with the client (Yontef & Simkin, 1989).

Shoulds

Arbitrary regulation creates "shoulds" that can control the client's thoughts, feelings, actions, and relationships. Regulation of human behavior and experience is to a greater or lesser degree organismic, coming from within individuals themselves, or it is "shouldistic," based on arbitrary imposition of what some controlling agent believes it should be (Yontef & Simkin, 1989). Any counselor or therapist who has worked with clients has often seen the strong pull between clients' sense of what they should think, feel, or do and the emerging awareness of what they, in actuality, do think, feel, and/or want to do. It is apparent that Gestalt therapy places a high value on autonomy and self-determination. Although Gestalt therapy maintains a "no should" ethic, there is one exception. The exception is the situation. Perls believed that when clients understand the situation they find themselves in and allow it to shape their actions, then they have begun to learn how to cope with life (Yontef & Simkin, 1989).

I-Thou, What and How, Here and Now

A shorthand of sorts for Gestalt therapy is reflected in the phrase "I-thou, what and how, here and now," which was derived from the philosophical writing of Martin Buber (Oaklander, 1999; Oaklander, 2000; Portnoy, 1999; Yontef & Simkin, 1989). The counselor or therapist and client form an alliance based on self-responsibility and an agreement to strive to be present with one another during their time together. Furthermore, the focus of counseling and therapy is the "what and how" of a client's experience in the present, in the moments that counselor or therapist and client are together (Corey, 2001; Hazler, 2001; McBride, 1998; Seligman, 2001). Client and counselor or therapist explore together through **experiments** that reveal what the client does and how it is done. In this light, *why* is viewed as a diversion, not as illuminating. A here-and-now focus on the what and how of the client's internal and external processes increases awareness, a necessity for growth.

Furthermore, the counselor or therapist is aware of the centrality of the client-counselor/therapist relationship and tends to it by being present, respectful of the client's capacity to heal and grow, and willing to be an authentic person in the therapeutic relationship (McBride, 1998). The client-counselor/therapist relationship is viewed as horizontal, not vertical. Thus the two parties seek equality in relation to one another (Oaklander, 2000). In this process, the counselor or therapist may choose, when appropriate, to share his or her own experience in the moment as it helps to facilitate the client's awareness. Yontef and Simkin (1989) state that counselor or therapist and client speak the same language of present-centeredness, emphasizing the direct experience of both participants, which helps counselor or therapist and client to show their full presence to one another. In this process, the counselor or therapist may share observations of the client that, for whatever reason, are not directly accessible to the client's awareness. Thus, the client shares awareness of what is experienced internally while this process is observed externally by the counselor or therapist.

Direct experience is the tool used to expand awareness, while the focus on the client's present experience is made deeper and broader as counseling or therapy unfolds. Awareness is viewed as occurring now; it takes place now, although prior events can be the object of present awareness. While the event took place in the past, the focus is on the awareness of it that is taking place in the now, in this moment. Therefore, the present is understood as an ever-moving transition between past and future (Yontef & Simkin, 1989).

Applications

In recent years, the application of Gestalt counseling and psychotherapy has extended beyond the realm of individual and group therapy into the field of business—specifically, organizational development and team building. In the following section, several applications from business consulting will be highlighted in addition to the practice of Gestalt psychotherapy.

Overview

This section will be concerned with the goals of counseling and psychotherapy, the desired outcomes of Gestalt counseling or therapy, the process of change that leads to client growth, and the specific strategies used in the change process.

Goals of Counseling and Psychotherapy

According to Tillett (1991), "As creativity and spontaneity are central to Gestalt, and as there is intrinsic antipathy towards the concept of therapy as technique, it can be difficult to reach an acceptable definition of Gestalt therapy" (p. 290). This view is shared by many respected practitioners (Clarkson & Mackeron, 1993; Dryden, 1984; Yontef, 1981). However, practice may be illuminated by examining the goals of Gestalt therapy. According to Tillett (1991), they include the following.

- Development and expansion of both physical and emotional awareness are emphasized. Intellectual insight and interpretation are limited.
- The relationship between client and therapist is existential and is central to the counseling or psychotherapy process.
- Conversations between client and counselor or psychotherapist are useful only to the extent that they support enactment and experimentation.
- Change should occur as the result of heightened awareness of the interactional process between client and counselor/psychotherapist or by the activity and experimentation within the counseling or psychotherapy process (p. 291).

Yontef (1995) suggests that Gestaltists are not concerned with a "preset end goal" (p. 273). However, they do recommend, as most Gestalt therapists would, the particular goal of phenomenological exploration, rather than reconditioning of behavior or interpretation of the unconscious. This goal is valuable in that it places "ownership and responsibility" (Segal, 1997, p. 332) directly on the client and facilitates the client's engaging in an inherently natural process of growth.

Creative and spontaneous intervention is the method of the experienced counselor or psychotherapist. The major goal of Gestalt counseling or psychotherapy toward which interventions aim is autonomy and growth of the client through increased awareness. According to Yontef (1995), this can be "microawareness"—awareness of a particular content area—and "awareness of the awareness process" (p. 275). Through heightened awareness, clients can know what they are choosing to do and can ultimately accept responsibility for these actions, as well as discover available choices and alternatives they may not have recognized due to limited self-awareness. How the counselor or psychotherapist intervenes with the client to bring about this awareness is discussed in the next section.

To help facilitate client awareness and growth, the practitioner does the following.

- He or she identifies themes or presenting problems that are central to the client's self-organization.
- He or she conceptualizes the issues and concerns of the client that will guide the sequence, timing, and methods of the counseling or psychotherapy process.
- He or she establishes and maintains a safe and professional environment.
- He or she provides an atmosphere that invites contact between client and counselor or therapist and encourages interaction.

The Process of Change

> *Reality is nothing but*
> *The sum of all awareness*
> *As you experience here and now.* (Perls, 1969a, p. 30)

While this statement may appear overly simplistic, it is Perls' dismissal of the mind-body dichotomy in favor of holism, and it presents a challenge to the student of Gestalt counseling and psychotherapy (1969a). Understanding the process of change from a Gestalt perspective calls for an appreciation of Perls' goal for the process: "The Gestalt approach attempts to understand the existence of any event through the way it comes about, which is to understand becoming by the how and not the why; through the all-pervasive gestalt formation; through the tension of the unfinished situation (business)" (Perls, 1966, p. 361).

One of the major differences between the process of change in Gestalt therapy and Freudian psychoanalysis, for example, is that instead of being reductionistic and deterministic, as the Freudians were, the Gestalt therapist views the client as a whole person in the context of family, school, and work relationships, and as having an innate capacity for growth (Hazler, 2001). The methods of recognition, consideration, and working within are unique to Gestalt practitioners. Thus, "there are specific skills, techniques and knowledge that should not be overlooked by the Gestalt counselor" (Shepherd, 1975, p. 196). Another aspect of the process of change in the Gestalt approach is the excitement that is generated when the client contacts something new, leading to the creation of a new Gestalt or a new experience. In a tape recorded by Swanson, the client's excitement was demonstrated: "It's all so simple—all I have to do is to say what I really am feeling, be honest about it, and be willing to be responsible for the results" (Swanson, 1984).

Specifically, the process of change in Gestalt counseling and psychotherapy consists of the identification and working through of a variety of blocks or interferences that prevent the client from achieving a balance (Wallen, 1970). Perls (1969a) described clients who block: (1) those who cannot maintain eye contact, who are unaware of their own movements; (2) those who cannot openly express their needs; and (3) those who use repression, examples of which are insomnia and boredom (p. 72).

According to Levitsky and Perls (1970), the process of change, which is aimed at helping clients become more aware of themselves in the here and now, involves several precepts, including the following.

1. *A continuum of awareness.* Clients focus constantly on the *how, what,* and *where* in the body, in contrast to the *why*.
2. *Statements rather than questions.* Many theorists and practitioners have found the establishment of response-ability to be more helpful and respectful than expecting answers to questions (Gazda, 1986).
3. *Use of the first-person pronoun "I" rather than "it" or "they."* If a client says that people feel "thus and so," the counselor or therapist asks the client to restate this sentence using "I." Then the client owns his or her feelings instead of distancing himself or herself from them by saying "I feel thus and so."
4. *The contact issue of addressing someone directly.* Clients are helped to express themselves, their feelings, thoughts, needs, and concerns, as they occur in the moment directly to the counselor or therapist. Talking about and/or "beating around the bush" are discouraged.

The process of change in Gestalt counseling and psychotherapy involves experience and activity. Yontef (1981) believes that all Gestalt techniques are a means of experimentation. He further states that experimentation in the change process can be used to study any phenomenon that the client has experienced. According to Gestalt therapy as postulated by Perls, as clients change and grow, they move through five layers of neurosis (Corey, 2001; McBride, 1998; Perls, 1969a).

1. *The cliché layer:* one of noncontact with others; the "Hello, how are you?" "Fine, how are you?" routine. Also includes acting or appearing to be what you are not (Thompson & Rudolph, 2000).
2. *The phony layer:* the role-playing layer; the boss, the victim, the good boy/bad girl layers; the superficial and pretend layers; Perls believed that people devote much of their active lives to this game-playing layer.
3. *The impasse layer:* the place between dependence on outside support (parents, for example) and the ability to be self-supportive; an avoidance of autonomy. People often become stuck while at the same time have become aware that they do not know a better way of coping with their fears and dislikes (Thompson & Rudolph, 2000).
4. *The implosive layer:* all the previous roles in the process are exposed, stripped, and seen for what they are: roles. This layer involves "pulling oneself together, contracting, compressing, and imploding" (Perls, 1969a, p. 60).
5. *The exploding layer:* tremendous energy is released at this stage. The "death layer comes to life and this explosion is the link-up with the authentic person who is capable of experiencing and expressing his emotions" (Dye & Hackney, 1975, p. 89).

This complete process, particularly from impasse to explosion, is often difficult for the client to comprehend. Yet most people have at one time or another reached that soul-searching depth that leads to getting in touch with values and self-perceptions that form the core of existence. The process, according to Dye and Hackney (1975), is best understood "only after it has been experienced" (p. 40).

Finally, the process of change in Gestalt counseling and psychotherapy contains a crucial feature that is both a valuable asset and a critical handicap: its open-endedness. Gestalt counselors and psychotherapists rarely use techniques or tools that can be quantified from a "proof of theory" perspective. However, this open-endedness is the very quality that encourages creativity, inventiveness, response-ability, and spontaneous change and growth by the client.

As Gestalt therapy continues to evolve, an emphasis has been placed more heavily on a dialogic approach as opposed to the traditional use of experimentation. This is not to say that the Gestalt counselor or psychotherapist has forgone tried and true experiments to facilitate change, but that it has been recognized that the contact between client and counselor/psychotherapist in the therapeutic relationship is a key process to change. Therefore, this dialogic approach is used more today than it has been used traditionally in the past when the experiments took center stage (Warwar & Greenberg, 2000).

Intervention Strategies

Specific interventions are the concrete behaviors of experimentation that emerge from the cooperation that exists between the client and the practitioner. They are labeled *experiments* because they are procedures aimed at discovery, rather than exercises (in the traditional sense). They are not designed to control or initiate behavior change. Instead, experiments are conducted through counselor or therapist recommendations or suggestions for focusing awareness that clients can use to heighten intensity, power, flexibility, and creativity. The action in the experiment is seen as the natural completion of awareness (Wolfert & Cook, 1999).

Yontef (1995) provides the following examples of experiments.

- To clarify and sharpen what the client is already aware of and to make new linkages between elements already in awareness.
- To bring into focal awareness that which was previously known only peripherally.
- To bring into awareness that which is needed but systematically kept out of awareness.
- To bring into awareness the system of control, especially the mechanism of preventing thoughts or feelings from coming into focal awareness (p. 280).

Miriam Polster (1987) sees experiments as a way of bringing out internal conflicts by making the struggle an actual process. She aims at facilitating a client's ability to work through the stuck points in his or her life. The strategies of experimentation can take many forms, according to Polster, such as imagining a threatening encounter, setting up dialogue with a significant other, dramatizing the memory of a painful event, and reliving a particularly profound past experience in the present through role-playing, exaggerated gestures, posture, body language, or other signs of internal expression.

Most theories value the personhood of the counselor or psychotherapist. In Gestalt counseling and psychotherapy, however, practitioners are particularly important as persons because of the active nature of the helping relationship. The following views about counseling and psychotherapy are particularly appropriate for Gestalt practitioners. "The most important element in counseling is the personhood of the counselor or psychotherapist. The most powerful impact on the client may be that of observing what the counselor is and does" (Gilliland, James, & Bowman, 1994, p. 7). Zinker (1978) focuses on the importance of the counselor or psychotherapist as a creative agent of change who must be both caring and compassionate as a human being. Polster and Polster (1973) see the "therapist as his own instrument" (p. 19). Further, Yontef and Simkin (1989) stress that *who* the counselor or psychotherapist is as a person is more important than *what* he or she is doing to or with the client.

Perls believed that counseling and psychotherapy were means of enriching life (Dye & Hackney, 1975). From his perspective, it is clear that "well people can get better" (Bates, Johnson, & Blaker, 1982). Intervention strategies suggested in this section are for clients who are fundamentally well but who need assistance in "making it" in a complex world (Maples, 1996). The main purpose, then, of intervention with persons who are seeking counseling or psychotherapy is to "simply sit down and start living" (Enright, 1970, p. 112). According to Dye and Hackney (1975), the aim of Gestalt counseling and psychotherapy is to take advantage of all dimensions of humanness by "achieving an integration of the thinking, feeling and sensing processes. The goal is to enable *full experiencing* rather than merely a cognitive understanding of certain elements" (p. 44).

Given the goals of completeness, wholeness, integration, and fulfillment of the essentially healthy but needy individual (in the sense of an incomplete Gestalt), the following intervention strategies may be used (see Table 8.1). We would like the student to have the opportunity to learn about as many Gestalt experiments as is feasibly possible. Unfortunately, the restrictions upon this chapter cannot allow for an in-depth discussion on all the Gestalt experiments available to the practitioner. Therefore, we have provided a comprehensive chart that provides details—albeit brief ones—on several of these experiments.

Table 8.1
Intervention Strategies

Experiment	Purpose	Technique
Locating Feelings	To encourage the client to directly experience sensations in the body that are connected to his or her current feelings.	Instead of asking the client, "What are you feeling?" the therapist tells the client, "Show me where you are feeling this anxiety, apprehension, or nervousness."
Confrontation and Enactment	The client confronts old behaviors, feelings, or expressions by acting out the various parts. This confrontation of self and then the enactment of disowned thoughts, feelings, sensations, or actions allows the client to discover and then re-own neglected parts of the self.	The client is told to "be your hand," "be your sorrow," "be your hatred." This forces the client to own what has been disowned. By identifying with all his or her "parts," the client can become what he or she truly "is," and be able to take responsibility for the self.

Empty Chair or Two-Chair Strategy; Also Called the "Hot Seat"	This is an extension of the confrontation and enactment intervention. This allows the client to become cognizant of how his or her behavior may be affecting others and to gain insight into all the pieces of the problem or issue. It helps the client to achieve clarity.	The client is asked to play one or more roles in addition to his or her own self. The client speaks the part of each person connected to the problem by moving back and forth between the chairs. This technique can also be used for issues that are internal within the client by having the client move back and forth among opposing forces and play out all the roles pertinent to the internal conflict. For example, in a conflict making a decision the client can role-play both the "pro" and "con" sides of the decision-making conflict.
Dream Work	To help the client in the present to understand what may be going on in the here and now. Because images, fantasies, and dreams are the projections of the person, dreams can be seen as the metaphoric expressions of the content and can reveal certain aspects of the person. The dream is not interpreted or symbolized in Gestalt therapy. The dream is simply reenacted to bring awareness to the client regarding the different parts of the self.	This technique asks the client to reenact the dream in the present and to play out the parts of the dream as if it were happening in the here and now. The client is told to animate the dream and give voice to all of the people and parts. This allows the counselor or therapist to help the client come into contact with, own, and accept responsibility for parts of the self that may not be well known or accepted, as every part of the dream represents some aspect of the self.
Making the Rounds	This is a group therapy technique whereby a group member makes some form of contact with other group members or practices a new way of being with each group member.	The client is asked to engage each member of the group. For example, this engagement may be soliciting feedback from each member, or making a statement to each member.
Unfinished Business	To resolve the unresolved feelings that have been left over from interpersonal relationships, most notably feelings of worry, resentment, grief, guilt, or rage. This exercise is designed to bring incomplete gestalts to closure.	The counselor or therapist helps the client to recognize his or her "stuck" points. The emphasis is upon helping the client recognize and accept what "is" rather than what "could be."
Rehearsal	Helps the client to bring clarity out of confusion and enables the client to practice change. This experiment seeks to break the client from the habit of playing the prescribed role(s) he or she continues to play within society.	The client is asked to rehearse new sentences or actions that are different from his or her status quo.

(*continued*)

Exaggeration	The client is asked to exaggerate some aspect of feeling or expressive act (e.g., a gesture, posture, voice inflection, or verbal statement). This intensifies the client's awareness of feelings behind the gesture or expression and eliminates his or her ability to minimize. It also enables clients to become aware of subtle signals and cues they are sending through their body language.	The client is asked to exaggerate repetitively some element of his or her being, which includes, but is not limited to, a motion or a speech pattern. By using exaggeration, feelings that the client has but has not been aware of can become more apparent and the focus of attention. The client gains awareness of inner meaning of his or her experiences.
Minimization	This technique eliminates the client's ability to minimize self-expression such as with the conjunction "but," as in "I would like to do this, but" or "I am a good person, but" and it prevents the client from disqualifying or taking away validity by adding ambiguity.	An example of minimization is when the counselor or therapist removes the client's use of the word *but* from his or her expressions by changing it to the word *and*. As in, "I am a good person, but …" to "I am a good person, and…" This removes the ambiguity, which allows the client to be noncommittal.
Reversal	To help the client bring out polarities that exist within the self, such as "good girl" and "bad girl," the "caring person" and the "selfish person," "the puritanical person" and the "sexual person," "top-dog and "under-dog," and so on. The client is able to directly address parts of the self that have caused anxiety and, therefore, have been repressed.	The client is asked to reverse a statement or a way of being. If the client says, "I hate myself," he or she will reverse that statement to "I love myself." If the client were shy and inhibited, he or she would be asked to play the part of a gregarious exhibitionist. The truthfulness of this polarity is then explored for relevance, as overt behavior often represents latent impulses.
Exposing the Obvious	To bring out into the open the deep structures and processes going on within the client of which the client may be unaware.	The counselor or therapist pays close attention to the client in the here and now and exposes aspects of the client of which the client may be unaware. For example, "Are you aware that you are clenching and unclenching your hands?"
Explicitation or Translation	The client gives voice to a nonverbal expression—a bodily movement, visual image, physical symptom, and so on, which helps him or her to turn the explicit content into implicit reality. This enables the client to experience internally what has only been looked at externally.	The client is asked to verbalize or make explicit something affecting him or her. Example, "If your tears could talk, what would they say?" "If your body spoke words, what would they be?" "If the person who molested you as a child could really tell you his/her feelings, what would he or she say to you?"

Retroflection; Also Known as "Playing the Projection"

To help a client redirect his or her actions, thoughts, or energy, and regain lost power, energy, and self-support, by determining those aspects of self that have been projected onto others and then facilitate bringing those back to the self. This enables the client to release his or her inhibitions, stop holding back impulses and choking off behavior, and stop projecting unwanted parts or disowned attributes of the self onto others.

The counselor or therapist has the client redirect to himself or herself what he or she has previously directed outward toward others. This splits the person into two, the giver and the receiver. When projecting, a person places onto someone else the traits, feelings, motives, and so on, that he or she does not want to face within himself or herself. When a client makes a statement such as "I don't trust you," the projection is retroflected or "played with" and the client is asked to act out the role of the untrustworthy person.

Let the Little Child Talk

To enable the counselor or therapist to talk to the client's "inner child." As part of the personality is formed in childhood, many aspects of that child are still found within the adult and influence the "adult" in all of us.

The counselor or therapist begins by asking the client's permission to speak to his or her inner child. The client is then encouraged to "be a child" and express feelings, thoughts and behaviors that have been repressed by adulthood. This allows the "adult" to listen to the opinions and feelings of the child and let go of restraints and allow the self to be nurtured.

Say It Again; Also Called "The Repetition Game"

To disrupt a patterned habit of expression and to call attention to ways of perceiving. This technique disables the client's ability to get emotional distance from sensitive feelings by rote expression. This technique makes the client stop to experience the full impact of words and feelings.

The counselor or therapist instructs the client to keep repeating a sentence over and over again. For example, a client says, "Nobody likes me." Through repetition, other messages come to the forefront. The end result is that the client may become aware that what he or she was really trying to express is that he or she has never felt loved.

I Take Responsibility For…

This is to help clients accept and recognize their feelings and actions, and take responsibility for them instead of projecting them onto others.

The counselor or therapist facilitates this by making the statement, "I take responsibility for…" and then asks the client to fill in the blank. Typically, the client will make a statement such as, "I am uncomfortable in social situations and *I take responsibility for* my own feelings of dis-ease."

"I Have a Secret."

To explore feelings of guilt and shame and identify what attachments the client holds that keep him or her from resolving this conflict.

A group therapy technique. Group members are encouraged to think of a personal dark secret (but not disclose it to the group) and then imagine (project) how others would react to this secret if it were known.

(continued)

Contact and Withdrawal	Enables the client to understand the polar nature of existence and that it is okay for these polarities to exist. This experiment helps the client to understand it is okay to withdraw from situations in order to preserve our attention. For example, one must rest to have energy. This is a polarity, just as one must periodically withdraw from others in order to maintain closeness. Just as resting enhances energy, so, too, does temporary withdrawal enhance closeness.	The client is told that when he or she feels like withdrawing from a situation, he or she should close his or her eyes and fantasize about a place where he or she feels secure and safe. When the client feels this safety and security, the client then should open his or her eyes, having rested and enhanced energy, continue on, and reestablish contact.
Can You Stay with This Feeling?	Used to keep clients from running away from uncomfortable feelings or glossing them over without examination. It prevents the client from avoiding.	When the client expresses a feeling, mood, or state of mind that is unpleasant or uncomfortable and that he or she tries to discount, dispel, or minimize, the client is then asked to elaborate on the "what" and "how" of his or her feelings.

Clients with Mental Disorders

The practice of Gestalt therapy in today's managed-care world can be difficult at times. It should be reiterated here that Gestalt therapy is existential and phenomenological, and therefore the focus is not on facilitating behavioral changes within the client, but is on helping the client to develop insight and interpersonal awareness. As a result of this insight and awareness, the client can achieve lifestyle changes. Gestalt therapy is also holistic; it does not break a person down into separate "pieces" or variables, and, therefore, it is difficult to "classify" clients in the same manner as is required by the *Diagnostic and Statistical Manual* (DSM-IV) (Wolfert & Cook, 1999). Gestaltists do not believe in disease, but rather in dis-ease, and to suggest that disorders are of the mind is inimical to the Gestalt approach, as Gestaltists believe disorders are holistic and organismic. It should also be noted that, within a managed-care setting, it is difficult for administrators to accept the types of "treatment goals" set in Gestalt therapy because insight is neither concrete nor measurable—two criteria for treatment planning within the managed-care setting (Haley & Carrier, 2002; Thompson & Rudolph, 2000).

All of this makes it difficult to have a discussion regarding the uses of Gestalt therapy for clients with mental disorders in the traditional sense within a mental health pathology parameter. Imes (1998) differentiates the definition of psychopathology and explains it from a Gestaltist point of view. Gestalt theory relates the development of pathology to the habitual self-interruption along the contact/withdrawal continuum. Contact/withdrawal is a concept that explains our interactions with others. We make contact with others from the outside boundary of our selves. When a person has a bad experience or experiences making contact with others, then he or she begins to withdraw in order to protect the self (Oaklander,

1999). This self-protection prevents appropriate interaction with others, and therefore interactions that could be classified as pathological result instead.

As a result of this hindered progress along the contact-withdrawal cycle, our needs are not met and we become inhibited in our awareness and expression. As a consequence, we begin to internalize to meet our needs satisfaction (Mandelbaum, 1998). Part of the process of this internalization is that we begin to introject that which we cannot get from ourselves and we internalize messages given to us by others that we begin to see as "truth." Believing we are bad encourages our fear of abandonment by others, and we then begin to block our awareness, put up defenses, and retroflect (turn back upon the self) to prevent expressing our wants or needs and to keep others from leaving us. This is the Gestalt theory of pathology.

Conversely, normal, healthy behavior occurs when people act and react as total organisms—unfragmented, self-regulating, and able to converse along the contact/withdrawal continuum by not self-interrupting (Imes, 1998; Thompson & Rudolph, 2000). The healthy person concentrates on one need (the figure) at any present time, delegating other needs to the background. When the need is met, the gestalt closes and is completed, and no business is left unfinished. When the need is unmet, the gestalt remains open and the person accumulates unfinished business.

Research claims that Gestalt therapy works best for overly socialized, restrained, and constricted individuals (Thompson & Rudolph, 2000). After having defined the above, and stated that Gestalt therapy does not categorize clients upon the DSM criteria, it can also be said that Gestalt therapy has not been limited by the above constraints. In fact, Gestalt therapy has been adapted to be used for a variety of modalities and issues. It has been used in art therapy (Manns, 1998; Rhyne, 1970), play therapy (Oaklander, 1999/2000), couples therapy (Hazler, 2001; Schwartz, 2000; Shane, 1999b; Zinker & Cardoso-Zinker, 2001), group therapy (Oaklander, 1999), crisis counseling (O'Connell, 1970), and career counseling (Martz, 2001), and has been foundational in many of the touch therapies (Zimmer & Dunning, 1998).

Gestalt therapy has been used for a variety of issues, including but not limited to, alcoholism (Carlock, Glaus, & Shaw, 1992; Ramey, 1998; Shane, 1999b), phobias (Imes, 1998), depression (Furnham, Pereira, & Rawles, 2001), sexual abuse (Imes, 1998; Mandelbaum, 1998), psychosomatic complaints (Wolfert & Cook, 1999), sexual dysfunction and sexuality (Kleinplatz, 1998; Melnick, 2000), body image (Imes, 1998; Kepner, 2001), issues with self-esteem (Shub, 2000), grief and mourning (Oaklander, 2000; Sabar, 2000), developmental issues (Wolfert & Cook, 1999), terminal illness (Baker, 2001), geriatric issues (O'Leary & Nieuwstraten, 1999), and with special populations such as those who have been institutionalized (e.g., long-term hospitalization and hardcore criminals) (Wolfert & Cook, 1999). Gestalt techniques have been used with those individuals suffering from schizophrenia (Furnham, Pereira, & Rawles, 2001; Harris, 1992; Shane, 1999b), and personality disorders including borderline personality disorder (Melnick & Nevis, 1992; Polo, 1993; Shane, 1999b).

It should be noted that caution has been mandated for the use of Gestalt experiments. While these experiments may seem simple and easy to apply, many are not suitable for all clients, especially those clients who are emotionally fragile, as most of these techniques are very intense. The same cautions are espoused when counselors work with clients who are severely psychotic (Shepherd, 1970; Thompson & Rudolph, 2000).

The skill of the Gestalt counselor or psychotherapist is at issue when working with these types of clients. Improper methods or the inability to work with the client through the trauma, grief, rage, or other intense emotions brought up by these techniques can leave the client in a very vulnerable position (Thompson & Rudolph, 2000). Individuals with more severe issues or disturbances will need long-term intensive counseling or psychotherapy. While this can be done within the bounds of Gestalt therapy, it must be done with caution and skill. Thompson and Rudolph (2000) advise that when working with clients who are, for example, severely psychotic, paranoid, or schizoid, it is prudent to limit activities to those that strengthen a client's contact with reality. Gestalt therapy may also be contraindicated for some issues and populations. These might include those clients with a problem with impulse control, those who act out, or those who are delinquent. For these individuals, Gestalt therapy may reinforce those behaviors. In addition, Gestalt therapy may not be suited for all cultures because its sometimes confrontational nature can make clients from some non-Western cultures uncomfortable (Seligman, 2001).

Evaluation

Overview

Several unique contributions have been made by the Gestalt counseling and psychotherapy model. One is the emphasis on the client's inherent wholeness and capacity for self-awareness. The work of the counselor or therapist is to help clients use focused awareness of their own to free up energy for health and growth. A second contribution is the application of dialogue in the counseling or psychotherapy relationship. The counseling or psychotherapy dialogue provides contact between the client and the counselor/psychotherapist. Dialogue is used to engage clients, not to manipulate or control them. The goal of the Gestalt therapist is to embody authenticity and responsibility in conversations with the client (Yontef & Simkin, 1989).

A third contribution is the emphasis on the counseling or therapy *process* rather than reliance solely on *techniques*. Beginning practitioners often depend on techniques more than process to help their client. In the application of Gestalt therapy, this creates difficulties because the process of counseling or psychotherapy must accommodate itself to the personalities and experiences of the counselor/psychotherapist and client. This often makes it difficult for the novice counselor or therapist to pinpoint an appropriate technique to apply to a particular problem. In Gestalt therapy, any activity that contributes to clients' awareness of self, others, and their experience of the larger world is seen as useful.

A fourth contribution of Gestalt counseling involves dream work. The confrontation with "unfinished business" through dream work or other interventions allows the practitioner to challenge the client's past in a lively and provocative manner. The purpose of engaging the past is for the client to become aware of and work with concerns, even those from the past, that are a part of present experience and therefore undermine the client's current functioning.

The use of dream work in Gestalt counseling or psychotherapy is often confused with the technique of dream interpretation as practiced by counselors or psychotherapists using other psychotherapy models, such as psychodynamic approaches in which dream content is interpreted by the counselor or therapist. Dream work in Gestalt counseling and psychotherapy is action-oriented. Clients are encouraged to bring specific parts of the dream to life and experience their meaning directly. They participate actively in understanding the dream's meaning while sharing significant aspects of the dream with the counselor or psychotherapist. The aim is to increase awareness of the important themes in their lives.

Finally, in this age of requirements for accountability to those who pay for services, such as third-party payers, the Gestalt approach lends itself well to treating certain diagnoses. According to Seligman (1986), Gestalt therapy is appropriate for treating certain affective disorders, including anxiety, somatoform, and adjustment disorders as well as occupational and interpersonal problems.

Supporting Research

Yontef and Simkin (1989) point out that Gestalt therapies focus on phenomenology, and the subjective experience of the client does not lend itself well to nomothetic psychotherapy outcome studies. However, evaluation of client outcomes in Gestalt therapy is idiographic—that is, assumed to be based on individual experiences unique to the subject of evaluation. Thus, outcome research on Gestalt therapy is sparse. Although individuals can be questioned about their unique experience of growth in Gestalt therapy, these reports do not lend themselves well to empirical research and the summation of findings via statistical analyses of group data (Wolfert & Cook, 1999).

Much has been done to extend Perls' individual approach to group work (Frew, 1984; Gladding, 1995; Staemmler, 1994; Yontef & Simkin, 1989). Applying Gestalt principles to families, Nevis and Harris (1988) highlight and reinforce the three constructs of awareness, contact, and withdrawal. For example, in one videotape, the counselor or psychotherapist demonstrates the pattern she has in mind: how the family arranges itself physically, how they talk to each other, and what theme emerges in the counseling or psychotherapy process. In this case, the theme involves the family members' abilities to provide clean, clear, positive messages of support for each other.

Applications of Gestalt therapy are cited in works by Alexander and Harman (1988) and Enns (1987). Alexander and Harman used Gestalt therapy as a means of dealing with the surviving classmates of a student who committed suicide. Through the task process of enhancing students' awareness of their feelings, of the choices for how they would respond both to the student's death and their own feelings, and of the experiences that would keep them in the present and not the past, the authors contended that the students experienced a more long-lasting and effective healing process. The authors believe, however, that this contention cannot be easily measured beyond self-report. They further caution that using a Gestalt approach with traumatic events such as suicide should be done only with "support of comparable theory, knowledge and skill" (1988, p. 283).

Enns presented a proposal for integrating the Gestalt goals of self-responsibility with a feminist perspective that values the web of relationships in women's lives and focuses attention on the "environmental constraints and socialization that affect women's lives" (1987, p. 93). Her use of Gestalt therapy included the empty-chair technique and the exploration of polarities or fantasy journeys. Enns' work parallels the position of Laura Perls, linking feminism with self-responsibility (Shane, 1999b).

Yontef and Simkin (1989) note that Perls provided no research to support his model of psychotherapy. Although traditional research on groups of clients is viewed by Gestalt therapists as having limited value in guiding the practice of Gestalt therapy with specific individual clients, they conclude that Gestalt therapy is not opposed to outcome research per se. Gestalt therapists are skeptical of the value of outcome research for informing practice because it fails to account well for therapy process variables. The interested student of Gestalt therapy practice may want to review the contributions many recent researchers (e.g., Baker, 2001; Prosnick, 2000; Yontef, 1993, 1995, 1998) have presented in the *Gestalt Journal* and the *Gestalt Review*. These add significantly to the work of earlier theorists, including the German psychologists.

Research does show a great deal of support for the efficacy of Gestalt therapy. Shane (1999b) notes that several recent studies have found efficacy in using Gestalt therapy when working with the body, including issues relating to body image and distress relating to coping with rheumatoid arthritis. Johnson and Smith (1997) also found Gestalt therapy to be efficacious when working with clients who had phobias.

Limitations

One of the limitations related to Gestalt counseling and psychotherapy has little to do with the theory itself, but with Perls (Shane, 1999b). The reliance on the workshop format developed during the 1960s seemed to lead to a reliance on Perls himself as a sort of guru who could answer any problem by demonstrating Gestaltism in a workshop, almost like an actor with an adoring audience. According to Miriam Polster (1987), "We, as Gestalt therapists, often became identified with burlesques of our principles with no possibilities of clarification [other] than [what] is available in any spread of rumor" (p. 34). Another criticism is that Gestalt therapy lacks an expressed model of personality and development (Shane, 1999b).

Ciorni (1994) suggests the difficulty in applying Gestalt theory across cultures. She indicates that Perls' emphasis (and that of most white American therapists) on "I-ness" may prove a challenge to clients of other cultures (p. 14). However, she makes some suggestions for adapting Gestalt to the Hispanic/Latino culture. Perhaps the crucial factor in applying any Euro-American theory, including Gestalt, is that the counselor or psychotherapist be familiar with and perhaps experienced in working with clients of various cultures before selecting an appropriate theory (Torres-Rivera, Maples, & Thorn, 1999). For many non-Western cultures, Gestalt therapy and its often confrontational nature can be intimidating (Bowman, 2000; Seligman, 2001).

The temptation for novice counselors or psychotherapists is to employ such Gestalt "techniques" (i.e., processes) as empty chair, top dog/underdog, figure-ground, and locating feelings without sufficient practitioner training. However, these processes alone can be of little value in helping the client. For example, the empty-chair or two-chair process was developed by Perls (1969a) to deal with the five layers of neurosis mentioned earlier in this chapter. However, if the practitioner lacks knowledge and understanding of those layers, the client may be misled. In addition, the intense emotional responses that some Gestalt experiments evoke can be harmful to the client if misused or abused by an inexperienced counselor or psychotherapist (Seligman, 2001).

Other limitations of Gestalt counseling and psychotherapy are discussed briefly below.

- How does a counselor or therapist prove that the client has achieved "understanding," "meaning," or "organization" in the helping relationship? While this question is difficult to answer with most theoretical counseling or psychotherapy approaches, it is a particular challenge for Gestaltists.

- Perls' work is sometimes seen as a potpourri of various theories—a little Freud, a little Jung, and a lot of the Berlin school—yet Perls seldom credits them for their contributions. In addition, in her later years and upon reflection, Laura Perls noted that there were as many ways to do Gestalt therapy as there were Gestalt therapists, which further dilutes the practice of the theory (Wolfert & Cook, 1999).
- According to Yontef (1993), some practitioners believe the client's cognitive process is important in counseling or psychotherapy work, yet many Gestaltists tend to deemphasize cognition, focusing more on feeling.
- The holistic nature of Gestalt counseling and psychotherapy and its allowances for therapist creativity in developing treatments flies in the face of today's trend toward specialization in the medical field (i.e., medical specialists such as cardiovascular surgeons who treat very specific diseases such as heart disease). However, holism fits the human condition better, so there is something to be said for bucking this medical trend.
- Perls' here-and-now orientation could limit the freedom that a counselor or psychotherapist might like to use in exploring the history of an issue, problem, or concern fully.
- Some current Gestalt therapists believe the issue of sexuality, historically thought to be something abused in Gestalt training programs, has been virtually left out of the current training of Gestalt therapists. Several articles have criticized this shift in focus from earlier days and claim Gestalt therapy has gone to the other extreme and this has the potential to harm clients (Becker, 2000; Bowman, 2000; Clemmens, 2000; O'Shea, 2000; Thompson, 2000). In addition O'Shea (2000) believes there is a strong heterosexual bias in which the issues pertaining to gays, lesbians, and bisexuals have largely been ignored.

Despite the limitations that may exist in Gestalt counseling and psychotherapy, its holistic nature is one of its most appealing features. Contrasted with more empirical scientific approaches, it offers a wide variety of opportunities to facilitate the client's journey toward greater health and development.

Summary Chart—Gestalt Theory

Human Nature

Rooted in existentialism and phenomenology, Gestalt counseling and psychotherapy focuses attention on the holistic nature of humankind. Gestalt counselors and psychotherapists strive to encompass the whole organism and operate from the perspective that human beings have the capacity and strength to grow, to develop, and to become the persons they want to be. A basic assumption is that individuals can deal with their life problems if they are fully aware of what is happening in and around them.

Major Constructs

There are a number of major constructs connected with Gestalt counseling and psychotherapy: holism, the concept of unifying wholes, which includes mind and body, past and present, and individual and environment; field theory, the idea that the individual in his or her environment produces a psychological field in which self-regulation can take place; figure-ground, the idea that the client's unfinished business becomes "figure" or foreground during the therapeutic process and everything else temporarily recedes to "ground" or background; here-and-now orientation, emphasis on the present rather than on the past or the future for the purpose of promoting the growth process; boundaries and polarities, the client's "definition" in relation to the environment and traits existing on the opposite ends of the same continuum (Corey, 2001).

Goals

1. Identifying themes that are central to the client's self-organization.
2. Conceptualizing the issues and concerns of the client that will guide the sequence, timing, and methods used.
3. Establishing and maintaining a safe professional environment.
4. Providing an atmosphere that invites contact between client and counselor or psychotherapist.

Change Process

Change results from the identification and working through of a variety of blocks or interferences that prevent the client from achieving a holistic integration of all aspects of self and the capacity to achieve responsibility for self. Clients work through the cliché, phony, impasse, implosive, and exploding layers of neurosis during this process.

Interventions

Usually labeled as "experiments" because they are procedures aimed at discovery and not exercises in the traditional sense, interventions are designed to control or initiate behavior change. Gestalt interventions may include locating feelings, enactment and confrontation, empty-chair, dream work, dialogue, making the rounds, unfinished business, playing the projection, rehearsal, and exaggeration.

Limitations

1. Gestalt theory deemphasizes the cognitive components of the counseling and psychotherapy process.
2. It is often seen as a potpourri of theories and philosophies.
3. Holistic approaches are incompatible with today's emphasis on time-limited, brief approaches.
4. The theory places too much emphasis on the here and now.

The Case of Jonathan: A Gestalt Approach

It should be understood that the goal of Gestalt therapy is not to facilitate direct change within the client through planned intervention, but is, instead, to facilitate the client's awareness and insight into himself or herself using creative experiments. Specifically, from the existential perspective, the goal is to help the client become aware of his or her subjective experience as fully as possible. The desired outcome is that the client will become more authentic as a person, will shed his or her "false self" and the "shoulds" that make up his or her life, will make better choices that lead to a better life situation, will develop the ability for growth, and will become more integrated within the self, with others, and between the self and the environment. Through this enhanced awareness of the self, the client gains self-acceptance and can take responsibility for his or her choices and be in charge of his or her own destiny.

The therapy objective for any client is to help the client become response-able and break through his or her stuck points. The therapy is not directive, but is experiential and is conducted through a conduit of the here and now and through the client/therapist (I/Thou) relationship. The focus is on the process and not the content.

Case Conceptualization

Jonathan is exhibiting a great deal of avoidance surrounding the issues of his brother's death, his role as a Native American within the majority white society, his role as a husband and father, his role as a man, and his obligations to his reservation and his family. These unresolved issues are creating stuck points in Jonathan's life and have left him with quite a residual of unfinished business or unexpressed feelings, which are causing him anger, depression, frustration, pain, anxiety, grief, guilt, and feelings of helplessness that he has turned into resentment and self-defeating behaviors. Corey (1996) observed that resentment left unexpressed and undealt with turns to guilt. Jonathan expresses severe guilt when he states, "I have ruined the lives of three families plus my own life and who knows what I am doing to my children."

Instead of expressing his feelings to those people directly involved, Jonathan has instead run away. He has quit (1) both his marriages, (2) the University, (3) the Bureau of Indian Affairs school, (4) his family and the reservation by running to Arizona, (5) his hospital job, and (6) his children. If he follows this same pattern, Jonathan will also quit the residential treatment facility at which he is currently employed.

There is evidence that Jonathan is avoiding his feelings and creating unfinished business for himself.

- He is uncertain as to whether or not his family blames him for his brother's death.
- He avoids confronting his wives regarding marital problems and instead engages in extramarital affairs and heavy drinking.
- He desires to avoid any other relationships with women of the type he had with his wives.
- He leaves the reservation and his family.

This unfinished business is driving his self-defeating behaviors of anger, alcohol consumption, broken relationships, and the inability to maintain employment or a permanent residence.

Adding to his burden, Jonathan is also living under an umbrella of oppressing expressed and unexpressed "shoulds" that he has internalized.

- He should have been able to prevent the car accident that killed his brother.
- He should have been a better husband to his wives.
- He should be a better father to his children.
- He should be a better son to his parents.
- He should have the answers to "make all of this better."

Treatment Plan

Jonathan will have the following therapeutic goals.

- *Learn about himself and the situations in which he is currently enmeshed.* This will include exploring his unfinished business in the context of the here and now, and experiencing his feelings and expressing them in real time during the session rather than just talking about them from the safe perspective of the past. This will allow Jonathan to get to the root of his frustrations and see them for what they really are.
- *Recognize that he has choices, that his choices affect his life, and that he can accept things as they are rather than for what he might want them to be.* Jonathan needs to let go of what could have been and start living in what is right now.
- *Learn that he can influence his environment rather than letting his environment control him.* He can learn this by focusing on the here and now rather than living in the past, a past that he can neither control nor change. He can only affect the "right now" by making choices in the present that will facilitate his own self-growth and enhance his ability to make better choices.

Experiments

Gestalt counselors and psychotherapists do not use interventions in the classical usage of this term. Instead, with the client, experiments are designed that will bring about great self-knowledge and insight that will allow the client to complete unfinished business by bringing the situation from the past and "into the right *now*" whereby the client can use words, actions, or fantasy to complete the unfinished event. This allows the unfinished business to become complete and slip into the background rather than continue to occupy the client's mind and the foreground of his or her field. Some of the experiments that could facilitate the goals outlined above for Jonathan are listed below. There are many experiments as can be found within the context of this chapter, but space prohibits using more than one or two for this section. The following is an attempt to give the reader insight into how these experiments might be used and how they might enhance the client's awareness.

Empty Chair   This technique can be used to help Jonathan express his feelings regarding his brother's death and deal with the unfinished business that continues to plague him surrounding this event. The counselor/psychotherapist will ask Jonathan his permission to proceed with the experiment. With his approval, the counselor or psychotherapist will have Jonathan sit in one chair with another empty chair directly across from him. The counselor or psychotherapist then has Jonathan speak both parts. This allows Jonathan to not only express his repressed and avoided feelings regarding his brother and the events leading up to his death, but also to express what Jonathan imagines his brother would say to him in response. This experiment takes the emotion out of the safety of referring to it in the past and brings it into the present where it can be worked through. Through the empty chair, Jonathan can speak directly to his brother and tell him of his pain and guilt. In this way, Jonathan can complete his unfinished business with his brother. This same technique can be used to work through his feelings of failure and rejection regarding his past relationships with his wives and family.

Dream Work   Because images, fantasies, and dreams are the projections of the person, dreams can be seen as the metaphoric expressions of the content and can reveal certain aspects of the person. Jonathan has a particularly poignant dream that can be worked with in the counseling or psychotherapy relationship, and this work can aid him in understanding rejected aspects of himself. The counselor or psychotherapist can set up chairs to represent the seating in a bus. With Jonathan's permission for this experiment, the counselor or psychotherapist will then instruct Jonathan to act out all the parts of his dream. Through this reenactment, Jonathan will gain insight into the feelings he has repressed. Through this work, a clearer image should emerge that will help Jonathan understand in the here and now why he has behaved in the manner that he has. Through this gained insight into his self, Jonathan can begin to make different choices, live in the here and now, and stop letting his past control his future.

Cognitive-Behavioral Theories

Cynthia R. Kalodner
Towson University

Background

Cognitive-behavioral theories (CBT) are best conceptualized as a general category of theories, or a set of related theories, that have evolved from the theoretical writings, clinical experiences, and empirical studies of behavioral and cognitively oriented psychologists and other mental health workers. The hyphenated term *cognitive-behavioral* reflects the importance of both behavioral and cognitive approaches to understanding and helping human beings. The hyphen brings together behavioral and cognitive theoretical views, each with its own theoretical assumptions and intervention strategies. Cognitive-behavioral is the hybrid of behavioral strategies and cognitive processes, with the goal of achieving behavioral and cognitive change (Dobson & Dozois, 2001).

Throughout this chapter, the blending of aspects of behavioral and cognitive approaches into cognitive-behavioral counseling and psychotherapy can be seen. There is no single definition of cognitive-behavioral theory because there are so many different cognitive-behavioral theories. There are three major types of cognitive-behavioral therapies: **cognitive restructuring**, **coping skills**, and **problem-solving** (Dobson & Dozois, 2001). **Beck's cognitive therapy** (Beck, 1976; Beck, Rush, Shaw, & Emery, 1979; DeRubeis, Tang, & Beck, 2001) is an example of a cognitive restructuring technique. **Meichenbaum's stress inoculation training** (1985) and **self-instruction training** (1977) are examples of coping skills therapies. Problem-solving therapy (D'Zurilla & Nezu, 2001) is, as its name implies, an example of the problem-solving type of CBT.

Although there are differences among the cognitive-behavioral approaches, all of these theorists value the role cognitions play in the development and maintenance of psychological problems (Dobson, 2001). In order for a therapy to be "cognitive-behavioral," it must be based on the idea that cognitions mediate (lead to) behavioral change. Therapists using this model use treatments that target cognitions in the service of changes in behavior and that outcomes of treatment are based on cognitive, behavioral, and emotional changes (Dobson, 2001). This chapter provides an overview of the highlights of cognitive-behavioral approaches to helping people.

Watson and the Beginnings of Behavior Theory

To understand cognitive-behavioral theories, it is necessary to study the history of the development of behavioral theory, various cognitive models, and the union of these approaches into cognitive-behavioral theories.

Early behaviorism was based on learning theory, the development of clearly defined techniques, and systematic, well-designed research (Hayes & Hayes, 1992). The behavioral history of cognitive-behavioral theory began with the behavioral approaches developed by **John B. Watson,** who is usually recognized as the most influential person in the development of behaviorism (Craighead, Craighead, & Ilardi, 1995). **Behaviorism** was formed as a reaction against the Freudian emphasis on the unconscious as the subject matter of psychology and introspection as the method of its investigation. Watson (1930) claimed that behavior should be the sole subject matter of psychology, and that it should be studied through observation. Furthermore, according to Watson, conscious processes (e.g., thinking) were determined to be outside the realm of scientific inquiry.

Using **Pavlov's** principles of classical conditioning, in which unconditioned stimuli (loud bell) paired with conditioned stimuli (white rat) lead to a conditioned response (startle), Watson trained Little Albert to fear a white rat, white cotton, and even Watson's white hair! This demonstration is important because it indicates that human emotions can be learned and modified using learning principles. There are several other well-known conditioning model behaviorists, including Eysenck, Rachman, and Wolpe, who developed treatments such as systematic desensitization and flooding, based on classical conditioning and counterconditioning (Kazdin & Wilson, 1978). The relationship between stimulus and response is essential to these classical behavioral paradigms.

A critical contribution Watson brought to psychology is the methodology for conducting research. Methodological behaviorism is concerned with procedures for scientific inquiry and data collection. It has the following characteristics: an assumption of determinism; an emphasis on observation of behavior and environmental stimuli; the use of specific operational definitions of independent and dependent variables such that measurement is reliable; the necessity to be able to falsify the hypotheses through research; use of controlled experimentation; and replication of research findings allows generalization to other subjects or situations. Methodological behaviorism continues to have a strong influence on cognitive-behavioral research.

Skinner and Operant Conditioning

The work of **B. F. Skinner** on the principles of reinforcement and operant conditioning further developed the school of behaviorism. Skinner is the best-known and most controversial figure in the field of behaviorism (Craighead et al., 1995). Despite the fact that, until his death in 1991, Skinner maintained an adamant denial of the importance of cognitions and affect in understanding human behavior, his work has been tremendously influential in the field of counseling and psychotherapy. Skinner developed applied behavioral analysis, which is based on **operant conditioning.** In operant conditioning, reinforcers shape behavior by being contingent on the response (Kazdin & Wilson, 1978;

Miller, 1980). Skinner's schedules of reinforcement (1969) define how different amounts of reinforcement can be delivered to continue to support behavioral changes. Key interventions in applied behavior analysis include reinforcement, punishment, extinction, and stimulus control, each of which involves a search for environmental variables that will lead to changes in behavior.

In operant conditioning, reinforcement is used to increase behavior. Examples of positive reinforcement include praise or money. Negative reinforcement, which also increases behavior, involves the removal of a negative stimulus, such as electric shock or a ringing bell. An example of negative reinforcement is turning off a loud bell after a rat presses a bar. Punishment and extinction decrease behavior by the addition of an aversive stimulus or the removal of a positive reinforcer, respectively. An example of punishment involves following cigarette smoking with electric shock. In extinction, a behavior to be decreased is ignored; a person who has the habit of interrupting conversation is ignored by friends when he or she interrupts, but friends listen when the comment is made in conversation without interrupting. These and many other applied behavior analysis techniques are included in Miller's (1980) text, which is a programmed learning manual designed to demonstrate the role of behavioral techniques in everyday situations.

Wolpe and Systematic Desensitization

Joseph Wolpe is another major contributor in the development of behavior therapy. **Systematic desensitization,** a behavioral procedure used to treat phobias, is the most thoroughly investigated behavioral procedure to treat simple phobias (Emmelkamp, 1994). According to the theory of reciprocal inhibition, which underlies systematic desensitization, when a response incompatible with anxiety (i.e., relaxation) is paired with an anxiety-evoking stimuli (whatever the client reports is anxiety-producing), then the association between the anxiety-producing stimulus and anxiety will be lessened (Wolpe, 1958). Through the use of systematic desensitization, clients are "desensitized" to their fears. First, clients are taught to use progressive relaxation to become completely relaxed. Using a hierarchy of stimuli arranged with the least anxiety-provoking first and the most anxiety-provoking last, the counselor or therapist asks the client to imagine each stimulus while remaining relaxed. Kalodner (1998) provides details on the technique of systematic desensitization.

A Brief History of Cognitive Therapy

The earliest cognitive-behavioral therapies emerged in the early 1960s, but it was not until the 1970s that major works on cognitive-behavioral therapy were written (Dobson & Dozois, 2001). The cognitive revolution brought forth by Beck and Ellis and others began as clinicians found that the available systems of therapy were not satisfactory. (Ellis's contributions are reviewed in Chapter 10). Aaron Beck (1976) was dissatisfied with psychoanalysis and behavior therapy. Though trained as a psychoanalyst, Beck objected to the unconscious aspects of Freud's theory, asserting that people can be aware of factors that are responsible for emotional upsets and blurred thinking. Beck indicated that his work with depressed individuals did not substantiate the psychoanalytic theory (Weinrach, 1988). At the same time, he found the radical behavioral explanation for human emotional disturbance to be too limited to adequately explain human emotional difficulties. For Beck, psychological disturbances may be the result of "faulty learning, making incorrect inferences on the basis of inadequate or incorrect information, and not distinguishing adequately between imagination and reality" (1976, pp. 19–20). Beck's work in cognitive therapy has been extremely influential in the treatment of depression and has been expanded to other psychological problems. The basics of his theory will be presented later in this chapter.

Human Nature: A Developmental Perspective

One wonders what "development" is for behaviorists and cognitive-behaviorists. Early behavioral theory, with its emphasis on learning, seems somewhat antithetical to developmentalism. Early behaviorists' view of the development of human nature was limited to the learning concepts of operant and classical conditioning. Individuals, born with a **tabula rasa** (blank slate), learn to associate stimuli and responses; development can be seen as the sum total of these associations.

Cognitive-behavioral theories are not developmental in the same sense that stage theories are. There is a stated assumption that behavior is learned (Kazdin & Wilson, 1978). This applies equally to the explanation of how problem behaviors and adaptive behaviors are developed. Behavior is assumed to be developed and maintained by external events or cues, by external reinforcers, or by internal processes such as cognition. Development is based on each individual's different learning history, the unique experiences provided by the environment, and the individual's cognitive understanding of the world.

The use of the here-and-now, a historical perspective in cognitive-behavioral therapy, highlights the emphasis on the present in understanding the presenting problems of a client. Childhood learning experiences are not usually the variables that are functionally related to current behavior, and the functional relationship is critical to assessment and treatment. Except as they may relate to present problems, past problems are not attended to in the same way as they might be within other counseling and psychotherapy systems (Beck et al., 1979). Because current problems are influenced by individual social learning history, past problems are not ignored, though it is clear that there is a relative lack of importance of early childhood experiences.

Major Constructs

Because cognitive-behavioral theories are an amalgamation of behavioral and cognitive approaches, cognitive-behavioral theoretical constructs contain aspects of both behavioral and cognitive theory. Considering the separate behavioral and cognitive roots may illustrate the key constructs in cognitive-behavioral theories. Kendall and Hollon (1979) consider the treatment target, treatment approach, and treatment evaluation for behavioral, cognitive, and cognitive-behavioral theories (see Table 9.1). For behavioral interventions, purely behavioral terms such as *behavioral excesses* or *deficits, learning theory,* and *observed changes in behavior* are used. Likewise, cognitive interventions are based on purely cognitive terms such as *cognitive excesses* or *deficits, semantic interventions* (cognitive), and *changes in cognitions.*

Cognitive-behavioral interventions are considered to encompass a range of approaches limited by the purer behavioral and cognitive interventions (Kendall & Hollon, 1979). Treatment targets range from behavioral excesses and deficits to cognitive excesses and deficits, and cognitive-behavioral interventions target both cognitive and behavioral excesses and deficits. The treatment interventions also range from an emphasis on behavioral interventions, to an emphasis on cognitive interventions with some behavioral strategies included, to a full integration of cognitive and behavioral strategies. The evaluation strategy associated with cognitive-behavioral counseling and psychotherapy interventions includes an emphasis on behavior changes, to an emphasis on cognitive changes; in the middle of this spectrum are observed changes in behavior and cognition with methodological rigor. What cognitive-behavioral theories provide, given this amalgamation model, is greater flexibility in treatment targets and interventions, with an emphasis on rigorous standards in measurement of change and research evaluation (Kendall & Hollon, 1979).

The Importance of Cognitions

The unifying characteristic of cognitive-behavioral counseling and psychotherapy approaches is the fundamental emphasis on the importance of cognitive workings as mediators of behavior change (Craighead et al., 1995; Dobson & Dozois, 2001). All cognitive interventions attempt to produce change by influencing thinking, which is assumed to play a causal role in the development and maintenance of psychological problems (Dobson & Dozois, 2001). The relationship between thoughts and behavior is a major aspect of cognitive-behavioral theory and counseling and psychotherapy. Thus, all cognitive-behavioral therapies share these three fundamental propositions.

- Cognitive activity affects behavior.
- Cognitive activity may be monitored and altered.
- Desired behavior change may be affected through cognitive change (Dobson & Dozois, 2001, p. 4).

The Importance of Learning

The cognitive-behavioral model of psychological disturbance asserts that abnormal behavior is learned and developed the same way that normal behavior is learned, and that cognitive-behavioral principles can be applied to change the behavior. The importance of this statement lies in the focus on learning as the way behavior is acquired, rather than underlying intrapsychic conflicts. It rejects the psychodynamic and quasi-disease models of development, which assume that underlying intrapsychic conflicts cause maladaptive behavior.

The Importance of Operational Definitions and Functional Analysis

In cognitive-behavioral approaches, problems are viewed operationally. The definition of the presenting problem must be concrete and specific, and observable whenever possible. It is assumed that problems are functionally related to internal and external **antecedents** and **consequences.** This assumption means that, in order to understand behavior, it is necessary to know the events that precede (antecedents) and follow (consequences) the behavior. These events may be external and observable behaviors or internal thoughts and feelings. The functional relationship conceptualization of problems necessitates a clear understanding of the internal and external antecedents that contribute to a problematic behavior, as well as the internal and external consequences that maintain behavior. This also means that the causes and treatments of problems should be multidimensional. Causes might include behaviors, environmental circumstances, thoughts, beliefs, or attitudes. Treatments are addressed in the intervention section of this chapter. Because there is rarely a single cause for a problem, treatments are comprehensive and designed to address the multiple issues.

The Importance of Therapeutic Empathy

Often when cognitive-behavioral counseling or psychotherapy is described, the techniques and theory are emphasized while the importance of the relationship between the client and the counselor or therapist is underemphasized. This inaccuracy is unfortunate; although cognitive-behavioral treatment manuals focus on the specific treatment techniques, the helping relationship is also addressed. Beck and Meichenbaum describe the importance of the relationship and include strategies for developing a therapeutic relationship in their manuals. Burns and Auerbach (1996) highlight the necessity for a warm, empathic therapeutic relationship in cognitive therapy. They provide an empathy scale that patients can use to rate how warm, genuine, and empathic their counselors or therapists were during a recent session. The necessary and sufficient conditions for personality change developed by Carl Rogers are included in Beck's cognitive therapy as "necessary, but not sufficient." In other words, these factors form the basis for the relationship, but the techniques of cognitive therapy are viewed as necessary to produce therapeutic change. The efficacy of the intervention is dependent on a relationship that is characterized by counselor or therapist warmth, accurate empathy, and genuineness (Beck, Wright, Newman, & Liese 1993).

Applications

Overview

There is great variability in the interventions practiced in cognitive-behavioral counseling and psychotherapy. Cognitive-behavioral interventions include various combinations of cognitive and behavioral techniques and are aimed at changing either cognitions, behavior, or both (Kendall & Hollon, 1979; see Table 9.1). Cognitive-behavioral interventions are directive, structured, goal-directed, and time-limited treatment, and most types involve the client in collaborative relationship with the counselor or therapist. The use of homework assignments and skills practice is common, along with a focus on problem-solving ability.

The Association for the Advancement of Behavior Therapy (AABT) describes therapy as goal-oriented, generally short-term, and often drug-free (AABT web page: *http://www.aabt.org/ABOUTAAB/ABOUTAAB.HTM*). Importantly, the treatments used by counselors or therapists who use CBT are research-based and designed to help clients reach specific goals. For example, AABT indicates that a goal might include each of the following.

- Acting—smoking less or being more outgoing
- Feeling—helping a person to be less scared, less depressed, or less anxious
- Thinking—learning to problem-solve or get rid of self-defeating thoughts

Goals of Counseling and Psychotherapy

Case Conceptualization   Before selecting a goal for counseling or psychotherapy or conducting any intervention with a client, a counselor or therapist using a CBT orientation

Table 9.1

General Characteristics of Cognitive-Behavioral Interventions

		Treatment Target	Treatment Approach	Treatment Evaluation
Behavioral {		Behavioral excesses or deficits	Behavioral "learning theory" interventions. Environmental manipulations (e.g., token economies, contingency management)	Observed changes in behavior with rigorous evaluation
	Cognitive-Behavioral {	Behavioral excesses or deficits	Behavioral interventions. Skills training, information provision (e.g., modeling, role playing)	Observed changes in behavior with rigorous evaluation
		Behavioral and cognitive excesses or deficits	Broadly conceived behavioral and cognitive methods	Observed changes in behavior and cognition with methodological rigor
Cognitive {		Cognitive excesses or deficits	Cognitive interventions with adjunctive behavioral procedures	Examination of cognitive and, to a lesser extent, of behavioral changes
		Cognitive excesses or deficits	Semantic interventions	Changes in cognitions, "integrative changes," often, but not always, nonempirically evaluated

Source: From Hollon, S. D., & Kendall, P. C. (1979). Cognitive-behavioral interventions: Theory and procedure. In P. C. Kendall & S. D. Hollon (Eds.), *Cognitive-behavioral interventions: Theory, research, and procedures* (pp. 445–454). New York: Academic Press. Copyright 1979 by Academic Press. Reprinted by permission.

begins with developing a conceptualization, or understanding, of the case. CBT case formulation has five components: **problem list, diagnosis, working hypothesis, strengths and assets,** and **treatment plan** (Persons & Davidson, 2001). These are illustrated in the case presented at the end of this chapter. The problem list is a comprehensive list of the difficulties stated in concrete behavioral terms. Usually there are five to eight problems identified in a variety of areas, such as psychological symptoms, interpersonal, occupational, medical, financial, housing, legal, and leisure (Persons & Davidson, 2001). Relationships between the problems may become clear when all of the issues are listed in this way. It is also useful to see a list of all the issues so that a prioritization of issues can be used when preparing the treatment plan.

A comprehensive problem list requires a detailed assessment and involves asking clients about areas that they may not have initially discussed. An important issue that clients may not report is substance abuse. It is for this reason that a global assessment is recommended. The counselor or therapist can use information derived from a standardized, structured interview along with the initial description of the presenting problem to develop an accurate picture of the problem. This usually begins by asking the client to describe the problem. However, clients do not always describe the most important problem in initial sessions. Sometimes they may not be ready to reveal the true problem until they have developed trust and confidence in the practitioner.

The second component in this case formulation plan is diagnosis, which refers to the *Diagnostic and Statistical Manual – IV-TR* (APA, 2000) method of presenting information along five axes. Diagnosis is not always included in CBT conceptualizations, but it is important because it provides a link to the type of treatment that may be selected. (It is beyond the scope of this chapter to describe diagnosis in detail.)

The working hypothesis section is considered the most critical part of the case conceptualization. It is a way to present the connections between the issues on the problem list. There are subsections, including schemata, precipitating or activating situations, and origins. The schemata section concerns the core beliefs held by the client. Core beliefs are those thoughts that are central to the problem, and that may cause or maintain the problems. Usually, they are negative thoughts about themselves, the world, others, or the future. Precipitating or activating situations refer to the specific external events that produce the symptoms or problems. They refer to the things that may have happened just before the problem began. Origins refer to early history that might be related to the problems. Origins might explain how the client learned the schemata that maintain the current situation. For example, belonging to a family with poor communication skills may explain why a client might have problems expressing herself or himself.

Strengths and assets refer to the positive aspects of a person's current situation. For example, a client may have good social skills, the ability to work collaboratively, a sense of humor, a good job, financial resources, a good support network, regular exercise, intelligence, personal attractiveness, and/or a stable lifestyle (Persons & Davidson, 2001). It is always useful to know what is *not* a problem in a client's life. These strengths can be used when developing the treatment plan.

The Treatment Plan   The treatment plan is the outcome of the case conceptualization. It must be related to the problem list and working hypothesis. The treatment plan tells about the goals for counseling or psychotherapy. Treatment plans are complex and require attention to goals and obstacles, as well as modality, frequency, interventions, and adjunct therapies. The goals of treatment must be reviewed with both the client and the counselor or therapist, and the client must agree on these goals. It is also important to know how progress in counseling or psychotherapy can be measured and monitored. Because cognitive-behaviorally oriented counselors or therapists are often focused on measuring outcome, it is important to know how the changes will be noted. For example, perhaps the counselor or therapist will ask the client to keep a diary of maladaptive thoughts, or a count of binge-eating episodes. Obstacles are to the potential difficulties that may arise during treatment. An awareness of obstacles may assist the counselor or therapist and client cope more effectively with them. Modality refers to the type of counseling or psychotherapy that will be used; in this case, cognitive-behavioral therapy. Frequency refers to the number of sessions a week; most often CBT is offered once a week. Initial interventions are the specific strategies that will be used in sessions. An example of initial interventions appears in the case study. Finally, adjunct therapies are those used in addition to cognitive-behavioral therapy. An example of an adjunct therapy is pharmacotherapy.

The Process of Change

The process of change is concerned with understanding how the theory explains the mechanisms for therapeutic change. This is particularly important in the cognitive-behavioral arena because there are many different theories and many different interventions.

Self-Efficacy   The self-efficacy theory of Albert Bandura (1977, 1986) has been used to provide a cognitive-behavioral theoretical explanation for how people change. It has been proposed as a common pathway to explain how people change despite using different therapeutic techniques. Self-efficacy theory asserts that individuals develop expectations for their success in performing specific behaviors and that these expectations influence their decision to try new behaviors and maintain behavioral changes (Bandura, 1977, 1986). Self-efficacy may be thought of as a sense of personal competence or feelings of mastery. The degree to which a person feels efficacious influences the amount of effort that he or she will apply in given situations. Thus, cognitive-behavioral therapy may work through increasing self-efficacy of clients.

Bandura (1986) described four mechanisms through which self-efficacy can be developed: enactive attainments, vicarious experience, verbal persuasion, and recognition of physiological states. Enactive attainments, the most powerful contributors to self-efficacy development, relate to the individual's own experience with achieving a goal. Vicarious experiences are those involving observing others as they succeed or fail. Through the process of observing, individuals are provided with a basis for making comparisons to their own competence to perform the task. Verbal persuasion is a less powerful way to influence self-efficacy. The final source of self-efficacy, physiological states, refers to the emotional arousal or degree of apprehension one feels. Feelings of fear may lead to decreased performance, whereas a moderate amount of anxiety may be helpful when performing a new task.

Examples of how clients learn assertive behavior can be used to apply these sources of self-efficacy. When clients are taught assertiveness skills, they practice making appropriate assertive comments. Enactive attainments are the experiences of success that lead clients to feel able to repeat the assertive behavior. In assertiveness training groups, clients watch each other perform new behaviors; this is an example of vicarious experience. Verbal persuasion is the source of self-efficacy based on telling clients "You can do it"; like encouragement, it might increase self-efficacy, but other sources are more powerful. The physiological states mechanism can be used in assertiveness training to inform clients that a moderate amount of anxiety may be helpful as they attempt to make changes in their behavior.

It is important to recognize that when applying the self-efficacy model to how cognitive therapy and other cognitive-behavioral interventions work, all four of the sources of self-efficacy are involved. In the process of learning that cognitions contribute to behavior and affective difficulties, enactive attainments, vicarious experiences, verbal persuasion, and physiological states play major roles.

Does Changing Beliefs Lead to Change in Behavior?   Addressing the question of how people change, Beck (1976) asserts that behavioral and affective change are hypothesized to occur through the change in cognitions. The assumption is clearly that changing beliefs is the key to helping people. Research has demonstrated that cognitive therapy does indeed change thoughts and that there are reductions in psychological disturbances. However, it has not been clearly demonstrated that changes in cognitions cause changes in behavior or affect. In fact, changes in cognition occur in behavioral programs not designed to change thoughts (DeLucia & Kalodner, 1990) and in pharmacological treatment (see Hollon & Beck, 1994).

Intervention Strategies

Because cognitive-behavioral interventions include aspects of both behavioral and cognitive interventions, this section will provide a few examples of some commonly used intervention strategies. The separation of behavioral, cognitive, and cognitive-behavioral techniques is rather artificial, as most cognitive procedures include behavioral components and some behavioral interventions also contain cognitive elements (Emmelkamp, 1994). However, in spite of this, a sample of some techniques most often associated with behavioral approaches follows. In addition, cognitive interventions are described briefly. The greatest attention is devoted to providing detail of several cognitive-behavioral theories of counseling and psychotherapy.

Behavioral Interventions   Behavioral interventions focus primarily on changing specific behaviors. Examples of purely behavioral interventions include reinforcement, extinction, shaping, stimulus control, and aversive control (Miller, 1980).

Reinforcement is a well-known behavioral strategy. **Positive reinforcement** is a procedure in which some behavior is increased by following it with something rewarding; for example, children who clean their room are given praise and attention, a gold star, or a new toy. It is important that the receiver views the reinforcer as positive. **Negative reinforcement** is the removal of something aversive to increase behavior. The buzz most cars make when the key is put in the ignition is a negative reinforcer designed to increase seat belt use. Both positive and negative reinforcement increase behavior and can be applied when clients want to increase a behavior.

Extinction is a behavioral intervention designed to decrease a problematic behavior. In this case, a reinforcer that has followed the behavior in the past is removed, and the problem behavior decreases. Think about the child who repeatedly gets out of his or her seat in a classroom. When the teacher notices and asks the child to sit down, the child may return to his or her seat. However, the attention of the teacher is reinforcing and the problem of out-of-seat behavior usually continues. Extinction is the procedure by which the teacher ignores the behavior until it stops. Extinction is characterized by **response burst,** an increase in the undesirable behavior that may occur before extinction. The child may get out of the seat, wander around, and continue to engage in negative behavior, still trying to get the attention of the teacher. If the teacher gives in and attends to the behavior now, negative behavior is actually being reinforced. Response burst is to be expected, and usually subsides when the individual learns that no amount of negative behavior will get the attention that has been reinforcing.

Shaping is a behavioral intervention used to gradually increase the quality of a behavior. Often used to teach a new skill, shaping works by reinforcing successive approximations of the desired behavior. Shaping is used when there is a clearly identified behavior to be changed and when differential reinforcement (reinforcing the behavior that gets closer and closer to the target, while ignoring the other behavior) can be applied.

In **stimulus control,** some event in the environment is used to cue behavior. When a stimulus leads to behavior that is desirable and will be reinforced, the cue is called a **discriminative stimulus.** For example, seeing exercise shoes in the living room may act as a cue to use an exercise tape to do aerobics. The exercise shoes are a discriminative stimulus for exercise.

One example of **aversive control** is punishment, which is defined as the addition of an unpleasant event following a negative behavior to decrease the occurrence of that behavior. Punishment is not used often by behaviorists, but it has been used to eliminate dangerous behavior such as head banging or other self-mutilative behaviors in severely emotionally disturbed children.

Cognitive Interventions   Cognitive interventions focus on the role of cognitions in the life of clients. One excellent self-help book written by Burns (1999) can be especially useful for clients using a cognitive-behavioral approach to recover from depression. This book, *Feeling Good: The New Mood Therapy,* was strongly recommended in a national study of psychologists who rated self-help books (Norcross, Santrock, Campbell, Smith, Sommer, & Zuckerman, 2000). The book is a source of information about the different types of **cognitive distortions** that can be identified and changed through the process of cognitive therapy. Some types of cognitive distortions include all-or-nothing thinking, disqualifying the positive, and catastrophizing (Burns, 1999). **All-or-nothing thinking** is characterized by assuming that things are either 100% perfect or absolutely terrible; there is no grey area. Because few things are perceived as perfect, all-or-nothing thinking usually leads to depression. **Disqualifying the positive** is defined as the rejection of any positive experiences (i.e., compliments) and assuming that these positive events do not really count. The person using this type of distortion may say, "I only received an A because the test was so easy" or "She is only complimenting me because she wants a ride in my new car." **Catastrophizing** is the exaggeration of a negative event so that it has much more impact than it deserves. Making a mistake at work or receiving a B on a quiz may be catastrophized into losing the job or failing the course.

Cognitive therapy utilizes many kinds of procedures, including thought stopping and positive self-statements, to change negative or maladaptive thoughts. **Thought stopping** is a procedure designed to interfere with thoughts that run through the mind of the client and make it difficult to change behavior. In this procedure, the client imagines the troublesome thought running through his or her mind, and the counselor or therapist shouts "Stop!" While the client may be a bit surprised, the shout does usually stop the thought. The client can then replace the thought with a more adaptive one, like "I can handle this situation." Clients can learn to do this procedure on their own, and can stop their self-defeating thoughts and substitute more useful ones.

The use of **positive self-statements** can go along with thought stopping. Statements such as "My opinion is important" or "I am an assertive person" can be practiced over and over. It is normal that these thoughts may not feel quite right at first. The important point is that what clients tell themselves influences their feelings and behavior. The counselor or therapist may use the self-statements as a way to cue assertive behavior by saying, "If it were true that your opinion was important, how might you behave?" The client might be encouraged to try acting as if the statements were true.

Cognitive-Behavioral Interventions   The essence of cognitive-behavioral therapies is the union of behavioral and cognitive strategies to help people. Often cognitive-behavioral strategies include the use of treatment manuals or guidelines for the implementation of interventions, with counseling and psychotherapy strategies clearly described and evaluated. Other advantages of treatment manuals include facilitation of counselor or therapist training and an increased ability to replicate research (Dobson & Shaw, 1988). Manuals for cognitive-behavioral treatment of a variety of psychological problems (Sanderson & Woody, 1995; Woody & Sanderson, 1998) are available. These manuals are specific for clinical problems; thus, the list contains cognitive-behavioral manuals for bulimia nervosa (Fairburn, Marcus, & Wilson, 1993), chronic pain (Turk, Meichenbaum, & Genest, 1983), depression (Beck et al., 1979), anxiety disorders (Brown, O'Leary, & Barlow, 1994), and panic disorder (Barlow & Cerny, 1988). (Note that this list is not exhaustive; interested readers are referred to *http:www.apa.org/divisions/div12/est/ manual60.html*).

Beck's Cognitive Therapy.   The primary principle underlying **cognitive theory (CT)** is that affect and behavior are determined by the way individuals cognitively structure the world. In an interview with Weinrach (1988), Beck described CT as "based on the view of psychopathology that stipulates that people's excessive affect and dysfunctional behavior are due to excessive or inappropriate ways of interpreting their experiences" (p. 160). First developed to treat depression, CT was later extended as a treatment for anxiety and is now being used to treat other psychological problems such as panic disorder, agoraphobia, drug abuse, and eating disorders. Interested readers are referred to full descriptions of CT in *Cognitive Therapy of Depression* (Beck et al., 1979), *Anxiety Disorders and Phobias* (Beck & Emery with Greenberg, 1985), *Cognitive Therapy of Personality Disorders* (Beck, Freeman, & Associates, 1990), and *Cognitive Therapy of Substance Abuse* (Beck, Wright, Newman, & Liese, 1993). Beck and Emery (1985) identified the following major principles of CT.

1. It is based on the cognitive model of emotional disorders.
2. It is brief and time-limited.
3. It is based on a sound therapeutic relationship, which is a necessary condition.
4. It is a collaborative effort between the client and the counselor or therapist.
5. It uses primarily the Socratic method.
6. It is structured and directive.
7. It is problem-oriented.
8. It is based on an educational model.
9. Its theory and techniques rely on the inductive model.
10. It uses homework as a central feature.

The cognitive model of disturbance asserts that cognitions play a central role in human emotional problems. In CT, there is an emphasis on internal thoughts, feelings, and attitudes rather than on behavior, although behavioral techniques are used in conjunction with cognitive therapy to help clients test their maladaptive cognitions and assumptions. Cognitive restructuring is used to identify automatic thoughts, evaluate their content, test the hypothesis that is generated, and identify underlying assumptions.

Unlike some dynamic therapies, CT is time-limited; treatment of anxiety disorders may take from five to twenty sessions (Beck & Emery, 1985), and treatment for moderate to severe depression may take 20 sessions over 15 weeks (Beck et al., 1979). The pace of intervention is rapid, and longer-term therapy is viewed as unnecessary to facilitate change. Some guidelines useful for keeping the counseling and psychotherapy process brief include keeping treatment specific and concrete, stressing homework, and developing the expectation that intervention will be brief for both the client and the counselor or therapist (Beck & Emery, 1985).

The therapeutic relationship is highly valued in CT. In order for the cognitive methods to work well, the counselor or therapist must work to establish good rapport with the client. Accurate empathy and warmth are necessary to enable the client to engage in a relationship with the practitioner such that cognitive techniques can be implemented. Using CT requires a collaboration between the counselor or therapist and the client. It is the practitioner's role to provide structure and expertise in solving the problems presented by the client, but this process involves teamwork. CT has been described as using collaborative empiricism, which is a continual process used by the counselor or therapist and the client to identify, reality-test, and correct cognitive distortions. Clients are encouraged to be active in the process of learning how maladaptive thoughts interfere with desirable behavior change.

The Socratic (or inductive) method is one in which the counselor or therapist leads the client through a series of questions in order to become aware of thoughts, identify the distortions in thinking, and find and implement more adaptive replacements for the distortion. Beck et al. (1979) provide the following interaction, which illustrates the use of questions to assist the client in disputing irrational thoughts.

> PATIENT: I think anyone who isn't concerned with what others think would be socially retarded and functioning at a pretty low level.
> THERAPIST: Who are the two people you admire most? (The therapist knew the answer from previous discussion.)
> P: My best friend and my boss.
> T: Are these two over-concerned with others' opinions?
> P: No, I don't think that either one cares at all what others think.
> T: Are they socially retarded and ineffective?
> P: I see your point. Both have good social skills and function at high levels. (pp. 265-266)

This example shows how the counselor or therapist can use examples and questions to guide the client to the conclusion that the initial statement was inaccurate.

CT is a structured and directive approach to counseling and psychotherapy. Treatment manuals have been developed that are used to structure the counseling and psychotherapy process. Treatment plans are developed for each individual, and each session has an agenda to organize the discussion of specific problems. It is clear that CT is problem-oriented, which means that the focus is on solving present problems. CT is based on an educational model; because it assumes that people learn inappropriate ways of coping with life, the process of change involves developing new ways of learning and thinking.

The inductive method is essential to CT because it involves a scientific way of thinking about problems (Hollon & Beck, 1994). This means that clients are taught to think of their beliefs as hypotheses that require testing and verification. Counselors or therapists are trained to help clients disconfirm maladaptive beliefs by confronting them with evidence contrary to those beliefs. Hypotheses often require behavioral assignments to test assumptions outside of the counseling or psychotherapy session, and clients report on their experiences. In addition, CT requires the client to do regular homework assignments. This involves applying the techniques learned in the counseling or psychotherapy office in the client's world and reporting the results to the counselor or therapist. Homework is used to reinforce learning and to give the client a place to try out new behaviors.

Meichenbaum's Self-Instructional Training and Stress Inoculation Training.   Meichenbaum's work has been described as the prototype of cognitive-behavioral work because it is a full integration of cognitive and behavioral elements (Hollon & Beck, 1994). Meichenbaum began his work on self-talk by studying schizophrenia (1969). He found that when individuals with schizophrenia were trained to use "healthy" self-talk (self-statements) such as "Be relevant," they were able to repeat these phrases and behave more appropriately. He continued to consider the role of self-statements in his work with impulsive children (Meichenbaum & Goodman, 1969) and developed the procedures for self-instructional training, which he published in a treatment manual in 1977.

Self-instructional training (Meichenbaum, 1977) is a technique in which clients learn to keep track of self-statements and to substitute more adaptive statements. Clients learn to make these adaptive statements through homework assignments and practice in nonstressful situations. It is important that the statements be phrased in the words of the client to be personally meaningful. Later, the adaptive statements are practiced in increasingly stressful situations to deal with anxiety or phobia. Self-instructional training has been used alone and within the stress inoculation treatment package.

Stress inoculation training (SIT) is a cognitive-behavioral intervention package that combines "didactic teaching, Socratic discussion, cognitive restructuring, problem-solving and relaxation training, behavioral and imaginal rehearsal, self-monitoring, self-instruction and self-reinforcement, and efforts at environmental change" (Meichenbaum, 1985, p. 21). The name of this strategy highlights the emphasis on stress as the problem, inoculation as an analogy to the medical concept of inoculation against biological disease as a way to develop the "psychological immunities" to cope with stress, and training as part of the clinical technique.

SIT consists of three phases: conceptualization, skills acquisition and rehearsal, and application and follow-through (Meichenbaum, 1985). The conceptualization phase has as its primary focus the development of a therapeutic relationship between the client and the counselor or therapist, and provides the client with the background to understand stress and its effects on human life. The second phase—skills acquisition and rehearsal—consists of learning a variety of coping skills and practicing these skills in session and in vivo. In cases in which clients have coping skills they are using, the practitioner might assist the client to understand the intra- and interpersonal issues raised by using the skills and help the client to remove inhibitors to using appropriate coping skills. The final phase, application and follow-through, is included to bring attention to the importance of a booster session, follow-up activities, and relapse prevention.

The specific goals and objectives for each phase of SIT are clearly outlined in Meichenbaum's *Stress Inoculation Training* (1985) and in Meichenbaum and Deffenbacher (1988). The conceptualization phase of SIT is structured to tie assessment of the problematic situation to the development of the helping relationship. This phase is educational and conceptual (Meichenbaum & Deffenbacher, 1988). The therapeutic relationship is critical to mediate the behavioral changes because SIT, like CT, is a collaborative intervention. Meichenbaum highlights the need for warmth, accurate understanding, and acceptance in developing a trusting relationship. Assessment consists of a semi-structured interview in which the client is asked to describe the problem and provide concrete examples of stressful events. A cognitive-behavioral analysis of stressful reactions is obtained by asking about specific antecedents (What was going on the last time the problem occurred?) and consequences (What happened afterward?). Assessment may include imagery-based recall, a procedure in which clients are guided through an imaginal reexperiencing of a stressful event. This is done to collect information about the thoughts, feelings, and behaviors associated with stress. Self-monitoring and open-ended diaries or stress logs can be used to bring valuable information back to the sessions. Other sources of information include in vivo behavioral assessments and psychological testing. It should be clear that the conceptualization phase is important because it provides the background necessary for the implementation of coping strategies and helps the practitioner choose the types of coping skills to be introduced in the next phase.

The second phase of SIT (skills acquisition and rehearsal) is designed to ensure that the client learns and can implement various coping skills (Meichenbaum & Deffenbacher, 1988). Clients should complete this phase with a repertoire of strategies to cope with stressful situations. Relaxation training is a very commonly used technique. Meichenbaum does not present a single type of relaxation technique; instead, he highlights the need to work with individual clients to ensure that the relaxation training procedure will be practiced regularly and used in anticipation of stressful situations. Cognitive restructuring strategies such as Beck's CT may be used to make clients aware of the role that thoughts and feelings have in maintaining stress. Problem-solving training is another intervention that may be implemented. Self-instructional training (Meichenbaum, 1977) is often used to help clients learn to make and use adaptive self-statements.

The major objective of the third phase of SIT (application and follow-through) is to facilitate the use of the coping strategies learned in the skills acquisition phase. Clients practice more than one strategy and learn to identify the circumstances under which a particular strategy is likely to work well. Imagery rehearsal is an important part of this phase of SIT. Imagery is used to practice the coping strategies in stressful situations. Clients might imagine themselves becoming stressed and having stressful thoughts and feelings, and then use the coping skills they have learned to handle the stress. Behavioral rehearsal, role playing, and modeling can also be used in sessions to practice coping skills and to evaluate the effectiveness of those skills for specific situations. Greater generalization to clients' real-life experiences may be facilitated through the use of homework assignments in which clients try out the new strategies and report on the outcomes.

Marlatt and Gordon (1984), who have developed strategies for relapse prevention, assert that clients are likely to have slips in their ability to practice new skills. To counter the negative effects of relapse, clients are told that it is very likely that they will make mistakes and want to give up trying the coping skills they have learned. This is viewed as a normal part of the process of change, and strategies are planned to deal with these events. Because stress is a part of life, clients should expect to continue to face stress, but through the use of the coping skills, they can learn to manage the effects of stress. Follow-through is included as a reminder that treatment effects may deteriorate after formal treatment ends. Booster sessions may be helpful to refresh the skills and the principles of SIT.

Clients with Mental Disorders

Cognitive-behavioral therapies have been developed and used with clients with a wide range of clinical problems. A great deal of research supports the use of CBT with a variety of clinical problems. The work on empirically supported treatments (EST; see Chambless, Sanderson, Shohan, Bennett-Johnson, Pope, Crits-Christoph et al., 1996) is indicative of the efficacy of CBT with people with generalized anxiety disorder, obsessive-compulsive disorder, panic disorder, social phobia, specific phobia, depression, eating disorders, and others (Sanderson & Woody; 1995; Woody & Sanderson, 1998). The list of EST contains references for the specific treatments and manuals for conducting each type of therapy, along with training opportunities for each of the treatments. Interested readers are referred to *http://www.apa.org/dividions/div12/est/manual60.html* for further information. Additionally, those interested in applying CBT to adolescents may review Braswell and Kendall (2001), which describes the application of CBT to youth.

Evaluation

Overview

A tremendous amount of research has been conducted on the effectiveness of various cognitive-behavioral interventions for different types of disorders. As indicated earlier, the whole body of work on empirically supported treatments is indicative of research that demonstrates the efficacy of cognitive-behavioral therapy for a variety of problems. Hollon and Beck (1994) and Emmelkamp (1994) provide comprehensive reviews. The following review will be limited to research on Beck's work. Readers interested in CBT with other clinical issues are advised to look in the publications described here. Other reviews can be found in the *Annual Review of Behavior Therapy and Progress in Behavior Modification*. Research on cognitive-behavioral treatment is ongoing; readers may find interesting articles published in several professional journals such as *Behavior Therapy, Cognitive and Behavioral Practice, Cognitive Therapy and Research*, and *Addictive Behaviors*.

Supporting Research

Beck's Cognitive Therapy for Depression   The treatment of depression has received a great deal of attention from cognitive-behavioral researchers. Beck's CT, developed for the treatment of depression, has been the subject of numerous treatment outcome studies. It has been compared to waiting list controls, nondirective therapy, behavior therapy, and various antidepressant medications with favorable findings. In an older but often-cited study, Shaw (1977) compared Beck's CT to behavior therapy treatment for depression developed to restore an adequate schedule of positive reinforcement (including activity scheduling, verbal contracts, and communication and social skill development), nondirective therapy, and a waiting list control. Those treated by CT had the best outcomes on self-report measures of depression. In addition, ratings by clinicians unaware of the type of therapy received by individual clients also were more favorable for the CT treatment group.

A meta-analysis of treatment studies comparing CT to no-treatment controls yielded the finding that CT clients had lower final depression scores than 99% of the no-treatment control subjects (Dobson & Shaw, 1988). It is clear that CT is better than no treatment.

The next test involved a comparison of the effects of CT with antidepressant medication. In a landmark comparative outcome study, Rush, Beck, Kovacs, and Hollon (1977) compared the use of CT to pharmacotherapy based on the tricyclic antidepressant imipramine. The clients were moderately to severely depressed individuals seeking treatment for depression. Clients were randomly assigned to CT or drug treatment. CT consisted of no more than 20 sessions in 12 weeks, and the imipramine treatment consisted of 12 weekly sessions. Weekly self-report depression ratings were obtained. In addition, an independent (though not unaware of the treatment being received) clinician interviewed the subjects to provide a clinical rating of depression. Although both interventions led to a reduction in depression, the results indicated that CT outperformed medication in client self-report ratings and in clinician evaluations. Over 78% of the clients treated with CT showed marked reductions in depression, whereas only 22% of those treated with medication experienced similar reductions in depression. In addition, there was a greater drop-out rate associated with the medication treatment. These results are particularly astounding in light of the fact that many of the therapists were psychoanalytically oriented and relatively inexperienced in conducting CT. (Therapists did follow a specified CT treatment manual and received weekly supervision.) It seems that CT is an effective intervention for depression.

Another study that also used medication and CT to treat depression found that the use of drugs and CT was no better than CT alone (Beck, Hollon, Young, Bedrosian, & Budenz, 1985). CT and drug treatment were better than drug treatment alone, leading Beck to conclude that if a client needs antidepressant medication, he or she should get CT with the medication. More recently, DeRubeis, Gelfand, Tang, and Simons (1999) reanalyzed individual patient data from four studies of CT treatment for depression, and concluded that cognitive therapy is as effective as medication for treatment of severely depressed patients. Another recent study (Jarrett et al., 1999) also concluded that CT and medication are effective treatments for depression. Thus, conclusions from this research indicate that CT is as effective as medication in the treatment of depression, even in cases of severe depression.

Limitations

The union of cognitive and behavioral counseling and therapy into "cognitive-behavioral" has been able to overcome many of the limitations of either type of therapy alone. However, those individuals who are more inclined toward psychodynamic interpretations continue to object to the lack of attention to unconscious factors in determining behavior and to concepts such as ego strength and insight, which are not included in this approach. In addition, experiential counselors and therapists indicate that cognitive-behavioral strategies do not pay enough attention to feelings. Insight and an emphasis on the past are features of other types of counseling and therapy that do not fit within the purview of cognitive-behavioral theory.

The behavior therapy roots of current cognitive behavioral theory may be criticized as lacking attention to the role of thoughts and feelings, ignoring the historical context of the present problem, and allowing the counselor or therapist too much power to manipulate the client. Because the origins of behavioral theory emphasized operationally defined behaviors and functional analysis, these are features that define the approach. These are the things that make behavioral counseling behavioral. The idea that behavioral counselors and therapists are manipulative comes from the use of external reinforcers and stimulus control types of treatments. It seems that this notion is maintained by token economy systems. In individual practice, behavioral counselors or therapists use informed consent to make changes in the contingencies of behavior.

The cognitive therapy roots may be described as too difficult to study empirically and as paying too much attention to cognitive factors while minimizing affective ones. Cognitive therapies focus to a large extent on internal events (thoughts) that cannot be directly observed. Although the radical behaviorists object to this, most other types of counseling or psychotherapy would also fit this criticism. Cognitive therapy researchers have continued to develop thought-listing and monitoring strategies to alleviate this criticism. In addition, cognitive strategies have been challenged for the lack of sufficient attention to affective factors. It seems that the emphasis on cognitions may lead to an intellectual understanding of the problem, but may not help change the feelings associated with the thoughts. This limitation is related to the fact that the mechanism for understanding how behavior, thoughts, and feelings change is still not understood.

Summary Chart—Cognitive-Behavioral Theories

Human Nature
Cognitive-behavioral theories are not developmental in the same sense that stage theories are. There is a stated assumption that behavior is learned, which applies equally to the explanation of how problem behaviors and adaptive behaviors are developed. Behavior is assumed to be developed and maintained by external events or cues, by external reinforcers, or by internal processes such as cognition. Development is based on each individual's different learning history, experiences, and cognitive understanding of the world.

Major Constructs
The major constructs of cognitive-behavioral theories are an amalgamation of behavioral and cognitive approaches and include emphasis on behavioral and cognitive excesses or deficits, learning theory, observed changes in behavior, semantic interventions, and changes in cognitions. Operational definitions, functional analysis, and therapeutic empathy also serve as major constructs.

Goals
The goals of cognitive-behavioral theories are best viewed in terms of understanding the nature of the presenting problem from a behavioral, affective, cognitive, and social perspective; how progress in counseling and psychotherapy can be measured and monitored; the environmental contingencies maintaining the behavior; and which interventions are more likely to be effective.

Change Process
Because many different theories and interventions comprise the cognitive-behavioral arena, the process of change is best understood in terms of how the theory explains the

mechanisms for change. For example, Bandura's self-efficacy theory asserts that individuals develop expectations for their success in performing specific behaviors and that these expectations influence their decisions to try new behaviors and maintain behavioral changes, whereas Beck asserts that behavioral and affective change occur through the change in cognitions.

Interventions

The interventions used in cognitive-behavioral theories are best viewed in terms of behavioral interventions (reinforcement, positive reinforcement, negative reinforcement, extinction, shaping, and stimulus control) and cognitive interventions (identifying cognitive distortions, thought stopping, the use of positive self-statements, cognitive restructuring, use of the empathic therapeutic relationship, the Socratic method, disputing, reframing, role playing, modeling, humor, homework, risk-taking exercises, systematic desensitization, bibliotherapy, shame-attacking exercises, self-instructional training, stress inoculation training, and relapse prevention).

Limitations

Based upon the views of the critics of cognitive-behavioral theories, the theories are limited as a result of their lack of attention to unconscious factors in determining behavior and to concepts such as ego strength and insight, which are not included in the approach. Experiential counselors and therapists indicate that cognitive-behavioral strategies do not pay enough attention to feelings. Insight and an emphasis on the past (often seen as important in other theories) do not fit within the purview of cognitive-behavioral theory.

▪▪▪ The Case Of Jonathan: A Cognitive-Behavioral Approach

Using Persons and Davidson's (2001) case conceptualization model as the basis of this discussion, I begin with a problem list. The case study provides bits and pieces of the kind of information necessary to understand the problems faced by Jonathan. It would be best to have the client explain the problem, which Jonathan does not do in this case description—at least, not directly.

Jonathan's "problem list" follows.

1. *Depressed, feels hopeless and lonely.* A Beck Depression Inventory score would be a useful bit of information. Depression is evidenced by sad affect, sleep disturbances, and disturbing dreams. His statements "I have little to live for. I have ruined the lives of three families plus my own life and who knows what I am doing to my children" are indicative of his depressed affect and sense of hopelessness.

2. *Interpersonal difficulties at work.* Jonathan reports problems at work that involve both his supervisor (who made the recommendation that Jonathan seek counseling) and his co-workers. He feels misunderstood and unliked. He perceives his work as less than what his supervisor and co-workers expect. He responds with anger to these situations.

3. *Interpersonal difficulties in relationships with women (ex-wife and second wife).* Jonathan is currently separated from his second wife and young daughter. He was previously married and has three other children. The first marriage ended in divorce when Jonathan began to drink heavily and had an affair. His second marriage is also in jeopardy

because of Jonathan's drinking and extramarital relationships. He feels like a failure in relationships with women and expresses guilt for being an absent father.

4. *Acculturation issues.* Jonathan grew up on the Navajo reservation, but left after his separation from his second wife. He is currently living in the city. He is separated from his culture, family, and heritage. He feels alienated, a victim of racism and prejudice, and "not wanted in the white man's world."

Note: The multicultural issues that are present when working with Native American individuals may be complicated by the view that many believe that mental illness is a justifiable outcome of human weakness or the result of avoiding the discipline necessary for the maintenance of cultural values and community respect (LaFromboise, 1998). I include acculturation issues on the problem list and highlight the unique aspects of working with a client of a Native American background. The reader is encouraged to note that multicultural counseling requires a set of skills that goes beyond that which can be presented in this cognitive-behavioral case conceptualization.

5. *Alcohol abuse.* Jonathan has a history of drinking heavily and using alcohol as an escape from interpersonal problems.

6. *Grief issues.* Jonathan feels guilty about being the driver in the accident that led to his brother's death. This appears to be unresolved grief. In addition, he feels a loss (grief) about being away from his four children.

Working Hypothesis

Schemata   Jonathan's thoughts about self, others, the world and the future can be summarized in this fashion.

1. I am inadequate, irresponsible, inferior, ashamed, and guilty.
2. Others are demanding, disrespectful, and do not understand me.
3. The world is unfair, demanding, and racist.
4. The future is hopeless.

Precipitating and Activating Situations   The immediate precipitant was his supervisor's suggestion that he talk to someone about the problems he was having at work. He has looked for other employment, but has been unable to find another job, which he attributes to prejudice toward Native Americans. When Jonathan feels helpless and lacking in control of his life, he often drinks alcohol or seeks inappropriate relationships with women, both of which create additional problems in his life.

Origins   The onset of Jonathan's problems appears to have occurred when his brother was killed as a result of a car accident in which he was the driver. We do not know much about this accident: Was Jonathan drinking? How has the family resolved their grief about this loss? How do they deal with loss in general? (There was also a loss of a sister during childbirth.) Jonathan may have learned that feelings are not to be discussed, which leaves him with sadness and guilt and no outlet for these emotions.

Summary of Working Hypothesis   When Jonathan was challenged to take responsibility for himself, his family, and his tribe, he began to feel "less than." His cognitive schema of inadequacy, irresponsibility, inferiority, shame, and guilt brought about unhealthy coping strategies, such as alcohol abuse and seeking sexual comfort in women. He feels angry and frustrated. These patterns have occurred in his personal and professional relationships over many years.

Because Jonathan is a Native American who recently left the reservation, several issues are relevant. These include feelings of inadequacy and low self-esteem as indicators of depression. Stress is associated with relocating to an urban area among Native Americans who leave the reservation.

Strengths and Assets

Jonathan is intelligent, resilient, and caring. He has an intact family who appear to want him to be involved with the immediate family and the tribe. He completed 2 years of a nursing degree and was employed on the reservation at the Bureau of Indian Affairs Hospital. He is part of a culture that values the family and social group.

Treatment Plan
Goals
1. Reduce depressive symptoms.
2. Increase self-esteem and confidence.
3. Increase social support through family or extra-family support.
4. Reduce anger.
5. Develop relaxation strategies.
6. Join AA affiliated with a reservation or tribal community.
7. Return to school to finish nursing degree.

Modality
1. Individual CBT that is culturally sensitive.
2. AA that is affiliated with Native Amercian values.

Initial Intervention
1. Focus on the present by assessing current depression and suicidality using BDI and clinical interview.
2. Refer to culturally sensitive AA group. (Alcoholism is a critical issue with Native Americans and it is associated with suicide and violence in this group.)
3. Incorporate meditative relaxation.
4. Develop an anger management plan.
5. Do not discuss medication as a treatment option. Many Native Americans believe that synthetic medication is not good for their health (Paniagua, 1998).

Asking Jonathan to describe his problem would help the counselor or therapist identify the primary presenting problem and provide the basis for deciding on goals for counseling or psychotherpy. This is not clearly presented in the case description, which is telling in that Jonathan may not understand what he might be able to get out of counseling or psychotherapy. A first step might be to help Jonathan describe how he wants his life to be different than it currently is. The goals can be expressed in cognitive, behavioral, or affective statements. For example, Jonathan might indicate that he wants to get a new job, return to school, or move back to the reservation. He may express an interest in feeling less depressed or angry. He may want to discuss his drinking and target that for change. What Jonathan wants is not clear from the case description provided.

How can progress in counseling or psychotherapy be measured and monitored? The counselor might select cognitions, behaviors, or feelings to monitor. Jonathan could complete thought diaries or record the kinds of maladaptive thoughts he has during the day. He might be asked to keep track of how often he drinks, or some other target behavior. He could record a rating of his feelings, which would provide useful information about how his behaviors and thoughts contribute to his negative affect. The counselor or therapist could also use a variety of self-report measures such as the Beck Depression Inventory to provide a record of depression.

What are the environmental contingencies maintaining the behavior? In this arena, it is important to study Jonathan's issues in the particular contexts of his daily life. What happens at work that contributes to his negative thoughts and feelings? It could be that he is telling himself that he is not performing as his supervisor thinks that he should, and this contributes to his problems at work. Likewise, what are his thoughts about his children? Does he think that they miss him and want him to be present in their lives, or is he thinking that they are glad that their dad is far away? We don't know, other than that he wonders if his absence is harmful to their development.

Which interventions are likely to be effective? It seems that the cognitive-behavioral interventions described in this chapter would be valuable for working with Jonathan. I have selected Beck's cognitive therapy to demonstrate how a particular approach would be used. Establishing rapport is a critical part of Beck's approach. The counselor or therapist will have to take special steps to establish good rapport with Jonathan. Because of his Native American cultural background, this may be a particularly important part of the counseling or psychotherapy process. Jonathan may have difficulty with the notion of counseling or therapy. He may be more accustomed to medicine men and other Native American healers and their practices (Paniagia, 1998). I would encourage Jonathan to bring this type of healing into our work, and I would be most interested in collaborating with a Native American healer to work with Jonathan. (Additionally, it would not be appropriate to question or interpret Jonathan's lateness to the session; rather, it is noted that the orientation to time is different among Native Americans.) Accurate empathy and warmth conveyed throughout the assessment and intervention are necessary to engage Jonathan in collaborative efforts to test some of the thoughts he identifies and to try new strategies in his work setting and personal relationships. A strong therapeutic relationship is necessary to allow therapeutic effects to be maximized.

A cognitive-behavioral counselor or therapist would establish a plan that focused on developing an understanding of the role Jonathan's thinking is having in his current situation. Jonathan would be challenged to identify the thoughts that go through his mind at work and at home, especially thoughts that are tied to depression, alcohol abuse, and anger. Patterns of thoughts might be classified into general categories of cognitive distortions, such as all-or-nothing thinking, overgeneralization, or disqualifying the positive. As Jonathan learns how to identify thoughts, he may also begin to talk about some feelings and see that the thoughts and feelings are related to his problems. It is the primary task of the counselor or therapist to demonstrate that the thoughts, feelings, and behaviors are interrelated and that the counseling or psychotherapy will work through changing the maladaptive thoughts.

Once there is an understanding of some of the thoughts that Jonathan may be having, the counselor begins the process of changing the thoughts. Questions like "What's the evidence?" "What's another way of looking at the situation?" and "So what if it happens?" (Beck & Emery, 1985, p. 201) are useful. Hypothesis testing, generating alternative interpretations, and decatastrophizing are some cognitive strategies that might be used. Self-monitoring thoughts might be used as a homework assignment to help Jonathan focus on thoughts and how they affect his behavior and feelings. One of the ways Jonathan copes with depression is to drink alcohol. Although this withdrawal behavior is a consequence of the depression, it ultimately increases the depressed feeling he has because it isolates him from making real connections with others. The extramarital relationships are outcomes of this situation, and they create a situation in which he feels more isolated and unhappy.

There are other features of Jonathan's case study that a counselor or therapist would address, including a potential risk of suicide and his parental, family, and tribe relationships. I have focused primarily on depression, as it seems that it is the primary problem, and one for which there is great motivation to seek solutions. As Jonathan learns the strategies in cognitive therapy, he may be better equipped to address the other problem areas in his life.

10

Rational Emotive Behavior Therapy

Ann Vernon
University of Northern Iowa

Background

Albert Ellis, the grandfather of **cognitive-behavior therapy** and the founder of **rational-emotive therapy,** currently known as **rational emotive behavior therapy (REBT),** is considered as a mentor by more counselors and psychotherapists throughout the world than perhaps anyone else alive (Broder, 2001). Although he has a reputation for being abrasive and abrupt and often seems to delight in being flamboyant and somewhat eccentric, comments about his harsh manner reflect overgeneralizations. In fact, there is another side to Albert Ellis that is often ignored, which is his ability to be compassionate and personable—characteristics to which numerous clients, colleagues, and personal friends can attest. Although he is an energetic professional who literally never wastes a minute, he reveals his human-ness by being unassuming, witty, supportive, and encouraging (Di-Mattia & Lega, 1990). The fact that he donates all his income from his therapy sessions, lectures, and workshops to the **Albert Ellis Institute** attests to his generous nature.

Ellis was born in Pittsburgh in 1913, but has spent most of his life in New York City. The eldest of three children, Ellis was frequently hospitalized when he was young and had a great deal of social phobia throughout his childhood and teen years (Nelson-Jones, 2000, p. 182). Ellis was a very bright student who began writing stories, essays, and comic poems at the age of 12. Prior to becoming a psychologist, Ellis worked as an accountant while he pursued his interests in philosophy, music, literature, and politics. He wrote novels and operas, and as a political activist, he overcame his fear of public speaking by giving political talks (DiGiuseppe, 1999).

As a young man, Ellis was also very interested in romantic and sexual relationships, in part because he was anxious about dating. To overcome his shyness toward women, he forced himself to talk to a hundred girls in the Bronx Botanical Gardens (Ellis, 1997a). When others began asking him for advice about romance, friends encouraged him to enroll in a clinical psychology doctoral program. After graduating from Columbia University, he started intensive psychoanalytic training. Although he had reservations about Freud's theory of personality, he retained his belief in the efficacy of psychoanalytic techniques and spent

2 years in intense analysis. At the conclusion of his therapy, he worked under supervision with his own clients, sitting behind them on the sofa and practicing orthodox psychoanalysis. However, he soon became disillusioned with this approach and began to question the validity of interpretation, as well as the effectiveness and efficiency of psychoanalysis (DiGiuseppe, 1999; Ellis, 1994). In 1950, he began to experiment with different forms of therapy, including psychoanalytically oriented psychotherapy and eclectic-analytic therapy. Although he achieved better results with his clients, he still felt dissatisfied. He began putting his psychological and philosophical knowledge together in a different way, and in 1955 developed rational-emotive therapy, which is now known as rational emotive behavior therapy (Broder, 2001).

As an innovator, Ellis is often criticized, but asserts that he probably "gets more criticism than most because I do some original things" (Broder, 2001, p. 78). He does not let criticism stop him because he sees his motive as being effective and efficient. Therefore, he continues to change his ideas and revise his theory, striving to make it comprehensive and intensive so that "clients wouldn't just *feel better,* but they would also *get* better" (Broder, 2001, p. 78). As a therapist, Ellis sees his goal as solving personal and social problems. As a problem solver, he tries to figure out better solutions. He notes that had he not been a therapist, he would have been an efficiency expert. His intolerance for inefficiency can be summarized in his statement that he "recognized the fact that life is short and the one thing you never get back is time" (Broder, 2001, p. 78). For this reason, Albert Ellis does most things quickly and efficiently, and often does several things at once, such as exercising or reading while he listens to music. He also is not a procrastinator, as he views that as a waste of time. As a high school student, he did his homework in the 10 minutes between classes, and to this day, he always submits articles several months before they are due. He attributes his ability to accomplish so much to his persistence, lack of procrastination, and the fact that he does not have to do everything perfectly (Broder, 2001).

As the founder of REBT, Ellis generally practices what he preaches. Not long ago he fell and was hospitalized for several days. Although it was a major inconvenience because he was scheduled for an out-of-town speaking engagement, he characteristically did not complain, but instead videotaped his lecture from his hospital room and continued reading and writing during his stay. He has been diabetic since the age of 40, and is assiduous about testing his blood and giving himself insulin. Rather than being victimized by his fate, he deals with the disorder and makes the necessary accommodations by exercising high-frustration tolerance.

Rational emotive behavior therapy was the first cognitive-behavioral therapy to be introduced into clinical practice (Ellis, 1957). In its over 46 years of existence, it has been applied successfully to individual, group, marital, and family therapy for a wide array of problems. It is a well-established form of counseling or therapy that has been used very successfully with children and adults in hospital and mental health facilities, as well as in educational, industrial, and commercial settings (Ellis & Dryden, 1997). Although over 12,000 counselors or therapists throughout the world have been trained in REBT (DiGiuseppe, 1999), Ellis himself is one of the most significant promulgators of his theory. At 88 years of age, he works from 9:30 A.M. until 10:30 P.M., seven days a week, only interrupting his schedule for a brief afternoon nap in his office. In a given week, he may see as many as 80 clients, conduct at least five group therapy sessions, supervise trainees, and give lectures and workshops throughout the world. He still writes prolifically, having published over 65 books and 800 articles, primarily on the theory and applications of REBT.

Dr. Ellis is a frequent guest on radio and television shows, and has been featured on ABC, NBC, CBS, and CNN. He is a charismatic speaker who has given over 2,500 lectures and workshops throughout the world. He is one of the most controversial figures in modern psychology and has received numerous awards, including Distinguished Psychologist, Scientific Researcher, and Distinguished Psychological Practitioner from various associations (DiMattia & Lega, 1990). His books have been translated into more than 20 languages, and he is famous for his **rational humorous songs** that he has written and sung at his public talks and workshops and on numerous radio and television programs in the United States and abroad. Dr. Ellis is President of the **Albert Ellis Institute** in New York City, which has affiliated training centers throughout the world.

Human Nature: A Developmental Perspective

Rational emotive behavior therapy is based on the assumption that humans have a biological tendency to think irrationally or dysfunctionally, as well as rationally or functionally. Therefore, even though they have an inborn propensity toward growth and actualization, human beings can readily sabotage their growth by their unrealistic, illogical, or other types of defeatist thinking (Dryden, 1996; Dryden & Ellis, 2001; Ellis, 1994, 1998). Ellis and Dryden (1997) noted that, while social influences exist, even people with the most rational upbringing show evidence of major irrationalities and often adopt new irrationalities after giving up previous ones. Nevertheless, REBT theory clearly asserts that despite the tendency to think irrationally, humans have the ability to construct self-enhancing thoughts, feelings, and behaviors and are strongly motivated to change things for the better (Ellis, 2001a; Ellis & Dryden, 1997).

Fundamental to REBT is the notion that our contradictory nature, along with our social upbringing, not only impels us to create happier and more fulfilling lives, but also encourages us to elevate strong goals, desires, and preferences into absolutistic and unrealistic shoulds, oughts, and musts that lead to emotional and behavioral difficulties. Ellis (1994) noted that these shoulds, oughts, and musts fall under three main categories: **self-demandingness, other-demandingness,** and **world-demandingness.** Self-demandingness refers to the idea that we must always perform well and win others' approval; and if we do not, we are incompetent, unworthy, and deserve to suffer. Self-hatred, anxiety, and depression often result from self-demandingness, along with procrastination, withdrawal, and obsessiveness. Other-demandingness implies that people with whom we associate must always treat us kindly, considerately, and fairly; and if they do not, they are unworthy, bad, rotten, and deserve to be punished. Anger, rage, hurt, jealousy, vindictiveness, and violence develop as a result of other-demandingness. World-demandingness means that the conditions in which we live must be enjoyable, hassle-free, safe, and favorable; and if they are not, it is awful and horrible and unbearable. This form of demandingness often leads to anger, depression, self-pity, and low-frustration tolerance, as well as withdrawal, procrastination, phobias, and addictions (Ellis, 1994).

Major Constructs

REBT has a strong philosophical basis (Dryden & Ellis, 2001; Ellis & Dryden, 1997). In fact, Ellis relied heavily on the teachings of Epictetus, a Stoic philosopher, who believed that "men are disturbed not by things, but by the view which they take of them" (as cited in Walen, DiGiuseppe, & Dryden, 1992, p. 3). However, REBT is not a form of Stoicism because the true Stoic attempts to develop an immunity to feelings, whereas REBT recognizes that rational thinking leads to the healthy expression of feelings. Contrary to what many people believe, emotions are a significant component of this theory.

In developing REBT, Ellis was also influenced by several psychologists, including Karen Horney and Alfred Adler (Ellis, 1994; Ellis & Dryden, 1997). Karen Horney's "tyranny of the shoulds" (Ellis & Dryden, p. 3) lead to Ellis' emphasis on how absolutistic thinking creates and maintains emotional disturbance. Adler's work was important because he used active-directive teaching and emphasized people's goals, purposes, values, and meanings, concepts also inherent in REBT (Dryden & Ellis, 2001). Also, Adler was one of the first well-known therapists to focus on inferiority feelings (Ellis & Dryden, 1997), and REBT similarly addresses the concept of inferiority with its emphasis on self-rating and ego anxiety.

Developing a **rational philosophy of life** is a major construct of this theory. A rational philosophy is designed to help people increase their happiness and decrease emotional distress. Walen, DiGiuseppe, and Dryden (1992) noted that the purpose of a rational philosophy is to identify beliefs that lead to survival, satisfaction with living, positive ways of relating to others, intimate involvement with a few others, and personally fulfilling endeavors.

Commitment to the scientific method is also a central aspect of REBT. Applying the scientific method to one's personal life will help people give up dysfunctional beliefs that can lead to emotional disturbance and ineffectual behavior, according to Ellis (DiGiuseppe, 1999). Testing one's assumptions and examining the validity and functionality of beliefs are important, as well as developing flexibility in adopting new beliefs to guide behavior. Ellis' theory includes some elements of constructivism, specifically in the sense that humans would be better off if they understood that they themselves create their images of how the world is or should be (Ellis, 1998). However, whereas modern constructivists assert that people should be allowed to find their own reality and develop alternative beliefs on their own, REBT posits that there are some constructions—namely, rational beliefs—that are more functional and lead to emotional adjustment. Therefore, REBT and counselors or therapists focus on helping clients develop rational, as opposed to irrational, constructions (Dryden & Ellis, 2001).

According to this theory, certain values promote emotional adjustment and mental health. These values include the following (DiGiuseppe, 1999; Ellis & Dryden, 1987):

1. *Self-acceptance.* Healthy people accept themselves unconditionally and do not measure their worth by their achievements. They try to enjoy themselves rather than try to prove themselves.
2. *Risk-taking.* Emotionally healthy people take risks and tend to be rather adventurous, but not foolish.
3. *Non-utopian.* Healthy people realize they are unlikely to get everything they want, nor do they attempt to avoid everything they find painful. They accept

the fact that there is no such thing as utopia, and, therefore, do not strive for the unattainable or for unrealistic perfectionism.

4. *High-frustration tolerance.* Healthy people recognize that there are problems they can do something about and those they cannot change. Their goal is to modify the negative conditions that can be changed, accept those that cannot, and have the wisdom to know the difference between the two.

5. *Self-responsibility for disturbance.* Healthy individuals do not blame others, the world, or fate for their distress. Instead, they accept a good deal of responsibility for their own thoughts, feelings, and behaviors.

6. *Self-interest.* Emotionally healthy people tend to put their own interests somewhat above the interests of others. Although they sacrifice themselves to some degree for those for whom they care, they do not do this completely.

7. *Social interest.* Most people choose to live in social groups, and, therefore, they understand that it is important to act morally, protect the rights of others, and contribute to society in order to help create the kind of world in which they would like to live.

8. *Self-direction.* Emotionally healthy people generally assume responsibility for their own lives, but at the same time, cooperate with others. They do not need or demand considerable support or nurturance from others.

9. *Tolerance.* Healthy individuals allow themselves and others the right to be wrong, recognizing that they may not like unpleasant or obnoxious behavior but do not condemn humans for behaving that way.

10. *Flexibility.* Mature, healthy people are unbigoted, open to change, and flexible in their thinking. They do not make rigid rules for themselves or others.

11. *Acceptance of uncertainty.* Healthy individuals acknowledge and accept the fact that we live in a world where absolute certainties do not exist. Although they like some degree of order, they do not demand to know exactly what will happen.

12. *Commitment.* Individuals tend to be happier and healthier if they are involved in something outside themselves and have at least one strong, creative interest around which they structure part of their lives.

Theoretical Assumptions

Ellis would argue that REBT is more theoretical than most therapies and that the theory not only structures, but also drives the entire therapeutic process (Trower & Jones, 2001). Like most generic cognitive behavior therapies, REBT ascribes to the notion that cognitions or beliefs cause emotions and behavior, and REBT theorists stress the interconnectedness of thinking, feeling, and behaving (DiGiuseppe, 1999; Nelson-Jones, 2000). Because people think, feel, and act simultaneously, it is logical that what people think affects how they feel, that people usually do not feel or act without thinking, and that how they behave influences what they think and how they feel (DiGiuseppe, 1999).

Central to this theory is the idea that events and other people do not make us feel bad or good. Rather, emotional distress results from dysfunctional thought processes such as exaggeration, overgeneralization, oversimplification, illogic, faulty deductions, absolutistic rigid schema, and unvalidated assumptions (DiGiuseppe, 1999; Ellis, 1994, 1996). Therefore, the best way to reduce emotional distress is to change the way people think.

According to this theory, irrational beliefs emanate from multiple environmental and genetic factors. Although these factors contribute to the acquisition of irrational beliefs, they are maintained because people rehearse them and continue to reindoctrinate themselves without reevaluating their thinking (DiGiuseppe, 1999). REBT theorists emphasize that irrational beliefs can be changed, but acknowledge that this is often difficult and takes persistent practice. Ellis (cited in Nelson-Jones, 2000) stated that "People are born, as well as reared, with greater or lesser degrees of demandingness, and therefore they can change from demanding to desiring only with great difficulty" (p. 186).

Ellis and Dryden (1997) identified five major theoretical concepts: goals, purposes, and rationality; a humanistic emphasis; the interaction of psychological processes and the place of cognition; basic biological tendencies; and fundamental human disturbances.

Goals, Purposes, and Rationality   This theory proposes that humans are happiest when they have goals and purposes that give meaning to their lives. As they strive to attain their goals, they need to adopt a philosophy of self-interest, where they put themselves first and others a close second, as opposed to being selfish and disregarding others. Given that they are interested in goal attainment, **rational** implies "that which helps people to achieve their basic goals and purposes, whereas **irrational** means that which prevents them from achieving these goals and purposes" (Dryden, 1984, p. 238).

Humanistic Emphasis   Although REBT is rational and scientific, it is not "purely objective, scientific or technique-centered, but takes a definite humanistic-existential approach to human problems and their basic solutions" (Ellis & Dryden, 1997, p. 4). The importance of human will and choice is emphasized, while at the same time recognizing that some behavior is biologically or socially determined (Ellis, 1994, 1996).

The Interaction of Psychological Processes and the Place of Cognition   REBT theory emphasizes an interactive view of psychological processes in that cognitions, emotions, and behaviors do not exist in isolation, but actually overlap considerably. This theory, however, especially emphasizes the cognitive aspect of the psychological process. In fact, REBT is best known for the concept of rational and irrational beliefs.

Two Basic Biological Tendencies   This theory acknowledges that social influences have some impact on humans' tendency to think irrationally, but stresses a strong biological basis to irrationality. According to Ellis and Dryden (1997), even if everyone had an exceptionally rational upbringing, all humans would eventually think irrationally and dysfunctionally to varying degrees. Ellis also noted that many of our self-destructive behaviors are not advocated by parents, educators, or the media, which strengthens the argument for a biological basis. For example, parents do not encourage their children to procrastinate or seek immediate gratification, yet that does not stop children from doing it. Furthermore, even though people give up irrationalities, they often develop new ones and it is very easy to revert back to self-defeating behaviors even after working hard to change them. Unfortunately, it is sometimes easier to learn and practice self-defeating rather than self-enhancing behaviors.

Two Fundamental Human Disturbances   Dryden and Ellis (2001) identified two major categories of psychological disturbance: ego disturbance and discomfort disturbance. Ego disturbance occurs when individuals make demands on themselves, others, and the world. If these demands are not met, they put themselves down by assigning a global negative rating to themselves and identifying themselves as bad or less worthy. This is in contrast to the concept of **unconditional self-acceptance (USA)** that does not involve rating but acknowledges human fallibility.

Discomfort disturbance, or **low-frustration tolerance (LFT),** occurs when individuals make demands on themselves, others, and the world relative to comfort and life conditions. When these demands are not met, individuals begin to "awfulize" and develop an "I-can't-stand-it" attitude.

Applications

Overview

The following section describes the goals of the counseling or therapy process and how change occurs, with specific emphasis on the therapeutic relationship and the A-B-C process that is a hallmark of this theory. A wide array of cognitive, emotive, and behavioral interventions that illustrate the multimodal nature of the theory are also presented.

Goals of Counseling and Psychotherapy

The goal of rational emotive behavior therapy is to help clients develop a rational philosophy of life that will reduce their emotional distress and self-defeating behavior and result in their ability to be happier and live more meaningfully (Dryden, 1996; Walen et al.,1992). To achieve this goal, REBT counselors or therapists help clients identify how they prevent themselves from being happy by focusing on their irrational beliefs that lead to emotional and behavioral disturbance. They encourage clients to think more rationally (logically and flexibly), feel healthier, and act more efficiently in order to achieve their basic goals and purposes (Dryden, 1996). Consequently, the counselor or therapist employs cognitive, emotive, and behavioral interventions that help clients feel better and get better.

A basic premise of this theory is that it is educative and preventative. Therefore, another goal of the REBT counseling or psychotherapeutic process is to educate clients about how they disturb themselves and to actively teach them the A-B-C model so they can ultimately help themselves. REBT counselors or therapists encourage clients to read self-help books and listen to tapes. They share worksheets and articles that describe cognitive distortions and emotional disturbance. They do not hesitate to use themselves as models to teach the concept of self-acceptance by self-disclosing about how they have made mistakes or learned to overcome low-frustration tolerance, for example. With children and adolescents, they employ developmentally appropriate interventions that teach young clients the basic REBT concepts and how to help themselves overcome their problems (Vernon 1989a,b; 1998a,b,c; Vernon, in press).

The Process of Change

The REBT theory of change is basically optimistic in that although humans have a biological tendency to think irrationally, they also have the ability to choose to change their irrational thinking and self-defeating emotions and behavior (Dryden & Ellis, 2001). According to this theory, there are several levels of change. The most long-lasting and elegant change involves philosophic restructuring of the irrational beliefs (Dryden & Ellis, 2001, Ellis & Dryden, 1997). At this level, change can be specific or general. According to Dryden and Ellis, "Specific philosophic change means that individuals change their absolutistic demands ("musts," "shoulds") about given situations to rational relative preferences. General philosophic changes involve adopting a nondevout attitude toward life events in general" (p. 310). Dryden and Ellis also distinguished between **superelegant** and **semielegant** philosophical change at the general level (p. 310), noting that superelegant change implies that under almost all conditions for the rest of their lives, people will not upset themselves about anything, whereas semielegant change means that most of the time they will employ a rational-emotive philosophy that will enable them not to upset themselves when bad events occur. Superelegant change rarely happens, as people "fall back to musturbating and thereby disturbing themselves" (p. 310).

DiGiuseppe (1999) stressed that it is far better to help clients change their core irrational beliefs at the philosophic level rather than their automatic thoughts. Challenging automatic thoughts or inferences, reframing, or reattributions are considered **inelegant** solutions, and although they may be a coping strategy for a particular event, they do not do so across a wide range of stimuli.

The REBT theory of change is quite simple (Dryden, 1996). Specifically, if clients choose to overcome their emotional and behavioral problems, they first must acknowledge that they have a problem. They also need to realize that, to a large extent, they create their own disturbance. Although environmental conditions can significantly contribute to their problems, it is how they think about those conditions that primarily influences their degree of disturbance (Ellis & Dryden, 1997). Second, they must identify any **meta-disturbances,** which means being disturbed about the original disturbance. For example, clients often are depressed about being depressed, or denigrate themselves for having a problem. Unless clients tackle these meta-emotional problems before they deal with the original issues, they will often fail to overcome the original disturbance. Third, they need to identify irrational beliefs and understand why the belief is illogical and irrational. Fourth, they must recognize why the rational beliefs would be preferable and give them better results. Fifth, they need to learn how to challenge their irrational beliefs and replace them with rational alternatives. Finally, they need to keep working on their tendencies to think and act irrationally.

The Therapeutic Relationship   In order for change to occur, REBT counselors or therapists are active and involved as they educate clients and help them develop a rational perspective and effective problem-solving skills. According to Dawson (1991), the relationship between client and counselor or therapist is very important, and while counselors or therapists are building rapport with clients, they can also begin to help them recognize both their practical and emotional problems.

It is critical to note that although Ellis himself prefers an active, directive therapeutic style with most clients (Ellis & Dryden, 1997; Ellis & MacClaren, 1998), he does not dogmatically insist that there is one specific type of relationship between client and counselor or therapist, stressing that the degree to which one is active-directive is a choice (Dryden & Ellis, 2001; Ellis & MacClaren, 1998; Grieger, 1991). However, Ellis and MacClaren stated that there are several advantages of an active-directive approach, including the fact that some disturbed people have low-frustration tolerance and will not put forth the sustained effort needed for change to occur.

Dryden (1996) emphasized that rational emotive behavioral counselors or therapists are encouraged to be flexible, and both he and Ellis (1997, 2001) concurred that even though not all REBT practitioners agree with the active-directive style, it is possible to vary the style and, at the same time, adhere to the theoretical principles upon which it is based. According to Dryden (1999), "effective rational emotive behavioral counselors vary their therapeutic styles and can adopt a variety of therapeutic styles to fit with the therapeutic requirements of different clients" (p. 20). With children and adolescents, establishing a good therapeutic relationship is particularly important. Being patient, flexible, and less directive are essential, in addition to employing a wider variety of techniques (Vernon, in press; Vernon, 1999).

In accordance with this theory, REBT counselors or therapists believe that because clients come to counseling or therapy for problems and want help, that part of establishing a good relationship is to help them work on their problems immediately (DiGiuseppe, 1991). Thus, part of the rapport-building process involves coming to an agreement on the goals for change (Dryden, 1991), as well as being active and helping clients discover what they are doing to upset themselves. In this way, they can leave the first session with some insight and hope, which in turn enhances the client-counselor/therapist relationship.

Contrary to what many believe, this theory has been influenced by Rogers' core conditions. The concept of unconditional acceptance and genuineness is endorsed by REBT counselors or therapists (Dryden, 1999). REBT counselors or therapists encourage their clients to accept themselves unconditionally as fallible human beings and endeavor to accept their clients unconditionally as well. In fact, Dryden (1996) posited that unconditional acceptance is more important than counselor or therapist warmth because too much warmth may inadvertently reinforce clients' demands for love and approval, which is irrational.

Because they feel free to be themselves and at times self-disclose their own fallibilities, REBT counselors or therapists are genuine. This genuineness has therapeutic purposes because it indicates to clients that counselors are humans, too, and it also teaches them what the counselor did to overcome his or her own problems. Obviously, it is inappropriate to self-disclose when counselors or therapists think it inappropriate or think the client might use such self-disclosure against the counselor.

REBT counselors or therapists are also empathic, both affectively and philosophically, communicating that they understand how clients feel and also showing them that they understand the beliefs underlying the feelings (Dryden, 1999). They may also be appropriately humorous, as many clients tend to take life too seriously. Dryden stressed that humorous interventions are not directed at the clients themselves, but at their irrational beliefs and self-defeating feelings and behaviors. He cautioned that the use of humor may not be appropriate with all clients, which is why it is so important to be flexible.

Dryden (1999) noted that the preferred counseling or therapy relationship is egalitarian in that the client and counselor or therapist are equal in their humanity. From another perspective, however, the relationship is unequal because the counselor or therapist has more expertise and skills and needs to help clients in their personal problem solving. This changes, however, as clients gain more insight and the counselor or therapist encourages them to assume more responsibility for change. Thus, as the counselor or therapist becomes less directive and clients become more effective problem solvers, the relationship becomes more egalitarian.

The A-B-C Model   Ellis developed a conceptual model to illustrate the major constructs of this theory, as well as the process of change (Dryden, 1999; Dryden & Ellis, 2001; Ellis & MacClaren, 1998). In essence, the nature of emotional disturbance can be explained by recognizing that as people attempt to fulfill their goals, they encounter an **activating event (A)** that either blocks or helps them achieve these goals. Activating events may be positive or negative; may refer to real or perceived events; can be past, present, or future-oriented; and can be an individual's own thoughts or feelings. When individuals seek counseling or therapy, they strongly believe that the activating event has caused their negative **emotional and behavioral consequences (C).**

REBT theory posits that it is not the activating event (A) that creates the emotional and behavioral consequences (C), but rather the **beliefs (B)** people hold about these activating events. While the activating event may certainly contribute to the consequence, two individuals can experience the same event and feel and react differently, which explains the relationship between the A, B, and C. For example, consider two students who both studied hard for a test and failed it. Assume that one student was devastated and the other student was just disappointed. The difference in how they felt can be attributed to what they were thinking about the event. The devastated student equated her failure with her self-worth, thinking that this proved how stupid she was. The disappointed student wished that he would have gotten a better grade, but realized that this in no way proved his ignorance.

Beliefs (B) are either rational or irrational. **Rational beliefs** are self-enhancing and help people achieve their goals. They are realistic preferences that typically result in constructive behavior patterns and moderate negative emotions when the activating events (A) fall short of the desired outcome (Dryden, 1999; Ellis & MacClaren, 1998). **Irrational beliefs** emanate from absolutistic evaluations that ultimately sabotage goals. They result in negative emotions such as depression, anger, anxiety, resentment, self-pity, worthlessness, and rage, as well as in maladaptive behaviors such as withdrawal, avoidance, violence, and procrastination.

Originally Ellis identified 11 irrational beliefs (Ellis, 1962), but now there is one core belief, which is a "must" with several derivatives.

1. I must be successful at important performances and relationships, or I am inadequate and worthless.
2. Other people must treat me considerately and fairly, or else they are bad and deserve to be punished.
3. The conditions under which I live must be absolutely comfortable and pleasurable or I can't stand it (Ellis, 1996, p. 13).

These basic irrational beliefs share four key elements: demanding, awfulizing, low-frustration tolerance, and global rating of self or others. Irrational beliefs are illogical and are not validly inferred, whereas rational beliefs are logical and can be validly inferred from earlier premises. For instance, if a student wanted to get a good grade on his test, his rational and logical conclusion would be that studying and doing homework would help him achieve that goal. However, if he assumed that studying for tests and doing his homework meant that he absolutely must get a good grade and that the teacher cannot give him anything except a top grade, he would be thinking irrationally because his conclusions are illogical.

Counselors or therapists can detect irrational beliefs in several ways: cognitively, emotionally, and behaviorally. Cognitively, irrational beliefs can be identified by listening for "shoulds, oughts, and musts," as well as phrases such as "I can't stand it," or "that is horrible" (Nelson-Jones, 2000, p. 204). Emotionally, irrational beliefs are present when there are extreme negative emotions such as panic, depression, or intense anger. Specifically, when clients report feelings of depression, guilt, or extreme sadness, they are probably engaging in self-downing. When they are angry, look for "musts," and are demanding. Frustration and anxiety are often present with low-frustration tolerance. Behaviorally, self-defeating actions signal the likelihood of irrational beliefs. Once the emotional and behavioral consequences and the irrational beliefs have been identified, the next step in the A-B-C-model is **disputation (D),** which is what REBT is probably best known for. Disputation is an active process that helps clients assess the helpfulness of their belief system (Ellis & MacClaren, 1998). The purpose of challenging these rigid and inflexible beliefs is to replace them with rational alternatives.

Disputing can be **didactic,** which is informational. In this process, the counselor or therapist explains the difference between rational beliefs, which are flexible and adaptive and help in goal attainment; and irrational beliefs, which are rigid, illogical, and interfere with goal achievement (Ellis & MacClaren, 1998). The **Socratic** approach, another common form of disputation, involves questioning that gives clients insight into the irrationality of their thinking (Dawson, 1991).

During the disputation process, several different types of cognitive disputes are employed. In a **functional dispute,** the purpose is to question the practicality of the client's irrational beliefs. Because irrational beliefs result in self-defeating behaviors and unhealthy emotions, questions such as "How is what you are doing helping you?" or "How is continuing to think this way affecting your life?" are helpful (Ellis & MacClaren, 1998, p. 60). Another type of dispute is the **empirical dispute,** which helps clients evaluate the factual aspects of their beliefs. Examples of empirical disputes include: "Where is the evidence that you are no good simply because you failed an exam?" "Where is the proof that life is not worth living if you do not get into graduate school?" "So you did not get the job you wanted. Where is it written that you will never be employed for the rest of your life?"

A third type of dispute is the **logical dispute,** which helps clients see how illogical it is to escalate their desires and preferences into demands (Nelson-Jones, 2000). Typical questions could include: "How does it follow that just because you'd like this to be true and it would be very convenient, it *should* be" and "How does it follow that failing at an important task makes *you,* a person who may fail at many tasks and succeed at many others, a failure? How does *it,* failing, make *you,* worthless?" (Ellis & MacClaren, 1998, p. 64). **Philosophical disputing** is another approach that helps clients look at meaning and satisfaction in life. Because clients often focus on specific problems and lose perspective on other aspects of their life, a philosophical dispute such as the following will help them develop that perspective: "Despite the fact that things will probably not go the way you want some/most of the time in this area, can you still derive some satisfaction in your life?" (Ellis & MacClaren, 1998, p. 66).

Clients readily can recognize that their beliefs are not rational, but as Dryden (1999) cautioned, even if counselors or therapists are successful in helping them achieve this understanding, it does not mean that they have a strong conviction in the rational alternative. Although intellectual insight indicates some progress, it is not sufficient to promote emotional and behavioral change. Therefore, counselors or therapists must persist in helping clients give up their irrational beliefs by continuing to use directive questions, as well as other cognitive, emotive-evocative, imaginal, and behavioral techniques to help change irrational ideas. The ultimate goal is to help them develop **effective new beliefs or philosophy (E)** (Ellis, 2001a; Ellis, 1996) and **effective new feelings (F)** (Corey, 2001).

The 13-Step Model　Dryden and DiGiuseppe (1990) identified 13 steps that counselors or therapists can use in each session to help them implement the critical aspects of REBT in order to effect client change. They noted that these steps can be applied to all age groups, even though the techniques used at each step may differ.

The first step is to ask clients to describe the problem; the second is to reach agreement about the goals for the counseling or therapy session. In each session, clients may present different issues, and it is important to have consensus on what is to be addressed. The third step is to assess the emotional and behavioral consequences, followed by an assessment of the activating event, step 4. At step 5, the counselor or therapist determines whether there are any secondary emotional problems that must be dealt with first (for example, being anxious about being anxious). In the sixth step, the counselor or therapist teaches the connection between beliefs, feelings, and behaviors, followed by an assessment of irrational beliefs at step 7.

Step 8 involves connecting the irrational beliefs to the disturbed emotions and behaviors and connecting the rational beliefs to the healthy emotions and behaviors. Disputing the irrational beliefs, using a combination of logical, empirical, and functional disputes, is step 9. Proposing alternative rational ideas and using direct teaching are also appropriate. In step 10, the counselor or therapist helps clients deepen their conviction in the rational beliefs through continued disputing and by helping them describe how they would behave differently by adopting this new belief. Step 11 involves encouraging clients to practice new learning through the use of homework assignments that may include worksheets or various types of behavioral activities. In step 12, the counselor checks the homework assignments. The final step (13) is to help clients generalize to other situations by reviewing other examples of activating events that have been upsetting. This model is particularly helpful to counselors or therapists who are just beginning to practice REBT. The steps can be written in the form of a checklist to serve as a guide throughout the session.

Maintaining Change　REBT counselors or therapists recognize that clients will backslide, and therefore teach them that it will take work and practice to maintain change. Throughout the counseling or therapy process, they use bibliotherapy, homework assignments, and self-help materials to help clients develop skills to use inside and outside of counseling or therapy (Ellis & MacClaren, 1998; Vernon, in press). They also help clients review the A-B-C model to determine what caused them to fall back into their old patterns and then encourage them to practice disputing again and again until they can replace their irrational beliefs with rational alternatives (Nelson-Jones, 2000). Recording counseling or therapy sessions so that clients can listen to them again can also be very effective (Ellis & Velten, 1992).

Intervention Strategies

Dryden (1999) pointed out that REBT has a multimodal emphasis because REBT counselors or therapists utilize so many cognitive, emotive, and behavioral interventions to bring about change. Although REBT counselors or therapists employ techniques from other schools of therapy, it is important to realize that REBT "is based on a clear-cut theory of emotional health and disturbance" (Dryden & Ellis, 2001, p. 325), and that the techniques are consistent with the theory.

Cognitive Interventions   The most common cognitive intervention is the disputation of irrational beliefs, which involves helping clients detect the beliefs, debating with them about whether their beliefs are true or logical, and helping them discriminate between rational and irrational beliefs (Dryden & Ellis, 2001). Although Socratic questioning is often used, skillful counselors or therapists use a variety of disputing methods (DiGiuseppe, 1991).

Other cognitive interventions include written homework forms that help clients dispute their irrational beliefs between sessions (Ellis & MacClaren, 1998), and **referenting,** which is making a list of the advantages and disadvantages of changing their irrational beliefs and behaviors (Ellis & MacClaren, 1998). **Rational coping statements,** which are factual, encouraging phrases such as "I can accomplish this task," or "I will work toward accomplishing this task, but if I don't succeed it doesn't make me a failure as a person" (Ellis & MacClaren, 1998, p. 67) can also be very effective, particularly if they are implemented after more forceful disputing has been done.

Semantic methods are also employed, such as helping clients change "I can't" statements to "I haven't yet" (Dryden & Ellis, 2001, p. 327). Other methods to introduce or reinforce a rational philosophy include bibliotherapy, where clients are assigned books and materials to read (Ellis & Harper, 1997), using REBT with others to practice using rational arguments (Dryden & Ellis, 2001), and age-appropriate worksheets that help clients identify and dispute irrational beliefs (Vernon, 1989a,b; Vernon, in press).

Emotive Interventions   As Dryden and Ellis (2001) pointed out, "REBT therapy has often been falsely criticized for neglecting the emotive aspects of psychotherapy" (p. 328). In fact, there are numerous emotive techniques that are routinely employed by REBT counselors or therapists.

Humor, in the form of exaggeration, is often used to help clients avoid taking themselves so seriously (DiGiuseppe, 1991; Ellis, 2001a; Nelson-Jones, 2000), but must be used cautiously (Vernon, in press). It is never appropriate to make fun of clients or joke only about their thoughts and behavior (DiGiuseppe, 1991). Another popular form of humor is to use rational humorous songs that Ellis and others have written. Songs such as the following are available at the New York Institute and are frequently used in REBT workshops.

Love Me, Love Me, Only Me (Tune: "Yankee Doodle Dandy")

Love me, love me, only me
Or I'll die without you!
Make your love a guarantee
So I can never doubt you!
Love me, love me totally–really, really try, dear;
But if you demand love, too
I'll hate you till I die, dear!
Love me, love me all the time

Thoroughly and wholly!
Life turns into slushy slime
'Less you love me solely!
Love me with great tenderness
With no ifs or buts, dear.
If you love me somewhat less,
I'll hate your goddammed guts, dear!

Rational role playing is also a very effective emotive intervention (Ellis, 2001a; Ellis & MacClaren, 1998; Vernon, in press). Role playing can help clients express feelings and can help resolve various emotionally laden issues. Ellis cautioned that even though feelings are expressed through role playing, the relief may be temporary because clients have not explored the basic beliefs that resulted in the feelings. Therefore, it is important to do rational role playing that not only helps clients express feelings but also identifies the beliefs that created those feelings.

A variation of rational role playing is to do a **reverse role play,** in which the counselor or therapist takes the role of the client and the client assumes the role of counselor or therapist. In this way, the client learns to dispute his or her own irrational ideas as played out by the counselor or therapist.

Rational emotive imagery (REI) is one of the key REBT emotive interventions (Dryden, 1999; Ellis, 2001a; Ellis & MacClaren, 1998). The purpose of REI is to help clients identify more rational and appropriate emotions in a particular problematic situation, as well as provide an opportunity for them to experientially identify self-statements and coping techniques that could work for them in stressful situations. In implementing this technique, the counselor or therapist invites the client to close his or her eyes and imagine a difficult situation that evoked strong negative emotions. After the client reconstructs this image and labels the upsetting feelings, the counselor or therapist asks the client to change the upsetting feelings to a more reasonable negative emotion. When the client signals that this has been accomplished, the counselor or therapist invites the client to return to the present and describe the healthy emotions, exploring how thoughts helped contribute to these less-upsetting emotions. Clients are usually encouraged to practice REI for 30 days to help them learn how to change unhealthy negative emotions.

Other emotive interventions include **forceful coping statements,** where clients formulate rational coping statements and then practice them forcefully during and between sessions (Ellis, 1996; Ellis, 2001a; Ellis & Velten, 1992). Ellis and MacClaren (1998) noted that because clients have usually practiced irrational statements for a long time, powerfully repeating such statements as "When I fail it NEVER, NEVER makes me a complete failure as a person" (p. 78) over and over helps them replace the irrational statements with rational alternatives.

Experiential exercises are also used by many REBT counselors or therapists in individual counseling or therapy as well as in classroom settings and small groups (Ellis & MacClaren, 1998; Vernon, 1989a, b; Vernon, in press). These exercises help clients learn new skills and give them an opportunity to explore problematic areas. For example, Ellis and MacClaren described an exercise in which clients wrote irrational beliefs on one side of an index card, and on the other side, five negative things that have happened to them because they think that way. Vernon (in press) discussed helping clients with procrastination by having them list things they typically put off doing and giving the list to the counselor or therapist. As the client lies on the floor, the counselor reads the items one by one. As each one is read, the counselor or therapist puts a stack of newspapers on the client's body. After the final item is read and the pile of newspapers is quite high, the client is invited to talk about how he or she feels with everything "all piled up" and what steps to take to get out from under the pile of procrastination.

Behavioral Interventions   Behavioral interventions have always played an important role in helping clients change and are used to supplement and reinforce cognitive and emotive interventions. Oftentimes behavioral interventions are incorporated into homework assignments or are used in conjunction with other techniques.

One of REBT's most unique behavioral interventions is the **shame attacking exercise** (Ellis & Dryden, 1997; Walen et al., 1992). Ellis (1996) realized that shame is at the core of a significant amount of our emotional disturbance, and that when people do something they consider shameful, they criticize their actions and think that they should never repeat them. Consequently, "In REBT we try to help people to stop putting themselves, their whole person, down no matter how badly they behave and no matter how much other people look down on them for so behaving" (Ellis, 1996, p. 92). To help clients understand this concept, they are encouraged to do things in public that they regard as shameful or embarrassing, such as yelling out the stops on elevators (Nelson-Jones, 2000), asking strangers for dollar bills (Ellis, 1996), or singing in the street (Ellis, 2001a). Shame attack exercises should not be illegal, harmful, immoral, or bothersome to others. Rather, they are "foolish, silly, and ridiculous" (Ellis, 2001a, p. 153) and are intended to help clients understand that, while they may act "bad" or "foolish," they are not bad persons. After doing shame attacks, clients often feel much less uncomfortable and anxious; at the same time, they realize that they can stand not having others' approval.

Another behavioral intervention is **skills training** (Dryden, 1999). Although considered an inelegant solution if clients do not work on identifying and disputing irrational beliefs, many clients need practical skills to help them overcome deficits that can range from trade skills to interpersonal or social skills such as assertion (Ellis & MacClaren, 1998).

Other behavioral interventions include rewards and penalties, where counselors or therapists help clients arrange reinforcement for achieving a goal, or penalties if they do not (Dryden, 1999). Penalties often involve contributing money to a cause clients do not believe in as a forceful way to modify behavior (Ellis, 2001a); rewards include things the client truly enjoys. Paradoxical homework, which involves prescribing the symptom the client is attempting to work on, is also used with some clients (Ellis & MacClaren, 1998). Ellis and MacClaren (1998) cautioned that there are some risks with this approach and it is not appropriate for all clients.

Clients with Mental Disorders

REBT has been applied to a wide variety of mental disorders, including the treatment of anxiety (Warren, 1997), depression (Hauck & McKeegan, 1997; Walen & Rader, 1991), obsessive compulsive disorder (Ellis, 1997b), and panic disorder and agoraphobia (Yankura, 1997). A brief description of REBT applications to these disorders follows.

Anxiety   From an REBT perspective, clients with generalized anxiety disorder are more likely to "interpret ambiguous information as threatening, overestimate the probability of the occurrence of potentially dangerous events, and rate the feared events as more aversive or costly" (Warren, 1997, p. 14). Furthermore, they may have issues related to approval and self-worth, or fear criticism and worry about making mistakes, which makes many life circumstances appear threatening.

After assessing the irrational beliefs, REBT practitioners would lead clients through the disputation process, paying special attention to their anxiety about being anxious (I can't stand this, I shouldn't be anxious), and also noting the shame and self-downing that clients often experience about their worry and anxiety (Walen & Rader, 1991). Teaching them to differentiate between the *possibility* of something occurring versus the *probability* of it happening is also an effective strategy.

Depression   Ellis (1987) maintained that REBT is an effective therapy with depressed individuals because it specifically focuses on addressing irrational beliefs as opposed to correcting distorted negative inferences. For this reason, it may result in more pervasive and long-lasting change. According to Hauck and McKeegan (1997), "Depression can be caused by (a) self-blame (the "bad me" approach), (b) self-pity ("poor me"), and (c) other-pity ("poor you")" (p. 49). Each of these factors is accompanied by underlying irrational beliefs that, if effectively disputed, can help alleviate depression. However, Hauck and Mc-Keegan stressed that this is generally true only when the depression is preceded by a negative life event as opposed to depression that is primarily organic in nature. These authors concurred with Walen and Rader (1991) that when depression is primarily biological in origin, a combination of cognitive therapy and antidepressant medication are most likely needed.

Walen and Rader (1991) suggested that the basic principle of cognitive therapy—how you feel is based on what you think—may send an erroneous message to clients with serious depressive illnesses that they are responsible for their illness. These authors strongly suggested that counselors or therapists differentiate among the different types of depression. Furthermore, they stressed the importance of letting clients with acute depression know that they have an illness and help them reframe depression as a disease, not a character flaw.

Obsessive Compulsive Disorder (OCD)   Ellis (1997b) indicated that the need for certainty contributes to individuals' tendency to develop rituals or obsessions, but noted that OCD may be the result of biological deficiencies, in which case medication may be needed in combination with REBT procedures. Although techniques such as activity homework and **in vivo desensitization** are often used successfully with OCD clients, clients with severe OCD are so obsessed with their repetitive behaviors that they find it very difficult to adhere to the behavioral, emotive, or cognitive techniques and fail to persist in changing their ritualizing.

Foa and Wilson (1991) identified several important considerations in treating OCD clients, including helping them recognize that the anxieties that underlie their OCD behaviors are unrealistic, illogical, and self-defeating. These authors also stressed the importance of helping clients develop high-frustration tolerance so that they can work harder to overcome their repeated rituals. Ellis (1997b) pointed out that these clients often put themselves down for having OCD and indicated that REBT counselors or therapists must help these clients accept themselves unconditionally with their OCD and use REBT techniques to help them dispute their anxiety, depression, and self-hatred about having this disorder.

Panic Disorder and Agoraphobia   Some individuals have a biological predisposition to panic disorder as a result of their genetic makeup (Clum, 1990), in which case psychotropic medications are often very helpful in reducing symptoms. However, Yankura (1997) stressed that it is not sufficient to treat panic disorders with medication alone, noting that it is far more effective to also use approaches such as REBT that teach coping skills to increase clients' sense of self-efficacy.

REBT treatment for anxiety disorders "involves helping clients to identify, dispute, and replace the irrational beliefs that underpin their anxiety problems" (Yankura, 1997, p. 126). Typical irrational beliefs include thinking that they must not experience uncomfortable feelings or a panic attack, and that something terrible may happen if they do. For example, clients may think it would be awful if they fainted or lost control, and that they could not stand the embarrassment.

It follows, then, that clients would tend to avoid going to places where they have had a panic attack, which results in their agoraphobia. These clients also tend to put themselves down, thinking they should be better able to control the panic and avoidant behavior, and they are weak and inadequate if they cannot.

REBT counselors or therapists would employ a number of interventions, including helping clients distribute their catastrophizing and awfulizing about their anxiety and teaching them how to use distraction techniques by focusing on their breathing or tensing and relaxing muscles (Clum, 1990). They would also use other approaches such as **flooding**, where clients are encouraged to confront what they fear (Yankura, 1997).

Evaluation

Overview

Ellis (1996) acknowledged that he was prejudiced, but maintained that REBT is more likely to help people achieve "deeper and more lasting emotional and behavioral change than other methods of therapy" (p. 1). He noted that usually clients can improve significantly in 10–20 sessions, in individual as well as group therapy. In the following sections, supporting research and limitations will be addressed.

Supporting Research

Smith and Glass (1977), in their meta-analytic review of psychotherapy outcome studies, concluded that RET was the second-most effective psychotherapy, with systematic desensitization being first. However, because Ellis has focused on theory and practice rather than research, REBT has a reputation of having insufficient empirical support. In an attempt to address this limitation, Lyons and Woods (1991) reported results from a meta-analysis of 70 outcome studies. They made a total of 236 comparisons of REBT to baseline, control groups, cognitive behavior modification, behavior therapy, or other psychotherapies. Results indicated that subjects receiving REBT showed significant improvement over baseline measures and control groups. Many of these studies supported the efficacy of REBT for a wide array of problems including stress, depression, anger, social anxiety, assertion, alcohol abuse, weight issues, behavior problems, school underachievement, test anxiety, sexual fears and dysfunction, and performance and public speaking anxiety. However, Lyons and Woods cautioned that the majority of studies did not report on follow-up data, making it difficult to determine the long-term effects of this counseling or therapy.

Several more recent studies suggested that REBT can be useful for practitioners in school or clinical settings. Sapp, Farrell, and Durand (1995) improved academic performance of African American children using an REBT program. Graves (1996) demonstrated that a parent training program reduced stress and improved parenting skills in parents of Down syndrome children. Shannon and Allen (1998) showed that students who participated in an REBT-based skill training program had better grades than peers in a control group and scored higher on a standardized math test.

Ellis (2001b) noted that there are numerous reasons for the lack of solid outcome studies. First, because REBT endorses the use of many cognitive, emotive, and behavioral techniques, it is more difficult to test the effectiveness of these techniques, and this has been discouraging for researchers. Furthermore, paper-and-pencil tests are an inadequate way to get at clients' beliefs and their unconscious shoulds and musts. A compounding problem is the fact that Albert Ellis's Institute, which could have been a significant instigator of solid outcome research, has traditionally been a counseling or therapy training institute as opposed to an academic research institute. As such, it has attracted mental health practitioners who are more interested in learning how to effectively help others than in doing research. At the present time, however, several efforts are underway at the Institute to promote quality research.

Limitations

In an interview with Michael Broder (2001b), Ellis stated, "My basic goals are to push REBT, and to improve it so as to help more people use it...I want REBT to be successful in the world...I think that REBT and Cognitive Behavior Therapy (CBT) are going to help more people more of the time in an efficient manner than other therapies" (p. 85). While he acknowledges that considerable research needs to be done, he firmly stands behind two predictions he made at the American Psychological Association Convention in 1956 (Ellis, 1994, p. 418): that "REBT . . . will prove more effective with more types of clients than any of the other kinds of psychotherapy that are now being widely employed" and that "A considerable amount of . . . REBT will prove to be the most effective type of psychological treatment that helps to minimize the basic neuroses . . . of many clients, and particularly of many with whom other types of therapy have been shown to be relatively ineffective."

While there are limitations to this theory, Ellis (1994) maintained that REBT is not alone—"even the most effective forms of psychotherapy are, as yet, distinctly limited" (p. 331) because clients continue to hold onto their irrationalities and repeatedly behave in self-defeating ways even though they may have insight into the cause of their disturbances and improve slightly. Therefore, no matter how hard the counselor or therapist works, client resistance is often difficult to overcome.

Perhaps one of the biggest limitations of REBT has been the negative influence of Ellis himself, as he acknowledged (2001b). In his opinion, professionals have slighted or opposed REBT because "I am a charismatic individual, with characteristics which many of them find distasteful" (p. 69). He admitted that his public manner and use of four-letter words is controversial and unconventional and that his use of the term *rational* may be aversive to empirically minded psychologists. Because it is irrational to demand that Ellis change his style, professionals must recognize that they can adhere to the basic principles of this theory that has been used very effectively with adults as well as with children (Vernon, in press) without emulating Ellis's style.

Summary Chart—Rational Emotive Behavior Therapy

Major Constucts

REBT has a strong philosophical basis as well as commitment to the scientific method. The interconnectedness of thinking, feeling, and behaving is central to this theory, as is the notion that emotional distress results from dysfunctional thought processes.

Goals

The goal is to help clients develop a rational philosophy that will allow them to reduce their emotional distress and self-defeating behaviors.

Change Process

Change occurs as counselors or therapists help clients work through the A-B-C model of emotional disturbance, replacing irrational beliefs with rational alternatives that result in more moderate, healthy emotions and self-enhancing behaviors.

Interventions

A wide variety of cognitive, emotive, and behavioral interventions including disputing, rational-emotive imagery, rational role playing, bibliotherapy, shame attack exercises, and rational coping self-statements are employed.

Limitations

Limitations include the lack of outcome research and the overgeneralization that REBT *is* Albert Ellis. Although he is the founder of the theory, numerous practitioners all over the world integrate the basic principles of this effective theory in their own style.

▪▪ ▪ The Case of Jonathan: A Rational Emotive Behavior Therapy Approach

Following the Dryden-DiGiuseppe (1990) 13-step model, the REBT counselor or therapist would first ask Jonathan to describe his problem, using active listening skills and conveying genuine interest in him by asking pertinent questions to help focus the interview. Jonathan and the counselor or therapist would come to some agreement about the goals for the session. Next, the counselor or therapist would assess emotional and behavioral consequences. In this case, Jonathan indicates that he is depressed and lonely, as well as angry and frustrated. Consequently, his drinking has increased and he has taken his anger and frustration out on his co-workers and supervisor, which has resulted in suspension without pay.

After assessing emotional and behavioral consequences, the counselor or therapist would assess the activating event (A): Jonathan's difficulties at work, financial problems, marital separation, and moving off the reservation. At this point, the counselor or therapist would want to teach Jonathan how these events themselves do not create his negative feelings and behaviors, explaining that his thoughts about these events create the emotional upset. The counselor or therapist would then assess Jonathan's irrational beliefs (B), helping him understand how his anger at his supervisor and co-workers is stemming from his irrational belief that they should not be so demanding and perfectionistic and should not treat him so unfairly. The counselor would also help Jonathan see how his depression is related to his self-downing: that his work is never good enough, that he is not wanted in the 'white man's' world, and that nothing ever seems to work out for him in terms of job and family. Even his dream reflects his self-downing: the bus driver does not hear him, laughs at him, and ignores him.

After helping Jonathan identify his irrational beliefs and how they connect to his feelings and behaviors (C), the REBT counselor or therapist would use a combination of logical, empirical, and functional disputes (D) to help him replace his irrational beliefs with rational alternatives. For example, the counselor or therapist might ask: "Where is the evidence that you are not wanted in the 'white man's' world? And even if you aren't, does that make you a bad person? Or, suppose it is true that your supervisor is expecting too much and treating you unfairly. How is getting angry helping you improve the situation?" The counselor or therapist would continue to help Jonathan dispute his irrational beliefs with the goal of helping him adopt a more effective rational philosophy (E) and reduce the intensity of the negative emotions (F), which in turn would help him behave in less self-defeating ways.

In addition to disputing, the REBT counselor or therapist would help Jonathan by using a combination of other techniques, either in session or as homework assignments. Examples could include teaching him how to be assertive rather than aggressive, implementing a reward and penalty system with regard to his drinking, teaching him how to use rational coping self-statements, and employing rational emotive imagery.

Although REBT counselors or therapists would not deal with a lot of family or origin issues, they would help Jonathan deal with his guilt and self-downing relative to his parents' feelings about his decision to leave the reservation, his guilt over his brother's death, and his failure to succeed in marriages. In addition, they would deal with his low-frustration tolerance that leads to his drinking and exacerbates his problems ("Life is too hard; I can't stand the pain and discomfort—I need an escape") through disputing as well as other psychoeducational approaches.

The goal of counseling or therapy is to help Jonathan learn more effective ways of thinking, feeling, and behaving that will enable him to deal not only with present problems, but also with future issues. The REBT counselor or therapist supports, challenges, educates, and empowers the client by employing a variety of cognitive, emotive, and behavioral strategies.

Reality Therapy Theory

Robert E. Wubbolding
Xavier University, Cincinnati

Background

William Glasser, M.D., the originator of reality therapy, first began to develop this approach to counseling and psychotherapy while working in a correctional institution and a psychiatric hospital. A board-certified psychiatrist, Glasser had been trained in the traditional methods of psychiatry. He was taught to help clients gain insight so that after transference was worked through, they could achieve a higher degree of sanity. However, his experience had shown that even if these goals of the analytic approach were achieved, clients did not necessarily change their behavior, and many continued to have difficulty making productive decisions. With support and input from a sympathetic professor named G. L. Harrington, Glasser formulated the early principles of his new treatment modality.

The watershed year for reality therapy came in 1965, when Glasser published *Reality Therapy*. In this then-controversial book, Glasser emphasized that people are responsible for their own behavior and that they cannot blame the past or outside forces and at the same time achieve a high degree of mental health. He asserted that behavior involves choices and that there are always options open to most people. Consequently, the objective of counseling and psychotherapy should be measurable behavioral change, not merely insight into and understanding of past events or current unconscious drives.

Though not greeted enthusiastically by the medical profession, Glasser's theory was well received by many, including corrections personnel, youth workers, counselors, therapists, and educators. He was asked to consult in schools to help students take more responsibility for their behaviors and to blame others less, and out of this work came his book *Schools Without Failure* (1968). In this work, he discussed how reality therapy can be used in large groups—what he called "class meetings." While not the same as group counseling or psychotherapy, the meetings have some of the same goals, such as increased self-esteem, feelings of success, and group members' involvement with and respect for each other.

At that time, many professionals saw reality therapy as a method rather than a theory. Then Glasser (1972), in *The Identity Society,* formulated what might be called the theory's sociological underpinnings. He explained that three forces had contributed to the radical changes in Western civilization in the 1950s and 1960s: the passage of laws that guaranteed human rights, increased affluence that satisfied the basic need of survival for the majority of people, and the advent of instant communication via electronic media. These three gradual but important changes facilitated the arrival of the "identity society"—a world in which persons are more focused on their identity needs than on their survival needs. Most people want an opportunity to move beyond economic and political serfdom. Therefore, reality therapy found acceptance because it is a theory that facilitates personal empowerment by means of self-evaluation and positive planning for the future.

Still, this pragmatic and culturally based method needed solid theoretical grounding. Such a foundation was provided by a relatively unknown theory of brain functioning. Powers (1973) described the brain as an input control system similar to a thermostat that controls the temperature of a room. Glasser (1984) extended Powers' **control theory** (or control system theory) by incorporating a system of needs to explain human motivation, and then molded the theory to the clinical setting and the practice of counseling and psychotherapy. With the addition of these and many other ideas, it was no longer appropriate to call Glasser's theory "control theory," and consequently the recognized name is now **choice theory.** The delivery system is **reality therapy.**

Another major development in reality therapy is the extended application described by Wubbolding (2000). The WDEP formulation provides a pedagogical tool for learning and practicing the process of reality therapy. Wubbolding has also extended the theory to multicultural counseling based on his experience working in Asia, Europe, and the Middle East. Additionally, he has provided credibility for the system by emphasizing research data and scientific validation. The system now is elevated beyond the work of one man and has reached the level of universal applicability.

Human Nature: A Developmental Perspective

Reality therapy provides a comprehensive explanation of human behavior as well as a methodology for addressing the vicissitudes of the human condition. Choice theory explains why and how human beings function; and the **WDEP system** (Wubbolding, 1989, 1991, 2000), explained briefly in the following paragraph and in greater depth later in the chapter, provides a delivery system for helping oneself and others to remediate deficiencies, make better choices, and become more fully self-actualized.

W implies that the counselor or therapist helps clients explore their *wants. D* means that clients describe the *direction* of their lives as well as what they are currently doing or how they spend their time. *E* indicates that the counselor or therapist helps in the client's *self-evaluation* by asking such questions as "Are your current actions effective?" Clients are then helped to make simple and attainable action *plans,* as implied by *P.* Thus, reality therapy is not a theory of developmental psychology per se. Still, as discussed in detail later, it contains ideas that harmonize with various stages of development.

Fundamental to reality therapy is the principle that human needs are the sources of all human behavior. An infant as well as a senior adult seeks to control or mold the world around himself or herself in order to fulfill his or her inner drives. But here the commonality among persons at various stages ends. For as persons grow, they develop specific wants unique to themselves. An infant, child, adolescent, young adult, middle-aged person, or senior adult has formulated a wide range of wants that are unique to that person, yet similar to needs experienced by others of the same age and culture.

Similarly, though the behavior of all human beings is designed to fulfill inner needs, it differs according to age and culture. Human behavior has an impact on the external world and, in a sense, shapes it, as a sculptor molds clay. As a result, the input or perception that one gets from the world—a person's worldview (perception)—is dynamic, always changing, and unique to each person depending on age and culture. A developmental implication of the principles of choice theory is that the perceptual system or worldview is a storehouse of memories. Because human problems at many levels of development are rooted in relationships, Ford (1979) and Wubbolding (1988) emphasize the necessity of interpersonal **quality time** as a facilitative component of healthy development. When parent and child, friend and friend, spouse and spouse, or colleague and colleague spend quality time together, they build a storehouse of pleasant and healthy perceptions of each other. In order for quality time to serve as a solid support for effective growth and development, it must be characterized by the following traits.

- *Effort.* The activity requires effort. Watching television and eating together can help, but they are less effective than other activities because they require little or no energy.
- *Awareness.* The persons are aware of each other. Playing a game or engaging in a hobby is very useful in facilitating the relationship and individual development. Again, watching television without talking to each other qualifies only minimally.
- *Repetition.* The activity is not an isolated event, but is performed on a regular basis. Consistent walking with a friend deepens the relationship and enhances the growth of both.
- *Free of criticism and complaint.* While the activity is being carried out, there should be no criticism of the other person. For instance, child development is enhanced if a parent creates an accepting atmosphere and encourages positive conversation.
- *Need-fulfilling for all persons.* The activity is geared to the interest and ability of all concerned. Attending a rock concert with an adolescent might be so painful for the parent that the relationship—and, therefore, the development of both—fails to improve.
- *Performed for a limited time.* Persons of various age levels require various amounts of time to ensure appropriate development. A child obviously requires more quality time than an adult.

Quality time is a crucial component of human growth and development. Moreover, the application to various individuals of activities labeled "quality time" is determined by the persons' interests and levels of intellectual functioning as well as their ages and degree of mental health.

Development of Mental Health

Besides looking at development from a chronological point of view, Glasser (1996) and Wubbolding (2000) have described mental health in terms of both regressive and positive stages.

Regressive Stages   The stages in which mental health is seen as regressive are not viewed in terms of pathology. Rather, in reality therapy the stages are seen as ineffective ways to fulfill needs. They are sometimes called *failure-directed* or *irresponsible,* but the most useful way to describe them is as a person's best but quite ineffective effort to fulfill human needs.

STAGE 1: *I Give Up.* This person has attempted to fulfill human needs effectively, but has not been able to do so. The only alternative that appears reasonable is to cease trying. The person is characterized by behaviors such as listlessness, withdrawal, and apathy. This stage is quite temporary and is followed by the symptoms of the more identifiable second stage.

STAGE 2: *Negative Symptoms.* The following behaviors, like all choices, are seen by clients as their best efforts to fulfill their wants and needs. However, they lead to more frustration. The following behaviors are descriptive of these symptoms.

- *Actions.* Someone exhibiting this negative symptom chooses destructive actions harmful to self or others. These range from mild acting out to severe antisocial behavior such as murder, rape, or suicide.
- *Thinking.* Cognitive disturbances are also attempts to fulfill needs. Such efforts often succeed in controlling others; nevertheless, they are self-destructive or harmful to others. The word *disturbance* is used in a wide sense to include negative cognition, ranging from the chronically pessimistic and negativistic thinker to a person with severe psychotic conditions.
- *Feelings.* Negative emotions include a spectrum ranging from mild to severe depression, from chronic aggravation to habitual anger or rage, and from the "worried well" (Talmon, 1990) to phobic disorders.
- *Physiology.* Other ineffective attempts to fulfill needs, used when other choices do not appear to be available to a person, include physical ailments. Many such maladies are best treated not only with good medical care but also through counseling or psychotherapy designed to help the client make better choices—that is, to choose positive symptoms.

STAGE 3: *Negative Addictions.* Negative addictions to, for example, drugs, alcohol, gambling, and work represent another regressive stage of ineffective behaviors that attempt to fulfill needs.

These three stages of regressively ineffective behaviors are not seen as rigid and exclusive of one another. On the contrary, they provide a way to conceptualize ineffective human behavior related to need-fulfillment. They also represent the reverse of effective behaviors.

Positive Stages   The positive stages of mental health are seen as effective ways to fulfill human needs. They serve to balance the negative stages and can be presented to clients as goals for the counseling or therapy process.

STAGE 1: *I'll Do It; I Want to Improve; I Am Committed to Change.* Such explicit or implicit statements made by clients represent the first stage of effective choices. This stage, like its negative mirror image, is quite temporary.

STAGE 2: *Positive Symptoms.* The following behavioral choices are effectively need-fulfilling and lead to less frustration.

- *Actions.* Effective choices aimed at fulfilling human needs include both assertive and altruistic behaviors. Healthy individuals know how to get what they want, yet they contribute to society through family life, employment, and so on.
- *Thinking.* The mirror image of cognitive disturbance is rational thinking. Among the many rational thinking patterns implicit in reality therapy are a realistic understanding of what one can and cannot control, acceptance of what is unchangeable, and knowledge that one is responsible for one's own behavior. Therefore, the perception that all early childhood traumas must of their nature continue to victimize a person's adulthood is rejected.
- *Feelings.* Patience, tolerance, sociability, acceptance, enthusiasm, trust, and hope are among the emotions that are positive behaviors and useful goals in the practice of reality therapy.
- *Physiology.* Another symptom of an effective lifestyle is the effort to attend to one's physical needs. Care of one's body, proper diet, and reasonable exercise are symbols of effective need-fulfillment.

STAGE 3: *Positive Addictions.* Glasser (1976) has identified activities that he calls **positive addictions** that enhance mental health and are intensely need-satisfying. Included are running and meditation. Such behaviors, as well as others that approach positive addiction, are the opposite of negative addictions. Rather than being self-destructive, positive addictions add to psychological development and increase feelings of self-worth and accomplishment. Such addictions are the result of habitually but noncompulsively choosing the behavior for 12 to 18 months, for a limited time such as 45 minutes per day (or at least on a regular basis), and in a noncompetitive way.

Like the negative stages, the stages of growth are not absolutely discrete categories. Human beings exhibit many characteristics and can float back and forth from the negative to the positive. No one lives entirely in a world of ineffective or effective choices. Even the most disturbed person occasionally chooses effective behaviors, just as even the most well-adjusted person makes unhealthy or ineffective choices at times.

In summary, the principles of reality therapy allow for applications to any stage of a person's chronological and psychological development. The use of quality time, for instance, can be adapted to persons of any age at any stage of development. Furthermore, development is seen as a series of choices leading to stages of regression or the stages of effective need-satisfaction (Wubbolding & Brickell, 2001).

Major Constructs

The underlying theory that justifies the methodology of reality therapy is called **choice theory**. While choice theory is separate and existed before reality therapy was developed, the terms *choice theory* and *reality therapy* are now sometimes used interchangeably. Norbert Wiener, a Harvard University mathematician, formulated many of the principles that have been subsumed under the name **control theory** (Wubbolding, 1994). Wiener described the importance of feedback to both engineering and biological systems (1948), as well as the sociological implications for human beings (1950). However, Wubbolding (1993) has emphasized that the more proximate basis for the clinical applications was formulated by Powers (1973). Powers rejected the mechanism of behaviorism by emphasizing the internal origins of the human control system.

Most significant in the development of choice theory, however, is the work of Glasser (1980b, 1984, 1986, 1996, 1998, 2001), who expanded Powers' work and adapted it to the clinical setting. Human beings, Glasser states, act on the world around them for a purpose: to satisfy their needs and wants. He speaks of **total behavior,** which is comprised of action, thinking, feelings, and physiology. All behaviors contain these four elements, although one element or another is more obvious at a given moment. Such behaviors, negative or positive, are the output generated from within a person in order to gain a sense of control or to satisfy needs.

Wubbolding (2000) has provided a summary of Glasser's choice theory as it applies to counseling and psychotherapy.

1. Human beings are born with five needs. These needs are belonging, power (competence, achievement, recognition, self-esteem, and so on.), fun or enjoyment, freedom or independence (autonomy), and survival. These needs are general and universal. Along with wants, which are specific and unique for each person, needs serve as the motivators or sources of all behavior.

2. The difference between what a person wants and what one perceives one is getting (input) is the immediate source of specific behaviors at any given moment. Thus, reality therapy rests on the principle that human behavior springs from internal motivation, which drives the behavior from moment to moment (Glasser, 1998; Wubbolding, 1985a, 2001; Wubbolding & Brickell, 1999). Another consequence of this principle is that human behavior is not an attempt to resolve unconscious early childhood conflicts. The sources of effective behaviors ("I'll do it," positive symptoms, and positive addictions) as well as ineffective behaviors ("I give up," negative symptoms, and negative addictions) are current, internal, and conscious.

3. All human behaviors are composed of doing (acting), thinking, feeling, and physiology. Behaviors are identified by the most obvious aspect of this total behavior. Thus, someone counseled for poor grades in school is seen as presenting an action problem. People are labeled "psychotic" because the primary and most obvious aspect of their total behavior is dysfunctional thinking. Depression, anger, resentment, and fear are most obvious in other persons, so their behavior is called a feeling behavior. For others, the most obvious component of behavior is the physiological element, such as heart disease or high blood pressure.

Because behavior is total—that is, made up of four components—and because it is generated from within, it is useful to see behavior not as static but as ongoing. Therefore, total behavior is often expressed in "-ing" words. Feelings, for example, are described as "depressing," "guilting," "anxiety-ing," and so on. Another implication of this principle is that all behavior has a purpose. Human choices are not aimless or random. They are all teleological; in other words, they serve a purpose: to close the gap between the perception of what a person is getting and what he or she wants at a given moment.

4. Because behavior originates from within, human beings are responsible for their behavior. In other words, we are all capable of change. This change is brought about by choosing more effective behaviors. The aspect of human behavior over which we have the most direct control is that of acting, and secondarily, that of thinking. Therefore, in counseling and psychotherapy, the focus is on changing total behavior by discussing current actions along with the evaluation of their effectiveness in fulfilling needs, by discussing current wants and the evaluation of their realistic attainability, and by discussing current perceptions or viewpoints along with their helpfulness to the individual.

5. Human beings see the world through a perceptual system that functions as a set of lenses. At a low level of perception, the person simply recognizes the world, giving names to objects and events, but does not make judgments about them. At a high level of perception, the person puts a positive or negative value on the perception. Exploring the various levels of perception and their helpfulness is part of the counseling or psychotherapy process.

In summary, choice theory is a psychology built on principles that emphasize current motivation for human choices. It stands in opposition to both psychological determinism and what Glasser (1998) calls **external control psychology.** Human beings are free to make choices; thus, although the past has propelled us to the present, it need not determine our future. Similarly, our external world limits our choices but does not remove them.

Applications

Overview

Reality therapy is a practical method based on theory and research. It aims at helping people take better charge of their lives. In order to help clients make such changes, the counselor or therapist focuses on realistic choices, especially those touching on human relationships. It is first necessary to establish a safe therapeutic environment similar to that espoused in most theories, although choice theory offers some unique ways to accomplish this. The WDEP system details the specific reality therapy procedures used to help accomplish these goals.

Goals of Counseling and Psychotherapy

The goal of reality therapy is to help clients fulfill their needs. Consequently, the counselor or therapist helps clients explore current behaviors and choices related to belonging, power, fun, and freedom. More specifically, the precise wants related to each need are examined so as to help clients fulfill their specific objectives or their **quality world** wants. Therefore, assisting clients to make more effective and responsible choices related to their wants and needs is the aim of the counselor or therapist. These choices are seen as motivated by current needs and wants, not by past traumas, unresolved conflicts, peer pressure, or previous training.

The Process of Change

To understand how change can occur in the life of a client, it is necessary to understand the following principles in the theory and practice of reality therapy.

Present Orientation   Choice theory, the theoretical basis for reality therapy, rests on the principle that the human brain functions like a control system—for example, like a thermostat—seeking to regulate its own behavior in order to shape its environment so that the environment matches what it wants. Therefore, human behavior springs from current inner motivation and is neither an attempt to resolve past conflicts nor a mere response to an external stimulus. In other words, human beings are not controlled by past history or victimized by the world around them; rather, they have control—to varying degrees—over current and future behavior.

Emphasis on Choice   One of the goals of counseling and psychotherapy for the practitioner of reality therapy is to help clients make positive choices. Therefore, it is useful to see behavior as a result of one's choices, to treat it as such, and to talk to clients as if they have choices. While no human being has total freedom to make better choices easily, it can still be helpful to see even severe emotional disturbance as a person's best choice for a given period of time. The work of the counselor or therapist is to reveal more choices to clients, and to help clients see that better choices are possible. Of course, the word *choice* is not used with the same meaning for every behavior. Choosing to keep an appointment is quite precise and specific and is more within one's control than becoming free of drugs or more assertive. Even though it is empowering to the client to see the latter options as *choices,* they can also be called *goals* comprised of many short-range *objectives* (wants) and more specific *steps* (choices).

Control of Action   In bringing about change, it is useful to recognize that the component of one's total behavior over which a human being has the most control and, therefore, choice is the action element. Although some persons have an amazing amount of direct control over their physiology (some can stop bleeding when they are cut), people seen in counseling and psychotherapy can rarely change their blood pressure, their ulcer condition, or their headaches by an act of will. Also, they can rarely change their feelings of depression, guilt, anxiety, or worry merely by choosing to do so. And though they have some control over their thoughts, it is still not easy for them just to begin thinking differently from the way they have in the past.

Because people have the most control over the action element, helping them change their actions is more efficacious than helping them think differently or helping them feel better. It is more productive to help spouses choose to talk politely to each other than to help them feel better about each other. Increasing self-esteem is possible if a client chooses to act in ways that are different from ways in which he or she has acted previously. The reason for this is that all four elements of behavior are connected. Total behavior is like a suitcase containing four levels of behavior. The handle of the suitcase is attached to the action. Beneath it are thinking, feeling, and physiology. When the suitcase is moved, it is seized by the handle, the part most easily grabbed. Yet when this occurs, the entire suitcase changes location. So, too, when we help a client change actions, there is a change of all behaviors.

Importance of Relationship   The specific procedures of the WDEP system are based on the establishment of an empathic relationship. As is abundantly clear from research, the relationship between the client and the counselor or therapist is critical in effecting change. Reality therapy offers specific interventions aimed at helping clients make more effective choices, and these are most effective when there is a genuine relationship established. Counselors and therapists who use reality therapy effectively employ many of the same skills and possess the same qualities as other counselors and therapists: empathy, congruence, and positive regard. Reality therapy offers specific ways, some unique to reality therapy and some incorporated from general practice, for establishing and maintaining a therapeutic relationship (Richardson & Wubbolding, 2001).

Metacommunication   The procedures of reality therapy are straightforward and direct. Yet when these procedures are used repeatedly, clients seem to gain more than the surface meaning allowed for by the questioning. The art of helping clients define what they want for themselves, examining what they are doing to get it, and making plans is based on an underlying belief that is often heard and incorporated by clients: namely, that they have the innate ability to make changes, to feel better, and to take better charge of their own lives. They gain self-confidence and a sense of hope, messages that extend beyond the mere asking of questions. (Specific questioning procedures are discussed in the following section.) Yet it is best for the practitioner to refrain from trying to send a metamessage to clients. Rather, client attitudinal changes will often occur if the WDEP system is skillfully used.

Reality therapy developed out of a desire to see change happen in clients rather than have clients merely gain insight and awareness. Contributing to the efficacy of reality therapy is its emphasis on present orientation, choice, action, the relationship, and the underlying message that is communicated through skillful questioning.

Intervention Strategies

The methodology employed in reality therapy consists of establishing an appropriate environment or psychological atmosphere and then applying the procedures that lead to change: the WDEP system. Together these constitute the "cycle of counseling" (see Figure 11.1). This cycle illustrates that the specific interventions summarized as WDEP are built upon a trustful relationship. Trust-destroying and trust-building ideas (see "Do" and "Don't") are listed. The process is described as a cycle because there is no single place to start when it is applied to clients. Counselors need to use their creativity to match the system to each client.

Create a Positive Environment   An atmosphere that provides for the possibility of change is characterized by specific guidelines and suggestions about what to do and what to avoid. These are designed for use by counselors, therapists, and case managers as well as supervisors and managers in the workplace. They can also be taught to clients, parents, teachers, and others for use in improving their interactions with clients, students, employees, and children. The specific applications vary slightly, but the principles are quite consistent.

CYCLE OF MANAGING, SUPERVISING, COUNSELING AND COACHING

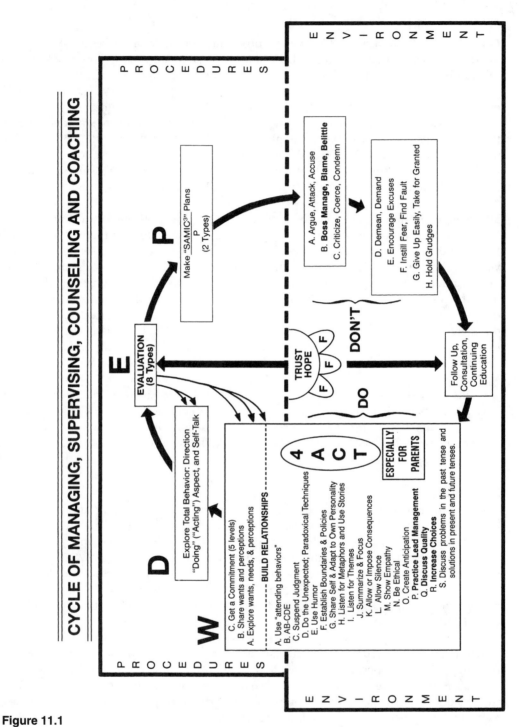

Figure 11.1

Cycle of Counseling

Adapted by Robert E. Wubbolding, EdD from the works of William Glasser, MD. Copyright 1986 Robert E. Wubbolding, EdD. 13th Revision 2002.

SUMMARY DESCRIPTION OF THE
"CYCLE OF MANAGING, SUPERVISING, COUNSELING AND COACHING"

(The Cycle is explained in detail in books by Robert E. Wubbolding:
Employee Motivation, 1996: *Reality Therapy for the 21st Century*, 2000
A Set of Directions for Putting and Keeping Yourself Together, 2001

Introduction:

The Cycle consists of two general concepts: Environment conducive to change and Procedures more explicitly designed to facilitate change. This chart is intended to be a **brief** summary. The ideas are designed to be used with employees, students, clients as well as in other human relationships.

Relationship between Environment & Procedures:

1. As indicated in the chart, the Environment is the foundation upon which the effective use of Procedures is based.

2. Though it is **usually** necessary to establish a safe, friendly Environment before change can occur, the "Cycle" can be entered at any point. Thus, the use of the cycle does **not** occur in lock step fashion.

3. Building a relationship implies establishing and maintaining a professional relationship. Methods for accomplishing this comprise some efforts on the part of the helper that are Environmental and others that are Procedural.

ENVIRONMENT:

DO: Build Relationship: a close relationship is built on TRUST and HOPE through friendliness, firmness and fairness.

A. Using Attending Behaviors: Eye contact, posture, effective listening skills.

B. AB = "Always **B**e . . ." **C**onsistent, **C**ourteous & **C**alm, **D**etermined that there is hope for improvement, **E**nthusiastic (Think Positively).

C. Suspend Judgment: View behaviors from a low level of perception, i.e., acceptance is crucial.

D. Do the Unexpected: Use paradoxical techniques as appropriate; Reframing and Prescribing.

E. Use Humor: Help them fulfill need for fun within reasonable boundaries.

F. Establish boundaries: the relationship is professional.

4 A C T

- Affirm feelings
- Accept
- Show affection
- Action consequences
- Conversation (WDEP)
- Time together

G. Share Self: Self-disclosure within limits is helpful; adapt to own personal style.

H. Listen for Metaphors: Use their figures of speech and provide other ones. Use stories.

I. Listen to Themes: Listen for behaviors that have helped, value judgements, etc.

J. Summarize & Focus: Tie together what they say and focus on them rather than on "Real World."

K. Allow or Impose Consequences: Within reason, they should be responsible for their own behavior.

L. Allow Silence: This allows them to think, as well as to take responsibility.

M. Show Empathy: Perceive as does the person being helped.

N. Be Ethical: Study Codes of Ethics and their applications, e.g., how to handle suicide threats or violent tendencies.

O. Create anticipation and communicate hope. People should be taught that something good will happen if they are willing to work.

P. **Practice lead management, e.g., democracy in determining rules.**

Q. **Discuss quality.**

R. **Increases choices.**

S. Discuss problems in the past tense, solutions in present and future tenses.

DON'T:

Argue, **Boss Manage,** or Blame, Criticize or Coerce, Demean, Encourage Excuses, Instill Fear, or Give up easily, Hold Grudges.

Rather, stress what they **can** control, accept them as they are, and keep the confidence that they can develop more effective behaviors. Also, continue to use "WDEP" system without giving up.

Follow Up, Consult, and Continue Education:

Determine a way for them to report back, talk to another professional person when necessary, and maintain ongoing program of professional growth.

PROCEDURES:

Build Relationships:

WDEP

A. Explore **W**ants, Needs & Perceptions: Discuss picture album or quality world, i.e., set goals, fulfilled & unfulfilled pictures, needs, viewpoints and "locus of control."

B. Share Wants & Perceptions: Tell what you want from them and how you view their situations, behaviors, wants, etc. This procedure is secondary to A above.

C. Get a Commitment: Help them solidify their desire to find more effective behaviors.

Explore Total Behavior:

Help them examine the **D**irection of their lives, as well as specifics of how they spend their time. Discuss ineffective & effective self talk.

Evaluation – The Cornerstone of Procedures:

Help them evaluate their behavioral direction, specific behaviors as well as wants, perceptions and commitments. Evaluate own behavior through follow-up, consultation and continued education.

Make **P**lans: Help them change direction of their lives.

Effective plans are **S**imple, **A**ttainable, **M**easurable, **I**mmediate, **C**onsistent, **C**ontrolled by the planner, and **C**ommitted to. The helper is **P**ersistent. Plans can be linear or paradoxical.

Note: The "Cycle" describes specific guidelines & skills. Effective implementation requires the artful integration of the guidelines & skills contained under Environment & Procedures in a spontaneous & natural manner geared to the personality of the helper. This requires training, practice & supervision. Also, the word "client" is used for anyone receiving help: student, employee, family member, etc.

For more information contact:

Robert E. Wubbolding, EdD, Director

Center for Reality Therapy
7672 Montgomery Road, #383
Cincinnati, Ohio 45236

(513) 561-1911 • FAX (513) 561-3568
E-mail: wubsrt@fuse.net • www.realitytherapy.com

The Center for Reality Therapy provides counseling, consultation, training and supervision including applications to schools, agencies, hospitals, companies and other institutions. The Center is a provider for many organizations which award continuing education units.

This material is copyrighted. Reproduction is prohibited without permission of Robert E. Wubbolding. If you wish to copy, please call.

Among the behaviors to be avoided is arguing. The counselor or therapist is quite active when applying the procedures; thus, there is danger that in helping clients evaluate their behavior, the practitioner will overstep the proper use of reality therapy by arguing about the best choice for the client. This mistake results only in resistance. Also, bossing, criticizing, demeaning, or finding fault with clients only creates resistance and poisons the atmosphere. In fact, even "constructive criticism" is best avoided in relationships with clients.

One of the most important counselor and therapist behaviors to avoid is that of accepting excuses. Too much empathy or sympathy reinforces the perceived helplessness and powerlessness of clients. For instance, clients often describe how they did something harmful to themselves or someone else not because they made a choice, but because of an outside force. For example, the teacher gave an unfair test. Someone rejected me. Another person got me into trouble. They are depressed because of some unfavorable outside event. The alternative to the quicksand of excuses is the effective use of the WDEP system. Asking about wants or goals gets quickly beyond the discussion of a perceived external locus of control.

In the early stages of the development of the reality therapy delivery system, the advice was to never give up. A more realistic formulation is to stay with the person as a helper past the time he or she expects to be abandoned. In other words, do not give up easily. Similarly, the counselor or therapist might be tempted to give up on the WDEP system if it fails to render the desired results immediately. Wubbolding (1996) emphasizes that this is because the principles appear to be easy to practice, in view of the fact that the vocabulary is uncomplicated. Yet to be proficient in the practice of the skills, repeated practice and supervision are required.

A positive environment that serves as the basis for the WDEP system is built not only on avoiding the uncongenial behaviors of arguing, criticizing, or giving up, but also on the global admonition to "be friends." Such efforts to establish an agreeable and harmonious atmosphere are sustained and nourished by the use of the following intervention strategies.

Use Attending Behaviors.   **Attending behaviors (ABs)** described by Ivey (1980) are especially useful in the practice of reality therapy. Eye contact and facial expression include looking at the client without staring and displaying a genuine interest. Physical posture includes sitting in an open, receptive position. Verbal following includes tracking the client's comments and reflecting in a manner that communicates that you are listening. Nonverbal behavior includes attending to the client's manner of expression, such as tone of voice. Paraphrasing means restating the client's comments occasionally. These skills serve as an effective foundation for an enhanced relationship between the client and the counselor or therapist. The acronym **AB-CDEFG** stands for the following interventions.

- *Always be* **courteous.** Being courteous is a behavior that counseling theory rarely mentions, perhaps because it is assumed to exist in the helping relationship. Authority figures are well served by treating the client with respect while refraining from venting anger.
- *Always be* **determined.** The determination of the counselor or therapist is perceived as an explicit and implicit belief or attitude. The metamessage,

relayed to the client by the verbal and nonverbal behavior of the practitioner, is simply that no matter what the circumstances of the client's life, no matter how dreadful the past history, a better life is possible.

- *Always be* **enthusiastic.** In this context, enthusiasm is not cheerleading. Nor is it a naive belief about longstanding disturbances and the difficulty in dealing with them. Rather, it is the continuous effort to look at the bright side; to emphasize what the client can do; to discuss possibilities, not merely problems; and to take a problem-solving approach. The session thus need not degenerate into an empty venting of negative feelings. Thomas Edison, a man who dealt with towering obstacles, once remarked that if we leave our children nothing but enthusiasm, we leave them a legacy of incalculable value.
- *Always be* **firm.** In establishing an empathic environment, the counselor or therapist remains firm. There is no contradiction between seeing the client's point of view and taking a stand for honesty and sobriety while disclosing opposition to dishonesty, drunkenness, or abusive behaviors. Moreover, disclosure that the counselor or therapist supports the policies of the practitioner's employer and applies them unapologetically does not damage the relationship. Rather, it facilitates the establishment of boundaries. However, firmness is not intended to serve as an excuse for the authoritarian personality to impose his or her whims on clients.
- *Always be* **genuine.** Personal authenticity and congruence are seen as necessary prerequisites in reality therapy as well as in other helping methods. Those personal qualities are summarized in Glasser's often-repeated statement, "The counselor must be healthier than the client."

The above attending behaviors are intended to serve as guidelines that can be adapted not only by professionally qualified counselors and therapists, but also by anyone who wishes to use the principles of reality therapy. It is important to remember that they constitute an ideal that few people can attain 100% of the time. They can be among the personal, internal goals of the counselor or therapist.

Suspend Judgment.   As stated earlier, all behavior is a person's best effort at a given time to fulfill his or her needs. Consequently, a counselor or therapist who keeps this principle in mind can more easily see quite harmful choices from a low level of perception, without approval or disapproval. Balancing such suspension of judgment with "always be firm" is a tightrope on which every counselor or therapist walks daily.

Do the Unexpected.   Unpredictability is a quality that facilitates a helpful counseling or psychotherapy environment. Focusing on a strength, a success, or a time when the client felt good often generates the type of discussion that clients do not expect. Nevertheless, clients who are characterized by negative symptoms also choose positive symptoms (Wubbolding, 1981, 2001). Therefore, it is good to discuss in detail the circumstances when clients chose effectively, felt good, and remained in effective control of their lives. Wubbolding has described other ways for doing the unexpected and has incorporated paradoxical techniques such as reframing, redefining, and relabeling into reality therapy (1984, 1988). However, in order to be effective using these and other paradoxical techniques, it is necessary to invert one's thinking. Causes are seen as effects; the objectionable is now a strength (Dowd & Milne, 1986; Fay, 1978; Seltzer, 1986; Weeks & L'Abate, 1982). Wubbolding (1993) states:

> A depressed child is seen as pensive, gentle, and thoughtful. An angry child is outgoing and has deep conviction. The bully is a leader and has ambition, while a submissive child is kind and cooperative. This paradoxical technique is, therefore, a technique that is useful to establish a relationship and can even serve as a procedure leading to change. However, it is not to be used indiscriminately and manipulatively. Rather, it is a psychological condiment, to be used sparingly. And like the other "guidelines" it is primarily a way to establish a safe counseling environment. (p. 293)

Use Humor.   A healthy and democratic sense of humor is a curative factor for the mental health specialist. Victor Borge once remarked that laughter is the shortest distance between two people. Peter (1982) states that laughter is helpful in dealing with anxiety, depression, and loss. Children learn by having fun. One of Aristotle's definitions of human beings is that we are risible; that is, we can laugh. Consequently, to function fully as a human being, as a person in effective control who is characterized by positive symptoms, it is advantageous to have a sense of humor. Indeed, an effective counselor or therapist using the principles of reality therapy can enhance the counseling or psychotherapy environment by laughing with the client.

Be Yourself.   Though it is to be expected that students learning counseling and psychotherapy skills will adopt the style of their teachers or that of the leaders in each theory, they also need to adapt the skills that fit their own personality. Whether they are assertive, placid, exuberant, dispassionate, expressive, restrained, confrontational, or laid back, they can practice the method effectively. It is a matter of practicing and assimilating the skills and thereby adapting them to a personal style.

Share Yourself.   The creation and maintenance of a trusting relationship is facilitated by appropriate self-disclosure. According to a Swedish proverb, "A joy shared is twice a joy. A sorrow shared is half a sorrow." While self-disclosure by a counselor or therapist can be helpful, caution is necessary. Cormier and Cormier (1998) warn that there can be a danger of accelerating self-disclosure to the point where the client and the counselor or therapist spend time swapping stories about themselves. As with all the techniques for building a trusting relationship, self-disclosure is best used moderately.

Listen for Metaphors.   Metaphors in this context are figures of speech, analogies, similes, and anecdotes that serve to quantify problems and thereby make them manageable. Barker (1985) states that if properly constructed, stories and other metaphors offer choices to clients. He observes that they are often helpful because "psychotherapy is essentially a process of providing people with more choice in the matter of how they behave, or respond emotionally, in various situations" (p. 17). Also, stories and anecdotes can be humorous and thus help clients perceive their problems and decisions in a different light. Metaphors used by clients are often overlooked by counselors and therapists, or they are paraphrased. It is better, however, to use the metaphor, to extend it, and to return to it in subsequent sessions. The following metaphors might be stated by clients or initiated by counselors and therapists.

> "I feel like a floor mat."
>
> "Cleaning my desk is like climbing Mount Everest."

"You sound like you've been on a merry-go-round."

"It sounds like warfare in your house."

"I don't know if I'm going up or down."

"I feel like I'm winning."

"Our relationship has gone sour."

"You seem to be back on track, heading in an upward direction."

Using these metaphors, the counselor or therapist can offer clients specific choices, such as "Would you like to get off the floor?" "Do you want to get off the merry-go-round?" and "What would you be doing today if you were on solid ground, away from the merry-go-round?" As with all such techniques used to enhance the counseling and psychotherapy environment, metaphors do not constitute the essence of reality therapy. They do serve, however, to build trust between the client and the counselor or therapist.

Listen for Themes.   Tying together the ideas, feelings, and actions of clients helps them to gain a sense of direction and control. The practitioner using reality therapy listens carefully for themes such as previous attempts to solve problems, wants that are fulfilled, and what has helped and not helped the client. This technique is not exclusive to the practice of reality therapy, but in using it the counselor or therapist listens for themes that are linked to the WDEP interventions (see "Procedures: The WDEP System").

Summarize and Focus.   Similar to the identification of themes, this technique helps the counselor or therapist listen carefully and communicate to clients that they are being heard. Unlike summaries used in other theories, this one concentrates on components of the WDEP system. A counselor or therapist might summarize a client's statements by responding, "You've stated that you've tried to get a promotion at work and been unsuccessful, that you've approached your boss and described what you want, that you've put in extra hours. Nothing so far has gotten you what you want." The counselor or therapist has summarized what the client has done that has not worked and has omitted many other details.

Focusing means to center the conversation on the client rather than on outside forces over which neither involved party has control. Very little can be done to cause changes in other people. Nothing can be done to change the past. Thus, it is most helpful if the counselor or therapist gently and positively assists clients to discuss their own here-and-now wants, total behaviors, plans, hopes, frustrations, and perceptions.

Allow or Impose Consequences.   Professional counselors and therapists have fewer opportunities to use this element of the environment than those who wish to integrate reality therapy into their work. Probation and parole officers, halfway-house workers, and others often function in a supervisory role and are required to impose consequences. It is assumed that the consequence is reasonable and not punitive, and also that it is imposed to help rather than merely control the client.

Even counselors and therapists occasionally impose consequences when life-threatening or evidently dangerous situations are described by the client. The code of ethics of the American Counseling Association states: "The general requirement that counselors keep information confidential does not apply when disclosure is required to prevent clear and imminent danger to the client or others or when legal requirements demand that confidential information be revealed. Counselors consult with other professionals when in doubt as to the validity of an exception" (Herlihy & Corey, 1996, p. 34).

Allow Silence.   The use of silence in reality therapy, if timed properly, allows the client to conduct inner self-evaluation, reassess wants, think about what is controllable and, therefore, uncontrollable, and in general take responsibility for the direction of the session. Trainees learning reality therapy tend to ask questions nervously in rapid-fire order. They are well advised to slow down and allow a few incisive questions to reverberate inside the client.

Be Ethical.   The ethical principle concerning clear or imminent danger is one of many that the practitioner of reality therapy practices. A trusting relationship and a professional atmosphere conducive to helping are built around solid ethical principles. Anyone using reality therapy properly knows, understands, and practices the ethical standards of various professional organizations. Professional disclosure is often required, as in Ohio (State of Ohio, 1984). Thus counselors, therapists, and social workers must provide clients with a written description of their professional qualifications. Wubbolding (1986) emphasizes that counselors and therapists should provide clients with information about the nature of reality therapy. These details help clarify the boundaries of the relationship as well as the advantages and limitations of the assistance that the practitioner can offer. He also emphasized the importance of knowing how to assess suicidal threats and how this assessment is used in the practice of reality therapy (1990). Informed consent, dual relationships, confidentiality, and proper record keeping are among the many ethical issues impinging on the relationship between counselor or therapist and client.

Be Redundant or Repetitious.   Often the same questions are asked in various ways. When a client is defensive and offering excuses in the form of denial, the counselor or therapist sometimes repeats the same question in a different way. It becomes a theme aimed at helping clients evaluate their own behavior. "When you made that choice, did it help?" "Did it work for you?" "What impact did that action have on you and on others?" "Did it help you enough?" "Was the action the best you were capable of?" Such questions asked at various times become a haunting theme that gradually and supportively lessens denial and facilitates the clients' assumption of responsibility. Yet like the overall art of counseling or therapy, the skill of being redundant is developed through practice and self-evaluation.

Create Suspense and Anticipation.   In a counselor or therapist's effective use of reality therapy there can be an element of drama. A counseling or psychotherapy session should be a significant event in the lives of clients. An authentic buoyancy on the part of the counselor or therapist and a desire to reassure can elicit a feeling of curiosity and a sense of impending success. The ability to communicate a sense of optimism is an advanced skill and is developed with practice and training.

Establish Boundaries.   There are limits within which a counselor or therapist operates, and these should be clarified. The ethical principle of dual relationships, discussed earlier, is clearly part of boundary classification. Further, the client might wish to shield certain areas from discussion. A useful question for counselors or therapists to ask is, "Is there any topic you would prefer we not discuss?" Such questioning empowers clients to choose what they want to work on. If clients have numerous topics that are forbidden territory (which is rarely the case), the counselor or therapist can ask them if it is helpful for them to conceal or mask potential topics. In any event, the wishes of the client are paramount and are respected.

The previous guidelines are designed to help the counselor or therapist using reality therapy to establish rapport, mutual trust, and a safe atmosphere by being aware of obstacles and barriers to involvement. They also consist of positive interventions that facilitate the client's expectation that the experience is worthwhile and significant. Moreover, a truly skilled practitioner of reality therapy engages in an ongoing self-evaluation process by means of follow-up with past clients, consultation with peers, and continuing education. These environmental building blocks aimed at establishing and deepening the relationship provide a fundamental prerequisite for what is essentially the practice of reality therapy: the WDEP system.

Procedures: The WDEP System   The specific interventions that are the essence of reality therapy are based on the trusting relationship described as *environment*. The procedures or determinations (Wubbolding, 1985b) are most appropriately formulated as the WDEP system as described in Figure 11.1 (Glasser, 1990; Wubbolding, 1989, 1991, 2000, 2002; Wubbolding & Brickell, 1999). They should not be seen as steps to be used sequentially or mechanically; and although they are described in simple, jargon-free language, they can be difficult to implement. For instance, a counselor or therapist working with a student referred for a school discipline problem would probably not begin with a lengthy discussion of W (wants), but rather with an exploration of D (doing): in other words, what happened to bring about the referral? Thus, in conceptualizing the entire process, it is useful to see it as a cycle that can be entered at any point.

W: Discussing Wants, Needs, and Perceptions.   Because human beings are motivated to fulfill their wants and needs, it is important for the counselor or therapist to take the time to explore the specific wants of the client. The questions might include: "What do you want from your spouse? From your school? Your job? Your career? From your friends? Your parents? Your children? Your supervisor? From yourself? What do you want from me? From your church?" Thus, there are at least 11 generic questions that can be asked. These are multiplied threefold if the counselor or therapist asks more precisely about each category: (1) "What do you want that you are getting?" (2) "What do you want that you are not getting?" (3) "What are you getting that you don't want?" The areas for exploration and clarification become almost endless when the counselor or therapist adds, "How much do you want it?" "What would you need to give up to get what you want?" "What will you settle for?"

All wants are related to the five needs: belonging, power or achievement, fun or enjoyment, freedom or independence, and survival. Therefore, it is useful to help clients link their wants explicitly to their needs by asking, "If you had what you wanted, what would you have?" or "If your wants were met, what would that satisfy inside?" Such questioning of a parent often elicits the following: "I want my child to keep the curfew, get good grades, stay away from drugs, do the house chores, and be pleasant to the rest of the family. If I had that, I would have peace of mind. I would know that I am a good parent." The parent has specific wants and has identified the underlying need: achievement or power.

Discussing perceptions is also an important part of W. Questions about clients' perceptions are slightly different from those specifically relating to wants. A parent might be asked, "What do you see when you look at your child?" The answer might be, "I see a child who is rebellious at times and cooperative when she wants something from me." Asking about perceptions is especially useful in groups and in family counseling and psychotherapy because arguments can be prevented. A counselor or therapist can intervene by reminding all present that they are discussing their viewpoints—what they see, not what "is."

W: Sharing Wants and Perceptions.   Counselors and therapists using reality therapy share their own wants and perceptions when such disclosure is helpful to clients. They share their wants regarding such issues as how many sessions are necessary and remind clients that the practitioner's role is to help clients make decisions but not to remove responsibility. On occasion, the counselor or therapist might even make a specific suggestion about what kind of action would be helpful. In the case of a parent, the counselor or therapist might say, "When I look at your child, I see similar things, but I also see a person struggling to grow up, one who doesn't need lectures but quality time from parents." Counselors and therapists who share wants and perceptions do not take responsibility for clients, nor do they lecture or admonish clients. They lead but do not coerce.

W: Getting a Commitment to Counseling.   Change and growth will occur only if the client is committed to making changes in his or her actions. Thus, it is imperative that the counselor or therapist discuss the client's **level of commitment** to the process and its outcomes. The question "How hard do you want to work at changing your situation?" gives the client an opportunity to look inward and reflect on the degree of responsibility he or she wishes to assume.

Wubbolding (1988) has identified five levels of commitment as described by clients.

1. *"I don't want to be here."* This statement clearly illustrates that the client is at best reluctant and resistant. It is even possible that he or she has been coerced into counseling or psychotherapy. In fact, this level of commitment is actually no commitment at all, but it is included because it seems to fit an increasing number of clients who are seen by practitioners.

2. *"I want the outcome, but not the effort."* This level indicates that the client does want to change and is perhaps at stage 1 ("I'll do it") in gaining effective control and taking personal responsibility. It is a higher commitment than the first level, but it will still result in no change until a higher level is achieved.

3. *"I'll try; I might."* Trying to make a change for the better constitutes the middle level of commitment to change. Still, trying to get out of bed early is not the same as doing it.

4. *"I will do my best."* At this level, a person goes beyond trying and commits to specific action. However, such a commitment still allows the possibility of failure.

5. *"I will do whatever it takes."* The highest level of commitment represents an outcome centered on a no-excuses level of commitment. It is the most desirable level from the view of the counselor or therapist.

The levels of commitment are developmental. The higher levels are more helpful than the lower ones. Yet for some clients, "I'll try" is a major improvement. They should not be pushed too vigorously or too quickly to move to a higher level. Rather, the skillful counselor or therapist helps clients to evaluate their level of commitment and gently leads them to the next level.

D: Discussing Behavioral Direction and Doing (Total Behavior).   The counselor or therapist helps the client review his or her overall direction by inquiries such as "Where do you think you're going if you continue on the same path?" A child might be asked, "If you continue to flunk in school, resist your parents' requests, and continue on the same pathway, where will you be in 2 or 3 or 12 months?"

The exploration of the overall direction is only the embarkation point for further questioning about current total behavior. More time and effort are needed to help clients examine their specific actions. The counselor or therapist helps the client verbalize exactly what he or she did for a specific amount of time. The client becomes a television camera, as it were, relating not typical events but what happened that was specific and unique.

Similarly, clients might describe their thoughts and feelings at the time of the actions as well as what they now think and feel about them. Likewise, they could even describe how their overall direction and specific actions are affecting the physiological component of their total behavior.

So important is the generic question "What are you doing?" that a book of reality therapy cases has that name (Glasser, 1980). Each word in the question serves as a signpost for the practitioner (Wubbolding, 1990, 2002). "What" implies that the counselor or therapist asks for precise details. When clients take refuge in generalities, they should be encouraged to be more specific. "Are" emphasizes the importance of stressing the present rather than indulging in endless discussions of past behaviors that are beyond the client's control. "You" focuses on the client rather than on other people, excuses, and uncontrollable events. Finally, "doing" connotes total behavior: the exploration of direction, specific actions, thoughts, feelings, and physical symptoms accompanying the client's choices.

E: Helping Clients Conduct Evaluations.   In the cycle of counseling and in the WDEP system of procedures, the element of evaluation occupies the central position (see Figure 11.1). Like a keystone in an arch, its pivotal place supports the entire structure. If it is absent, the arch crumbles. The practice of reality therapy is firm and effective to the degree that the counselor or therapist assists clients in evaluating their own behavior, wants, perceptions, level of commitment, and plans.

Because of the prominent place of self-evaluation in the cycle of counseling, reality therapy is properly placed among the cognitive counseling theories. It is here, especially, at the cardinal point of self-evaluation, that cognitive restructuring takes place. Clients look inward and examine the effectiveness of their lifestyle and its specific aspects. Only now, when they have concluded that some part of their control system (wants, behaviors, perceptions) is not helping them or is not as beneficial as it could be, do clients see that a change is necessary.

More specifically, evaluation contains the following elements.

1. *Evaluation of behavioral direction.* After helping the client describe the overall direction of his or her life, the counselor or therapist assists in evaluating the significance of this direction. Is it the best direction in the mind of the client? Is it helpful or harmful, and does the direction have what, for the client, is high quality?

2. *Evaluation of specific actions.* The questions about specific actions are geared to the descriptions provided in the client's explanation of how a specific segment of his or

her day was spent. Such questions as the following might be asked: "Did sleeping until 10:00 in the morning help or hurt your effort to find a job?" "What were the consequences of hitting your brother?" "When you shout at the kids, do you get what you want?" "Even if they obey for a while, does it help both in the short run and in the long run?" "Does it help to the degree you were hoping for?" "If you continue to eat a diet of ice cream, sweets, and starch, will you ever attain the weight you said you wanted?"

3. *Evaluation of wants.* The client is assisted in making judgments about the appropriateness and the attainability of his or her wants: "Is what you want truly good for you?" "How realistic is it for you to get your parents totally off your back?" "How realistic is it for your adolescent child to become 100% cooperative or perfect in your own eyes?"

4. *Evaluation of perceptions or viewpoints.* Perceptions are not easily changed. Rarely are they changed by a simple decision to view a person, a situation, or an event differently. Yet they can be changed by changing behavior (Glasser, 1980b, 1984; Powers, 1973). But because perceptions involve what people want, they occupy an important place in the evaluation process. So even though they are not directly changed, their desirability and appropriateness should be evaluated. More specifically, human beings seek the perception of being adequate, popular, skilled, in control, helpful to others, and comfortable. They also have more specific perceptions relative to each generic perception. Thus, the client is helped to evaluate general and specific perceptions or viewpoints. Evaluative questions for perceptions might include: "Does it help if you see your son only as rebellious and lazy?" "What is accomplished if you see only the negative aspects of your parents' behavior?" "When you nurse a negative attitude toward your boss, does it help you to improve your situation at work?"

5. *Evaluation of new direction.* As new possibilities unfold for clients, it is useful to help them determine whether those possibilities are need-satisfying. The rebellious student is asked, "How will cooperation at home benefit you and your family?" "If you were to make an effort to learn, do your homework, ask questions in class, and, in general, do what 'successful' students do, would you feel better?" "What impact would this approach have on your friends and family?"

6. *Evaluation of plans.* After a new direction is defined, and often even before clients have committed to a change of direction, they can be encouraged to make plans. At first glance these plans might appear to be meager and insignificant, but they often represent the first steps toward more effective and positive need-satisfaction. In working with an adolescent, Wubbolding (1980) was able to help him make a modest plan of action. This high school student had shut himself in his room on the weekends with the curtains and drapes closed. Although resistant at first, he eventually made plans to open the blinds and let the light in. He subsequently developed a healthy social life by making rudimentary changes in his overall direction. Thus, the evaluation of plans is based not on whether they solve the basic problem but on whether they address the problem and aim toward the more effective fulfillment of belonging, power, fun, and freedom.

P: Planning.   According to one saying, "To fail to plan is to plan to fail." Glasser (1980a) states that plans vary; some are detailed, while others are quite simple, yet he emphasizes that "there must always be a plan. People who go through life without some sort of a long-term plan, usually divided into a series of small plans to reach larger goals, are like ships floundering without rudders" (p. 52).

The procedure of planning is often mistakenly viewed as the essence of the practice of reality therapy. And though it is important, it is effective only if based on a client's inner self-evaluation. Plans that are truly efficacious, or at least more likely to be carried out by the client, have at least eight qualities, which can be summarized by the acronym SAMI^{2}C^3 (Wubbolding, 2002):

S	***Simple:***	The plan is uncomplicated.
A	***Attainable:***	If the plan is too difficult or too long range, the client will become discouraged and not follow through.
M	***Measurable:***	The plan is precise and exact. The client is encouraged to define a clear answer to the question, "When will you do it?"
I	***Immediate:***	The plan is carried out as soon as possible.
I	***Involved:***	The helper is involved if such involvement is appropriate. The involvement is, of course, within the bounds of ethical standards and facilitates client independence rather than dependence.
C	***Controlled by the client:***	An effective plan is not contingent on the actions of another person but is, as much as possible, within the control of the client.
C	***Committed to:***	The counselor or therapist helps the client to pledge firmly to put the plan into action.
C	***Consistent:***	The ideal plan is repetitious. A single plan can be a start, but the most effective plan is one that is repeated.

The common denominator to all planning is **persistence** on the part of the counselor or therapist. This coincides with the injunction "Don't give up."

Planning and follow-through are crucial elements in personal growth, enhanced mental health, decision making, and remediation of problems. Helpful plans aimed at achieving these ultimate goals are not forced on clients. Rather, clients are taught that the achievement of their goals will be the result of their own positive choices and plans. Clients are accordingly led to discover within themselves desirable plans aimed at their own need-satisfaction.

In summary, the cycle of counseling or psychotherapy is a design for understanding reality therapy and an outline for knowing how to apply it. The environment consists of specific recommendations for building a firm but friendly atmosphere in which a client can feel safe and confident while realizing that the counselor or therapist actively seeks to be of help. The WDEP formulation is not a system that is intended to be followed in a mechanical manner, but rather a system from which the proper intervention is selected at a given time because of its apparent appropriateness.

Clients with Mental Disorders

The diagnostic labels described in the *Diagnostic Statistical Manual* are not static conditions. They are negative symptoms (i.e., behaviors generated for a purpose—to fulfill wants and needs). As goal-directed behaviors, they can be replaced by more effective behaviors (i.e., positive symptoms). The skilled reality counselor or therapist spends little time discussing diagnostic symptoms such as hallucinations, compulsions, psychoses, or depression. Rather, the counselor or therapist and client search for specific solutions related to effective need and want satisfaction especially directed toward a better sense of belonging and healthier relationships.

Consequently, reality therapy applies to virtually every kind of behavior and, when necessary, medication assists in making reality therapy more effective. The theory began in a mental hospital and a correctional institution and is widely used in corrections. Though not describing diagnostic categories, Lojk (1986) demonstrated that reality therapy is still used successfully with prisoners. Bratter, Bratter, Maxym, Radda, and Steiner (1993) have successfully used reality therapy for delinquent youth whose diagnosis ranged from attention deficit hyperactivity disorder and conduct disorder to affective disorders, both depression and bipolar.

The reality counselor or therapist treats all behaviors as if some element of choice is present. In this way, clients feel both hope and empowerment. They realize that a better life is accessible and they are not irretrievably doomed to a life of mental illness.

Evaluation

Overview

While more research could be conducted to validate the use of reality therapy, the widespread interest in the theory indicates that many practitioners have confidence in its efficacy. From 1975 to 2002, more than 7,000 persons worldwide completed the 18-month training program and were certified in reality therapy. Anecdotal evidence points toward the theory's usefulness with a wide variety of issues, such as eating disorders, child abuse, marriage, aging, elective mutism, career satisfaction, study habits, self-esteem, assertive behavior, and many others (Glasser, 1980, 1989).

Supporting Research

Practitioners of reality therapy represent virtually every helping profession: counselors, therapists, educators, managers, chemical dependency workers, corrections specialists, and many others. This overview of research represents a sampling of some such studies.

Glasser (1965) described the dramatic effect of a reality therapy program in a psychiatric hospital. The average stay in a ward of 210 men was 15 years. Within 2 years, 75 men had been released with only three returning. According to Shea (1973), the use of reality therapy produced significant results in increasing self-concept and lowering court referrals. Gang (1975) showed that the use of reality therapy resulted in more socially acceptable student behavior in the classroom. The teachers in the study also believed that the relationship skills resulting from the use of reality therapy were essential if change were to result.

German (1975) investigated the effects of reality therapy in group counseling or psychotherapy with institutionalized adolescents. In relation to a comparative group, the students displayed significantly fewer behaviors requiring disciplinary action. Poppen, Thompson, Cates, and Gang (1976) found that after reality therapy was used with disruptive students, appropriate behavior increased 18 to 47%. In a study of juvenile offenders, Yarish (1986) found significant differences in the participants' perceived locus of control. They became aware that they made their own choices rather than being controlled by external forces.

Gorter-Cass (1988) studied the use of reality therapy in an alternative school and stated that the overall trend was toward "less severe behavior" and that there were significant changes in self-worth and self-concept among students. Elementary school students ages 9 to 11 were studied by Hart-Hester, Heuchert, and Whittier (1989). The students were counseled in groups, and action plans were formulated. The study showed a "pronounced increase in the percentage of time-on-task for each targeted student" (p. 16).

In a study of the effects of reality therapy in a rural elementary school, Bowers (1997) found improvements in relationships and self-concept, but little change in school attendance. The author noted that school attendance was not a significant problem at this school.

Studying the effects of reality therapy in a therapeutic community in Ireland, Honeyman (1990) found significant changes in the residents' self-esteem, awareness of their inability to control their drinking, and insight into living in a more inner-controlled manner. Positive effects have also been shown when reality therapy has been used with teachers (Parish, 1988, 1991; Parish, Martin, & Khramtsova, 1992), undergraduate students (Peterson & Truscott, 1988), graduate students (Peterson, Chang, & Collins, 1997; Peterson, Woodward, & Kissko, 1991), foster parents (Corwin, 1987), negatively addicted inmates (Chance, Bibens, Cowley, Prouretedal, Dolese, & Virtue, 1990), and student athletes (Martin & Thompson, 1995). Y. S. Kim (2001) found a positive correlation between the use of group reality therapy with parents and self-esteem as well as parent-child relationships. Similarly, in a 1-year follow-up study of previous research, Kim and Hwang (2001) found constant, positive, long-term effects on middle-school students' sense of internal control.

This brief selection of research studies illustrates the value of reality therapy as a reliable tool for counselors and therapists. However, many areas for possible study remain. Researchers could investigate further the effects of reality therapy on the areas already mentioned, as well as on other issues dealt with by counselors and therapists.

Limitations

Reality therapy should be seen as an open system that will grow and change. It is not a narrow theory that is rigidly applied. Yet as a free-standing cognitive behavioral theory and practice of counseling and therapy, it has limitations. Some of these are inherent in the theory, and some reside in the skill of the practitioner.

Many clients believe that in order to make changes in their lives or to feel better, they need to gain insight into their past, resolve early conflicts, describe the negative aspects of their lives, or tell how they arrived at their present state. Many of these clients could be successfully encouraged to emphasize their present behavior, but some believe that no change can result without dealing specifically with past pain, and for them reality therapy will appear to avoid the real issues.

Part of this limitation resides in the skill of the counselor or therapist rather than the theory, but in the minds of clients it is often difficult to separate the theory from the practitioner. For such clients, the practitioner needs to adjust the therapy rather than cling to the principle of discussing current behavior. Practitioners who have been trained to emphasize a discussion of feelings as the true test of effective counseling or therapy find the quick emphasis on clients' actions premature if not hasty. However, a skillful reality counselor or therapist is aware of all aspects of clients' behavior—actions, thinking, and feelings—and responds to them as a unit rather than as disconnected from one another. Still, if feelings such as anger are seen as the root cause of problems rather than as feelings caused by unmet needs, the counselor or therapist will probably be less effective when using the WDEP system of reality therapy.

The concrete language of reality therapy may be another limitation. It contains little jargon or technical terminology, and the theory and practice employ words like *belonging, power, fun, freedom, wants, plans, self-evaluation,* and *effective control.* Because the language of reality therapy is easily understood, its practice can appear to be easily implemented. Nevertheless, the effective use of reality therapy requires practice, supervision, and continuous learning.

Because reality therapy is straightforward and deals with present issues, its subtlety often is obscured. The discussion of current and future actions and plans is the most obvious part of the counseling or therapy process, yet the most important components are the clarification of clients' wants and their self-evaluation. In learning reality therapy, practitioners who are in a hurry to see results frequently proceed too rapidly to action planning. Such efforts to help clients make decisions, solve problems, or take more effective control of their lives result in resistance because of the inappropriate use of reality therapy principles.

Summary Chart—Reality Therapy Theory

Human Nature
Human beings are motivated by current drives, not by past events, fixations, or external stimuli. They have choices related to their motivation. Often human beings make choices that are ineffective, even harmful to themselves. Through counseling or therapy and education, they can learn to achieve inner harmony and happiness without infringing on the rights of others.

Major Constructs
Human needs are the basis for the practice of reality therapy. Inner motivation is rooted in the ever-present search for and effort to gain survival or self-preservation, love and belonging, power or achievement, fun or enjoyment, and freedom or independence. These motivators are made concrete and specific through wants or desires unique to each individual. People choose specific behaviors to fulfill these wants and needs. Thus the purpose of behavior is to gain the perception that we are getting what we want— that is, that needs are fulfilled.

Goals
The primary goal of reality therapy is to help clients make more effective choices to meet their needs more efficiently and effectively. Specific goals, formulated with clients, depend on their stage of development, their perception of what they want, and their ability to realistically fulfill their specific wants. When clients learn to make better choices, they can relinquish the prison of the past and the current pressures of their environment.

Change Process
Change occurs when clients decide to change. When counselors or therapists believe clients have the power to change, they communicate this to clients. They present realistic choices and proceed on the assumption that a better life is possible. Developing a relationship based on this unshakable belief enables clients to make more effective choices and to gain a sense of inner control and need-satisfaction.

Interventions

Two generic kinds of interventions are used: first, establishing a firm but friendly environment that enables clients to spontaneously explore their control systems; and second, utilizing the WDEP procedures, which consist of helping clients explore their wants, discuss all aspects of their current behavior, evaluate the attainability of wants and the effectiveness of their choices, and finally formulate realistic and repetitive plans.

Limitations

For clients who believe that they need to gain insight into their past or resolve early conflicts in order to change or feel better, reality therapy will appear to avoid the real issues. In order to use the principles effectively, the counselor or therapist needs to genuinely believe in them and be trained in them; this poses a problem for practitioners who have an inadequate understanding of the principles or practice of reality therapy. Finally, the simple language of reality therapy can be a barrier to its effective implementation. The system is easy to understand but more difficult to practice.

The Case of Jonathan: A Reality Therapy Approach

It is evident that Jonathan feels rejected by co-workers, family, and society in general. This alienation manifests itself in his total behavior: actions, thinking, feelings, and physiology. His excessive drinking, self-talk ("They're all against me"), anger, and insomnia are symptoms of unmet wants and needs. Because he is unable to connect with other people, achieve success at work, enjoy life, and make desirable or satisfying choices, he has extracted from his internal behavioral suitcase choices that have proven to be highly ineffective and destructive.

A skilled reality therapist would establish an empathic, ongoing but time-limited relationship with him to help him to especially satisfy his need for belonging at work and with his family, resulting in an internal sense of control. A primary goal of such counseling or therapy is to help him abandon his negative symptoms and choose positive ones. Accomplishing this might involve systemic interventions such as conferences with the employer as well as couple counseling or therapy with his estranged wife.

Establishing the Environment

As in any counseling or therapy, a warm, caring relationship is the foundation for change. It is important to listen carefully to Jonathan, allowing him to tell his story in his own words. Reflective listening and empathy are crucial at this stage. However, the user of reality therapy does not listen passively, but rather attempts to identify themes related to the procedures. For example, Jonathan's frustrations can be translated into wants. Because he is a verbal client, he will probably use metaphors to describe how he feels as well as other aspects of his current plight. Such metaphors might include, "I feel like I'm in prison," "I'm really down," "I'm at the end of my rope," and "I feel like a floor mat." These can be used later in the counseling or therapy to help him gain a sense of inner control.

In establishing the environment, the reality therapist intervenes directively and emphatically but does not encourage "venting of feelings" in such a way as to indirectly communicate that merely talking will solve a problem. Feelings are always connected to actions. Such questions as "What did you do yesterday when you felt so depressed?" are very useful. The counselor or therapist also helps the client to speak of problems in the past tense and solutions in the present or future tense. This results in addressing an immediate goal—communicating hope (i.e., Jonathan can improve his life and achieve some degree of happiness).

After a friendly atmosphere has been established, the counselor or therapist uses the WDEP system more explicitly.

Using the Procedures

The use of the WDEP system is not a step-by-step process. In fact, there is no absolute delineation between environment and procedures (see Figure 11.1). At the beginning of the session, Jonathan was encouraged to talk about actions (D) when he described his anger, alienation, pain, guilt, loneliness, and depression. Still, there are many more explicit interventions that are built on the friendly, warm, helping relationship and these interventions should not be used precipitously in the session.

Exploration of Wants and Locus of Control   Jonathan would be asked to describe what he wants (W) from the counseling or psychotherapy process. He would discuss how he thinks the counselor or therapist could help him. The counselor or therapist would disclose how he or she can be of assistance, what is realistic, and so forth. The counselor or therapist would explain that the myriad of problems can be less painful if his interpersonal relationships improve. Even his nightmares are normal expressions of frustrations resulting from unmet needs, especially belonging.

The counselor or therapist would help him describe what he wants from the employer, co-workers, wife, and so on, and help him describe exactly what a pleasant and satisfying day would look like. More than likely he would have difficulty describing such a day, but the counselor would patiently help him to be very specific.

The exploration of his perceived locus of control is especially relevant for Jonathan. The counselor or therapist leads him to the conclusion that his own behavior is all that he can control, and that effective counseling or psychotherapy will empower him to make more need-satisfying choices. This emphasis does not minimize the impact of the external world on Jonathan or the systemic issues that limit his options.

The counselor or therapist further elicits a high level of commitment, a willingness to try new behaviors such as communicating with his wife in new ways, utilizing the traits of quality time with his children and his wife. Interspersing statements about the hopefulness of his future, the counselor or therapist assures Jonathan that his reactions to his circumstances are normal and not unusual.

Exploring His Specific Actions and Self-Evaluation   After this exploration of the overall direction of his life with emphasis on belonging, Jonathan would describe how he spends his time regarding the other psychological needs: power or achievement, fun or enjoyment, and freedom or independence.

He would go into detail about the last time he chose to do something that provided a sense of accomplishment, even if it was for a brief time. While discussion of fun might seem superficial, there is almost always a "fun-deficit" in clients who are absorbed in anger, resentment, guilt, alienation, self-pity, loneliness, shame, depression, or any other negative symptom. The counselor or therapist would ask him to evaluate his own behaviors. Did they work for him? Were they helpful and satisfying? Self-evaluation (E) is a major part of this dialogue. If he doesn't allow time for fun, is he helping or hurting himself? The counselor or therapist would interject humor into the session to help Jonathan laugh. When he reflects on his laughter and says he felt better for a few seconds, he will come to realize that he can feel better for longer periods of time if he chooses to insert some fun into his schedule.

He would explore the feeling of being trapped and discouraged about his choices or options. Again his current actions would be the focus of the discussion. When was the last time he felt freedom or independence? What was he doing at that time? If he does not do the same things that helped him feel some degree of freedom earlier, how will anything change for him?

Planning   The planning phase (P) is always dependent on the clients' judgments. Thus, it is assumed that the plans described below fit with Jonathan's wants. It is also assumed that he is committed to them and that he has made firm evaluations that his current direction and specific activities are not helping. He is, therefore, ready for a new series of choices. The planning is connected with the four psychological needs: belonging, power, freedom, and fun.

Belonging

1. He will contact his wife to see if he can spend a brief time with her and the child. He would ask her to agree that the time be free of arguing, blaming, criticism, and all discussion of divisive topics.
2. He will look for opportunities to establish friendly, casual, and temporary relationships. He will look for opportunities to *go out of his way* to engage as many people in conversation in church groups, stores, neighborhood, and so on.
3. Upon return to work he will do the same: engage in agreeable conversations. The counselor or therapist explains that this is not an avoidance of unpleasantness. This plan is a temporary attempt to build relationships with co-workers.

Power

1. He will agree to an alcoholism assessment.
2. If necessary, he will join a 12-step program.
3. He will investigate opportunities for furthering his education: courses, financial aid, and so on.
4. He will begin to read for discussion during counseling books such as *A Set of Directions for Putting and Keeping Yourself Together* (Wubbolding, 2002).
5. The counselor or therapist will arrange for a conference with his work supervisor and co-workers to address cultural issues for the purpose of resolving disagreements.

Freedom   He will think about the counselor's or therapist's comments that nightmares are normal for him and that each nightmare experience means he will need to have one less after that. They are not a sign of sickness, but are the way he releases tension. He might even be encouraged to try to have a nightmare when he goes to bed.

Fun

1. He will schedule brief periods of enjoyable activities. At first these might not seem like fun, but eventually he will find them need-satisfying.
2. When he returns to counseling or psychotherapy, he must tell the counselor two jokes found in books, magazines, or on the Internet.

Summary   The goal of this process is to help Jonathan fulfill his needs more effectively, not merely to remediate problems. The plans must be his, not those of the counselor or therapist who suggests them. The plans are also developmental. Not all of them are formulated at the same time. Perhaps in the first session only one plan is selected.

Finally, using the WDEP system built on the proper atmosphere or relationship, Jonathan can make significant changes in his life in eight to ten sessions.

Family Theory

Valerie E. Appleton
Eastern Washington University

Cass Dykeman
Oregon State University

Background

Up to this point, the chapters in this textbook have focused on counseling and psychotherapy with individuals. Why care about the application of counseling to families? After all, the fathers and mothers of counseling did not seem to care about applying their ideas to whole families. In this chapter, we will present reasons why the counselor or therapist should care about the familial applications of counseling and psychotherapy. In addition, we will define key terms, detail prominent theories, and discuss practical applications of these theories.

So why should the counselor or therapist care about family therapy? The following questions suggest possible reasons: What would family therapy theories add to his or her clinical reasoning? What would family therapy techniques add to his or her clinical "tool bag"? At the end of this chapter, we hope the reader can list many answers to both questions. Right now, let us start with the assertion that family therapy can enlarge the scope of clinical reasoning and practice. Specifically, it can enlarge the practitioner's scope from individuals to families and the larger sociocultural contexts that make up an individual's environment. Family therapy can help the counselor or therapist look at the patterns of communication and relationship that connect people to each other and to their social and physical environments.

Definitions

In elementary school education, there is a principle that in grades 1 through 3 a child learns to read, and in grades 4 through 6 a child reads to learn. In other words, literacy must precede the acquisition of ideas and their applications. This principle is especially true when it comes to learning about family therapy. Family therapists have a maddening habit of both coining new terms and using common terms in unique ways. This habit can sometimes leave neophytes to family therapy in a daze. So, to enhance the reader's understanding of the theoretical and applied discussions in this chapter, we present the following family therapy terms.

- **Centripetal** and **Centrifugal.** These terms were borrowed from physics to describe different relational styles in families. Centripetal families look inward to the family as the source of pleasure, joy, and satisfaction. As such, these families seek to maintain rigid boundaries and harmonious familial interaction. Centrifugal families look outside the family for pleasure, joy, and satisfaction. As such, familial boundaries and interactions are minimized (Beavers & Hampson, 1990).
- **Cybernetics.** This term refers to the study of the processes that regulate systems, especially the control of information (Barker, 1995).
- **Dyad.** This term denotes a two-person system (McGoldrick & Carter, 2001).
- **Family Boundaries.** This term denotes the explicit and implicit rules within a family system that govern how family members are expected to relate to one another and to non-family members (Barker, 1995).
- **Family Homeostasis.** This term is used to describe a family system's tendency to maintain predictable interactional processes. When such processes are operating, the family system is said to be in equilibrium (Sauber, L'Abate, Weeks, & Buchanan, 1993).
- **Family Projection Process.** This term refers to the transmission of a problem in a marital dyad to one of the children. Such a process helps maintain the illusion of a harmonious marital relationship. However, this process occurs at the expense of transmitting the symptoms of the problem to one of the children. Typically, this child is presented at the beginning of family therapy as the "problem to be fixed" (Sauber et al., 1993). Among family therapists, this child is called the "identified patient" or "IP."
- **Family System.** A family system is a social system built by the repeated interaction of family members. These interactions establish patterns of how, when, and to whom family members relate (Sauber et al., 1993).
- **Family Therapists.** Family therapy is practiced either as a specialty within a profession (e.g., counseling, clinical psychology) or as a stand-alone profession (e.g., marriage and family therapy). Persons who practice family therapy usually possess at least a master's degree (Dykeman, 2001).
- **Family Therapy.** This is an umbrella term for therapeutic approaches in which the whole family is the unit of treatment. This term is theoretically neutral, as one can conduct family therapy using a variety of frameworks (Reber, 1986).
- **Family.** This term applies to two or more people who consider themselves family. These persons generally share a common residence and assume the obligations, functions, and responsibilities essential to healthy family life, such as economic support (Barker, 1995).
- **Feedback Loop.** This term identifies the process by which a system gets the information required to correct itself. This self-correction is exerted either to maintain a steady state (i.e., homeostasis) or to move toward a goal (Nichols &

Schwartz, 1995). A system that receives negative feedback attempts to maintain a steady state. Positive feedback increases deviation from the steady state, enabling the family to evolve to a new state (Kaslow & Celano, 1995).

- **Holon.** Koestler (1967) coined this term to name whole units nested in larger whole units; for example, the marital dyad in a nuclear family.
- **Marital Dyad.** This term denotes a relationship composed of a husband and wife (Sauber et al., 1993).
- **Nuclear Family.** The nuclear family is the kinship group that consists of a father, a mother, and their children (Barker, 1995).
- **Triangulation.** The process of a third person or thing being added to a dyad in order to divert anxiety away from the relationship of the twosome (McGoldrick & Carter, 2001).

The goal of the previous section was to add some new terms to the reader's professional vocabulary. Now let us take a closer look at some major family theories and their clinical applications.

Human Nature: A Developmental Perspective

As with individual development, the family system can be seen as a developmental process that evolves over time. Developmental models of family life include the **family life cycle**, the **family life spiral**, and the **family genogram**.

The Family Life Cycle

Jay Haley (1993) offered the first detailed description of a family life cycle. He identified six developmental stages, stretching from courtship to old age. Haley was interested in understanding the strengths families have and the challenges they face as they move through the life cycle. He hypothesized that symptoms and dysfunctions appeared when there was a dislocation or disruption in the anticipated natural unfolding of the life cycle: "The symptom is a signal that a family has difficulty in getting past a stage in the life cycle" (p. 42).

Over time, tension inevitably emerges in families because of the developmental changes they encounter (Smith & Schwebel, 1995). Family stress is most intense at those points where family members must negotiate a transition to the next stage of the family life cycle (Carter & McGoldrick, 1999). On one level, this stress may be viewed as part of the family's response to the challenges and changes of life in their passage through time. For example, a couple may encounter tension while making the transition to parenthood with the birth of their first child. On another level, pressures may emerge from the family's multigenerational legacies that define the family's attitudes, taboos, expectations, labels, and loaded issues. For example, over several generations a rule that men cannot be trusted to handle the money may impose stress when the female is absent. When stress occurs on both levels, the whole family may experience acute crisis.

Family therapists can find it difficult to determine the exact sources of stress on a family. Papp and Imber-Black (1996) present an interesting vignette describing the power of illuminating a wide spectrum of stressors for a family. In this vignette, Papp and Imber-Black connect what was viewed as the developmental struggle between a mother and an adolescent son to a three-generation theme of "footsteps." In this case, the adolescent's grades had plummeted and he was both depressed and argumentative. Furthermore, he had engaged in some stealing activity. On the surface, these behaviors can be understood as either symptomatic of family life with an adolescent or symptomatic of life after creation of a blended family. However, by teasing out a specific theme, Papp and Imber-Black discovered that the family's fears emerged as a story about the son "following in the footsteps"—in particular, the footsteps of a drug-dealing father and a larcenous grandfather. The therapists skillfully challenged three generations of the family to tell the family myth about their men who chose the "wrong path." Sorting out the current stressors on the family through the lens of the family scripts encouraged the adolescent to leave behind the old stories to develop his own story. The process also helped his mother to realize how these historic scripts hid her son from her. This multigenerational storytelling intervention worked to free the young man from a catastrophic prophecy while bringing all members of the family into better communication.

The Family Life Spiral

Combrinck-Graham (1985) constructed a nonlinear model of family development referred to as the family life spiral. The spiral includes the developmental tasks of three generations that simultaneously affect one another. Each person's developmental issues can be seen in relation to those of the other family members. For example, midlife crisis involves the reconsideration of status, occupation, and marital state for adults in the middle years of their lives. This crisis may coincide with their adolescent children's identity struggles and the parents' plans for retirement. Similarly, when a family's childbearing experience is viewed in terms of grandparenthood, the birth of a child "pushes" the older generations along the timeline, whether or not the grandparents are prepared for their new roles.

The family life spiral looks like an upside-down tornado. This spiral is compact at the top to illustrate the family's closeness during centripetal periods. Also, it is spread out at the bottom to represent centrifugal periods of greater distance between family members.

Centripetal Periods   The close periods in family life are called *centripetal* to indicate the many forces in the family system that hold the family tightly together (Combrinck-Graham, 1985). Centripetal periods (CPs) are marked by an inner orientation requiring intense bonding and cohesion, such as early childhood, child rearing, and grandparenting. Both the individual's and the family's life structure emphasize internal family life during these periods. Consequently, the boundaries between members are more diffuse so as to enhance teamwork among the members. In contrast to diffuse internal boundaries, external boundaries may become tightened, as if to create a nest within which the family can attend to itself.

Centrifugal Periods   By contrast, the distant or disengaged periods have been called *centrifugal* to indicate the predominance of forces that pull the family apart (Combrinck-Graham, 1988). Centrifugal periods (CFs) are marked by a family's outward orientation. Here the developmental focus is on tasks that emphasize personal identity and autonomy, such as adolescence, midlife, and retirement. As such, the external family boundary is loosened, old family structures are dismantled, and distance between family members typically increases.

The Family Merry-Go-Round   The terms *centripetal* and *centrifugal* are derived from physics and indicate the push and pull of forces on and within things—in this case, families. These forces might also be compared to the process of riding a merry-go-round. On a merry-go-round, the centripetal force is the push one will need to keep oneself on the horse. One pushes against the spinning ride toward the center of the rotation. The centrifugal force is what tries to pull the rider off and out into the world away from the spinning direction. For example, if the rider lets go of the horse's pole, this force will pull him or her away from the merry-go-round.

It is important to recognize that families are also in a constant process of pushing and pulling in order to adapt to life's events. Families move between centripetal and centrifugal forces depending on the developmental tasks required of them at various stages of the family life cycle. A family will typically move through one cycle every 25 years. This period is the time required to produce a new generation. Within each family cycle, different members will experience the following.

1. One's own childhood (CP) and adolescence (CF).
2. The birth (CP) and adolescence (CF) of one's children.
3. The birth (CP) and development (CF) of one's grandchildren.

These developmental shifts have been called *oscillations* that provide opportunities for family members to practice intimacy and involvement in the centripetal periods and individuation and independence in the centrifugal periods (Combrinck-Graham, 1985).

Implications for Practice   Neither the centripetal nor the centrifugal direction defines a pathological condition. These directions describe the relationship styles of the family at particular stages of the family life spiral. Symptom formation often occurs when the family is confronted with an event that is out of phase with the anticipated development of the family life spiral. Such events include untimely death, birth of a disabled child, chronic illness, or war. For some families, stress will develop around typical developmental demands, such as children's needs for dependency as infants, or adolescents' demands for more autonomy. The intensity and duration of family anxiety will affect the family's ability to make the required transitions. The purpose of family therapy is to help the family past the transitional crisis so that they can continue toward the next stage of family life.

The Family Genogram

Genograms give family therapists another useful way to conceptualize family development. Typically, genograms are used to chart the progression of a particular family through the life cycle over at least three generations. The genogram is like a family tree that includes information about birth order, family members, their communications, and issues of relationships. The work of McGoldrick and Gerson (1985) provides an excellent resource for clinicians unfamiliar with the use of genograms. Genograms often provide the basis of clinical hypotheses in family work and offer a culturally sensitive method for understanding individual or family clients. For example, Magnuson, Norem, and Skinner (1995) recommend mapping the relationship dynamics in the families of gay or lesbian clients. They point out the importance of mapping the relationship markers of gay or lesbian couples that are not recognized by general society (e.g., marriage). Ann Hartman (1995) has developed a similar tool called an *eco-map*. The advantage of the eco-map is that it allows the client and therapist to diagram family and community interactions in tandem. An eco-map is included as an organizing element in the case study presented later in this chapter.

Major Constructs

Theoretical Antecedents

The present family systems theories emerged out of the ideas and debates in the social and physical sciences after World War II. In the next two sections, we will outline the specific ideas that led to the development of a systems approach to counseling and psychotherapy.

Bateson   **Gregory Bateson** is acknowledged by many as the pioneer in applying cybernetic systems thinking to human interaction. He saw that cybernetics provided a powerful alternative language for explaining behavior—specifically, a language that did not resort to instinct or descriptions of the internal workings of the mind (Segal, 1991). Bateson began to use these ideas to understand social interaction (Bateson, 1951). For instance, he applied cybernetic principles to the study of families of schizophrenics (Haley, 1976). Bateson considered pattern, process, and communication as the fundamental elements of description and explanation. He believed that by observing human systems he could formulate the rules governing human interaction.

The Palo Alto Group   In 1952, while based in Palo Alto, Bateson received a grant from the Rockefeller Foundation to investigate the general nature of communication. He was joined on this project by Jay Haley, John Weakland, William Fry, and Don D. Jackson. This research team defined the family as a cybernetic, homeostatic system whose parts (i.e., family members) co-vary with each other to maintain equilibrium by means of error-activated negative feedback loops (Jackson, 1957). For example, whenever deviation-amplifying information is introduced (e.g., an argument between two family members or the challenge of a new stage in the family life cycle), a designated family member initiates a counter-deviation action (e.g., a family member exhibits symptomatic behavior), such that the family's existing equilibrium is restored (i.e., threatened changes are defeated). The emphasis on homeostasis prevailed in family therapy theory into the 1980s.

The recognition of the **symptomatic double bind** as a homeostatic maneuver regulating family patterns of relationship is considered the definitive contribution of the Palo Alto Group. The symptomatic double bind most often cited is Bateson's classic example of the interaction between a mother and her son who had "fairly well recovered from an acute schizophrenic episode." Bateson described this interaction as follows.

> [The son] was glad to see her and impulsively put his arm around her shoulders, whereupon she stiffened. He withdrew his arm and she asked, "Don't you love me any more?" He then blushed, and she said, "Dear, you must not be so easily embarrassed and afraid of your feelings." The patient was able to stay with her only a few minutes more, and following her departure, he assaulted an aide and was put in the tubs. (Bateson, Jackson, Haley, & Weakland, 1976, pp. 14–15)

The Palo Alto Group noted both the incongruence of the mother's message and the fact that the son could not clearly and directly comment on it. They concluded that the son's craziness was his commentary on his mother's contradictory behavior. Bateson's work in the 1950s spawned the development of many family therapy models, including the strategic model of Haley (1991) and Madanes (1991). An examination of this model will follow our discussion of the ideas of another Palo Altoan, **Virginia Satir.**

Conjoint Theory

Virginia Satir is among the best-loved of all theorists in the field of family therapy and, arguably, beyond. After leaving a career as a schoolteacher, she first practiced as a psychiatric social worker, then engaged in private practice work with families. In 1959, she joined the Mental Research Institute in Palo Alto. Satir gained international recognition with the publication of her first book, *Conjoint Family Therapy,* in 1964.

Satir acknowledged the impact of a diverse group of theorists on her life's work (Satir & Bitter, 1991). These included Fritz Perls (Gestalt therapy), Eric Berne (transactional analysis), J. J. Moreno (psychodrama), Ida Rolf (life-posturing reintegration), Alex Lowen (bioenergetics), and Milton Erickson (hypnosis). Her family therapy model reflects a growth perspective rather than a medical model for assessing and working with families. In her frame, illness was seen as an appropriate communicative response to a dysfunctional system or family context. Health, therefore, is developed when the system is changed so as to permit healthy communication and responses.

Like other communication theorists such as Bateson, Satir defined **congruence** as the use of words that accurately match personal feelings. In other words, congruence is where direct communication and meta-communication are the same. When using congruent communication, the person is alert, balanced, and responsive to any question or topic without needing to hold back. In contrast, **incongruence** is seen as communication wherein the nonverbal and verbal components do not match. Examples of incongruent communication include double messages, assumptions, ambiguous messages, and incomplete communication. Satir saw self-esteem as the basis for family emotional health. Her perspective was that there is a correlation between self-esteem and communication. Low self-esteem is associated with poor communication because low self-esteem affects behavior and interactions among the members of the system. She also held that maladaptive communication can be both learned and unlearned.

To demonstrate concretely to a family how incongruence occurs and is a source of pain and poor self-esteem, Satir would ask them to enter into a game. The communication game would typically be used to work with two members. She observed that when a person delivers an incongruent or mixed message, there is little skin or eye contact. It is as though the sender is "out of touch" with the other person. In the communication game, Satir taught families to improve their communication through a series of interactions that concretely show people what happens when they do not look, touch, or speak congruently. Satir (1983) outlined these steps as follows.

1. Place two persons back to back and ask them to talk.
2. Turn them around and have them "eyeball" each other without touching or talking.
3. Direct them to "eyeball" and touch without talking.

4. Have them touch with eyes closed and without talking.
5. Have them "eyeball" each other without touching.
6. Finally, have the two talk and touch and "eyeball" and try to argue with each other.

By the last stage of the game, the couple usually finds it impossible to argue with one another. The problem of delivering an incongruent message is clear to the family when one is touching, talking, and looking at the listener.

Besides the inherent humor of this process, the provocative nature of this game encourages a deeper examination of the ways family members suffer and feel inadequate or devalued when engaged in incongruent communication patterns. These revelations are supported through steps toward increasing self-esteem and communication as the family moves from a "closed" to a more "open" system. Satir believed that a functional family is an **open system** wherein there is a clear exchange of information and resources both within the system and with the others outside the family. In contrast, a **closed system** is rigid and maladaptive.

Satir observed that family pain is symptomatic of dysfunction. She did not believe that the problems the family brought to her were the real difficulty. Rather, she saw that methods of coping within the family and rules for behavior that were fixed, arbitrary, and inconsistent decreased the family's ability to cope over time. Her approach involved the following treatment stages.

1. Establish trust.
2. Develop awareness through experience.
3. Create new understanding of members and dynamics.
4. Have family members express and apply their new understandings with each other.
5. Have the family use their new behaviors outside therapy.

As the family moves through this cycle of change, they feel less anxious and more fully valued and valuing of each other (Satir & Bitter, 1991). In this way, self-esteem, communication, and caring are raised and pain is decreased.

Strategic Theory

Jay Haley left Palo Alto in 1966 and joined **Salvador Minuchin** in Philadelphia to pursue his growing interest in family hierarchy, power, and structure. In 1974, he established the Washington Institute of Family Therapy, where he was joined by **Cloe Madanes.** Their family therapy model has three roots: the strategic therapy of Milton Erickson, the theories of the Palo Alto Group, and the structural therapy of Minuchin.

Haley (1991) and Madanes (1981) asserted that a family's current problematic relational patterns were at some point useful because they organized family members in a concerted way to solve an existing problem. These patterns persisted because they protected the family from the threat of disintegration. Haley held that therapeutic change occurs when a family's dysfunctional protective patterns are interrupted. He noted that the role of family therapists, through the use of directives, is to provoke such interruptions. Haley offered therapist provocations such as the following.

- A husband and wife with sexual problems may be required to have sexual relations only on the living room floor for a period of time. This task changes the context and so the struggle.
- A man who is afraid to apply for a job may be asked to go for a job interview at a place where he would not take the job if he got it, thereby practicing in a safe way.

For Haley (1990), therapist directives served three purposes: to facilitate change and make things happen; to keep the therapist's influence alive during the week; and to stimulate family reactions that give the therapist more information about family structure, rules, and system. Haley held that the goal of therapy was not client insight—in fact, the actual mechanisms of change need not be understood by the family. Furthermore, the therapist should act without trying to convince the family that the set of hypotheses guiding the therapy is valid. Haley commented that "the goal is not to teach the family about their malfunctioning system but to change the family sequences so that the presenting problems are resolved" (p. 135).

Haley's ideas have direct consequences for the family therapist wishing to practice a strategic approach. First, a strategic family therapist attends to what is defined by the family members experiencing the problem as the "nature of the problem." Second, the therapist focuses on how the family is responding in attempting to resolve the problem. The assumption here is that it is often the very ways in which families are defining a problem and responding to it that may "keep it going" in a vicious problem-solution cycle.

Structural Theory

Structural family therapists do not "sit on the sidelines" during therapy. Rather, they become involved with family members, pushing and being pushed. Minuchin put a strong emphasis on action in his own work as a family therapist. His justification for this emphasis was his belief that "if both I and the family take risks within the constraints of the therapeutic system, we will find alternatives for change" (Minuchin & Fishman, 1981, p. 7). He commented that observers of his structural family therapy work would notice (a) his concern with bringing the family transactions into the room; (b) his alternation between participation and observation as a way of unbalancing the system by supporting one family member against another; and (c) his many types of response to family members' intrusion into each other's psychological space (Minuchin & Fishman, 1981).

Minuchin's therapeutic maneuvers were based on his theoretical schema about family structure and family transformation. He carried out his vision by being uniquely himself. He stated:

> In families that are too close, I artificially create boundaries between members by gestures, body postures, movement of chairs, or seating changes. My challenging maneuvers frequently include a supportive statement: a kick and a stroke are delivered simultaneously. My metaphors are concrete: "You are sometimes sixteen and sometimes four"; "Your father stole your voice"; "You have two left hands and ten thumbs." I ask a child and a parent to stand and see who is taller, or I compare the combined weight of the parents with the child's weight. I rarely remain in my chair for a whole session. I move closer when I want intimacy, kneel to reduce my size with children, or spring to my feet when I want to challenge or show indignation. These operations occur spontaneously; they represent my psychological fingerprint. (Minuchin & Fishman, 1981, p. 7)

For Minuchin, family therapy techniques are uniquely integrated in the person of the counselor or therapist who goes beyond technique to wisdom, specifically, wisdom concerning "knowledge of the larger interactive system—that system which, if disturbed, is likely to generate exponential curves of change" (Bateson, 1972, p. 439).

Transgenerational Theory

Murray Bowen's approach to family therapy, like Haley's, had many roots. Specifically, Bowen merged concepts such as Freud's unconscious id and Darwin's theory of evolution with his own observations of schizophrenics at the Menninger Clinic and the National Institute of Mental Health. His core idea was the concept of the **differentiation** of self. It was through this concept that Bowen addressed "how people differ from one another in terms of their sensitivity to one another and their varying abilities to preserve a degree of autonomy in the face of pressures for togetherness" (Papero, 1990, p. 45).

Bowen also posited that there were two different systems of human functioning: an emotional and reactive system that humans share with lower forms of life, and an intellectual and rational system that is a more recent evolutionary development. The degree to which these two systems are fused or undifferentiated is the degree to which the individual is vulnerable to the impulses of his or her emotional system and less attentive to his or her intellectual and rational system. For example, people are more likely to react emotionally rather than rationally when they are anxious. Bowen asserted that the extent to which persons have differentiated their thinking system from their emotional system will determine how able they are to maintain a sense of self in relationship with others, particularly members of their family.

Bowen believed that emotional illness was passed from one generation to another through the **family projection process (FPP).** FPP theory suggests that the ego differentiation achieved by children will generally approximate that of their parents. However, FPP often distributes the capacity for differentiation unevenly among family members. For example, one child may grow up with a high level of ego differentiation, while a sibling may grow up with a low level of differentiation. The hallmark of a high level is a well-defined sense of self and low emotional reactivity, whereas a low level is characterized by a poorly defined sense of self and high emotional reactivity.

Low levels of ego differentiation occur when parents "triangulate" a child into their conflicts in order to dissipate the stresses of their relationship. Bowen (1978) held that "triangles" were the natural consequence of two poorly differentiated people who are overwhelmed by anxiety and seek relief by involving a third party. Triangulation is how parents' low level of differentiation is passed on to the next generation. Bowen's work has influenced many of the present family therapy theorists. One of the best examples of the extension of Bowen's ideas is McGoldrick's and Gerson's (1985) work on genograms. This work was discussed earlier in the chapter.

Narrative Theory

Long before *constructivism* or *narrative* became common terms in counseling, family therapists used story-making. Papp and Imber-Black (1996) cite various names coined to identify the role of story in family work, including *family myth, family paradigm,* and, more recently, *landscape of consciousness.*

The narrative therapy approach of family therapist **Michael White** (1992) was built on the writings of French philosopher and social historian Michel Foucault (1980), who described the process whereby knowledge is embedded in language and serves the values of the dominant culture. Narrative has become a popular method for therapy based on the notion that individuals, families, and entire cultures are given a different level of power as creators of their realities.

Concerning reality creation, White and Epston (1990) asserted that the social sciences classify and minimize people around a norm that becomes internalized. People take on these objective categorizations and see themselves as "a schizophrenic" or as "having a behavior disorder." Solutions to such internalized and normative problems are limited. To overcome this internalization, narrative family therapists work to help families "externalize" problems through storytelling. This **externalization** can give a family the ability to construct a story wherein the problem is subject to manipulation or change because it exists as a separate entity. Also, externalization can break the retelling of complaint-saturated stories and offer a sense of personal agency. A common question asked in narrative family therapy is "How has the problem affected your life?" Such a question works to separate the family from their problem.

Families have styles for telling their stories. Roberts (1995) defined six types of story styles: intertwined, separated, interrupted, secret, rigid, and evolving. For example, family members may offer intertwined stories so the events described at one time are used to make sense of other circumstances. Conversely, a rigid story is frozen and told over and over in the same way without interpretations. Everyone in the family knows these stories by heart because they have been told so often. Once the type and goals of the story style are determined, the counselor or therapist can work with the family to see what resources they have available and open possibilities for making new meaning out of personal histories. Roberts' work offers another method for assessing the types of stories told and their possible therapeutic uses.

The major constructs discussed in this section were developed by clinicians to understand how families function. As we have seen, family theorists conceptualized the communication patterns, structures, relationship dynamics, and story-making processes of their client families. The concepts they developed reflected their own therapeutic interventions. In this way, family theory is a rich resource to students and family practitioners. Table 12.1 provides an overview and comparison of these major theoretical constructs.

Applications

Overview

All counseling and psychotherapy approaches share a common goal of producing change in clients. In this section, we will differentiate family therapy applications from the applications of the individualistic approaches presented in the previous chapters. Our goal is to help the reader find ways to add systems-level interventions to both his or her reasoning and his or her counseling or therapy tool bag.

Table 12.1
Major Family Therapy Theoretical Constructs

	Conjoint	Strategic	Structural	Transgen-erational	Narrative
Major theorists	*Satir*	*Haley, Madanes*	*Minuchin*	*Bowen, McGoldrick*	*White*
What family members participate in therapy?	flexible	everyone involved in the problem	whoever is involved and accessible	the most motivated family member(s)	flexible
What is the theory of dysfunction?	low self-esteem; poor communication; triangulation	confused hierarchy; rigid behavioral sequences	enmeshed or disengaged boundaries; intrafamilial coalitions	emotional fusion (symbiosis with family of origin); anxiety; triangulation	disempower-ment by the dominant cultural narrative
What are the primary goals of therapy?	improved communication; personal growth	problem solving; restore hierarchy	change the family structure; increase flexibility	greater differentiation of self; reduced anxiety	empowerment through reauthoring the family's life story
How is family functioning assessed?	family life chronology	structured initial interview; intervene and observe the reaction	joining the family to experience its process; chart family structure	genogram	narration of family history and myths
What is the temporal focus of therapy?	present	present	present	past	present and past
What are common intervention practices?	modeling and coaching; clear communication; family sculpting; guided interaction	directives are used to change behavior; they may be straightforward, paradoxical, or ordeals	reframing is used to change the perception of the problem; structure is changed by unbalancing and increasing stress	reducing anxiety by providing rational, untriangulated third party; coaching to aid in differentiation from family of origin	externalization of family problems through narration
What characterizes the therapist's approach to the family?	active, directive, matter-of-fact, nonjudgmental; models open communication	active, directive, but not self-revealing; planned, not spontaneous	active, directive, personally involved; spontaneous; humorous	interested but detached; reinforces calmness and rationality	active partnership; encourages the telling of family history and myths

Table 12.2
Worldview Comparison

Individual Psychotherapy	Family Systems Psychotherapy
asks "why?"	asks "what?"
linear cause/effect	reciprocal causality
subject/object dualism	holistic
either/or dichotomies	dialectic
value-free science	subjective/perceptual
deterministic/reactive	freedom of choice/proactive
laws and lawlike external reality	patterns
historical focus	here-and-now focus
individualistic	relational
reductionistic	contextual
absolutistic	relativistic

Goals of Counseling and Psychotherapy

Family therapy represented a watershed in the history of counseling or therapy. Before family therapy, the focus of counselors or therapists had been solely on the individual. The goal of counseling or therapy was always to change some cognitive, affective, or behavioral component of an individual. In contrast, family therapists aim to change systems within which individuals reside. Becvar and Becvar (1999) compared how the worldview of individual psychotherapy differed from that of family systems psychotherapy. Table 12.2 details the major differences they mentioned.

The Process of Change

Family therapists use cybernetics to understand change—specifically, the cybernetic control processes involving information and feedback. Information in the form of feedback precipitates shifts that either amplify or counteract the direction of change. Family therapists differentiate between **first-order change** and **second-order change.** Lyddon (1990) succinctly defined these different types of change as follows: "First-order change is essentially 'change without change'—or any change within a system that does not produce a change in the structure of the system. In contrast, second-order change is 'change of change'—a type of change whose occurrence alters the fundamental structure of the system" (p. 122). At any given moment, counselors or psychotherapists can only bring about one or the other type of change in their clients. Now let us look at these change types more closely.

First-Order Change   First-order change occurs when a family modifies problem behaviors yet maintains its present structure. An example of a first-order change intervention is a family therapist's instructing parents when they can fight with their son over bedtime. By this intervention, the family therapist hopes to give the family relief from their problem behavior; radical change of the present family system is not a goal. Family therapists call the process of bringing about this type of change *negative feedback.*

Second-Order Change   In contrast to first-order change, second-order change refers to transformations in either the structure or the internal order of a system. Family therapists often seek to generate or amplify change processes that will alter the basic structure of a family system (Nichols & Schwartz, 1995). This goal embodies second-order change. An example of a second-order change intervention is a family therapist's directing the more passive parent to take over bedtime compliance responsibility with the goal of changing the power dynamics in the marital dyad. Family therapists call the process of bringing about second-order change *positive feedback.*

Intervention Strategies

The case study for this chapter will illustrate in detail one way to conduct family therapy. Besides the strategies presented in the case study, there are two additional points on family therapy applications to which we would like to draw the reader's attention. The first is an understanding of the significance of nonspecific factors in family therapy outcomes. The second is how to structure the first session so that family therapy can get off to a good start.

Specific Versus Nonspecific Factors   A strong current trend in individual-focused counseling or therapy research is an examination of the specific and nonspecific factors involved in treatment outcomes. **Specific factors** are those counseling or therapy activities that are specific to a particular approach—for example, a strategic family therapist's use of a "proscribing-the-symptom" intervention. **Nonspecific factors** are those change-producing elements present in counseling or therapy regardless of theoretical orientation. Many nonspecific factors have been proposed, but few have withstood empirical testing. One exception is working alliance. In fact, working alliance scores are the best-known predictor of counseling or therapy outcomes (Horvath, 1994).

The modern transtheoretical definition of **working alliance** was promulgated by **Edward Bordin** (1994), who posited that there were three components of working alliance: **task, goal,** and **bond.** He conceptualized these three components as follows.

1. *Task* refers to the in-therapy activities that form the substance of the therapeutic process. In a well-functioning relationship, both parties must perceive these tasks as relevant and effective. Furthermore, each must accept the responsibility to perform these acts.
2. *Goal* refers to the counselor or therapist and the client mutually endorsing and valuing the aims (outcomes) that are the target of the intervention.
3. *Bond* embraces the complex network of positive personal attachments between client and counselor or therapist, including issues such as mutual trust, acceptance, and confidence (adapted from Horvath, 1994).

Overall, Bordin's working alliance model emphasized "the role of the client's collaboration with the therapist against the common foe of the client's pain and self-defeating behavior" (Horvath, p. 110).

Family therapists have been slower to examine the nonspecific factors involved in positive treatment outcomes (Blow & Spenkle, 2001). One exception was **William Pinsof** of the Family Institute (Evanston, Illinois). In his research, Pinsof (1994) found a positive relationship between working alliance and family therapy outcomes. The few other studies conducted on working alliance in family therapy produced similar results to Pinsof's research (Friedlander, Wildman, Heatherington, & Skowron, 1994).

Given the effectiveness of working alliance concerning treatment outcomes, persons practicing family therapy would be wise to attend carefully to such alliances. However, such attention would run counter to the preeminence family therapists give to technique. Coady (1992) noted that the emphasis in family systems theory on homeostasis has led to family therapists' viewing family members as being dominated by the family system. Thus, family therapists "often expect families to exert an oppositional force against change efforts, and they feel compelled to manipulate the family into change" (p. 471). Unfortunately, such a perspective runs exactly counter to formation of strong working alliances. We want to be careful to note that a commitment to build strong working alliances with client families does not mean the counselor or therapist has to dismiss technique. Rather, it means acknowledging that techniques should not be separated from the interpersonal and cultural contexts in which they occur (Coady, 1992).

The Family Interview   From the start, Haley (1991) advocated brevity and clarity in counseling or therapy work with families. He stated that "if therapy is to end properly, it must begin properly—by negotiating a solvable problem and discovering the social situation that makes the problem necessary" (p. 8). To help family therapists start on a good note, Haley outlined a structured family interview for use during an initial session. The five stages of this structured family interview follow.

1. *Social*—the interviewer greets the family and helps family members feel comfortable.
2. *Problem*—the interviewer invites each person present to define the problem.
3. *Interaction*—the interviewer directs all members present to talk together about the problem while the interviewer watches and listens.
4. *Goal setting*—family members are invited to speak about what changes everyone—including the "problem" person—wants from the therapy.
5. *Ending*—directives (if any) are given and the next appointment is scheduled.

The information gained from the first interview helps the family therapist form hypotheses about the function of the problem within its relational context. Moreover, this information can help the family therapist generate directives to influence change. For Haley, "the first obligation of a therapist is to change the presenting problem offered. If that is not accomplished, the therapy is a failure" (p. 135).

Clients with Mental Disorders

Family therapy has been found to be applicable to persons with mental disorders. Two major family therapy researchers, William Pinsof and Lyman Wynne (2000), conducted an exhaustive review of published family therapy research. Based upon a criterion of at least two controlled studies with significant positive results and no studies with negative results, they concluded that there was sufficient scientific evidence to support the fact that couple therapy (CT) or family therapy (FT) is more effective than therapy that does not involve a family member in treating the following mental disorders.

- adult schizophrenia (FT)
- depression in women in distressed marriages (CT)
- adult alcoholism and drug abuse (FT)
- adolescent conduct disorders (FT)
- anorexia in young adolescent females (FT)
- childhood autism (FT)
- aggression and non-compliance in ADHD (FT)
- dementia (FT)
- childhood conduct disorders (FT)

Pinsof and Wynne concluded their listing with the powerful and instructive conclusion that "for most disorders, therapists are likely to be more effective if they include relevant and appropriate family members in treatment" (p. 2).

Evaluation

Overview

The emergence of managed care has radically altered the delivery of mental health services. Increasingly, those who pay for treatment are demanding proof of efficacy. This demand for efficacy has extended to those professionals practicing family therapy (Kaslow, 2000). In this section, we will review what is known about the efficacy of family therapy.

Supporting Research

Historically, empirical research has not been a strong component of family therapy (Gladding, 2001). Lebow and Gurman (1995) noted that "at one time, most research on couples and families was conducted with little or no connection to the outstanding clinical developments in the field. Alternative modes of investigation such as inductive reasoning, clinical observation, and deconstruction have dominated in the development of methods and treatment models. Some couple and family therapists have even been reluctant to acknowledge that empirical research has an important role" (p. 29). Fortunately, this reluctance was overcome and solid research evidence for the efficacy of family therapy now exists—evidence that professionals practicing family therapy can use to defend their work in the world of managed care.

Pinsof and Wynne (2000) concluded that there was sufficient scientific evidence to support the fact that couple therapy (CT) or family therapy (FT) is more effective than therapy that does not involve a family member in treating these areas in addition to those listed earlier.

- marital distress (CT)
- cardiovascular risk factors (CT)
- adolescent drug abuse (FT)

In addition, they found that couples therapy or family therapy is more effective than no treatment for all of those areas previously mentioned as well as the following.

- adult obesity (CT)
- adult hypertension (CT)
- adolescent obesity (FT)
- anorexia in younger adolescents (FT)
- childhood obesity (FT)
- almost all childhood chronic illness (FT)

Based upon the findings of Pinsof and Wynne and their strong recommendation regarding the inclusion of relevant and appropriate family members in effective treatment, it would seem obvious that counselors or therapists would rapidly adapt to this process. The truth, however, is that professional counselors or therapists have been slow to adopt this practice in their work. In fact, the latest study of the practice patterns of family therapists revealed that approximately half of their client load was individuals (Doherty & Simmons, 1996).

Research on treatment outcome predictors is useful to family therapy practitioners. Unfortunately, little credible research has been conducted in the area. One notable exception is a study by Hampson and Beavers (1996), who studied family and therapist characteristics in relation to treatment success. Their subjects were 434 families treated at an actual family therapy clinic in Dallas. Hampson and Beavers reported the following predictors of successful treatment.

- number of family therapy sessions attended
- third-party ratings of family competence
- self-ratings of family competence
- therapists' ratings of working alliance

Hampson and Beavers' measure of family competence included items on family affect, parental coalitions, problem-solving abilities, autonomy and individuality, optimistic versus pessimistic views, and acceptance of family members. The two reported that the six-session mark was the breakpoint in increasing the probability of good results. However, a sizable subset of families did well with fewer than six sessions. What distinguished this subset of families was their strong self-ratings of competence. Hampson and Beavers were careful to note that family size, family income, family structure (e.g., blended), family ethnicity, and counselor or therapist gender did not predict outcome.

Limitations

One of the basic ethical principles in health care is the principle of non-maleficence—that is, "above all, do no harm." To carry out this ethical principle, one must make oneself aware of the limitations of each counseling or therapy approach contained in this textbook. To that end, we now present three limitations to family therapy approaches.

First, the early language chosen for describing family systems was "combative and bellicose, often suggesting willful opposition: double bind, identified patient, family scapegoat, binder, victim, and so on" (Nichols, 1987, pp. 18–19). The choice of language emphasized the destructive power of families and contributed to an assault on the family by several pioneers in family therapy (Cooper, 1970). This assault has continued to the present because many family therapy educators and practitioners have overread this language and adopted a directive, manipulative approach to treatment. This overreading led to unfortunate consequences. For instance, Green and Herget (1991) discovered that at their family therapy clinic many families found "paradoxical prescriptions as signs of therapist sarcasm or incompetence, that engender massive resistance, sometimes destroying altogether the clients' faith and cooperative attitude in therapy" (p. 323). Also, Patterson and Forgatch (1985) uncovered, in their study of families in treatment, a direct relationship between client resistance and frequency of counselor or therapist directives.

Second, family is a culturally determined phenomenon. Kaslow, Celano, and Dreelin (1995) correctly noted that "the dominant American definition, reflecting white Anglo Saxon Protestant (WASP) values, focuses on the intact nuclear family unit. African Americans' definition of family refers to a wide network of kin and community. For many Italian Americans, family implies a strong, tightly knit three-or-four generation unit including godparents and old friends. The traditional Chinese definition of family includes ancestors and decedents" (p. 622).

In a review of the literature on cultural competence and family interventions, Celano and Kaslow (2000) found family therapy to be the treatment of choice for culturally diverse clients. They noted that family therapists can be efficacious and culturally competent only in the following contexts.

1. They recognize the effects of their own culture(s) on the therapy.
2. They acknowledge that family therapies, theories, and techniques reflect the culture in which they were developed.
3. They attend to the dynamic interplay of the cultural influences that affect the individual's and family's functioning.
4. They devise and implement problem-resolution strategies that are culturally acceptable.

In another review, Bean, Perry, and Bedell (2001) noted that there was wide conceptual and empirical support for the use of family therapy with Latinos.

Third, family therapists have ignored the different socialization processes operating for men and women. Thus, family therapists have not adequately considered how these socialization processes have disadvantaged women (Friedlander et al., 1994). Walters, Carter, Papp, and Silverstein (1988) called for family therapists to review all family therapy concepts through the lens of gender socialization in order to eliminate the dominance of male assumptions. Their hope was that such a review would promote the "recognition of the basic principle that no intervention is gender-free and that every intervention will have a different and special meaning for each sex" (p. 29).

Summary Chart—Family Theory

Human Nature

Like models used to explain individual development across the life span, the creation and maintenance of a family system can be viewed as a developmental process that evolves over time. Developmental models of family life include the family life cycle, the family life spiral, and the family genogram.

Major Constructs

A variety of constructs are associated with family theory, and each theory contributes discrete concepts. Conjoint theory, strategic theory, structural theory, transgenerational theory, and narrative theory are overviewed in this chapter as points of departure for some of the major constructs connected with counseling and psychotherapy with couples and families.

Goals

The goals of individual counseling or therapy are usually aimed at changing cognitive, affective, or behavioral components of the individual. In contrast, family counselors and psychotherapists aim to change whole systems.

Change Process

Family counselors and psychotherapists use cybernetics to understand change. Specifically, the cybernetic control processes involve information and feedback. Information in the form of feedback precipitates shifts that either amplify or counteract the direction of change. Family counselors and therapists differentiate between first-order and second-order change.

Interventions

Strategies and interventions associated with systemic change in families are varied; many were first introduced in the context of a specific family theory. Because systemic change can be difficult to precipitate, family therapists must be schooled and supervised in the application of interventions. In addition, practitioners must be able to set boundaries and limits with couples and families and be "powerful" and strategic in their choices and development of treatment plans.

Limitations

The choice of language connected with couples and family counseling and psychotherapy often emphasizes the destructive power of families and contributes to an "assault" on the family. At times, practitioners forget that the proper use of interventions always involves consideration of cross-cultural variations that may limit applicability. Often, practitioners have ignored the different socialization processes operating for men and women and how these processes have disadvantaged women.

The Case of Jonathan: A Family Theory Approach

Presenting Problem

Jonathan Benally (age 36) was referred by a human resources counselor at work to a mental health service agency in Phoenix. Jonathan was suspended for difficulty at work including anger and arguments with his co-workers. It was clear during the intake process that he was feeling overwhelmed with his life and feelings of isolation from his estranged wife and daughter. Jonathan's workplace offered to provide the cost of the counseling session as part of the employee assistance program (EAP).

Therapists

Jenny Smith and Mr. Tsome are the co-therapists assigned to work with Jonathan and his family. They are both staff therapists with mental health services in Phoenix. Mrs. Smith possesses a national certification in family therapy. Mr. Tsome holds a national certification as an art therapist and is state certified in chemical dependency counseling. Both therapists have worked extensively with families in the Four Corners region. Mr. Tsome is also a member of the Navajo Nation. The agency is aware that counseling or therapy goals with diverse clients are better met when the client is matched with therapists with understanding of the cultural heritage of the clients.

Family Demographics and History

Jonathan lives in a blue-collar neighborhood of Phoenix, Arizona. His parents, Charley Benally (age 66) and Rita Benally (age 64), live on the reservation near Shiprock where his first wife and three children reside. Jonathan's wife, Glenna (age 34), also lives in Phoenix. Glenna's parents, Nelson Tsossie (age 57) and Gladys Tsossie (age 55), live on the Navajo reservation near Canyon de Chelley. Both sets of grandparents interact with Jonathan's children in their respective villages and come together for community events. The children from both of his marriages know each other and will visit or live with a variety of extended family members including aunts and second cousins in respective areas of the reservation. This pattern of residence is common on the reservation and reflects a different process of child rearing than is typically seen in the dominant culture. Besides these grandparents, all of Jonathan's siblings live on the reservation. These include Herbert (age 42), Slim (age 40), and Ethyl (age 37). The deaths of two siblings, L. C. and Bea, and their ages are noted on the eco-map. Jonathan's eco-map appears in Figure 12.1 and reflects purely fictional names and places developed with respect for Navajo people and customs.

Family Therapy Process

Intake Interview: Building Working Alliances   Mrs. Smith and Mr. Tsome have both worked extensively with Native American families. This experience influenced the selection and application of their interventions. For instance, they initiated the first sessions with Jonathan and with Glenna by discussing tribal affiliation and clan names. They developed an eco-map with Jonathan of his family that includes the spiritual and types of bonds that the various members of his family have (see Figure 12.1). The eco-map is a pen-and-paper depiction of the family's existential relationship with the environmental systems (Hartman, 1995).

Case Conceptualization and Treatment Planning   Mrs. Smith and Mr. Tsome diagnosed Jonathan as suffering from late-onset Dysthymic Disorder (Axis I: 300.4) and Alcohol Abuse Disorder without physiological dependence (Axis III: 303.00). Jonathan has experienced a growing sense of loneliness, failure, and worthlessness in life. His depression was demonstrated by the symptoms of alcohol abuse, unsatisfying liaisons with women, and anger toward others at work. Jonathan's statement of love for his wife and fear that he had ruined three families helped the counselors to determine the over-arching framework for their intervention. The therapists decided to address three levels of Jonathan's family life: (1) the immediate family of Glenna and Amber, (2) the family of origin, and (3) the tribe and extended family. Mrs. Smith and Mr. Tsome prioritized the first level for immediate intervention with attention to the alcohol use. To address Jonathan's alienation from his wife and daughter, the two therapists proposed that Jonathan bring them to the

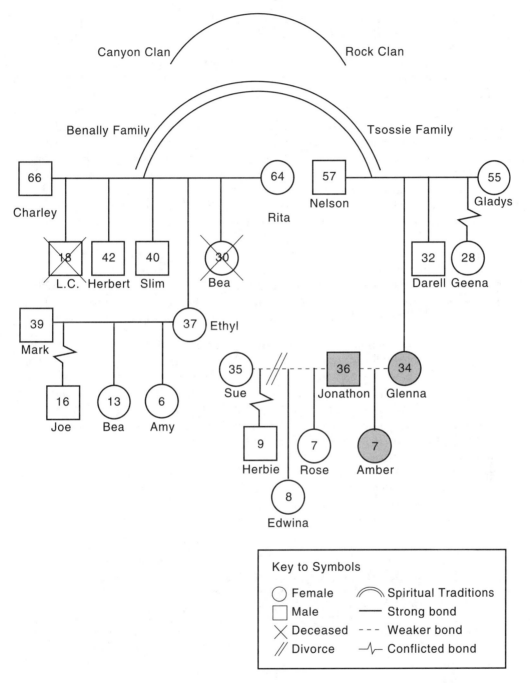

Figure 12.1
Jonathan's Eco-map (all names and places are fictional)

next session. Mr. Tsome offered to invite Glenna to the session and successfully obtained her agreement to attend the following Wednesday.

Combining Conjoint Family Therapy with Art   Art allows individuals to project both personally and culturally relevant images that can transcend the limitation of spoken language and dominant cultural frames. Art is also an effective method for assessing family interactions and communication patterns (Kwiatkowska, 1978). During her years at the National Institute of Mental Health (NIMH), where family therapy was being developed, Hanna Yaxa Kwiatkowska devised a series of art tasks useful for therapists to evaluate and disrupt non-productive family structures. Later, Helen Langarten (1987) combined Virginia Satir's (1983) conjoint family therapy approach with Kwiatkowska's art task series to help family members examine problems in a symbolic way.

Mr. Tsome and Mrs. Smith used these conjoint therapy art tasks to begin their work with Jonathan and Glenna while Amber participated in a separate playgroup. The goal was to strengthen the couple's relationship to provide a foundation for supporting the next steps of counseling. As in narrative therapy approaches, the metaphors that would emerge from the art processes would provide a valuable method to help the couple to rediscover their interconnectedness to each other. Mr. Tsome and Mrs. Smith planned that the information obtained through the art products would be used to set goals and plan directives for integrating families and tribal members as appropriate and over time.

Session 1   The first session involved building a working relationship with the couple by engaging them in a series of four art tasks to help them reconnect and begin to communicate with each other. Mr. Tsome and Mrs. Smith alternately directed the art tasks so that both therapists would have an opportunity to direct/support and observe the couple. The first drawing task eased the couple into the art-making process by introducing the material with a warm-up process (individual free drawing). The second and third drawings focused specifically on the problems and resolutions identified by Jonathan and Glenna. The final art process put the couple together to create a family mural on one piece of paper. Through the art task sequence, the couple was encouraged to move from a distant to a closer physical proximity. At the end of the art process, the therapists reviewed all of the drawings with the couple. The assignments given for each of the tasks were adapted from Kwiatkowska (1978) and are presented here.

- "Make an individual free drawing of anything that comes to mind."
- "Make an individual drawing of why you think you are here."
- "Make an individual drawing on how you would like the 'problem' to change."
- "Now together, make a joint mural about your family."
- "At this time we will review the drawings you have made."

The therapists often use this series of tasks with families like Jonathan's who play lethal games with one another through hurtful communication patterns and alienation. The use of such tasks allows a family therapist to do the following.

- Elicit metaphorical information for planning future intervention.
- Provide drawing tasks that disrupt dysfunctional family communication patterns (e.g., a family's covert blaming rule).
- Help family members discover and clarify values through the understanding of personal symbols.

Given the tension present between the couple, they welcomed Mr. Tsome's initial suggestion that they start out by working on their own drawing. The therapists had a wide array of drawing materials available to use, including oil and chalk pastels and felt marker pens.

Free Drawing Art Task   Jonathan's free drawing depicted a man in a hazy cloud with two tiny *Yei* figures in the left corner. The images of *Yei* figures are used in Navajo sandpaintings and represent supernatural beings translated from the Navajo word *god*. Jonathan's drawing reflected his confusion and hinted at his affiliation to tribal beliefs. Glenna drew a large heart with herself, Amber, and Jonathan inside it. Across the heart was a broken line depicting that the heart was broken. Tears fell from the heart. Her drawing reflected her feelings of abandonment and difficulty raising Amber alone.

After 20 minutes, Mrs. Smith had the couple stop their drawings and share them. As the couple discussed their drawings and the pain of their separation, they made eye contact for the first time in the session. Mr. Tsome read these nonverbal behaviors as a sign that the couple was ready for closer proximity. To concretize this new connection to Jonathan, Mr. Tsome directed Glenna to add to Jonathan's drawing through the production of a joint mural.

Couple Mural Art Task   After the mural was completed, Mrs. Smith asked Jonathan and Glenna to discuss the feelings the mural evoked about reconciliation. Mrs. Smith helped to reflect the statements the couple made that they had fallen into a family communication style described as the "blaming cycle" (Satir, 1983). In this communication style, family members are stuck in a lethal cycle of blaming others for their problems. Jonathan blamed the "white man's world" for his troubles, Glenna blamed Jonathan for abandoning her and Amber, and the Benally and Tsossie families blamed Jonathan for leaving the family and tribal ways. The therapist stated that this style of communication avoids the expression of deeper feelings, which produces low self-esteem and defeats the potential for growth and change. After the art sessions and expressing how unhappy they were, Glenna and Jonathan made a commitment to return for several counseling or therapy sessions to explore ways to communicate differently with one another. These sessions were planned to include Amber as soon as the couple were able to provide joint parental support for her. Between sessions, Mr. Tsome also recommended that Jonathan examine how often he used alcohol in the next week and think about whether he would like to cut down on his drinking.

Sessions 2–5   The next four sessions involved rebuilding family connectedness between the couple and their child by "trying on" new styles of communication. Again, the therapists used art tasks to facilitate culturally salient modes of communication as well as other techniques developed by Satir such as family sculpting. Both Jonathan and Glenna were able to declare their love for one another and commitment to the marriage. To develop dissonance about the use of alcohol, Mr. Tsome asked Jonathan to draw a picture of what he valued in his roles in his family. Jonathan's drawing reflected how important his wife and children are to him and how he misses the Benally family. Mr. Tsome then encouraged Jonathan to experience the dissonance between his use of alcohol and his view of being a good father or family member. This technique is a useful approach to encourage a motivation to change and has proven effective with addictive behaviors (Miller & Rollnick, 1991). Weeping, Jonathan declared that he wanted to change but did not know how. Mr. Tsome next worked with Jonathan to examine a menu of options for change and the underlying issues of his alcohol use.

Despite this work, Jonathan's desire to gain reentry to his family life remained blocked by his belief that he could not live in two worlds simultaneously, the "white man's world," as he called it, and the Navajo Nation. This belief left Jonathan feeling marginalized from the Benally and the Tsossie family and prevented building alliances with his children from his first marriage.

During one of these middle sessions, the art tasks served as a potent stimulus for self-discovery. Jonathan's chalk pastel drawing recounted his early learning of the blessing songs and the blessing way offered in his own Navajo traditions and revealed in sandpaintings. Jonathan recognized that he kept putting *Yei* figures in all the drawings he made in the counseling or therapy sessions and that they were getting larger in size with each drawing. *Yei* figures, used in the Navajo sandpainting ceremonies, are believed to offer protection, strength, and healing. Seeing his own artwork, it was clear to Jonathan that to try to ignore his heritage was impossible. Glenna suggested that the *Yeis* might be offering their family a way to resolve the imbalance in their lives. Amber said she hoped the *Yeis* would bring her cousins together for a party.

Mr. Tsome asked Jonathan and Glenna to consider holding an option in mind—the idea of how Jonathan could be a member of two worlds at the same time. He asked Jonathan how he might integrate the two seemingly disconnected value systems of the "white man's world" and the Navajo blessing way. This question prompted a revelation about Jonathan's life. He had always imagined he might become a healer, a *hatathli* (i.e., medicine man). When he decided to go to nursing school, it was his intention to be a healer in the "outside world" away from the reservation. After his failure in the nursing program, Jonathan sought work helping others at the adolescent facility. However, the split between his first wife, his parents, and then his second wife overwhelmed his belief in himself that he could be a healer.

With Jonathan's agreement, Mrs. Smith set up an appointment for him with a member of his tribal community, Hosteen Begay, a nurse who works with respected *hatathli* from local clans. It was decided that Jonathan would meet with Hosteen to discuss his work at the Blessingway Physician's Clinic where Western medicine and Native American practices are combined in the care of patients. When the Benally and Tsossie families heard of Jonathan's meeting with the *hatathli,* they hosted a special family dinner for him, Glenna, and Amber. They invited the elders and all members of the Benally and Tsossie clans in honor of Jonathan and Glenna's work to rebuild their family. After the dinner, Jonathan and Glenna decided to try living together to jointly support their family with their daughter.

Session 6: Termination   As Jonathan began to reenter family life, his dysthymia lifted and he began to have more satisfaction in his work. Consequently, he stopped the abuse of alcohol. The meetings with Hosteen Begay and the *hatathli* at the clinic gave Jonathan a renewed sense of purpose and direction. He decided to finish his degree in nursing at the University of New Mexico. By the final session of family therapy, Jonathan reported that he was discovering a new peace in his life. In addition, the renewed consistency in Jonathan's parenting had begun to help the couple build a productive relationship. Glenna and Jonathan also developed a plan with the Benally and Tsossie families to set up regular co-parenting sessions arranged with his first wife and their children to bring together the grandparents, cousins, aunts, and uncles.

13

Brief Theories

Rolla E. Lewis
Portland State University

Background

Brief Counseling and Psychotherapy

Brief counseling and psychotherapy has often been talked about as if only one question mattered: How do the results of **brief therapy** compare with those of **long-term therapy**? As important as the query might be, the question dichotomizes a subject that does not lend itself to such dualistic thinking. Defining the processes and outcomes of counseling and psychotherapy is rarely an either/or, cured/not cured process. As human beings, we all have good days and bad days. As counselors and therapists, we find some interventions prompt individuals to change thoughts and actions around problems, while the same interventions do not work with other individuals. Pitting brief approaches against long approaches misses the point, and professionals are beginning to understand that the crucial issue in counseling and therapy is determining the common factors that bring about change (Hubble, Duncan, & Miller, 1999). Understanding those common factors of change points professionals toward approaches that have efficacy and efficiency; that is to say, counseling and psychotherapy approaches that work for clients and in a timely manner.

Of the over 400 different forms of counseling and therapy, there are over 50 different brief therapy approaches (Bergin & Garfield, 1994; Cooper, 1995). In the previous edition of this book, this chapter attempted to balance divergent brief approaches in order to show the variety of theories that make up what is referred to as *brief therapy* (Sieber & Lewis, 1999). The chapter focused on showing how the many forms of brief therapy are characterized by intentional use of concepts and principles that guide practice in a purposeful way (Cooper, 1995). This updated chapter will follow the same path that characterizes brief therapy as intentionally using principles to guide practice, but will highlight

The author wishes to thank Conrad Sieber for his collaboration in developing the previous version of this chapter.

strength-based brief therapies that place counselors and therapists in a collaborative role with their clients. The reason for this choice is to offer helping professionals-in-training an opportunity to consider an emerging philosophy in working with clients that changes the professional focus from client pathology to client strengths (Hoyt, 2001; Lewis, 2000; Peavy, 1998; Saleebey, 1997; Walter & Peller, 2000; Winslade & Monk, 1999).

Before embarking on a deeper explanation of the emerging **strengths-based brief counseling and psychotherapy approaches,** it is important to see how brief therapy is looked at and defined in the profession. Although brief therapy was previously described as intentionally using principles to guide practice, defining *brief therapy* can get slippery. For instance, in the landmark *The Handbook of Counseling* (Locke, Myers, & Herr, 2001), *brief therapy* is listed five times in the subject index, whereas the same subject index presents solution-focused approaches and therapists as separate categories not cross-referenced to brief therapy. In one section in the *Handbook's* text, **solution-focused therapy** is presented as a viable, strategic, family, therapeutic approach, whereas in another section, solution-focused therapy is described as a postmodern, constructivist approach. Both descriptions are accurate, but neither portrayal highlights solution-focused therapy as a brief therapy; solution-focused therapy is a viable, strategic, family, therapy approach, and it is a postmodern, constructivist approach, and it is a brief therapy. The *Handbook* is an extremely valuable resource for professional counselors or therapists, but the text's descriptions of brief therapy are mainly limited to (1) pointing out brief counseling or psychotherapy usefulness in the schools, (2) describing a variety of theoretical orientations that use time-limited approaches, and (3) considering who is best served by brief approaches because managed care is going to press professionals to minimize sessions with clients. The *Handbook* is correct; brief counseling is useful in the schools (Bertolino, 1999; Davis & Osborn, 2000; Durrant, 1995; Lewis, 2000; Metcalf, 1995; Mills, Dunham, & Alpert, 1988; Murphy, 1997; Sklare, 1997; Winslade & Monk, 1999). Brief therapy can be viewed and practiced from a number of divergent theoretical perspectives (Cade & O'Hanlon, 1993; Cooper, 1995; Hoyt, 2001; Pransky, Mills, Sedgeman, & Blevens, 1997; Saleebey, 1997). Brief counseling or psychotherapy will continue to be pushed by managed care to press helping professionals to minimize sessions, but as described in this chapter, brief therapy is not a bag of techniques merely responding to managed care's desire to minimize sessions with clients. Certainly, the pressure toward using brief therapy, at least in part, has grown out of the context of having limited resources for mental health care, but brief therapy or short-term encounters with clients is not new. Freud and other pioneers saw numerous patients for a few visits (Cooper, 1995). The reality of **behavioral health care** puts counselors on notice to consider what works to promote successful therapeutic change and how efficiently it works, but simple dualisms that weigh brief therapy against longer therapy should be avoided. More importantly, as O'Hanlon (1990) asserts, "The issue isn't whether therapy is brief or not, but whether it is effective. Brief therapy can teach us much about how to do effective therapy" (p. 88).

Brief counseling or psychotherapy is mindful and intentional practice guided by principles that focus on therapeutic efficacy and efficiency. Brief counselors or therapists listen carefully, define clear goals, and focus on client strengths (Hoyt, 2001). What works guides brief therapists, and this chapter will explore the possibilities inherent in effective and efficient therapies that can be described as brief. Sometimes brief interventions have been trivialized by an excessive focus on the issue of treatment length. Focusing primarily on treatment duration to define an intervention is a very blunt instrument and the wrong focus (Beutler, 1994). At its extreme, this means that client resources, counselor or therapist knowledge, and interventions are less important than the time itself. It is analogous to saying that the most important thing physicians offer patients is time, not what is done with that time. For example, would it make sense to allot six 30-minute office visits to all medical patients regardless of diagnosis? This very equation has been used in mental health treatment by mental health agencies and insurance providers that establish maximum session limits without enough regard for client problems and resources. Who our clients and we are, including their resources and difficulties, and how we work with them, are the important domains.

There are limited resources. Limited resources translate into limited time, and limited time means counselors or therapists must use what works and be efficient as possible in their practice. The push for greater efficiency should not rule out therapeutic efficacy. There is no need to emphasize either a brief or a long approach if neither works. The helping professions show wisdom by directing their attention toward what works. Hubble et al. (1999) are among the theorists and researchers who are beginning to utilize the underlying common factors that cross theoretical boundaries. Brief therapies are frequently criticized for being about technique. Rather than creating a menu of techniques highlighting the common factors inherent in the therapeutic enterprise and sharing techniques that can inform professionals concerned with practices that have efficacy and efficiency, I will explore strength-based brief counseling or psychotherapy approaches that claim to have efficacy and efficiency. **Solution-focused brief therapy (SFBT), narrative therapy,** and **Health Realization** focus on client strengths and challenge our profession to move beyond what Gergen (1990) calls the language of mental deficit that leads to dependency on the helping professions and to progressive infirmity and self-enfeeblement.

Solution-Focused Brief Therapy

Steve de Shazer (1994) describes the historical roots of SFBT. In the 1950s, **Don Jackson, Gregory Bateson, John Weakland,** and **Jay Haley** worked in a research group that applied the scientific model of its time to psychotherapy. John Weakland, de Shazer's mentor, worked at the **Mental Research Institute (MRI),** which was founded by Don Jackson in 1958. The MRI group consulted regularly with **Milton Erickson,** who had a profound influence on the development of brief therapies. Although Bateson and Erickson were not a part of the MRI group, their ideas influenced MRI's thinking about the role of systems in creating and sustaining problems (Cade & O'Hanlon, 1993; Cooper, 1995). Erickson is one of the principal innovators in the therapeutic field because he challenged the medical model's dominant problem-classification system, with its problem-solving premises guided by a linear, cause-and-effect view of clinical practice. His success as a counselor or therapist and hypnotist emerged from using people's strengths. People were not fundamentally flawed or needing to be repaired; people had resources within themselves or within their social systems to make the changes they needed to make to improve their lives (O'Hanlon & Weiner-Davis, 1989). Erickson broke through the convergent reasoning that viewed client problems as medical puzzles with single answers; he viewed people as having untapped resources that could help them solve the problems they faced. Erickson helped brief counselors or therapists see the importance of using **divergent thinking** to see problems as having more than one correct solution and taking the position that believes clients have answers within themselves to solve most problems they face in living.

In 1966, **Richard Fisch** initiated the brief therapy project at MRI that focused on **problem solving.** In essence, the MRI tactic was to resolve problems by narrowing the treatment focus and helping clients change specific behaviors that were connected to their difficulties (Fisch, 1990; Fisch, Weakland, & Segal, 1982). The MRI model emphasized systems, **homeostasis, redundancy,** communication, relationships, and **circular causes.** Problems were maintained because people continued unsuccessful solutions to the problems.

Steve de Shazer co-founded the **Brief Family Therapy Center** with **Insoo Kim Berg** in Milwaukee, Wisconsin, where they moved beyond the focus on problem-sustaining factors to develop a model focused on preferred futures and strengths rather than deficits and problems. The shift to seeing solutions as independent from problems came to de Shazer in 1982 when working with a family with a litany of difficulties. Faced with a growing list of problems as a session with the family unfolded, de Shazer asked a key question: "What is happening in your lives that you want to continue to have happen?" Two weeks later, when the family came in, they reported that things were improved; at that point, de Shazer and his colleagues realized that they could promote change by focusing on developing solutions rather than concentrating on how to solve problems (De Jong & Berg, 2002). By asking clients questions and prescribing tasks to clarify their needs, goals, and personal resources for finding solutions, the therapeutic process shifted emphasis toward solution talk that helps clients look forward to changes, solutions, and to strive to promote positive growth. SFBT continues to grow and evolve, and inform the strength-based counseling or therapy practice worldwide (De Jong & Berg, 2002; de Shazer, 1990; Davis & Osborn, 2000; Durrant, 1995; Durrant & Kowalski, 1993; Hart, 1995; Hoyt, 2001; Walter & Peller, 2000). SFBT points to an alternative view in the counseling or therapy profession.

The process is not about counselors or therapists helping clients correct objectively defined problems; instead, counseling and therapy is a collaborative process that promotes the creation of meaning, personal responsibility, and agency (Cade & O'Hanlon, 1993; De Jong & Berg, 2002; de Shazer, 1994; Mahoney, 1995; Neimeyer & Mahoney, 1995; O'Hanlon, 1999; Sarbin & Kitsuse, 1994; Walter & Peller, 2000). Understanding the value placed on **solution talk,** utilizing client resources, creating an expectation of change, and using appropriate interventions are crucial to becoming competent as a SFBT counselor or therapist. Narrative counselors or therapists address common factors inherent in effective and efficient counseling and therapy as well, but they focus on helping clients discover preferred stories that empower them to live their lives according to preferred ways of living.

Narrative Counseling and Therapy

The **narrative counseling** or therapy notion of helping clients focus their resources and solutions developed from understanding the storied nature of life. The term *narrative* can create some difficulties: first, narrative refers to a general theoretical perspective that draws upon **constructivist** approaches and **epistemologies;** second, narrative refers to a specific therapeutic perspective associated with **Michael White** and **David Epston** (Hevern, 1999). In this chapter, narrative counseling or therapy will refer largely to the practice that has emerged from the work of Michael White and David Epston (Monk, Winslade, Crocket, & Epston 1997; White & Epston, 1990). Simply put, narrative counseling or therapy is best summarized by the belief that our lives are stories in progress and that they can be told from any number of perspectives. Narrative counselors' or therapists' essential credo is that "the person is never the problem; the problem is the problem" (O'Hanlon, 1994, p. 23). For instance, if a father told his son the story that he was a failure, it would not rule out the possibility that the son might find another person in his life experience who would offer him an alternative story that described him as kind and tenacious. One story highlights the son's deficits, whereas the other recognizes strengths and possibilities. Stories that clients find impoverishing and subjugating do not have to be embraced by clients. The therapeutic challenge in narrative counseling or therapy is to help clients **re-author** their lives according to alternative and preferred stories.

There is common ground and there are differences between SFBT and narrative counseling or therapy (Hart, 1995). In this chapter, we will begin to explore narrative counseling or therapy by investigating a common philosophical root that influences SFBT and narrative therapeutic theory and practice (De Jong & Berg, 2002; Durrant, 1995; Durrant & Kowalski, 1993; Hart, 1995; Metcalf, 1995; Murphy, 1997; Selekman, 1993; Walter & Peller, 2000; Zimmerman & Dickerson, 1996). Although they have divergent philosophical sources and practices, both SFBT and narrative have been influenced by a **social constructionist** philosophy. Social constructionism is a well-established perspective in the discipline of sociology that asserts people make meaning of reality through their interactions with others (Sarbin & Kitsuse, 1994). Given individual, family, and group relationships, individual and social meanings develop, evolve, and persist over time. Any historical-personal-theoretical construct encompasses a complex narrative that lends itself to multiple truths and alternative interpretations (Sarbin, 1993; Sarbin & Kitsuse, 1994). That is, when we use such constructs as "shy" or "introverted," we should recognize that these terms have meanings that are influenced by the historical, personal, and theoretical context where both their creators and their consumers exist. Our meanings are **linguistic** and meanings do not exist in vacuums; they exist in social and ecological contexts. Any story or narrative serves two functions by providing forms for interpretation and guides for action (Sarbin, 1993). From a constructivist vantage point, counseling or psychotherapy can be defined as a variegated and subtle interchange that involves the negotiation of (inter) personal meanings (Neimeyer, 1995). For counselors and therapists, **constructivism** is a concept used in theories of psychotherapy that focus on the centrality of meaning-making to human experience and how meaning is co-created by the individual in relationship with others, including counselors or therapists.

White and Epston (1990) promoted a narrative approach to help clients understand "knowledges" and "stories" that give meaning to their experiences while assisting clients in taking authorship of their lives. White and Epston were influenced by Bateson's (1972, 1979) argument that there is a subjective quality inherent in how we view reality and how we learn. Ontology and epistemology are connected. All understanding requires acts of interpretation on the part of individuals, and the cultural milieu influences the "reality" we see. In other words, reality is not separate and distinct from the observer. We participate in the construction of our social realities. Lives and relationships are shaped by "knowledges and stories" that communities of people negotiate and engage in to give meaning to their experiences and by "certain practices of self and of relationship that make up ways of life associated with knowledges and stories" (White, 1995). Basically, some stories are better than other stories for clients, and counselors and therapists can help clients re-story their self-limiting, problem-saturated life stories in an effort to help them find preferred stories of identity and live preferred ways of life.

The view of self-limiting stories deserves further explanation because it is a key feature that sets narrative apart from SFBT, and reveals a fruitful and sometimes heated dialogue that has occurred over the years (Hart, 1995). The neo-Nietzschean French historian and philosopher **Michel Foucault** has influenced White and Epston. Foucault is suspicious of claims of universal truths and critiques how power is used to subjugate persons, and White and Epston argue that counselors and therapists are wise not to claim they have some universal truth and that they must be mindful of the role that power plays in relationships between persons, especially between clients and counselors and therapists. White challenged the mental health profession to question its "move, deliberately or inadvertently, into the role of classifying, judging, and determining what is a desirable, appropriate, or acceptable way of life" (Monk, 1997, p. 8). Narrative counselors and therapists are alert for multiple truths; they avoid trying to find a singular, objective, universal truth that would determine what is best for clients. Clients are the best experts regarding preferred ways of living their lives. By breaking from notions of objective truth, narrative counselors and therapists enter conversations with clients that offer different explanations for lived experience. Counselors and therapists help clients discover "unique outcomes" or "sparkling moments" (i.e., successes) that challenge self-limiting, problem-saturated views of their lives. In the process, narrative counselors and therapists collaborate with clients to re-author alternative stories for describing life experiences, and help clients recognize their **personal agency** and **power**—their capacity to author their own life story.

Such a position points to one difference between SFBT and narrative counseling and therapy: solutions constructed in the narrative approach help people understand how power is negotiated and how stories give meaning to the experiences in their lives (Bruner, 1986, 1990; Durrant & Kowalski, 1993; Epston & White, 1995; Hart, 1995; Hoyt, 2001; Monk et al., 1997; Parry & Doan, 1994; White, 1995; White & Epston, 1990; Zimmerman & Dickerson, 1996). Narrative counselors and therapists might be curious and query a female client who constructed a solution that left her in an oppressive relationship that she expressed as "the way it is; men control women," whereas SFBT counselors and therapists might not explore the solution if the solution was okay for the client. Hence, there is a more political and cultural dimension to narrative work. Narrative counselors and therapists are mindful regarding their cultural assumptions and the power they have in their role as helpers. Thus, they explore the possible political implications inherent in some conversations with clients. They are sensitive to their own power, make adjustments, and learn from clients, such as First Nation, Maori, and other native peoples (Peavy, 1998).

A common theoretical ground should be recognized and appreciated by beginning brief therapy students. Rather than focusing on past problems and current deficits, both SFBT and narrative counselors and therapists enter into conversations in order to help clients draw upon strengths so they may move toward preferred futures. In a similar vein, Health Realization highlights strengths and possibilities, and goes further by asserting that there is a capacity for innate mental health.

Health Realization

Health Realization is a brief approach that assumes people have the innate capacity for mental health, common sense, and the ability to live in a mature and responsible manner regardless of past experiences or current circumstances (Pransky, Mills, Sedgeman, & Blevens, 1997). As brief approaches, Health Realization and its cousin, **Psychology of Mind,** view their therapeutic process as educational in nature (Marshall, 1998; McCombs & Pope, 1994; Mills & Spittle, 2001; Pransky, 1998; Pransky, Mills, Sedgeman, & Blevens, 1997). Counseling and therapy entails teaching people about how to access their health rather than treating psychological illness. Most radically, Health Realization "argues that the resource which alleviates mental anguish and dysfunction is already fully intact within every person… [and] can be drawn to the surface and applied directly to resolving a wide range of human problems" (Pransky, 1998, p. 205–206).

Using a principle-based paradigm for understanding human beings, Health Realization counselors and therapists look closely at the client's moment-to-moment psychological functioning because whatever is on his mind is his experience of reality or the world at that moment. The principles turn attention away from exploring the content of thinking and toward understanding the process of how thought and experience are created moment-to-moment (Sedgeman, 2001). Rather than investigating multiple outside forces that influence psychological life, the move is toward helping clients understand that the experience of life is created from the inside out. An "objective" and singular reality can never be known by persons because the only reality any person experiences is one emerging from his or her unique and individual thoughts. The point is not a solipsistic denial of external reality; it is the simple recognition that each person's psychological experience of the world occurs moment-to-moment. Different persons will see the same event in different ways because experience of the world emerges from thoughts about the world. In a family consisting of two parents and two children, the same event will be understood from different developmental and personal perspectives. For instance, if one parent is a Muslim and the other parent is Jewish, each will see events and issues in different ways. If one child is 10 years old and another is 17 years old, each will understand the same event in different ways. At the same time, if all family members understand the principles underlying the formation of their moment-to-moment thought, they might understand and appreciate the separate realities existing within the same household. Rather than a singular reality, there are multiple ways to see and appreciate our experience of the world. Rather than fighting about the truth of one reality, family members might attempt to listen, learn, and appreciate the multiple perspectives inherent in the family. They might even listen deeply to each other and become curious about the divergent points of view and experiences within the family.

The principles work together, cannot be separated, and can be grasped at a commonsense level of understanding. Because of this commonsense understanding, Health Realization breaks from attempts to intellectualize about such truth. Health Realization has been applied in a wide variety of settings, including public schools, housing projects, mental health agencies, prisons, universities, and businesses (Health Realization Institute, 2001). In fact, the University of West Virginia has committed to a research effort exploring the efficacy of the approach as a result of changes university leaders observed in faculty and students exposed to the understanding.

Interventions at the housing projects and other challenging communities initiated by **Roger Mills'** teams begin by helping a small community group understand their thinking process and how their reality is an inside-out affair. Project success grows from that small beginning that teaches clients to see and understand the link between their thinking and their life experiences (Health Realization Institute, 2001; Mills, 1995; Mills & Spittle, 2001; Pransky, 1998). What seemed to be a fixed, external reality shifts to become moment-to-moment thoughts about circumstances. Interventions concentrate on teaching clients about separate realities, moods, feelings and emotions, levels of understanding, and natural, healthy human functioning and self-righting capabilities. Clients become more engaged and aware of their own innate capacity for mental health, and their own capacity to take actions to change the circumstances around them. Thus, as they change their internal understanding, clients are able to take more positive steps toward transforming their circumstances, even those as oppressive as housing projects and prisons (Health Realization Institute, 2001).

Human Nature: A Developmental Perspective

Solution-Focused Brief Therapy

Although SFBT does not offer a developmental perspective, it clearly states that people create meaning in their lives. People construct reality with language, and many of their problems are maintained as the result of a **construction of reality** that discounts their natural competence and resources. The emphasis on creating meaning appears to be rooted in an understanding of how language works to help people perceive and define the world around them. Thus, de Shazer (1994) draws upon **postmodern philosophy, linguistics,** and **epistemology** in developing his theory.

Solution-focused counselors and therapists believe that **objective reality** does not exist because the act of describing experience itself requires **subjective interpretation.** As such, this non-objectivist view challenges the belief that language describes reality, and points to a perspective where meaning and understanding of reality are negotiated: "Neither authors (or speakers) nor readers (or listeners) can be assured that they can get at what the other person meant with any certainty because they each bring to the encounter all their previous and unique experiences. Meaning is arrived at through negotiation within a specific context" (Berg & de Shazer, 1993, p. 7). In other words, reality is not out there to be grasped; rather, we continually negotiate meanings in our conversations with others. People are natural storytellers trying to make sense of and take action in the world.

Narrative Counseling and Therapy

SFBT's emphasis on story making to understand and define experience creates the context for the current exchange of ideas with narrative counselors and therapists. SFBT and narrative counselors or therapists would agree with the storied nature of human existence. However, narrative counselors or therapists are very mindful of the larger social context within which their work is embedded and the inherent potential for counselors and therapists to reproduce, in the helping relationship, patterns of domination and oppression that exist in society. Narrative counselors and therapists see the political dimensions embedded in human nature, and they are aware that some human stories are oppressive. Gender, race, culture, and power are aspects of human nature and play a part in the therapeutic relationship, whereas some of these issues are not deemed central by solution-focused counselors or therapists.

Health Realization

Health Realization capitalizes on client strengths, expertise, and innate mental health (Mills, 1995, 1996; Saleebey, 1997). Human nature is innocent and emerges from the operation of the three principles: **Mind, Thought,** and **Consciousness** (Mills, 1995, 1996; Mills & Spittle, 2001; Pransky, 1998; Sedgeman, 2001). Arguing that there is innate mental health assumes that an incredible potential for well-being exists in each person (Pransky, 1998). It is human nature to think; our thoughts create our experience of the world. Problems of living are the result of **dysfunctional thinking;** worried thought, frantic thought, and angry thoughts create a certain experience of the world. Thoughts occur, one after the other. Thought recognition aids healthy thinking and desirable feelings that lead people away from merely coping and toward a greater appreciation of themselves as active participants in their world. The point is not to pretend that individuals can control their thoughts or have to feel guilty about their thoughts. The key is recognizing that thoughts are thoughts that change moment-to-moment.

Health Realization moves human nature into a realm that is beyond most current counseling and psychotherapy theories by presenting the approach as addressing our "psychological-spiritual make-up as human beings" (Health Realization Institute, 2001, p. 2). Theories normally avoid **psychological-spiritual fusion,** but Health Realization's notion of Mind places a **life-force** behind people's moment-to-moment psychological functioning. As a principle, Health Realization simply points out that a life-force moves through each person. The life-force has a spiritual quality that can be appreciated if recognized, but trivialized via over-analysis or intellectualizing because understanding emerges from insight. Commonsense understanding exists naturally within each person, and it is facilitated or tapped by others who have the same commonsense understanding.

The emphasis on competence rather than pathology, and on counselors or therapists collaborating with clients to help them draw upon their inherent resources, is fundamental to a strength-based understanding of human nature (Avis, 1987; Cade & O'Hanlon, 1993; de Shazer, 1994; Hoyt, 2001; Lewis, 2000; Mahoney, 1995; Mills, 1995, 1996; Mills & Spittle, 2001; Monk et al., 1997; Neimeyer & Mahoney, 1995; Peavy, 1998; Pransky, 1998; Saleebey, 1997; Sarbin & Kitsuse, 1994; Walter & Peller, 2000).

Major Constructs

Solution-Focused Brief Therapy

SFBT is not a cookbook of techniques, but it is the approach in this chapter that foregrounds technique the most. As a constantly evolving theory and philosophy of counseling and psychotherapy, SFBT practice requires an optimistic orientation (Hoyt, 2001; Walter & Peller, 1992). Its main assumptions include the following.

1. People are constantly making sense of their experience. The beliefs they have guide their actions and how they view the world.
2. Problems are experienced as problems, and people want to make things in their lives better.
3. Problems do not equal pathology. Problems are an inherent part of life; generally, problem patterns include how persons are "viewing" and "doing" the problem.

4. People try to solve their problems, but not all their attempts are successful. Not solving problems leads people to feel stuck and focused on problems rather than generating alternative solutions.
5. People have abundant resources that are both known and unknown.
6. The problem is the problem; the person is not the problem.
7. Change is constant and inevitable, and one small change can lead to another.
8. There are exceptions to any problem pattern. The problem does not always occur.
9. There are different ways to look at any problem.
10. If it works, don't fix it.

Counseling and psychotherapy conversations de-emphasize problems, pathology, and **objectification** of people and instead lead to a **collaborative dialogue** that creates positive alliances in which the counselor or therapy co-creates solutions with clients (De Jong & Berg, 2002; Walter & Peller, 1992, 2000). The focus is on helping people in social contexts to enhance their sense of responsibility and power in their lives. Like narrative counselors and therapists, SFBT counselors and therapists point out that the person is not the problem; the problem is the problem. For example, saying the client is a person with depression is different from describing the client as a depressed person. SFBT is concerned with competence and assumes that there are inherent resources to be found in the experiences and stories of clients, and that clients have competence to find solutions with the help of the counselor or therapist. Counseling or psychotherapy begins by respecting **clients as experts** on their own lives, and noticing the times when a client's life is not affected by the problem. The counselor or therapist enters a collaborative dialogue by respecting the client's lived experience, incorporating what clients are saying into the therapeutic conversation, and identifying exceptions to the occurrence of the problem in the client's life (O'Hanlon, 1993).

SFBT contrasts with psychotherapies that require clients to enter the practitioner's experiential realm. For instance, clients are not asked to see their problems in terms of DSM diagnoses or to understand their coping behaviors as defenses and resistance to change. The collaborative nature of the counseling or therapy relationship helps solution-focused counselors and therapists make use of what is going right in clients' lives rather than trying to "fix" what is wrong. Instead of asking, "What is the cause of the problem?" or even "What maintains it?" solution-focused counselors or therapists ask, "How do we construct solutions?" This counseling stance or perspective helps the practitioner enable clients to use their resources instead of focusing on and defining their pathology. In fact, de Shazer (1990) sees no need during counseling or therapy to return to conversations about problems, and concentrates instead on behaviors and goals that will lead to and maintain solutions. Emphasizing strengths may prompt more rapid change than focusing on pathology and problems.

Narrative Counseling and Therapy

Rather than a set of techniques or formulas, narrative counselors and therapists see their practice as emerging from a way of being with clients by using co-creative practices that require them to see their clients as partners (Monk et al., 1997). Winslade and Monk (1999) summarize narrative counseling's basic assumptions.

1. People live their lives in accordance to the stories in which they participate. Talk to any person about his life. He will tell a story that connects one stage to another.
2. People are not the only authors of their stories. Stories occur in **social contexts,** not in an individual vacuum. Life stories are created and acted out socially.
3. Discourses are embedded within stories, and a way of talking about events and a person's influences. If a social discourse defines girls as not being athletic, then there is an embedded way of talking about young women.
4. Surveillance and scrutiny are part of the social norms within the modern world. Current efforts to assess and compare children by using standardized instruments point to a desire to "gaze" at, measure, and scrutinize worth. In a similar manner, young women who compare their bodies to the "ideal" bodies found in tabloids are involved in self-scrutiny.
5. Alternative discourses and stories are always present. There is no single way to view a discourse or story. There are alternatives to any story, including oppressive ones.
6. Severe limits can be imposed on persons who try to change dominant social stories. African American Rosa Parks suffered arrest and ridicule by white members of her community when she refused to give up her seat to a white patron.
7. By breaking down oppressive stories, clients can create new possibilities for living. For instance, a counselor or therapist might explore how the African American dialect has the same grammatical complexities inherent in standard American dialect. The ability to use the standard dialect will open certain economic doors, but it is not a sign of intelligence.
8. There are always experiences that do not get into the stories being told. The work of the counselor or therapist is to help clients find untold stories that capture elements of an untold story that helps clients see events in a new light.
9. Counselors or therapists work to help clients develop more satisfying stories about their lived experience.

Clients possess local knowledge and expertise about their life experiences, and counselors or therapists use curiosity about clients' experience in order to open up space for new possibilities to emerge from the therapeutic conversation. In being sensitive to focusing on the problem and not the person as the problem, narrative counselors or therapists have developed externalizing conversations by separating the person from the problem. For instance, with a young client who has been referred because of "anger issues," the narrative counselor or therapist would describe anger as external to the young client during their conversation. A typical way of framing such a conversation would be, "How long has anger been pushing you around?" Thus, anger is an external force to be talked about with the client, rather than an internalized state within the client. Externalizing conversations enable the counselor or therapist working with this client to join with the client to figure out how they can outwit anger and prevent anger from tricking or causing the client additional difficulties.

Health Realization

The three principles underlying the formation of moment-to-moment functioning are **Mind, Consciousness,** and **Thought.**

1. Mind is the source of thought and consciousness; it is the power that makes thought and consciousness possible and can be likened to terms like *life force.* "Mind is the energy of all creation, the origin of the infinite flow of thought and experience. It can only be defined by inference because our thinking is a part of the creative process we call Mind, but it is not all of it, nor can we separate ourselves from it to see it whole" (Sedgeman, 2001, p. 10).

2. Consciousness is the capacity for people to be aware of experience and how thinking shapes our experience via the senses. Consciousness is the ability to be aware of reality (Health Realization Institute, 2001). "What we know as life becomes experienced as real via our senses" (Sedgeman, 2001, p. 10). Consciousness places the experience of our thoughts in our bodies. Our reality is constantly being formed moment-to-moment via thought plus consciousness.

3. Thought is the capacity to create via mental activity. Thought is the ability to form ideas and to create images, such as beliefs, values, and opinions, in our heads (Health Realization Institute, 2001). The function and ability to think are universal but the contents of our thoughts emerge within each person. We know and experience life via thought (Mills, 1995; Mills & Spittle, 2001; Pransky, 1998; Sedgeman, 2001). Thought is the "fabric of personal reality" (Health Realization Institute, 2001).

The principles of Mind, Consciousness, and Thought are the constructs guiding Health Realization. One principle without the other two falls short of describing moment-to-moment psychological functioning.

Applications

Overview

In the following sections, the use of SFBT, narrative counseling, and Health Realization are examined as theories applied to practice. The goals of counseling and psychotherapy, the change process, and intervention strategies are discussed.

Solution-Focused Brief Therapy   Clients are viewed as partners in a collaborative relationship concerned with facilitating solutions to problems (Cade & O'Hanlon, 1993; De Jong & Berg, 2002; Hoyt, 2001; Walter & Peller, 2000). A consolidation of the assumptions previously enumerated leads to three basic rules that guide application. First, "if it ain't broke, don't fix it." Second, once you know what works, do more of it. Find exceptions to problems and help the client do more of the same. This means that the counselor or therapist does not need a great deal of information about the problem in order to help. It is important to recognize the power of solution talk, such as asking about positive pretreatment changes, and that frequently small changes bring about larger changes. Third, if it doesn't work, don't do it again; do something different. This means that practitioners help clients to stop doing what is not working. Take what is not working as information and avoid doing it. Counseling or psychotherapy is about helping the client do something differently (De Jong & Berg, 2002; de Shazer, 1990).

Narrative Counseling or Psychotherapy   Narrative counseling or psychotherapy assumes that the counselor or therapist does not have privileged access to the truth. In an effort to help clients author their lives according to preferred ways of life, the counselor or therapist must be curious about the client's experience and possible alternative stories regarding problems (Monk et al., 1997). For narrative counselors or therapists, the problem is the problem, and the client is the expert with the resources to solve the problem. The counselor's or therapist's job is to help clients explore the problems they have defined as problems, and to facilitate clients in identifying parts of their lives that are not dominated by problems.

Health Realization   Health Realization views clients as possessing innate mental health. The approach is educative in nature, and attempts to facilitate insight into understanding the consequences inherent in operating from the principles of Mind, Consciousness, and Thought. The source of experience emerges from the ability to think and is brought to life by the continual experience of thought as reality (Sedgeman, 2001). Looking at multiple external forces to understand experience orients people to the outside, whereas human experience is an inside-out affair. Understanding the inside-out nature of our experience liberates clients to understand the source of their experience and to take actions that can transform their circumstances.

Goals of Counseling and Psychotherapy

Solution-Focused Brief Therapy   O'Hanlon (1990) describes two essential tasks for brief counseling or psychotherapy: **changing the viewing** and **changing the doing.** SFBT highlights various ways to help clients recognize their own resources (De Jong & Berg, 2002; Hart, 1995). It is concerned with goals and behavior. In essence, the goal of counseling or psychotherapy is to help clients develop a view of themselves as competent and capable of change. De Shazer's (1990) psychotherapy focuses on defining goals with the client in the present or future when the problem is not occurring.

Narrative Counseling or Psychotherapy   Narrative counseling or psychotherapy enables clients to separate their lives and relationships from knowledges and stories they find impoverishing, assists them to challenge ways of living they find to be subjugating, and encourages them to re-author their own identities and lives according to ways they would prefer to be living (White, 1989, 1995).

Health Realization   Health realization seeks to help clients to see every moment as new and to understand that each moment holds potential for new thoughts that can change one's life. Insight into the moment-to-moment nature of experience grows from an understanding of the three principles of Mind, Consciousness, and Thought. Fear, hopelessness, gratitude, and euphoria are all thought-events (Sedgeman, 2001).

The Process of Change

Solution-Focused Brief Therapy   The change process begins with solution talk and other techniques directed toward enhancing client competence and seeing possibilities for creating a successful future. The process begins by socializing and getting to know the client, then proceeds to **setting the agenda** and assessing the client's wishes and complaints. Change begins by exploring what the client noticed was going right since she made her appointment, what brought her to counseling or therapy, where she thinks she is going, and what she thinks would be helpful for the counselor or therapist to know. During counseling or therapy, the counselor or therapist keeps in mind the client's desired changes. Practitioners use **solution talk,** choose a series of future-oriented questions, ask **miracle questions** and **scaling questions,** or explore exceptions and past successes. If the problem appears too large, the practitioner helps a client to define the problem in a solvable manner. These solutions generated in collaboration with the practitioner lead clients to see themselves as doing things differently as they move toward a preferred reality with the problem solved. Then, future-oriented questions are used to keep the changes going. For SFBT counselors and therapists, there is no specific formula for change because the practitioner wants to avoid rigid and inflexible practice.

Narrative Counseling and Psychotherapy   As a basic stance, narrative counselors or therapists embody a compassionate curiosity about the client's lived story rather than the certainty promoted in modernist therapies (Monk et al., 1997). Narrative counselors and therapists use externalizing conversations as a key intervention. Externalizing conversations place problems outside the client. This helps clients discover exceptions to their problems and/or sparkling moments that illuminate past successes. The change process leads to conversations that promote a separation between the person and the problem in order to help clients become active agents in their own lives. Clients are invited to entertain ideas about their own agency and to re-author new stories about themselves and their experiences. The therapeutic conversation promotes self-exploration and understanding by discovering clients' concerns and alternative stories. The therapeutic conversation involves deconstructing clients' stories in such a way that hidden meanings, gaps, and evidence of conflicting, more empowering information are found. By focusing discourse on the problem rather than on the person, the client's resources are mobilized against the problem and toward contributing to solutions. This may be particularly helpful to clients who are ashamed of their difficulties or who blame themselves for struggling with their concerns. Therefore, the change process is fluid because people are not fixed entities in need of repair; instead, they are works in progress that can be revised as they go.

Health Realization   Health Realization understands that the change process involves an insight into the moment-to-moment nature of thought. Counselors or therapists teach and model quieting themselves down, listening deeply, and speaking from their own understanding. Counselors or therapists teach the three principles and enter into therapeutic conversations with clients to facilitate the personal insight that comes from understanding that experience is one thought after another. Anger is a wave of thoughts. Fear is a wave of thoughts. By quieting oneself, other thoughts become available, and such thoughts can change the experience of reality.

Intervention Strategies

Solution-Focused Brief Therapy   SFBT's "apparent faith in technique" sets it apart from other strength-based approaches (Parry & Doan, 1994, p. 18). **Client selection criteria** for SFBT are not dealt with directly by the creators of this model, but it is generally accepted that client and counselor or therapist must be able to create a contract for change through early collaboration in the counseling and therapist process. It is acknowledged that some clients may enter into a **visitor relationship** with the counselor or therapist and not de-fine a problem or goals that can be addressed (De Jong & Berg, 2002). With no real agree-ment regarding what counseling or therapy is for, there is no basis for engagement in SFBT.

During the first session, SFBT asks about pretreatment improvements clients have noticed since calling to request counseling or therapy (de Shazer, 1985, 1988). Checking for pretreatment changes helps clients take into account steps they have taken to improve the situation and steps they might want to continue taking. Although used throughout counseling and therapy, solution talk and change talk are techniques SFBT counselors or therapists use to explore pretreatment improvements and help clients notice differences between times the problem is occurring and times when the problem is not occurring (de Shazer, 1988, 1994).

SFBT uses a number of questioning strategies. **Exception-oriented questions** help the client find examples of situations where the problem is not occurring (De Jong & Berg, 1998; de Shazer, 1988, 1991; Walter & Peller, 1992). For instance, when the client has de-scribed an overwhelming experience, the counselor or therapist can respond, "That's in-credible. There is so much going on for you. Just one of those problems would be enough to knock most people for a loop. How have you managed to do things as well as you have?" Clients are asked questions such as, "How did you manage to take this important step?" "How did you turn that around?" and "What does this tell you about yourself?" (Se-lekman, 1993). **Presuppositional questions** convey the inevitability of change (De Jong & Berg, 1998). For instance, "If you were to show me a movie about how things would look as soon as the problem is solved, what would we see?" and "What would you be do-ing differently?" **Miracle questions** help the client see the possibility of finding a solution to the problem and help to clarify their counseling or therapeutic goals (De Jong & Berg, 1998; de Shazer, 1985, 1988, 1991). De Shazer (1988) offers the classic question: "Suppose that one night, while you were asleep, there was a miracle and this problem was solved. How would you know? What would be different?" (p. 5).

Scaling questions help clients reflect on and discuss their own perspective regard-ing the problem, themselves, or others (Berg & de Shazer, 1993; De Jong & Berg, 2002), as in the following example: "Let's say that on a scale of 1 to 10 that 10 means being brave in social situations and 1 means acting timidly. If in a month from now you will be able to go to the dance and ask someone to dance, how brave would you be on that scale be-tween 1 and 10?" Different questions are used to invite clients to break out of restrictive beliefs or rules they have about themselves (Walter & Peller, 1992). Typical **difference questions** are "How did you get the problem to go away?" and "What is different about the times when the problem is not as intense?"

Solution-focused counselors or therapists provide specific tasks for clients to perform. **Formula first-session tasks** are designed to be used at the end of the first session to help clients with vague complaints (de Shazer, 1985). **Observation tasks** require clients to look, pay attention to, and observe, whereas **behavior tasks** (or "do something different" tasks) direct clients to take action (De Jong & Berg, 2002; de Shazer, 1988; O'Hanlon & Weiner-Davis, 1989). An observation task would be presented in the following manner: "Between now and the next time we meet, I would like you to observe, so that you can describe to me, what happens in your family that you want to continue to have happen" (de Shazer, 1985, p. 137). A behavior task might be: "I would like each of you to do something different, no matter how strange, weird, or off-the-wall what you do might seem" (de Shazer, 1985, p. 123). Goals that are clearly defined are critical and frequently must be broken down into smaller steps or sub-goals (Cade & O'Hanlon, 1993; De Jong & Berg, 2002). Important questions to ask are, "What would be the first sign that things are getting back on track?" "What do you want?" and "What would you be doing differently?"

Narrative Counseling and Therapy   Narrative counselors and therapists see themselves as taking a position in relation to their clients that is based on a philosophy of human experience and meaning-making. They do not see themselves as technicians merely using a series of procedures to promote client change. They explore clients' problem-saturated stories with the intention of helping clients develop their own preferred alternative stories. Positions they take include **externalizing conversations,** and redefining the difficulty as an object outside of the client (White, 1989; White & Epston, 1990). For instance, rather than using language that internalizes problems within the individual by talking about the individual as a "depressed client," the counselor or therapist will ask "How long has depression been pushing you around?" They would also look for **unique outcomes** and sparkling moments that are exceptions used to describe when the problem has not dominated the client's actions (Monk et al, 1997; White & Epston, 1990). Because the term *unique* implies that the outcome is not a normal, everyday event, Monk (1997) uses the term *sparkling moments* to emphasize the regularity of these occurrences.

Health Realization   Health Realization does not have a menu of techniques. "Therapeutic power has a one-to-one correlation with the exact level of well-being of the therapist" (Pransky, 1998, p. 202). The counselor or therapist is the instrument and the intervention because therapeutic effectiveness is mediated by the counselor or therapist's well-being. The primary technique is to talk about the three principles as understood by the counselor or therapist. Such moment-to-moment understanding is recognized as evolving and never complete, but those with greater understanding can assist those who are beginning to learn. In the area of techniques and modeling understanding, the approach can be seen as having parallels with Buddhist psychology or connected ways of knowing described in feminist psychology (Clinchy, 1996; Watson, Batchelor, & Claxton, 2000).

Clients with Mental Disorders

There is a dearth of research regarding how these brief approaches have been used with clients who have mental disorders. Health Realization practitioners frequently work in collaboration with psychiatrists to help such clients slow down enough to become aware of their own thought-generated reality. In Santa Clara County, California, an Alliance for Community Care Study used random group assignment with 89 patients diagnosed with severe, chronic mental illness. Data and follow-up interviews with staff and clients found "treatment group participants were more present and aware, were more involved in social activities, were more connected to their families, and more positive about being able to make progress in their lives and increase their level of self sufficiency" (Health Realization Institute, 2001, p. 6). Thus, there is reason for caution and hope in using brief approaches with clients with mental disorders.

Evaluation

Overview

In the following sections, after a discussion regarding the common factors in successful therapy, the research regarding the brief therapies is examined. Limitations of the theories are also explored.

Supporting Research

It is important to recognize the current state of affairs with regard to the common factors influencing practice and the challenges of doing **outcome research** (Hubble et al., 1999). For instance, O'Hanlon (1990), a brief solution-focused therapist, states, "You'd think I'd be happy that my side seems to be winning, but something about the newfound popularity of brief therapy worries me. After all, the real question is not how long therapy takes but how effective it is and whether it serves those who seek it. I believe effective therapy is usually brief, but not in every case. Although I see clients on the average of about five sessions, I occasionally do long-term work. Sometimes I see people for several years" (p. 48). In summarizing the research on the efficacy of brief therapy, Koss and Shiang (1994) acknowledge the difficulty of conducting outcome research. They note Garfield's (1990) conclusions that outcome research presents "extreme and varied challenges," including selecting therapies, counselors and therapists, and clients; training the counselors and therapists; selecting criteria to measure outcome; and finding control groups and resources to pay for the study. Thus, it is appropriate to have a healthy level of skepticism in reviewing outcome studies and to be critical in evaluating their claims. However, outcome research, although imperfect, must help inform practice as the ability to evaluate counseling or psychotherapy processes and outcomes improves. Investigating the common factors inherent in all successful counseling or therapy may be one avenue for moving toward a greater understanding of what works in therapy. Two important points should be made about brief counseling and therapy. First, most clients begin therapy expecting it to be brief, whereas counselors and therapists tend to prefer long-term therapy (Koss & Shiang, 1994; McKeel, 1996). Second, studies comparing brief counseling and therapy to long-term therapy show no difference in success rates (Hubble et al., 1999; Koss & Shiang, 1994). But does counseling and therapy work?

Research shows counseling and therapy works. Overall, therapeutic treatment works for 80% of clients (Asay & Lambert, 1999). Current research indicates that at least 50% of clients can benefit from counseling and therapy in 5 to 10 sessions, whereas 20-30% of clients require treatment lasting more than 25 sessions (Asay & Lambert, 1999). In exploring what works, based on a review of the extant literature, Lambert (1992) divided common therapeutic factors influencing successful counseling and therapy into four broad areas: client and extratherapeutic events, therapeutic relationship, expectancy and placebo effects, and therapeutic technique factors. Client and extratherapeutic events accounted for 40% of improvement in counseling and psychotherapy clients. The therapeutic relationship accounted for 30%, expectancy and placebo effects accounted for 15%, and therapeutic technique accounted for 15% of improvement in counseling or psychotherapy clients.

Common factors are crucial and will be used as a connecting thread in describing the brief therapies depicted in this chapter. Students wishing to explore the significance of each of the common therapeutic factors in greater depth should refer to Hubble et al. (1999). Koss and Shiang (1994) note the prevalent belief that outcomes of different psychotherapies are equivalent, but conclude that this may be an artifact of methodology limitations and lack of equivalence in the measurement of outcome criteria across therapies.

Client/Extratherapeutic Factors   Lambert's (1992) review of the literature described client factors as accounting for 40% of change in counseling and therapy. Their strengths, support found in the environment, and positive (even chance) change events account for the largest percentage of therapeutic change. What clients bring into the counseling and therapy room and the resources they have outside of therapy have a profound impact on the success of counseling and therapy (Garfield, 1994; Lambert, 1992). Tenacity, faith, caring mentors and allies, social connections, and a sense of personal responsibility are just a few client/extratherapeutic factors. The crucial point is that clients are not damaged goods who need a heroic counselor or therapist to fix them. In fact, rather than celebrating the counselor or therapist or technique as the crucial factor, Tallman and Bohart (1999) take the position that clients are self-healers and should be described as heroes who account for 70% of what works in counseling or therapy. Counselors' and therapists' main function is to set a stage and to "serve as assistants" in helping clients access their own magic. In a number of brief therapies, we find a mental health resource model that emphasizes client strengths and innate capacity for mental health (De Jong & Berg, 2002; de Shazer, 1990; Durrant, 1995; Durrant & Kowalski, 1993; Hart, 1995; Lewis, 2000; Mills, 1995, 1996; Mills, Dunham, & Alpert, 1988; Paris, 2000; Pransky, Mills, Sedgeman, & Blevens, 1997; Saleebey, 1997).

Relationship Factors   Lambert's (1992) review of the literature details relationship as accounting for 30% of change in counseling or therapy. Warmth, caring, empathy, acceptance, mutual respect, and encouragement are a few factors that contribute to a positive relationship. Relationship factors such as caring, empathy, credibility, and supportiveness are common to many counseling and psychotherapeutic approaches and are often described as affecting treatment outcomes (Garfield, 1980; Parloff, 1986). Bachelor and Horvath (1999) summarize research that illustrates positive therapeutic relationships are necessary to effective counseling and therapy. Just as the client comes to be changed in the relationship, the counselor or therapist must be prepared to face the unknown and uncertainty inherent in remaining open to understanding the client's world. As in any genuine relationship, the therapeutic relationship invites parties to join together in conversations where the other can change each party. Illustrating one movement toward relationship in brief counseling or therapy, Walter and Peller (2000) no longer use the terms *therapy* and *therapist;* they now refer to the *conversational event* as a consultation and themselves as consultants. The point is not merely semantic. In their effort to create space for dialogue and wonder, Walter and Peller seek to have conversations with persons rather than interviews with therapeutic objects. In other words, the process of helping others has shifted toward evolving conversations that facilitate persons in finding strengths in themselves and resources in their environment. The role of relationship is important in brief counseling and therapy (Cade & O'Hanlon, 1993; De Jong & Berg, 2002; Walter & Peller, 2000).

Expectancy and Placebo Effects   Lambert's (1992) review of the literature details expectancy and placebo effects as accounting for 15% of change in counseling and therapy.

Hope is a necessary part of this process. Both counselor or therapist and client must believe in the restorative power inherent in the therapeutic process. They must be alert to the questions: Does the client believe that he can reach the goals defined in counseling and therapy? If he does not, obviously the counselor or therapist must collaborate with him to define goals that he has faith he can achieve. Hope is vital in brief counseling and therapy (Cade & O'Hanlon, 1993; De Jong & Berg, 2002; Monk et al., 1997; Peavy, 1998; Saleebey, 1997; Walter & Peller, 2000).

Model/Therapeutic Technique   Lambert's (1992) review of the literature describes therapeutic technique as accounting for 15% of change in counseling and therapy. With the expectation that clients will do something different in their lives, the techniques counselors or therapists use prepare clients to take action to help themselves (Hubble et al., 1999). In comparing outcomes of counselors and therapists from various theoretical orientations, no differences are found. Rosenzweig (1936) and then Luborsky, Singer, & Luborsky (1975) used the "dodo bird verdict," a line borrowed from *Alice in Wonderland,* "to illustrate the empirical conclusion that all the different therapies appeared to be equal in effectiveness" (Tallman & Bohart, 1999, p. 92). Subsequent research came to the same conclusion; the dodo bird verdict is accurate.

Solution-focused Brief Therapy   SFBT makes maximum use of a number of the common factors influencing successful counseling and therapy. Interventions highlight client strengths, create a sense of hope, and offer an array of techniques to promote change. De Shazer (1985, 1990, 1991, 1994) offers abundant case material, and a limited but growing body of outcome research (George, Iveson, & Ratner, 1999; Gingerich & Eisengart, 2000; Lindforss & Magnusson, 1997; McKeel, 1996). As a non-normative model, clients are considered the best judges of their own success (De Jong & Berg, 2002; de Shazer, 1991). Early on, de Shazer (1991) summarized a Brief Family Therapy Center evaluation of clients' perceptions of treatment efficacy. Clients reported an 80.4% success rate initially and an 86% success rate 18 months later. De Jong and Berg (1998, 2002) studied clients receiving SFBT who were categorized by DSM-V-TR diagnoses. Overall outcome results indicated that 39% met treatment goals, 40% made some progress, and 21% made none; that is, 79% met or made some progress as the result of SFBT. The average number of sessions was 2.9. Research summaries regarding SFBT include McKeel, 1996; George et al., 1999, and Gingerich and Eisengart, 2000. In a summary of research regarding SFBT, McKeel (1996) is critical of the lack of outcome studies, but indicates that the early research results are promising. George et al. (1999) summarized 25 studies across a range of referrals that show good outcomes for between 65% and 85%. Gingerich and Eisengart (2000) reviewed 15 controlled studies, concluding that there is preliminary support indicating SFBT may be helpful to clients. Thus, studies fall short of establishing the efficacy of SFBT, but studies also report that SFBT may be beneficial to clients.

Narrative Counseling and Therapy   Narrative counseling and therapy make maximum use of a number of the common factors influencing successful counseling or therapy. Beginning with the strengths inherent in clients' alternative stories, exploring how relationships are shaped, creating a sense of hope, and offering a way to look at problems as problems are ways narrative counselors or therapists promote change. Narrative counselors or therapists offer abundant case material (Monk et al., 1997; White, 1989, 1995; White & Epston, 1990; Winslade & Monk, 1999), but little in the way of experimental design and outcome research. Lack of such group design is due partly to the collaborative nature and co-constructive process inherent in defining issues related to counseling or therapy. Narrative counselors or therapists use the ethnographic and case study methods more akin to anthropology than to modernist empirical science (Hevern, 1999). There is no normative position. All knowing requires interpretation that persons bind into stories. Case study data regarding narrative may be found in the texts written by clinicians (Epston & White, 1995; Monk et al., 1997; Parry & Doan, 1994; White, 1989, 1995; White & Epston, 1990; Zimmerman & Dickerson, 1996).

Health Realization   Health Realization makes maximum use of a number of the common factors influencing successful counseling or therapy. The assumption that there is innate mental health highlights client strengths. Health Realization counselors or therapists create relationships that focus on hope and the expectancy for change. Health Realization has been conducting research into the effectiveness of its practices for nearly two decades.

The wide range where Health Realization interventions have been applied is most impressive. Efforts to apply Health Realization have taken place in communities where many counselors or therapists would not want to work, such as prisons and housing projects. Impressive outcomes resulted from a 2-year project started by Roger Mills at the Coliseum Gardens, a 200-unit housing project that had the highest homicide rate and the highest frequency of drug-related arrests in Oakland, California. An independent evaluation conducted by Dr. Kathleen Roe at San Jose State University and Dr. Benjamin Bowser at University of California, Santa Cruz, concluded, "Community building, and interpersonal activities have given residents new tools for dealing with symptoms of the deeper problems facing their community. Their emerging self-confidence and self-efficacy as a community have fueled their interest in tackling bigger issues" (Roe & Bowser, 1993). After two years, a short list of what was reported at the Coliseum Gardens indicated the following.

- Homicides dropped by 100% (none reported in year 2).
- Violent crimes were reduced by 45%.
- Drug possession/sales were reduced 16%.
- Assaults with firearms were reduced by 38%.
- Youth attendance in Boys and Girls Club increased 110%.

The data are impressive. At the same time, there is a great need to conduct other, more rigorous studies using experimental designs. Surveys used in a number of Health Realization studies are limited and point to a need for more experimental designs and for even more rigorous use of single case-study designs. Current research includes an experimental design with the Alliance for Community Care Study in Santa Clara County, California, where patients diagnosed with severe, chronic mental illness were randomly assigned to experimental and control groups. "The treatment group showed significant positive changes in positive affect, behavioral emotional control, self esteem, self efficacy, with significant decreases in anxiety and depression" (Health Realization Institute, 2001, p. 6).

Limitations

The practice of brief counseling and therapy demands flexibility, and rarely do counselors or therapists limit themselves to one way of doing things. The trap becomes using techniques without a sound basis and rationale for their use. If the philosophy of not pathologizing clients by focusing on diagnoses is adhered to too rigidly, some clients who can benefit from referrals to psychiatrists might not be referred for medication. However, Health Realization counselors or therapists have traditionally worked with psychiatrists to help clients get the medication necessary for them to begin recognizing their thought as thought.

Current research indicates that at least 50% of clients can benefit from therapy in 5 to 10 sessions, whereas 20-30% of clients require treatment lasting more than 25 sessions (Asay & Lambert, 1999). Not every client will benefit from brief counseling or therapy.

Solution-Focused Brief Therapy   Although De Jong and Berg (2002) offer outcome data regarding SFBT, the lack of additional and more comprehensive research continues to limit claims of efficacy. Overall, two client limitations that affect practice are generally cited by solution-focused counselors or therapists: clients not interested in changing the problem, and those lacking a clear goal (Walter & Peller, 1992). In other words, counseling or therapy will not work unless there is some agreement between the counselor or therapist and client about defining a problem to be changed. Other limitations involve the manner in which counselors or therapists apply SFBT in practice. Those who use this treatment in a formulistic way without understanding the underlying philosophy and theory may strike clients as simplistic and/or lacking an understanding of their problems. Counselors or therapists should not use techniques advanced by this theory without fully understanding how and why they are being used, as this is clearly counterproductive. Also, there are clients who can benefit from referrals to psychiatrists for medication; being too rigid about not pathologizing clients is not helpful to them.

Narrative Counseling or Therapy   Narrative counselors or therapists offer abundant case materials, but still lack quantitative research that will point to the approach's general efficacy and efficiency. Narrative research largely emerges from case studies, and the use of qualitative research comes from a core belief that the human capacity to talk and use language limits the use of quantitative methods of research. Human beings exist in cultural and social contexts that quantitative methodologies do not take into account. Thus, the limit comes from perspectives of rigor. Obviously, practitioners want to evaluate the efficacy and efficiency in any approach, but the challenge with therapies emerging from anthropological perspectives involves studying one case or group at a time.

Health Realization   Health Realization has a variety of studies dating back nearly 20 years. A large part of the research has consisted of self-report and surveys. The more recent experimental designs, such as those in the Alliance for Community Care Study, indicate more rigorous designs are forthcoming.

Summary Chart—Brief Theories

Human Nature

Solution-Focused Brief Therapy. People construct reality with language, and many of their problems are maintained as the result of a construction of reality that discounts their natural competence and resources.

Narrative Counseling or Therapy. Language and meaning-making define humanness. People are social beings who co-create meaning through their social interactions.

Health Realization. It is human nature to think; our thoughts create our experience of the world. Problems of living are the result of dysfunctional thinking; worried thought, frantic thought, and angry thoughts create a certain experience of the world. Thoughts occur one after the other.

Major Constructs

Solution-Focused Brief Therapy. A consolidation of the major assumptions that guide application of SFBT leads to three principles.

1. If it ain't broke, don't fix it.
2. Once you know what works, do more of it. Finding exceptions where the problem does not dominate the client's life is important in helping the client "do more of the same."
3. If it doesn't work, don't do it again. Do something different.

Narrative Counseling or Therapy. Narrative counseling and therapy asserts that people's lives are storied. The client is not the problem; the problem is the problem. The clients are the expert about their lives and counselors and therapists work with clients to help them find preferred ways of living their lives.

Health Realization. Three principles guide Health Realization.

1. Mind is the source of thought and consciousness; it is the power that makes thought and consciousness possible, and can be likened to terms like *life force.* "Mind is the energy of all creation, the origin of the infinite flow of thought and experience. It can only be defined by inference because our thinking is a part of the creative process we call Mind, but it is not all of it, nor can we separate ourselves from it to see it whole" (Sedgeman, 2001, p. 10).
2. Consciousness is the capacity for people to be aware of experience and how thinking shapes our experience via the senses.
3. Thought is the capacity to create via mental activity. The function and ability to think are universal, but the contents of our thoughts emerge within each person. We know and experience life via thought.

Goals

Solution-Focused Brief Therapy. Help clients change how they view their problem (interpretation) and what they do around the complaint. The latter means changing behavior, taking action that is new, different, and more effective in response to the problem.

Narrative Counseling or Therapy. Narrative counseling or therapy enables clients to separate their lives and relationships from knowledges and stories they find impoverishing, assists them to challenge ways of living found to be subjugating, and encourages them to re-author their own identities and lives according to ways they would prefer to be living.

Health Realization. Health realization seeks to help clients see every moment as new and to understand that each moment holds potential for new thoughts that can change one's life. Insight into the moment-to-moment nature of experience grows from an understanding of the three principles of Mind, Consciousness, and Thought.

Change Process
Solution-Focused Brief Therapy. Focusing on the problem is unnecessary; change involves collaborating with clients to define solutions. Counselors or therapists help clients stop focusing on problems and to shift their attention to creating solutions.

Narrative Counseling or Therapy. As a basic stance, narrative counselors or therapists embody a compassionate curiosity about the client rather than the certainty promoted in modernist therapies of Health Realization.

Health Realization. This strategy understands that the change process involves an insight into the moment-to-moment nature of thought.

Interventions
Solution-Focused Brief Therapy. In SFBT, counseling or therapy interventions include solution talk, exception-oriented questions, presuppositional questions, miracle questions, scaling questions, difference questions, formula first-session tasks, observation tasks, and "do something different" tasks.

Narrative Counseling or Therapy. Narrative counselors or therapists explore clients' problem-saturated stories with the intention of helping clients develop their own preferred alternative stories. Positions narrative counselors or therapists take include externalizing the problem, and redefining the difficulty as an object outside of the client.

Health Realization. The counselor or therapist is the instrument and the intervention because therapeutic effectiveness is mediated by the counselor or therapist's well-being. The primary technique is to talk about the three principles as understood by the therapist. Such moment-to-moment understanding is recognized as evolving and never complete, but those with greater understanding can benefit those who are beginning to learn.

Limitations
At least 50% of clients can benefit from counseling or therapy in 5 to 10 sessions, but 20-30% of clients require treatment lasting more than 25 sessions. Brief counseling and therapy are not a cure-all. In general, although growing in volume, there is a lack of outcome research on the efficacy of SFBT, narrative counseling and therapy, and Health Realization. In part, this is a result of each theory's focus on the subjective experience of clients and eschewing rigidity on the part of counselors or therapists in helping clients construct their own solutions. If the philosophy of not pathologizing clients by focusing on diagnoses is adhered to too rigidly, some clients who can benefit from referrals to psychiatrists might not be referred for medication. However, Health Realization counselors or therapists have traditionally worked with psychiatrists to help clients get the medication necessary for them to begin recognizing their thought as thought.

◼️ The Case of Jonathan: A Brief Therapy Approach

In order to illustrate brief theories in action, a fictionalized case will draw primarily from the narrative work of John Winslade (2001) and utilize the Collaborative Story model, an integrative approach to strength-based brief counseling or therapy (Lewis, 1999). As an integrative approach, the Collaborative Story could be criticized by brief counseling or therapy orthodoxies as not being truly SFBT, narrative counseling or therapy, or Health Realization, but it is an approach that integrates elements found in all three brief approaches described in this chapter. Like any contextual approach, its truth is based on what works (Hayes, Hayes, Reese, & Sarbin, 1993). Readers should analyze this case study as a story that concentrates on exchanges between a fictional client and a fictional counselor or therapist.

Jonathan is described as a 36-year-old Native American male with an array of personal and professional difficulties, and he has been referred to the mental health clinic by his supervisor at work. Drawing on the wisdom found in Garrett and Herring (2001) for working with Native American adults, and leaving abundant time for silence between exchanges, this description takes place some time after Jonathan has exclaimed, "I am not wanted in the 'white man's' world, and have no future in my own."

COUNSELOR OR THERAPIST: "Jonathan, it must be strange and even uncomfortable being referred here by your supervisor who is white and having a white counselor as well. After all, you do not even feel wanted in the white man's world. But here you are because you have a story to tell me. Here we are together in the same room sharing breath. My job is to listen to learn, and not to dictate and command. We're in this together. I'll hear some of your story and you'll hear some of mine. Here's what I am wondering. Many times people notice, in between the time they make the appointment for counseling and the first session, that some things seem different—even better. What have you noticed in your situation?"

CLIENT: "It is strange, but like you say, here we are sharing breath. There was one thing that was different. There are a couple kids at the treatment facility who really listen to me, who maybe I can help heal. As disturbing as work, my relationship, and my dreams are, I remember something Uncle Andrew told me when I went into nursing. He said I was a healer—a young one with power. The words are still woven there."

COUNSELOR OR THERAPIST: "Still woven there?"

CLIENT: "Like part of a weaving."

COUNSELOR OR THERAPIST: "'Weaving' seems to have something more to it."

CLIENT: "Uncle Andrew's mother wove a rug we would sit upon when he told stories. He told us the stories about the people of the Colorado Plateau—the Ute, Paiute, Hopi, Hualapai, Havasupai, Zuni, and Navajo. Our people's vocabulary is based on kinship, shared stories, and a long history of inhabiting the desert. He helped us to see how we were connected; those small stories are part of a larger story. What bothers me is that now I'm just some failure in Phoenix with nothing."

COUNSELOR OR THERAPIST: "Do you mind if I ask some questions about this?"

CLIENT: "No, go ahead."

COUNSELOR OR THERAPIST: "When did this notion of failure first enter your life?"

CLIENT: "When I dropped out of the Indian Affairs school after my brother got killed in the car I was driving, when I got a divorce, when I got drunk, when I got angry. You want more?"

COUNSELOR OR THERAPIST: "Failure has pushed you around quite a bit. What effect has it had on you?"

CLIENT: "Right now, it gets me pissed off."

COUNSELOR OR THERAPIST: "Yes, I can see. How has failure affected your relationships with others?"

CLIENT: "My wife isn't with me. I got a divorce from my first one. My supervisor is making me come here because I am having 'difficulty getting along' with others."

COUNSELOR OR THERAPIST: "Failure has really jerked you around, hasn't it? I mean, what influence has failure had on your feelings about yourself?"

CLIENT: "I feel down, depressed."

COUNSELOR OR THERAPIST: "What sort of life does failure want you to have?"

CLIENT: "Just like I'm having. Miserable."

COUNSELOR OR THERAPIST: "How wide has its influence spread in your life?"

CLIENT: "Over everything."

COUNSELOR OR THERAPIST: "Are you happy with failure having this sort of influence?"

CLIENT: "No."

COUNSELOR OR THERAPIST: "Why not?"

CLIENT: "Because it makes everything bad."

COUNSELOR OR THERAPIST: "How have you resisted the influence of failure?"

CLIENT: "There are times at work when I feel like a healer. When the kids look up to me like I had some wisdom to give them. I quiet myself down. I go down, real slow, and listen within, and I tell them to do the same thing."

COUNSELOR OR THERAPIST: "How did you know to do that?"

CLIENT: "Uncle Andrew. He taught me to be real quiet, to slow down when praying to Father Sky and Mother Earth. He used to get us up before dawn to greet the Morning Spirits."

COUNSELOR OR THERAPIST: "Has failure not affected you in some other areas?"

CLIENT: "There were some times when I greeted the Morning Spirits with my kids. They'd laugh, but those were good times."

COUNSELOR OR THERAPIST: "How did you prevent failure at those moments?"

CLIENT: "I just quieted down. I knew what we wanted for the kids. I listened within. Our personal story was part of a larger story. My wives. Both my first wife and my second wife used to laugh a lot with us at those times. We could feel the Spirit."

COUNSELOR OR THERAPIST: "That's powerful. When you take a stand against failure, what knowledge do you call to mind?"

CLIENT: "The knowledge of elders, like Uncle Andrew. Go slow. Quiet down. Trust the Spirit. We are Children of the Earth. Problems are only part of a larger story."

COUNSELOR OR THERAPIST: "How does that help?"

CLIENT: "I dunno. It just does. Maybe it just takes me back to the rug and being with Uncle Andrew and other elders."

COUNSELOR OR THERAPIST: "You feel connected and see your capacity for having wise thoughts. Who has noticed and appreciated these achievements in your life?"

CLIENT: "My wife and kids. The kids at work, even a couple of co-workers a couple of times. When they happen."

COUNSELOR OR THERAPIST: "What does this mean to you?"

CLIENT: "I can feel connected."

COUNSELOR OR THERAPIST: "Tell me a story about being connected to the past and future of your people, your family, and the elders."

14

Feminist Theories

Barbara Herlihy
University of New Orleans

Vivian McCollum
University of New Orleans

Background

Feminist theory evolved from the feminist movement of the 1960s. The feminist movement allowed women to actively articulate their dissatisfaction with their second class citizenship in a patriarchal social system. One of the most vocal feminists, Betty Friedan, put a face to feminism with her book, *The Feminine Mystique* (1963). **Feminism,** which is the philosophical basis for feminist counseling and therapy, has been described as "the collection of political philosophies that aims to overthrow patriarchy and end inequities based on gender through cultural transformation and radical social change" (Brown, 1994, p. 19). The **National Organization for Women (NOW)** was instrumental in rallying the charge to reform social structures and traditional roles for women and was a strong voice for feminism during the 1960s and 1970s.

As the feminist movement grew, many women formed groups for the purpose of **consciousness-raising** and to discuss their lack of a collective voice in politics, the work place, economics, education, and other significant socio-political arenas (Kaschak, 1992; Kirsh, 1987). Consciousness-raising groups began as loosely structured meetings of women who met to discuss common themes, but soon developed into sophisticated self-help groups that empowered women.

Feminist counseling or therapy grew from these consciousness-raising groups of the 1960s as women began to discuss their shared experiences of oppression and powerlessness. These groups played important roles in the education, radicalizing, and mobilization of women in the early 1970s. Freeman (1989) indicated that, although consciousness-raising groups were instrumental in helping women gain personal insight, they were not as effective in producing political change. Thus, these groups became a chief mechanism for effecting personal change and support for their members (Lieberman, Solow, Bond, & Reibstein, 1979), but left a void where broader change at a societal level was needed.

As the therapeutic value of consciousness-raising groups became evident, and the need for more structured groups grew, the 1970s marked the beginning of feminist counseling or psychotherapy as a recognized approach to psychotherapy. Feminist counseling or psychotherapy evolved, however, without being founded by a specific person, theoretical position, or set of techniques (Enns, 1997). This early phase of feminist counseling or psychotherapy was predicated on the assumptions that women had shared experiences of oppression and victimization and that only a proactive approach could be effective. Early feminist counselors or therapists helped name other issues facing women and worked to adapt traditional therapies to meet the needs of women.

Early feminist theory called for a radical form of counseling and psychotherapy, using techniques that were designed to help women see that a patriarchal society was at the center of many of their problems and that change would be virtually impossible until they were empowered to feel equal and act with equal voice. **Radical feminist** counselors or therapists vigorously communicated the goals and tenets of feminism. These early goals included (a) encouraging financial independence, (b) viewing women's problems as being influenced by external factors, and (c) suggesting that the client become involved in social action (Enns, 1997). Radical counseling or psychotherapy encouraged active participation in social action groups and other social justice causes to ensure societal change that embraced gender equity.

Walstedt (as cited in Enns, 1993) called feminist counseling or psychotherapy a "radical therapy of equals," which made it dramatically different from traditional counseling or psychotherapy with its hierarchical composition. The activist phase of feminist counseling theory lasted approximately 10 years and was the catalyst for the development of other grassroots counterinstitutions, such as rape crisis centers, that offered a wide range of services to women (Enns, 1993).

Not all feminists welcomed the new feminist counseling and psychotherapy. Some feminists during this period implied that feminism and counseling and psychotherapy were incompatible because counseling or therapy involved "one up/one down politics that encouraged women to focus on pleasing the therapist rather than assuming responsibility for themselves" (Enns, 1993, p. 8). Groups became the preferred method for feminist counselors or therapists. The balance of power between the counselor or therapist and clients was more equal, with both counselor or therapist and clients receiving and giving emotional support. Many more women could be reached through groups, thus effecting more sweeping social change (Kaschak, 1981).

The 1980s saw a further infusion of feminist thought with other counseling theories in what has been termed the "mainstreaming era" (Dutton-Douglas & Walker, 1988). The idea was to put traditional theories to a political gender "litmus test" and remove those parts of the traditional approach that promote a dichotomous view of men and women (Elliott, 1999). Many early practitioners of feminist counseling or psychotherapy promoted the goal of **androgyny,** integration of both traditional masculine and feminine characteristics as an ideal of mental health (Enns, 1997). Androgyny research (Bem, 1976, 1987) and behavioral skills training (Brown, 1986) became the standard for feminist counseling. Feminist counselors or therapists were encouraged to choose from all traditional intervention methods that did not support gender-biased outcomes (Enns, 1993).

Contrarily and simultaneously, during this same era feminist counseling or psychotherapy was being defined as a separate entity (Enns, 1993). During this time, stages of feminist counseling and psychotherapy were articulated and skills for implementing feminist counseling and psychotherapy were presented (Ballou & Gabalac, 1984; Fitzgerald & Nutt, 1986). Also, feminist personality theory was proposed to support and integrate feminist therapeutic practices (Enns, 1993).

Feminist counseling and psychotherapy became more liberal and less radical. **Liberal feminists** emphasize different goals than the radical feminists. Liberal feminists view counseling and psychotherapy as a process to gain self-understanding and see the necessity for flexibility in helping the client solve problems (Enns, 1997).

Since the late 1980s, there has been a movement within feminist theory that acknowledges feminine potential, focuses on equality, and acknowledges that many of the shared problems of women are created by a society that does not value them or allow them to exercise their free will. Unlike the earlier years of feminist counseling and psychotherapy, the tone of feminist counseling or psychotherapy has become more moderate, adapting goals espoused by both radical and liberal feminists. During the 1980s, the demand for groups decreased, and individual counseling and psychotherapy became the most frequently used form of feminist practice (Kaschak, 1981). Enns (1993) and Shreve (1989) posited that a "second wave" of consciousness-raising is necessary to provide knowledge and resources for women and to effectively impact many of the same social issues that plagued women in the past. This third phase is in continuous development and helps to further define and clarify the work of the feminist counselor or therapist (Enns, 1997; Walker, 1990).

Like the feminist movement itself, feminist counseling and psychotherapy has its supporters and its critics. Critics are often those who are unfamiliar with the precepts of the theories and those who harbor erroneous concepts that feminist counseling or therapy is anti-male just because it is pro-female (Elliott, 1999). According to Ballou and Gabalac (1984) and Enns (1992), a feminist counselor or therapist is a self-professed feminist who is not prejudiced based on gender or sexual orientation and who works toward social equality for women.

Because many traditional counseling or psychotherapy practices have been harmful when used with women (Hooks, 2000), feminist counselors or therapists are encouraged to continually examine their theoretical orientations from a feminist perspective (Enns, 1993). According to Dutton-Douglas and Walker (1988), a wide variety of counseling or psychotherapy theories can be incorporated within a feminist approach.

Human Nature: A Developmental Perspective

The feminist perspective is grounded in the belief that traditional theories of human nature and human development, created by Western males in their own image, are not universally applicable. Rather, feminists believe it is essential to recognize that women and men are socialized differently and that gender role expectations begin to influence human development from the moment a child is born. These expectations are strongly embedded in the fabric of our society and have such a profound impact that they become deeply ingrained in the adult personality.

Gender-role socialization has been defined as a multifaceted process, occurring across the life span, of reinforcing specific beliefs and behaviors that a society considers appropriate based on biological sex (Remer, Rostosky, & Wright, 2001). This process has limiting effects on both women and men. For example, our myths and the stories we tell our children abound with sex-role stereotypes that send subtle but powerful messages that men are strong, clever, and resourceful, while women are passive, dependent, and help-less. Oedipus solved the riddle of the Sphinx; David slew the mighty Goliath with only a slingshot; Arthur pulled the sword, Excalibur, from the rock to demonstrate that he was king; and Jack climbed the beanstalk to wealth and fortune. By contrast, Rapunzel was trapped in a tower with no exits, fated to await her male rescuer; Cinderella's lot in life depended on the prince to place the glass slipper on her foot; Sleeping Beauty could awaken only when kissed back to life by a man; and Little Red Riding Hood had to be saved by the brave woodsman (Polster, 1992). There are lifelong consequences for grow-ing girls who learn that femininity is incompatible with strength, assertiveness, or compe-tence, and for boys who learn that masculinity is incompatible with expressions of fear, dependency, emotionality, or weakness (Lerner, 1988). Some of these consequences in-clude the following.

- Men are encouraged to be intelligent, achieving, and assertive, and to go after what they want. Females, however, may have a kind of wisdom called "women's intuition," but are discouraged from being intellectually challenging, competitive, or aggressive. They are expected to thread their way through a middle ground where they are encouraged to be smart enough to catch a man, but never to outsmart him (Lerner, 1988). Although women in today's society are less likely than they were decades ago to be discouraged from pursuing a career, they often are still expected to put family first and subordinate their careers to the male "breadwinner."
- Men are encouraged to be independent; expression of dependency needs in men may be regarded as weak or "effeminate." By contrast, women's dependency on others is less likely to be viewed in a negative light. The attractiveness of "girlish" qualities in women is reflected in the common practice of affectionately referring to women as "chicks," "girls," "dolls," or "babes" (Lerner, 1988).
- Men are expected to be rational, logical, and stoic. Women, although they are expected to be emotional, may be labeled "hysterical" when they overtly express strong emotions. For men, anger may be the only emotion that can be expressed acceptably, and then primarily as a means of control, while it is more acceptable for women to cry or to ask for help.
- Stereotyped ideals of women's sexuality value naivete and innocence, while "experience" enhances a man's sexual attractiveness. Our culture sends mixed messages to young women: they are expected to be sexually attractive, with their bodies on display, yet they are discouraged from making sexual choices and developing a healthy sexual identity (Elliott, 1999). Tolman (1991) described a "missing discourse of desire" in our society, in which discussion and exploration of adolescent female sexuality are absent or discouraged.

Feminist scholars have challenged the assumptions on which gender-role socializa-tion and **sex-role stereotyping** are based. Notable among those who have reformulated our understanding of human development are Nancy Chodorow, Carol Gilligan, Jean Baker Miller, and other women affiliated with the Stone Center in Massachusetts such as Sandra Bem and Ellyn Kaschak. Their contributions are discussed in the following section.

The Mother-Child Relationship

Nancy Chodorow (1978) attributed the differences between women and men to the fact that women are primarily responsible for early childcare. Thus, a girl's **identity formation** occurs in a context of ongoing relationships: girls experience themselves as being like their mothers, which fuses the process of attachment with the process of identity development. For boys, separation and individuation are tied to gender identity; thus, separation from the mother is essential to the development of masculinity. Because masculinity is defined through separation while femininity is defined through attachment, "male gender identity is threatened by intimacy, while female identity is threatened by separation" (Gilligan, 1982, p. 8).

A Different Voice

Carol Gilligan's work as a research assistant with Lawrence Kohlberg prompted her interest in women's moral development. After conducting and analyzing extensive interviews with women, she concluded that Kohlberg's model of moral development was less applicable for women than for men. She saw differences in the way women and men responded to moral dilemmas. Men generally reacted with a morality of justice that emphasized individual rights, while women tended to approach the dilemmas with a **morality of care and responsibility** that emphasized a concern that no one would be hurt. Noting that these concerns are embedded in a cultural context, Gilligan was concerned that traits such as compassion and caring are prized in women but at the same time are seen as a deficit in their moral development. In her book, *In a Different Voice* (1982), she asserted that concern for connectedness is central to women's development. Exploring developmental crises faced by girls at adolescence, she concluded that it is difficult for girls to maintain a strong sense of identity and "voice" when doing so would be to risk disconnection to a society that does not honor their needs and desires for relatedness and connectedness. Thus, it is necessary for women to recover and reclaim their lost voices so that they can move forward along the pathway to healthy growth and development.

Toward a New Psychology of Women

Jean Baker Miller's (1976) pioneering work focused on gender inequality and the implications for personality development of membership in dominant and subordinate groups. In her view, because women are the subordinate group in society, they develop characteristics such as passivity and dependency to help them cope with this status. Focusing on relationships of dominance and subordination, Miller concluded that women differ from men in their orientation to power. Thus, the distinctive psychology of women arises from their position of inequality. She noted that psychology has no language to describe the structuring of women's sense of self, which is organized around being able to make and maintain affiliations and relationships. Miller conceptualized this difference as holding the potential for more cooperative, more affiliative ways of living. She called for a "new psychology of women" that would recognize that women have a different starting place for their development, that they "stay with, build on, and develop in a context of attachment and affiliation with others" (p. 83).

Self-in-Relation

Jordan and Surrey's (1986) self-in-relation theory reflects a collaborative effort among women at the Stone Center in Massachusetts to reformulate women's development and psychology. Their work followed in the tradition of Miller and Gilligan, who argued for the development of new concepts, language, and theories to describe and understand female development. Jordan and Surrey paid particular attention to the positive, adaptive aspects of the mother-daughter relationship, and offered a new model of female development that positively redefined the mother-daughter dyad and affirmed traditional female values of nurturance and connectedness. Their model challenged the traditional psychoanalytic tendencies to pathologize female development, particularly the mother-daughter relationship, and to engage in "mother-blaming" as a way to explain adult psychological dysfunction. Postulating that mother-daughter sameness facilitates the development of empathy and the capacity for relatedness, they saw the core self of women as including an interest in and an ability to form emotional connections with others. According to self-in-relation theory, "women organize their sense of identity, find existential meaning, achieve a sense of coherence and continuity, and are motivated in the context of a relationship" (Jordan & Surrey, 1986, p. 102).

Gender Schema

Sandra Bem's gender schema theory provides another perspective on the powerful influence of gender-role expectations on identity development. *Schema* is a term used by cognitive psychologists to describe an organized set of mental associations used to interpret perceptions (Sharf, 2000). Bem (1981, 1993) has argued that gender schema is one of the strongest perceptual sets we use when looking at society and our place in it. When children learn society's views of gender and apply it to themselves, stereotypes of masculinity and femininity are reinforced. Children learn very early that certain behaviors are desirable for girls to be considered "feminine" and boys to be seen as "masculine." In adolescence, boys and girls tend to become highly gender focused as they become concerned with physical attractiveness and exploring their emerging sexuality. By adulthood, these gender schemas are deeply ingrained and they are limiting to both sexes.

Engendered Lives

According to **Ellyn Kaschak, gender** is the organizing principle in people's lives. In *Engendered Lives* (1992), she focused on the societal impact on gender-role development. She argued that the masculine defines the feminine; that is, men determine the roles that women play. Because women are socialized to feel rather than to act, and because society values action more than feeling, women are placed in a subordinate role.

Conclusions

Feminist scholars, by positing different models of development for women and men, have provided us with a better understanding of relationships and a more comprehensive portrayal of human development over the life span (Gilligan, 1982). At the same time, they have been concerned that their work might be interpreted as dichotomizing the sexes. Although the validation of women's relational skills and the recognition of the needs for connectedness and individuation are important contributions of feminist scholars, Lerner (1988) has noted that it is crucial to keep in mind that *all* people develop within the context of ongoing relationships and fail to thrive in the absence of human connectedness. A circular and reciprocal relationship exists between men and women, and an appreciation of the different filters through which they perceive and experience the world can broaden our understanding of human nature and human growth and development.

Major Constructs

Although feminist counselors and therapists practice in various ways, depending on their approach, generally they share a commitment to a core set of principles (Enns, 1997). Perhaps the most fundamental of these principles is that **the personal is political.** The basis for this belief is that the personal or individual problems that women bring to counseling or psychotherapy originate in social and political oppression, subordination, and stereotyping. Thus, the goal of feminist counseling and therapy is not only individual change, but also social transformation. Clients' responses are not viewed as **dysfunctional** or as having an **intrapsychic** origin, but are seen as ways of coping with an oppressive environment in which they have a subordinate status. Because the environment is a major source of pathology in the lives of women and other oppressed minorities, the toxic aspects of the environment must be changed if individual change is to occur. "The goal is to advance a different vision of societal organization that frees both women and men from the constraints imposed by **gender-role expectations**" (Herlihy & Corey, 2001, p. 351).

A second principle, intertwined with the first, is that feminist counselors and therapists share a **commitment to social change.** Feminist counselors or therapists work to help clients achieve a "revolution from within" and a "revolution from without" (Prochaska & Norcross, 1994). Their goal is to assist women not only to make internal, psychological changes, but also to join with others in working toward social change that will liberate all members of society from subordination, oppression, and gender-role stereotyping. In feminist counseling and psychotherapy, clients are encouraged to become active in furthering social change through such means as joining political action groups or confronting sexism in their workplace. Feminist counselors or therapists work with individual clients, couples, and families, but they also have an overarching commitment to broader social change. They are themselves involved in social change in their own communities and sometimes in larger spheres.

Third, feminist counselors and therapists are committed to the establishment of **egalitarian relationships** (Ballou & West, 2000; Herlihy & Corey, 2001; Remer, Rostosky, & Wright, 2001). One of the roots of women's problems is the unequal distribution of power between women and men, and between other dominant and subordinate groups. Thus, it is important for feminist counselors or therapists to establish counseling or psychotherapy relationships in which clients are viewed as equal partners in the therapeutic endeavor, who have the capacity to change in directions that they themselves select and to decide on therapeutic goals and strategies. The counselor or therapist is viewed as another source of information rather than an "expert" in the relationship. Feminist counselors or therapists employ a variety of means for sharing power with the client, including demystifying the process, self-disclosing appropriately, and paying careful attention to informed consent issues. Their two-fold aim in building egalitarian therapeutic relationships is to empower the client and to model collaborative ways of being in relationship. It is important to feminist counselors and therapists that they do not replicate in the therapeutic relationship the power disparity that the client experiences in her larger social, economic, and political worlds.

A fourth principle of feminist counseling or psychotherapy is to **honor women's experiences** and to appreciate their perspectives, values, and strengths. The belief that underlies this tenet is that only women's unique experiences can provide a foundation of knowledge for understanding women (Elliott, 1999). Forcing women's experiences into a traditional framework that ignores their voice and status would devalue and distort both the experiences and the women themselves (Ballou & West, 2000). Instead, theories of feminist counseling and therapy evolve from and reflect the lived experiences of women that include a number of gender-based phenomena such as sexual assault, domestic violence, eating disorders, and sexual harassment. The voices of the oppressed are acknowledged as authoritative, valued, and valuable sources of knowledge (Worell & Johnson, 1997).

Fifth, feminist counselors and therapists **recognize all types of oppression,** not only those based on gender. Feminist counselors and therapists respect the inherent worth and dignity of every individual and recognize that societal and political inequities are oppressive and limiting to *all* people. Feminist principles have been expanded to encompass an awareness of the multiple interactions of gender with other variables that impact the lives of clients who are not members of the dominant class or race or ethnicity. Feminists strive to be cognizant of the ways in which all people, depending on their position in a complex social matrix, are both oppressed and oppressor, both dominant and marginalized. When psychological distress is placed within a socio-cultural context, it is apparent that experiences of oppression based not only on gender—but also on race, ethnicity, class, physical ability, age, religion, and sexual orientation—are interrelated in complex ways (Ballou & West, 2000; Remer, Rostosky, & Wright, 2001).

Sixth, a goal in counseling or psychotherapy is to help clients **challenge the androcentric norms** that compare women to men and embrace the idea of a "woman-defined woman" (Sturdivant, 1980, p. 92) rather than for women to allow themselves to be defined by others. One of the ways that our society has tended to devalue women's voices has been to prize the patriarchal norm of "objective truth" over subjective experience. Feminists call for an **acceptance of feminist consciousness,** which acknowledges diverse ways of knowing. Within this new paradigm, women are encouraged to express their emotions, trust their intuition, and use their personal experience as a touchstone for determining what is reality (Herlihy & Corey, 2001).

Finally, the feminist approach calls for a **reformulated understanding of psychological distress.** Feminist counselors and therapists reject the medical or disease model of psychopathology. The notion of psychological distress is **reframed** so that it is viewed as a communication about the experience of living in an unjust society. From this new perspective, psychic pain is not seen as a symptom of disease or deficit. Instead, it is defined as evidence of resistance and the will and skill to survive (Worell & Johnson, 1997). According to Brown (1994), *resistance* is a term that describes a person's ability to remain alive and strong in the face of oppression. Thus, a client's problems in living are not assumed to arise from within that individual, but to derive instead from multiple sources within a complex social context.

Applications

Overview

Counselors and therapists practice multiple forms of feminist counseling and psychotherapy today, basing their work on the unique combination of their feminist orientation and their counseling or psychotherapy approach (Dutton-Douglas & Walker, 1988). Therefore, feminist counseling or psychotherapy is highly personal for the counselor or therapist, as it originates in the counselor's or therapist's personal beliefs concerning the empowerment of women and changing social norms that inhibit women from self-direction. The goals of feminist counseling and psychotherapy are basically two-fold: to help clients understand that socio-political forces influence their lives and to understand how women's problems can be interpreted as methods of surviving rather than as signs of dysfunction. The overall purpose of feminist counseling and psychotherapy, however, is to help clients change by making choices based upon their own personal experiences and strengths (Enns, 1997). The process of change includes the development of self-help skills and tools that allow clients to problem-solve in the absence of the counselor or therapist. The feminist counselor or therapist helps the client explore how problems exist in both personal and social contexts (Enns, 1997), thus demonstrating that change must occur at both a personal level and a social level.

Feminist counseling or psychotherapy can be particularly effective with certain "mental disorders" that are commonly diagnosed among women in our society. Feminist counselors and therapists use a feminist analysis with alternative diagnostic systems (Kincade, Seem, & Evans, 1998). They consider the social meanings of diagnosis, broadening the focus to a more complex understanding of the client's experience and distress within a cultural context. The client is the expert member of the therapeutic dyad who is knowledgeable about her or his own distress and its social meaning (Brown, 1994).

The basic tenets of feminist counseling and psychotherapy are widely accepted. Feminist counselors and therapists practice from self-chosen models developed from their philosophical views about social justice and equality coupled with their theoretical orientation to counseling or psychotherapy. Feminist counselors and therapists operate from a complex knowledge base that includes the psychology of women; counseling and psychotherapy theory; perspectives on gender, race, and class; socio-political change strategies; and multicultural issues (Enns, 1997). This knowledge base is reflected in the goals, intervention strategies, and research agendas of feminist practitioners.

Goals of Counseling and Psychotherapy

Change often involves developing new attitudes toward the circumstances and realities of women's and men's lives, not just adjusting to those circumstances and realities. It is the responsibility of the feminist counselor or therapist to help clients explore a full range of options available to them, rather than concentrating solely on what is to be perceived to be the right course to take because of one's gender. This might take the form of self-analysis for the client, exposure to feminist literature, or participation in consciousness-raising groups or other gender-homogenous support groups. At a societal level, uncovering emotional distress, anger, or outrage to promote social change, and participating in social activism, may benefit the client. Involvement in community action programs and social action activities can help the client gain both experience and confidence. Enns (1997) proposed six goals for feminist counseling or psychotherapy: equality, independence/interdependence, empowerment, self-nurturance, and valuing diversity.

Equality as a goal of feminist counseling or psychotherapy is designed to help the client gain freedom from traditional gender roles. Gaining equal status in personal relationships, economic self-sufficiency, and work equity are all components of equality. It is the counselor's or therapist's role to encourage the client to negotiate greater equality in intimate relationships, with friends, and with work colleagues. This is done through exposing the client to information regarding the unequal status and power of women and men in Western society (Enns, 1997).

Balancing **independence** (personal attributes) and **interdependence** (relational skills) has proven to be one of the most difficult goals to operationalize for feminist counselors or therapists. Balancing personal attributes and relational skills moves feminist counseling and psychotherapy away from the notion of androgyny as the model for mental health and focuses on the importance of valuing the relational skills of women. To accomplish this balance, the counselor or therapist helps the client to separate traits related to independence and interdependence from traditional perceptions about gender roles and what is considered masculine and feminine.

Empowerment is a major goal of feminist counseling or psychotherapy in that it helps clients see themselves as having control over themselves and the ability to actively advocate for others. Empowerment involves recognition that powerlessness is a learned behavior. Once clients become aware of gender role socialization and how it relates to oppression, it is important for them to develop mechanisms to counteract the effects of socio-political forces that have limited their choices in life.

Self-nurturance is a pivotal goal in feminist counseling or psychotherapy. A lack of self-care causes self-doubt, lack of self-esteem, an inability to develop trust relationships, and difficulty in expressing needs (Enns, 1997). Development of self-nurturance involves becoming more self-aware—aware of personal needs, personal goals, desires, and self-identity. The aim of the counselor or therapist is to help the client to experience the sense of pleasure and mastery that comes with discovering self-value.

Valuing diversity is a recent goal of feminist counseling and psychotherapy designed to create a more inclusive feminist approach. This goal helps the counselor or therapist and client to recognize the many ways that gender intersects with other factors in a multicultural society. Historically, feminism and feminist counseling or psychotherapy responded to the concerns of white women. However, although women of color may experience oppressive "isms" similar to those experienced by their white counterparts, they may also suffer from a lack of power and self-direction due to racism. Feminist counselors or therapists work to become educated about the cultural plurality among the oppressed. "Learning about women of diverse backgrounds is important not only for providing non-biased treatment, but also for enriching our knowledge of women's lives in general" (Enns, 1997, p. 30).

The Process of Change

Empowerment to change is the most essential aspect of feminist counseling or therapy. In order to change, the individual must understand and remove socialized conditioning that restricts decision making based upon societal expectations of what is appropriate for men and women. A process of **resocialization** allows clients to value themselves and realize that their lived experiences are important. What was once considered pathology can be renamed as **coping mechanisms.** The client then begins a process of relearning and practicing new behaviors that promotes egalitarian relationships. An indicator of change is when the client actively advocates for herself or himself and for other oppressed groups while participating in social action groups that promote societal change.

Intervention Strategies

All feminist counseling and psychotherapy interventions seek to empower clients. The goal is to mobilize the client's resources to effect change at the personal, relational, and socio-political levels. Two important empowerment strategies are demystifying counseling or psychotherapy and self-disclosure.

Feminist counselors and therapists strive to create an egalitarian relationship with their clients so that the inequities found in society are not replicated in the counseling or psychotherapy relationship. For example, if the counselor or therapist calls the client by his or her first name, the counselor or therapist introduces herself using her first name. A strategy for empowering clients is to **demystify** the counseling and psychotherapy process at the outset of the relationship by paying careful attention to informed consent issues. It is important that clients participate in identifying and naming their problems; understand and agree to goals and procedures; realize that they are in charge of the direction, length, and choices of techniques to be implemented; and know their rights as consumers of counseling and psychotherapy services. Feminist counselors and therapists provide their clients with information about their theoretical orientation, competencies, and alternatives to counseling and psychotherapy so that the clients can make fully informed choices (Enns, 1997).

Feminist counselors or therapists engage in **self-disclosure** and state their values explicitly to emphasize the commonalities among women and decrease the client's sense of isolation. Brief and timely self-disclosures about the counselor's or therapist's own struggles with issues serve the purposes of modeling coping responses to difficult issues and equalizing the therapeutic relationship. Feminist counselors and therapists share with counselors and therapists of other theoretical orientations the commitment to ensuring that self-disclosures are in the client's best interests and are relevant to the client's needs.

Gender-role analysis is an intervention strategy used to help clients learn about the impact of culturally prescribed gender-role expectations on women and how their lives are affected by them (Israeli & Santor, 2000). In a collaborative effort, the counselor or therapist and client examine the client's values and how these values are reflected in the client's role expectations for herself and others. They identify the explicit and implicit sex-role messages the client has experienced and internalized. They then decide which of these messages the client wishes to change.

According to Brown (1986), this analysis should include exploration of (1) gender meanings in light of family values, the client's life stage, cultural background, and present conditions of living; (2) past and present rewards and penalties for gender role conformity or noncompliance; (3) how the counselor- or therapist-client relationship mirrors these issues or provides insight into them; and (4) the client's history relative to victimization. During this process, clients learn that their methods of coping have been adaptive for living in an oppressive society rather than symptoms of pathology. They develop an empathic rather than self-blaming attitude toward themselves. Thus, gender-role analysis serves to help clients gain self-knowledge, increase their awareness of the socio-cultural basis for distress, and identify areas for desired change. Following the analysis, a plan for implementing changes is developed, which may draw on cognitive-behavioral or other strategies as appropriate to the client's needs.

Power analysis is an assessment and intervention strategy that aims to help women understand their devalued status in society and to help clients of both sexes become aware of the power difference between men and women. The counselor or therapist may begin by educating the client about various kinds of power and women's limited access to most kinds of power. Women are often uncomfortable with the term *power* because of their limited experience or exposure to only aggressive aspects of it. The counselor or therapist may help the client understand the differences among *power over* (which implies dominance or oppression), *power within* (which involves feeling that one has inner strength), and *power to* (which refers to goal-directed behavior that respects the rights of all involved) (Gannon, 1982). The client can then offer her own definition of power and consider how it fits for her and her way of being in the world. Together, the counselor or therapist and client identify the client's usual means of exerting her power and the effectiveness of those means. Next, they identify ways in which the client's internalized gender-role messages impact her use of power, which synthesizes gender-role and power issues for the client (Remer, Rostosky, & Wright, 2001). Finally, the client is encouraged to increase her repertoire of **power strategies** by experimenting in areas of her life where lack of power previously prevented change. Power analysis empowers clients to challenge and change the oppressive environments in which they live (Worell & Remer, 1996).

Over the last 10 to 15 years, feminist counselors and therapists have developed a more complex, **integrated analysis of oppression** that recognizes that "gender cannot be separated from other ways in which a culture stratifies human difference, privileging some at the expense of others" (Hill & Ballou, 1998, p. 3). In an integrated analysis, procedures utilized in gender analysis and power analysis are expanded to consider the impact of other variables such as race or ethnicity, class, sexual orientation, age, size, and religion. Because diversity is a central concern of the feminist approach, a multicultural, multidimensional analysis considers variables in addition to gender in examining personal, group, and institutional oppression in clients' lives.

Reframing and relabeling are intervention strategies frequently used in feminist counseling and psychotherapy. To *reframe* is to change the frame of reference for looking at an individual's behavior. When feminist counselors or therapists reframe a client's behavior, they consider the sociopolitical and cultural contributions to the client's issues, which shifts the etiology of the problem from the individual to the environment. This change in perspective avoids "blaming the victim" for her problems. Negative labeling, such as defining a behavior as "dysfunctional," is relabeled as a "positive coping strategy." "Feminine" characteristics such as sensitivity, compassion, or subjectivity, which may be devalued as weaknesses when viewed through an androcentric lens, are revalued as strengths through the feminist lens. Thus, through reframing and relabeling, symptoms can be seen as coping mechanisms and weaknesses can be seen as strengths.

Bibliotherapy, although not unique to feminist counseling or psychotherapy, is another strategy that feminists often find useful. Bibliotherapy involves reading and processing books or articles, carefully chosen by the counselor or therapist, to help the client understand societal influences that impact her personal experiencing (Remer, Rostosky, & Wright, 2001). This literature may address issues such as women's body image and appearance, sexual violence, relationships, and aspects of the lifespan. For example, a client concerned about her relationship with a significant other might be asked to read Lerner's *The Dance of Intimacy* (1989). Such reading assignments serve to empower the client by increasing the client's expertise on topics of concern to her.

Another intervention strategy that has been associated with feminist counseling and psychotherapy is **assertiveness training.** Because some women do not feel powerful, they may not act assertively and thus give up some control over their lives (Sharf, 2000). Feminist counselors and therapists teach these clients assertiveness skills using direct teaching methods, bibliotherapy, and role-play. Through assertiveness training, women learn to stand up for their rights without violating the rights of others. The aim of this training is to facilitate women's use of personal power to achieve personal change and effectively challenge their environments (Remer, Rostosky, & Wright, 2001).

Although much feminist counseling or psychotherapy is conducted with individual clients, **group work** is often a preferred modality for some issues that women experience in our culture (Herlihy & Corey, 2001). For example, group approaches have been recommended for dealing with incest and sexual abuse, body image issues, battering, eating disorders, and sexual functioning (Enns, 1997). Feminist counselors and therapists may also encourage clients to participate in consciousness-raising groups to increase their awareness of sexism and other forms of oppression. Consciousness-raising groups offer women a supportive environment in which they can share personal experiences with gender-role stereotyping and expectations, experience the commonalities among women, and see more clearly the link between their own experiences and the sociopolitical structure (Remer, Rostosky, & Wright, 2001). Other types of groups, such as advocacy groups or political action groups, may also be recommended to empower women and allow them to experience their connectedness with other women.

Clients with Mental Disorders

Feminist counselors and therapists are concerned about problems inherent in the prevailing DSM medical model diagnostic system. Phyllis Chesler, in *Women and Madness* (1972), articulated the view that the DSM approach pathologizes any difference from the standards established by the dominant group in society. Since the publication of this groundbreaking work, feminists have argued that it is important to assess not just symptoms and behaviors, but also the context of women's lives (Brown, 1994; Santos de Barona & Dutton, 1997). Within this broader context, many symptoms can be understood as coping strategies rather than as evidence of pathology (Worell & Remer, 1996). Thus, feminist counselors and therapists use a broad, bio-psycho-socio-cultural-structural model of assessment and diagnosis (Ballou & West, 2000). Using this broader approach to assessment, feminist counselors and therapists have obligations to familiarize themselves with the literature on gender and its relationship to clinical judgments of mental health and to examine their own gender biases and expectations. They actively inquire into the meaning of gender for the client, assess the rewards and penalties of gender-role compliance or noncompliance for the client, attend to the client's responses to the counselor's or therapist's gender and their own responses to the client's gender, and check their diagnoses to guard against inappropriately imposing gender-stereotyped values of mental health. Arriving at a diagnosis is a shared process in which clients are the experts on their distress and its social meaning. Clients' understanding of the meaning of their behaviors is considered equally with the counselor's or therapist's interpretations. Some of the types of distress commonly experienced by women are discussed in the remainder of this section.

According to the DSM-IV, women are twice as likely as men to suffer from **depression.** From a feminist perspective, women have twice as many reasons as men to experience depression. Women, taught to be helpless and dependent and to please others, may feel that they are not in control of their lives or their environments. Their subordinate position—along with their experiences of domestic violence, sexual or physical abuse, poverty, or harassment or sex discrimination in the work place—can result in a sense of powerlessness that can manifest as symptoms of depression. Feminist counselors and therapists view women's depression as revealing the "vulnerabilities of a relational sense of self within a culture that dangerously strains a woman's ability to meet basic needs for interpersonal relatedness while maintaining a strong sense of self" (Jack, 1987, p. 44). They work to help clients reframe their understanding of the causes of their depression so that they can move away from blaming themselves for the problem and from believing that they must "adjust" to their circumstances. They help clients become aware of external forces that limit their freedom so clients can release self-blame and focus their energies on circumstances they can influence (Enns, 1997).

As a result of conflicting societal messages and multiple pressures and demands, women may experience symptoms of **anxiety** disorders. Ballou and West (2000) relate the example of Beth, a working-class, single mother who presented with "fear, worry, and the experience of racing and jumpy energy, all symptoms of an anxiety disorder" (p. 279). Beth was struggling to juggle at least three responsibilities: parenting young children, maintaining a home, and working at a job she did not enjoy, all within a cultural context that isolated her and devalued her status. A feminist counselor or therapist, rather than recommending an antianxiety medication, might work with Beth to help her develop concrete ways of challenging her gender-role expectations, establish a self-nurturing program, join a support group for women who are experiencing role strain, develop relaxation skills, and identify and mobilize resources that are available to help her meet ongoing responsibilities and demands.

One specific anxiety disorder that has received considerable attention in the feminist literature is **post-traumatic stress disorder** (PTSD). Feminist counselors and therapists have identified rape trauma syndrome and battered woman syndrome as women's typical responses to traumatic environmental events. They connect the personal to the political by stressing that violence influences the psychological self, and that the symptoms are normal responses to abnormal events. They have proposed new diagnostic categories, such as "complex post-traumatic stress disorder" (Herman, 1992) and "abuse and oppression artifact disorders" (Brown, 1994), to describe reactions to a history of subjugation over a period of time. A feminist counselor or therapist, in working with clients who present with symptoms of PTSD, addresses the connection between abuse and sexism and behavior patterns of learned helplessness, avoidance, and rescuing. The counselor or therapist listens respectfully to the client and does not minimize the extent to which the client has been wounded (Chesler, 1990). In the therapeutic relationship, the counselor or therapist and client explore the ways in which emotions and **cognitions** have become constricted or distorted by fear or gender stereotyping, self-blame, or shame. The process involves naming the distress accurately, identifying the complex **contextual factors** that contribute to the client's problems, and transforming possibilities for oppression into opportunities for liberation and social change.

A feminist approach to working with clients with **eating disorders** focuses on messages conveyed by society—and by the mass media in particular—about women's bodies and androcentric standards for attractiveness. Feminist counselors or therapists use gender-role analysis to help clients examine the messages about body image that are found in magazines, advertisements, movies, and television. They help clients challenge the stereotyped ideal of a woman with large breasts and pencil-thin thighs that is held up as the standard toward which they should strive. Power analysis may help women understand how they relinquish their personal power when they diet and dress to please men, as well as how their preoccupation with weight, size, and shape contributes to a lack of power (Sharf, 2000). Group work can be effective with women who suffer from anorexia, bulimia, and other eating disorders because it provides a supportive environment for examining, challenging, and reframing body image.

Feminists have drawn attention to the high rate of sexual and physical abuse in the histories of women who have been diagnosed as having **borderline personality disorder** (BPD) (Brown & Ballou, 1992). In the traditional diagnostic system, the link between these traumatic experiences and the symptoms that lead to a diagnosis of BPD is ignored and the problem is placed within the individual. Viewed from a feminist framework, BPD is seen as a long-term chronic effect of post-traumatic stress. Feminist counselors and therapists, rather than focus on a client's problematic behaviors, frame the symptoms as indicators of the client's strength as a survivor. The counseling or psychotherapy process involves strategies such as establishing a contract that defines expectations for both counselor or therapist and client and sets limits in non-punitive ways. Careful consideration is given to the client's level of readiness to explore past abuse, to help the client strengthen her fragile sense of control over her inner and external worlds. Symptoms such as dissociation and mood swings are reframed as ways of coping. The counselor or therapist helps the client understand the needs beneath behaviors that seem impulsive and self-defeating, so that the client can find new ways to meet these needs. Feminist counselors and therapists continue to propose new conceptualizations of reactions to abuse with the goal of changing the way the mental health professions deal with disorders that affect so many women (Enns, 1997).

Evaluation

Overview

The feminist approach to counseling and psychotherapy has not been researched extensively. However, studies that have been conducted generally show positive results. Additional quantitative and qualitative research is needed to clearly establish the effectiveness of feminist counseling and psychotherapy.

Feminist counseling and psychotherapy has not been defined as clearly as some of the more traditional approaches. It is difficult to find adequate training programs. Mistaken perceptions continue to exist that feminist counseling and psychotherapy is conducted only by women and for women.

Supporting Research

The theory and practice of feminist counseling and psychotherapy have grown rapidly, outpacing their empirical support (Remer, Rostosky, & Wright, 2001; Worell & Johnson, 2001). Therefore, validating the effectiveness of the feminist approach remains an ongoing challenge. Studies that have been conducted, however, generally show encouraging results.

In comparison studies, feminist counseling and psychotherapy has been found to be as effective as other, more traditional forms of counseling and psychotherapy (Follingstad, Robinson, & Pugh, 1977; Johnson, 1976). Recently, controlled outcome studies have assessed whether feminist counseling and psychotherapy is effective in meeting the goals it espouses. Cummings (in press) found that both brief (less than four sessions) and extended (more than seven sessions) feminist counseling or psychotherapy positively impacted clients' sense of personal empowerment. In a long-term follow-up study of feminist counseling or psychotherapy outcomes, client self-ratings of improvement over time were assessed; results indicated that clients' resilience increased over time (Chandler, Worell, Johnson, Blount, & Lusk, 1999).

Israeli and Santor (2000) evaluated existing research on several components of feminist counseling or psychotherapy practice. They concluded that consciousness-raising appeared to be the most studied feminist counseling or psychotherapy intervention and that the research literature suggests consciousness-raising provides therapeutic benefit by allowing women to feel supported. Israeli and Santor recommended that future studies focus on evaluating the efficacy of other interventions and tenets of feminist counseling or psychotherapy, such as gender-role analysis and social activism.

Further research is needed to assess the effectiveness of feminist counseling and psychotherapy using not just traditional empirical methods, but also qualitative techniques which are more synchronous with feminist principles. A major challenge for the future of feminist counseling or psychotherapy is to validate the efficacy of its applied practices with research that demonstrates client or social change (Worell & Johnson, 2001).

Limitations

One limitation of feminist counseling and psychotherapy is that it is not as clearly defined as some of the more traditional theories. It has been argued that feminist counseling or psychotherapy is not so much a theory as it is a philosophy or belief system about the importance of gender (Rampage, 1998), and that it is better defined as politics than as counseling or psychotherapy. Because feminist counseling and psychotherapy practitioners are diverse, reaching consensus on its scope and definition will be a challenging task.

It is difficult to obtain adequate training in feminist counseling and psychotherapy. There are few feminist counseling or psychotherapy training programs per se, although many counselor education programs have faculty members who contribute feminist principles and practices to the training of prospective counselors and therapists (Rave & Larsen, 1995). There is no official credentialing of feminist counselors and therapists.

The erroneous perception continues to exist that feminist counseling or psychotherapy is conducted only by women and for women. This may discourage male clients from seeking counseling and psychotherapy services from counselors and therapists who identify themselves as feminist practitioners. The historical association of feminism with some of the more radical elements of the women's movement may discourage some prospective clients, both female and male, from entering into counseling or psychotherapy relationships with feminist counselors and therapists.

Important to the future of feminist counseling and psychotherapy will be the ability of its theorists, scholars, and practitioners to more clearly articulate its definition, make training more widely available, correct mistaken perceptions, and demonstrate its effectiveness through research.

Summary Chart—Feminist Theories

Human Nature
Gender role expectations have a profound impact on human development. Because women and men are socialized differently, models of psychological development based on male development fail to recognize that women's identity develops in a context of connectedness and in relationship with others.

Major Constructs
The five major tenets of feminist counseling and therapy are (1) the personal is political, (2) commitment to social change, (3) egalitarian relationships, (4) women's experiences and voices are honored, and (5) all types of oppression are recognized.

Goals
Based on the work of Enns (1997), major goals of feminist counseling or psychotherapy are change, equality, balancing independence and interdependence, empowerment, self-nurturance, and valuing diversity.

Change Process
External forces are recognized as the root of problems for women. Clients learn self-appreciation and self-value. Women rename pathology as coping mechanisms. They learn to change their environments rather than adjust to them. They learn to advocate for social change, and to develop egalitarian rather than hierarchical relationships.

Interventions
Although feminist counselors and therapists adapt interventions from a wide range of theoretical orientations, several strategies that have been developed specifically for feminist counseling and psychotherapy are empowerment, gender-role analysis, power analysis, and integrated analysis of oppression. Other frequently used interventions are reframing and relabeling, bibliotherapy, assertiveness training, and group work.

Limitations
Feminist counseling or psychotherapy is often incorrectly perceived as being for women only. It is not as well grounded in research as some of the more traditional theories. It is difficult to find adequate training in feminist counseling and psychotherapy.

The Case of Jonathan: A Feminist Approach

Jonathan's presenting issues include poor relationships with his co-workers and his supervisor, anger management issues, depression, sleep deprivation, loneliness, stressors related to separation from his family, financial hardship, abuse of alcohol, alienation from his cultural support system, and feelings of oppression and discrimination. Jonathan appears to be subscribing to a traditional male role.

A feminist counselor or therapist will describe to Jonathan the goals of feminist counseling or psychotherapy and her personal philosophy concerning client empowerment and the need for an egalitarian client-counselor or therapist relationship. The counselor or therapist will help Jonathan see that he has been socialized to believe things about being a man that may not be congruent with his needs or his cultural values.

During counseling or psychotherapy, Jonathan will be allowed to articulate, in his own words, the anger and frustration he experiences due to his poor work-place relationships. Expression of this anger may be cathartic when in a controlled environment. Additionally, his anger may be representative of his overall lack of self-appreciation and powerlessness. Jonathan exhibits symptoms of poor self-esteem and a sense of powerlessness in trying to prove himself as a valued employee to his supervisor and a good husband and father. The counselor or therapist may use a power analysis with Jonathan so that he can see the power differential between majority members of society and minority groups. The counselor or therapist will guide Jonathan through some empowerment exercises based upon the reality therapy approach so that he can understand the difference between what is in his personal control and what is not. She will ask Jonathan such questions as, "What in yourself or your environment can you control or change?" After some probing by the counselor or therapist, Jonathan might say he has control over his drinking, how he sees himself, and his sleep environment.

For the drinking issue, the counselor or therapist may recommend a 12-step program and give Jonathan verbal and written information on such programs. To improve self-esteem, Jonathan can make a list of his positive attributes and positive things that other people have said about him. The counselor or therapist will encourage the client to concentrate on these positive attributes by making verbal affirmations.

A cognitive approach can be used to help Jonathan make some personal changes and changes in his environment. Jonathan might be instructed to name one thing that he would like to change about himself or his environment. The counselor or therapist and Jonathan consider the change together to ensure that what Jonathan wants to change is in his control and that the result would be evident in a relatively short time. This will show Jonathan that he can effect change, and that some things can be changed immediately. Small, immediate changes will encourage Jonathan and keep him from doubting himself.

To improve sleep, the counselor or therapist can remind the client of the benefit of sleep in developing **holistic wellness.** Suggestions might include (1) reserving the bed for sleep only, not for watching television or working; (2) entering the bedroom only to go to bed; (3) developing bedtime rituals; (4) abstaining from napping; and (5) reserving sleep for the bed only. **Dream analysis** is also an appropriate technique to help Jonathan understand what his dreams mean and how they affect his interactions with people in his work environment.

Group support can help Jonathan deal with many of his issues, including lack of job opportunities, loneliness, alienation, societal pressures, and family issues. Jonathan has problems in his important relationships. A **homogenous group** composed of Native American men would be ideal to help Jonathan reconnect with his cultural group and gain support from their shared experiences.

Jonathan feels incapable of fulfilling commitments to marriage and to his work. It seems to be easier for him to leave than to try to change his behavior or the behavior of others. Feminist family counseling or psychotherapy with Jonathan and his wife can help them both deal with family roles, child-rearing practices, and visitation issues. This will help Jonathan deal with his guilt concerning his responsibility as a father.

Individual career and financial counseling or psychotherapy may also be helpful for Jonathan as well as contact with Jonathan's tribal council, Bureau of Indian Affairs, or other advocacy group for Native Americans. Contact with advocacy groups can help Jonathan with job seeking, finances, and feelings that external pressures are responsible for his plight. This reconnection with his tribe and cultural group will also help to improve his relationship with his family and other reservation Native Americans. This may help him reconcile his departure from the reservation.

The counselor or therapist may suggest to Jonathan that he get involved with community groups that advocate for Native Americans and other oppressed groups so that he can make a greater impact on society-at-large. His involvement can have a dual benefit, as it can increase his self-worth as well as engage him in making societal changes. Perhaps Jonathan's efforts can help with the issue of unemployment among Native Americans living on the reservation.

The most important thing to consider about feminist counseling and psychotherapy with Jonathan is the need for an egalitarian counseling or psychotherapy relationship. Jonathan must feel that he has some important contributions to make to the counseling or psychotherapy sessions. The counselor or therapist considers Jonathan's culturally reinforced behavior and helps him to reconnect with his cultural group. Jonathan's self-worth will improve when he understands that his behavior is not a symptom of pathology, but in fact may be a part of the solution to some of his problems. Jonathan's successes in understanding and reframing his anger will assist him with relationship building and be helpful to him in maintaining employment. Generally, Jonathan is aware that there are sociopolitical issues that cause roadblocks to a better life for him and his family. By better understanding what these sociopolitical issues are, Jonathan will be empowered to change his behavior and encouraged to help make broader societal changes that can benefit Native Americans and other oppressed groups.

Eastern and Nontraditional Approaches

A textbook focused on the topic of counseling and psychotherapy would not be complete without the perspectives contained in Part III. Because all of the theoretical positions presented in Part II of this text have a foundation in Western culture, we believe it is important for our readers to be exposed to counseling and psychotherapeutic orientations stemming from Eastern philosophy and religion. It is our hope that such exposure will broaden the reader's perspective by presenting diverse viewpoints regarding human nature, theoretical constructs, and their application based upon a philosophical and religious perspective too often missing from current educational programs in counseling and psychotherapy. Chapter 15, "Eastern Theories," provides this type of exposure together with an overview of Eastern theories and their application to individual counseling and psychotherapy. Chapter 16, "Body-Centered Counseling and Psychotherapy," offers the reader a comprehensive view of selected somatic and six related body-centered modalities and psychotherapy methods and highlights Hakomi Body-Centered Psychotherapy developed by Ron Kurtz. In the chapters that follow, the reader is exposed to a multitude of non-Western ideas and modalities that we hope will provide the practitioner and student alternatives to helping the culturally different client.

Eastern Theories

Catherine Buffalino Roland
University of Arkansas

Larry D. Burlew
University of Bridgeport

Background

A recognition is growing within the discipline of Western mental health counseling and psychotherapy that counselors or therapists and counselors-in-training must consider theoretical approaches from diverse cultures and areas of the world. Understanding how different cultural groups comprehend and value life, as well as their worldviews, facilitates the practice of counseling and psychotherapy within our society. The vast differences between clients and client groups availing themselves of mental health services today require that counselors and therapists cultivate a broadened understanding and acceptance of cross-cultural philosophical and psychological beliefs so that they may offer the best service to clients. Knowledge of Eastern thought concerning mental health counseling and psychotherapy practices for the traditional Western-culture counselor or therapist expands traditional Eurocentric worldviews of counseling and psychotherapy. This chapter explores the basic philosophies of Eastern psychological thought and mental health practice, with a focus on **Morita therapy** as a specific approach, and on the integration of meditation and meditative interventions from the Eastern, or Buddhist, perspective.

Eastern Psychological Thought

When we speak of Eastern therapies, we are referring to the three major cultural/religious traditions of Asia, India, China, and Japan, which focus mainly on the transpersonal and existential beliefs that are grounded in the philosophy of the East. Traditionally, Westerners have perceived a lack of analysis in contemporary Eastern psychotherapies regarding pathology (Murphy & Murphy, 1968). Westerners perceive the Eastern focus on mental health to be strictly religious or philosophical in nature, concentrating mainly on states of consciousness and stages of enlightenment that could not be practiced by unenlightened people.

The three Eastern systems of thought have their roots in religion. They approach the psychological tradition through the definition of various ethical and religious practices that embrace as goals the understanding of the mind as well as the liberation of the mind from negativity, misery, and delusion (Murphy & Murphy, 1968; Walsh, 1995). To acquire a working knowledge of Eastern mental health core values, one must delve into Eastern psychological thought as it relates to practice.

Therefore, it is impossible to discuss Eastern mental health practice and core values without looking toward Eastern religious and philosophical thought. The ancient and traditional philosophy of the East is fused with the basic principles of Eastern mental health practices. A basic concept of all Eastern ideas about psychological health is a focus on calm and contemplation in everyday life, and acceptance of life as it is.

Meditation and yoga are the two traditional approaches one typically finds mentioned when researching the Asian quest for ideal psychological health, comprised of advanced enlightenment or liberation (Walsh, 1995). Although it is sometimes argued that meditation and yoga are not pure forms of psychological counseling and therapy because of their individual nature, the broad definitions of meditation as a means to cultivate awareness, concentration, love, and compassion, and of yoga as having similar goals (with the addition of ethical and intellectual capacities) indicate that both meditation and yoga are the mainstays or underpinnings of Asian therapies. Practiced for several thousands of years, and by tens of millions of people, meditation and yoga remain an integral part of almost all of the Eastern therapies utilized today (Bankart, 1997; Kutz, Borysenko, & Benson, 1985; Walsh, 1995; West, 1987).

Eastern philosophy has influenced Eastern psychological therapies through such concepts as high regard for ethical thought and conduct, unselfishness and generosity to self and others, and an understanding of personal well-being. Within the Eastern tradition, **individual will** is often thought of as selfish, immature, and out of sync with the societal and familial loyalties and goals inherent in Eastern culture (De Vos, 1980). A close and necessary relationship exists between body and mind in Eastern thought. Japanese philosopher Eriken Kaibara (1630–1714) recognized and wrote of the traditional *Ki* concept, which represents psychological energy or mental force. For mental energy or *Ki* to be fluid and consistent, the individual must rid himself or herself of things harmful to the body, such as desires and unhealthy conditions (e.g., consuming desire for food, sex, or sleep, and feelings of sorrow, joy, anger, or anxiety). Deep anger may induce the *Ki* to go too high, and extreme or excess pleasure may induce it to lose strength (Murphy & Murphy, 1968). Several Eastern therapies utilize this concept in the acceptance of life as it is and support the practice of deep contemplation coupled with cleansing.

Eastern Mental Health Practice

Eastern mental health practice has as a broad goal the transformation of attitude concerning self. As observed in the meditative and yogic training, shifts in lifestyle, mirrored by changes of the mind, body awareness, relationships, and self-awareness, require commitment (Walsh, 1995). Just as the counselor or therapist is committed to the best ethical practice for the good of the client, so are clients committed to an ethical, honest assessment of their lives and to an openness to the avenues that might be taken to reach a self-fulfilled, calm state.

Therapeutically, the first shift is a basic tenet of ethical behavior (i.e., not engaging in lying, stealing, sexual misconduct, murder, or ingesting mind-altering drugs) (Walsh, 1995). The quest for **purification** is a vital step in the Eastern model of the mental health journey. Through the preliminary skill development of concentration and cultivation of calm, the mind-body focus goes on to incorporate **agape** (unconditional love) for the purpose of self-awareness and the therapeutic processes of introspection and evaluation.

Within the Asian tradition, positive mental health is most characterized by a mind that is peaceful. From that peace can subsequently flow the tranquility and empathy of the continuum of human suffering and joy (Walsh, 1995). The controlled, homeostatic state of the mind, devoid of anger, is essential to the Eastern therapies and to Eastern philosophical thought. Contemplation and quiet isolation allow the individual's positive nature to emerge toward enlightenment and tranquility. Once this occurs, individuals can participate in the fullness and positiveness of the natural being of self as connected to all others, unselfishly and securely.

De Vos (1980) presented the Buddhist perspective concerning counseling and therapy as including an emphasis on the sense of connectedness and obligation to family, self-discipline, and an inherent need to express gratitude. Eastern philosophical thought relative to mental health encourages strength of mind and body, a positive outlook that does not dwell upon personal sorrow, and a self-efficacious belief that the "illness" can be controlled through allowing natural and flowing pain and joy to permeate the mind. As De Vos writes, "In Buddhism the self is an illusion, and the sense of separateness so painfully a part of becoming human is transitory, in that it will not persist through all eternity. . . . One's ultimate duty, as well as one's ultimate psychological security, is to be found in family or group continuity, not in the continuity of the self" (p. 121).

In this chapter, we will discuss two major therapeutic models from the Eastern tradition. The first is Morita therapy, and the second is the Zen Buddhist approach to counseling and psychotherapy, emphasizing meditation as a therapeutic underpinning and intervention.

An Introduction to Morita Therapy

Morita therapy, a Japanese example of an Eastern approach to counseling and psychotherapy, has gained recognition in North America, Europe, and Asia. **David Reynolds** studied Morita therapy intensively and has been its principal proponent in the United States. He immersed himself in the therapy, actually going through the traditional "bed rest" version as a client. From his experiences and studies, he developed his own adaptation of Morita therapy in a book titled *Constructive Living* (1984a). As many as 80 certified Constructive Living instructors have been trained and are using the principles here and in other countries (Hedstrom, 1994). However, other practitioners (e.g., Bankart, 1997; Fujita, 1986; Ishiyama, 1990; Walsh, 1995) have also described and promulgated the concepts and practice of Morita therapy.

Readers may eventually use Morita concepts with Western clients, but we remind you that Morita therapy is not a Eurocentric approach to counseling and psychotherapy. It was developed to address the needs and cultural beliefs of the Japanese people. Therefore, we urge readers not to make comparisons between this Eastern approach to counseling and psychotherapy and Western approaches such as existential, person-centered, or cognitive-behavioral theories. By not comparing, your study of Morita therapy begins with *arugamama* (i.e., accepting reality as it is) (Iwai & Reynolds, 1970; Kitanishi & Mori, 1995), the foundation of this approach. For our purpose, experiencing *arugamama* as you read means that Morita is a reality in and of itself; it stands alone and can be accepted, studied, and incorporated into your counseling and psychotherapy approach if it feels right. Figure 15.1 lists terms frequently used in Morita therapy and their definitions.

History of Morita Therapy

Shoma Morita (1874–1938) was trained as a psychiatrist and taught at the Jikei University School of Medicine in Tokyo. He initially called his approach **experiential therapy**, **natural therapy**, or **awakening therapy** (Kitanishi & Mori, 1995). Only later did it become known as Morita therapy. He first wrote about this approach in 1917 for treating a condition he called *shinkeishitsu,* a form of anxiety and obsession disorder. However, he worked since the early 1900s (i.e., for at least 15 years) trying to find an effective treatment for "clients with a nervous predisposition" (Ishiyama, 1990, p. 566).

Morita's initial knowledge about *shinkeishitsu* stemmed from his own experience with this condition. Fujita (1986) labeled "understanding" as the critical factor in the client-counselor or therapist relationship and claimed that "understanding comes from the counselor's or therapist's personal experience of suffering from *shinkeishitsu*" (p. 224). Despite his training, Morita's experiential counseling or therapy clearly deviated from traditional psychoanalysis. He initially tried three therapeutic interventions—Weir Mitchess's "rest therapy," Otto Binswanger's method of "life normalization," and Dubois' "persuasion method"—without much success (Kitanishi & Mori, 1995, p. 245). However, Mitchess's and Binswanger's approaches are particularly evident in Morita therapy. Using these approaches convinced Morita to disregard the psychoanalytic tradition of examining childhood etiologies for neurotic symptoms. Morita counselors or therapists are not concerned with the cause of neurotic symptoms, but rather focus only on the present moment, accepting reality as it is, whether good or bad, and working in spite of one's neurotic symptoms (Ishiyama, 1990; Kora & Ohara, 1973; Reynolds, 1981a).

Interestingly, Morita first counseled clients in his own home with his family present. His family, particularly his wife, was crucial to the therapeutic process as assistant counselor or therapist (Kitanishi & Mori, 1995). In Japan, the family is sacrosanct and a "haven of security and protection in times of trouble" (Reynolds & Kiefer, 1977, p. 398), so counseling psychotherapy clients within the day-to-day life of a real family made sense. Additionally, because the major symptom of *shinkeishitsu* is selfish preoccupation (i.e., *toraware*), these clients avoid their intuitive social obligations (i.e., *on*) to family and society (Bankart, 1997; Ishiyama, 1990; Reynolds, 1980, 1981a; Walsh, 1995). Rather than talk about *on* with clients and have them respond respectfully within their families, the *on* was stimulated experientially by incorporating clients into the life of Morita's own family. The in-home counseling or therapy began with complete bed rest and minimal contact with the family; eventually the client would assume work responsibilities within the family. Although it is no longer practiced, this in-home method was a rare form of experiential counseling and psychotherapy whereby clients learned about *on* and *work* phenomenologically.

Agape	unconditional love
Amae	passive or unconditional love
Arugamama	accepting reality as it is
Bodhi	term meaning wisdom that is a way of being or experiencing
Eightfold Path	factors that are embedded in the Buddhist spiritual training or code of conduct for living each day; lie within the path to enlightenment
First Noble Truth	posits that suffering or dissatisfaction is inherent in life
Fourth Noble Truth	posits that by leading a life filled with compassion, virtue, wisdom, and meditation, liberation is possible
Fumon	an attitude of completely cutting off the counselor or therapist as a listener to the client's complaints
Giri	the assurance of belonging to a group
Homophobia	undue or irrational anxiety, fear, and discomfort in or in the prospect of interaction with other human beings
Honne	the stream of personal thoughts and feelings that make up the private, inner world of the individual
Ittaikan	the family as a unit, merging with each other
Ki	represents psychological energy or mental force
Ki-kubari	attentiveness
Klesha	affliction, misconception of thought, or contamination by the passions
Kowa	an educational, philosophical lecture used in Morita therapy
Ma	when the counselor or therapist cuts off discussion of the client's problems by "pausing" the therapy; this puts a proper distance between counselor or therapist and client
Meditative moment	a moment of silence whereby the counselor or therapist and client sit quietly after a statement or word is spoken that may have caused pain or disturbance for the client
Miuichi	being a member of the inner circle
On	social obligations to family and society
Onozu-kara-naru	natural or spontaneous
Second Noble Truth	posits that we go through life with a desire or craving for satisfaction to a degree that is impossible to obtain
Sei no chikara	the strength of life
Sei no yokubo	the desire to live
Shinkeishitsu	a form of anxiety or obsession disorder
Tanin	recognized outsiders to the family
Tatemae	the social part of the self that emphasizes role performance and dependence on others
Third Noble Truth	suggests that suffering can be diminished or even eradicated, enabling *on* to reach a sense of liberation
Toraware	selfish preoccupation
Un	fate
Wa	harmony of the whole
Work	an assertion to be active, to pay attention to the outside

Figure 15.1
Eastern Theories Terms and Definitions

Morita's original method of in-home counseling and psychotherapy with his family present would shock the mental health profession should a practitioner attempt it today—in fact, the practice would likely be reported as an ethical violation, particularly regarding dual relationships and boundary issues. Eventually, Morita therapy moved from the counselor's or therapist's home to inpatient work in a hospital or clinic, with absolute bed rest still required. The clinic's task, however, is to create a family-like environment, as much as that can occur with staff and other patients. A clinic does provide a social setting for the therapeutic process, and this setting is a critical phenomenological requirement for tapping into Japanese character (Kitanishi & Mori, 1995; Reynolds & Kiefer, 1977).

The traditional method of absolute bed rest is not much in practice today, and Reynolds reported "only about a dozen hospitals still practicing it in the mid-1980s" (cited in Hedstrom, 1994, p. 154). More frequently, Morita therapy occurs on an outpatient basis, in group counseling and psychotherapy and group meetings as well. Additionally, innovative forms of the approach are in practice, including correspondence counseling or therapy, cassette tapes, and bibliotherapy (i.e., monthly magazines) (Hedstrom, 1994; Reynolds, 1981a).

Because Morita therapy is considered a philosophy of life, its principles are used for public education. A self-help organization called *Seikatsu no Hakkenkai* (The Discovery of Life Organization) has about 5,000 members, many of them former clients, who meet and support living life according to Morita principles (Hedstrom, 1994; Reynolds, 1981b). Krech (1989) also uses Morita principles in consulting with organizations and businesses. He teaches the principles to individual employees, helps work groups operate as teams, and conducts workshops on conflict resolution. Morita principles extend beyond the traditional client-counselor or therapist setting because "Morita therapy is a system of therapeutic instruction through which the [client] is taught a *lifeway* which focuses on living fully in each moment" (Reynolds, 1981b, p. 201).

Human Nature: A Developmental Perspective

Morita therapy was developed to address a particular type of neurosis, *shinkeishitsu*. Understanding the nature of the Japanese character may help the reader understand what contributes to the occurrence of *shinkeishitsu* in a Japanese individual. Keep in mind, however, that a Morita counselor or therapist would not be concerned with causes. Neither etiology nor causes are explored with clients, because such introspection would only cause clients to turn further inward and obsess more on themselves rather than focus on the outer world and what needs to be done (Reynolds, 1981a, 1984a, 1989). However, knowing the nature of the Japanese character that is admired, respected, and desired may help you appreciate the *shinkeishitsu* client's "urgent" desire to be cured. One must also understand the nature of *shinkeishitsu* as an entity in and of itself within the Japanese character. Aldous (1994) described *shinkeishitsu* clients as "nervous, anxious, hypochondriacal, behaviorally avoidant and procrastinating" (p. 239). If they cope by avoiding, then they cannot be facing reality *arugamama*. As long as they remain in a cycle of ideal, avoidance, and obsessing on self (i.e., *toraware*), they can never truly contribute to the good of all. They do not fulfill their *on* because their *toraware* controls their behavior. These clients seem unusually sensitive to the fact that their drives are not constructive and not contributing to society. Therefore, they are unusually anxious to be cured (Reynolds, 1976).

We have chosen three constructs of family and *amae,* collectivism, and naturalism that we believe contribute to the healthy development of the respected Japanese character. However, our review is a generalization culled from the literature and viewed through the experience and perceptions of Westerners. We have, therefore, excluded many constructs due to lack of space and of greater familiarity. Additionally, differences also exist within the Japanese culture of which we are most likely not even aware. To completely describe the Japanese character, these differences would also need to be considered, but this is not our goal. Rather, the three concepts included should help you better understand the nature of *shinkeishitsu* neurosis, and the client's desire to be cured.

Family and *Amae*

The Japanese are raised to see the family as sacrosanct and something to which they "belong" (Bankart, 1997; Reynolds & Kiefer, 1977). This belonging to the family is represented by the term *miuichi,* which means "being a member of the inner circle," as distinguished from *tanin,* who are "recognized outsiders" (Bankart, 1997). The family is a unit, its members merging with each other (called *ittaikan*) within the hierarchical structure to promote harmony of the whole (or *wa*) (Bankart, 1997; Pelzel, 1977; Weisz et al., 1984). Children learn that the family will protect them from "dangerous outsiders" and is thus a safe place (Pelzel, 1977). Being a productive working member of the family, or eventually of small primary groups, in order to promote *wa* is highly respected.

Within this safe *miuichi,* the child experiences *amae* (or learns to "use" *amae,* depending on how one is defining this term) with the family. Bankart (1997) defines *amae* as "passive love," which means that one does not actively seek love; it is provided no matter what. This, in turn, taps into a family member's *on* (i.e., intuitively experienced obligation) to all members of *miuichi,* which eventually yields *giri,* which is the "assurance of belonging to a group" (Bankart, 1997). Being alone, isolated, and separate, and thus without *giri* is an insufferable condition that induces pity for those caught in such a situation.

Collectivism

Because of the prevalence of childhood teachings promoting respect for and harmony with the family in Japanese society, Weisz, Rothbaum, and Blackburn (1984) claimed that the Japanese character has an "orientation to persons and society [in general]" (p. 958). The Japanese tend to be very polite, try not to hurt or insult others, and keep hostile feelings to themselves (Abel, 1977). Bankart (1997) believes that "communal groups such as the family, coworkers, and the nation as a whole take precedence in everyday life over needs and desires of the individual" (p. 440). Therefore, dominant individualism or selfish egotism would be avoided because such behavior is not for the good of the whole. According to Reynolds and Kiefer (1977), "The resulting sense of self has two distinct facets: *tatemae,* or the social self, emphasizing role performance and dependence on others, and *honne,* or the stream of personal thoughts and feelings that makes up the private, inner world. The ideal in Japan is to be sensitive to others' *honne,* and to try to adjust one's own *honne* so that it resonates in harmony with the *tatemae*" (pp. 408–409). The *tatemae,* then, promotes social harmony, and the Japanese are keenly aware of their social obligations. They have a sense of "contributing to the common good" (Bankart, 1997, p. 446).

The respected Japanese individual, then, is group-oriented and unusually socially sensitive. Social cues are important because "every act is defined in terms of its social consequences" (Hedstrom, 1994, p. 155). Generalizing from family interactions, the same principles of *on* and *giri* are also expected in the larger context of society. For example, if one does one's job well and meets obligations (i.e., *on*) at work, then one has accomplished for the whole company because one "belongs" (i.e., *giri*) to that particular work group (Weisz et al., 1984). Individuals who cannot meet *on* and who do not experience *giri* are considered unfortunate and in need of help (perhaps reeducation).

Naturalism

This final construct is inherent in Zen Buddhism and relates to "an acceptance of the world as it is" (Pelzel, 1977, p. 306). Many writers (e.g., Aldous, 1994; Hedstrom, 1994; Iwai & Reynolds, 1970; Reynolds, 1976, 1980, 1981a, 1989) discuss **naturalism** as reality with connections to *un* (i.e., fate), and wise individuals align themselves to reality, whether good or bad (Weisz et al., 1984). Reynolds and Kiefer (1977) refer to this as "the interdependence of self and environment" (p. 409). One cannot control realities because they simply are, and one should not waste time on ideals or "shoulds" because they are not real. Weisz et al. claimed that "an ability to peacefully accept one's outcomes *arugamama* (as they are) is considered a sign of great maturity and wisdom" (1984, p. 962).

Morita's view of human nature was optimistic and naturalistic, most likely in consideration of the Japanese character. He believed that "most human beings have basically decent, constructive drives" (Kora & Ohara, 1973, p. 68). People desire to live, grow, and work despite the many obstacles they face in life (Hedstrom, 1994; Kondo, 1953; Walsh, 1995). They "seek self-preservation and self-actualization by the compatible forces of fears and desires" (Ishiyama, 1990, p. 568). They face reality *arugamama* and make adjustments to themselves as necessary. They express *sei no yokubo* (the desire to live) and have *sei no chikara* (the strength of life) (Fujita, 1986).

Major Constructs

Walsh (1995) claims that Asian psychotherapies do not focus much on pathology, but instead "contain detailed maps of states of consciousness, developmental labels, and stages of enlightenment" (p. 388). Morita therapy fits this description as a "natural therapy" that helps individuals become more conscious of the mind and body as natural phenomena over which we have no control (Fujita, 1986). Once clients accept the environment *arugamama*, they can do what needs to be done to create "a meaningful life for self and a usefulness to society" (Reynolds, 1981a, p. 500). Morita considered this stimulation of consciousness a reeducation process for clients, who might be called "students" (Reynolds, 1984b).

We have selected seven major constructs to help the reader better appreciate this "natural therapy": neurosis, misfocused mind, homophobia, *arugamama*, meaningful life, *work*, and cure.

Neurosis

Neurosis is not viewed from a pathology perspective in Morita therapy. Like other natural phenomena, it is a response to one's environment, only it is one that clients "have gener-

ated within themselves in the fruitless struggle to avoid inevitable and natural psychological and physiological reactions" (Bankart, 1997, p. 456). Neurotics respond more to the
"what ifs and shoulds" (i.e., the ideal) than to what is (i.e., reality). Reynolds (1981a) referred to this as "mental overspinning" that results in too much thinking and not enough
action. Neurotics act based on the ideal (e.g., "I'll take care of it when I feel happier"), while
the mental overspinning is focused on feelings and thoughts—things over which they have
no control. Their character becomes misfocused *toraware* and thus requires a form of
"character education and the essence of the character is learning to accept the world as it
is—not as you would like, hope, wish, or force it to be" (Bankart, p. 458).

As early as 1953, Asihisa Kondo listed seven characteristics of the neurotic personality: hypochondriasis; attempting to make the impossible possible; trying to avoid anxiety; not accepting facts and learning from them; thinking of oneself and one's experiences
as different from others' and their experiences; wishing to have happiness without effort;
and feelings of inferiority and incapacity (pp. 31–32). The umbrella term Kondo used for
these terms was "egocentricity." Egocentricity, then, is a form of neurosis because the
tatemae is de-emphasized, which disrupts the potential for *wa*. Morita developed his approach to help *shinkeishitsu* clients who were deep in the throes of egocentricity.

Shinkeishitsu   *Shinkeishitsu* neurosis generally includes three clinical groups: neurasthe-
nia, anxiety neurosis, and obsessional fears. These clients are introverted, pessimistic, socially inhibited, perfectionistic, oversensitive, critical of self, have somatic and psychologic
complaints, and feel inferior (Aldous, 1994; Chang, 1980; Hedstrom, 1994; Kitanishi &
Mori, 1995; Kondo, 1953; Kora & Ohara, 1973; Reynolds, 1981a; Walsh, 1995). They can
experience anthropophobia, a form of debilitating shyness (Reynolds & Kiefer, 1977), and
they experience anxieties with a strong social focus, often with concomitant social phobias (Hedstrom, 1994; Reynolds, 1981a). In Japan, this condition centers around *toraware*,
which has been defined as a selfish preoccupation, fixation of attention, and prepossess-
ion (Bankart, 1997; Kitanishi & Mori, 1995; Kora & Ohara, 1973). *Toraware* is conceptualized as a flight from reality to an obsessive turning inward of attention (Reynolds &
Kiefer) that inhibits the performance of *on* to family and society.

However, *shinkeishitsu* clients are described as demonstrating the Japanese concept
of *sei no yokubo* (i.e., the desire to live fully) (Fujita, 1986). They tend to be brighter than
normal, ambitious, high achievers, intellectually oriented, and anxious to be rid of their
symptoms (Fujita, 1986; Kora & Ohara, 1973; Reynolds, 1981a). Morita believed that the
shinkeishitsu symptoms indicate just how strongly they have *sei no yokubo*. These individuals have *sei no chikara* (i.e., the strength of life) that obsessively drives them to seek
a "cure" (i.e., to be rid of their symptoms). Morita conceptualized the *shinkeishitsu* condition as a vicious cycle that will intensify without intervention (see Figure 15.2). The
shinkeishitsu temperament might be genetically predisposed (i.e., "Disposition" in the figure). Such persons emotionally respond to experiences (i.e., "Opportunity" in the figure)
like other people, but their responses are "a negative reaction to [their] own survival and
adaptation and [focus their] attention on this reaction" (Kitanishi & Mori, 1995, p. 246). The
emotional reaction is felt more intensely and for longer periods of time, and the client fix-
ates attention on the anxious feelings (i.e., "Psychic Interaction" in the figure). Morita
(cited in Kitanishi & Mori, 1995) referred to this as "the conflict between the ideal [e.g.,
dreading having to go to school because others might ridicule you] and real [i.e., school

Figure 15.2
The *Shinkeishitsu* Condition
Adapted from Kitanishi & Mori,
1995, p. 246.

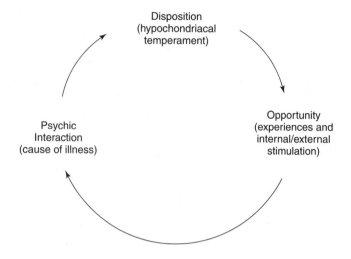

is an experience and you can go despite your dread]" (p. 246). What then happens in the cycle? *Shinkeishitsu* clients' hypochondriacal/neurotic symptoms become exaggerated, and they begin to dread the next opportunity that might occur and try to avoid it, thus being controlled by their anxious feelings, the psychic interaction (Kitanishi & Mori, 1995).

Misfocused Mind

Writing about Zen, Bankart (1997) has described its central idea as "focusing the misfocused mind away from preoccupation with self and toward the accomplishment of what needs to be done" (p. 458). The "curing" process in Morita therapy embodies this Zen belief as a central concept. *Shinkeishitsu* clients suffer with *toraware*, or selfish preoccupation (Bankart, 1997; Ishiyama, 1990; Kitanishi & Mori, 1995; Reynolds, 1976). This condition causes a misfocus of attention, and "clients become less aware of the situation at hand and suffer from the lack of appropriate action and reduced effectiveness in living" (Ishiyama, p. 567). The misfocused attention is on all the anxieties and concerns about self, "an internal subjective world" (Reynolds, 1981b, p. 201), rather than on reality and the outer world.

Toraware causes the client to become "individualistic, alienated, and selfish" (Bankart, 1997, p. 442), and part of the "cure" in Morita therapy is for "the ego to lose power" (Kitanishi & Mori, 1995, p. 251). To accomplish this, clients' attention must be focused away from excessive self-absorption. The refocusing is not just an intellectual exercise of telling oneself, "Now quit thinking about me and my problems. What's going on today?" Rather, the refocusing is experienced as the counselor or therapist guides, instructs, and encourages clients to interact with the outer world while accomplishing *on*. Fujita (1986) writes: "Mental shifts take place within an *onozu-kara-naru* (natural or spontaneous) mentality in response to whatever conditions we confront, and this phenomenon cannot be manipulated intentionally, irrespective of our wishes" (p. 222). Most importantly, the refocusing helps clients learn to focus on reality *arugamama* (Bankart, 1997; Ishiyama, 1990; Kora & Ohara, 1973; Pelzel, 1977; Reynolds, 1981a, 1989; Reynolds & Kiefer, 1977; Weisz et al., 1984).

Control

A major part of *shinkeishitsu* clients' focus is on what they cannot control: feelings and thoughts (Bankart, 1997; Fujita, 1986; Hedstrom, 1994; Ishiyama, 1990; Krech, 1989; Reynolds, 1976, 1980, 1981a, 1984a, 1984b, 1989). Krech writes, "If we could control our moods why would we ever choose to be anxious, or depressed, or angry or unhappy?" (pp. 109–110). Rather, feelings are reality, come and go regularly, and should be experienced *arugamama*. Because we have no control over our feelings, the Morita counselor or therapist gives clients "permission" to feel or think whatever they are feeling or thinking. Therefore, one is not responsible for one's feelings (Hedstrom, 1994). These are good reasons for why "Morita explicitly questions the importance of emphasizing feelings in counseling or therapy" (Hedstrom, 1994, p. 157).

However, "one is morally, socially, and personally responsible for what one does" (Reynolds, 1981a, p. 492) because we have complete control over our behavior and actions. Krech (1989) explains that "since we can't control our feelings and thoughts we should simply accept them and get on with doing what needs to be done. This brings us to what is controllable—Doing" (p. 110). While feelings are not focused on in counseling and psychotherapy sessions, neither are they avoided. Clients are reeducated to consider them a natural reaction of the mind and body to stimulation (Kitanishi & Mori, 1995). More importantly, clients experientially learn that doing and accomplishments equal life satisfaction (Fujita, 1986; Reynolds, 1980), in spite of how one feels.

For example, one of our clients once said, "I get so worked up and anxious about my boss after work that I just sit in the garage and smoke pot, even though I know my wife gets mad because I don't do anything around the house. I don't even take out the garbage." Imagine the power this client assigned to the feelings of "worked up and anxious." My response at the time was, "What's getting you so worked up and anxious?" This response kept the client ruminating on a feeling state, thus reinforcing his "bad habits of thinking and not acting" (Reynolds, 1984b, p. 13). From a Morita therapy perspective, a more instructive response might have been, "It is natural to feel worked up and anxious because you and your boss aren't getting along. Now what is it that needs doing around the house?"

Homophobia

Bankart (1997) used the term *homophobia* to describe the common social focus of the *shinkeishitsu* anxieties. In Japanese usage, the term refers to "undue or irrational anxiety, fear, and discomfort in or in prospect of interaction with fellow human beings" (Bankart, p. 455).

Shinkeishitsu clients are generally overly sensitive, have problems relating to people, and are self-conscious in public (Ishiyama, 1990; Reynolds, 1981a, 1981b; Reynolds & Kiefer, 1977). They can be anthropophobic. Reynolds (1980) claimed they bombard themselves with questions such as "What do people think of me?" "Does everyone see my weaknesses?" "Why don't I accomplish more?" (p. 6). Their response to this, of course, tends to be avoidance of social situations, when possible, and more of a flight inward. They fail to meet their *on* because they have become "spoiled, pampered, self-indulgent, isolated, egotistical, uncooperative burdens on the rest of society" (Bankart, 1997, p. 456). Counseling and therapy, therefore, is conducted in a social setting that eventually restimulates the *tatemae* to help *shinkeishitsu* clients once again become productive members of society.

Arugamama

Arugamama is a pivotal construct in Morita therapy. The term technically means "accepting reality as it is," or "accepting things as they are" (Bankart, 1997; Pelzel, 1977; Reynolds, 1976; Weisz et al., 1984). In Morita therapy, *arugamama* becomes a means to a more constructive *lifeway*. Kora and Ohara (1973) define *arugamama* as "accepting one's symptoms as they are and accepting one's life as it is" (p. 68). In order to do this, clients learn to overcome "attitudinal blocks" preventing them "from implementing desirable actions" (Ishiyama, 1990, p. 566). Thus, we are back to the basic principle of working despite debilitating thoughts and feelings.

Meaningful Life

Morita considered the *shinkeishitsu* condition to involve two sides of the same coin (Aldous, 1994). Although *shinkeishitsu* clients are filled with excessive worries and anxieties, this excessiveness may actually be an indicator of desire to grow and develop or for *sei no yokubo* (Fujita, 1986; Weisz et al., 1984). Part of character reeducation, then, is helping clients move away from *toraware* enough to experientially align themselves with the other side of the coin, *sei no yokubo*.

What, then, is this other side of the coin directed toward? Perhaps "having a purpose in the physical world that holds one's attention" (Reynolds & Keifer, 1977, p. 406). Notice that "attention" is directed toward the outer world, which certainly includes *on* to family and society. Therefore, a meaningful life provides service to others and a "usefulness to society" (Reynolds, 1981a, p. 500). As clients experientially learn that they can become more sociocentric, then healthy qualities such as mindfulness, love, compassion, concentration, and calm emerge (Walsh, 1995).

Work

Work is a vital construct in Morita therapy, only not work as the Western reader might be thinking. Kitanishi and Mori (1995) describe *work* as "an assertion to be active, to pay attention to the outside" (p. 250). "Work [then] allows the self-centered person to lose [himself or herself]," that is, to transcend [himself or herself]" (Reynolds, 1976, p. 32).

Work is a therapeutic technique used to (1) focus attention on something other than self; (2) become aware of the outer world; (3) acknowledge experiences moment-by-moment; (4) take control over behavior and become involved in life activities; and (5) eventually realize that one can work in spite of one's feelings (Aldous, 1994; Hedstrom, 1994; Ishiyama, 1990; Reynolds, 1976, 1980, 1981a, 1984b). The experiential learning of *work* actively helps clients move toward a major goal: "[to] achieve satisfactory control over what they do in life, regardless of their feeling state" (Hedstrom, 1994, p. 157). Additionally, by actually doing something and accomplishing, "we learn our true capabilities, our true limitations, and, invariably, what needs to be done next" (Reynolds, 1984b, p. 36).

Cure

Shinkeishitsu clients come to counseling or therapy to be "cured" of their symptoms. However, what clients mean by "cured" is being anxiety free, not fearful, able to be social without extreme self-consciousness, and self-confident (i.e., free of their symptoms). The cure through Morita therapy is exactly the opposite. Weisz et al. (1984) cited Reynolds' idea that "a [client] is considered cured when [he or she] has stopped groping for means to relieve [his or her] symptoms" (p. 964).

Cured clients, then, realize that their attention has been obsessively internal and self-focused, thus prohibiting them from doing what needs to be done. Morita therapy leads them through experiential learning so they can (1) transcend their symptoms; (2) accept self, feelings, and thoughts *arugamama*; (3) direct attention outward, seeing what needs to be done (*work*); and (4) take responsibility and actively *work* (i.e., accomplish). *Cured*, then, "does not mean removing symptoms but living productively in spite of them" (Reynolds, 1980, p. 7). Living productively means accomplishing. However, accomplishment is not viewed from a Western perspective (i.e., meaning we accomplished in terms of "doing well or great"). Instead, accomplishment is just that one did what one set out to do. When clients learn to "work, socialize and behave normally in spite of [their symptoms]" (Weisz et al., 1984, p. 964), they are "cured" and discharged or terminated.

Applications

Overview

We consider Morita therapy to be a phenomenological approach to counseling and psychotherapy. Some researchers (e.g., Hedstrom, 1994) noted the behavioral aspects of Morita therapy, giving Morita credit for introducing Eastern behavioral counseling or therapy before Western behavioral counseling or therapy came to Japan. However, we caution the reader not to parallel Morita therapy too closely with the Western idea of behavioral counseling and psychotherapy.

While Morita therapy does concentrate on taking action, the action is not conditioning any particular behavior (e.g., asking people out on dates). The action is part of the natural experience of living that *shinkeishitsu* clients tend to overlook—and thus avoid—because of their intense self-absorption. There would be no rhyme or reason to what activity occurs in a given day because, phenomenologically, each day unfolds as a new flower with new responsibilities. On a particular day, one might scrub the kitchen floor, buy a new coffeemaker, and guest lecture in a friend's class. The next day, he or she might fly to Washington, DC, and visit the Department of Education about a grant, visit with friends, and eat at a favorite bagel shop in Dupont Circle. No systematic conditioning of a particular behavior deficiency occurs; instead, the whole experience of the individual is considered as each day unfolds.

Researchers (e.g., Kitanishi & Mori, 1995) have addressed the de-conditioning of *toraware*. From our perspective, this de-conditioning may take place by a technique called "disregarding method" (Kitanishi & Mori, 1995), in which the counselor or therapist does not respond—thus does not reinforce—discussions about symptoms, the past, or the etiology of clients' neuroses. However, Morita counselors or therapists would not think of it this way (from our perspective). *Toraware* is a form of awareness gone astray (Reynolds, 1976) because, in the *shinkeishitsu* condition, one is egotistically self-absorbed. As counseling and psychotherapy progresses and clients become experientially involved in activities in the outer world, they discover that they lose themselves in work, in the moment, and forget about their symptoms (Hedstrom, 1994). Rather than undergo any type of systematic de-conditioning, clients learn through their experiencing to shift their attention to the outer world and accomplish things in spite of symptoms (Ishiyama, 1990; Reynolds, 1976, 1980). The shift seems to be toward accepting symptoms *arugamama* and doing what needs to be done.

Goals of Counseling and Psychotherapy

As we mentioned earlier, the overall goal of Morita therapy is reflected in the Zen concept of "focusing the misfocused mind away from the preoccupation with self and toward the accomplishment of what needs to be done" (Bankart, 1997, p. 458). Clients strive to become aware of the outer world to determine what needs to be done and to act in spite of feelings such as hopelessness, depression, anger, and frustration (Abel, 1977; Hedstrom, 1994; Kitanishi & Mori, 1995; Kondo, 1953; Kora & Ohara, 1973; Reynolds, 1976, 1980, 1981a, 1984b; Reynolds & Kiefer, 1977). The following example may make this goal clearer.

Jorge had a bad day at work because he did not complete a major report, had to work through lunch, and found out he was not getting the promotion he thought he deserved. He came home feeling angry, tense, and disappointed with the way his life was going.

Jorge walked into his urban condo, grabbed a container of ice cream from the freezer, flopped on the sofa, ate the ice cream, and sulked. He ruminated on the day and his frustrations: "I'm never going to succeed like everyone else. Maybe they're never going to be as fair with Latinos as they are with Anglos. It's not right that I get the long, complex reports to write. I'm too timid to ask my supervisor to lessen my work."

As one can see, Jorge's "mental overspinning" leads to (1) complete self-absorption; (2) failure to act in any meaningful way; (3) increased anxiety; and (4) dread of the situation yet to come. Jorge represents a typical *shinkeishitsu* client. If he were in Morita therapy, he might react differently to his difficult situation. He might come home accepting his anger, disappointment, and depression. He might even acknowledge that he has no control over these feelings, and that they make sense based on his work day. Then he might examine his environment (both physical and mental) and actively engage in *work* (i.e., see what needs to be done and do it). The hallway closet might need to be reorganized. He might call his mother to see how she's doing and to ask if there is anything he can do to help her. He might plan a quiet time to talk with his supervisor about workload despite his fear and stuttering. Then he might practice what he wants to say.

Jorge's outer-world focus and physical/mental work lead to (1) accepting symptoms and feelings *arugamama*; (2) living in the present moment; (3) becoming aware of the outer environment to see what needs to be done; and (4) working (i.e., doing) alongside his feelings and symptoms. As he focuses on tasks at hand and works on them, his symptoms fade into the background.

Obviously, to achieve the broader goal of "focusing the misfocused mind," other goals must also be met. These goals are not separate or even sub-goals, but rather form the *wa*. This harmony of the whole allows clients to eventually work productively. The other goals follow.

1. Accept self and the world *arugamama* (Aldous, 1994; Bankart, 1997; Hedstrom, 1994; Ishiyama, 1990).

2. Learn that one has complete control over one's behavior and be socially and morally responsible by doing what needs to be done (Hedstrom, 1994; Pelzel, 1977; Reynolds, 1976, 1980, 1981a, 1981b).

3. Learn to live in reality experientially. Reality is moment-by-moment as one experiences one's environment and world (both internal and external). Only by living in reality can one live fully (for each moment brings new challenges), experience constructive living patterns (Hedstrom, 1994; Reynolds, 1984a, 1984b), and build a history of success with life (Reynolds, 1981a).

4. Recognize one's purpose. Purpose comes from living life fully, and one accomplishes this by developing more effective work habits, which leads to a more organized life (Hedstrom, 1994).

The Process of Change

The counseling or psychotherapy process in Morita therapy is based on phenomenological and experiential concepts. Clients don't "talk" about their symptoms in an effort to gain insight into "why" they are the way they are, hoping not to be. Rather, the "chief treatment process in Morita therapy is centered on the actual life activities of a [client]; the counselor or therapist-[client] relationship is secondary and serves only as a setting in which the [clients'] activities may be stimulated" (Fujita, 1986, p. 223). Clients learn how to refocus attention and accomplish life activities mostly through experiential learning. The actual therapeutic intervention with the client is considered short-term, lasting anywhere from 40 to 60 days (Iwai & Reynolds, 1970; Kitanishi & Mori, 1995; Kondo, 1953; Kora & Ohara, 1973; Reynolds & Kiefer, 1977). However, Morita therapy is a lifeway or life path, and clients live by Morita principles after termination. Guidance can continue via self-help groups, follow-up visits with the counselor or therapist, and reading materials sent from the counselor/therapist or clinic.

Traditionally, four phases occur in the counseling and psychotherapy process: absolute and complete bed rest; light work therapy; heavier mental and physical work therapy; and life activities training therapy (Fujita, 1986). Each phase is briefly described below. We also describe a pre-counseling or psychotherapy phase that others include as part of Phase 1. However, we believe that it is critical enough in establishing the client-counselor or therapist roles to include as a separate phase.

To fully understand the richness of Morita therapy and the phases it progresses through, we urge the reader to seek such resources as David Reynolds' (1976) original and first English-language text on this topic, titled *Morita Psychotherapy;* Takehisa Kora and Kenshiro Ohara's (1973) original article in *Psychology Today,* titled "Morita therapy"; or more current overviews of the phases, such as L. James Hedstrom's (1994) article in *Psychotherapy* titled "Morita and Naikan Therapies: American Applications."

Pre-Counseling or Therapy Phase   Once an individual is diagnosed as appropriate for Morita therapy, the counseling or psychotherapy process begins. The counselor or therapist meets with the client and describes the process counseling or therapy will take. If Morita therapy is a form of character education (Bankart, 1997), then the counselor or therapist is a type of teacher or guide who has "surmounted [his or her] own self-imposed limitations through this method" (Reynolds, 1981a, p. 493).

The counselor or therapist-client relationship is beginning to conform to the Japanese hierarchical structure familiar to the Japanese client. Although the counselor or therapist exhibits understanding, empathy, and an accepting attitude, the relationship itself is only secondary to the process (Fujita, 1986). While a positive relationship is the goal, it is not a necessary condition for counseling or therapy to continue and be successful. However, trust seems to be a necessary factor—trust that the counselor or therapist is knowledgeable and experienced enough to help "stimulate" life activities (Fujita).

During this phase, the counselor or therapist, like a helpful and concerned guide, explains the following.

1. The *shinkeishitsu* condition as a psychological problem, and the client's experience with this condition up to this point
2. The phases that counseling or therapy progresses through
3. The client's feelings and reactions to various phases (e.g., the counselor or therapist predicts that ultimate experience of bed rest will not be pleasurable) (Reynolds, 1980)
4. What the client can or cannot do during each phase (e.g., if counseling or therapy is inpatient, outside visitors cannot come until Phase 4) (Fujita, 1986)
5. The role of the counselor or therapist, such that "the [client] must entrust the [counselor or therapist] to apply effective counseling or therapy" (Fujita, p. 200)
6. The role of the client to "begin life activities in this new direction and to cooperate in the therapeutic procedure" (Fujita, p. 200)

Phase 1: Absolute, Isolated Bed Rest   In the traditional form of Morita therapy, the inpatient counseling and psychotherapy process started with isolated bed rest that lasted anywhere from four to seven days (Fujita, 1986; Hedstrom, 1994; Kitanishi & Mori, 1995; Kondo, 1953; Kora & Ohara, 1973; Reynolds, 1976, 1980, 1981a; Reynolds & Kiefer, 1977). Fujita described this process: "The [client] must be completely isolated, with visitors, conversation, reading and smoking prohibited and with bed rest imposed at all times except for use of the lavatory, washing the face or eating at mealtimes" (p. 201). Clients are instructed to focus on any and all thoughts and feelings as they occur. The counselor or therapist checks on clients' progress daily (Hedstrom, p. 155). This form of absolute bed rest is the ultimate experiential learning of how "unnatural" complete self-absorption is. The process makes concrete what is occurring (i.e., isolation from outer world) with *toraware.*

Phase 2: Light Work Therapy   Phase 2 lasts approximately 3 to 7 days (Reynolds, 1980; Reynolds & Kiefer, 1977). During this phase of inpatient counseling or therapy, clients are introduced to the facility and assigned light tasks such as weeding a garden, sweeping a floor, or washing clothes (Hedstrom, 1994). Walking outside is allowed, as is reading serious material; however, no daytime napping is permitted (Aldous, 1994).

Clients keep a diary from now on, write approximately a page a night, and focus on what they "saw and did during the day," but they are instructed "not to write about [their] symptoms or [their] subjective feelings" (Reynolds, 1976, p. 36). The diary is collected each morning, and the counselor or therapist comments in red ink, providing "guidance and encouragement." Reynolds and Kiefer (1977) describe the theme of the counselor's or therapist's comments as "life must be lived constructively regardless of one's feelings" (p. 399).

While clients may not yet socialize or converse with other clients, each week they are required to attend an educational, philosophical lecture called a *kowa.* The lecture is conducted by a counselor or therapist and focuses on the Japanese character and ideas related to Morita therapy (Reynolds, 1976). The second phase is designed for the client to experience taking "attention away from himself or herself and toward the task at hand. Activity is required to be purposeful and careful" (Aldous, 1994, p. 242). Directing clients' attention toward simple tasks is a form of redirecting their awareness to the outer world and "[substituting] constructive living patterns" (Hedstrom, 1994, p. 155). Yet clients must ultimately develop attentiveness (i.e., *ki-kubari*) spontaneously, choosing work that interests them (Fujita, 1986).

Phase 3: Heavier Mental and Physical Work Therapy   The third phase lasts anywhere from 3 to 7 days or longer (Reynolds, 1980). Clients become involved in more strenuous work, such as chopping wood or building something, with more of an emphasis on "what needs to be done" (Hedstrom, 1994). Hedstrom suggests that clients may work with others at this time, while Fujita (1986) suggests that work is still done alone. In either case, clients cannot be involved in idle social interaction. Interaction that occurs is likely to be around some work activity. Clients can read anything now and take care of personal business (e.g., going to the store to purchase toiletries) outside the facility (Fujita, 1986). They still attend the *kowa*, which presents "work as intrinsically good, and an aid to the growth of the individual and society" (Hedstrom, p. 155). The diary is still maintained, but now with a stricter focus on daily activities and what was done (Reynolds, 1980). The experience of heavy work and of work that clients may usually not do (e.g., building something) gives clients a sense of "confidence and joy in accomplishment" (Aldous, 1994, p. 242).

Clients learn experientially that arduous activity causes one's attention to shift, leaving symptoms in the background. When one is actively involved, the symptoms are no longer a problem. As Reynolds (1984a) states, "A neurotic symptom is only a problem when we are noticing it" (p. 13). The important shift from *toraware* is occurring as clients experience "doing what needs to be done and putting things in order" (Hedstrom, 1994, p. 155) and focus on the outer world. They are beginning to live a more organized, constructive life. Clients no longer wait for suggestions about what to do, but spontaneously see what needs to be done and do it.

Phase 4: Life Activities Training Therapy   The last phase in inpatient Morita therapy prepares clients to reenter their environments, deal with the social realities, and continue to work productively. Hedstrom (1994) writes: "At the time of discharge, there may still be symptoms, including fears and unhappiness, but the [client] should be ready to carry out the tasks of life irrespective of [his or her] symptoms" (p. 155). All restrictions on activities are removed. Therapy now involves working clients into the social environment of the clinic and having them learn to interact with other clients regardless of their symptoms. Clients continue the heavy work, but may work directly with other patients on projects. They become involved in group excursions and sports and recreational activities with other clients. They can be sent on errands within the community (Kora & Ohara, 1973; Reynolds, 1976, 1980).

Clients continue to see their counselors or therapists on a daily basis, and receive additional guidance provided by comments in their diary. Fujita (1986) believes that the "chief objective is to get a [client] to participate in everything spontaneously as the need arises and, further, to make the [client] feel, in this manner, that he or she can do whatever he or she wants to do" (p. 207).

Morita therapy is a *lifeway*, so upon discharge, clients can attend ex-patient meetings, which may be in the form of the self-help organizations called *Seikatsu no Hakkenkai* ("The Discovery of Life Organization"). Additionally, they receive the clinic's magazine, which contains articles about Morita life principles as well as comments about treatment. They have their diary, can always refer back to the counselor's or therapist's comments, and will continue to keep the diary for as long as it is useful. Finally, they might correspond with the counselor or therapist, share their diary again, or set up follow-up appointments (Reynolds, 1980). The experiential treatment becomes the stepping stone for a change in life pattern that is more constructive, outwardly focused, and of benefit to self and society.

Intervention Strategies

Most researchers (e.g., Aldous, 1994; Hedstrom, 1994) describe the inpatient Morita therapy process, but have little comment on the outpatient process. Through his own adaptation of Morita therapy in his text *Constructive Living,* Reynolds (1984a) shared his own techniques and practice with clients outside a clinical setting. A separate section on outpatient Morita therapy is not necessary because the goals are the same regardless of the setting in which they are applied. The counseling or therapy is also still based on experiential learning, not traditional talk counseling or therapy.

Bed Rest   While bed rest is an inpatient strategy, the experiential learning that occurs through this strategy must also be accomplished in outpatient counseling or therapy. Reynolds (1984b) suggests exercises and activities, both in and out of sessions, that allow clients to experience the moment and refocus on the outer world. For example, during a first session clients may converse for 40 minutes on their symptoms. When clients finish, Reynolds (1984b) asks them to close their eyes and describe what is in his office. This exercise starts the important teaching process typical for Phase 1: (1) symptoms will be neither ignored nor reinforced in session; (2) clients' attention is directed toward *toraware*; and (3) when their attention is directed toward *toraware*, they are not attending to the many things going on in the outer world, moment-by-moment.

Refocusing clients' attention starts immediately with various guided activities. Meditation (explained in a later section) is also used in lieu of bed rest. Homework is frequently used to help clients focus on the outer world. Reynolds (1984b) asked a client to drive home via the same route, but to focus on every detail of the environment. She was asked to journal about this. Clients soon learn via experience that *toraware* isolates them from the outer world, and a sense of urgency develops to act on this awareness.

Personal Counseling and Psychotherapy: Guidance and Instruction   Reynolds (1981a) described Morita counselors or therapists as "explicitly directive. They are teachers, experienced guides who, for the most part, have surmounted their own self-imposed limitations through this method" (p. 493). During inpatient work, guidance and instruction begin during the pre-counseling or therapy phase, when the counselor or therapist explains and predicts what will happen if clients cooperate with the counseling or psychotherapy. Clients are checked daily during bed rest for progress reports only, and as counseling or psychotherapy progresses, "informal" (Abel, 1977) sessions occur during which guidance is provided for daily activities, instruction is provided about living via Morita principles, and encouragement is given to help clients continue living constructively.

A unique type of counseling or psychotherapy relationship is then formed between the counselor or therapist and client. This relationship is hierarchical in nature, with the counselor or therapist becoming the guide/master to his or her clients, the students. The counselor- or therapist-guide must, through his or her own experience, help the client-student refocus *toraware* to a more meaningful, outer-world focus. Like any guide, the counselor or therapist is directive, keeping the client's attention away from symptoms and on daily activities. This is partly accomplished through a "human relationship situation" called *fumon* (Fujita, 1986). Fujita defined *fumon* as "an attitude of completely 'cutting off' the counselor or therapist as a listener to the [client's] complaints" (1986, p. 226). If a client presents complaints around "uncontrollable" feelings and thoughts, the counselor or therapist cuts off the discussion by *ma* (i.e., "pause"). *Ma* creates a "proper distance" initiated by the counselor or therapist so that clients can gain "control" of themselves. Most likely the "control" gained is to dialogue on what clients have control over (i.e., behavior and life activities), not on what they do not have control over (i.e., feelings and thoughts). In other words, the counselor or therapist at times completely ignores dialogue about symptoms (Fujita, 1986). Kitanishi and Mori (1995) called this the "disregard method." The counselor or therapist "disregards [by] not exploring the pathology" (i.e., either etiology or symptoms), but instead discusses "the importance of clarifying the patient's *toraware*" (p. 251). Overall, *fumon* "is an opportunity to open up the self and to grow by means of a momentary silence in the mutual relationships that take place between human beings" (Fujita, p. 225).

In outpatient work, clients are seen on a weekly basis. However, the personal counseling or psychotherapy is similar to inpatient work. The counselor or therapist explains and reinforces the principles of Morita therapy. Reynolds (1981a) believes that "counseling or therapy sessions focus on the application of these understandings [i.e., Morita principles] and suggestions for living to the patient's daily life" (p. 494).

Work   In both inpatient and outpatient Morita therapy, work, physical activity, and acting/doing are at the heart of treatment (Aldous, 1994; Hedstrom, 1994; Fujita, 1986; Kitanishi & Mori, 1995; Reynolds, 1976, 1980, 1981a, 1984b). Along with explicit instructions about behavior being the only thing we control, counseling or therapy is built around experiencing how symptoms can fade into the background when one is involved in some activity (i.e., life). Kitanishi and Mori describe the significance of work as follows: "(1) the exertion of the desire to be active, which is part of human nature (the exertion of the desire to live fully); (2) experiencing a situation in which one finds that it is possible to work despite the existence of symptoms; and (3) paying attention to the outside (change from self-serving attitude to matter-oriented attitude)" (p. 250).

Even in outpatient work, the activities should at first be simplistic and somewhat meaningless, leading to more complex, important, and meaningful physical and mental work (Reynolds, 1976, 1981a, 1984a, 1984b). Work stimulates a focus away from *toraware* to what needs to be done. Reynolds (1984b) suggests using "physical activity to accomplish tasks when we feel overwhelmed by feelings" (p. 51). Although initially the counselor or therapist can recommend or suggest activities, particularly during inpatient work, ultimately clients must develop *ki-kubari* (attentiveness) as Fujita (1986) described, thus choosing activities of personal interest.

Diary   The diary is an important therapeutic tool for both the counselor or therapist and clients. Clients monitor their experiences, begin to realize what is and is not controllable, organize themselves better by more carefully detailing the diary, and learning from the comments provided by the counselor or therapist. The counselor or therapist uses the diary as an instructional method via comments made in the diary, as a progress check, and, particularly for outpatient work, as a form of counseling or therapy continuation (i.e., work extends beyond the counseling and psychotherapy session) (Fujita, 1986; Hedstrom, 1994; Krech, 1989; Reynolds, 1976; Reynolds & Kiefer, 1977).

Reynolds (1980) describes how clients might organize their diaries. On the left side of the paper, the client might write what he or she felt like doing at any given moment, including feelings, moods, and fancies. On the other side, the client might write what he or she actually did at the moment. For example, one client had finished writing in the diary for the day. On the left side, the client had written: "I dreaded getting up because I knew I had to finish reading this book (feeling). I wished I could have just stayed in bed and forgotten about finishing that reading (fancy)." On the right side, the client had written: "I got up, did my morning exercises, sat at the table and read for two hours. I did forget my dread feeling after all." (This last sentence should have been on the left side because we have no control over the dread feeling.) Reynolds claimed that from the diary we "can learn that much of daily life is carried out regardless of one's felt needs at a given moment, and even in spite of them" (p. 17).

Meditation   Meditation is probably not used in inpatient Morita therapy. This may even be contraindicated for a counseling or therapy milieu aimed at having clients focus on the outer world and become re-involved in a social setting. However, Reynolds (1984b) suggests its use in outpatient counseling and psychotherapy "to still the mind in order to allow subsequent attention to moving about in ordinary life" (p. 23). He is not interested in the enlightenment aspect of meditation. He also uses it to teach clients to focus on one thing over a period of time. Focusing is important because clients must learn to choose an activity and then do it, which requires an outer-world focus. Eventually, one must also be observant enough of the world, and of one's life, to see what needs to be done. Additionally, as clients meditate, Reynolds (1984b) asks them to think of (1) knowing their purpose, (2) accepting their feelings, and (3) doing what needs to be done.

Readings   Bibliotherapy is a strategy used in both inpatient and outpatient Morita therapy. Assigned readings take the form of education, both about Morita principles and about life pathways/morals. Hospital magazines are provided to ex-clients for outpatient follow-up. Reynolds (1976) described them as "professional-looking journals which appear at least twice a year. The forty pages or so in a typical issue contain articles about Morita therapy by counselors or therapists and patients, excerpts from diaries, *kowa* notes, records of symposia, testimonies, advice, poetry, slogans, news of meetings and trips, and human-interest stories about inpatients and therapists" (p. 38). The magazines serve as reminders about Morita principles, thus reinforcing clients' following a constructive *lifeway*.

For outpatient work, the counselor or therapist might assign articles about Morita therapy to educate clients about the process and principles of a Morita *lifeway*. Clients might be instructed not to read fantasy or fictional material of any sort during counseling or therapy. Such reading material could easily precipitate a flight inward, an escape to another form of *toraware*. Again, whatever they read, they must be instructed not to worry about the meaning, just to accomplish the reading. Readings can be discussed in session, if appropriate.

Homework and Guided Activities   Both of these strategies are geared to clients experientially learning about *arugamama, toraware*, refocusing, and doing/behavior. An example of a guided activity in an outpatient session is the one Reynolds (1984b) uses when asking clients to close their eyes and describe his office. This activity forces clients to experience the moment, thus turning their focus away from *toraware* and all the isolation it brings. Rather than telling clients, "I bet you don't realize you're not experiencing your moment-by-moment reality," the counselor or therapist helps clients realize this fact via experiential learning, a powerful therapeutic strategy.

Homework assignments can be anything that helps clients experience life rather than ruminate on feelings and thoughts (i.e., symptoms). An early assignment might be to do a very simple task like picking up newspapers one has allowed to pile up, or forcing oneself to be sad all day (paradoxical intention). As clients learn that they are unable to control their feelings and thoughts but can work in spite of them, less homework is needed because they develop *ki-kubari,* act on the world *arugamama*, and figure out what needs to be done.

Kowa   This strategy is used during inpatient counseling or therapy. Clients attend a lecture once a week, even though outpatients may come back for the lectures. Abel (1977) describes the *kowa* as having "sort of [a] philosophical, perhaps, semi-religious, moral, and esthetic tone which may make a deep impression on patients" (p. 557). This method fits well with Morita therapy because the counselors or therapists usually give the *kowa*, and they are "honored" teachers after all (Reynolds & Kiefer, 1977).

In *Morita Psychotherapy*, Reynolds (1976) described the following as sample topics for the *kowa*.

1. We cannot control our likes. One cannot make oneself like snakes. But we can control our behavior. That is important.
2. If we cannot *gaman* ("stick it out") we cannot be cured.
3. One should not focus so much on the past. One must focus instead on what he or she will do from now on.
4. If we are always talking about ourselves, we cannot listen.
5. We all feel afraid of cancer. It is sensible to fear cancer. People die from cancer, and we do not want to die. But we can work anyway. (p. 88)

Goal Setting   This strategy is not to be confused with plans of action. In fact, Morita "[discouraged] the constructing of elaborate plans for recovery" (Reynolds & Kiefer, 1977, p. 410). Too rigid a plan of action is unnatural in some ways and disregards the "interdependence of self and environment" (Reynolds & Kiefer, p. 409). Each day is different and may bring new challenges to act on, thus a new purpose. This purpose is what produces daily goals, and for both inpatient and outpatient work, clients find a purpose each day with *ki-kubari* (Fujita, 1986). Ultimately, "purposive, goal-directed behavior must be reestablished in order to reorient the life pattern" (Kora & Ohara, 1973, p. 68).

Clients with Mental Disorders

There are, of course, many individuals who have benefited and continue to benefit from the therapeutic process that combines some form of Buddhist or mindful intervention, many of whom will never be reflected in any research study or attend a clinical trial to test the effectiveness of that model. There are several specific issues that have been considered in research practice however, and there is a great need for more.

Bringing calm and purpose to the mind through mindful meditation has been shown to promote a self-regulatory component to the treatment of several, more serious mental health issues (Shapiro, Schwartz, & Bonner, 1998). Jack Kornfield (1993) suggested,

> Just as we heal the body and heart through awareness, so can we heal the mind . . . as we notice our thoughts in meditation, we discover that they are not in our control—we swim in an uninvited constant stream of memories, plans, expectations, judgments, regrets. . . . While thoughts can be enormously useful and creative, most often they dominate our experience with ideas of likes versus dislikes, higher versus lower, self versus other . . . this dualistic nature of thought is a root of our suffering. (pp. 49)

At the University of Massachusetts Stress Reduction clinic, several thousand individuals have completed a clinical program designed to reduce stress and enhance relaxation (Kabat-Zinn, 1996; Shapiro et al., 1998). Clinical mental health issues such as chronic depression, anxiety, panic disorders, hypertension, and sleep disorders represent a wide range of mental health concerns, with a common thread running through: that stress may be a factor in all of the aforementioned issues, and the need to control stress as a common goal (Kabat-Zinn, 1996; Kristeller & Hallett, 1999; Shapiro et al., 1998).

In a 1999 study on women and eating disorders, specifically binge eating, Kristeller and Hallett found that a component of mindful meditation training and practice may be an effective means of treating a diagnosed Binge Eating disorder (BED). In the study, 18 women participants met the criteria for a BED diagnosis, and over a period of 6 weeks, participated in a three-pronged process of general mindful meditation, eating meditation, and mini-meditations. Although the researchers noted as a limitation the same sample size, the results reported suggested a need for attention to the model of inclusion of meditation for BED-diagnosed clients. According to Kristeller and Hallett (1999),

> The number of binges reported per week dropped significantly over treatment. Nine participants reduced binges to less than one per week, and five reported one to two per week. . . . Perceived levels of eating control, sense of mindfulness, and awareness of hunger cues and satiety cues all increased significantly . . . there was no overall change in weight. Both depression, as measured by the BDI (Beck Depression Inventory) and anxiety, as measured by the BAI (Beck Anxiety Inventory), fell significantly. (pp. 361)

Clients presenting with disorders of an obsessive nature may benefit from the inclusion of meditation intervention. Thought patterns of an unintended or intrusive nature that have been negative or disruptive influences can cause pain, anxiety, and depression (Freestone, Ladouceur, Thibodeaux, & Gagnon, 1991; Mikulas, 2002). The very "practice" of meditation or meditative techniques can cause the individual to be more in the here and now, not in the past, therefore allowing her or him to either stop a thought that is negative or disturbing, or to meet that thought with immediacy. Mikulas (2002) avers:

> With the development of concentration and mindfulness, a person gradually disidentifies with the contents of the mind and learns how to stand back and objectively observe the contents. . . . For many people, it is often personally quite significant when they eventually disidentify with and disengage from the contents of their minds, even for a short period. (p. 94)

The inclusion of meditative interventions may yield more success for clients as researchers design and conduct more clinical studies. It does seem apparent that the concepts of mindfulness, purpose of thought, and concentration have the potential to enhance a therapeutic process for clients who have presented with a cognitive-type disorder, stress-related issue, behavioral disorder, or a clinical depression/dysphoric disorder. More research would be necessary to continue the discussion of further efficacy of the model with any confidence.

Evaluation

Overview

Morita therapy was developed in Japan by Shoma Morita. Since he first wrote about his approach in 1917, the counseling or therapy has consistently been practiced in Japan (Hedstrom, 1994; Kitanishi & Mori, 1995). While Morita therapy has gained recognition in Western cultures, its use is not as common. Therefore, most of the research and evaluation on effectiveness is published in Japanese. The available reports on the effectiveness of the approach are mostly small parts of articles summarizing the results of Japanese reports. However, the summaries are sufficient to suggest the continued use of Morita therapy.

Supporting Research

As Morita therapy is recognized and more frequently practiced in Western cultures, more research on its effectiveness will occur and be reported in the English language. Hedstrom (1994) claims that "familiarity with Morita therapy in the Western world is increasing as English language accounts of the counseling or therapy grow" (p. 154). Until then, we will have to accept Morita therapy *arugamama* and believe in its worth if for no other reason than the fact that it is still a reality after 70 years.

Research is available in Japan on the effectiveness of Morita therapy and is summarized in English-language publications. The reported rate of "cured" and "improved" clients ranges from 60% to 90% (Kondo, 1953; Kora & Ohara, 1973; Reynolds, 1980). The higher effectiveness rates seem to occur "when selecting the treatment population" (Kitanishi & Mori, 1995, p. 247). Two important facts must be considered about higher effectiveness rates. First, "cured" or "improved" means that clients have "stopped groping for a means to relieve symptoms" (Weisz et al., 1984, p. 964) and have learned to work in spite of them (Aldous, 1994; Reynolds, 1976, 1980, 1981a, 1984a, 1984b). Second, Morita developed his theory for *shinkeishitsu*, not for all types of neurosis (Aldous, 1994; Reynolds, 1976). Clients with the requisite diagnosis, then, were originally included in treatment and apparently were successfully treated through Morita therapy.

As the use of Morita therapy became more common, however, effectiveness rates changed, revealing important information about the types of clients who are best helped.

Kitanishi and Mori (1995) included their own summary of "cured" and "improved" rates through the years: 1919–29, 93.3%; 1929-37, 92.9%; 1963-74, 92.7%; 1972-91, 77.6% (p. 247). They attribute the lower 1972–91 effectiveness rate "to the fact that [they] have been actively attempting to treat atypical cases [i.e., not diagnosed with *shinkeishitsu*]" (p. 247). They conclude that Morita therapy works best with young males who (1) exhibit typical *shinkeishitsu* symptoms; (2) allow an appropriate amount of time to be treated; and (3) voluntarily want to be treated with this approach. Clients who seem not to benefit as much from Morita therapy include those who are delusional, those with obsessive-compulsive behavior, those with borderline personality, and some schizophrenics.

Suzuki and Suzuki (1981) examined the long-term effects of Morita therapy. They surveyed 1,287 ex-clients who had been discharged for at least 2 years, with 6.3 years as the average length of discharge. A majority (81.1%) of these clients were diagnosed with *shinkeishitsu*. They received a 71.1% usable survey return rate (914 surveys). Their results shed interesting light on Morita therapy, particularly in support of its being a *lifeway* or life path. Upon discharge, approximately 78.6% of the clients felt that they were fairly or highly improved in terms of being able to "live either an active daily life or a relatively normal life" (Suzuki & Suzuki, p. 207). However, 96.1% of the clients reported being able to live an active life, as compared to only 3.7% reporting being unable to do so, as their current status (i.e., 2 or more years after discharge). The greatest change between immediate discharge and long-term reports occurred in the top two categories related to a highly improved condition. Immediately upon discharge, only 12.1% put themselves in these categories; by 2 or more years after discharge, 59.4% included themselves in these categories. Clearly, the initial 40- to 60-day active counselor or therapist intervention is only the beginning for putting Morita principles into practice and experience to produce change.

The Suzuki and Suzuki (1981) study had unique qualities with regard to the sample of clients. The clients' mean age was 26 years, with a range of 16–30 years involving 76.2% of the whole sample. A majority (75.9%) were male and unmarried (78%). Overall, those clients with hypochondriasis and anxiety neurosis improved over time more than those with obsessive and depressive neurosis. Suzuki and Suzuki again reinforce that the "willingness to do what needs to be done in spite of one's symptoms is an important criterion for discharge" (p. 211).

The results available in the English language support the use of Morita therapy, particularly with *shinkeishitsu* clients. Therefore, careful diagnosis may be required if one intends to use this approach with clients. Kora and Ohara (1973) state only two reasons why Morita therapy might not help clients change: injudicious selection of patients and lack of client motivation to follow the regime. They conclude that "only a very few show no progress at all" (p. 66).

Limitations

Based on research findings and written reports describing Morita therapy, practitioners need to be cautious in using it with all clients. The approach was developed for *shinkeishitsu* and seems to be most effective with this population of clients. Therefore, a careful diagnosis of any client's condition should occur to determine if the client falls under this rubric or some aspect of *shinkeishitsu*. The approach does not seem as effective and may even be contraindicated for children, addicts, mentally challenged individuals, sociopaths, depressives, psychotics, borderlines, compulsives, and schizophrenics (Kitanishi & Mori, 1995; Reynolds, 1980; Suzuki & Suzuki, 1981).

More research and practice need to occur with populations other than young males. Although Reynolds (1980, 1984b) is working with a much more varied client population, caution must be used when using Morita therapy with women of all ages and midlife and older adults. This caution is given not because the therapy will not be useful; rather, it relates to the lack of reports from practitioners or researchers about Morita therapy's effectiveness with these populations. Additionally, clients who have difficulty sticking to a regimen or who are unmotivated may not do well with this approach (Kora & Ohara, 1973). Finally, more practitioner reports need to occur with specific populations like people of color, low-income groups, gay men and lesbians, and special populations like prison inmates to determine the full potential of this counseling and psychotherapy approach. Until then, nobody can, with complete confidence, say that it crosses racial, ethnic, geographic, and socioeconomic boundaries.

Summary Chart—Morita Therapy

Human Nature
Morita therapy suggests that humans are optimistic, naturalistic, and basically decent, with constructive drives. They face reality *arugamama* and make adjustments as necessary. They express *sei no yokubo* and have *sei no chikara.*

Major Constructs
Morita therapy is a natural, experiential counseling or therapy. Its major constructs include neurosis and egocentricity; *shinkeishitsu* (a form of anxiety and obsession disorder); misfocused mind; *toraware* (selfish preoccupation); giri (assurance of belonging to a group); *arugamama* (accepting reality as it is); *onozu-kara-naru* (natural or spontaneous); control; *homophobia* (irrational anxiety, fear, and discomfort in or in prospect of interaction with fellow human beings); *amae* (passive love or take advantage of); *on* (intuitively experienced obligation); meaningful life; *work*, and cure (stop groping for means to relieve symptoms and live productively in spite of them).

Goals
1. Focus the misfocused mind away from preoccupation with self.
2. Accept self and world *arugamama.*
3. Be socially and morally responsible for behavior.
4. Live a full and constructive life.
5. Recognize one's purpose.

Change Process
The change process involves reeducation of character, experiential learning, phases, precounseling and psychotherapy, complete bed rest, light work therapy, heavier mental and physical work therapy, life activities training therapy, follow-up contact, and *lifeway* and life path constructive living.

Interventions

Interventions in Morita therapy include bed rest, guidance and instruction, work, diary, meditation, readings, homework and guided activities, *kowa*, and a family-like environment in a social setting.

Limitations

Morita therapy is most useful with *shinkeishitsu* clients. It is not typically used with children, addicts, or the mentally challenged, and is not as effective with sociopaths, depressives, psychotics, borderlines, and schizophrenics. More practitioner reports are needed on its use with women, midlife and older adults, people of color, and members of low-income groups.

■.■■ ■ The Case of Jonathan: A Morita Therapy Approach

Overview

Jonathan's case fits the profile of clients successfully treated with Morita therapy: he is young, displays typical *shinkeishitsu* symptoms, and is voluntarily seeking treatment (Kitanishi & Mori, 1995). Jonathan's suicide potential and level of depression must be assessed. If he is not actively suicidal, then counseling and psychotherapy could proceed.

Morita therapy might work well with Jonathan because his symptoms resemble those of *shinkeishitsu* neurosis. He is angry, anxious, and pessimistic. His comment "I am not wanted in the white man's world . . ." illustrates a negative, "poor-me" attitude. His attention is misfocused, *toraware*. Jonathan seems fearful of women and relationships, which is a form of social inhibition. Ultimately, he has lost his purpose (i.e., "I have little to live for") because of *toraware*.

Counseling and Psychotherapy Process

Jonathan is separated from his second wife; therefore, his children are not with him. Marriage counseling or psychotherapy is not indicated at this time. However, in the future, it should be considered. Jonathan has work to do in regard to himself and his purpose for living. After Jonathan "tells his story," I instruct and explain (i.e., as "teacher") about the Morita process and principles. I explain the basic principles of his neurosis (e.g., *toraware*, avoidance, *on*, constructive living, *work*, purpose). Additionally, I congratulate him on his strong desire to live life fully (i.e., *sei no yokubo*), evident in his seeking help. Finally, I give him hope of "cure" with the condition that he cooperate fully with my guidance, counseling and psychotherapy, and instruction, despite questions and doubts he may have about Morita therapy. At this time, I give him an article to read (i.e., scan lightly) about Morita therapy.

Goals of Counseling and Psychotherapy

1. Jonathan will become aware that he is selfishly preoccupied (i.e., *toraware*), which is causing the psychic interaction shown earlier in Figure 15.1. He will realize that *toraware* causes him to isolate himself even more from the outer world (i.e., "opportunities" such as healthier interactions with his family of origin). He will become focused on

the outer world so that he can live life fully, moment-by-moment, instead of being focused on himself, in guilt: "I have ruined the lives of three families plus my own. . . ."

2. Jonathan is not accepting feelings and thoughts *arugamama*. Instead, he is living life as if the feelings are reality and is allowing them to run his life. Feelings of depression, sadness, and guilt are a part of living; they come and go based on life situations. He will find that he can live a constructive life of benefit to himself and society in spite of those feelings.

3. Jonathan will get back on track and be responsible for his behavior. He has responsibilities and obligations (i.e., *on*) to his children, his marriage, his family of origin, and work. As he focuses more on the outer world, he will begin to see what those responsibilities are and "work" at them (e.g., visit his family on the reservation; address the issues around his infidelity with his wife). He has a responsibility to himself and will begin to take care of himself physically, deal with his alcohol misuse, and come to grips with feelings concerning the death of his brother.

4. As he lives life constructively, he will begin to find purpose in living again because each day brings purpose. Each day brings new goals and activities that must be accomplished.

Interventions

How will Jonathan accomplish his goals? I have included several examples of the counseling and psychotherapy process below. I would guide Jonathan from the simple to the complex as counseling and psychotherapy progresses and as he is ready for more complex responsibilities.

1. Jonathan is not accepting feelings and thoughts *arugamama*. Instead, he is living life as if the feelings (particularly the negative ones) are the only reality, and he is allowing them to run his life. In some ways, he is acting out his "depressing" and "giving-up" feelings. I tell him that he is not responsible for his feelings and thoughts; they just are. I ask him to try to feel extremely happy right now, in the session. When he cannot, I explain that "just like you cannot make yourself happy, you cannot control when you are sad or depressed. Otherwise, I assume you would not let yourself be sad or depressed." I explain that because he cannot control his feelings, the best he can hope for is to live life constructively in spite of them.

2. Jonathan begins to keep a diary immediately. On the left half of a page, he writes his feelings and thoughts, and on the right side he writes what he accomplished. As he reads the diary in session, we discuss what he learned (e.g., that he does live despite negative feelings; that these feelings are not always present; that he is letting his internal focus and selfish preoccupation with feelings guide his behavior). From the diary, he learns that feelings come and go during the week, and that he does accomplish things (e.g., eating out with his children in lieu of picking up women) despite those feelings. I review the diary each week and make instructive comments related to Morita principles. The diary is also a means to organize Jonathan's life. Therefore, he writes for no more than 30 minutes at the end of each day and uses no more than one sheet of paper. Initially, he writes anything that he wants. Eventually, I ask him to focus more on what he has learned from *working* and *doing* as well as what he accomplished, and less on the feelings.

Additionally, I conduct my counseling and psychotherapy from a *fumon* framework. As Jonathan presents complaints in session, I use *ma* (the disregarding method) at times until he gains control of himself and discusses what he has control over: his work and behavior. I might also instruct. If Jonathan says, "This guy I work with was absolutely horrible to me yesterday—always on my back, telling me I wasn't working hard enough" I might respond, "You gave up too easily on your work obligation. Perhaps you can speak to your superior, and find out exactly what you are doing or not doing that is productive in the workplace. Think of what you do when you are suspended from your job. You drink more, get more depressed, and feel horrible. Go to work tomorrow and talk with your boss, and listen to what he says. Think about what you can do a little differently at work, so that you feel more of a sense of acceptance and accomplishment. They were very happy when you began to work there—think about that. Then, make a pact with your boss that if he finds your work lacking, or your attitude slipping into a negative place, you will talk with him and work on it."

3. Jonathan has given up and totally immersed himself in *toraware*. He does not "see" the reality around him and what needs to be done, both for himself and for his social groups (i.e., *on*). Therefore, I am initially directive about getting Jonathan actively involved in reality until he develops *ki-kubari* (i.e., attentiveness) and spontaneously chooses activities (i.e., work, family) that interest him (Fujita, 1986).

I ask him to get up 30 minutes earlier than usual and read one page aloud from Reynolds' *Constructive Living*. He does not have to make sense out of the words, even though we discuss the principles in session. He must do the same right before going to bed. I advise him to plan an outing with his children for the next weekend, where he will pick them up, plan the day, and return them home. I ask him to sit down and think of fun things the children enjoy, and to plan on doing some of those specific things. I suggest he invite his wife for at least one of the activities of the day. Then, I suggest he begin to include his children in activities involving his family of origin on a fairly regular basis. I encourage Jonathan also to plan on spending time with his children from his first marriage. His drinking and his anonymous "dates" with women should decrease in frequency.

Another activity that helps Jonathan realize that he can work in spite of his feelings is the assignment that he go to work every day regardless of how he is feeling physically or emotionally. Eventually, he develops *ki-kubari* and chooses his own activities, but it is important to start slowly and to help him learn to focus on one accomplishment at a time. The following activities seem important to Jonathan.

- It is vital that he keep his job so that he can support his lifestyle and children.
- He must meet his *on* to his children and his wife. As he builds an outer-world focus, he will realize the needs of all his children and meet them, and perhaps will meet the needs of his wife as well.
- He must meet his *on* to his family of origin. Jonathan's Native American culture places high value on family and connection to family. His moving from the reservation might have been a significant insult to his family. However, the past is past, and Jonathan's activities with his family of origin, as well as with his children and wife, must center on the present and establishing a satisfying working relationship with them. He will determine what activities might work toward this goal.
- Finally, Jonathan will develop goals and activities that lead to a more organized, constructive life. This will involve eating appropriately, curbing his drinking, resting, and working on his marriage as much as possible. This goal in itself re-

quires special attention. For example, Jonathan suffers from intense guilt about his brother's accident, and he has always wondered if he was blamed by his family. He might discuss this with his family as well as in counseling or therapy, allowing for the emotions and sadness to surface.

Buddhist Meditation Approach in Counseling and Psychotherapy: An Addendum

Buddhist teaching tells us that our thoughts comprise who we are as human beings, and that if we are able to control our thinking, many of life's trials will either disappear or not appear at all (Walsh, 2000). Awareness of being, awareness of thought, and correction of thought are at the heart of the quest for **enlightenment**, and the practice of meditation creates the beginning of the path toward freedom and openness. Within an Eastern view, "Health is defined in terms of three fundamental parameters: (1) the relinquishment of unhealthy mental qualities such as attachment, aversion, and delusion; (2) the development of specific healthy mental qualities and capacities; and (3) maturation to transpersonal levels" (Walsh, 2000, p. 423).

While the mention of what specific mental qualities are "healthy" according to the Eastern tradition is somewhat vague, we can turn to our knowledge and experience with more Western cognitive constructs of personality that lead to psychological or emotional distress for some clarity. For example, anxiety, feelings of low self-esteem, abandonment fears, or self-destructive thought patterns are issues with which Western counselors or therapists are familiar; therefore, we are able to notice the parallels with issues from the Eastern tradition. The concept of thought and cognition relative to behavior and mental health are familiar to us as Western counselors or therapists. We work with clients every day who embark on the therapeutic journey in order to feel good, to learn to love themselves, to lead more satisfying lives, to engage in more meaningful relationships, or to end addictive, self-harming behaviors. The desire for direction toward awareness, freedom, and serenity is common to clients seeking our assistance and services. From here, we will discuss an Eastern path, one that has as an underpinning the very essence of the Buddhist tradition and framework for existence, and that can be effective in helping clients to reach their goals.

Background

When reviewing an Eastern therapeutic approach, the blend of meditation, counseling or therapy, and the psychological/philosophical aspects of **mindfulness** have been recognized by several well-respected masters in the field of counseling and psychotherapy. Historical figures such as Karen Horney, Erich Fromm, and especially Carl Jung have written about the worth and efficacy of Buddhist teachings relative to counseling and psychotherapy practice (Fulton, 2001; Michalon, 2001).

According to Paul Fulton of the Institute for Meditation and Psychotherapy in Newton, Massachusetts, meditation and psychotherapy both deal with "salvation from psychological suffering, both rest on the power of insight or understanding, both value truth and 'wakefulness' which is truly in the here and now" (July, 2001). The quest of the client for some level of life satisfaction, happiness within a personal definition, and forward growth is similar to the desire to embark on the path toward fulfillment, wisdom, and ultimate enlightenment. Without comparing Western and Eastern counseling and psychotherapy philosophies, it is important to set the stage for use of meditative interventions in the process of counseling and psychotherapy. Counseling and psychotherapy students have hopefully moved beyond the misconception that client-centered therapy, for example, is non-directive and non-confrontive—indeed the intentionality of Rogers is very close to a mindfulness approach, a rich focus, as may be seen in the Eastern tradition (Bankart, 1997; Rogers, 1980).

Many translations and interpretations of Eastern Buddhist teachings are pertinent to counseling and psychotherapy. The belief in the **Four Noble Truths**, or the **Middle Way**, as a way to live life on the path of enlightenment should be examined by the counselor or therapist on a personal as well as philosophical level prior to learning and using any meditative interventions (Lama Surya Das, 1997; Michalon, 2001). Inclusion of Zen Buddhist teachings in the counseling and psychotherapy process is not simply using certain techniques; the entire scope of the Eastern view must be understood as a life path, a quest for awareness and focus with a mindful nature—an enlightened existence. This may require reevaluation on the counselor's or therapist's part of her or his beliefs in the areas of spirituality, therapeutic consciousness, or even personal life path—all worthwhile journeys.

The Path

We cannot discuss the process that embodies living life through the Four Noble Truths, the Middle Way, without a discussion of the reason one would have that as a goal: enlightenment! The seven factors of enlightenment, or great wisdom, as outlined by Brazier (1995) are (1) mindfulness; (2) energy and effort; (3) investigating; (4) rapture; (5) concentration; (6) tranquility; and (7) equanimity. Wisdom, or *bodhi*, "does not refer to a form of learning or knowledge, but to a way of being or experiencing. To have *bodhi* means to be in the flow of existence just as it is" (Brazier, 1995, p. 180).

The quality of mindfulness—acute awareness of surroundings, feelings, and the world around us—is integral in the attainment of mind-balance, indeed, life-balance. The here-and-now conceptual framework fits nicely with the Eastern tradition of mindful attention (Brazier, 1995; Goldstein & Kornfield, 1987). The essence of attention to our bodies, our world, our emotions, and our thoughts is cultivated through mindfulness. Zen teachings posit that the spiritual life must be in concert with all of our existence through awareness and mindful practice. Jack Kornfield (1987) offers:

> Through attention to our bodies and minds and our reactions to outer circumstances, practice will deepen. This can be done through mindfulness while driving, in family life, at work or alone . . . we will see more and more clearly the patterns of habits and fears that have often run our lives. In coming more into the moment, we can actually experience the dynamic energy of our bodies and hearts. We can feel the difference between when we live with attachment and when we are at ease, when we are caught in compulsion and identification and when there is wisdom . . . mindfulness brings us the possibility of being free. (p. 80)

The Middle Way (Four Noble Truths)

The **First Noble Truth** posits that suffering or dissatisfaction is inherent in life, and that at times life seems difficult to bear. Freedom in the Buddhist view is somewhat similar to personal growth, gaining positive self-esteem, or engaging the ability to transcend (Michalon, 2001; Morgan, 2001). A major obstruction to that freedom is the concept of *Klesha,* translated as affliction, misconception of thought or cloudy thought, or contamination by the passions (Bankart, 1977; Epstein, 2001). One view of how *Kleshas* work is offered by Mark Epstein: "*Kleshas* work by grabbing hold of consciencelessness and taking it over. When I am enraged . . . I am completely caught up in my anger. There is no space in my mind. The reason that *Klesha* is so difficult to translate is that it connotes something that underlies both state of mind and emotion. . . . *Kleshas* are so intense they propel us mindlessly into actions that cause suffering" (2001, p. 127).

A parallel can be drawn between the Eastern concepts of *Klesha* and the First Noble Truth with the more Western concepts of behavior, mindset, low self-esteem, depression—indeed, the presentation and diagnosis of the presenting issue within the therapeutic process.

The **Second Noble Truth** posits that we go through life with the desire or craving for satisfaction to a degree that is impossible to attain because it is closely related to a negative attachment. The Eastern tradition suggests that our mental state cannot reach a balance because of attachments or cravings; therefore, we suffer. Freedom from the insatiable cravings that entangle us will allow us to celebrate healthy desires on many levels (Goldstein & Kornfield, 1987; Michalon, 2001; Salzberg, 1995).

The Second Noble Truth can be likened to the intense craving for, or addiction to, a substance or behavior that manifests from "suffering," and that affects the client in a negative manner.

The **Third Noble Truth** suggests that suffering can be diminished or even eradicated, empowering one to reach a sense of liberation (Michalon, 2001; Morgan, 2001). A parallel can be drawn between the Eastern belief of the Third Noble Truth and the more Western therapeutic concepts of recovery, after-stages of addiction concerning loss of pleasure, and behavior change as a result of counseling or therapy.

The **Fourth Noble Truth** posits that by leading a life filled with compassion, virtue, wisdom, and meditation, liberation is possible. The treatment for the aforementioned maladies of initial suffering is within the construct of the Fourth Noble Truth, as a result of the Eastern teachings of living a mindful life with purpose and awareness (Michalon, 2001; Morgan, 2001).

How do we attain awareness of self, or embark on the path to enlightenment, so that the Middle Way, the Four Noble Truths, become a part of our existence? Within the path to the achievement of liberation and awareness, there are eight factors embedded in the Buddhist spiritual training, or code of conduct, for living every day. This is called the **Eightfold Path**, and includes the following factors: (1) **right view** or understanding of human behavior and the universe; (2) **right intention** or thought; (3) **right speech**, using language in a positive manner, not telling lies; (4) **right action** or conduct, action of honor, peace and compassion; (5) **right livelihood**, or doing good things through your occupation; (6) **right effort**, using your energy and motivation toward compassionate ends; (7) **right mindfulness**, and (8) **right concentration**, leading to focused attention and liberation (Bankart, 1997; Michalon, 2001; Morgan, 2001). All eight factors have a place on the path to freedom and wisdom. Right mindfulness and right concentration lead us naturally into a discussion of meditation and meditative interventions in the practice of counseling and psychotherapy.

Meditation as Practice in Counseling and Psychotherapy

The study and interpretation of Buddhist meditation is broad and eclectic. Two types of meditation often written about in the context of personal growth and development are **concentration meditation**, or *Samadhi,* and **insight meditation (mindfulness meditation)**, or *Vipassana.* In concentration meditation, the focus is narrow, with attention typically on one object or concept. *Vipassana*, insight meditation, has a broad attention focus, with the aim of ultimate awareness through moment-to-moment awareness, leading to wisdom and change (Brown, 1984; Goleman, 1977). It is the emphasis on broad awareness and trait or behavior change that suggests an impact on the therapeutic process. In insight meditation, suppression of feelings or emotions is a negative. Goleman (1977) offers that the mind must not get lost in concentration or be abducted by it, for how else could we live in the moment and be aware of that moment?

Some qualities that can be cultivated in meditation fit nicely with the goals and inherent relationship between counselor or therapist and client, such as (1) warmth, or a holding environment; (2) interest, or engagement or willingness to re-engage; (3) steadiness/balanced effort, which offers continuity and stability; and (4) attention to detail, meaning a precise, intentional view of life behavior. These four qualities cultivate a widening of the ability for self-acceptance, a complete reception of whatever "state of mind" arrives (Goldstein & Kornfield, 1987; Goleman, 1977; Morgan, 2001).

It is important to note at this time that best practice suggests that a counselor or therapist should not assume the role of her or his client's meditation teacher (Epstein, 2001; Fulton, 2001; Morgan, 2001). To do so would constitute as much of an ethical duality as that of, for instance, a massage counselor's or therapist's practicing counseling and psychotherapy on her or his clients. Boundaries would be blurred at best, and the transferential issues arising from either the counseling or psychotherapeutic relationship or the meditation teacher/guru relationship might prove less than helpful, and indeed possibly harmful. The use of meditative techniques within the counseling or therapy construct, however, allows for some exercises to become part of that process, and might encourage the conjoint practice of the client's meditation practice and the personal counseling or therapy.

Creation of Inner Space

In counseling or therapy, the creation of physical space is vital: space must be warm, safe, and inviting. The counselor or therapist who desires to begin the inclusion of meditative intervention must create an inner space that will be felt by the client and conductive to openness and awareness. Brazier (1995) suggests:

> . . . space is a womb: room to grow . . . according to Buddhism, we are all 'embryo buddhas.' For our original buddha nature to become apparent, we need a womb in which to mature. The counselor's or therapist's acceptance of the client has to be profound and vast, encompassing their world, not just their self . . . the client seeks to bolster the self against the world. Zen shows us that when we look more deeply, self is a reflection of the world and to reject one is also to reject the other . . . Zen is more interested in emptying than filling; letting go is enlightenment. (pp. 24–25)

As one can see, it would be difficult for the counselor or therapist to include a meditation component without adhering to the principles and teachings of the Eastern tradition mentioned earlier. Mark Epstein (2001) shares his journey relative to the "space within" as a counselor or therapist, and how meditation impacted his clinical practice:

> Through my meditation I have seen how openness can contain and transform fear, and how desire interferes with this process. Without quite knowing how it was happening, I found an approach to psychology that puts less of an emphasis on understanding and more of a focus on experiencing than I was ever taught . . . having learned to jump into my own reality, I am no longer shy about jumping into another's. But it is Buddhism, with its emphasis on the Eightfold Path, that has taught me how not to be an interference in my own right. (pp. 58–59)

Deep breathing exercises, a **meditative moment** where the counselor or therapist and the client sit quietly after a statement or word comes up in session that might have caused pain or disturbance for the client, or a carefully chosen guided visualization are some interventions to consider. The following vignette illustrates a meditative moment included in a counseling or therapy session.

Before counseling and psychotherapy, Lilly had suppressed feelings of fear and loss concerning the impending loss of her grandmother to cancer. Lilly would typically come to counseling or therapy and discuss family conversations and activities, rarely allowing herself to go to the feeling level. Lately, she is allowing herself to feel more in-the-moment and to deal with her loss as a part of the life process, not as some type of punishment. She would express anger because she feels abandoned, alone, and cheated: she is a young adult, too young to lose a loved family member. Her grandmother was taken to the hospital last night, and Lilly is tense, angry, and anxious. She was previously referred to a meditation teacher and has been attending the sittings for over 6 months. Lilly has come to know that the therapeutic space we have created is womb-like, accepting, and conducive to the emptying process in her quest for letting go of the fear, anger, and anxiety.

Lilly represents a typical client for whom suffering and tightness is common. She struggles with the idea that all of life will not be perfect and pain-free. Conjointly with her reading on Buddhist teachings and Eastern tradition, she has journaled throughout the 6 months. Today, she brings a passage she penned early this morning after visiting her grandmother. The words are reflective of the calm she began to feel as she sat with the older woman, feeling the warmth of her hand and seeing her even breaths. Lilly asked if she could read some of those words. "The breathing—it's so even, it's more calm than mine. What does Grandma know that I don't? She's not upset. She asked me to be ready to accept that she is dying. . . . Dying. *Dying*—I've never used that word. . . ."

The word *dying* was repeated, then there was a silence, a meditative moment that lasted almost 2 minutes, during which time Lilly did the deep breathing she was being taught. The equanimity of the silence allowed her to breathe, to practice the mindful intention she was learning. She began to relax: her shoulders untensed, her hands unclasped her journal. "I feel much calmer right now. I'd like to talk about my grandma, if I could."

Given the space, the patience, and the opportunity to intentionally increase her awareness, Lilly was on the road to accepting a life issue that was here-and-now for her, not allowing that issue to dictate behavior and cognition.

Supporting Research

There have been numerous studies in the past 25 years that have discussed the efficacy of introducing meditation to the counseling or therapy process. Some articles have focused on the use of meditation for the benefit of the therapeutic relationship, for the benefit of the client, or for the benefit of the counselor or therapist—indeed, the subjective experience in all three scenarios would likely prove helpful (Shapiro & Giber, 1984). Studies have found that the inclusion of a meditation process or intervention positively affected the mental health of the client, and those researchers encouraged Western counselors or therapists to explore the Eastern Buddhist teachings as an enhancement of practice (Alexander, Rainforth, & Gelderloos, 1991; Davis & Gold, 1998; Goleman & Schwartz, 1976; Kristeller & Hallett, 1999; Shapiro, Schwartz & Bonner, 1998; Solberg & Halvorson, 2000; Walsh, 1999).

Limitations

There are, of course, cautions concerning the use of meditation and meditative interventions. Clients presenting with histories of psychosis would perhaps not be the best clients for this approach because of the reality constructs that are necessary in order to gain the most from the Eastern philosophical teachings. Also, clients with a propensity for "moving into a state of deep terror or psychosis . . . deep panic" (Michalon, 2001, p. 211), might actually regress through the use of meditation or meditative intervention, especially while in the throes of the panic or psychosis.

For the student who wishes to learn more about Eastern Buddhist teachings, their blend with counseling and psychotherapy, and meditation in particular, there are a number of good resources available. We urge those interested in taking the initial step on the path to integrating Eastern teachings with a practice of counseling and psychotherapy to (1) learn on a personal, "doing" level about meditation, and (2) seek respected resources such as Suzuki's *Zen Mind, Beginner's Mind;* Hanh's *Guide to Walking Meditation;* Brazier's *Zen Therapy: Transcending the Sorrows of the Human Mind;* and Epstein's *Thoughts Without a Thinker: Psychology from a Buddhist Perspective.*

Body-Centered Counseling and Psychotherapy

Donna M. Roy
Portland State University

Background

Ways of alleviating psychic pain and supporting the full flowering of humanness continue to evolve and change. More than 50 types of **non-traditional** or **alternative counseling or psychotherapy methods** are currently practiced (Corsini, 2001). Many non-traditional approaches are grounded in years of clinical experience, although they may have a limited empirical research base. Three sometimes-overlapping categories of alternative counseling or psychotherapy disciplines are **somatic** or **body-centered, expressive,** and **transpersonal.**

Somatic or body-centered counseling and psychotherapy, highlighted in this chapter, focuses on reuniting the body and mind and stems from both classical theories and ancient healing approaches (Caldwell, 1997; Kurtz, 1987; Mindell, 1982). Expressive counseling and psychotherapy center on externalizing, understanding, and processing internal urges, trauma material, and untapped capacities through images, sound, movement, or words. They include art, dance, drama, poetry, sand tray, play, music, writing, and reading therapies. Transpersonal methods focus on the evolution of the individual in both spiritual and personal terms and can employ meditation, shamanic healing, spiritual counseling and psychotherapy, and mystical, altered state, or trance experiences. In this chapter, expressive and transpersonal approaches to psychological and spiritual healing will be discussed only as they relate to somatic counseling or psychotherapy.

Somatic approaches to healing have broad roots in classical psychological theories, in shamanism and Eastern philosophy, in physics and systems theory, in medicine, and in education and the arts. (Caldwell, 1997; Kurtz, 1987, 1990; Mindell, 1982) This eclectic foundation evolved into a paradigm that stresses holism, inclusivity, and partnership and that is less reductionistic than the classical Aristotelian worldview, which emphasizes the breaking down of the whole into parts in order to identify, isolate, and manipulate (Kurtz, 1987; 1990). Somatic psychotherapies may complement, integrate, and sometimes diverge from conventional methods and may overlap with expressive and transpersonal work.

Body-centered counseling or psychotherapy takes various forms that share certain common principles. Among these is the idea that a return to health requires embracing the whole human being and giving special attention to the place where the body and mind meet, the **body-mind interface** (Kurtz, 1987). Another key idea is that the primal expression of self, or life-energy, cannot be bad. Disease is created, from this perspective, when life force is repressed or unexpressed (Caldwell, 1997). Somatic counseling or psychotherapy assumes that body posture and movement, as well as the ways we speak of and imagine the body, are clues to how we organize our experience and relate to the world. Our bodies receive and communicate information. Central to the concept of the mind-body interface is a belief in the profound effect of the body's early experiences (pre- and perinatal) on psychological and social development (Caldwell, 1997; Keleman, 1985; Kurtz, 1990; Pesso, 1997).

This chapter, while presenting an overview of selected somatic counseling or psychotherapy methods, will highlight **Hakomi Body-Centered Psychotherapy,** developed by **Ron Kurtz** (1987, 1990, 2000), and introduce aspects of six related body-centered modalities, including one often integrated into Hakomi practice. Although a myriad of transformational methods exists, Hakomi can serve as a primer on body-centered counseling or psychotherapy. An original and highly eclectic body-centered counseling and psychotherapy modality, Hakomi is active and vital throughout the Americas, Europe, New Zealand, Australia, and parts of Asia.

The Roots of Somatic Counseling and Psychotherapy

Somatic counseling or psychotherapy owes part of its development to traditions outside the realm of conventional psychology, such as **shamanic healing** and the spiritual disciplines of the East. Shamanistic cultures throughout the world have operated for millennia from the premise that the mind and body are not in fact divided, that health comes from balance of mind, body, and spirit, and that there is a direct relationship between mental and physical health. Shamans practice with respect for and understanding of the connection between the body, mind, and spirit and use the generation of trance and altered states of consciousness to facilitate what essentially is a journey within to the source of healing (Halifax, 1979; Hammerschlag, 1988; Harner, 1980). This view of wholeness and the use of meditative states such as **mindfulness** are also fundamental to somatic counseling and psychotherapy. The importance of increasing awareness through mindfulness—a non-reactive self-observation of internal experiences—is central to the Buddhist path. In a similar way, somatic counseling or psychotherapy (and other current therapies such as Dialectic Behavior Therapy) recognize the value of developing non-judgmental self-observation capacities and related self-reflection skills (Kurtz, 1990; Linehan, 1993).

Body-centered counseling and psychotherapy have learned much from the East. Spiritual disciplines such as Buddhism recognize the unity and interrelationship of all things; they see a fundamental delusion in the idea of separateness on any level. This means that we are not separate from each other, our bodies are not separate from our minds, and further, our minds are not divided within themselves. All things are connected. The splits we perceive between others and ourselves, between mind and body, and even within our minds, are delusions. Our bodies are bridges to the unconscious as well as to the outside world. Somatic counseling or psychotherapy encourages communication not only between therapist and client, but also, and equally as important, between the various internal parts of the mind, all with the goal of recognizing wholeness and interconnections within and without (Johanson & Kurtz, 1991; Kurtz, 1990).

In addition to Eastern thought and shamanistic perspective, the somatic field is heavily influenced by psychology's more conventional theorists. **Freud** (1955) began as a physician and saw the body, through its sensations, as directly related to psychological states. The ego, according to Freud, was a body ego. With his eventual emphasis on talking in therapy, however, the body never became central to his work; the only place it remained in analysis was on the couch as a way to reduce the client's defenses (Caldwell, 1997). Some of Freud's contemporaries gave the body more attention. **Josef Breuer,** a long-time colleague of Freud's (Boadella, 1987), related neurotic symptoms to currents of energy in the body and was the first to connect the discharge of energy—**catharsis**—with analysis. **Georg Groddeck,** also practicing during Freud's time, recognized that physical illness and psychological states were related. He pioneered the combined use of diet, massage, and psychoanalysis. **Sandor Ferenczi,** another of Freud's peers, used what he saw his patients doing with their bodies to create techniques that associated movement and posture with memories and the unconscious (Caldwell, 1997; Smith, 1985).

Considered by many to be the father of somatic counseling and psychotherapy, **Wilhelm Reich** (1974), a student of Freud and Ferenczi, saw a person's psychological history in his or her body. He believed that the repression of **universal life energy** (psychic and physical energy) caused neuroses and psychoses, which in turn caused **character armoring** (rigid and chronic physical manifestations of psychological defense mechanisms). To address this armoring and treat physical rigidity, he had his clients breathe heavily. He then used their breathing and his touch to identify and work with blocks in the flow of body energy. The fact that he had patients lie down, breathe, move, and vocalize as early as the 1950s made him a controversial figure (Caldwell, 1997).

The Evolution of Somatic Counseling and Psychotherapy

Somatic counseling and psychotherapy have evolved since Reich, with **bodywork** one of its offshoots. The bodywork branch of the family tree grew from the work of practitioners like **Frederick Alexander** (1974), **Ida Rolf** (1978), and **Moshe Feldenkrais** (1972). Their work focused on body alignment in space as well as physical balance, and was not counseling or psychotherapy, nor were their bodyworkers trained as counselors or psychotherapists, but they held a strong belief that bodywork would improve mental as well as physical health. Their contributions significantly influenced somatic counseling and psychotherapy (Caldwell, 1997; Kurtz, 1987, 1990).

Practitioners in body-centered psychotherapy often blend and synthesize modalities. **Dance/Movement Therapy** evolved from the work of **Marian Chace** in the 1940s, and over time, became grounded in Jungian, Freudian, and object relations' depth psychology. One of these modern movement practices is **Authentic Movement** (Boughton, 2001).

Robert Hall studied under **Fritz Perls** (1969) and co-founded the **Lomi School,** where Gestalt therapy and many forms of bodywork are combined (Hall, 2001). Hall suggests that the mind and body are functionally the same and both must energetically release for healing to happen. **Thomas Hanna** (1970, 1987) combined psychotherapy with teaching clients new ways to move their bodies freely. **Stanislav Grof** (1985) developed **Holotropic Breathwork,** which has clients breathe deeply to attain an altered state of consciousness in which they move or speak or express themselves physically, and later, make mandalas to process and physically manifest their experience (Caldwell, 1997). Grof's work has some similarities with the inward journey of shamans and stemmed partially from his research using LSD in counseling and psychotherapy (Metzner, 1998).

So-called "**hard techniques**" (Smith, 1985) of somatic counseling and psychotherapy that evolved from Reichian theory include **bioenergetics** and **core energetics.** These methods support the expression of strong emotions and are intense forms of therapy. Therapists use exercises with clients that intensify body tensions and force their release. In 1952, **Alexander Lowen** (1976) and **John Pierrakos** (1987), students of Reich, together developed bioenergetics, based on Reich's universal life energy and armoring theories. Bioenergetics studies the personality through the body, using a systemic description of five character types (schizoid, oral, psychopathic, masochistic, and rigid) based on body movement and form (holding together, holding on, holding up, holding in, and holding back). Core energetics, developed by Pierrakos when he later split from Lowen, also focuses on intensifying clients' core feelings and energy in order to release blocks to fulfillment (Caldwell, 1997).

The Gentler Forms of Body-Centered Counseling and Psychotherapy

Currently, there is a profusion of "softer," less aggressive modalities. These approaches use awareness techniques and meditation and rely less on counselor and therapist analysis of body structures and movement and more on the client's experience and self-awareness. Clients are not encouraged to work toward explosive catharsis, are not put into stressful physical positions or touched invasively, and are not led into altered states through intensive breathing (Caldwell, 1997). These methods still assume that transformation is the goal, and have faith in the human organism's natural tendency to unfold. They are also informed by feminist theory, seeking to create therapeutic relationships that are based on interdependence (Jordan & Surrey, 1986) and a sharing of power (Espin & Gawelek, 1992). Many of these forms were created either by women or in cross-gender partnerships. Six of these forms of somatic counseling and psychotherapy are briefly described below.

Pat Ogden's Hakomi Sensorimotor Psychotherapy (1997; Ogden & Minton, 2001) evolved from Hakomi Body-Centered Psychotherapy and Ogden's personal training as a bodyworker, and has become one of the preeminent alternative methods for working with symptoms of trauma (Van der Kolk, McFarlane, & Weisaeth, 1996). Aligned with Hakomi philosophically, Hakomi Sensorimotor Psychotherapy is grounded in the use of mindfulness to study present experience, the belief in the client's capacity for self-regulation in response to new information, and faith in the client's ability to unfold toward wholeness. Hakomi Sensorimotor Psychotherapy differentiates between treatments for trauma and developmental wounds, and thus is especially effective in working with trauma survivors. Its methods offer specific interventions to improve regulation of emotional and sensorimotor states, a common difficulty among traumatized individuals. Integrating body awareness and trauma work requires high levels of counselor or psychotherapist somatic awareness and counseling and psychotherapy skills.

Gay and Kathlyn Hendricks' Body-Centered Therapy (1993) stems from Kathlyn's background in movement and transpersonal counseling and therapy and Gay's training in counseling and clinical psychology, as well as his own transformative experiences. Hendricks' Body-Centered Therapy focuses on healing the body-mind split that leads to a disconnection from our fundamental **essence,** or pure consciousness. They contend that to be fully alive and aware of the unity of existence, we must listen to and fully experience our feelings. Counselors and therapists act like teachers as much as healers and make therapeutic strategies transparent to clients. The Hendricks assert that this changes the dynamic in the relationship and gives more power to clients (Hendricks, 1997).

Understanding **Amy and Arnie Mindell's Process Work** (1997) requires the ability to look softly and indirectly. Deeply grounded in Jungian psychology, this modality defines reality more like a shaman might. A fundamental concept is the **dreambody,** the experience of oneself as an evolving process, as a flow of timeless experience. This can be thought of as a changing process of expression whose form depends on the context. In sleep, it is experienced as dream images; in dancing, the impulse behind movements; in extreme states, waking visions; in ordinary consciousness, physical or emotional sensations; in relation to others, instances of synchronicity or accidents. The Mindells suggest that the more we are aware of our dreambodies, the more we are truly ourselves. Process Work strives to awaken this awareness. The Mindells also work with groups and individuals around conflict resolution, chronic and terminal illness, and extreme states of consciousness, such as coma (Mindell, 1982).

Integrative Body Psychotherapy (IBP), developed by **Marjorie Rand and Jack Rosenberg,** has the goal of increasing connections with the self and others while maintaining clear personal boundaries. Self in IBP is perceived energetically, as a felt body sense of continuity, well-being, and identity. IBP contends that effective personal boundaries lead to a clear sense of self, which allows for the development of intimate relationships; intimacy grows best when people have a definite sense of self and maintain that in coming together with another. Developmentally, IBP sees experiences *in utero* and early childhood as formative and held in the physical body. Consequently, it puts emphasis on a safe, boundaried, therapeutic relationship; the client's present body experience; and the development of effective personal boundaries (Rand & Fewster, 1997; Rosenberg, Rand, & Asay, 1985).

Pesso Boyden System Psychomotor (PBSP) is one of the earliest of these gentler methodologies. Developed in the 1960s by **Albert Pesso** and **Diane Boyden Pesso,** the method is grounded in their backgrounds as dancers. PBSP suggests that memories of past experiences are not hard facts but subjective experiences as assessed by the individual. These body memories live in our tissue and powerfully influence our present and future. Such personal memory is active in every moment of our lives, as is **evolutionary memory,** which is held in our genes and contains all the species' knowledge of how to further life. Our evolutionary memory knows what each of us longs for and needs, and when the need or longing is best met, in order to develop fully. Our personal memory tells us whether our developmentally driven needs and longings have been met adequately and appropriately or not. Typically practiced in group settings, PBSP helps clients undergo

structures—client-controlled re-experiences of the body sense of not getting a developmental need met, as well as the symbolic satisfaction of the need. These unmet developmental needs and longings revolve around place, nurture, support, protection, and limits. As a result of the structures, new **virtual memories** can be formed that offer alternatives to the painful past (Pesso, 1969, 1973, 1997).

Re-Creation of the Self (R-CS), developed by Hakomi Institute founding member **Jon Eisman** (1995, 2001), is rooted firmly in Hakomi and is taught in Hakomi/R-CS training programs in the United States, Canada, and Europe. This counseling and psychotherapeutic method adds a detailed map of the psyche and offers an existential alternative to doing regressive work. It focuses on the innate wholeness of people, and sees each of us as being formed from Divine wholeness yet experiencing human separateness and fragmentation. It contends that the failure to integrate our Divine nature with our human nature, coupled with later unyielding life events, leads to a fragmented perception of self. As humans, we experience trance-like states of consciousness through whose eyes we perceive our lives. The R-CS approach to counseling and psychotherapy accesses and encourages a state of aware consciousness that recognizes our innate wholeness, allows the full expression of humanness and human resources, and supports freedom from trance. Its interventions assist clients in stepping out of the illusion of limitation and fragmentation and into the felt experience of wholeness and unlimited potential. Because it recognizes the differences among clients in strength of inner resources, R-CS sets goals based on client readiness and present capacity. When needed, it uses Hakomi and other R-CS techniques to do regressive work—the exploration of the various trance selves—to build inner resources and to foster client self-reorganization.

These six approaches, as well as Hakomi Body-Centered Psychotherapy, represent an evolving orientation of counseling and psychotherapy strategies that value and regard the whole person in the healing process.

Hakomi Body-Centered Counseling and Psychotherapy

Hakomi Therapy is one of the original "softer" somatic psychologies and is rooted in the experiential therapies of the 1960s, Eastern philosophy, and systems theory. Its founder, Ron Kurtz, has been called a "therapeutic wizard" and an irreverent pragmatist (Johanson, 1987). Kurtz's postgraduate work in psychology was in learning and perception; the major influences on his early professional development included experiential learning, sensitivity training, Gestalt therapy, bioenergetics, Buddhism, Taoism, yoga, and the work of Reich, Milton Erickson, Feldenkrais, Rolf, Pesso, and Pierrakos. He taught at San Francisco State University in the 1960s, immersed himself in the evolving experiential psychology community of the time, and then worked in New York for 7 years in private practice. After his first book, *The Body Reveals* (Kurtz & Prestera, 1976), was published, he and a small group of dedicated students co-founded the **Hakomi Institute** in 1980 in Putnam, Connecticut. The Institute later moved to Boulder, Colorado, and Kurtz began a career as a leader of workshops and professional training. He continues to teach and write throughout the United States and abroad (Jon Eisman, personal conversation, September 10, 2001; Kurtz, 1987, 1990, 2000).

The word *Hakomi* comes from the Hopi language and means roughly, "How do you stand in relation to these many realms?" It emerged from a dream of one of the original founders. The distinct relevance to the heart of Hakomi inspired the original institutional founders to embrace the dream name, and it continues to both reflect and inform the work (Kurtz, 1990).

The Western psychological roots of Hakomi, including Person-Centered Therapy and Gestalt Therapy, emphasize the counseling or therapeutic relationship and the role of experience and its study. They see value in talking, but unlike their Freudian and neo-Freudian predecessors, they place more value on having experiences and expressing feelings. Perls' (1969; Perls, Hefferline, & Goodman, 1977) encouragement of clients to exaggerate movements or voices was a way to interrupt "any attempt to head trip" (Kurtz, 1987, p. 10) and to ground people in their present experiences. Perls' and Rogers' experiential therapies and the encounter movement of the 1960s were much less about analyzing the past and more about being in and aware of the present, and making clients more responsible for their own change processes. The body therapies (e.g., Feldenkrais) of the 1980s added the study of present experience to the recipe. Their goal was to study how experience was organized in order to make fundamental life changes (Kurtz, 1990).

Another key aspect of Hakomi is drawn from the work of master therapists like Milton Erickson (Erickson & Rossi, 1976) and Virginia Satir (1983). They had fundamentally positive assumptions about people and their suffering. They believed that the pain of existence comes from how a person responds to the world and that changing the way he or she perceives and responds to life also changes the experience of pain. This assumption about the nonpathology of existence is critical to Hakomi and greatly influenced its development (Kurtz, 1987, 1990).

The main Eastern philosophical influences on Hakomi came from awareness practices of yoga, Taoism, and Buddhism. These traditions are meditative and contemplative and use the practice of **mindfulness** to explore consciousness and its relationship to matter. They also concentrate on using present experience and its study to inform action. They are based on a nonviolent worldview that supports the potential for change without force. The reliance on the Buddhist meditative technique of mindfulness is central to Hakomi, and it is this aspect of the method that Kurtz says he would like to be remembered for integrating into the field of counseling and psychotherapy (Johanson & Kurtz, 1991; Kurtz, 1987, 1990; Batchelor, 1997).

Kurtz has a background in physics and information theory and a lifelong passion for systems theory, which constitutes Hakomi's third major influence. Systems theory assumes that living systems are nonlinear, fluid, interdependent, self-regulating, and can create and heal themselves. Living systems are complex and actively respond to their environments by organizing themselves. They are alive with uncertainty, participation, variety, and change. This is an organismic and contextual, nonmechanistic view; it asserts that dynamic, multiinfluenced systems concern wholes with interrelated parts, not separate parts fabricated into wholes (Capra, 1982; Kurtz, 1990). Hakomi embraces this paradigm.

Human Nature: A Developmental Perspective

Hakomi has an unabashedly optimistic view of human nature. It assumes that people are fundamentally whole and, when wounded, have the innate capacity to redirect themselves back toward wholeness. It begins with the view that people are not problems that need to be fixed, but complex systems that are prone to self-correction when obstacles are removed. Although this self-correction may need periodic updating, it is the best a person can do at any moment, given his or her disposition, level of awareness, and existing life conditions. Like the person-centered theory of Carl Rogers, Hakomi assumes that people are fundamentally trustworthy, naturally move toward greater awareness and self-actualization, have the needed inner resources to do this, and experience unique worlds (Hazler, 1999). It does not judge someone's response to life as being deficient or fault-ridden; nor does it see defects that need curing. Hakomi assumes that people can accomplish a natural self-expansion through mindfully studying how they organize their experience and making choices based on the new perspective gained from this self-study (Kurtz, 1987, 1990).

Hakomi presumes an underlying interconnectedness among people and in the natural world and that, at the individual level, humans have a self-healing capacity. Based on the interactive integration of the mind and the body, Hakomi is at home with individual complexity and mystery. It contends that the human "default" mode of interaction is to embrace partnership rather than domination, and that people would rather peacefully cooperate than use violence to dominate. While acknowledging the special role of early childhood in fostering strategic responses to the world, Hakomi theory rests on the premise that psychological woundings and limitations have multiple causes. Finally, while recognizing the multiplicity of influences on human development, it celebrates the power of the individual in the creation of his or her own life (Kurtz, 1990).

Like Reich, and consistent with a holistic orientation, Hakomi counselors and psychotherapists function from the premise that a "person's character is the fractional sum total of all past experiences" (Reich, 1974). Although Hakomi counselors and psychotherapists use information about character to inform their interventions, the nature of character etiology, as defined in Hakomi, is currently in a state of flux as counselors and psychotherapists become increasingly aware of new findings—and further questions—regarding human development and the mind from researchers such as Daniel Siegel (1999). Although character strategies help clarify why and how people learned to be, feel, and act as they do, character theory remains secondary to honoring the gradual unfolding of individual uniqueness (Eisman, personal communication, September 26, 2001; Kurtz, 1990, personal communication, August 20, 2001).

From a Hakomi perspective, character strategies evolve from interruptions of natural growth; they are primarily the result of a child's natural responses to his or her environment over time. They develop for very good reasons—as ways to deal with innate dispositions and situations of childhood—and are the ghosts of early experiences. Hakomi concurs with developmentalists who suggest normal development requires having certain experiences within critical time periods in order to proceed with healthy growth. Without critical psychological or social "experiences that need and want to happen" (Kurtz, 1990, p. 30), children miss something important: they either do not learn, or inaccurately learn, or partially learn the human social skills and attitudes that childhood is meant to teach. As a result, they develop a fear of particular current experiences because of the pain associated with the original incomplete or skewed learning experiences. They enter a kind of trance that keeps them blind and powerless in the face of the original experiences' present day reflections. These **missing core experiences** cause pain, blocks, and limiting ways of being in the world. They contribute to the creation of character patterns whose purpose is to soothe the pain of the original experience or contend with the still-present, unmet natural longing around the issue (Eisman, personal communication, September 27, 2001; Kurtz, 1987, 1990, personal communication, June 20, 2000).

People are internally complicated and use a variety of character strategies to respond to the world, so individuals cannot be defined by one strategy; they are combinations of various patterns. Different character patterns develop around different developmental learning tasks so people evolve as "constellations of character," rather than as one fixed type (Eisman, personal communication, September 26, 2001). Life unfolds, beliefs develop, experimentation happens, strategies develop, and eventually character strategies reach a certain degree of homeostasis. Functionally, they are strengths, because they helped the child deal with his or her life; practically, they can become weaknesses if overused. In Hakomi, they are not treated as defenses to be overcome, but as processes to be understood. These "organized, habitual patterns of reaction" (Kurtz, 1990, p. 42) can be consciously employed or not, once their roots are uncovered and the missing core experiences are reclaimed (Eisman, 1987; Kurtz, 1987, 1990). Hakomi character typologies follow a developmental model influenced by both Freud and Lowen. Hakomi incorporates Freud's tactile, oral, anal, and genital stages, applied to the developmental period from *in utero* to about 7 years of age, as well as Lowen's body movement and form-derived types, and suggests eight major strategic responses to the world (Eisman, 2001; Kurtz, 1990). Table 16.1 outlines Freud's and Lowen's terms and Hakomi's character typologies, developmental time frames, related core beliefs, strategies, and longings.

To provide further definition for what the self is and how it evolves, the aligned Re-Creation of the Self method is helpful. R-CS embraces all the major constructs of Hakomi and subscribes to the concept of individual development over time, with childhood having the deepest impact. In addition, however, it delineates a model of the self that puts an emphasis on recognizing limiting psychological states of consciousness and making existential choices. Eisman describes an **Organic Self,** the original and most pure form of self, as the unique and true expression of individual humanity and Divine consciousness. Its purpose is to live, learn, grow in wisdom, and develop into a unique, fully human person. It does this through the ongoing pursuit of what it wants moment-to-moment: the **Organic Wish**—an intention rising from a reservoir of **core knowledge** about how the world is ideally supposed to be (Eisman, 2001).

In life circumstances when this core knowledge is betrayed, or the Organic Wish meets unresolvable resistance by some kind of limiting experience, the Organic Self is caught between its innate desire to continue to expand its experience further and its natural impulse to avoid the painful experience by contracting. To resolve this dilemma, it uses the "trick it knows from incarnating," which is "to divide its own consciousness" (Eisman, personal communication, October 3, 2001). It then fragments itself into several substates of consciousness. Each of these substates represents some aspect of the dilemma and is like a self-sustained trance with its own limited view of reality (Eisman, 2001).

In those situations when present experience echoes the original wounding—those particular developmental challenges that were not mastered, or perceived or real traumas that were experienced—these individual trance selves are activated into what Eisman calls an **inner committee** (2001–2002, p. 26). These selves do not communicate freely or see the whole truth of any situation, nor are they true to the wishes of the Organic Self. This leads to a sense of confusion and disharmony, a lessening of inner resources, and acting

Table 16.1
Character Strategies in Hakomi

Neo-Freudian Terms	Lowen's Terms	Hakomi Terms (Kurtz/Eisman)	Relevant Developmental Period	Core Belief	Character Strategy	Natural Longing
tactile	schizoid	sensitive/analytic (K) hypersensitive/withdrawn (E)	*in utero* to 1 year	I am not safe, so I have to withdraw from experience.	Minimize self-expression and contact with others. Take refuge in thought and fantasy.	I have a right to be alive, safe, and welcome.
oral	oral	dependent/endearing (K) abandoned/endearing (E)	birth to 2 years	I cannot get what I need, so I have to depend on others.	Seek support by acting childlike.	I have a right to need.
oral	compensated oral	self-reliant (K) alienated/self-reliant (E)	birth to 2 years	No one will help me, so I have to do it myself.	Mobilize self-support and rely on yourself. Seek challenges.	I have a right to have my needs met.
anal	psychopathic 1	tough/generous (K) hurt/invulnerable (E)	2 to 4 years	My needs will be used against me, so I have to be invulnerable and in charge.	Hide your weakness, insecurity, and fear. Look tough, act important.	I have a right to be a separate person.
anal	psychopathic 2	charming/seductive (K) betrayed/manipulative (E)	2 to 4 years	If I am honest, they will trick me, so I have to maneuver secretly around them.	Hide your true intentions. Charm others and use them to get what you need.	I have a right to be a separate person.

anal	masochistic	burdened/enduring	18 months to 4 years	If I do what I want, I will hurt them, so I have to control myself and resist them to feel free.	Bear up and wait it out.	I have a right to assert myself.
genital	phallic	industrious/overfocused (K) ignored/industrious (E)	3 to 7 years	They do not see my talent, so I have to work hard to show them my worth.	Work hard, keep going, and let nothing distract you. Take refuge in action.	I have a right to relax and be loved.
genital	hysteric	expressive/clinging (K) rejected/dramatic (E)	3 to 7 years	They do not appreciate me, so I have to work hard to get their attention.	Dramatize events and feelings to get attention and avoid separation.	I have a right to be heard and understood.

Derived from Eisman, J. (2000-2001, 2001-2002), *The Hakomi method and re-creation of the self: Professional training* (available from the Hakomi Institute of Oregon, 6836 HWY 66, Ashland, OR 97520) and Kurtz, R. (1990), *Body-centered psychotherapy: The Hakomi method.* Mendocino, CA: Life Rhythm.

in the world as an "**assumed adult**" (Eisman, 2001–2002, p. 26). An adult operating from this position is on automatic pilot, in and out of various trances, unable to fully evolve. In circumstances where supportive experiences allow a child to fully embody his or her Organic Wishes, barring other psychic insults, fragmentation is not a necessary resolution to a psychic dilemma. Because R-CS acknowledges the common human experience of being wounded and reverting to perceptions of fragmentation, it focuses on helping clients reclaim the underlying innate sense of wholeness and aliveness (Eisman, 2001).

Major Constructs

The Organization of Experience

Foundational to all experiential approaches, and fundamental to Hakomi, is the tenet that experience is organized and has meaning. Bateson, in *Mind and Nature* (1979), describes the organization of systems and suggests that experience is more than free-flowing emotion or energy: it is information. Further, information is contained in all parts of the experiencing organism, whether it be a fruit-fly or all of nature, and all parts are in communication with each other. These parts are organized into wholes—hierarchical systems that exhibit increasing levels of complexity. Minds are these kinds of information systems (Kurtz, 1990). Bateson goes on to say that everything in nature, indeed, nature itself, has mind. From a Hakomi perspective, this supports the celebration of complexity and underscores the importance of holding the highest order of possibility for clients.

Additionally, humans have life experiences from conception through old age that have emotional and cognitive (and spiritual) impact, and from which we make generalizations about the world. These generalized beliefs, especially those from early childhood events and traumatic or other life-altering experiences, comprise **core organizing material** that resides deep in our psyches and forms a base upon which we continue to perceive and act in the world. We create feeling and meaning from these events; we begin to believe we are loved or unloved, safe or unsafe, strong or weak. We gather and meld our responses into our own truths that rule our lives. This means that each of us is the lead player in our own life story. Each of us gathers and groups events and experiences in order to keep the flow of experience moving in particular directions. Although we are each very active in this creation of our lives, we usually are unaware of much of it (Kurtz, 1990; Eisman, 2001).

This lack of awareness of our own role in creating our lives is not surprising. People have learned through millennia to speed progress by developing habits that reduce the time needed to attend to repetitive actions. We are skilled in many areas of our lives at responding without having to think. Many of these automatic life responses flow from memories, beliefs, images, neural patterns, and attitudes that do not need to reach consciousness to profoundly influence our actions (Kurtz, 1990). Studying this core organizing material allows us to make these automatic habits conscious and make choices about changing the actual flow of our experience. Hakomi works toward helping clients uncover their organizing core beliefs and influences and wake up to themselves and their creative power. Although this study is often accompanied by strong emotions, which Hakomi honors, it emphasizes the uncovering of meaning rather than the release and expression of emotion (Kurtz, 1990).

The Principles

Hakomi has seven basic principles that inform all of its techniques and therapeutic strategies. A counselor or psychotherapist operating in congruence with these principles, even without knowing any Hakomi techniques, could still be an effective partner in healing. The principles provide an attitudinal foundation that communicates to the client that he or she is free, alive, and of exquisite interest. This experimental attitude of curiosity, invitation, acceptance of uncertainty, receptivity, and faith in the client's unfolding invites the unconscious to reveal itself and collaborate in the process. In contrast, working outside of these principles is, as Kurtz says, like "working blind" (1990).

The **unity principle** states that everything is interconnected; that the idea of a separation between people and within people is false. Unity is associated with belonging and bonds because, as Kurtz says, "...the universe is fundamentally a web of relationships" (1990, p. 33). Unity is also reflected in primal psychic wholeness, rather than brokenness. It assumes there is a basic healing drive toward unity in all of us. This view is very different from a mechanistic orientation that focuses on separation and isolation as a fundamental human construct. The unity principle assumes that we have to actively split ourselves internally and from others in order to perceive a world of separation. The unity principle proclaims the underlying belief, instead, in the interconnectedness of existence. It recognizes the interdependence of everything, and that the whole is greater than the sum of the parts (Kurtz, 1990; Wilbur, 1977).

The **organicity principle** affirms that each living system has its own organization and is self-regulating. As such, it is not possible to "heal" another person, only to assist (or hinder) his or her own self-healing through a therapeutic relationship and appropriate interventions. This underscores the importance of looking within the client, within the client/counselor or therapist relationship, and/or within related systems to find insight and answers. It also reminds counselors and therapists to follow natural processes that want to unfold, rather than assume authority over the client's process. It respects the client's innate capacity for health, self-determination, and personal responsibility (Kurtz, 1990).

Mindfulness is a state of consciousness that allows nonjudgmental awareness of present experience. Some have called its use in Hakomi "assisted meditation" (Kurtz, 1990, p. 23). It is also a principle that assumes the path of consciousness is the preferred way. In Hakomi, the **mindfulness principle** involves waiting and noticing, without taking automatic action, in order to allow what wants to happen to actually happen. Mindfulness allows a client to stay with his or her immediate experience long enough to gather the information needed for true change to be possible. In a mindful state, a client maintains a connection to both conscious and normally unconscious experience. Awareness becomes crystallized and offers the person a broader, witnessing view of his or her inner and outer world while also allowing awareness of his or her immediate surroundings. Mindfulness is not the same as hypnosis, which intentionally bypasses the conscious mind to go straight to the unconscious. Hakomi welcomes the conscious and unconscious as equal partners, using mindfulness to witness internal events.

The **principle of nonviolence** involves a basic respect for life and engenders an attitude of inclusiveness and regard for the "inevitable presence of unity and organicity" (Eisman, 2001–2002). It eschews the use of force against a living system because force creates resistance, which hinders growth. Hakomi has a special definition of nonviolence that goes beyond the conventional interpretation of the term; violence, for example, does not have to be blatant. Violence can be a counselor or psychotherapist thinking he or she knows what's best for a client, or failing to truly accept a client as a self-determining, whole living system (Kurtz, 1990). Hakomi affirms this basic concept of Buddhism and implements it within the therapeutic relationship.

One way Hakomi operates within this principle is its support of, rather than active opposition to, client "defenses." By supporting the client's tried and true ways of managing and protecting himself or herself, Hakomi creates a safe space for exploring these possibly outdated mechanisms, and does not increase the client's need to protect himself or herself further. Another nonviolent aspect of Hakomi is its focus on experience over problem solving. This allows choices to unfold naturally, and the client to be the "doer" of his or her own change process. Another example is the way Hakomi invites both the client's conscious and unconscious mind to be present in sessions. This ensures that the client is not tricked or manipulated and retains full power of choice (Kurtz, 1987).

The **principle of mind-body holism** recognizes that the mind and the body influence one another and that the mind-body system is complex and unpredictable. It is an orientation that "sees patterns and interactions and non-linear influences" (Kurtz, 1990), and is intrigued and expectant about complexity and mystery. In Hakomi, the mind-body interface is the territory most explored because it is the place where information is accessible and can evolve. This is where the counselor or psychotherapist can have a direct relationship with the unconscious. At the mind-body interface, it is possible to communicate in terms of body experiences that give clues to the client's inner world. Movements like a person's automatic head-ducking upon thinking about his or her father merit noticing and exploring because they hold information about the client's response to and organization of past and present experience. This is the place to work with interactions and feedback loops, between sensations and memories, emotions and images, experience and belief (Kurtz, 1990).

Two additional principles have been added to Hakomi training literature that were not part of Kurtz's original concept. They both, however, evolved naturally from the principles and came from the experience of long-time Hakomi practitioners.

Hakomi therapist Halko Weiss first suggested the **principle of truth.** It speaks to the importance of not making false promises to clients, especially to those in the altered state of consciousness called the **child state** (see Intervention Strategies). It is related to recognizing our own limits as counselors or therapists, as well as our mistakes, and about being ethical and honest. This principle also emphasizes the significance of the existential pursuit of the question "What is the truth?" for both counselor or therapist and client, and assumes there is such a thing as universal truth. This includes championing such values as human wholeness, goodness, worth, and right to exist (Eisman, 2001–2002).

The **mutability principle** contends that change is an inherent and absolute characteristic of reality. This means that things change, and will continue to change. People can effect certain changes, such as stopping the building of prisons, but some things are out of human control, such as death and the seasons. Hakomi therapy, like all psychotherapies, is built on the assumption that people can and want to change, and will do so under certain circumstances. Hakomi embraces this principle by supporting clients in transforming their core beliefs and fully embodying and acting from their truths (Eisman, 2001–2002).

The Healing Relationship

The Hakomi method assumes that it is the counselor's or psychotherapist's job to create the therapeutic relationship. The process of counseling or therapy in Hakomi is embedded in the context of the relationship between counselor or therapist and client. This means that maintaining the relationship and holding an emotional attitude grounded in the principles is paramount to doing good therapy. This attitude is one of "resting in nonviolence" (Kurtz, 1990) and being a "loving presence" (Kurtz, 2000), and is necessary to gain the cooperation of the client's unconscious. The counselor or therapist needs to be warm, accepting, honest, nonjudgmental, and respectful of the client's self-management. This requires a level of psychological maturity on the part of the counselor or therapist that comes from deep self-awareness. It offers the client the chance to engage with someone who has the strength to back off and let the process unfold.

An understanding of the client's world is also needed, as is the ability to communicate that understanding to the client in a way that rings true (Eisman, 2000; Kurtz, 1990). Expressions of intuitive insight and other verbal and nonverbal communication need to be grounded in the same honesty and nonjudgmentalism referred to earlier.

A therapeutic relationship is also founded on self-awareness on the part of the counselor or therapist, and the cooperation of his or her own unconscious. In Trungpa Rinpoche's words, "full human beingness" (1983) is critical to counselor and psychotherapist effectiveness. Hakomi realizes that for counselors and psychotherapists to develop skills like intuition and holistic seeing, it is essential to be self-aware and self-trusting. Practitioners may not need to be enlightened, but it is crucial that they be on the road toward greater self-understanding and acceptance (Kurtz, 1990).

Applications

Overview

Hakomi is a body-centered approach to counseling and psychotherapy that focuses on helping people internally reorganize and thereby change how they live their lives. A therapeutic relationship based on a partnership worldview is key to success, as are techniques geared toward honoring all aspects of the client and his world. The following section presents Hakomi's goals, change assumptions, intervention strategies, and client characteristics.

Goals of Counseling and Psychotherapy

Hakomi's primary healing intention is to facilitate the unfolding of a client's experience toward core material, to offer a related transforming experience (missing experience), and to support the reorganization of the self. Interventions are aimed at affecting core material's influence on a client so he or she has the chance to transform his or her life. In order to do this, Hakomi techniques focus on opening and enhancing communication between mind and body, as well as unconscious and conscious. The counselor's or therapist's task is to, without force, ". . . bring together all aspects of the person: mind/mind, mind/body and self/universe . . ." (Kurtz, 1990, p. 33), so that change happens at the level of core material, allowing the information systems of the mind and of the body to live in harmony (Kurtz, 1990).

The Process of Change

Hakomi sees change as a natural life process, like the growth of a seed into a plant. Transformative change is more than just simple growth, however; Hakomi interventions encourage the client's evolution into his or her full humanness, into his or her greatest complexity as a system, much the same way that water braids under pressure, allowing more to flow through the system. Hakomi recognizes that this kind of change requires the willingness to be vulnerable and the courage to move forward in spite of danger, uncertainty, and past traumas. It requires the existence of a safe and caring environment for the journey and the presence of an honest, supportive, loving therapist willing to wait and call forth what is true (Kurtz, 1990). Hakomi supports change unfolding in life-affirming ways, and recognizes, as the mutability principle states, that change is inevitable, happens in the present, and occurs when the principles are honored.

Intervention Strategies

Hakomi is called the "method of evoked experiences in mindfulness" (Kurtz, 1990). Although there are numerous counseling and psychotherapy methods that are humanistic, client-centered, partnership-oriented, and supportive, Hakomi is unique in its combined use of the principles to ground the counselor or therapist, a compassionate therapeutic relationship to hold the work, and mindfulness to empower the client.

Present Orientation   All Hakomi techniques operate in the now, whatever the actual timeframe of the event or issue under study. Although respecting the profound effect past experiences have on a person's perception of reality and interaction in the everyday world, Hakomi methods are based on the assumption that the present moment is where life is happening and where insight, perceptual shifts, and new intentions can be formed. Rather than only talking for an hour about the past, a client undertaking Hakomi counseling and psychotherapy might mindfully study current physical or emotional or energetic responses to a body event, or a statement from the counselor or therapist, or some other intentional experiment that evolves from what is happening in the session. This mindful study of experience in the present is one of the aspects of Hakomi that Kurtz suggests makes it quicker than other methods, positing that observation and examination of present experience are more efficient than discussion and speculation (2001).

Experimental Attitude   Hakomi is a process-oriented method of assisted self-study that assumes the goal is transformation. The ebb and flow of the process involves working with created experiments that help the client spiral closer and closer to the core material that wants to be uncovered and understood. As it is the client's organicity, the natural tendency to re-organize, that is being supported, an attitude of receptivity, openness, non-judgmentalism, and flexibility is needed. The counselor or psychotherapist has to have faith in, curiosity about, acceptance of, and eagerness for the client's natural unfolding, and be able to invite, not insist (Kurtz, 1990). The counselor or psychotherapist needs to be comfortable with his or her own uncertainty in the face of the complexity of another human being, and be willing to table preconceived notions of what is right for the client, trusting that the person has an innate desire and propensity to evolve (Eisman, 2001). When experimentation is done, the counselor or psychotherapist first has a hypothesis; then the counselor or psychotherapist, or the counselor or psychotherapist and client together, create an experimental process, get client permission to proceed, and implement the experiment. The client and counselor or psychotherapist, noticing what transpires, can process or adjust to the response, develop new experiments, and further access core material.

Managing the Process   Managing the therapeutic process using a method that emphasizes the client's organicity can be tricky, but it is as important as being in relationship with the client, and more important than gathering information. This is because the counselor or psychotherapist's main role is to facilitate and support the client's unfolding, not develop a diagnosis. Within this intent, the counselor or psychotherapist has to be active at times and passive at others. Active taking charge directs the process by offering interventions for inducing mindfulness, and for contacting, accessing, deepening, processing, transforming, and integrating client experiences. Passive taking charge creates spaciousness and an environment of letting be and allowing; it responds to the client's leads and requires the counselor or psychotherapist to be silent at critical times (Kurtz, 1990).

Managing the process brings the counselor or psychotherapist fully into the therapeutic relationship as a leader, not a dictator. Phrases such as "If it's okay with you," and "I might be off, but how about trying" indicate this to the client. Taking charge in Hakomi is not about controlling, ordering, or being violent toward another. It is quite the opposite of violence, in fact, for it can be violent not to act when action is called for. Taking charge in the Hakomi sense is nonviolent because it provides clear support for what the client deeply wants to happen. How the counselor or psychotherapist manages the process looks different at different points in a session: he or she creates safety and cooperation of the unconscious at the start; helps the client access and deepen his or her experience and try on new options in the middle; helps him or her learn to use the new ways in his or her life toward the end; and lets go of being in charge at the completion of the session (Eisman, 2001).

Managing Consciousness   Managing consciousness is critical to Hakomi because it is a state-of-consciousness-driven modality. Without the client's ability to maintain some degree of mindfulness, self-study does not happen, so being able to induce and help a client maintain mindfulness is one of the counselor or psychotherapist's main management jobs. Mindfulness can exist with eyes closed or open, but it is usually characterized by a slowing of breathing, a deliberation of reaction, and the ability to perceive, describe, and choose to align with or neutrally witness inner experiences. To manage the immersion in this state of consciousness, the counselor or psychotherapist may need to teach the client how to be mindful, consistently return him or her to inner-directed study and body experiences, remind him or her to notice whatever happens in his or her inner world, and encourage him or her to give ongoing reports. When the client is in a state of mindfulness—an already altered state, and one in which minimal input has maximal results—other non-ordinary states that contain core material, such as the **child state** and **emotional rapids,** are more likely to occur. When this happens, the counselor or psychotherapist needs to manage the client's immersion in them as well. The final management task related to states of consciousness is to ensure the client's transition back to ordinary consciousness and safe reentry into the outside world (Eisman, 2001; Kurtz, 1990).

Gathering Information   Gathering information, although important in Hakomi, is secondary to supporting the client's natural unfolding. Gathering information is not only done verbally, but also comes from tracking the client, confirming accuracy of counselor or psychotherapist perceptions, getting reports from the client, and "listening" with ears and eyes, as well as energetic, intuitive, and spiritual bodies. Information comes from clients who are in mindful, highly emotional, or normal states of consciousness, from the counselor or psychotherapist's internal reactions, or from a supervisor's input subsequent to the session. Information about personal history, culture, the physical and energetic bodies, thoughts, emotions, and spirituality can be sought, as well as information on life themes and beliefs, core longings and desires, automatic defenses and strategies, degrees of congruence with the self and the outside world, and expectations and assumptions (Eisman, 2001).

Categories of Experience   Hakomi values experience above all else as the door into the unconscious and core material. It works with specific **categories of experience** that people encounter in their inner journeys: thoughts, sensations, emotions, memories, images, meanings, and beliefs (Kurtz, 1990). Accessing and exploring these experiences involves being aware of clues and choosing appropriate language. The counselor's or psychotherapist's question "What are you thinking?" is bound to evoke the description of a thought; the statement "Notice exactly where you feel that tension" focuses the client on his or her body sensations. Emotions can be explored with statements such as "Let that sadness get as big as it wants"; memory can be elicited with a simple "Familiar, huh?" Images may be generated by the suggestion to "Notice what you see as you stay with that." The statement "Something important about that" leads to meaning and insight; beliefs show up with a phrase such as "You start believing something about the world from this." General exploration happens with asking "What are you noticing?" or "What happens when you...?" Physical contact (always done with permission), such as a touch on the hand when the client is in a mindful state, may elicit a response from any of the categories of experience. Experiences come in different types, represent different aspects of a person's world, and communicate in specific ways.

The Flow of the Process   Hakomi has a flow to it that both varies and stays the same. It varies in that each person has his or her own way of self-exploration and expression; it stays the same in that there are common steps that typically occur in practicing Hakomi. Below is a summary of the process.

Establish a Therapeutic Relationship.   In order for a healing relationship to be established, safety, trust, and cooperation of the conscious and unconscious are required. The counselor or psychotherapist's initial task is to create this therapeutic container. Ways of doing this include making **contact statements** that show understanding of the client, his or her story, and his or her world, direct him or her into his or her present experience, and invite the unfolding of the unconscious. A contact statement may be as simple as "Sad, huh?" Meeting the client in his or her world is what is important. The counselor or psychotherapist needs to respect the client's integrity as well as the integrity of the counselor or psychotherapist-client system; he or she must be willing to be in charge of the therapeutic process, while respecting the client as the ultimate controller of his or her own life, in and out of the sessions. This presumes careful **tracking,** or continuous following, of the client's experience—what he or she is saying and doing, what he or she is consciously and unconsciously communicating. It requires going at the client's pace, holding the best interests of the whole person, not interrogating for information, and waiting for the right time to deepen experiences (Eisman, 2000; Kurtz, 1990).

Establish Mindfulness.   With contact established, a state of relaxed, inner-directed, non-judgmental, aware, quiet mindfulness is possible. This may occur simply because of the calm, simple, focused, nonjudgmental, inclusive way the counselor or psychotherapist speaks and acts; it also may require teaching the client how to be mindful. Aspects of mindfulness such as orientation in the present, internal focus, contextual awareness, non-judgmental self-observation, non-doing, and receptivity may be described, demonstrated, and practiced. It is also important to note that the counselor or psychotherapist needs to be in a state of inner and outer mindfulness in order to be fully present, able to track the client, and wisely serve his or her needs (Kurtz, 1990).

Evoke Experiences in Mindfulness.   Hakomi returns again and again to the study of present experience because it faithfully leads to core material, the organizer of experience. Counselors and psychotherapists do this by tracking clients' present experience and listening for themes that want attention, and by offering ways to mindfully explore these experiences and themes. Specific types of interventions to evoke experience include **little experiments, probes,** and **taking over** (Eisman, 2001; Kurtz, 1987).

A little experiment is a way to set up a test of what happens inside a mindful client when he or she or the counselor does something, or one of them does not do something. It helps insert a degree of detachment in the process of self-study, can reduce the effects of transference, and allows space for lightness and flexibility. A little experiment could come, for example, from a client's difficulty with eye contact. The client might experiment with noticing his or her responses to the counselor's looking at him or her, or looking away from him or her or to himself or herself, slowly turning his or her eyes toward the counselor. He or she might have a memory, a sensation, a feeling, or see an image. Whatever happens is grist for the mill and an opportunity for further study (Kurtz, 1990).

A probe is a specific kind of little experiment that is a statement or physical touch by the counselor or psychotherapist delivered when the client is in a mindful state. Its wording (e.g., "Your life belongs to you") or form (e.g., a gentle touch on the arm) is based on stating the opposite of a limiting client belief, and is nourishing or potentially nourishing (although it is not the primary intent of the probe to nourish). The intent is to be truthful, and to give the client's unconscious the chance to either take in some important truth or notice that he or she rejects what is offered (and perhaps how and why it is rejected). It should be geared toward the particular client's process, and is used to evoke an experience worth studying. Although probes are most effective if customized from observing body movement, gestures, posture, and listening to a client's story, there are generic probes that relate directly to specific character strategies. For example, operating from one pattern described in Hakomi character theory—hypersensitive/withdrawn—makes it very difficult to believe the following statement: "You are safe here." Upon hearing this probe, such a client may react strongly and immediately by shaking his or her head, crying, tightening up, freezing, or withdrawing into himself or herself more. Conversely, someone not stuck in this orientation, who at least feels safe in the counselor's or psychotherapist's office, would react differently, perhaps nodding, saying he or she agrees, and visibly relaxing. Whatever the response, it provides either an opportunity for conscious integration of an important truth, or material for deeper study (Kurtz, 1990).

The concept of taking over grew from the Taoist idea of supporting the natural flow of things, Feldenkrais' application of physics to therapy, Pesso's use of structures, and Kurtz's experience of spontaneously supporting the arched back of a woman in a workshop and feeling his assumptions about how to work with "defenses" transformed by her response. Taking over assumes that supporting a client's defenses—which are the natural result of struggle and serve as protection—rather than fighting them leads to awareness, without re-traumatizing the client. Taking over is based in the principles, and frees the client from the work of managing or blocking some past painful experience, or from having to protect himself or herself from the associated feelings. It gives him or her the chance to safely experience the original event and focus deeply and singularly on its effects. It is also based on the physics of background noise and signal detection. Lowering background noise allows a specific signal to be detected more clearly. If we think of core material as a signal we are trying to tune into, and our worries, tensions, anxieties, and confusions as the background noise that gets in the way, it is clear that we can either increase the signal or **lower the noise** to access core material. Hakomi tends toward noise lowering, which is what taking over does. A counselor or psychotherapist takes over something that the client is already doing consistently for himself or herself, like clenching his or her fist each time he or she talks about his or her spouse. Other experiences to take over might be chronic body posture, temporary body events or sensations, spontaneous gestures, familiar limiting thoughts, beliefs or inner voices, internal conflicts, or impulses or resistance to impulses. Taking over can be done verbally or nonverbally, and always includes client involvement in developing and permitting the experiment (Eisman, 2001; Kurtz, 1990).

Access and Deepen.   Most clients' lives reflect all the categories of experience, with some clients favoring certain ways of experiencing life over others. Hakomi respects a client's natural ways of being and doing while encouraging deepening toward core material. This deepening is sought because core beliefs, meanings, and images can be said to live "underneath" memories and emotions, which are thought of as underneath sensations and thoughts (Kurtz, 1990). A deepening spiral into core material might flow from thought (*I hate my job*), to sensation (*My neck feels tense and my stomach hurts*), to emotion (tears of sadness), to a memory (*My father died when I was 10*), to an image (*I see my father sitting at his desk late at night, rubbing his neck; his hand looks bloodless*), to meaning (*My father's job drained his life from him*), to belief (*I believe work will kill me, just like it killed my dad*). The process of deepening varies, of course, depending on what and how the client presents himself or herself and his or her story, and may take numerous interconnected spirals and periods of sustaining and processing experiences.

The **3-Step Method** of accessing meaning and facilitating the unfolding of experience is used over and over in a Hakomi session. It typically engenders the spiraling process described above that can steer the client toward deeper meaning or, at the least, toward the continuation of "what wants to happen next." The 3-Step Method directs the client to (1) notice the experience, (2) stay with/immerse himself or herself in the experience, and (3) study the experience (Eisman, 2001).

Accessing phrases serve to maintain the inward spiral, increase focus and/or foster broadening of awareness, encourage a deeper felt sense of an experience, uncover meaning, and lead to further experience. Staying fully engaged in this process leads to delving deeper and deeper through the categories of experience until the core is reached, and a missing core experience and/or felt sense of inner resource is identified. Previously described techniques, such as little experiments, probes, and taking over, as well as others, can all be used to access and deepen (Eisman, 2001).

Process and Work at the Core.   Powerful experiences happen when core material is reached. There is a shift from thoughts, sensations, and feelings about the present to beliefs, memories, images, and holistically felt experiences that come from the past but are awakened in the moment. This is what a shaman might consider to be the creation level of existence. The actual felt sense of a limiting core belief as well as its transformed version may occur. Shifts out of mindfulness into other altered states of consciousness such as the child state or the rapids are common. This is where deep character issues and the client's long held habits of self-protection may arise. Finally, a felt sense of wholeness, with no awareness of brokenness, may occur as a deep core experience, and may or may not come about from retracing history, accessing painful memories, or experiencing trance states.

The **child state** is a felt experience of being young and perceiving the world from a child's orientation. It can occur, for example, when the process has evoked a body memory of a childhood experience. Sometimes it is elusive and hard to maintain; sometimes it is very intense, vivid, and full-bodied. Working with a client in this state offers the chance to help complete unfinished childhood business and have important missing experiences, such as being really seen, or listened to, validated, or held. Because it is not really a child in the counseling or psychotherapist's office, but an adult with adult capacities, the child can tap into the adult strengths and resources (and vice versa), and integration of new insights becomes possible for the whole person (Kurtz, 1990).

Emotions arise regularly in Hakomi sessions because the work centers on deep pain and strongly held beliefs. Hakomi counselors and psychotherapists want emotional release to be therapeutic, not just cathartic, so they support the release of feelings and provide a safe environment to express them in, but they do not force emotional expression. Any part of a client that wants to resist expressing feelings is accepted, and by this, counselors and psychotherapists offer a non-overwhelming, balanced way of working with emotions that allows inner study to continue. However, because supporting the resistance to expression can actually communicate safety and opportunity to the unconscious, there are times when chaotic and powerful emotions of grief, terror, or rage spontaneously and naturally explode. Their expression is then vital to the client's organicity, so Hakomi encourages counselors and psychotherapists to work differently when clients are "riding the rapids" of strong feelings than when they are in a mindful state. Kurtz suggests that, because these rapids are not compatible with mindfulness, when they occur the counselor or psychotherapist needs to fully support spontaneous behavior, let go of any attempt at self-study, and offer nourishing verbal or nonverbal contact. Return to mindful study may happen after the emotional release is complete (Kurtz, 1990).

Hakomi considers character strategies to be rooted in childhood missing experiences, and to be automatic and limiting responses to the world. There is a tendency for people to fixate on a few strategies in their everyday lives, the seeds of which show up when working at the core (Eisman, 2001). Although overreliance on character theory can fly in the face of organicity, knowledge of Hakomi's particular slant on Freud's and Lowen's concepts can offer a counselor or psychotherapist additional resources when working at the core.

Core material is not all painful; it also includes the experience of deep aliveness and wholeness. This felt sense can come from processing painful experiences or from making choices connected to innate aliveness. It is here that the R-CS method dovetails with Hakomi by providing a map of the psyche and ways for the counselor or psychotherapist to facilitate the tapping of client aliveness and inner resources. By recognizing the degree to which he or she feels fragmented internally and the extent of his or her longing to live differently, the client has the chance to tap into his or her innate aliveness and capacity for a fully empowered life. This energy of aliveness generally supports expansion, curiosity, existential responsibility, and truth, and provides a resource to combat fear. It is this aliveness that generates the capacity to reject limiting trances, and that, combined with clear intention and action, can lead to the Organic Self moving back in charge of the whole person, rather than the assumed adult staying mired in the trance of brokenness (Eisman, 2001; Morrissey, 2000). As a counselor or psychotherapist, working at a client's psychic core requires managing interrelated and complex variables, yet has the potential of bringing about transformational life change.

Transform, Integrate, and Complete.   Transformation in a Hakomi sense is reorganization that comes when the inner resources of the self are bigger than the woundedness. From the R-CS perspective, transformation can occur when aware aliveness generates the capacity to reject limiting trances. Transformation happens in both ways, and is both an event and a process. The event may happen in a session as working at the psychic core results in clarity about something important. It is not necessarily dramatic, although it may be accompanied with awe, joy, relief, relaxation, or strong emotions. The event is not the end; in order for real change to happen, newly realized truths need integration and nurturing both in the session and over time (Eisman, 2001; Kurtz, 1990).

It is not the counselor's or psychotherapist's responsibility to force change or insist on transformation. He or she is called to trust the client's organicity and to create an experiential context where change has a chance. When the client's inner resources seem big enough to tip the balance toward a new belief, Hakomi counselors and psychotherapists follow the same process of experimentation that is used over and over at all stages of therapeutic work. An experiment is offered that, for example, allows the client to experience the opposite of the old belief, get unexpected permission or support, have a reality check that supports the new belief, or have a missing experience. If the experiment produces an "Aha!" response on some experiential level, the counselor or psychotherapist tracks it and works to help the client stabilize the growing new belief. This requires time to anchor the new truth and to consider and work with any life challenges around the new belief. If the experiment meets resistance, the counselor or psychotherapist needs to help the client study and work with that, not push a client who is not fully ready to change beliefs. Techniques used at this stage include savoring, stitching (tying elements together), practicing new beliefs, discussion, fantasy/imagery, anchoring (reinforcing a felt sense), storytelling, rituals or ceremonies, and suggesting homework (Eisman, 2001).

Sessions often have a natural flow from ordinary consciousness to non-ordinary consciousness—from studying to processing to transformation to integration—and then back to ordinary consciousness (Kurtz, 1990). The term *completion* in Hakomi refers to resolution of issues, ending counseling or psychotherapy sessions, and terminating counseling or psychotherapy. Because Hakomi operates in a paradigm that does not look for "cures," completion is seen in a "for now" context. Although the point of counseling and psychotherapy is to eliminate its need in the long term, a person's life is an ongoing evolution with needs that ebb and flow throughout his or her life-span (Eisman, 2001).

Clients with Mental Disorders

Clients seeking Hakomi counseling and psychotherapy exhibit a wide range of presenting diagnoses and therapeutic needs, from personal fulfillment, to acute psychological disorders, to traumatic life events, to chronic mental illness. Clients with psychotic symptoms or other severe disturbances are referred for appropriate psychiatric help. Although Hakomi counselors and psychotherapists, with their principled theoretical foundation, are cautious about diagnosing or defining clients according to standard DSM-IV criteria, they consider traditional diagnoses along with many other immediate factors in assessing and offering therapeutic interventions. Hakomi counselors and psychotherapists work with clients looking for enhanced life skills, better relationships, fewer psychosomatic symptoms, reduced affective and cognitive disturbances, and a method that complements conventional treatments for trauma and addiction issues. Clients include children, adolescents, adults, couples, and families, and are usually seen in private practices in the United States, and in both private practice and counseling and psychotherapy centers and clinics in Europe (Schulmeister, 2000).

Evaluation

Overview

Hakomi has contributed significantly to the field of psychotherapy and counseling. Foremost among these contributions is its use of mindfulness for experiential self-study. Although it has much in common with other experiential, person-centered, and systems-oriented approaches, it has succeeded in a unique integration of a number of elements. This integration results in an efficient modality that is appropriate for a wide range of clients. The specific interconnected elements (Kurtz, 2000) include the following.

1. the mindful study of experience
2. the reliance on experimentation and non-violence
3. the creation of a clear and direct relationship to the unconscious while maintaining connection to the conscious mind
4. a systems approach to the person, his or her world, and the process
5. the development of a partnership-oriented therapeutic relationship
6. the emphasis on insight over catharsis, and nourishment over suffering
7. the nonjudgmental framing of "defenses" as the habitual management of experience

Supporting Research

In Europe, body-psychotherapy is a scientifically validated branch of mainstream psychotherapy. In 2000, the Hakomi Institute of Europe submitted evidence to and received validation from the European Association for Body-Psychotherapy (EABP) in support of Hakomi's inclusion within this framework. Criteria included evidence of theoretical coherence, clarity and organization, research and client assessment capacity, explicit relationship between methods and results, broad treatment applicability, and peer review (Schulmeister, 2000).

Empirical research on its efficacy is, however, sparse, as Hakomi focuses on clients' subjective experiences of reality. Counselors and psychotherapists and Hakomi Institutes are amenable to outcome research, as long as it considers the complexity of the individual and the therapeutic environment. An ongoing empirical study of Hakomi methods is currently underway with the Hakomi Institute of Europe and the Psychological Institute of the Universities of Tubingen and Heidelberg (Schulmeister, 2000).

Research and evaluation methods of conventional therapies are congruent with Hakomi. For example, Carl Rogers' use of session taping as a means of evaluation has been a standard tool of Hakomi counselors and psychotherapists since the Institute's inception, and is often used in counselor and psychotherapist certification. In addition, Hakomi professionals contribute regularly to the thinking in the field. Over the last 17 years, the **Hakomi Forum** has published scores of articles by both Hakomi practitioners and aligned professionals on topics related to the theory, techniques, and application of Hakomi and body-centered psychotherapy.

Limitations

Hakomi has controlled much of the "guru factor" sometimes attributed to methods created under charismatic leaders, and sometimes seen as affecting training of practitioners. Even though some of the original Hakomi founders, especially Kurtz, are known for their charismatic, almost magical, styles, the Hakomi Institute has succeeded in formalizing, standardizing, and teaching the theory and techniques of Hakomi in a way that meets professional and adult learning needs and turns out skilled practitioners. Moreover, Hakomi Institute training programs reach a wide domestic and international counselor or psychotherapist audience. There is a pedagogical emphasis on performance over seat time, though, which makes the counselor or psychotherapist assessment and certification process somewhat daunting. Consequently, although hundreds of professionals have been trained as of January 2002, there are only about 281 who have been certified as Hakomi Therapists (CHT) in the United States, New Zealand, Australia, Asia, and Europe—a problem currently under Institute review.

As it has developed, Hakomi has grown into and has grown out of itself and has stayed true to its open and inclusive nature. Gaps in or opportunities to improve methodology or theory have regularly surfaced, and Hakomi has either reorganized itself or given rise to new modalities. The method has not always worked well with all clients, especially those who are severely traumatized or who frequently dissociate (Ogden, 1997). As Ogden identified the need to hone classic Hakomi in a way that served traumatized clients, Hakomi Sensorimotor Psychology was developed. Another master Hakomi therapist, Eisman, also on the ground level of launching Hakomi, used his 20-year practice with hundreds of non-psychotic Hakomi clients to define a phenomenon not clearly delineated in Hakomi theory. His clients exhibited inner fragmentation as well as the capacity to shift into a state of wholeness. From this client-reported, persistent evidence, the complementary Re-Creation of the Self was born, which resulted in an alternative model and methodology of self-transformation. Another method used by counselors and psychotherapists to address this same limitation in Hakomi's model of the self is **Richard Schwartz's Internal Family Systems Therapy (IFS).** IFS grew out of family systems theory and posits the existence in each person of a core Self and internal parts. IFS works to reduce polarization of these parts and to increase inner harmony and what Schwarz calls "Self-leadership" (Schwartz, 1995). Finally, Hakomi trainers, with philosophical integrity, consistently emphasize the importance of counselors and psychotherapists developing their own unique way of doing counseling or psychotherapy, recognizing that no single modality has all the answers.

And finally, it has been at least 13 years since the publication of Kurtz's seminal Hakomi texts. As of the writing of this chapter, he continues to teach, write, and explore Buddhism, the development of the mind, attachment theory, affect regulation, sociobiology, and what it means to be human (*http://www.ronkurtz.com*). His work reflects this ongoing exploration, expands as his thinking evolves, and may look different from Hakomi as described in this chapter. Additionally, although Hakomi as practiced, taught, and elaborated on by Hakomi Institute trainers throughout the country and the world is reflected in this chapter, true to its core principles, it continues to evolve (*http://www.HakomiInstitute.com*).

Summary Chart—Hakomi Body-Centered Psychotherapy

Human Nature

Hakomi believes in the innate wholeness and interconnectedness of individuals, each a complex self-organizing system that can self-heal. Although early childhood strongly affects psychological development, psychological limitations have many causes, and each person has the capacity to create his or her own life. Past experience does inform personality, but each of us is constantly unfolding in a unique way. Increased mindful self-study can lead to increased awareness and self reorganization.

Major Constructs

Hakomi is grounded in the precept that experience is organized and has meaning. Core organizers—memories, images, beliefs—lie buried deep in our psyches and rule our lives until we wake up to their meaning and influence and transform our relationship to them. The foundational principles of Hakomi are more important than any technique. They are **unity** (everything is connected), **organicity** (organisms self-regulate), **mindfulness** (nonjudgmental self-observation increases awareness), **nonviolence** (going with the grain honors natural unfolding), **mind-body holism** (mind and body affect each other unpredictably), **truth** (be honest; seek Truth), and **mutability** (change will happen). The healing relationship needs to be partnership-oriented and is the safe container where change can happen.

Goals

1. Provide a safe context to do transformative work.
2. Increase communication between mind and body, conscious and unconscious.
3. Facilitate the unfolding of the client's experience toward core material.
4. Offer therapeutic missing experiences.
5. Support the reorganization of the self, the stepping out of limiting trances, and transformation.

Change Process

Change will happen, but for healthy change, individuals need to be courageous and vulnerable, take risks, feel safe, and experience a loving therapeutic relationship. People live and change in the present, so interventions need to be present-oriented. Change comes when inner resources are greater than inner pain.

Interventions

All interventions are done with an experimental attitude that is open and curious and that seeks the unfolding of experience as well as the gathering of information. The managing of the process and of client consciousness keeps the state of consciousness appropriate to what wants and needs to happen. Establishing a healing relationship comes from making meaningful client contact and tracking client experience. Helping the client turn inward comes from teaching mindfulness. Mindfulness allows accessing and deepening into core material, where processing can happen. Accessing and processing techniques include little experiments, probes, and taking over. Processing at the core and transformation can involve the child state, the rapids, character issues, missing experiences, and experiences of aliveness. Integration and completion can include savoring, practicing, imagining, role playing, and homework.

Limitations
1. Empirical research studies are sparse because of Hakomi's intrapsychic orientation.
2. Charismatic leaders create the potential for a "guru factor."
3. Not enough counselor or psychotherapists become certified.
4. The method is continually evolving and so is a challenge to quantify.
5. The method does not work for all clients, especially those who cannot attain a state of mindfulness or who frequently dissociate.

The Case of Jonathan: A Hakomi Approach

Assumptions

Because Hakomi interventions are based on experience that wants to happen in the moment, specific case planning is always hypothetical. Furthermore, Hakomi does not use a conventional diagnostic, cure-oriented approach to counseling and psychotherapy. Rather, it views clients as always on their own paths—not as broken beings who need fixing. However, working effectively with Jonathan requires considering a number of issues. A counselor or psychotherapist needs to assess his or her own awareness of the Navaho culture, consider Jonathan's sense of himself as a cultural being, and look at his or her own cultural self-awareness. He or she needs to be able to work outside the dominant cultural paradigm in shepherding the counseling and psychotherapy process, looking, for example, at such factors as his or her beliefs regarding the standard 50-minute hour, his or her assumptions about individual versus group identity, and his or her expectations regarding counseling and psychotherapy goals. Moreover, the counselor or psychotherapist needs to take the following into consideration.

- Jonathan's tribal roots are healthy, deep, and available.
- The Navaho culture is matrilineal, and, like other Native American tribes, organized around the responsibility to (and interdependence of) family and community, balance of opposites in the "world of shadows" (Hall, 2001), and the importance in life of wisdom and spiritual awareness.
- Indigenous cultures often see psychological, physical, family, social, and spiritual problems as interconnected. Their worldviews are holistic and organismic.
- Native American men may hesitate to express deep emotions or disclose private material, except in specially framed grieving or spiritual contexts.
- The Navaho respect healers.

Jonathan's World

As a member of the Navaho nation, a vital and large Native American tribe (Utter, 1993), and as a human being with varied life experiences, Jonathan is a man rich in inner and outer resources, with a unique and community-connected life purpose. He has managed his life based on his degree of connection with these inner and outer resources. His heritage, experiences, choices, and the larger environment have contributed to his current state of being.

It is apparent from his life-story that he values his Navaho culture and formal education, loves his immediate and extended families, and functions responsibly as a provider. Furthermore, he is able to consider and describe his own experience, recognizes connections between his feelings and his circumstances, pays attention to dream messages, is intelligent, and is able to self-critique. We can also infer that he feels trapped, afraid, angry, misunderstood, undervalued, unsuccessful, lacking in power, alienated from the "white man's world" and his own tribe, discriminated against, and deeply guilty about his brother's death. He is a complex man, as are all humans.

His life-story speaks of fragmentation and separation from his personal, community, and, perhaps, spiritual roots, as well as of bouts of self-medication with alcohol. Although he clearly longs for success in relationships, he believes he and his actions are never quite good enough for his brother, his wives, his boss, his children, his extended family, or his tribe. He persists in being a seeker of answers, even though he repeatedly leaves and returns to marriage and the reservation without finding answers that satisfy him. He hears his dreams, as they speak to him of his journey and frustration at not having the power to direct his life.

Congruence with Hakomi

Hakomi has much that lends itself to working effectively with Jonathan. The emphasis on relationship is, of course, primary. The principles of unity, organicity, non-violence, mindfulness, and mind-body holism are congruent with tribal values of interconnectedness and relationship, balance of opposites, seeking wisdom and spiritual awareness, spirit-mind-body interconnectedness, and responsibility to the whole. The idea that responsibility to the community and the family is greater than responsibility to the self is also congruent with Hakomi. The principle of organicity recognizes that wholes are made up of parts, and healing interventions done anywhere in the system affect the whole and each of the parts. Consequently, serving the community helps the individual (and vice versa).

The fact that Hakomi's main goal is uncovering information, not expressing emotions, also indicates congruence. Too much talk and emotional disclosing can go against the Navaho cultural norm and may not be seen as useful or appropriate. Thus, the centrality in Hakomi of *being in experience to gain insight*—not necessarily in the form of spoken words, but possibly through a felt sense, or a vision, or an inner voice—may be more acceptable, as this insight can lead to wisdom that serves the family and community.

Establishing a Therapeutic Relationship

Knowing as much about Jonathan's world as we do from the case description, the counselor or psychotherapist can immediately focus on establishing a therapeutic relationship through building trust and creating a "container" that helps Jonathan feel comfortable, valued, hopeful, and empowered. This involves listening to and honoring his story, as well as demonstrating patience, collaboration, respect, curiosity, integrity, acceptance, empathy, and awareness. Carefully tracking his experience in the session and contacting it in ways that show understanding and intuition can help build trust.

Mindfulness, Accessing, Processing

If congruent with Jonathan's beliefs, mindfulness can be re-framed as a way to gain knowledge by tapping into the dreamtime world of resources—of allies, personal memories, and tribal wisdom. The purpose, then, can become less centered on individual awareness as the presumptive counseling or psychotherapy goal, and more on community hopes and needs and Jonathan's connection to them. Mindfulness can also be presented as a way to identify and listen to important body language and messages, taking care to respect his cultural boundaries around physical contact. Using mindfulness to explore the interconnection in Jonathan's life of his body, mind, spirit, and community would honor his ongoing attempts to seek answers, while providing a life-affirming, trustworthy method.

The melding of present and past can occur in mindfulness and be therapeutic, an experience naturally congruent with a non-linear worldview. In a shaman's world, intervening today can change yesterday and tomorrow. This could be relevant in working with Jonathan's guilt about his brother. When the time is right, the counselor or psychotherapist might use an experiment that has Jonathan mindfully respond to a probe such as *"It's not your fault that your brother died"* to evoke Jonathan's experience of himself as a 16-year-old, horrified and filled with guilt over his brother's death. He or she might then invite Jonathan to witness this 16-year-old from the eyes and heart of his wise adult self, or another wise ally or elder. This could provide a missing experience of compassion and understanding, and allow self-forgiveness for the 16-year-old Jonathan, thereby shifting his sense of himself as responsible for his brother's death. He may also be able to align with spiritual resources in this self-forgiveness process.

Jonathan's use of alcohol, the anger that precedes it, and his pattern of quitting school, marriages, and life on the reservation, only to return to them, can also be studied mindfully, processed respectfully, and put in a larger perspective. Using mindfulness interspersed with a sharing of stories, issues of acceptance and alienation, being and producing, racism and power, the connection of anger and grief to each other and to alcohol use, fears about harming himself or others, and other life-limiting or life-enhancing possibilities can arise and be explored. To honor the dream message coming to him, Jonathan's dream can be explored through the technique of mindful dream re-entry—not analysis. The purpose would be to identify the dream people and dream elements and his relationship to them all; to help Jonathan—in an awake mindful dream state—to ask for and access the help that he needs to follow his inclinations; and then—again, in a mindful dream state—to act and respond to the results of his actions.

Integrating, Completing

Finally, work with Jonathan needs to involve helping him integrate non-limiting beliefs and empowering ways of being, acting, and connecting into his life. One task would be to consciously tie insights from the missing experience around his brother's death, his dream journey, and from other experiments in mindfulness to his everyday life. Another would be to encourage him to do reality checks with people in his life, and then explore their responses in sessions. These checks might be with his extended family concerning their belief about his innocence or guilt in his brother's death, with his wife and children regarding their sense of him as a husband and father, and with tribal elders about his value and purpose as a Navaho tribal member.

Multicultural Considerations

For the past three decades, writers, researchers, and professionals have been espousing the need for multicultural and cross-cultural strategies and approaches to counseling and psychotherapy. Traditional counseling and psychotherapies were developed for white, middle- and upper-middle-class clients. These theories were developed by white practitioners who were enmeshed in Western cultural values; hence the applicability of these theories, without modification, to multicultural populations is questionable. We agonized over the issue of whether to ask each contributing author to include discussion of multicultural and cross-cultural variations or to include a chapter focused solely on this topic and written by individuals known for their expertise in this area. We decided on the latter approach in order to avoid repetition throughout the text and to ensure content of the highest quality. We think you will find Chapter 17, "Counseling and Psychotherapy: Multicultural Considerations," extremely pertinent to your work with racial, cultural, and ethnic minorities. We recommend that you reevaluate the strengths and weaknesses of each of the theories presented in this text after you finish reading Chapter 17.

Counseling and Psychotherapy: Multicultural Considerations

G. Miguel Arciniega
Arizona State University

Betty J. Newlon
University of Arizona

Introduction

A significant amount of research and writing has addressed the impact of culture on counseling and psychotherapy; very few mainstream textbooks have incorporated **multicultural** themes into their discussions of theories of counseling and psychotherapy. Multicultural counseling is at a crossroads (Ponterotto, Casas, Suzuki, & Alexander, 1995), and in spite of the increased attention it has received, it is still considered to be in its infancy (Ponterotto & Sabnani, 1989).

The existence of **cultural bias** in counseling and psychotherapy has been documented by many authors (Atkinson, Morten, & Sue, 1993; Helms & Cook, 1999; Katz, 1985; LeVine & Padilla, 1980; Pedersen, Draguns, Lonner, & Trimble, 1996; Ponterotto & Casas, 1991; Sue & Sue, 1999). Wrenn (1962) first introduced the concept of the "culturally encapsulated counselor" by pointing out how practitioners protect themselves from the reality of change by "surrounding [themselves] with a cocoon of pretended reality—a reality which is based upon the past and the known, upon seeing that which is as though it would always be" (p. 446). More than 20 years later, Wrenn (1985) again addressed the issue of the encapsulated counselor with a broader view that dealt with practitioners who denied the reality of change.

The history and legitimacy of multicultural counseling and psychotherapy have paralleled sociopolitical movements in the United States. The civil rights efforts of the 1960s, 1970s, and 1980s produced a racial and cultural pride among minority groups, which in turn stimulated their demand for recognition and equality. This movement has pushed mental health professionals to consider cultural issues (Wehrly, 1991).

For the past three decades, writers, researchers, educators, and professionals in the field of counseling and psychotherapy have espoused the need for multicultural and cross-cultural awareness, knowledge, strategies, and approaches in order to serve the increasing number of racial, cultural, and ethnic minorities throughout the nation. The need for a minority perspective in counseling and psychotherapy has become one of the most important topics in professional journals. More recently, a topic that has become a major focus in multicultural counseling is the importance of cultural competencies (Arredondo, Toporek, Brown, Jones, Locke, Sanchez, & Stadler, 1996; Sue, Arredondo, & McDavis 1992). Between 1983 and 1988, the major counseling and counseling psychology journals (*The Counseling Psychologist, The Journal of Counseling Psychology, The Journal of Counseling and Development,* and *The Journal of Multicultural Counseling and Development*) published 183 conceptual and empirical articles in this area (Ponterotto & Casas, 1991). Since then, the number has grown considerably. *The Journal of Counseling and Development* published a special issue called "Multiculturalism as a Fourth Force in Counseling" (American Association for Counseling and Development, 1991). Numerous researchers have responded to Pedersen's (1991) fourth force in counseling, and a call to the professions has been made to establish multiculturalism as an integral part of counseling (Essandoh, 1996). Even more recently, unprecedented numbers of presentations and symposia on multicultural psychology have filled professional conferences (Sue, Ivey, & Pedersen, 1996).

Wehrly (1991) states, "In spite of the fact that the United States has been (and is) a nation of immigrants whose values differ, a major theme of Euro-American individualistic psychology seems to have been that of assimilation" (p. 4). She points out that writers in the field have been slow to recognize the cultural impact of American ethnic minorities. They have not broadened the theoretical base of counseling or psychotherapy beyond Western thought. Consequently, most training institutions, while they might offer a course on multicultural counseling or psychotherapy, still use theory texts that expound a monoethnic, monocultural theory.

Traditional theories are based on Western Euro-American assumptions that are considered to be morally, politically, and ethnically neutral. This foundation has also been perpetuated as culturally fair and unbiased. Atkinson et al. (1993), Ivey, Ivey, and Simek-Morgan (1993), Pedersen (1994), and Ponterotto et al. (1995) have noted that counseling and psychotherapy approaches and theories were developed for the white middle class and traditionally conceptualized in a Western individualistic framework.

To clarify this point, Katz (1985) presented a paradigm for viewing cultural dimensions of traditional therapy in terms of mainstream white cultural values and beliefs. Katz concluded that the "similarities between white culture and the cultural values that form the foundations of traditional counseling theory and practice exist and are interchangeable" (p. 619). These monocultural-based theories assume applicability to all populations, regardless of minority racial and cultural experiences. While these theories may be well intentioned, they have not systematically integrated the current sociopolitical nature of multicultural populations. They inadequately explain the complexities and experiences of racial/ethnic minority groups, are culture-bound and inflexible, focus on a single dimension of personality, and expound only one world view—Euro-American (Parham, 1996).

Further, Helms (1990) proposes the concept of white racial identity development, which contradicts the traditional paradigm that it is only about minority clients.

Native Americans, African Americans, Latinos, and Asian Americans

It is not possible in this space to provide a descriptive overview of all American minority groups. We have selected the following four groups because they have been identified for special attention by the American Psychological Association and the American Counseling Association: Native Americans, African Americans, Latinos, and Asian Americans. In order to understand the current experience of these populations, it is essential that counselors and therapists understand the groups' historical, educational, social, political, and economic development and climate in addition to their basic family characteristics and values. For a more thorough understanding of counseling these groups, see LeVine and Padilla (1980), Pedersen et al. (1996), Sue and Sue (1999), and Atkinson et al. (1993).

It is not our intent to provide a comprehensive analysis of all of the factors impinging on theories of counseling and psychotherapy, but rather to introduce the important social, ethnic, and cultural issues and considerations that practitioners must take into account when applying theory. This chapter addresses the following as they relate to the four previously mentioned racial, ethnic, and cultural groups: (1) definitions; (2) counselor and therapist self-awareness; (3) acculturation; (4) demographics; (5) racial and ethnic cultural considerations; and (6) racial and ethnic cultural components. In addition, we present a discussion of theories of counseling and psychotherapy and their appropriateness or adaptability to traditional minority groups. The chapter concludes with a discussion of how multicultural considerations can add breadth to prevailing theories. It encourages the reader to examine very critically the most current theory of multicultural counseling and psychotherapy (Sue et al., 1996).

Definitions

For the purpose of this chapter, we propose the following terms and definitions (Mio, Trimble, Arredondo, Cheatham, & Sue, 1999).

- **Race.** This is a controversial concept, the origin of which can be traced to the Swedish taxonomist Carolus Linneaus, who said that human beings are of four types: **Americanus, Asiaticus, Africanus,** and **Europeaeus.** Genetic studies by contemporary scientists indicate that traits assumed to be factors of "race" (i.e., hair texture, skin color, eye color, and facial features) are superficial and thus make attempts to classify persons into "races" a futile exercise. While many scientists believe *race* cannot be accurately defined, they also concede that this concept will continue to be used to categorize people into one of four groups: Asian, Black, White, or American Indian (p. 219).
- **Ethnicity.** Derived from the ancient Greek word *ethnos*, which referred to a range of situations in which a group of people lived and acted together, *ethnicity* more specifically refers to one's values and general lifestyle that is

shared with a particular ethnic group. Ethnicity is a fluid concept, while race is static. Sometimes the terms *race* and *ethnicity* are used interchangeably. *Race* refers to a person's genetic heritage, while *ethnicity* refers to the cultural values, beliefs, and norms that a person ascribes to and identifies with. Race is a matter of social categorization while ethnicity seems to be a matter of group identification (p. 110).

- **Culture.** This term denotes habitual patterns of behavior that are characteristic of a group of people and are transmitted from one generation to the next through symbolic communication. *Culture* implies a way of life. Culture is learned and represents the commonalities around which people develop norms, family lifestyles, social roles, and behaviors in response to historical, political, economic, and social realities. Culture consists of all that people have learned to do, believe, and enjoy in their history (p. 83).

It is necessary to point out that these three terms have often been used interchangeably in the literature and are often misunderstood. *Race* refers to a biological concept, while *ethnicity* and *culture* refer to shared and uniquely learned characteristics. Ethnic groups within races differ in their cultural specificity, and people of the same racial background and same ethnic group may differ in their cultural specificity. For example, African Americans may be part of a Latino ethnic group, but may identify with a number of cultural groups from their country of origin.

Other important terms and definitions posited by Mio and associates (1990) follow.

- **Minority.** "Meaning not of the majority or the dominant group," this term refers not necessarily to the lack of numerical dominance, but rather to the lack of dominance in terms of power and status (p. 187).

- **Multicultural counseling.** This term describes a counseling situation where a client and a therapist are of different ethnicities, races, cultures, and so on. Multicultural counseling suggests both a conceptual framework of and a tool for a process concerned with culturally appropriate attitudes, strategies, and skills that consider how individuals are influenced by their particular culture, the interlockings and interrelationships among the many microcultures to which they belong, and the many social forces that impact on their positions and situations at any given moment (p. 195).

- **Stereotype.** This term refers to a set of oversimplified generalizations of characteristics that typify a person, group, or situation. Social scientists use the term to describe the process by which individuals develop attitudes and judgments about an entire group based, usually, on limited information and experience with a member from a particular group or situation (p. 249).

- **White.** This is a general ethnic term that describes anyone whose ancestry traces to the Caucasians, a collective of ancient tribes who lived in the Caucasus Mountains, a range located between the Black and Caspian Seas in what today is Russia. The description is, of course, based upon skin color (p. 265). White culture may be considered as the synthesis of ideas, values, and beliefs coalesced from descendants of white European ethnic groups in the United States (Pedersen, 1988).

Counselor Self-Awareness

The development or modification of a theory of counseling or psychotherapy that is more responsive to racial and cultural groups requires that practitioners determine the appropriateness or inappropriateness of their basic assumptions and culture-bound nature (Sue, Ivey, & Pedersen, 1996). Counselors must have knowledge of the demographics of these groups and an awareness of their history, sociopolitical issues, communication styles, culture, class, language factors, world views, acculturation, and identity. In addition, practitioners must have an awareness of their own biases and beliefs. This requires critical examination of themselves and their theoretical frameworks in order to provide effective and ethically appropriate services.

This process is not an easy task. It also requires a **paradigm shift** in thinking—broadening personal realities with other world views and integrating them into counseling theory and practice. This paradigm shift gives the counselor conceptual clarity and provides a framework of thought to explain various aspects of reality (Kuhn, 1962). Midgette and Meggert (1991) propose such a paradigm shift: "Multicultural instruction represents an emergent synthesis—a somewhat new systematic outlook that benefits from knowledge of previously developed philosophies but is not an eclectic composite" (p. 136). Lee (1996) posits that as multicultural counseling continues to emerge as a primary mode of practice, a paradigm shift in the intervention is also needed. Ibrahim (1985) and Sue et al. (1996) propose that effectiveness in cross-cultural counseling is determined by how well the counselors are aware of their own world view and can understand and accept the world view of the client. The power of a dominant, traditional, preset paradigm can block the pursuit of knowledge through alternative approaches and thereby create major limitations by closing the system and not allowing further development. Traditional paradigms are the source of basic beliefs and attitudes that are difficult to modify. However, if counselors are to act with integrity and commitment, they must begin to take steps in shifting their theoretical paradigms to include racial and cultural world views.

This paradigm shift requires one to assess his or her personal values and beliefs and determine how others' views can be integrated into one's own. Newlon and Arciniega (1992, p. 286) proposed a process of cultural integration involving the following.

1. Confronting and challenging personal stereotypes held about cultural groups
2. Acquiring knowledge about the groups' cultures and, even more important, about heterogeneous responses of the groups
3. Understanding the traditional institutional interaction between the dominant society and minorities, and vice versa
4. Understanding the effects of institutional racism and stereotypes
5. Acquiring firsthand experience with focus minority groups
6. Challenging normative counselor and therapist approaches and understanding their cultural implications
7. Knowledgeably using a culturally pluralistic model

Sue and Sue (1999) posited similar observations in the form of characteristics of culturally aware counselors or therapists. These characteristics included "being aware and sensitive to their own values and biases; comfortable with differences between themselves and their clients in terms of race and beliefs; sensitive to circumstances dictating referral; and aware of their own racist beliefs and feelings" (p. 160). This shift offers an opportunity to expand theoretical frameworks (not necessarily to replace them) and to integrate a more comprehensive view of our world.

Sue, Arredondo, and McDavis (1992) developed a set of multicultural competencies that were presented to the American Counseling and Development Association and later refined and operationalized by Arredondo et al. (1996). This list of competencies responds to the aforementioned paradigm shift, reflecting a more comprehensive analysis of counselor self-awareness, knowledge, and skills. Additionally, Arredondo et al. (1996) propose a personal identity model that provides the framework for analyzing the various dimensions of an individual that are culturally responsive to these four groups.

Acculturation

Acculturation is an important phenomenon to be considered in relation to counseling theory and practice. It is composed of numerous dimensions, such as cultural values, ideologies, ethnic identity, beliefs, attitudes toward self and majority, language use, and cultural customs and practices. It has often been confused with the concept of **assimilation.** In this chapter, *acculturation* is defined as the degree to which an individual from a racial or ethnic minority uniquely incorporates, adds to, and synthesizes the values, customs, language, beliefs, and ideology of the dominant culture in order to survive and feel a sense of belonging. *Assimilation,* however, refers to a "process of acculturation in which an individual has changed so much as to become disassociated from the value system of his/her group or in which the entire group disappears as an autonomously functioning system" (Teske, 1973, p. 7907a).

Each racial ethnic group has its own distinct acculturation process, even though they all manifest similar concerns. Native Americans, who were here before the white settlers, were forced onto reservations and only later entered the majority mainstream. They differ from the Latinos and Asians, who came from another country. The history of African American acculturation also has unique characteristics, including slavery and economic and racial oppression.

Acculturation is not continuous from traditional to mainstream; rather, its origin might be best understood as a multidimensional, multifaceted phenomenon. Individuals may learn how to become acculturated to mainstream U.S. culture, but this does not imply that they reject their own culture. These values may be additive and not supplantive. Persons can retain the values of their culture of origin and simultaneously learn to operate with mainstream values. Minority individuals who have retained their identity and who still incorporate American values in a healthy way are those who have come to an understanding of self without losing their cultural self-concept.

Demographics

A century from now, the population of the United States is expected to be closer to the world balance: 57% Asian American/Pacific Islander, 26% white, 7% African American, and

10% Latino (Edmunds, Martinson, & Goldberg, 1990; Ibrahim, 1991). Judging from census information, researchers believe that by 2010 the white population will have marginal overall growth, while African American and Latino populations will grow at an accelerated rate. The most recent data indicate that Latinos are now the largest minority in the United States (U.S. Bureau of the Census, 2001c).

Population Profile

According to the 2000 census, 75% of the total population of the United States reported only white; 12% of the total population reported black or African American; approximately 0.9% of the total population reported only American Indian and Alaska Native; 3.6% of the total population reported Asian; 0.1% of the total population reported only Native Hawaiian and other Pacific Islander. Approximately 12.5%, or more than 35 million respondents, reported to be only Latino (U. S. Bureau of the Census, 2001a).

As of July 1, 1999, the resident population of the United States was 273 million, a 10% increase over the April 1, 1990 census count. However, not all segments of the population grew at the same rate. Rapid growth in the Asian and Pacific Islander and Latino populations was fueled by migration from abroad. However, the black and American Indian populations also experienced rapid population growth. The growth rate for whites was only 4%. Because other groups were growing faster, the white share of the total population dropped from 76% to 72% (U. S. Bureau of the Census, 1999).

With a growth rate of 45%, the Asian population was the fastest growing racial or ethnic group during this decade. Latino residents, who can be of any race, were the second fastest growing racial or ethnic group in the United States in the 1990s. Although American Indians were a small group, they also outpaced the national growth rate (U. S. Bureau of the Census, 1999).

Educational Attainment

Among the population 25 years old and older, 85% of Asian and Pacific Islanders had completed high school, compared to 88% of whites. However, 42% of Asians and Pacific Islanders in this age group held at least a bachelor's degree, compared to 28% of whites.

The proportion of the black population aged 25 and older with a high school diploma—77%—was 11 percentage points lower than the proportion among whites. This represents a significant improvement over 1989, when the difference was 16 percentage points. Furthermore, 15% of blacks held a bachelor's degree or more.

In addition, 56% of Latinos had a high school diploma or better, and 11% held at least a bachelor's degree. The share of Latinos holding a high school diploma increased 5 percentage points since 1989. The educational attainment level of Native Americans has improved significantly since the 1980s, but remains considerably below the levels of the total population. More than 66% of Native Americans 25 years old and over were high school graduates or higher (U. S. Bureau of the Census, 2000).

Poverty

Child poverty rates were higher than the total poverty rate for each group: 11% for whites, 18% for Asians, 34% for Latinos, and 37% for blacks. The share of families in poverty was about 23% for both black and Latino families.

Generally speaking, married couples have higher incomes than other types of families. Married couples represented 68% of Latino families and fewer than half of all black families. However, families maintained by women with no husband present are among the poorest. About 13% of both white and Asian families were of this type, as were 45% of black families and 24% of Latino families. Native American families maintained solely by women were more than 27% (U. S. Bureau of the Census, 1999).

Aging

The United States population is growing older. In July 1999, half of all people living in the United States were aged 36 or older, almost 3 years older than the median age in April 1990.

Age differences were evident by race and ethnicity. The two youngest groups were the Latino population and the Native American Indian population. About half of the people in both of these groups were aged 27 or younger. The median age was 30 for the black population and 32 for the Asian population. The white population was the oldest population group. The median age for this group was 38—more than 10 years higher than that of the youngest group (U. S. Bureau of the Census, 1999).

Native Americans

Native Americans include American Indians, Eskimos, and Aleuts (Alaska natives). Twenty-two percent of all Native Americans lived on reservations and trust lands in 1990 (U. S. Bureau of the Census, 1993). The number of Native Americans living on the 314 reservations and trust lands varied substantially. In 1990, only 22% of all Native Americans lived on reservations. Only 10 reservations had more than 7,000 Native Americans in 1990; most had fewer than 1,000. Seven of the 10 reservations and trust lands with the largest Native American populations were entirely or partially in Arizona. These state and federally recognized Native American tribes speak more than 200 distinct tribal languages.

The 10 states with the largest Native American population were California, Oklahoma, Arizona, New Mexico, Washington, Alaska, North Carolina, Texas, New York, and Michigan. Overall, nearly one-half of the nation's Native Americans lived in western states. Not every Native American is actually native to America (U. S. Bureau of the Census, 1998). In fact, in 1997, 6% of the nation's Native Americans were foreign-born. Three of every four of these residents were non-citizens who arrived in this country since 1980.

In the fall of 1995, approximately 131,000 Native Americans were enrolled in the nation's colleges and universities. This is an increase of more than 50,000 from the fall of 1980. Nearly 6 in 10 of these students were women, more than 8 in 10 attended public schools, and more than 9 in 10 were undergraduates. During the 1993-94 school year, more than 13,000 of the nation's Native Americans received an associate's, bachelor's, master's, doctor's, or professional degree (U. S. Bureau of the Census, 1998).

About one-third of the nation's Native American households had incomes that placed them below poverty level in 1995. In 1990, for every $100 U. S. families received, Native American families received $62 (U. S. Bureau of the Census, 1993).

In terms of educational, economic, and political power, Native Americans are at the lowest end of the spectrum. More often than not, they have little influence over what happens in the United States or in their own life (LaFromboise & Low, 1989). However, some tribes have become involved in reservation gaming. This new business seems to be changing the lives of many tribal members, resulting in an increase in employment opportunities, educational support, and social services.

American Indians are geographically dispersed throughout the United States. There are 511 federally recognized native entities and an additional 365 state-recognized American Indian tribes, with 200 distinct tribal languages (LaFromboise, 1988). Theory application must be sensitive to the tremendous heterogeneity and diversity existing among Native Americans. The 2000 national census reported the Native American and Alaska Native population as roughly 2.5 million (U. S. Bureau of the Census, 2000). States with relatively high Native American populations include (listed from most to least) California, Oklahoma, Arizona, New Mexico, Texas, North Carolina, Alaska, and Washington (U. S. Bureau of the Census, 2000). According to LaFromboise (1988), only 24% of the population lives on reservations, and that segment is remarkably young, with a median age of 20.4 compared to the U. S. median age of 36.0.

African Americans

African American refers to people having origins in any of the black racial groups in Africa. African Americans are represented by numerous diverse ethnic and cultural groups, including Spanish-speaking populations from Cuba, Puerto Rico, and Panama; groups from the Caribbean Islands and northern Europe; and Native American/African Americans (Wehrly, 1991).

Prior to the 2000 census, African Americans constituted the nation's largest racial and ethnic minority. According to the 2000 census, African Americans now represent 12% of the total U. S. population and number close to 35 million (U. S. Bureau of the Census, 2001). Most African Americans reside in the Southern states. States with more than 20% of the total resident population identifying as African American include Louisiana, Mississippi, Alabama, Georgia, South Carolina, North Carolina, Virginia, and Maryland. More than 60% of the residents in the District of Columbia are African American (U. S. Bureau of the Census, 2001).

The disadvantaged status, racism, and poverty impacting African Americans have been well documented. Although these statistics are grim, Ford (1997) points out that much of our literature is based on characteristics of individuals of the lower social class who are on welfare or unemployed and not enough on other segments of the African American population. More than one-third of African Americans are now middle-class or higher. They tend to be well educated, homeowners, and married. Many middle- and upper-class African Americans are receptive to the values of the dominant society, believe that advances can be made through hard work, believe race has a relative rather than pervasive influence in their lives, and embrace their heritage. However, they may feel bicultural stress and feelings of guilt at having "made it." Frustrations with the limitations imposed by the "glass ceiling" and feelings of isolation were also reported (Sue & Sue, 1999).

African American values have been shaped by cultural factors, social class variables, and experience with racism. As a group, African Americans tend to be more group-centered and sensitive to interpersonal matters, to have strong kinship bonds, be work- and education-oriented, and to have a strong commitment to religious values and church participation (Sue & Sue, 1999).

It is important for counselors and therapists to acknowledge and understand the tremendous diversity within the African American population in the United States. The African

American experience in America is unique. This group first arrived in the United States in the 1600s and, unlike immigrant groups who followed, came involuntarily as slaves. The group as a whole has been subjected to continuing majority-group oppression. In no case has the sheer brutality and evil of racism, prejudice, and penetrating hate been so evident and salient as in the white majority's treatment of African Americans throughout U. S. history.

Latinos

The group term *Hispanic* was created by federal order in 1978 by the Office of Management and Budget. Hispanic origin, in the 2000 census, is based on self-identification by respondents and includes people whose origin is Mexican, Puerto Rican, Cuban, Central or South American, or other. People of Hispanic origin may be of any race. While some consider the word *Hispanic* offensive, others merely see it as a bureaucratic government term with very little personal significance and prefer to be classified by their countries of origin (e.g., Puerto Rican, Dominican, Cuban, Mexican). The term *Latino* for a male and *Latina* for a female is growing in popularity among U. S.-born Latinos, which represents a political consciousness and a sense of ethnic pride (Santiago-Rivera, Arredondo, & Cooper, 2001). This is why the term *Latino(s)* rather than *Hispanic* is used throughout this chapter.

Latinos are now the largest minority in the United States (U. S. Bureau of the Census, 2001), representing 35.3 million or about 13% of the total population. The Latino population increased by 57.9% from 1990 to 2000. Population growth varied by group. Mexicans increased by 52.9%, Puerto Ricans increased by 24.9%, Cubans increased by 18.9%, and Latinos who reported other origins increased by 97%. "Other Latino origins" referred to Latinos from Central America, South America, and the Dominican Republic. Salvadorans were the largest Central American group, followed by Guatemalans and Hondurans.

More than three-quarters of Latinos live in the West or South. In 2000, 43.5% of Latinos lived in the West, and 32.8% lived in the South. Latinos accounted for 24.3% of the population in the West, the only region in which Latinos exceeded the national level of 12.5%.

Mexicans, Puerto Ricans, and Cubans were concentrated in different regions. Among Mexicans, 55.3% lived in the West. The largest Mexican populations (more than one million) were in California, Texas, Illinois, and Arizona. Among Puerto Ricans, 60.0% lived in the Northeast. The largest Puerto Rican populations (more than 250,000) were in New York, Florida, and Pennsylvania. Among Cubans, 74.2% lived in the South. About two-thirds of all Cubans were in Florida.

Half of all Latinos lived in just two states: California and Texas. Latinos in New Mexico accounted for 42% of the total state population, the highest proportion of any state. More than four million Latinos lived in Los Angeles County, California. In 2000, more than a million Latinos lived in the cities of New York and Los Angeles (U. S. Bureau of the Census, 2001). Latinos in East Los Angeles comprised 95.8% of the population, the highest for any place outside of the Commonwealth of Puerto Rico. Two of the top ten cities in terms of numbers of Latinos were El Paso and San Antonio, Texas.

Asian Americans

Asian Americans, in this chapter, include Chinese, Japanese, Filipinos, Koreans, Asian Indians, Southeast Asians, Vietnamese Laotions, Cambodians, Hmongs, Pacific Islanders,

Hawaiians, Guamanians, and Samoans. This group has been growing rapidly and has shown a large increase because of the changes in immigration laws that occurred in 1965 and the entry of over 1.5 million Southeast Asian refugees since 1975 (Chung, Bemak, & Okazaki, 1997). The immigration pattern changed the characteristics of the Asian American population. In fact, with the exception of Japanese Americans, Asian American populations are now principally composed of foreign-born individuals.

The Chinese and Japanese were the first Asians to settle in the United States in large numbers. Like other minority groups, they arrived with the hope of improving their economic conditions, lifestyles, and social and political life (Dillard, 1985). Today, Asian Americans are dispersed throughout the United States. A large percentage are located in urban areas on the west and east coasts. Although some Asian American groups have been portrayed as "model minorities" in terms of significant educational and economic success, large percentages of these groups live in poverty and suffer high levels of psychological stress (Sue & Sue, 1999). Between-group differences within the Asian American population may be quite great, as the population is composed of at least 40 distinct subgroups that differ in language, religion, and values (Hong & Ham, 2001). They include the larger Asian groups in the United States (Chinese, Filipinos, Koreans, Asian Indians, and Japanese), refugees and immigrants from Southeast Asia (Vietnamese, Laotions, Cambodians, and Hmongs), and Pacific Islanders (Hawaiians, Guamanians, and Samoans) (Sue & Sue, 1999). The tremendous heterogeneity both between and within various Asian American groups defies categorization and stereotypic description. This group has been subjected to continuing societal oppression, discrimination, and misunderstanding.

Cultural Considerations

Each of the specific racial and ethnic groups that we have addressed has cultural considerations that must be taken into account by counselors. These considerations should be evaluated with respect to minority groups' needs, values, and level of acculturation. Newlon and Arciniega (1983) addressed these considerations as "factors" to be considered by practitioners when gathering information and integrating them into counseling theory and process. Cultural considerations include language, cultural identity, generation, cultural custom styles, geographical location and neighborhoods, family constituency, psycho-historical aspects, and religious traditions. It should be noted that these are stated in a general sense and must be interpolated with information from each group.

Language

When working with minority clients who still use their language of origin, understanding the language is not enough. The practitioner must consider both content and contextual meaning. In addition, the counselor or therapist must be able to assess the language proficiency of the various minority groups: not all members will have the same degree of fluency in the language of origin or in English. Practitioners must be cognizant of the fact that the language of origin is where much of the affect is first learned. Although some minority clients may be fluent in English, the English words may have a different affective meaning from that of the language of origin. Meanings of some words may not have the same sense when translated.

Identity

Counselors must be aware of the **self-referent labels** that clients choose. Self-referent labels are a sensitive issue for many clients and may be different even for various members within the family. For example, to individuals of Mexican or Latin American descent, the identifiers may be *Mexican American, Latino, Chicano, Americans of Mexican descent,* or others. For clients of African descent, these may be *African American, Negro, black,* or *West Indian.* For Native Americans, identifiers may be *American Indian,* or important tribal names. For Asian Americans, the identifiers may be *Asian, Asian American, Oriental,* or specific countries of origin. One of the major contributions from multicultural researchers is the idea of **identity stage development models,** which provide a framework to help counselors understand an identity process that minorities may experience. For more detailed information, see Sue and Sue (1999) and Atkinson et al. (1993).

Generation

Clients' generational factors—that is, first, second, or third generation in this country—should be assessed by the counselor or therapist to assist in a thumbnail assessment of acculturation. Inherent in this is the history of the family from the country of origin. First-generation clients may have more ties to the traditional culture, and these ties may be reflected in the nuclear and extended family dynamics. The acculturation process is unique for each minority group and individual. Contrary to some current beliefs, as clients become acculturated they do not drop their former cultural ways but rather add new ones and synthesize both the new and the old in a creative manner.

Cultural Custom Styles

In addition to the obvious cultural customs of food, dress, and traditions, several cultural styles of responsibility and communication have to be considered. For example, the Mexican, Indian, and Asian cultures emphasize the responsibility an eldest child has for younger siblings. An Asian family's expectations for unquestioning obedience may produce problems when family members are exposed to American values emphasizing independence and self-reliance.

The style of communication in traditional Native American and Mexican American clients stresses patience and personal respect. Clients from traditional families may show respect by looking down and not making eye contact with authority figures. With African American clients, verbal interaction moves at a faster pace; sensitive confrontation is accepted more readily than with traditional Latino, Native American, or Asian families.

Geographical Location and Neighborhoods

Ethnic groups from different geographical locations exhibit distinct geocultural traditions and customs. Practitioners cannot assume that the same customs apply to seemingly similar cultural groups. They should also note rural and urban influences in the client's present situation within the family history.

Neighborhoods where the minority clients reside have a great deal to do with how clients see themselves. Minority clients living in a totally ethnic area have a different view than clients living in an integrated neighborhood or clients residing in a neighborhood where they are the only minority family.

Family Constituency

In most minority families, kinship networks help to satisfy important cultural needs for intimacy, belonging, and interpersonal relations. Extended families, where more than one generation lives in the same household and where formalized kinship relations exist, are common among minority groups. In many Latino and Native American families, significant adults may extend to uncles, grandparents, cousins, close friends, and godparents. Family holds a special place for most minority clients. Love, protection, and loyalty to the family are pronounced, creating an environment where members can develop strong feelings of self-worth despite the lingering effects of discrimination and racism.

Psychohistorical and Religious Traditions

The history of the client's ethnic group, along with the groups' history of that ethnic group in the United States, is information that counselors need. Minority clients reflect the psychohistory of the family through child-rearing practices. Many facets of child rearing are rooted in the history of minority groups and are distinct from the dominant culture in which the clients presently live. For example, Latinos and Native Americans may have been raised in a cooperative mode rather than the competitive mode of the dominant culture.

Spiritual and religious practices traditionally have been strong within most minorities. Religion provides the medium through which minority clients deal with forces and powers beyond their control. It also provides a basis for social cohesion and support. Historically, religious institutions and personnel have been a resource for personal counseling and a refuge from a hostile environment. For example, African Americans have traditionally gone to their religious leaders for advice and direction.

Racial and Ethnic Components

Specific racial and ethnic cultural components that are common to the traditional members of the four racial ethnic groups should be further clarified, as they are uniquely important. These components have been identified as critical when assessing minority relationships to the various counseling theories. It is important to have knowledge of these components in order to determine whether theories directly or indirectly address these racial and ethnic cultural components and, if not, whether they can be modified or adapted to the counselor's theoretical framework.

Racial/ethnic women's issues are not addressed because of space limitations of this chapter. Rather than provide scant information, the authors encourage you to read "The Woman Factor in Multicultural Counseling" (Arredondo, Psalti, & Cella, 1993); *Women of Color: Integrating Ethnic and Gender Identities in Psychotherapy* (Comas-Diaz & Greene, 1994); and "Gender Issues in Multicultural Counseling" (Hansen & Gama, 1996).

These racial and ethnic components are related to some of the cultural considerations discussed in the previous section. However, they are presented here in the light of counseling theory variables as opposed to counselor variables. This distinction is important in determining whether a theory allows for the extenuating manifestations inherent in each component. In addition, because these components and considerations manifest a holistic view, they have descriptive overlaps.

Language

In addition to the fact that minority groups may retain their language of origin, use black English, or use code switching (words from English combined with language of origin), there are other considerations that need to be taken into account. Counselors should be competent in the languages of particular diverse populations, but they must also be cognizant of the fact that affect is learned in the culture of origin through presymbolic and symbolic language at an early age. This affect reflects the minority member's world view and the inherent assumptions of the culture. The meanings of some words may not have the same sense when translated. Also, English is more linear than other languages of these four groups. Therefore, the theoretical framework employed must be able to allow for these considerations directly or indirectly.

Family and Social Relations

The importance of family is a major consideration for each of the four groups. Extended family kinship ties, respect for elders, defined gender roles, emphasis on the nurturing of children, the hierarchical nature of the family structure, primary responsibility to family, and identity are closely linked through strong family ties in all four groups. A counseling theory that does not incorporate this multifaceted component has limited value. The theory must be able to address this component in a familial, holistic sense because of the minority group's strong sense of belonging to and identity with the family group.

Time Focus

For these four groups, the concept of time may be distinct from the majority view, in which the focus is the future: one sacrifices for tomorrow and postpones gratification. The concept of rigid adherence to time is an artifact of Euro-American culture. For the four groups discussed in this chapter, the present and past may be more important than the future because of cultural or socioeconomic factors. World views that are based on past cultural history may still operate in the present. For these minority groups, time is viewed contextually as an artifact of mainstream society. Future predictions and time specificity are placed in the context of possibility, not fact. Social relations and obligations often have a higher priority than specific time-clock appointments. Theories that incorporate the planning of an individual's future behavior may be counterproductive if this is not taken into consideration. In addition, those theories that impose the "fifty-minute hour" at a specific time take a mainstream cultural view that is not responsive to the cultural world view of these groups. Events or situations that happen to these groups may be viewed as more important than being on time and, consequently, a client's behavior may be misinterpreted as resistance by a majority theoretical view (Ibrahim, 1991).

Nature–People Relationships

The relationship of people to nature has a distinct and unique value orientation for these four minority groups. Life may be determined by external forces such as fate, God's will, or "that's the way it is." Acceptance of (not subjugation) and harmony with nature—coexisting without control—may be part of an inherent cultural view for these groups. People are a priority, and relationships are important and primary. This view may often be in conflict with the majority view, which operates in terms of overcoming, controlling, or conquering nature and the environment, including one's own behaviors. Counseling theories that assume that the individual is greater than or separate from nature and the environment have limited effectiveness with these groups (Sue & Sue, 1999).

Collectivist and World View/Holistic View

A holistic view for these groups encompasses both a particularistic cultural perspective and a universal view. These groups operate from the interaction of their environment and themselves as a whole. Support of the interrelationship between individual and environment has been documented extensively (Katz, 1985). Therefore, this holistic component has both universal and particularistic (edic and emic) aspects for these minority groups. The framework of this view is based on a collectivistic rather than an individualistic world view. Life is based on a totality of this interaction and does not fragment and separate. Counseling theories that only address this component from either a universal view or a particularistic view have limitations in their theoretical application. A collectivistic and world view are utilized by the four groups as opposed to an individualistic world view (Trevino, 1996). The collectivistic world view focuses on group and family centeredness being the importance of relationships, and time is relative (Ibrahim, 1991).

Human Activity

Common to all four minority groups is the cultural component of cooperation, which includes connectedness and loyalty to respective groups. This component is part of the groups' socialization and child-rearing patterns, which are manifested in unique, complementary roles and tasks in the family and community. These groups emphasize the concept of "being" and not of having to become better in order to have status with one's own group. Contribution is seen from a collectivistic view, with members having value simply because of who they are. Counseling theories that emphasize only the growth of the individual, regardless of how it affects a minority individual's group and family, may meet with obstacles and confusion.

Identity

For these four groups, personal identity cannot be separated from each member's cultural identity. Theories that address the universal self or identity development alone bypass a very important cultural component. The process of minority identity has been addressed extensively by Sue and Sue (1999). Hall, Cross, and Freed (1971) have elaborated further on minority identity models. Cultural or ethnic identity is in the midst of much research developed by many authorities in cultural identity theory and addresses many other dimensions beyond what is presented here (Bernal & Knight, 1993; Cross, Parham, & Helms, 1995; Helms, 1990; Sue & Sue, 1999). A minority member may have distinct self-referent labels that vary even within each group, and these labels are related to both negative and positive identity. Additionally, most members struggle with imposed stereotypes from the majority culture, which affect the self-esteem and self-worth of each group member. The psychological costs of racism in identity cannot be stressed enough. Counseling theory and process must be able to address these complex identity components.

Spirituality and Religion

Each of these four groups deals with unique and distinct spiritual issues as part of its daily life. Spirituality and religion may be an integral part of each group and its members. Spirituality and religion have been a source of stability and hope for these groups for many generations and are part of their socialization. Few counseling theories address this component, and consequently they omit a major mainstay and refuge used by these groups in hostile environments.

Individuality and Responsibility

The concept of individual responsibility may be viewed differently by minority groups. Native Americans, for instance, judge their worth primarily in terms of whether their behavior serves to better the tribe. Tribal culture places a high value on the harmonious relationship between an individual and all other members of the tribe. This concept of cooperation within certain ethnic groups has been empirically documented (Kagan & Madsen, 1971). Responsibility to the family is a major value often found in African American, Latino, Native American, and Asian American clients and should be considered and encouraged. Individual responsibility is integrated as part of the value of the family.

The concept of responsibility in these four groups may be different from the mainstream majority view. For them, a concept of collective responsibility may be prioritized: first to family, then to their own group or community, and finally to self. Most theories deal with responsibility according to a different priority: first to individual, then to family, and finally to group and community. Neither approach implies a wrong or right, but when theories operate totally from the development of responsibility to self and do not consider the consequences of those implications to members of minority groups, they may meet with confusion and resistance. Individually centered theories, with their goal of individual responsibility, may work in counterproductive ways and are apt to discount the values of these groups. While some theories may espouse the concept of universal responsibility, they often fail to address cultural specificity.

Oppression and Racism

All four groups have experienced a history of oppression and racism that has affected them in terms of identity, alienation, and devaluation of their worth. While other American minority groups have experienced oppression, these four groups have distinct physical phenotypic traits that are readily identifiable. This factor alone has kept the differentness on the surface, no matter what may transpire within. Because of the United States' melting-pot philosophy, which is still in existence despite the culturally pluralistic views and values of cultural diversity being professed, racism continues to persist and affect these groups. Most counseling theories do not address this component in their frameworks, and this omission appears to discount their cultural reality (Sue & Sue, 1999).

A note of caution in addressing these components and considerations: the degree of acculturation plays an important role in that it may be possible that many of the minority group members will be able to operate contextually depending on whether they are in a majority environment or are within their own minority group. Therefore, these components and considerations need to address the context of the individual's own ability to adjust.

Assessment of Theories on Racial/Ethnic Components

Table 17.1 presents a framework to view diagrammatically whether nine traditional theories presented in this book address the proposed racial and ethnic components and considerations. It is important that the reader understand that feminist theory and Eastern theories were not included in this diagrammatic comparison, as these theories direct the majority of emphasis on one segment of the client population and comparison with more generic theoretical systems would be inappropriate. Brief therapy was also not included because it is not considered to be a "theory" (Hergenhan & Olson, 1999; Sue et al., 1999). The table lists the nine theories and identifies racial and ethnic components at the top, with their respective intercepting boxes marked as follows: (+) theory responds positively; (–) theory is contrary; (0) theory doesn't address; (P) theory responds partially.

Note that the table has been proposed as an outline to view how the various identified components correspond to the theories. We interject a note of caution here, pointing out that this figure is *not* intended to be definitive and closed but to facilitate an understanding of the relationship among the theories and the racial and ethnic components. Arbitrary assessments by the authors were made after reviewing the theories; other experts in the field might offer different interpretations.

We have given consideration to *traditional* racial and ethnic groups where *survival* is primary and where educational level may be lower than the general white population. For the four focus minority groups, a major segment of these populations have less than a high school education. In addition, many of these minority groups still hold on to the culture and language of origin and therefore still reflect different world views.

Summary and Critique of Theories

In light of the racial and ethnic components we proposed, our assessments indicate that very few of the theories discussed in this book address those components effectively. Our purpose is not to show the limitations of these theories with racial or ethnic minorities, but to point out that when the theories were developed, populations with differing world views were not taken into consideration.

Alderian, existential, person-centered, and family system theories—with some interpolation—could respond to specific components. However, such a response would result from counselor interpretation that is not necessarily inherent in the theory. It could be argued that existential and person-centered theories have much leeway in the universal sense; therefore, important components could be addressed with adaptations. Philosophically, there is merit in these approaches. However, in relation to the specificity of these components, both theories appear to be lacking. Alderian and family system theories hold the most promise with their holistic, sociocultural, and family-centered points of view with minority populations.

The appropriateness of cognitive-behavioral theories is subject to a counselor's awareness and sensitivity rather than inherent in the theory itself. For the most part, the rest of the theories have little to limited inherent relevance when dealing with minority populations unless the counselor adapts the theories to address these components.

Freudian Psychoanalytic Theory

One of the main limitations of Freudian psychoanalytic theory is its focus on intrapsychic conflict as the source of all dysfunction and its failure to consider interpersonal and sociocultural variables. It ignores social class, culture, ethnicity, and race as variables in the

Table 17.1
Counseling Theories in Terms of Racial and Ethnic Components

Theory	Racial and Ethnic Components								
	Language	Family and Social Relations	Time Focus	Nature-People Relationships	Holistic View	Human Activity	Identity	Spirituality and Religion	Oppression and Racism
Psychoanalytic	–	–	0	–	–	–	0	–	–
Jungian	0	–	P	0	P	P	0	+	0
Alderian	0	+	P	P	+	+	P	P	P
Existential	0	–	P	P	+	+	P	0	0
Person-centered	0	0	P	P	+	+	P	P	0
Gestalt	0	–	P	–	+	P	0	–	0
Cognitive-behavorial	0	P	+	0	0	0	P	0	0
Reality therapy	0	0	+	0	0	P	P	0	0
Family	P	+	P	P	+	+	P	0	P

+ Theory responds positively
– Theory is contrary

0 Theory doesn't address
P Theory responds partially

developmental process. The consequences of racism on the intrapsychic process are not addressed, and differential experiences or the values of being different in a white-dominated society are not acknowledged. Psychoanalytic theory is individualistic and does not deal with cultures that are group or family centered. Stage developments are based on a two-parent family, which is not always the case in many minority groups. The theory also involves a process in which clients are expected to be verbal and disclosing, which can be counterproductive and alien when used with Asian Americans, Native Americans, and Latinos, who are socialized not to readily disclose (Okum, 1990). The theory does not address the social, cultural, and political dimensions that impinge on these four focus minority groups. In addition, the anonymous role the counselor assumes can be restrictive for minority clients and is in direct conflict with minority clients' social framework and environmental perspective.

Most minority clients cannot afford to devote 5 years to intensive treatment when what they want is immediate response to specific issues. The goals of psychoanalytic therapy are not appropriate for minority clients when dealing with the practical concerns in their social environments. This theory, with modification, could have some application with diagnosed borderline minority clients if they were examined from a sociocultural and developmental perspective. Additionally, the diffused sense of ethnic identity could be addressed, but, again, would bring up the issue of long-term therapy. Based on these considerations, this model is inappropriate for the racial and ethnic groups we have discussed (Corey, 2001; Ivey, Ivey, & Simek-Morgan, 1993).

Jungian Analytical Theory

Jungian theory has limitations similar to those of Freudian theory for racial and ethnic minority groups. Jungian therapy is an intrapsychic process and does not address racism and discrimination as variables in the developmental process. Consequently, all problems lie within the individual. Jung's mystical approach, with its collective unconscious, archetypes, and unconscious factors, would have little appeal to those minority groups struggling to survive. It also emphasizes a model of healthy functioning—one that would take years of counseling. In addition to using impersonal treatment modalities, Jungian counselors are subject to their own beliefs about and interpretations of the symbols.

The racial and ethnic groups we have discussed may have their own distinct symbols and are not socialized to deal with abstract articulation as required by this model. The theory does not deal with the influence of either social class or institutional oppression and thus can be misinterpreted by practitioners. The methodology of this model does not provide a reality base congruent with these minority groups. While it is a holistic model and deals with universal symbols of spirituality, it is not culturally specific to these groups. The model would not be very relevant to or effective with these traditional groups.

Adlerian Theory

Strict Adlerian theory would have some limitations for minority clients who want quick solutions, for the clients would have little interest in exploring early childhood, early memories, or dreams. These clients may not see the purpose of dealing with life's problems by going through details of lifestyle analysis. However, of all the theories we will consider, this one holds great promise because of several characteristics: it focuses on the person in a familial and sociocultural context; it is involved in developing social interest in contributing to others; it emphasizes belonging, which supports the value system of these minority groups; and its emphasis on the role of the family and culture fits well with the values of these focus minority groups.

Adlerian assumptions that people are equal, social, and goal-centered, that they seek cooperation, and that they contribute to the common good of the group are holistic and are congruent with the cultural values of these racial and ethnic groups. The individual's unique subjective interpretation and perception are part of Adlerian theory, and the client's culture, values, and views are honored and accepted. Adlerian goals are not aimed at deciding for clients what they should change about themselves. Rather, the practitioner works in collaboration with clients and their family networks. This theory offers a pragmatic approach that is flexible and uses a range of action-oriented techniques to explore personal problems within their sociocultural context. It has the flexibility to deal both with the individual and the family, making it very appropriate for these racial and ethnic groups (Corey, 2001; Sherman & Dinkmeyer, 1987).

Existential Theory

Existential theory is based on an understanding of the individual and allows the freedom to use other systems and techniques that can be made applicable to racial and ethnic groups. The existential notions of **freedom** and **control** can be helpful in assisting clients to clarify their cultural values, identity, and meaning. Ibrahim (1985) has pointed out that an existential approach provides for the concept of "cultural relativity" and "relative objectivity" (p. 635). It is essential in this approach for practitioners to understand their own cultural heritage and world views so that they can more effectively help people with other world views.

It can, however, with much sensitivity and a knowledge of the components, enable minority clients to look at how their behavior is being influenced by social and cultural conditioning. Vontress, Johnson, and Epp (1999) argue that existential counseling is a useful approach for clients of all cultures in helping them find meaning and harmony in their lives because it focuses on human experiences.

However, a major criticism of this theory is that it is excessively individualistic with freedom of choice as a focus. Minority clients may not feel they have much choice because of their sociocultural and political environmental circumstances. The theory is based on the assumption of self determination, which does not consider the same sociopolitical dimensions in which these four groups operate. Because these client groups often seek counseling for specific direction, reflecting on freedom of choice and meaning may create frustration and misunderstanding. Lack of direction in terms of specificity, abstract meaning, and the concept of individual responsibility can be counterproductive to these focus minority groups (Corey, 2001; Seligman, 2001; Yalom, 1988).

Person-Centered Theory

In many ways, person-centered theory has made significant contributions to practice in multicultural settings. Carl Rogers used this approach in several countries throughout the world. The theory's emphasis is on humanness and the core conditions that infuse an egalitarian approach into the model. However, it does emphasize independence and self-direction, which may be contrary to the family-centered values of these four racial/ethnic groups.

The theory can allow clients to explore their own cultural reality, and if counselors do not understand how to integrate this, they need to be honest and develop a learning situation (Freeman, 1993). However, the core conditions of this theory are difficult to translate into the cultural framework of Latinos, Native Americans, African Americans, and Asian Americans. It is *incumbent upon the counselor* to go beyond core conditions of humanness and deal with the cultural relatedness of these minority groups. Because the theory originated in a white, middle-class milieu, it has inherent limitations unless counselors carefully look at their own beliefs and gain an understanding of the world views of these groups.

A limitation of person-centered theory is that many racial and ethnic groups want more structure and direction than is inherent in this theory. Person-centered theory values an internal focus, while many of these minority groups may still operate to some extent on the value of external evaluation—that of family and group identity. This theory emphasizes **self** and **real self,** which can be counterproductive because it obscures relational and broader environmental issues that may be a priority with these minority groups. Minority clients may focus more on the real world than the ideal (Corey, 2001; Ivey et al., 1993; Rogers, 1980; Sue & Sue, 1999). In addition, the focus on individual development can be at odds with cultural values that stress the common good and cohesion of a person's group. This model provides a foundation for a relationship to be developed if the counselor integrates cultural factors. Thus, the theoretical framework alone does not directly address these groups' identified racial and ethnic components. It is incumbent on the counselor to integrate these components into the theoretical application.

Gestalt Theory

Because of its emphasis on individual responsibility and techniques that may be too confrontational or out of the realm of reality for these minority groups, Gestalt theory has several limitations. Confrontation and the techniques used may produce intense feelings that minority clients may not be ready for or that are not culturally appropriate. Responsibility focuses on the self without connecting to the group relationship, which may have a higher priority for these minority groups. Native Americans, Asian Americans, and Latinos have strong cultural characteristics that prohibit them from expressing negative emotions about their parents and family. Where cooperation is a heavy cultural injunction, these individuating directions for self-responsibility might meet with opposition. Many members of these focus minority groups often begin counseling with the expectation of getting advice and direction, and are then confronted with looking at feelings and self-responsibility, which may be counterproductive with their group.

Another theoretical characteristic in Gestalt theory is that of "being in the present." This may not be understood by groups in which connectedness with the past is important to their world view. Additionally, this theory's emphasis on dreams, fantasies, and symbols may be incompatible with minority groups' world-view orientation. Again, the application of the model depends on its sensitive use by the counselor. Gestalt therapy may be useful for those minorities that may be more bicultural by utilizing Gestalt techniques for integration of polarities (Corey, 2001; Okum, 1990; Perls, 1973; Seligman, 2001; Sue & Sue, 1999).

Cognitive-Behavioral Theories

We discuss the various cognitive-behavioral theories together because they are closely related. Although there are some differences in technique, all hold to a basic cognitive-behavioral belief system. Albert Ellis's rational-emotive behavior theory does not deal with past history. It does address the client's view of the problem, yet only the cognition of specific events or incidents. This has the danger of devaluing the minority group members' feelings of frustration and their cultural view of self. The theory can be confrontational and dismiss the story around the event or incident that is part of the minority's holistic view, thereby devaluing the integrity and values of these four groups.

Inherent in this theory is the tenet that rational and irrational beliefs are the basis of client problems. These beliefs are based on white, middle-class values; hence, what is rational or irrational for the counselor may not be such for the minority client. The issue of how much power counselors have may be intimidating or even negatively challenging, creating a retreat from the practitioners, or even worse, acquiescence to their ideas.

This theoretical framework has a firm set of beliefs that are not culturally inherent and relevant and could create confusion. The beliefs the minority client holds may be interpreted as being different from those held by members of the mainstream and therefore inappropriate. Consequently, this may further exacerbate the client's feelings of insecurity. Unless the counselor deals carefully and sensitively with the client's cultural beliefs and world view, this model will meet with disaster.

The theory challenges dependency, which to these groups may be counterproductive to their concept of interdependency, an important part of their cultural values and one they view as essentially healthy. The theory does not deal with such factors as racism, sociocultural experience, and family roles, which are conditioned by the groups' culture (Corey, 2001; Okum, 1990).

There are other cognitive-behavioral theories that do not take such a dogmatic approach as Ellis's. Beck (1976) and Meichenbaum (1979), who take a collaborative and active approach, consider sociocultural determinants more closely. Their approaches posit the problem being defined as the client sees it. In addition, their approaches look at the cultural milieu before determining faulty beliefs, and they involve the client in mutually acceptable goals that can be culturally relevant. The counselor in this theory also functions as a teacher, and the focus on learning would appeal to these groups. It also gives the counselor an expertise that would be useful to some of the minority groups such as Latinos and Asians, who might look for more direction. Structure is still primary; and once goals are determined, the models proceed on their own. However, little room is left for people who do not possess mainstream ideas and are less articulate in majority mainstream logic. Behaviors and thoughts deemed culturally acceptable by the dominant culture may have unique and different meanings for these focus groups. Such values and meanings are not accounted for in cognitive-behavioral theory (Okum, 1990). Casas (1988) points out that cognitive-behavioral theory does not address racial ethnicity and culture in the development of research paradigms. He avers that the basic assumption of this model is that people are responsible for their own anxiety, contribute significantly to it, and can decide responsibly to act. This view may not be congruent with the life experiences of these minority groups. Casas further states, "Racism, discrimination, and poverty may have created a cognitive mindset antithetical to any self-control approach" (1988, p. 109). The practitioner's value system concerning race and class is eminently important. If it is incompatible with that of a minority group member, it may be imposed on the client and consequently affect him or her inappropriately. "The theory implies that the dominant therapist's value system is the correct one" (Corey, 2001; Ivey et al., 1993; Okum, 1990, pp. 200–201).

Reality Therapy Theory

The principles of this model, which incorporate care, respect, and rejection of the medical model, are that behavior is purposive and geared to fulfilling needs. This model has potential for use with minority clients, depending on the modification by the counselor. Reality counselors can demonstrate their respect for cultural values and assist minority clients in exploring how satisfying their current behavior is and in collaboratively forming realistic plans that are consistent with their cultural values. The focus is on acting and thinking rather than identifying and exploring feelings. It focuses on positive steps that *could* deal with cultural specificity, which would appeal to these minority groups. However, in this theory the responsibility lies totally with the individual. The counselor or therapist does not seek out the support systems and cooperation values that are part of these groups. The model itself does not address the very real aspects of discrimination and racism that limit these groups. If counselors do not accept these environmental restrictions as real, minority group members may resist and feel misunderstood. Accountability is a mainstream value and may be incompatible with the value of these focus groups.

Additionally, many minority group members may be reluctant to state what they need to an institutional counselor because of real paranoia or because their socialization has not reinforced self-assertiveness. Their socialization has been to think more in terms of what is good for the group than in terms of their individual needs. Again, as in other approaches, the effectiveness of reality therapy is based on the counselor's ability to be sensitive to cultural aspects rather than on the theory itself (Corey, 2001; Glasser, 1998; Wubbolding, 2000).

Family Theory

Family theory incorporates several of the leading family systems theorists and principles of holistic thinking. This theory considers the family as the basic social system and that understanding the system's environment is paramount to being an effective practitioner. By definition, a system's environment (institutional, societal, cultural) includes all that affects the basic family system. Consequently, this theory has great implications in its application to minority populations. However, in order for the theory to be effective, counselors must have a strong training base in multicultural counseling. This theory has the inherent ability to extend itself to racial and ethnic populations and address their cultural issues and considerations.

The basic premises of family theory deal with the individual, whole family system in its sociocultural contexts. It addresses extended family kinships and respects the concepts of cooperative functioning, an approach that would have much appeal to the racial and ethnic groups we have discussed. It sees the family as the basic unit of development and examines the alliances, subsystems, relationships, and cross-generational issues in their relationship to the larger whole. Minuchin's structural approach has been implemented with several minority groups, thereby demonstrating its cultural adaptability. Minuchin and Fishman (1981) have emphasized the reciprocal influences of the family and community and have focused on interventions that address this interdependence. They incorporate a broad world view and a knowledge that different cultural systems do affect the function of the family and individuals. However, it is noted that family systems theory has some value-laden terms that have their origin in mainstream thinking. The terms of *independence, enmeshment,* and *autonomy* are used to define all groups, and these four groups might find these terms antithetical to their values. The systems approach within family theory can be used with an individual or family, yet still deal with the extended family system. Although this approach does not directly address the concept of racism and discrimination in the larger sociocultural context, it lends itself well to the issues minority groups encounter (Aponte, Rivers, & Whol, 1995; Corey, 2001).

Special Note

In 1996, a new theory of multicultural counseling and therapy (M.C.T.) was proposed by Sue et al. (See *A Theory of Multicultural Counseling and Therapy.*) It provides counselors with a much needed theoretical framework that addresses all racial and ethnic considerations and components more comprehensively than those theories reviewed here. Although this new M.C.T. theory is not one of the theories covered in this text, we strongly encourage you to read this book and consider its ideas and conceptualization. This theory was developed over a period of time by theorists who have been in the multicultural counseling field for over two decades. Granted, it was developed with the whole concept of multiculturalism that is reflective of the authors' own *zeitgeist* and their views. Beside the authors' own chapters on the theoretical framework, comments from leading experts on multicultural theory from various perspectives are presented, including information on specific racial ethnic groups. Although this area is still in its "infancy," the book is timely and well worth reading.

Summary

This chapter discussed some of the multicultural issues facing our profession—in particular, the racial and ethnic considerations impinging on current theories of counseling and psychotherapy. The study of multiculturalism must consider many facets, including demographics, definitions, racial and ethnic cultural considerations, acculturation, identity, and socioeconomic and cultural distinctions. These considerations do not provide a prescriptive analysis for integration into existing theories, nor do they address all issues that are important, such as research, assessment, training, and ethics. But they have been included in this chapter because of their importance to the four focus minority groups. Table 17.1 was developed to facilitate the reader's understanding of these complex, interactive phenomena. We hope our critique of the chart and the general discussion of the theories will provide insight into the dilemma of how theories must be viewed in light of our changing population. Counseling theories are fundamental to the way in which counselors deliver services, but they carry inherent assumptions that need to be challenged. We need to critically evaluate them in light of minority concerns.

Current counseling theories reflect the spirit of the era and region in which the theorists lived. Therefore, traditional counseling and psychotherapies were developed for white, middle-, and upper-middle-class clients (Atkinson et al., 1996; Sue & Sue, 1999). As Katz (1985) noted, these Euro-American theories were developed by white practitioners enmeshed in Western cultural values, and the applicability of these theories to multicultural populations is questionable.

The onus for the development of cultural awareness and applicability has been shouldered by counselors. Only recently have training institutions begun to provide multicultural training, but those practitioners already in the field have had to rely on workshops and their own reading and experience to obtain this awareness. Many of them have tried to integrate multicultural factors into their own ingrained Euro-American theoretical frameworks, usually by looking for a "prescription."

In addition to the cultural milieu in which theories were developed, one also has to consider the theoretical framework that reflects practitioners' own *zeitgeist*. Theory cannot be considered apart from the context of its original background and its filtering through a counselor's interpretation. This may provide an even more distorted view, not only of the theory but also of its applicability to different cultural groups. Each of the major models of counseling and psychotherapy is based on its own unexamined assumptions. At best, theory can only lay a foundation from which to view client behavior and development. There is no one *fully acceptable* model that is considered unassailable.

Most theories reviewed here do not specifically address the racial, ethnic, and cultural considerations of American minority groups. However, it is possible to adapt some theories if certain cultural considerations are taken into account. So before one "throws the baby out with the bath water," it is essential to take a critical look at significant cultural components and adapt the theory to integrate these components.

Counselors are facing a critical impasse in the profession. Multiculturalism—what Pedersen (1991) called "the fourth force"—has gained tremendous momentum. Perhaps this fourth force will require a redefinition of current theories with a major integration of multicultural considerations, or newer multicultural theories that will be applicable to all clients will emerge, such as the one proposed by Sue et al. (1996). Only time, analysis, research, and exposure will tell. In the meantime, a paradigm shift in our thinking about how to deliver services based on a theoretical framework that incorporates multicultural aspects is no longer just an idea but a mandated reality. As counselors, we need to proceed with diligence and commitment with the information and research we have on hand. The reality of the rapidly changing demographics of our clientele presents our greatest challenge to integrate this information into our own evolving frameworks.

References

Abel, T. M. (1977). Review: David Reynolds's Morita Therapy. *Journal of Personality Assessment, 41,* 556–558.

Abreu, J. M., Gim Chung, R. H., & Atkinson, D. R. (2000). Multicultural counseling training: Past, present, and future directions. *The Counseling Psychologist, 28,* 641–656.

Abroms, E. M. (1993). *The freedom of the self: The bioexistential treatment of character problems.* New York: Plenum.

Adler, A. (1926). *Psychotherapie und Erziehung.* Retrieved April 1, 2002, from Alfred Adler Institute of San Francisco, Classical Adlerian Quotes: The Art of Encouragement. Web site *http://ourworld. compuserve.com/homepages/hstein/qu-encou. htm.* Center City, MN: Hazelden Foundation.

Adler, A. (1935). The fundamental view of Individual Psychology. *International Journal of Individual Psychology, 1,* 1–8.

Adler, A. (1978). Cooperation between the sexes. In H. L. Ansbacher & R. R. Ansbacher (Eds.), *Writings on women, love, and marriage, sexuality and its disorders.* Garden City, NY: Doubleday.

Ahn, H., & Wampold, B. E. (2001). Where oh where are the specific ingredients? A meta-analysis of component studies in counseling and psychotherapy. *Journal of Counseling Psychology, 48*(3), 251–257.

Aldous, J. (1994). Cross-cultural counseling and cross-cultural meanings: An exploration of Morita psychotherapy. *Canadian Journal of Counseling, 28,* 238–249.

Alexander, C., Rainforth, M., & Gelderloos, P. (1991). Transcendental meditation, self-actualization and psychological health: A conceptual overview and statistical meta-analysis. *Journal of Social and Behavioral Personality, 6,* 189–248.

Alexander, F. M. (1974). *The resurrection of the body.* New York: Dell Publishing Company.

Alexander, J., & Harman, R. (1988). One counselor's intervention in the aftermath of a middle school student's suicide: A case study. *Journal of Counseling and Development, 66,* 283–285.

Allport, G. W. (1961). *Pattern and growth in personality.* New York: Holt, Rinehart, & Winston.

American Association for Counseling and Development. (1991). Special issue: Multiculturalism as a fourth force in counseling. *Journal of Counseling and Development, 70,* 4–76.

American Psychiatric Association. (1994). *Diagnostic and statistical manual of mental health disorders* (4th ed.). Washington, DC: Author.

Ansbacher, H. L. (1965). The structure of Individual Psychology. In B. B. Wolman (Ed.), *Scientific psychology* (pp. 340–364). New York: Basic Books.

Ansbacher, H. L. (1966). Gemeinschaftsgeguehl. *Individual Psychology News Letter, 17,* 13–15.

Ansbacher, H. L. (1968). The concept of social interest. *Journal of Individual Psychology, 24,* 131–149.

Ansbacher, H. L., & Ansbacher, R. (1956). *The Individual Psychology of Alfred Adler.* New York: Harper & Row.

Ansbacher, H. L., & Ansbacher, R. (1964). *Superiority and social interest.* Evanston, IL: Northwestern University Press.

Aponte, J., Rivers, R., & Whol, J. (1995). *Psychological interventions and cultural diversity.* Boston: Allyn & Bacon.

Arciniega, M., & Newlon, B. (1999). Counseling and psychotherapy: Multicultural considerations. In D. Capuzzi & D. Gross (Eds.), *Counseling and psychotherapy: Theories and interventions* (2nd ed.). (pp. 435–458). Upper Saddle River, NJ: Merrill/Prentice Hall.

Ardell, D. B. (1988). The history and future of the wellness movement. In J. P. Opatz (Ed.), *Wellness promotion strategies: Selected proceedings of the eighth annual National Wellness Conference.* Dubuque, IA: Kendall/Hunt.

Ariel, S. (1999). *Culturally competent family therapy: A general model.* Westport, CT: Greenwood Press.

Arredondo, P., Cooper, M., & Santiago-Rivera, A. (2002). *Counseling Latinos and la familia: A practical guide*. Thousand Oaks, CA: Sage Publications.

Arredondo, P., Psalti, A., & Cella, K. (1993). The woman factor in multicultural counseling. *Counseling and Human Development, 25,* 1–8.

Arredondo, P., Toporek, R., Brown, S., Jones, J., Locke, D., Sanchez, J., & Stadler, H. (1996). Operationalization of multicultural counseling competencies. *Journal of Multicultural Counseling and Development, 24,* 42–178.

Asay, T. P., & Lambert, M. J. (1999). The empirical case for the common factors in therapy: Quantitative findings. In M. A. Hubble, B. L. Duncan, & S. D. Miller (Eds.), *The heart and soul of change: What works in therapy* (pp. 23–55). Washington, DC: American Psychological Association.

Atkinson, D., Morten, G., & Sue, D. W. (1993). *Counseling American minorities* (4th ed). Madison, WI: Brown & Benchmark.

Attinasi, L. (1992). Rethinking the study of the outcomes of college attendance. *Journal of College Student Development, 33,* 61–69.

Avis, J. P. (1987). Collaborative counseling: A conceptual framework and approach for counselors and adults in life transitions. *Counselor Education and Supervision, 27,* 15–30.

Axelson, J. A. (1999). *Counseling and development in a multicultural society* (3rd ed.). Pacific Grove: Brooks/Cole.

Bachelor, A., & Horvath, A. (1999). The therapeutic relationship. In M. A. Hubble, B. L. Duncan, & S. D. Miller (Eds.), *The heart and soul of change: What works in therapy* (pp. 133–178). Washington, DC: American Psychological Association.

Baker, F. S. (2001). Healing in psychotherapy: Using energy, touch and imagery with cancer patients. *Gestalt Review, 4*(4), 267–288.

Baldwin, M., & Wesley, R. (1996). Effects of existential anxiety and self-esteem on the perceptions of others. *Basic and Applied Social Psychology, 18,* 75–95.

Ballou, M., & Gabalac, N. (1984). *A feminist position on mental health*. Springfield, IL: Thomas.

Ballou, M., & West, C. (2000). Feminist therapy approaches. In M. Biaggio & M. Hersen (Eds.), *Issues in the psychology of women* (pp. 273–297). New York: Kluwer Academic/Plenum Publishers.

Bandura, A. (1986). *Social foundations of thought and action*. Upper Saddle River, NJ: Prentice Hall.

Bankart, C. P. (1997). *Talking cures: A history of Western and Eastern psychotherapies*. Pacific Grove, CA: Brooks/Cole.

Bankart, C. P. (1997). Contemporary Japanese psychotherapies: Morita and Naikan. In C. P. Bankart, (Ed.), *Talking cures: A history of Western and Eastern psychotherapies* (pp. 440–462). Pacific Grove, CA: Brooks/Cole.

Barker, P. (1985). *Using metaphors in psychotherapy*. New York: Brunner/Mazel.

Barker, R. L. (1995). *The social work dictionary*. Washington, DC: National Association of Social Workers.

Barlow, D. H., & Cerny, J. A. (1988). *Psychological treatment of panic*. New York: Guilford.

Barrett-Lennard, G. T. (1998). *Carl Rogers's helping system: Journey and substance*. Thousand Oaks, CA: Sage.

Baruth, L. G., & Robinson, E. H. (1987). *An introduction to the counseling profession*. Upper Saddle River, NJ: Prentice Hall.

Batchelor, S. (1997). *Buddhism without beliefs: A contemporary guide to awakening*. New York: Riverhead Books.

Bates, M., Johnson, C., & Blaker, J. (1982). *Group leadership*. Denver: Love.

Bateson, G. (1951). The convergence of science and psychiatry. In J. Ruesch & G. Bateson (Eds.), *Communication: The social matrix of psychiatry* (pp. 257–272). New York: Norton.

Bateson, G. (1972). *Steps to an ecology of mind*. New York: Ballantine Books.

Bateson, G. (1979). *Mind and nature*. New York: Bantam Books, Inc.

Bateson, G., Jackson, D. D., Haley, J., & Weakland, J. G. (1976). Toward a theory of schizophrenia. In C. E. Sluzki & D. C. Ransom (Eds.), *Double bind: The foundation of the communicational approach to the family* (pp. 3–22). New York: Grune & Stratton.

Bateson, M. C. (1972). *Our own metaphor*. New York: Knopf.

Bauman, S., & Waldo, M. (1998). Existential theory and mental health counseling: If it were a snake, it would have bitten! *Journal of Mental Health Counseling, 23,* 13–27.

Bean, R. A., Perry, B. J., & Bedell, T. M. (2001). Developing culturally competent marriage and family therapists: Guidelines for working with Hispanic families. *Journal of Marital and Family Therapy, 27,* 43–54.

Beard, J. H., Propst, R. N., & Malamud, T. J. (1982). The Fountain House model of psychiatric rehabilitation. *Psychosocial Rehabilitation Journal, 5*(1), 47–53.

Beavers, W. R., & Hampson, R. B. (1990). *Successful families.* New York: Norton.

Beck, A. T. (1976). *Cognitive therapy and emotional disorders.* New York: International Universities Press.

Beck, A. T., & Emery, G. (1985). *Anxiety disorders and phobias.* New York: Basic Books.

Beck, A. T., Freeman, A., & Associates. (1990). *Cognitive therapy of personality disorders.* New York: Guilford.

Beck, A. T., Hollon, S. D., Young, J. E., Bedrosian, R. C., & Budenz, D. (1985). Treatment of depression with cognitive therapy and amitriptyline. *Archives of General Psychiatry, 42,* 142–148.

Beck, A. T., Rush, A. J., Shaw, B. F., & Emery, G. (1979). *Cognitive therapy of depression.* New York: Guilford.

Beck, A. T., Wright, F. D., Newman, C. F., & Liese, B. S. (1993). *Cognitive therapy of substance abuse.* New York: Guilford.

Becker, R. (2000). La femme n'existe pas (Jacques Lacan): L'hjomme non plus. *Gestalt Review, 4*(1), 26–28.

Becvar, D. S., & Becvar, R. J. (1999). *Family therapy: A systemic integration.* Boston: Allyn & Bacon.

Beecher, W., & Beecher, M. (1966). *Beyond success and failure.* Dallas, TX: Willard & Marguerite Beecher Foundation.

Belenky, M. F., Clinchy, B. M., Goldberger, N. R., & Tarule, J. M. (1997). *Women's ways of knowing: The development of self, voice, and mind* (10th ed.). New York: Basic Books.

Belkin, G. S. (1980). *An introduction to counseling.* Dubuque, IA: William C. Brown.

Belkin, G. S. (1984). *An Introduction to counseling* (2nd ed.). Dubuque, IA: William C. Brown.

Bem, S. L. (1976). Probing the promise of androgyny. In A. G. Kaplan & J. P. Bean (Eds.). *Beyond sex-role stereotypes: Readings toward a psychology of androgyny* (pp. 47–62). Boston: Little, Brown.

Bem, S. L. (1981). Gender schema theory: A cognitive account of sex typing. *Psychological Review, 88,* 354–364.

Bem, S. L. (1987). Probing the problem of androgyny. In M. Walsh (Ed.), *The psychology of women : Ongoing debates.* New Haven, CT: Yale University Press.

Bem, S. L. (1993). *The lenses of gender.* New Haven, CT: Yale University Press.

Bepko, C. (1989). Disorders of power. In M. McGoldrick, C. Anderson, & F. Walsh (Eds.), *Women in families* (pp. 406–426). New York: Norton.

Berg, I. K., & de Shazer, S. (1993). Making numbers talk: Language in therapy. In S. Friedman (Ed.), *The new language of change: Constructive collaboration in psychotherapy* (pp. 5–24). New York: Guilford.

Bergin, A. E., & Garfield, S. L. (Eds.). (1994). *Handbook of psychotherapy and behavior change* (4th ed.). New York: John Wiley & Sons.

Bernal, M., & Knight, G. (1993). *Ethnic identity: Formation and transmission among Hispanics and other minorities.* Albany: State University of New York Press.

Bertolino, B. (1999). *Therapy with troubled teenagers: Rewriting young lives in progress.* New York: John Wiley & Sons.

Beutler, L. (1994). *What psychotherapy outcome research can teach us in the age of managed care.* Salishan, OR: Oregon Psychological Association.

Binswanger, L., & Boss, M. (1983). Existential analysis and Daseinsanalysis. In T. Millon (Ed.), *Theories of personality and psychopathology* (3rd ed., pp. 283–289). New York: Holt, Rinehart, & Winston.

Blow, A. J., & Sprenkle, D. H. (2001). Common factors across theories of marriage and family therapy: A modified Delphi study. *Journal of Marital and Family Therapy, 27,* 385–401.

Blyski, N., & Westman, A. (1991). Relationships among defense style, existential anxiety, and religiosity. *Psychological Reports, 68,* 1389–1390.

Boadella, D. (1987). *Wilhelm Reich: The evolution of his work.* Boston, MA: Arkana.

Bohart, A. C. (1990). A cognitive client-centered perspective on borderline personality development. In G. Lietaer, J. Rombauts, & R. Van Balen (Eds.), *Client-centered and experiential psychotherapy in the nineties* (pp. 599–622). Leuven, Belgium: Leuven University Press.

Bohm, D. (1973). Quantum theory as an indication of a new order in physics. Part B: Implicate and explicate order in physical law. *Foundations of Physics, 2,* 139–168.

Bolen, J. S. (1996). *Close to the bone: Life-threatening illness and the search for meaning.* New York: Scribner.

Bordin, E. S. (1994). Theory and research on the therapeutic working alliance: New directions. In A. O.

Horvath & L. S. Greenberg (Eds.), *The working alliance* (pp. 13–37). New York: John Wiley & Sons.

Bottome, P. (1957). *Alfred Adler: A portrait from life.* New York: Vanguard Press.

Boughton, B. (2001). Dance therapy. *Gale encyclopedia of alternative medicine.* [Online]. Available: *www.findarticles.com.*

Bowen, M. (1978). *Family therapy in clinical practice.* New York: Jason Aronson.

Bower, J. E., Kemeny, M. E., Taylor, S. E., & Fahey, J. L. (1998). Cognitive processing, discovery of meaning, CD4 decline, and AIDS-related mortality among bereaved HIV-seropositive men. *Journal of Consulting and Clinical Psychology, 66,* 979–986.

Bowers, E. (1997). The effects of CT/RT "Quality School" programming on attendance, academic performance, student self-concept, and relationships in a rural elementary school. *Journal of Reality Therapy, 16*(2), 21–30.

Bowman. C. (2000). Commentary on Leanne O'Shea's "Sexuality: Old struggles and new challenges." *Gestalt Review, 4*(1), 29–31.

Boy, A., & Pine, G. J. (1982). *Client centered counseling: A renewal.* Boston: Allyn & Bacon.

Boy, A., & Pine, G. J. (1999). *A person centered foundation for counseling and psychotherapy* (2nd ed.). Springfield, IL: Charles C. Thomas.

Brabender, V., & Fallon, A. (1993). *Models of inpatient group psychotherapy.* Washington, DC: American Psychological Association.

Bradshaw, J. (1993). Never knowing who we are. *Lear's, 5,* 42.

Brammer, L. M. (1985). *The helping relationship: Process and skills* (3rd ed.). Upper Saddle River, NJ: Prentice Hall.

Brammer, L. M., Abrego, P., & Shostrom, E. (1993). *Therapeutic counseling and psychotherapy* (6th ed.). Upper Saddle River, NJ: Prentice Hall.

Brammer, L. M., & MacDonald, G. (1996). *The helping relationship: Process and skills* (6th ed.). Needham Heights, MA: Allyn & Bacon.

Braswell, L., & Kendall, P. C. (2001). Cognitive-behavioral therapy with youth. In K. S. Dobson (Ed.), *Handbook of cognitive-behavioral therapies* (2nd ed., pp. 246–294). New York: Guilford.

Bratter, B., Bratter, T., Maxym, C., Radda, H., & Steiner, K. (1993). The John Dewey Academy: A residential quality school for self-destructive adolescents who have superior intellectual and intuitive potential. *Journal of Reality Therapy, 12*(2), 42–53.

Brazier, D. (1995). *Zen therapy: Transcending the sorrows of the human mind.* New York: John Wiley & Sons.

Brazier, D. (Ed.). (1993). *Beyond Carl Rogers: Toward a psychotherapy for the 21st century.* London: Constable and Company Limited.

Brems, C. (2000). *Dealing with challenges in counseling and psychotherapy.* Belmont, CA: Brooks/Cole.

Brenner, C. (1974). *An elementary textbook of psychoanalysis.* New York: Doubleday.

Bretall, R. (Ed.). (1951). *A Kierkegaard anthology.* Princeton, NJ: Princeton University Press.

Broder, M. S. (2001). Dr. Albert Ellis–in his own words–on success. *Journal of Rational-Emotive & Cognitive-Behavior Therapy, 19*(2), 77–88.

Brown, D. P. (1984). A model for the levels of concentration meditation. In D. Shapiro & R. Walsh (Eds.), *Meditation: Classic and contemporary perspectives* (pp. 281–317). New York: Aldine Press.

Brown, D., & Srebalus, D. J. (1988). *An introduction to the counseling profession.* Upper Saddle River, NJ: Prentice Hall.

Brown, J. A., & Pate, R. H. (1983). *Being a counselor: Direction and challenges.* Monterey, CA: Brooks/Cole.

Brown, L. S. (1986). Gender role analysis: A neglected component of psychological assessment. *Psychotherapy: Theory, Research, and Practice, 23,* 243–248.

Brown, L. S. (1994). *Subversive dialogues: Theory in feminist therapy.* New York: Basic Books.

Brown, L. S., & Ballou, M. (Eds.). (1992). *Personality and psychopathology: Feminist reappraisals.* New York: Guilford Press.

Brown, T., O'Leary, T., & Barlow, D. H. (1994). Generalized anxiety disorder. In D. H. Barlow (Ed.), (pp. 137–188). *Clinical handbook of psychological disorders.* New York: Guilford.

Bruner, J. (1986). *Actual minds, possible worlds.* Cambridge, MA: Harvard University Press.

Bruner, J. (1990). *Acts of meaning.* Cambridge, MA: Harvard University Press.

Buber, M. (1970). *I and thou.* New York: Scribner.

Buchheimer, A. (1959). From group to "gemeinschaft." In K. A. Adler & D. Deutsch (Eds.), *Essays in individual psychology* (pp. 242–247). New York: Grove Press.

Bugental, J. (1978). *Psychotherapy and process: The fundamentals of an existential humanistic approach.* Reading, MA: Addison-Wesley.

Bugental, J. (1996). 1943–1996: Highly personal reflections. *American Journal of Psychotherapy, 50,* 133–135.

Burns, D. D. (1999). *Feeling good: The new mood therapy* (Rev ed.). New York: Avon Press. (See also Web site at *http://www.feelinggood.com*.)

Burns, D. D., & Auerbach, A. (1996). Therapeutic empathy in cognitive-behavioral therapy. In P. M. Salkovskis (Ed.), *Frontiers of cognitive therapy* (pp. 135–164). New York: Guilford.

Cade, B., & O'Hanlon, W. H. (1993). *A brief guide to brief therapy*. New York: Norton.

Cadwallader, E. (1984). Values in Fritz Perls's Gestalt therapy: On the dangers of half-truths. *Counseling and Values, 4,* 192–201.

Cain, D. J. (1986). Editorial: A call for the "write stuff." *Person Centered Review, 1*(2), 117–124.

Cain, D. J. (1987). Carl R. Rogers: The man, his vision, his impact. *Person Centered Review, 2*(3), 283–288.

Caldwell, C. (1997). *Getting in touch: The guide to new body-centered therapies*. Wheaton, IL: Theosophical Publishing House.

Campbell, J. M. (2000). *Becoming an effective supervisor: A workbook for counselors and psychotherapists*. Philadelphia, PA: Accelerated Development.

Cannon, B. (1991). *Sartre and psychoanalysis: An existentialist challenge to clinical metatheory*. Lawrence, KS: University Press of Kansas.

Capra, F. (1982). *The turning point: Science, society and the rising culture*. New York: Simon & Schuster, Inc.

Capuzzi, D., & Gross, D. (Eds.). (1998). *Introduction to group counseling* (2nd ed.). Denver: Love.

Carkhuff, R. (1969). *Helping and human relations: A primer for lay and professional helpers* (Vols. 1–2). New York: Holt, Rinehart, & Winston.

Carkhuff, R. R., & Berenson, B. G. (1977). *Beyond counseling and therapy* (2nd ed.). New York: Holt, Rinehart, & Winston.

Carkuff, R. R., & Berenson, B. G. (1967). *Beyond counseling and psychotherapy*. New York: Holt, Rinehart, & Winston.

Carlock, C. J., Glaus, K., & Shaw, C. A. (1992). The alcoholic: A Gestalt view. In E. C. Nevis (Ed.), *Gestalt therapy: Perspectives and applications* (pp. 191–237). New York: Gardner Press.

Carter, B., & McGoldrick, M. (1999). Overview: The expanded family life cycle: Individual, family and social perspectives. In B. Carter & M. McGoldrick (Eds.), *The expanded family life cycle* (pp. 1–26). New York: Gardner Press.

Casas, M. (1988). Cognitive behavioral approaches: A minority perspective. *Counseling Psychologist, 16,* 106–110.

Celano, M. P., & Kaslow, N. J. (2000). Culturally competent family interventions: Review and case illustrations. *The American Journal of Family Therapy, 28,* 217–228.

Chambless, D., Sanderson, W. C., Shoham, V., Bennett-Johnson, S., Pope, K. S., Crits-Cristoph, P., Baker, M., Johnson, B., Woody, S. R., Sue, S., Beutler, L., Williams, D. A., & McCurry, S. (1996). An update on empirically validated therapies. *Clinical Psychologist, 49,* 5–18.

Chance, E., Bibens, R., Cowley, J., Prouretedal, M., Dolese, P., & Virtue, D. (1990). Lifeline: A drug/alcohol treatment program for negatively addicted inmates. *Journal of Reality Therapy, 9,* 33–38.

Chandler, R., Worell, J., Johnson, D., Blount, A., & Lusk, M. (1999). *Measuring long-term outcomes of feminist counseling and psychotherapy*. Paper presented at the annual meeting of the American Psychological Association, Boston.

Chang, S. C. (1980). *Morita therapy*. In R. Herink (Ed.), *The psychotherapy handbook* (pp. 391–393). New York: Meridian.

Charny, I. (1992). *Existential/dialectical marital therapy: Breaking the secret code of marriage*. New York: Brunner/Mazel.

Chesler, P. (1972). *Women and madness*. New York: Doubleday.

Chesler, P. (1990). Twenty years since *Women and Madness:* Toward a feminist institute of mental health and healing. *Journal of Mind and Behavior, 11,* 313–322.

Chessick, R. D. (1996). Heidegger's 'authenticity' in the psychotherapy of adolescents. *American Journal of Psychotherapy, 50*(2), 208–216.

Chodorow, N. J. (1978). *The reproduction of mothering*. Berkeley, CA: University of California Press.

Chodorow, N. J. (1999). *The power of feelings: Personal meaning in psychoanalysis, gender, and culture*. New Haven, CT: Yale University Press.

Christopher, J. C. (1996). Counseling's inescapable moral visions. *Journal of Counseling and Development, 75,* 17–25.

Chung, R. C. Y., Bemak, F., & Okazaki, S. (1997). Counseling Americans of southeast Asian descent. In C. C. Lee (Ed.), *Multicultural issues in counseling* (2nd ed., pp. 207–231). American Counseling Association, Alexandria, Virginia.

Ciorni, S. (1994). The importance of background in Gestalt therapy. *Gestalt Journal, 18*(2), 7–34.

Clarkson, P., & Mackeron, J. (1993). *Fritz Perls*. Newbury Park, CA: Sage.

Clemmens, M. C. (2000). Response to Leanne O'Shea's article "Sexuality: Old struggles and new challenges." *Gestalt Review, 4*(1), 35–37.

Clinchy, B. M. (1996). Connected and separate knowing: Toward a marriage of two minds. In N. C. Goldberger, J. M. Tarule, B. M. Clinchy, & M. F. Belenky (Eds.), *Knowledge, difference, and power: Essays inspired by women's way of knowing*. New York: Basic Books.

Clum, G. A. (1990). *Coping with panic: A drug-free approach to dealing with anxiety attacks*. Pacific Grove, CA: Brooks/Cole.

Coady, N. F. (1992). Rationale and directions for the increased emphasis on the therapeutic relationship in family therapy. *Contemporary Family Therapy, 14*, 467–479.

Comas Diaz, L., & Greene, B. (1994). *Women of color: Integrating ethnic and gender identities in psychotherapy*. New York: Guilford.

Combrinck-Graham, L. (1985). A developmental model for family systems. *Family Process, 24*, 139–150.

Combrinck-Graham, L. (1988). Adolescent sexuality in the family life spiral. In C. J. Falicov (Ed.), *Family transitions* (pp. 107–131). New York: Guilford.

Combs, A., & Snygg, D. (1959). *Individual behavior*. (Rev. ed.). New York: Harper.

Combs, A., Soper, D., Gooding, C., Benton, J., Dickman, J., & Usher, R. (1969). *Florida studies in the helping professions*. University of Florida Monographs Social Sciences No. 37. Gainesville: University Press of Florida.

Combs, A. W. (1986). What makes a good helper? A person-centered approach. *Person Centered Review, 1*, 51–61.

Combs, A. W. (1988). Some current issues for person centered therapy. *Person Centered Review, 3*(3), 263–276.

Combs, A. W., & Avila, D. (1985). *Helping relationships: Basic concepts for the helping professions*. Boston: Allyn & Bacon.

Combs, A. W., & Gonzalez, D. M. (1994). *Helping relationships: Basic concepts for the helping profession* (4th ed.). Needham Heights, MA: Allyn & Bacon.

Cooper, D. (1970). *The death of the family*. New York: Pantheon.

Cooper, J. F. (1995). *A primer of brief psychotherapy*. New York: Norton.

Corey, G. (2001). *Theory and practice of counseling and psychotherapy* (6th ed.). Belmont, CA: Wadsworth Publishing.

Corey, M. S., & Corey, G. (1993). *Becoming a helper* (2nd ed.). Pacific Grove, CA: Brooks/Cole.

Cormier, W. H., & Cormier, L. S. (1991). *Interviewing strategies for helpers: A guide to assessment, treatment, and evaluation* (3rd ed.). Pacific Grove, CA: Brooks/Cole.

Cormier, W., & Cormier, L. (1998). *Interviewing strategies for helpers*. Pacific Grove, CA: Brooks/Cole.

Corsini, R. J. (2001). *Handbook of innovative therapy* (2nd ed.). New York: John Wiley & Sons.

Corwin, N. (1987). Social agency practice based on reality therapy/control theory. *Journal of Reality Therapy, 7*, 26–35.

Coster, J. S., & Schwebel, M. (1997). Well-functioning in professional psychologists. *Professional psychology: Research and Practice, 28*, 5–13.

Coward, D. (2000). Making meaning within the experience of life-threatening illness. In G. T. Reker & K. Chamberlain (Eds.), *Exploring existential meaning: Optimizing human development across the life span* (pp. 157–170). Thousand Oaks, CA: Sage Publications.

Craig, P. E. (1995). Being contrary, being human: The pregnant, paradoxical openness of resistance. *Humanistic Psychologist, 23*(1), 161–186.

Craighead, W. E., Craighead, L. W., & Ilardi, S. S. (1995). Behavior therapies in historical perspective. In B. Bongar & L. E. Beutler (Eds.), *Comprehensive textbook of psychotherapy: Theory and practice* (pp. 64–83). New York: Oxford University Press.

Cross, W., Parham, T., & Helms, I. E. (1995). Negrescence revisited: Theory and research. In R. L. Jones (Ed.), *Advances in black psychology* (pp. 1–69). Los Angeles: Cobb & Henry.

Csikszentmihalyi, M. (1992). *Validity and reliability of the experience sampling method*. Cambridge, MA: Cambridge University Press.

Cummings, A. (In press). Assessing the process and outcome of short-term feminist therapy. *Counselor Education and Supervision*.

D'Zurilla, T. J., & Nezu, A. M. (2001). Problem-solving therapies. In K. S. Dobson (Ed.), *Handbook of cognitive-behavioral therapies* (2nd ed., pp. 211–245). New York: Guilford.

Dass, R. (2000). *Still here: Embracing aging, changing, and dying*. New York: Riverhead Books.

Dass, R., & Bush, M. (1992). *Compassion in action: Setting out on the path of service*. New York: Bell Tower.

Dass, R., & Gorman, P. (1985). *How can I help?* New York: Knopf.

Davis, P. A., & Gold, E. B. (1998). The use of contemporary/alternative medicine for the treatment of asthma in the United States. *Journal of Investigative Allergological Clinical Immunology, 8,* 73–77.

Davis, T. E., & Osborn, (2000). *The solution-focused school counselor: Shaping professional practice*. Philadelphia, PA: Taylor & Francis.

Dawson, R. W. (1991). REGIME: A counseling and educational model for using RET effectively. In M. E. Bernard (Ed.), *Using rational-emotive therapy effectively: A practitioner's guide* (pp. 112–132). New York: Plenum Press.

De Jong, P., & Berg, I. K. (1998). *Interviewing for solutions*. Pacific Grove, CA: Brooks/Cole.

De Jong, P., & Berg, I. K. (2002). *Interviewing for solutions* (2nd ed.). Pacific Grove, CA: Brooks/Cole.

de Shazer, S. (1985). *Keys to solution in brief therapy*. New York: Norton.

de Shazer, S. (1988). *Clues: Investigating solutions in brief therapy*. New York: Norton.

de Shazer, S. (1990). What is it about brief therapy that works? In J. K. Zeig & S. G. Gilligan (Eds.), *Brief therapy: Myths, methods, and metaphors* (pp. 90–99). New York: Brunner/Mazel.

de Shazer, S. (1991). *Putting difference to work*. New York: Norton.

de Shazer, S. (1994). *Words were originally magic*. New York: Norton.

De Vos, G. (1980). Afterward. In D. K. Reynolds, *The quiet therapies: Japanese pathways to personal growth*. Honolulu: University Press of Hawaii.

DeLucia, J. L., & Kalodner, C. R. (1990). An individualized cognitive intervention: Does it increase the efficacy of behavioral interventions for obesity? *Addictive Behaviors, 15,* 473–479.

DeRubeis, R. J., Gelfand, L. A., Tang, T. Z., & Simmons, A. (1999). Medications versus cognitive behavioral therapy for severely depressed outpatients: Mega-analysis of four randomized comparisons. *American Journal of Psychiatry, 156,* 1007–1013.

DeRubeis, R. J., Tang, T. Z., & Beck, A. T. (2001). Cognitive therapy. In K. S. Dobson (Ed.), *Handbook of cognitive-behavioral therapies* (2nd ed., pp. 349–392). New York: Guilford.

Deurzen-Smith, E. (1991). Ontological insecurity revisited. *Journal of the Society for Existential Analysis, 3,* 15–23.

Diagnostic and statistics manual of mental disorders-IV-TR (4th ed.). (2002). American Psychiatric Association. Washington, DC.

DiGiuseppe, R. (1991). A rational-emotive model of assessment. In M. E. Bernard (Ed.), *Using rational-emotive therapy effectively: A practitioner's guide* (pp. 151–169). New York: Plenum Press.

DiGiuseppe, R. (1999). Rational emotive behavior therapy. In H. T. Prout & D. T. Brown (Eds.), *Counseling and psychotherapy with children and adolescents: Theory and practice for school settings* (pp. 252–293). New York: John Wiley & Sons.

Dillard, M. (1985). *Multicultural counseling: Ethnic and cultural relevance in human encounters*. Chicago: Nelson Hall.

DiMattia, D., & Lega, L. (Eds.). (1990). *Will the real Albert Ellis please stand up?* New York: Institute for Rational-Emotive Therapy.

Dinkmeyer, D. C., Pew, W. L., & Dinkmeyer, D. C., Jr. (1979). *Adlerian counseling and psychotherapy*. Monterey, CA: Brooks/Cole.

Dobson, K. S. (2001). *Handbook of cognitive-behavioral therapies* (2nd ed.). New York: Guilford.

Dobson, K. S., & Dozois, D. J. A. (2001). Historical and philosophical bases of the cognitive-behavioral therapies. In K. S. Dobson (Ed.), *Handbook of cognitive-behavioral therapies* (2nd ed., pp. 3–39). New York: Guilford.

Dobson, K. S., & Shaw, B. F. (1988). The use of treatment manuals in cognitive therapy: Experience and issues. *Journal of Consulting and Clinical Psychology, 56,* 673–680.

Doherty, W. J., & Simmons, D. S. (1996). Clinical practice patterns of marriage and family therapists: A national survey of therapists and their clients. *Journal of Marital and Family Therapy, 22,* 9–25.

Dowd, E., & Milne, C. (1986). Paradoxical interventions in counseling psychology. *Counseling Psychologist, 14*(2), 237–282.

Dreikurs, R. (1950). *Fundamentals of Adlerian Psychology*. New York: Greenberg.

Dreikurs, R. (1956). Adlerian psychotherapy. In F. Fromm-Reichmann & J. L. Moreno (Eds.), *Progress in psychotherapy* (pp. 111–118). New York: Grune & Stratton.

Dreikurs, R. (1961). The Adlerian approach to psychodynamics. In M. Stein (Ed.), *Contemporary psychotherapies* (pp. 60–93). New York: Free Press of Glencoe.

Dreikurs, R. (1967a). Psychotherapy as correction of faulty social values. In R. Dreikurs, *Psychodynamics, Psychotherapy and Counseling,* pp. 113–123. Chicago: Alfred Adler Institute of Chicago.

Dreikurs, R. (1967b). The function of emotions. In R. Dreikurs, *Psychodynamics, psychotherapy, and counseling: Collected papers of Rudolf Dreikurs, M.D.* (pp. 205–217). Chicago: Alfred Adler Institute of Chicago.

Dreikurs, R. (1967c). Adlerian psychotherapy. In R. Dreikurs, *Psychodynamics, psychotherapy, and counseling: Collected papers of Rudolf Dreikurs, M.D.* (pp. 63–72). Chicago: Alfred Adler Institute of Chicago.

Dryden, W. (Ed.). (1984a). *Individual therapies: A comparative analysis in individual therapy in Britain.* London: Open University Press.

Dryden, W. (1984b). *Rational-emotive therapy: Fundamentals and innovations.* Beckenham, Kent, England: Croom Helm.

Dryden, W. (1991). Flexibility in RET: Forming alliances and making compromises. In M. E. Bernard (Ed.), *Using rational-emotive therapy effectively: A practitioner's guide* (pp. 133–148). New York: Plenum Press.

Dryden, W. (1996). Rational emotive behaviour therapy. In W. Dryden (Ed.), *Handbook of individual therapy* (pp. 306–338). London: Sage.

Dryden, W. (1999). *Rational emotive behavioural counseling in action* (2nd ed.). London: Sage.

Dryden, W., & DiGiuseppe, R. (1990). *A rational emotive therapy primer.* Champaign, IL: Research Press.

Dryden, W., & Ellis, A. E. (2001). Rational emotive behavior therapy. In K. S. Dobson (Ed.), *Handbook of cognitive behavioral therapies* (pp. 295–348). New York: Guilford.

Duncan, B. L., & Moynihan, D. W. (1994). Applying outcome research: International utilization of the client's frame of reference. *Psychotherapy, 31*(2), 294–301.

Dupree, P. I., & Day, H. D. (1995). Psychotherapists' job satisfaction and job burnout as a function of work setting and percentage of managed care clients. *Psychotherapy in Private Practice, 14,* 77–93.

Durrant, M. (1995). *Creative strategies for school problems: Solutions for psychologists and teachers.* New York: Norton.

Durrant, M., & Kowalski, K. (1993). Enhancing views of competence. In S. Friedman (Ed.), *The new language of change: Constructive collaboration in psychotherapy* (pp. 107–137). New York: Guilford.

Dutton-Douglas, M. A., & Walker, L. E. (Eds.). (1988). *Feminist psychotherapies: Integration of therapeutic and feminist systems.* Norwood, NJ: Ablex.

Dye, A., & Hackney, H. (1975). *Gestalt approaches to counseling.* Boston: Houghton Mifflin.

Dykeman, C. (2001). Counseling couples and families. In D. Capuzzi & D. R. Gross (Eds.), *Introduction to the counseling profession* (pp. 357–385). Boston: Allyn & Bacon.

Dykeman, C., & Noble, F. C. (1997). Counseling couples and families. In D. Capuzzi & D. R. Gross (Eds.), *Introduction to the counseling profession* (pp. 357–385). Boston: Allyn & Bacon.

Eckstein, D., Baruth, L., & Mahrer, D. (1982). *Life style: What it is and how to do it.* Dubuque, IA: Kendall/Hunt.

Edmunds, P., Martinson, S. A., & Goldberg, P. F. (1990). *Demographics and cultural diversity in the 1990s: Implications for services to young children with special needs.* Washington, DC: Office of Special Education Programs, U.S. Department of Education.

Egan, G. (1975). *The skilled helper.* Monterey, CA: Brooks/Cole.

Egan, G. (1994). *The skilled helper* (5th ed.). Pacific Grove, CA: Brooks/Cole.

Egan, G. (1998). *The skilled helper* (6th ed.) *A problem-management approach to helping.* Pacific Grove, CA: Brooks/Cole.

Eisman, J. (1987). Character typologies. In R. Kurtz (Ed.), *Hakomi therapy* (pp. 19/1–19/14). (Available from the Hakomi Institute, PO Box 1873, Boulder, CO 80306.)

Eisman, J. (1995). *The re-creation of the self.* Manuscript submitted for publication.

Eisman, J. (2000–2001). *The Hakomi method and re-creation of the self: Professional training.* (Available from the Hakomi Institute of Oregon, 6836 HWY 66, Ashland, OR 97520.)

Ellenberger, H. F. (1970). *The discovery of the unconscious: The history and evolution of dynamic psychiatry.* New York: Basic Books.

Elliott, J. M. (1999). Feminist theory. In D. Capuzzi & D. R. Gross (Eds.), *Counseling and psychotherapy: Theories and interventions* (pp. 203–229). Upper Saddle River, NJ: Merrill Prentice Hall.

Elliott, R., Clark, C., Wexler, M., Kemeny, V., Brinker-hoff, J., & Mack, C. (1990). The impact of experiential therapy of depression: Initial results. In G. Lietaer, J. Rombauts, & R. Van Balen (Eds.), *Client-centered and experiential psychotherapy in the nineties* (pp. 549–577). Leuven, Belgium: Leuven University Press.

Ellis, A. E. (1957). *How to live with a neurotic: At home and at work.* New York: Crown.

Ellis, A. E. (1962). *Reason and emotion in psychotherapy.* Secaucus, NJ: Citadel.

Ellis, A. E. (1987). A sadly neglected cognitive element in depression. *Cognitive Therapy and Research, 11,* 121–146.

Ellis, A. E. (1994). *Reason and emotion in psychotherapy: A comprehensive method of treating human disturbances* (Rev. ed.). New York: Carol Publishing Company.

Ellis, A. E. (1996). *Better, deeper, and more enduring brief therapy: The rational emotive behavior therapy approach.* New York: Brunner/Mazel.

Ellis, A. E. (1997a). The evolution of Albert Ellis and rational emotive behavior therapy. In J. K. Zeig (Ed.), *The evolution of psychotherapy: The third conference* (pp. 69–82). New York: Brunner/Mazel.

Ellis, A. E. (1997b). REBT with obsessive-compulsive disorder. In J. Yankura & W. Dryden (Eds.), *Using REBT with common psychological problems: A therapist's casebook* (pp. 197–222). New York: Springer Publishing Company.

Ellis, A. E. (1998). How rational emotive behavior therapy belongs in the constructivist camp. In M. F. Hoyt (Ed.), *The handbook of constructive therapies: Innovative approaches from leading practitioners* (pp. 83–99). San Francisco, CA: Jossey-Bass Publishers.

Ellis, A. E. (2001a). *Feeling better, getting better, staying better.* Atascadero, CA: Impact Publishers.

Ellis, A. E. (2001b). Reasons why rational emotive behavior therapy is relatively neglected in the professional and scientific literature. *Journal of Rational-Emotive & Cognitive-Behavior Therapy, 19* (1), 67–74.

Ellis, A. E., & Dryden, W. (1987). *The practice of rational emotive therapy.* New York: Springer Publishing Company.

Ellis, A. E., & Dryden, W. (1997). *The practice of rational emotive behavior therapy* (2nd ed.). New York: Springer Publishing Company.

Ellis, A. E., & Harper, R. A. (1997). *A guide to rational living* (3rd ed.). North Hollywood, CA: Melvin Powers.

Ellis, A. E., & MacClaren, C. (1998). *Rational emotive behavior therapy: A therapist's guide.* Atascadero, CA: Impact Publishers.

Ellis, A. E., & Velten, E. (1992). *When AA doesn't work: Rational steps for quitting alcohol.* New York: Barricade Books.

Emanuel, E. J., & Emanuel, L. L. (1998). The promise of a good death. *The Lancet, 351,* 21–29.

Emerson, P., & Smith, E. (1974). Contributions of Gestalt psychology to Gestalt therapy. *Counseling Psychologist, 4,* 8–13.

Emmelkamp, P. M. (1994). Behavior therapy with adults. In S. L. Garfield & A. E. Bergin (Eds.), *Handbook of psychotherapy and behavior change* (4th ed., pp. 379–427). New York: Wiley.

Enns, C. (1987). Gestalt therapy and feminist therapy: A proposed integration. *Journal of Counseling and Development, 66,* 93–95.

Enns, C. Z. (1992). Self-esteem groups: A synthesis of consciousness-raising and assertiveness training. *Journal of Counseling and Development, 71,* 7–13.

Enns, C. Z. (1993). Twenty years of feminist counseling and therapy: From naming biases to implementing multifaceted practice. *The Counseling Psychologist, 21,* 3–87.

Enns, C. Z. (1997). *Feminist theories and feminist psychotherapies: Origins, themes, and variations.* New York: Haworth.

Enright, J. (1970). An introduction to Gestalt techniques. In J. Fagan & I. Shepherd (Eds.), *Gestalt therapy now: Theory, techniques, and applications.* Palo Alto: Science & Behavior Books.

Epp, L. R. (1998). The courage to be an existential counselor: An interview with Clemmont E. Vontress. *Journal of Mental Health Counseling, 20,* 1–13.

Epstein, M. (1995). *Thoughts without a thinker: Psychology from a Buddhist perspective.* New York: Basic Books.

Epstein, M. (2001). *Going on being: Buddhism and the way of change—A positive psychology for the West.* New York: Broadway Books.

Epston, D., & White, M. (1995). Termination as a rite of passage: Questioning strategies for a therapy of inclusion. In R. A. Neimeyer & M. J. Mahoney (Eds.), *Constructivism in psychotherapy* (pp. 339–354). Washington, DC: American Psychological Association.

Erickson, M. H., & Rossi, E. S. (1976). *Hypnotic realities*. New York: Irvington Publishers. Inc.

Erikson, E. (1963). *Childhood and society*. New York: Norton.

Erikson, E. H. (1968). *Identity: Youth and crisis*. New York: Norton.

Espin, O. M., & Gawelek, M. A. (1992). Women's diversity: Ethnicity, race, class, and gender in theories of feminist psychology. In L. S. Brown & M. Ballou (Eds.), *Personality and psychopathology: Feminist reappraisals* (pp. 88–107). New York: Guilford.

Essandoh, P. (1996). Multicultural counseling as the fourth force: A call to arms. *Counseling Psychologist, 24*, 126–137.

Evans, K. G. (1996). Chaos as opportunity: Grounding a positive vision of management and society in the new physics. *Public Administration Review, 56*(5), 491–494.

Evans, K. M. (1997). Wellness and coping activities of African American counselors. *Journal of Black Psychology, 23*(1), 24–35.

Evans, T. D. (1995). The encouraging teacher. In G. M. Gazda, F. S. Asbury, F. M. Blazer, W. C. Childers, & R. P. Walters (Eds.), *Human relations development* (5th ed., pp. 261–270). Boston: Allyn & Bacon.

Evans, T. D. (1996). Encouragement: The key to reforming classrooms. *Educational Leadership, 54*, 81–85.

Evans, T. D. (1997a). The tools of encouragement. *Reaching Today's Youth: National Educational Service, 1*(2), 10–14.

Evans, T. D. (1997b, February). Establishing goals in counseling. Paper presented at UT Permian Basin Spring Counseling Workshop, Odessa, TX.

Evans, T. D., & Milliren, A. P. (1999). Open-forum family counseling. In R. E. Watts & J. Carlson (Eds.), *Interventions and strategies in counseling and psychotherapy* (pp. 135–160). Levittown, PA: Accelerated Development.

Fairbairn, W. R. D. (1941). A revised psychopathology of the psychoses and psychoneuroses. *International Journal of Psychoanalysis, 22*, 250–279.

Fairburn, C. G., Marcus, M. D., & Wilson, G. T. (1993). Cognitive behaviroal therapy for binge eating and bulimia nervosa. In C. G. Fairburn & G. T. Wilson (Eds.), *Binge eating: Nature, assessment, and treatment* (pp. 361–404). New York: Plenum Press.

Farber, B. A., Brink, D. C., & Raskin, P. M. (Eds.). (1996). *The psychotherapy of Carl Rogers: Cases and commentary*. New York: Guilford.

Fay, A. (1978). *Making things better by making them worse*. New York: Hawthorne.

Feldenkrais, M. (1972). *Awareness through movement: Health exercises for personal growth*. New York: Harper & Row Publishers.

Fenichel, O. (1945). *The psychoanalytic theory of neurosis*. New York: Norton.

Ferguson, E. D. (1984). *Adlerian theory: An introduction*. Chicago: Adler School of Professional Psychology.

Ferguson, E. D. (1989). Adler's motivational theory: An historical perspective on belonging and the fundamental human striving. *Individual Psychology, 45*, 354–362.

Ferguson, E. D. (2000a). Individual Psychology is ahead of its time. *Journal of Individual Psychology, 56*, 14–20.

Ferguson, E. D. (2000b). *Motivation: A biosocial and cognitive integration of motivation and emotion*. New York: Oxford University Press.

Ferguson, E. D. (2001). Adler and Dreikurs: Cognitive-social dynamic innovators. *Journal of Individual Psychology, 57*, 324–341.

Finch, E. S., & Krantz, S. R. (1991). Low burnout in a high-stress setting: A study of staff adaption at Fountain House. *Psychological Rehabilitation Journal, 14*, 15–26.

Fine, M., Weis, L., Powell, L. C., & Wong, L. M. (1997). *Off-white: Readings on race, power, and society*. New York: Routledge.

Fine, R. (1979). *A history of psychoanalysis*. New York: Columbia.

Fisch, R. (1990). Problem-solving psychotherapy. In J. K. Zeig & W. M. Munion (Eds.), *What is psychotherapy? Contemporary perspectives* (pp. 269–273). San Francisco: Jossey-Bass.

Fisch, R., Weakland, J. H., & Segal, L. (1982). *Tactics of change: Doing therapy briefly*. San Francisco: Jossey-Bass.

Fisher, S., & Greenberg, R. (1977). *The scientific credibility of Freud's theories and therapy*. New York: Basic Books.

Fitzgerald, L. F., & Nutt, R. (1986). The division 17 principles concerning the counseling/psychotherapy of women: Rationale and implementation. *The Counseling Psychologist, 14*, 180–216.

Foa, E. B., & Wilson, R. (1991). *Stop obsessing: How to overcome your obsessions and compulsions*. New York: Bantam.

Folligstad, D. R., Robinson, E. A., & Pugh, M. (1977). Effects of consciousness-raising groups on measures of feminism, self-esteem, and social desirability. *Journal of Counseling Psychology, 24,* 223–230.

Ford, D. H., & Urban, H. B. (1998). *Contemporary models of psychotherapy: A comparative analysis.* New York: John Wiley and Sons.

Ford, D. Y. (1997). Counseling middle-class African Americans. In C. C. Lee (Ed.), *Multicultural issues in counseling* (2nd ed., pp. 81–108). Alexandria, VA: American Counseling Association.

Ford, E. (1979). *Permanent love.* Minneapolis: Winston.

Foucault, M. (1980). *Knowledge/power: Selected interviews and other writings.* New York: Pantheon.

Frankl, V. (1975). *The unconscious god.* New York: Simon & Schuster.

Frankl, V. (1984). *Man's search for meaning.* New York: Washington Square Press.

Freeman, J. (1989). Feminist organization and activities from suffrage to women's liberation. In J. Freeman (Ed.), *Women: A feminist perspective* (4th ed., pp. 541–555). Palo Alto, CA: Mayfield.

Freeman, S. (1993). Client-centered therapy with diverse populations: The universal within the specific. *Journal of Multicultural Counseling and Development, 21,* 248–254.

Freestone, M. H., Ladouceur, R., Thibodeaux, N., & Gagnon, F. (1991). Cognitive intrusions in a nonclinical population. I. Response style, subjective experience, and appraisal. *Behavioral Research & Therapy, 29,* 589–597.

Freud, A. (1966). *The ego and the mechanisms of defense.* New York: International Universities Press.

Freud, S. (1930). *Civilization and its discontents* (J. Strachey, Trans. & Ed.). New York: Norton.

Freud, S. (1940). *An outline of psychoanalysis* (Vol. 23). Standard Edition (J. Strachey, Trans.). London: Hogarth Press. (Original work published 1938).

Freud, S. (1955). *The interpretation of dreams.* New York: Basic Books.

Freudenberger, H. (1983). Hazards of psychotherapeutic practice. *Psychotherapy in Private Practice, 1*(1), 83–89.

Frew, J. (1984). Enlarging what is not figured in the Gestalt group. *Journal for Specialists in Group Work, 8,* 175–181.

Friedan, B. (1963). *The feminine mystique.* New York: Dell.

Friedlander, M. L., Wildman, J., Heatherington, L., & Skowron, E. A. (1994). What we do and don't know about the process of family therapy. *Journal of Family Therapy, 8,* 390–416.

Fromm, E. (1955). *The sane society.* New York: Rinehart.

Fujita, C. (1986). *Morita therapy: A psychotherapeutic system for neurosis.* Tokyo: Igaku-shoin.

Fulton, P. (2001, July). *Psychotherapy and meditation: Cultivating connection to others, ourselves, and our lives.* Paper presented at the New England Educational Summer Institute, Cape Cod, MA.

Funder, D. C. (1997). *The personality puzzle.* New York: Norton.

Furnham, A., Pereira, E., & Rawles, R. (2001). Lay theories of psychotherapy: Perceptions of the efficacy of different 'cures' for specific disorders. *Psychology, Health and Medicine, 6,* 77–85.

Furtmueller, C. (1946). Part VI: Alfred Adler: A biographical essay. In A. Adler (1979). *Superiority & social interest.* New York: W. W. Norton, pp. 311–394.

Gang, M. (1975). Empirical validation of a reality therapy intervention program in an elementary school classroom. *Dissertation Abstracts International, 35*(8B), 4216.

Gannon, L. (1982). The role of power in psychotherapy. *Women and Therapy, 1,* 3–11.

Garfield, S. L. (1980). *Psychotherapy: An eclectic approach.* New York: John Wiley & Sons.

Garfield, S. L. (1990). Issues and methods in psychotherapy process research. *Journal of Consulting and Clinical Psychology, 58,* 273–280.

Garfield, S. L. (1994). Research on client variables. In A. E. Bergin & S. L. Garfield (Eds.), *Handbook of psychotherapy and behavior change* (4th ed., pp. 190–228). New York: John Wiley & Sons.

Garrett, M. T., & Herring, R. D. (2001). Honoring the power of relation: Counseling Native American adults. *Humanistic Counseling, Education, and Development, 40,* 139–170.

Gay, P. (1988). *Freud: A life for our time.* New York: Norton.

Gazda, G. (1986). *Human relations development: A manual for educators.* Boston: Allyn & Bacon.

George, E., Iveson, C., & Ratner, H. (1999). *Problem to solution: Brief therapy with individuals and families* (2nd ed.). London: Brief Therapy Press.

George, R. L., & Cristiani, T. S. (1990). *Counseling theory and practice* (3rd ed.). Upper Saddle River, NJ: Prentice Hall.

Gerardi, S. (1990). Academic self-concept as a predictor of academic success among minority and low-socioeconomic status students. *Journal of College Student Development, 31,* 401–407.

Gergen, K. J. (1990). Therapeutic professions and the diffusion of deficit. *Journal of Mind and Behavior, 11,* 353–368.

German, M. (1975). The effects of group reality therapy on institutionalized adolescents and group leaders. *Dissertation Abstracts International, 36,* 1916.

Gill, M. (1996). Discussion: Interaction III. *Psychoanalytic Inquiry, 16*(1), 118–135.

Gilligan, C. (1982). *In a different voice.* Cambridge, MA: Harvard University Press.

Gilliland, B. E., James, R. K., & Bowman, J. T. (1989). *Theories and strategies in counseling and psychotherapy* (2nd ed.). Upper Saddle River, NJ: Prentice Hall.

Gilliland, B., James, R., & Bowman, J. (1994). *Theories and strategies in counseling and psychotherapy.* Upper Saddle River, NJ: Prentice Hall.

Gingerich, W. J., & Eisengart, S. (2000). Solution-focused brief therapy: A review of the outcome research. *Family Process, 39,* 477–498.

Giovacchini, P. (1987). *A narrative textbook of psychoanalysis.* London: Aronson.

Gladding, S. (1995). *Groups: A counseling specialty* (2nd ed.). Upper Saddle River, NJ: Merrill/Prentice Hall.

Gladding, S. (2000). *Counseling: A comprehensive profession* (4th ed.). Englewood. Cliffs, NJ: Prentice-Hall.

Gladding, S. (2001). *Becoming a counselor: The light, the bright, and the serious.* Alexandria, VA: American Counseling Association.

Gladding, S. T. (2001). *Family therapy: History, theory, and practice* (3rd ed.). Upper Saddle River, NJ: Merrill Prentice Hall.

Glasser, C. (1990). *My quality world workbook.* Los Angeles: The William Glasser Institute.

Glasser, N. (Ed.). (1980). *What are you doing?* New York: Harper & Row.

Glasser, N. (Ed.). (1989). *Control theory in the practice of reality therapy.* New York: Harper & Row.

Glasser, W. (1965). *Reality therapy.* New York: Harper & Row.

Glasser, W. (1968). *Schools without failure.* New York: Harper & Row.

Glasser, W. (1972). *The identity society.* New York: Harper & Row.

Glasser, W. (1976). *Positive addiction.* New York: Harper & Row.

Glasser, W. (1980a). Reality therapy. In N. Glasser (Ed.), *What are you doing?* (pp. 48–60). New York: Harper & Row.

Glasser, W. (1980b). *Stations of the mind.* New York: Harper & Row.

Glasser, W. (1984). *Control theory.* New York: Harper & Row.

Glasser, W. (1986). *A diagram of the brain as a control system.* Los Angeles: Institute for Reality Therapy.

Glasser, W. (1996). *Programs, policies, and procedures of the William Glasser Institute.* Los Angeles: The William Glasser Institute.

Glasser, W. (1998). *Choice theory: A new psychology of personal freedom.* New York: Harper Collins.

Glasser, W. (1999). *Choice Theory.* New York: Harper Collins.

Glasser, W. (2001). *Fibromyalgia: Hope from a completely new perspective.* Los Angeles: The William Glasser Institute.

Goldenberg, I., & Goldenberg, H. (2000). *Family therapy: An overview* (5th ed.). Pacific Grove, CA: Brooks/Cole.

Goldfried, M. R., Greenberg, L. S., & Maramar, C. (1990). Individual psychotherapy: Process and outcome. *Annual Review of Psychology, 41,* 659–688.

Goldstein, J., & Kornfield, J. (1987). *Seeking the heart of wisdom: The path of insight meditation.* Boston: Shambala.

Goleman, D. (1977). *The varieties of meditative experience.* New York: E. P. Dutton.

Goleman, D., & Schwartz, G. (1976). Meditation as an intervention in stress reactivity. *Journal of Consulting and Clinical Psychology, 44,* 456–467.

Goodyear, R. (1987). In memory of Carl Ransom Rogers. *Journal of Counseling and Development, 65,* 523–524.

Gorter-Cass, S. (1988). Program evaluation of an alternative school using William Glasser's reality therapy model for disruptive youth. *Dissertation Abstracts International, 49,* 1702A.

Gould, W. B. (1993). *Victor E. Frankl: Life with meaning.* Pacific Grove, CA: Brooks/Cole.

Graves, D. (1996). *The effect of rational emotive parent education on the stress of mothers of young children with Down syndrome.* Dissertation, University of Melbourne, Australia.

Green, R., & Herget, M. (1991). Outcomes of systemic/strategic team consultation: III. The importance of therapist warmth and active structuring. *Family Process, 30,* 321–335.

Greenberg, J. (1996). Psychoanalytic interaction. *Psychoanalytic Inquiry, 16*(1), 25–39.

Greenberg, J., Pyszcznski, T., Solomon, S., Rosenblatt, A., Veeder, M., Kirkland, S., & Lyon, D. (1990). Evidence for terror management theory II: The effects of mortality salience on reactions to those who threaten or bolster the cultural worldview. *Journal of Personality and Social Psychology, 58,* 308–318.

Greenberg, L. S., Elliott, R., & Lietaer, G. (1994). Research on humanistic and experiential psychotherapies. In A. Bergin & S. Garfield (Eds.), *Handbook of psychotherapy and behavior change* (4th ed., pp. 509–542). New York: John Wiley & Sons.

Greenson, R. (1967). *The technique and practice of psychoanalysis*. New York: International Universities Press.

Grieger, R. M. (1991). Keys to effective RET. In M. E. Bernard (Ed.), *Using rational-emotive therapy effectively* (pp. 36–66). New York: Plenum Press.

Grof, S. (1985). *Beyond the brain: Birth, death and transcendence in psychotherapy*. Albany, NY: SUNY Press.

Gross, A. (2000). Ram Dass: A Western guru finds peace while fighting to save his life. *Modern Maturity, 43*(4), 12–16.

Grunbaum, A. (1984). *The foundations of psychoanalysis: A philosophical critique*. Berkeley: University of California Press.

Hackney, H., & Cormier, L. S. (1994). *Counseling strategies and interventions* (4th ed.). Upper Saddle River, NJ: Prentice Hall.

Hackney, H., & Cormier, L. S. (1996). *The professional counselor: A process guide to helping* (3rd ed.). Needham Heights, MA: Allyn & Bacon.

Haley, J. (1976). Development of a theory: A history of a research project. In C. E. Sluski & D. C. Ransom (Eds.), *Double bind: The foundation of the communicational approach to the family* (pp. 59–104). New York: Grune & Stratton.

Haley, J. (1990). *Strategies of psychotherapy*. New York: Norton.

Haley, J. (1991). *Problem-solving therapy*. San Francisco: Jossey-Bass.

Haley, J. (1993). *Uncommon therapy*. New York: Norton.

Haley, M., & Carrier, J. W. (2002). Psychotherapy groups. In D. Capuzzi & D. Gross (Eds.), *Introduction to group counseling* (3rd ed., pp. 291–317). Denver: Love.

Halifax, J. (1979). *Shamanic voices: A survey of visionary narratives*. New York: E. P. Dutton.

Hall, R. H. (2001). *A shadow on the path*. [Online]. Available: *http://www.lomi.iohome.net/cgi-bin/Topic.pl?topic=20&public*.

Hall, W., Cross, W. E., & Freed, W. R. (1971). Stages in the development of black awareness: An exploratory investigation. In R. L. Jones (Ed.), *Black psychology* (pp. 156–166). New York: Harper & Row.

Hammerschlag, C. A. (1988). *The dancing healers: A doctor's journey of healing with Native Americans*. New York: Harper Collins Publishers.

Hampson, R. B., & Beavers, W. R. (1996). Measuring family therapy outcome in a clinical setting: Families that do better or do worse in therapy. *Family Therapy, 35,* 347–361.

Hanh, T. N. (1985). *A guide to walking meditation*. Berkeley, CA: Parallax.

Hanna, F. J., & Bemak, F. (1997). The quest for identity in the counseling profession. *Counselor Education and Supervision, 36,* 194–206.

Hanna, F. J., Hanna, C. A., & Keys, S. G. (1999). Fifty strategies for counseling defiant, aggressive adolescents: Reaching, accepting, and relating. *Journal of Counseling and Development, 77*(2), 395–405.

Hanna, F. J., & Ottens, A. J. (1995). The role of wisdom in psychotherapy. *Journal of Psychotherapy Integration, 5,* 195–219.

Hanna, T. (1970). *Bodies in revolt: A primer in somatic thinking*. Novato, CA: Freeperson Press.

Hanna, T. (1987). *The body of life*. New York: Alfred A. Knopf.

Hansen, J. C., Rossberg, R. H., & Cramer, S. H. (1994). *Counseling: Theory and process* (5th ed.). Needham Heights, MA: Allyn & Bacon.

Hansen, J. T. (1999). A review and critical analysis of humanistic approaches to treating disturbed clients. *Journal of Humanistic Counseling, 38,* 29–39.

Hansen, L. S., & Gama, E. M. (1996). Gender issues in multicultural counseling. In P. Pedersen, J. Draguns, W. Lonner, & J. Trimble (Eds.), *Counseling across cultures* (pp. 73–105). Thousand Oaks, CA: Sage.

Harner, M. (1980). *The way of the shaman: A guide to power and healing*. New York: Harper & Row, Publishers, Inc.

Harris, C. O. (1992). Gestalt work with psychotics. In E. C. Nevis (Ed.), *Gestalt therapy: Perspectives and applications* (pp. 239–261). New York: Gardner Press.

Hart, B. (1995). Re-authoring the stories we work by situating the narrative approach in the presence of the family of therapists. *Australian and New Zealand Journal of Family Therapy, 16,* 181–189.

Hart-Hester, S., Heuchert, C., & Whittier, K. (1989). The effects of teaching reality therapy techniques to elementary students to help change behaviors. *Journal of Reality Therapy, 8*(2), 13–18.

Hartman, A. (1995). Diagrammatic assessment of family relationships. *Families in Society, 76,* 111–123.

Hauck, P. A., & McKeegan, P. (1997). Using REBT to overcome depression. In J. Yankura & W. Dryden (Eds.), *Using REBT with common psychological problems: A therapist's casebook* (pp. 44–73). New York: Springer Publishing Company.

Hayes, S. C., & Hayes, L. J. (1992). Some clinical implications of contextual behaviorism: The examples of cognition. *Behavior Therapy, 23,* 225–249.

Hayes, S. C., Hayes, L. J., Reese, H. W., & Sarbin, T. R. (Eds.). (1993). *Varieties of scientific contextualism.* Reno: Context Press.

Hazell, C. (1984). Scale for measuring experienced levels of emptiness and existential concern. *Journal of Psychology, 117,* 177–182.

Hazell, C. (1989). Levels of emotional development with experienced levels of emptiness and existential concern. *Psychological Reports, 64*(3), 835–838.

Hazler, J. H. (1999). Person-centered theory. In D. Capuzzi & D. Gross (Eds.), *Counseling & psychotherapy: Theories and interventions* (pp. 179–201). Upper Saddle River, NJ: Prentice Hall, Inc.

Hazler, R. J. (2001). Humanistic theories of counseling. In D. Locke, J. Meyers, & E. Herr (Eds.), *The handbook of counseling* (pp. 151–158). Thousand Oaks, CA: Sage Publications.

Hazler, R. J., & Barwick, N. (2001). *The therapeutic environment: Core conditions for facilitating therapy.* Philadelphia, PA: Open University Press.

Health Realization Institute. (2001, July). *The understanding behind health realization, a principle-based psychology: Summary of clinical, prevention and community empowerment applications. Documented outcomes.* Saratoga, CA: Health Realization Institute.

Heard, W. G. (1996). The unconscious function of the I-it and I-thou realms. *Humanistic Psychologist, 23,* 239–258.

Hedstrom, L. J. (1994). Morita and Naikan therapies: American applications. *Psychotherapy, 31,* 154–160.

Heidegger, M. (1949). *Existence and being.* South Bend, IN: Regnery.

Heidegger, M. (1962). *Being and time.* New York: Harper & Row.

Hellman, I. D., & Morrison, T. L. (1987). Practice setting and type of caseload as factors in psychotherapist stress. *Psychotherapy, 24*(3), 427–432.

Helms, J. (1990). *Black and white racial identity.* Westport, CT: Greenwood.

Helms, J., & Cook, D. (1999). *Using race and culture in counseling and psychotherapy.* Needham Heights, MA: Allyn & Bacon.

Hendricks, G., & Hendricks, K. (1993). *At the speed of life: A new approach to personal change through body-centered therapy.* New York: Bantam.

Hendricks, K. (1997). The relationship dance. In C. Caldwell (Ed.), *Getting in touch: The guide to new body-centered therapies* (pp. 29–44). Wheaton, IL: Theosophical Publishing House.

Henle, M. (1978). Gestalt psychology and Gestalt therapy. *Journal of the History of Behavioral Sciences, 14,* 23–32.

Hepner, M. J., Multon, K. D., Gysbers, N. C., Ellis, C., & Zook, C. E. (1998). The relationship of trainee self-efficacy to the process and outcome of career counseling. *Journal of Counseling Psychology, 45*(4), 393–402.

Hergenhan, B., & Olson, M. (1999). *An introduction to theories of personality* (5th ed.). Upper Saddle River, NJ: Prentice Hall.

Herlihy, B., & Corey, G. (Eds.). (1996). *ACA ethical standards casebook.* Alexandria, VA: American Association for Counseling and Development.

Herlihy, B., & Corey, G. (2001). Feminist therapy. In G. Corey (Ed.), *Theory and practice of counseling and psychotherapy* (6th ed., pp. 340–381). Pacific Grove, CA: Brooks/Cole.

Herman, J. L. (1992). *Trauma and recovery: The aftermath of violence.* New York: Basic Books.

Hettler, B. (1984). Wellness: Encouraging a lifetime pursuit of excellence. *Health Values, 8*(4), 13–17.

Heuscher, J. (1987). Love and authenticity. *American Journal of Psychoanalysis, 47*(1), 21–34.

Hevern, V. W. (1999, January). *Narrative psychology: Internet and resource guide* [Online]. Syracuse, NY: Author. Available: *http://maple.lemoyne. edu/~hevern/narpsych.html.*

Hill, M., & Ballou, M. (1998). Making feminist therapy: A practice survey. *Women & Therapy, 21,* 1–16.

Hillman, J. (1989). *A blue fire: Selected writings by James Hillman.* New York: Harper & Row.

Hillman, J. (1996). *The soul's code: In search of character and calling*. New York: Random House.

Hinterkopf, E. (1998). *Integrating spirituality in counseling: A manual for using the experiential focusing method*. Alexandria, VA: American Counseling Association.

Hjelle, L. A., & Ziegler, D. J. (1992). *Personality theories*. New York: McGraw Hill.

Hoffman, E. (1994). *The drive for self: Alfred Adler and the founding of Individual Psychology*. Reading, MA: Addison Wesley.

Hoffman, I. (1991). Discussion: Toward a social constructivist view of the psychoanalytic situation. *Psychoanalytic Dialogues, 1,* 74–105.

Hogg, A., & Frank, M. L. (1992). Toward an interpersonal model of codependence and contradependence. *Journal of Counseling and Development, 70,* 371–375.

Holburn, S., & Vietze, P. (2000). Person-centered planning and cultural inertia in applied behavior analysis. *Behavior and Social Issues 10*(1), 39–70.

Hollon, S. D., & Beck, A. T. (1994). Cognitive and cognitive-behavioral therapies. In S. L. Garfield & A. E. Bergin (Eds.), *Handbook of psychotherapy and behavior change* (4th ed., pp. 428–466). New York: John Wiley & Sons.

Honeyman, A. (1990). Perceptual changes in addicts as a consequence of reality therapy based on group treatment. *Journal of Reality Therapy, 9*(2), 53–59.

Hong, G. K., & Domokos-Cheng Ham, M. D. (2001). *Psychotherapy and counseling with Asian American clients: A practical guide*. Thousand Oaks, CA: Sage Publications, Inc.

Hooks, B. (2000). *Feminist theory: From margin to center* (2nd ed.). Cambridge, MA: South End Press.

Hooper, A., & Holford, J. (1998). *Adler for beginners*. New York: Writers & Readers.

Horner, M. (1972). Toward an understanding of achievement related conflicts in women. *Journal of Social Issues, 28,* 157–175.

Horney, K. (1950). *Neurosis and human growth*. New York: Norton.

Horvath, A. O. (1994). Empirical validation of Bordin's pantheoretical model of the alliance: The Working Alliance Inventory perspective. In A. O. Horvath & L. S. Greenberg (Eds.), *The working alliance* (pp. 109–130). New York: John Wiley & Sons.

Howe, J. M. (1997). A crisis of meaning. *Choice, 35,* 1373.

Hoyt, M. F. (2001). *Interviews with brief therapy experts*. Philadelphia, PA: Taylor and Francis.

Hubble, M. A., Duncan, B. L., & Miller, S. D. (1999). *The heart and soul of change: What works in therapy*. Washington, DC: American Psychological Association.

Hubble, M. A., Duncan, B. L., & Miller, S. D. (1999). Directing attention to what works. In M. A. Hubble, B. L. Duncan, & S. D. Miller (Eds.), *The heart and soul of change: What works in therapy* (pp. 407–447). Washington, DC: American Psychological Association.

Ibrahim, F. (1985). Effective cross-cultural counseling and psychotherapy: A framework. *Counseling Psychologist, 13,* 625–637.

Ibrahim, F. A. (1985). Effective cross cultural counseling and psychotherapy: A framework. *Counseling Psychologist, 13,* 625–638.

Ibrahim, F. A. (1991). Contribution of cultural world view to generic counseling and development. *Journal of Counseling and Development, 70,* 13–19.

Imes, S. (1998). Long-term clients' experience of touch in gestalt therapy. In E. Smith, P. Clance, & S. Imes (Eds.), *Touch in psychotherapy: Theory, research, and practice* (pp. 170–200). New York: Guilford.

Ishiyama, F. I. (1990). A Japanese perspective on client inaction: Removing attitudinal blocks through Morita therapy. *Journal of Counseling and Development, 68,* 566–570.

Israeli, A. L., & Santor, D. A. (2000). Reviewing effective components of feminist therapy. *Counseling Psychology Quarterly, 13,* 233–247.

Ivey, A. (2002). *Counseling and psychotherapy: A multicultural perspective* (5th ed.). Needham Heights, MA: Allyn & Bacon.

Ivey, A. E. (1988). *Intentional interviewing and counseling: Facilitating client development*. Monterey, CA: Brooks/Cole.

Ivey, A., Ivey, M. B., & Simek Morgan, L. (1993). *Counseling and psychotherapy: A multicultural perspective*. Boston: Allyn & Bacon.

Iwai, H., & Reynolds, D. K. (1970). Morita psychotherapy: The view from the West. *American Journal of Psychiatry, 126,* 1031–1036.

Jack, D. (1987). Self-in-relation theory. In R. Formanik & A. Gurian (Eds.), *Women and depression: A lifespan perspective* (pp. 41–45). New York: Springer.

Jackson, D. D. (1957). The question of family homeostasis. *Psychiatric Quarterly Supplement, 31,* 79–90.

Jagers, R. J., & Smith, P. (1996). Further examination of the Spirituality Scale. *Journal of Black Psychology, 22*(4), 429–442.

Jahoda, M. (1958). *Current concepts of positive mental health.* New York: Basic Books.

Jarrett, R. B., Scheffer, M., McIntire, D., Witt-Browder, A., Kraft, D., & Risser, R. (1999). Treatment of atypical depression with cognitive therapy or phenelzine. *Archives of General Psychiatry, 56,* 431–437.

Johanson, G. (1987). Foreward. In R. Kurtz, *Hakomi therapy* (pp. i–vii). (Available from the Hakomi Institute, PO Box 1873, Boulder, CO 80306.)

Johanson, G., & Kurtz, R. (1991). *Grace unfolding: Psychotherapy in the spirit of the Tao-te ching.* New York: Bell Tower.

Johnson, M. (1976). An approach to feminist therapy. *Psychotherapy: Theory, Research, & Practice, 13,* 72–76.

Johnson, W. R., & Smith, E. W. L. (1997). Gestalt empty-chair dialogue versus systematic desensitization in the treatment of a phobia. *Gestalt Review, 1*(2), 150–162.

Jones, C. J., & Meridith, W. (2000). Developmental paths of psychological health from early adolescence to later adulthood. *Psychology and Aging, 15*(2), 351–360.

Jordan, J. V., & Surrey, J. L. (1986). The self-in-relation: Empathy and the mother-daughter relationship. In T. Bernay & D. W. Ballou (Eds.), *The psychology of today's woman: New psychoanalytic visions* (pp. 81–104). Hillsdale, NJ: Analytic Press.

Jung, C. G. (1953a). Two essays on analytical psychology. In *The collected works of C.G. Jung* (vol. 7). Princeton, NJ: Princeton, University Press.

Jung, C. G. (1953b). *Collected works 12: Psychology and alchemy.* New York: Pantheon.

Jung, C. G. (1954). *Collected works 16: The practice of psychotherapy.* New York: Pantheon.

Jung, C. G. (1954). *The development of personality.* Princeton: Princeton University Press.

Jung, C. G. (1959). *Collected works 9: The archetypes and the collective unconscious.* New York: Pantheon.

Jung, C. G. (1960). *Collected works 8: The structure and dynamics of the psyche.* New York: Pantheon.

Jung, C. G. (1963). *Memories, dreams, reflections.* New York: Pantheon.

Jung, C. G. (1964). *Man and his symbols.* Garden City, NY: Doubleday.

Jung, C. G. (1966). *Collected works 16: The practice of psychotherapy.* New York: Pantheon.

Jung, C. G. (1967). *Collected works 13: Alchemical studies.* New York: Pantheon.

Jung, C. G. (1968). *Collected works 18: Symbolic life.* New York: Pantheon.

Kabat-Zinn, J. (1996). Mindfulness meditation: What it is, what it isn't, and its role in health care and medicine. In I. Y. Haruk & M. Suzuki (Eds.), *Comparative and psychological study on meditation* (pp. 161–170). Netherlands: Eburon.

Kagan, S., & Madsen, M. (1971). Cooperation and competition of Mexican, Mexican-American, and Anglo children of two ages under four instructional sets. *Developmental Psychology 5,* 32.

Kalodner, C. R. (1998). Systematic desensitization. In S. Cormier & B. Cormier (Eds.), *Interviewing strategies for helpers* (4th ed., pp. 497–529). Pacific Grove, CA: Brooks/Cole.

Kaschak, E. (1981). Feminist psychotherapy: The first decade. In S. Cox (Ed.), *Female psychology: The emerging self* (pp. 387–400). New York: St. Martin's.

Kaschak, E. (1992). *Engendered lives.* New York: Basic Books.

Kaslow, F. W. (1986). Therapy with distressed psychotherapists: Special problems and challenges. In R. R. Kilburg, P. E. Nathan, & R. W. Thoreson (Eds.), *Professionals in distress: Issues, syndromes, and solutions in psychology* (pp. 187–210). Washington, DC: American Psychological Association.

Kaslow, F. W. (2000). Continued evolution of family therapy: The last twenty years. *Contemporary Family Therapy, 22,* 357–386.

Kaslow, F. W., & Schulman, N. (1987). How to be sane and happy as a family therapist, or the reciprocal impact of family therapy teaching and practice and therapists' personal lives and mental health. *Journal of Psychotherapy and the Family, 3*(2), 79–96.

Kaslow, N. J., & Celano, M. P. (1995). The families therapies. In A. S. Gurman & S. B. Messer (Eds.), *Essential psychotherapies* (pp. 343–402). New York: Guilford.

Kaslow, N. J., Celano, M., & Dreelin, E. D. (1995). A cultural perspective on family theory and therapy. *Cultural Psychiatry, 18,* 621–633.

Katz, J. (1985). The sociopolitical nature of counseling. *Counseling Psychologist, 13,* 615–624.

Katz, J. H. (1985). The sociopolitical nature of counseling. *The Counseling Psychologist, 13,* 615–624.

Kazdin, A. E., & Wilson, G. T. (1978). *Evaluation of behavior therapy: Issues, evidence, and research strategies*. Lincoln: University of Nebraska Press.

Keleman, S. (1985). *Emotional anatomy: The structure of experience*. Berkeley, CA: Center Press.

Kelly, E. W., Jr. (1995). Counselor values: A national survey. *Journal of Counseling and Development, 73*, 648–653.

Kelly, G. A. (1955). *The psychology of personal constructs*. New York: Norton.

Kempler, W. (1973). Gestalt therapy. In R. Corsini (Ed.), *Current psychotherapies* (pp. 251–286). Itasca, IL: Peacock.

Kendall, P. C., & Hollon, S. D. (1979). Cognitive-behavioral interventions: Overview and current status. In P. C. Kendall & S. D. Hollon (Eds.), *Cognitive-behavioral interventions: Theory, research, and procedures* (pp. 1–9). New York: Academic Press.

Kennedy-Moore, E., & Watson, J. C. (2001). How and when does emotional expression help? *Review of General Psychology, 5*(3), 187–212.

Kepner, J. (2001). Gestalt approaches to body-oriented theory: An introduction. *Gestalt Review, 4*(4), 262–264.

Kern, R., Snow, J., & Ritter, K. (In press). Making the lifestyle concept measurable. In D. Eckstein, & R. Kern (Eds.), *Lifestyle interventions*. Dubuque, IA: Kendall/Hunt.

Kerr, B., Cohn, S. J., Webb, T., & Anderson, T. (2001). *Smart boys: Talent, manhood, and the search for meaning*. Scottsdale, AZ: Gifted Psychology Press.

Kierkegaard, S. (1944). *The concept of dread* (W. Lowrie, Trans.). Princeton, NJ: Princeton University Press.

Kim, R. I., & Hwang, M. (2001). The effects of internal control and achievement motivation in group counseling based on reality therapy. *International Journal of Reality Therapy, 20*(2), 12–15.

Kim, Y. S. (2001). The development and effects of a reality therapy parent group counseling program. *International Journal of Reality Therapy, 20*(2), 4–7.

Kincade, E. A., Seem, S., & Evans, K. M. (1998). *Feminist therapy theory and practice: A model for social and individual change*. Paper presented at the American Counseling Association World Conference, Indianapolis, IN.

Kinnier, R. T. (1997). What does it mean to be psychologically healthy? In D. Capuzzi & D. R. Gross (Eds.), *Introduction to the counseling profession* (2nd ed., pp. 48–63). Boston: Allyn & Bacon.

Kirsh, B. (1987). Evolution of consciousness-raising groups. In V. Franks (Series Ed.) & C. M. Brady (Vol. Ed.), *Springer series: Focus on women: Volume 10: Women's therapy groups: Paradigms of feminist treatment* (pp. 43–54). New York: Springer.

Kitanishi, K., & Mori, A. (1995). Morita therapy: 1919 to 1995. *Psychiatry and Clinical Neurosciences, 49*, 245–254.

Kleinplatz, P. J. (1998). Sex therapy for vaginismus: A review, critique, and humanistic alternative. *Journal of Humanistic Psychology, 38*, 51–82.

Koestler, A. (1967). *The ghost in the machine*. London: Hutchinson.

Kogan, G. (1976). The genesis of Gestalt therapy. In C. Hatcher & P. Hililstein (Eds.), *The handbook of Gestalt therapy* (pp. 255–257). New York: Aronson.

Kohut, H. (1977). *The restoration of the self*. New York: International Universities Press.

Kondo, A. (1953). Morita therapy: A Japanese therapy for neurosis. *American Journal of Psychoanalysis, 13*, 31–37.

Kopp, S. (1972). *If you meet the Buddha on the road, kill him*. New York: Bantam.

Kora, T., & Ohara, K. (1973). Morita therapy. *Psychology Today, 6*(10), 63–68.

Kornfield, J. (1993). *A path with heart: A guide through the perils and promises of spiritual life*. New York: Bantam.

Koss, M. P., & Shiang, J. (1994). Research on brief psychotherapy. In A. E. Bergin & S. L. Garfield (Eds.), *Handbook of psychotherapy and behavior change* (4th ed., pp. 664–700). New York: John Wiley & Sons.

Kottler, J., & Brown, R. (1992). *Introduction to therapeutic counseling* (2nd ed.). Pacific Grove, CA: Brooks/Cole.

Kraus, N., & Shaw, B. A. (2000). Role-specific feelings of control and mortality. *Psychology and Aging, 15*, 617–626.

Kraut, R., & Lundmark, V. (1998). Internet paradox: A social technology that reduces social involvement and psychological well being. *American Psychologist, 53*(9), 1017–1031.

Krech, G. (1989). Kyoryoku: The application of Morita and Naikan principles to the work setting. In D. K. Reynolds (Ed.), *Flowing bridges, quiet waters* (pp. 108–122). Albany: State University of New York Press.

Kristeller, J., & Hallett. C. (1999). An exploratory study of meditation-based intervention for binge eating disorder. *Journal of Health Psychology, 4,* 357–363.

Krueger, M. J., & Hanna, F. J. (1997). Why adoptees search: An existential treatment perspective. *Journal of Counseling and Development, 75,* 195–202.

Kubler-Ross, E. (1975). *Death: The final stage of growth.* New York: Simon & Schuster.

Kuhn, T. (1962). *The structure of scientific revolutions.* Chicago: University of Chicago Press.

Kuiken, D. (1995). Dreams and feeling realization. *Dreaming: Journal of the Association for the Study of Dreams, 5*(3), 129–157.

Kurtz, R. (1987). *Hakomi therapy.* (Available from the Hakomi Institute, PO Box 1873, Boulder, CO 80306.)

Kurtz, R. (1990). *Body-centered psychotherapy: The Hakomi method.* Mendocino, CA: LifeRhythm.

Kurtz, R. (2000). *Highlights from a 4-day advanced seminar: Melbourne, Australia.* (Available from Rosemary McIndoe, 395 Station St., North Carlton, Victoria, Australia. 3054.)

Kurtz, R. (2002). *Hakomi experiential pychology.* [Online]. Available: *http://www.ronkurtz.com.*

Kurtz, R., & Prestera, H. (1976). *The body reveals.* New York: Harper & Row.

Kutz, I., Borysenko, J., & Benson, H. (1985). Meditation and psychology. *American Journal of Psychiatry, 142,* 1–8.

Kwiatkowska, H. Y. (1978). *Family therapy and evaluation through art.* Springfield, IL: Charles C. Thomas.

LaFromboise, T. (1988). American Indian mental health policy. *American Psychologist, 43,* 388–397.

LaFromboise, T. (1998). American Indian mental health policy. In D. R. Atkinson, G. Morten, & D. W. Sue (Eds.), *Counseling American minorities* (pp. 137–158). New York: McGraw Hill.

LaFromboise, T., & Low, K. G. (1989). American Indian children and adolescents. In J. T. Gibbs & L. N. Huang (Eds.), *Children of color: Psychological intervention with minority youth* (pp. 114–147). San Francisco: Jossey-Bass.

Lama Surya Das. (1997). *Awakening the Buddha within.* New York: Broadway Books.

Lambert, M. J. (1992). Implications of outcome research for psychotherapy integration. In J. C. Norcross & M. R. Goldstein (Eds.), *Handbook of psychotherapy integration* (pp. 94–129). New York: Basic Books.

Landgarten, H. (1987). *Family art therapy.* New York: Brunner/Mazel.

Lantz, J. (1993). *Existential family therapy.* Northvale, NJ: Jason Aronson.

Lantz, J., & Alford, K. (1995). Existential family treatment with an urban-Appalachian adolescent. *Journal of Family Psychotherapy, 6*(4), 15–27.

Lantz, J., & Gomia, L. (1995). Activities and stages in existential psychotherapy with older adults. *Clinical Gerontologist, 16,* 31–40.

Lantz, J., & Pegram, M. (1989). Casework and the restoration of meaning. *Journal of Contemporary Social Work, 70,* 549–555.

Laplanche, J., & Pontalis, J. B. (1973). The language of *psychoanalysis.* New York: Norton.

Lebow, J. L., & Gurman, A. S. (1995). Research assessing couple and family therapy. *Annual Review of Psychology, 46,* 25–57.

Lecours, S., Bouchard, A. M., & Normandin, L. (1995). Countertransference as the therapists mental activity: Experience and gender differences among psychoanalytically oriented psychologists. *Psychoanalytic Psychology, 12*(2), 259–281.

Lee, C. (1996). M.C.T. theory and implications for indigenous healing. In D. W. Sue, A. E. Ivey, & P. Pedersen (Eds.), *A theory of multicultural counseling and therapy* (pp. 86–96). Pacific Grove, CA: Brooks/Cole.

Leifer, R. (1996). Psychological and spiritual factors in chronic illness. *American Behavioral Scientist, 39*(6), 752–766.

Lerner, H. G. (1988). *Women in therapy.* New York: Harper & Row

Lerner, H. G. (1989). *The dance of intimacy.* New York: Harper & Row.

LeVine, E. S., & Padilla, A. M. (1980). *Crossing cultures in therapy: Pluralistic counseling for the Hispanic.* Monterey, CA: Brooks/Cole.

Levitsky, A., & Perls, F. S. (1970). The rules and games of Gestalt therapy. In J. Fagan & I. Shepherd (Eds.), *Gestalt therapy now: Theory, techniques, and applications* (pp. 140–149). Palo Alto: Science & Behavior Books.

Lewis, R. E. (1999, April). *The collaborative story.* Oregon Counseling Association Conference. Seaside, OR.

Lewis, R. E. (2000). Resiliency: Pathway to protective factors and possibilities for self-righting narratives.

In D. Capuzzi & D. R. Gross (Eds.), *Youth at risk* (3rd ed., pp. 41–80). Alexandria, VA: American Counseling Association.

Lewis-Fernandez, R., & Kleinman, A. (1995). Cultural psychiatry: Theoretical, clinical, and research issues. *Psychiatric Clinics of North America, 18,* 433–448.

Lieberman, M. A., Solow, N., Bond, G. R., & Reibstein, J. (1979). The psychotherapeutic impact of women's consciousness-raising groups. *Archives of General Psychiatry, 36,* 161–168.

Lindforss, L., & Magnusson, D. (1997). Solution-focused therapy in prison. *Contemporary Family Therapy, 19,* 89–103.

Linehan, M. (1993). *Skills training manual for treating borderline personality disorder.* New York: Guilford.

Lister, J. L. (1964). The counselor's personal theory. *Counselor Education and Supervision, 3,* 207–213.

Litt, S. (2000, March 31). The psychologists corner: Laura Perls (1905–1990) co-founder of gestalt therapy. *Positive Health Magazine, 14.*

Locke, D. C., Myers, J. E., & Herr, E. L. (Eds.). (2001). *The handbook of counseling.* Thousand Oaks, CA: Sage Publications.

Lojk, L. (1986). My experiences using reality therapy. *Journal of Reality Therapy, 5*(2), 28–35.

Lowen, A. (1976). *Bioenergetics.* New York: Penguin Books, Inc.

Loy, D. (1996). *Lack and transcendence: The problem of death and life in psychotherapy, existentialism, and Buddhism.* Atlantic Highlands, NJ: Humanities Press.

Luborsky, I., Singer, B., & Luborsky, L. (1975). Comparative studies of psychotherapies: Is it true that "everyone has won and all must have prizes"? *Archives of General Psychiatry, 42,* 602–611.

Luborsky, L., & Spence, D. P. (1978). Quantitative therapy. In S. L. Garfield & A. E. Bergin (Eds.), *Handbook of psychotherapy and behavior change* (2nd ed., pp. 220–246). New York: John Wiley & Sons.

Lyddon, W. J. (1990). First- and second-order change: Implications for rationalist and constructivist cognitive therapies. *Journal of Counseling and Development, 69,* 122–127.

Lyons, L. C., & Woods, P. J. The efficacy of rational-emotive therapy: A quantitative review of outcome research. *Clinical Psychology Review, 11,* 359–369.

Mackey, R. A., & Mackey, E. F. (1994). Personal psychotherapy and the development of a professional self. *Families in Society: The Journal of Contemporary Human Services, 75,* 490–499.

Madanes, C. (1981). *Strategic family therapy.* San Francisco: Jossey-Bass.

Madanes, C. (1991). *Strategic family therapy.* In A. S. Gurman & D. P. Kniskern (Eds.), *Handbook of family therapy* (Vol. 2, pp. 396–416). New York: Brunner/Mazel.

Magnuson, S., Norem, K., & Skinner, C. H. (1995). Constructing genograms with lesbian clients. *The Family Journal: Counseling and Therapy for Couples and Families, 3,* 110–115.

Mahoney, M. J. (1991). *Human change processes.* New York: Basic Books.

Mahoney, M. J. (1995). Continuing evolution of the cognitive sciences and psychotherapy. In R. A. Neimeyer & M. J. Mahoney (Eds.), *Constructivism in psychotherapy* (pp. 39–68). Washington, DC: American Psychological Association.

Malson, H. (1997). *Feminism post-structuralism and the social psychology of anorexia nervosa.* London: Routledge.

Malterud, K. (2001). The art and science of clinical knowledge: Evidence beyond measures and numbers. *Lancet, 358,* 397–400.

Manaster, G. J., & Corsini, R. J. (1982). *Individual psychology.* Itasca, IL: F. E. Peacock.

Mandara, J., & Murray, C. B. (2000). Effects of parental marital status, income, and family functioning on African American adolescent self-esteem. *Journal of Family Psychology, 14*(3), 475–490.

Mandelbaum, D. (1998). The impact of physical touch on professional development. In E. Smith, P. Clance, & S. Imes (Eds.), *Touch in psychotherapy: Theory, research, and practice* (pp. 211–219). New York: Guilford.

Manns, J. W. (1998). *Explorations in philosophy: Aesthetics.* Armonk, NY: M. E. Sharpe.

Maples, M. (1996). Cornerstones of a civilized society: Law, morality, faith and spirituality. *Juvenile and Family Court Journal, 47*(3), 41–60.

Maples, M., Dupey, P., Torres-Rivera, E., Phan, L., Vereen, L., & Garrett, M. T. (2001). Ethnic diversity and the use of humor in counseling: Appropriate or inappropriate? *Journal of Counseling and Development, 79*(1), 53–60.

Marlatt, A., & Gordon, J. (1984). *Relapse preventions: A self-control strategy for the maintenance of behavior change.* New York: Guilford.

Marshall, K. (1998). Reculturing systems with resilience/health realization: Promoting positive and healthy behaviors in children. *Fourteenth Annual Rosalyn Carter Symposium on Mental Health Policy* (pp. 48–58). Atlanta, GA: The Carter Center.

Martin, S., & Thompson, D. (1995). Reality therapy and goal attainment scaling: A program for freshmen student athletes. *Journal of Reality Therapy, 14*(2), 45–54.

Martz, E. (2001). Expressing counselor empathy through the use of possible selves. *Journal of Employment Counseling, 38,* 128–134.

Maslow, A. (1954). *Motivation and personality.* New York: Harper & Row.

Maslow, A. (1968). *Toward a psychology of being* (2nd ed.). New York: Van Nostrand.

Maslow, A. (1971). *The further reaches of human nature.* New York: Viking.

Maslow, A. H. (1970). *Motivation and personality* (2nd ed.). New York: Harper.

Mathews, L. G., & Atkinson, D. R. (1997). Counseling ethnic minority clients. In D. Capuzzi & D. Gross (Eds.), *Introduction to the counseling profession* (2nd ed., pp. 433–462). Needham Heights, MA: Allyn & Bacon.

May, R. (1953). *Man's search for himself.* New York: Dell Publishing.

May, R. (Ed.). (1961). *Existential psychology.* New York: Random House.

May, R. (1969). *Love and will.* New York: Norton.

May, R. (1979). *Psychology and the human dilemma.* New York: Norton.

May, R. (1983). *The discovery of being.* New York: Norton.

May, R. (1992). *The cry for myth.* New York: Delta.

McAuliffe, G., Eriksen, K., & Associates. (2000). *Preparing counselors and therapists: Creating constructivist and developmental programs.* Alexandria, VA: American Counseling Association.

McBride, M. C. (1998). The use of process in supervision: A gestalt approach. *Guidance and Counseling, 13,* 41–49.

McCombs, B. L., & Pope, J. E. (1994). *Motivating hard to reach students.* Washington, DC: American Psychological Association.

McCullough, J. E., Worthington, E. L., Maxey, J., & Rachal, K. C. (1997). Gender in the context of supportive and challenging religious counseling interventions. *Journal of Counseling Psychology, 44*(1), 80–88.

McFadden, J. (1988). Cross-cultural counseling: Caribbean perspective. *Journal of Multicultural Counseling and Development, 16,* 36–40.

McFadden, J. (1996). A transcultural perspective: Reaction to C. H. Patterson's "Multicultural counseling: From diversity to universality." *Journal of Counseling and Development, 74*(3), 232–235.

McGoldrick, M., & Carter, B. (2001). Advances in coaching: Family therapy with one person. *Journal of Marital and Family Therapy, 27,* 281–300.

McGoldrick, M., & Gerson, R. (1985). *Genograms in family assessment.* New York: Norton.

McKeel, A. (1996). A clinician's guide to research on solution-focused brief therapy. In S. D. Miller, M. A. Hubble, & B. L. Duncan (Eds.), *Handbook of solution-focused brief therapy* (pp. 251–271). San Francisco: Jossey-Bass.

Meichenbaum, D. (1969). The effects of instructions and reinforcement on thinking and language behaviors of schizophrenics. *Behaviour Research and Therapy, 7,* 101–114.

Meichenbaum, D. (1977). *Cognitive behavior modification: An integrative approach.* New York: Plenum.

Meichenbaum, D. (1979). *Cognitive behavioral modification.* New York: Plenum.

Meichenbaum, D. (1985). *Stress inoculation training.* New York: Pergamon Press.

Meichenbaum, D. H., & Deffenbacher, J. L. (1988). Stress inoculation training. *Counseling Psychologist, 16,* 69–90.

Meichenbaum, D., & Goodman, J. (1969). Training impulsive children to talk to themselves: A means of developing self-control. *Journal of Abnormal Psychology, 77,* 115–126.

Meier, S. T., & Davis, S. R. (2001). *The elements of counseling* (4th ed.). Belmont, CA: Wadsworth.

Meir, E. (1996). The contributions of modern thought to a psychoanalytic phenomenology of groups. *Psychoanalysis and Contemporary Thought, 19,* 563–578.

Melnick, J. (2000). Editorial: Sexual issues in therapy consultation and training. *Gestalt Review, 4*(1), 1–7.

Melnick, J., & Nevis, S. M. (1992). Diagnosis: The struggle for the meaningful paradigm. In E. C. Nevis (Ed.), *Gestalt therapy: Perspectives and applications* (pp. 57–78). New York: Gardner Press.

Meredith, C. W., & Evans, T. D. (1990). Encouragement in the family. *Individual Psychology, 46,* 187–192.

Metcalf, L. (1995). *Counseling toward solutions: A practical solution-focused program for working with students, teachers, and parents.* West Nyack, NY: Center for Applied Research in Education.

Metzner, R. (1998). *The unfolding self: Varieties of transformative experience.* Novato, CA: Origin Press.

Miars, B. D., Burden, C. A., & Pedersen, M. M. (1997). The helping relationship. In D. Capuzzi & D. Gross (Eds.), *Introduction to the counseling profession* (2nd ed., pp. 64–84). Needham Heights, MA: Allyn & Bacon.

Miars, B. D., & Halverson, S. (2001). The helping relationship. In D. Capuzzi & D. Gross (Eds.), *Introduction to the counseling profession* (3rd ed., pp. 50–68). Needham Heights, MA: Allyn & Bacon.

Michalon, M. (2001). "Selflessness" in the service of the ego: Contributions, limitations, and dangers of Buddhist psychology for Western psychology. *American Journal of Psychotherapy, 55,* 202–221.

Midgette, T., & Meggert, S. (1991). Multicultural counseling instruction: A challenge for faculties in the 21st century. *Journal of Counseling and Development, 70,* 136–141.

Mikulas, W. L. (2002). *The integrative helper: Convergence of Eastern and Western tradition.* Pacific Grove, CA: Brooks/Cole.

Miller, D. (1997). New physics at last? *Nature, 385,* 768–769.

Miller, G. (2001). Finding happiness for ourselves and our clients. *Journal of Counseling and Development, 79*(3), 382–384.

Miller, J. B. (1976). *Toward a new psychology of women.* Boston: Beacon Press.

Miller, L. K. (1980). *Principles of everyday behavior analysis* (2nd ed.). Monterey, CA: Brooks/Cole.

Miller, W. R. (Ed.). (1999). *Integrating spirituality into treatment: Resources for practitioners.* Washington, DC: American Psychological Association.

Miller, W. R., & Rollnick, S. (1991). *Motivational interviewing: Preparing people to change addictive behavior.* New York: Guilford.

Milliren, A. (1995). Foreword. In T. Reed (Ed.), *Lost days: Children from dysfunctional families in school.* Salt Lake City, UT: Northwest Publishing.

Mills, R. C. (1995). *Realizing mental health: Toward a new psychology of resiliency.* New York: Sulburger & Graham.

Mills, R. C. (1996, August). *Empowering individuals and communities through health realization: Psychology of mind in prevention and community revitalization.* Paper presented at the meeting of the American Psychological Association, Toronto, Canada.

Mills, R. C., Dunham, R. G., & Alpert, G. P. (1988). Working with high-risk youth in prevention and early intervention programs: Toward a comprehensive wellness model. *Adolescence, 23,* 643–660.

Mills, R. C., & Spittle, E. (2001). *The wisdom within.* Renton, WA: Lone Pine Publishing.

Milton, M. J. (1993). Existential thought and client centered therapy. *Counseling Psychology Quarterly, 6*(1), 239–248.

Mindell, A. (1982). *Dreambody: The body's role in revealing the self.* Boston, MA: Sigo Press.

Mindell, A., & Mindell, A. (1997). Dreams and the dreaming body. In C. Caldwell (Ed.), *Getting in touch: The guide to new body-centered therapies* (pp. 61–70). Wheaton, IL: Theosophical Publishing House.

Minuchin, S., & Fishman, C. (1981). *Family therapy techniques.* Cambridge: Harvard University Press.

Mio, J. S., Trimble, J. E., Arrendondo, P., Cheatham, H. E., & Sue, D. (Eds.). (1999). *Key words in multicultural interventions: A dictionary.* Westport, CT: Greenwood Press.

Mishara, A. L. (1995). Narrative and psychotherapy: The phenomenology of healing. *American Journal of Psychotherapy, 49,* 180–195.

Mitchell, S. (1988). *Relational concepts in psychoanalysis.* Cambridge: Harvard University Press.

Monk, G. (1997). How narrative therapy works. In G. Monk, J. Winslade, K. Crocket, & D. Epston (Eds.), *Narrative therapy in practice: The archaeology of hope* (pp. 3–31). San Francisco: Jossey-Bass.

Monk, G., Winslade, J., Crocket, K., & Epston, D. (Eds.). (1997). *Narrative therapy in practice: The archaeology of hope.* San Francisco: Jossey-Bass.

Morgan, B. (2001, July). *The Four Noble Truths and meditation: Understanding resistance.* Paper presented at the New England Educational Summer Institute, Cape Cod, MA.

Morrissey, B. (2000). The re-creation of the self: An overview. In J. Eisman (Ed.), *The Hakomi method and re-creation of the self: Professional training.* (Available from the Hakomi Institute of Oregon, 6836 HWY 66, Ashland, OR 97520.)

Mosak, H., & Dreikurs, R. (1973). Adlerian psychotherapy. In R. J. Corsini (Ed.), *Current psychotherapies.* Itasca, IL: F. E. Peacock.

Mosak, H. H. (1979). Adlerian psychotherapy. In R. J. Corsini (Ed.), *Current psychotherapies.* Itasca, IL: F. E. Peacock.

Moursund, J. M., & Kenny, M. C. (2002). *The process of counseling and psychotherapy* (4th ed.). Upper Saddle River, NJ: Prentice Hall.

Mozdzierz, G. J., Lisiecki, J., Bitter, J. R., & Williams, A. L. (1986). Role functions for Adlerian therapists. *Journal of Individual Psychology, 42*(2), 154–177.

Murphy, G., & Murphy, L. (1968). *Asian psychology*. New York: Basic Books.

Murphy, J. J. (1997). *Solution-focused counseling in middle and high schools*. Alexandria, VA: American Counseling Association.

Murray, D. J., & Farahmand, B. (1998). Gestalt theory and evolutionary psychology. In R. W. Rieber & K. D. Salzinger (Eds.), *Psychology: Theoretical-historical perspectives* (2nd ed., pp. 255–288). Washington, DC: American Psychological Association.

Myers, J. E. (1991). Wellness as the paradigm for counseling and development: The possible future. *Counselor Education and Supervision, 30*(3), 183–193.

Myers, J. E., Sweeney, T. J., & Witmer, J. M. (2000). The wheel of wellness counseling for wellness: A holistic model for treatment planning. *Journal of Counseling and Development, 78,* 251–266.

Neimeyer, R. A. (1995). An invitation to constructivist psychotherapies. In R. A. Neimeyer & M. J. Mahoney (Eds.), *Constructivism in psychotherapy* (pp. 1–10). Washington, DC: American Psychological Association.

Neimeyer, R. A., & Mahoney, M. J. (Eds.). (1995). *Constructivism in psychotherapy*. Washington, DC: American Psychological Association.

Nelson-Jones, R. (2000). *Six key approaches to counseling & therapy*. London: Continuum.

Nevis, S., & Harris, V. (1988). *A session of Gestalt therapy with families* [Videotape]. Cleveland: Gestalt Institute of Cleveland.

Newlon, B. J., & Arciniega, M. (1983). Counseling minority families: An Adlerian perspective. *Counseling and Human Development, 16,* 1–12.

Newlon, B. J., & Arciniega, M. (1992). Group counseling: Cross cultural considerations. In D. Capuzzi & D. Gross (Eds.), *Introduction to group counseling* (pp. 286–306). Denver: Love.

Nichols, M. P. (1987). *The self in the system: Expanding the limits of family therapy*. New York: Brunner/Mazel.

Nichols, M. P., & Schwartz, R. C. (1995). *Family therapies*. Boston: Allyn & Bacon.

Nichols, M. P., & Schwartz, R. C. (1998) *Family therapy: Concepts and methods* (4th ed.). Boston, MA: Allyn & Bacon.

Nietzsche, F. (1889). *Twilight of the idols* (W. Kaufmann, Trans.). New York: Viking.

Nietzsche, F. (1967). *The will to power* (W. Kaufmann & R. Hollingdale, Trans.). New York: Random House.

Norcross, J. C., Santrock, J. W., Campbell, L. F., Smith, T. P., Sommer, R., & Zuckerman, E. L. (2000). *Authoritative guide to self-help resources in mental health*. New York: Guilford.

Nord, D. (1996). The impact of multiple AIDS-related loss on families of origin and families of choice. *American Journal of Family Therapy, 24,* 129–144.

O'Connell, V. F. (1970). Crisis psychotherapy: Person, dialogue, and the organismic event. In J. Fagan & I. L. Shepherd (Eds.), *Gestalt therapy now: Theory, techniques, applications* (pp. 243–256). Palo Alto, CA: Science and Behavior Books.

O'Hanlon, W. H. (1990). A grand unified theory for brief therapy: Putting problems in context. In J. K. Zeig & S. G. Gilligan (Eds.), *Brief therapy: Myths, methods, and metaphors* (pp. 78–89). New York: Brunner/Mazel.

O'Hanlon, W. H. (1993). Take two people and call them in the morning: Brief solution-oriented therapy with depression. In S. Friedman (Ed.), *The new language of change: Constructive collaboration in psychotherapy* (pp. 50–84). New York: Guilford.

O'Hanlon, W. H. (1994, November/December). The third wave. *Family Therapy Networker,* 19–29.

O'Hanlon, W. H. (1999). *Do one thing different: And other uncommonly sensible solutions to life's persistent problems*. New York: William Morrow.

O'Hanlon, W. H., & Weiner-Davis, M. (1989). *In search of solutions: A new direction in psychotherapy*. New York: Norton.

O'Leary, C. J. (1999). *Counseling couples and families: A person-centered approach*. Thousand Oaks, CA: Sage.

O'Leary, E., & Nieuwstraten, I. M. (1999). Unfinished business in gestalt reminiscence therapy: A discourse analytic study. *Counseling Psychology, 12* (4), 395–412.

O'Leary E., Purcell, U., McSweeney, E., O'Flynn, D., O'Sullivan, K., Keane, N., & Barry N. (1998). The cork person centered Gestalt project: Two outcome studies. *Counseling Psychology Quarterly, 11,* 45–71.

O'Shea, L. (2000). Sexuality: Old Struggles and new challenges. *Gestalt Review, 4*(1), 8–25.

Oaklander, V. (1999). Group play therapy from a gestalt therapy perspective. In D. S. Sweeney & L. E. Homeyer (Eds.), *The handbook of group play therapy: How to do it, how it works, whom it's best for* (pp. 162–176). San Francisco, CA: Jossey-Bass.

Oaklander, V. (2000). Short-term gestalt play therapy for grieving children. In H. G. Kaduson & C. E. Schaefer (Eds.), *Short-term play therapy for children* (pp. 28–52). New York: Guilford.

Ogden, P. (1997). Hakomi integrated somatics: Hands on psychotherapy. In C. Caldwell (Ed.), *Getting in touch: The guide to new body-centered therapies* (pp. 153–178). Wheaton, IL: Theosophical Publishing House.

Ogden, P., & Minton, K. (2001). Sensorimotor psychotherapy: One method for processing traumatic memory. *Traumatology* (Vol. VI, Issue 3, Art. 3) [Online]. Available: *www.fsu.edu/~trauma/v6i3/v6i3a3.html.*

Okum, B. (1990). *Seeking connections in psychotherapy.* San Francisco: Jossey-Bass.

Okun, B. (1992). *Effective helping: Interviews and counseling techniques* (4th ed.). Pacific Grove, CA: Brooks/Cole.

Okun, B. F. (1987). *Effective helping: Interviewing and counseling techniques* (3rd ed.). Monterey, CA: Brooks/Cole.

Orlinsky, D. E., & Howard, K. I. (1978). The relation of process to outcome in psychotherapy. In S. L. Garfield & A. E. Bergin (Eds.), *Handbook of psychotherapy and behavior change* (2nd ed., pp. 283–330). New York: John Wiley & Sons.

Orlinsky, D. E., & Howard, K. I. (1986). Process and outcome in psychotherapy. In S. L. Garfield & A. E. Bergin (Eds.), *Handbook of psychotherapy and behavior change* (3rd ed., pp. 311–381). New York: John Wiley & Sons.

Osipow, S. H., Walsh, W. B., & Tosi, D. J. (1980). *A survey of counseling methods.* Homewood, IL: Dorsey.

Owen, H. (1997). *Expanding our now: The story of open space technology.* San Francisco, CA: Berrett-Koehler.

Owen, I. R. (1994). Introducing an existential-phenomenological approach: Basic phenomenological theory and research: I. *Counseling Psychology Quarterly, 7*(4), 261–273.

Paniagua, F. A. (1998). *Assessing and treating culturally diverse clients* (2nd ed.). Thousand Oaks: Sage.

Papero, D. V. (1990). *Bowen family systems theory.* Boston: Allyn & Bacon.

Papp, P., & Imber-Black, E. (1996). Family themes: Transmission and transformation. *Family Process, 35,* 5–20.

Parham, T. (1996). M.C.T. theory and African American populations. In D. Sue, A. Ivey, & P. Pedersen (Eds.), *A theory of multicultural counseling and therapy* (pp. 177–191). Pacific Grove, CA: Brooks/Cole.

Parham, T., & Helms, J. (1985). Relation of racial identity attitudes to self actualization and affective states of black students. *Journal of Counseling Psychology, 32*(3), 431–440.

Paris, J. (2000). *Myths of childhood.* Philadelphia, PA: Taylor & Francis.

Parish, T. (1988). Helping teachers take more effective control. *Journal of Reality Therapy, 8*(1), 41–43.

Parish, T. (1991). Helping students take control via an interactive voice communications system. *Journal of Reality Therapy, 11*(1), 38–40.

Parish T., Martin, P., & Khramtsova, I. (1992). Enhancing convergence between our real world and ideal selves. *Journal of Reality Therapy, 11*(2), 37–40.

Parloff, M. B. (1986). Frank's "common elements" in psychotherapy: Nonspecific factors and placebos. *American Journal of Orthopsychiatry, 56,* 521–530.

Parry, A., & Doan, R. E. (1994). *Story re-visions: Narrative therapy in the postmodern world.* New York: Guilford.

Passons, W. R. (1975). *Gestalt approaches in counseling.* New York: Holt, Rinehart, and Winston.

Patterson, C. H. (1958). The place of values in counseling and psychotherapy. *Journal of Counseling Psychology, 5,* 216–223.

Patterson, C. H. (1974). *Relationship counseling and psychotherapy.* New York: Harper & Row.

Patterson, C. H. (1989). Values in counseling and psychotherapy. *Counseling and Values, 33,* 164–176.

Patterson, C. H. (1996). Multicultural counseling: From diversity to universality. *Journal of Counseling and Development, 74*(3), 227–231.

Patterson, G. R., & Forgatch, M. S. (1985). Therapist behavior as a determinant for client noncompliance: A paradox for the behavior modifier. *Journal of Consulting and Clinical Psychology, 53,* 846–851.

Peavy, V. (1998). *SocioDynamic Counseling.* Victoria, BC, Canada: Trafford Publishing.

Pedersen, P. (1987). Ten frequent assumptions of cultural bias in counseling. *Journal of Multicultural Counseling and Development, 15,* 16–22.

Pedersen, P. (1988). *A handbook for developing multicultural awareness.* Alexandria, VA: American Association for Counseling and Development.

Pedersen, P. (1991). Multiculturalism as a generic approach to counseling. *Journal of Counseling and Development, 70,* 6–12.

Pedersen, P. (1994). *A handbook for developing cultural awareness* (2nd ed.). Alexandria, VA: American Counseling Association.

Pedersen, P. (1996). The importance of both similarities and differences in multicultural counseling: Reaction to C. H. Patterson. *Journal of Counseling and Development, 74*(3), 236–237.

Pedersen, P. (2000). *A handbook for developing multicultural awareness* (3rd ed.). Alexandria, VA: American Counseling Association.

Pedersen, P., Draguns, J., Lonner, W., & Trimble, J. (Eds.). (1996). *Counseling across cultures* (4th ed.). Thousand Oaks, CA: Sage.

Pederson, P. (2000). *A handbook for developing multicultural awareness* (3rd ed.). Alexandria, VA: American Counseling Association.

Pelzel, J. C. (1977). Japanese personality-in-culture: From the psychiatric aerie. *Culture, Medicine, and Psychiatry, 1*(3), 299–315.

Perls, F. (1966). The meaning of Gestalt therapy. Workshop presented in Atlanta, GA (cited in Fagan & Shepherd, 1970, pp. 360–362).

Perls, F. (1969a). *Gestalt therapy verbatim.* Lafayette, CA: Real Person Press.

Perls, F. (1969b). *In and out of the garbage pail.* Lafayette, CA: Real Person Press.

Perls, F. (1973). *The Gestalt approach and eyewitness to therapy.* New York: Bantam.

Perls, F., Hefferline, R., & Goodman, P. (1977). *Gestalt therapy.* New York: Bantam Books, Inc.

Persons, J. B., & Davidson, J. (2001). Cognitive-behavioral case formulation. In K. S. Dobson (Ed.), *Handbook of cognitive-behavioral therapies* (2nd ed., pp. 86–110). New York: Guilford.

Pesso, A. (1969). *Experience in action: A psychomotor psychology.* Albany, NY: SUNY Press.

Pesso, A. (1973). *Movement in psychotherapy.* New York: New York University Press.

Pesso, A. (1997). PBSP—Pesso Boyden system psychomotor. In C. Caldwell (Ed.), *Getting in touch: The guide to new body-centered therapies* (pp.

117–152). Wheaton, IL: Theosophical Publishing House.

Peter, L. (1982). *The laughter prescription.* New York: Ballantine.

Peterson, A., & Truscott, J. (1988). Pete's pathogram: Quantifying the genetic needs. *Journal of Reality Therapy, 8*(1), 22–32.

Peterson, A., Chang, C., & Collins, P. (1997). The effects of reality therapy on locus of control among students in Asian universities. *Journal of Reality Therapy, 16*(2), 80–87.

Peterson, A., Woodward, G., & Kissko, R. (1991). A comparison of basic week students and introduction to counseling graduate students on four basic need factors. *Journal of Reality Therapy, 9*(1), 31–37.

Pierrakos, J. C. (1987). *Core energetics.* Mendocino, CA: LifeRhythm.

Pine, F. (1985). *Developmental theory and clinical process.* New Haven: Yale University Press.

Pine, F. (1990). *Drive, ego, object, and self.* New York: Basic Books.

Pines, A., & Maslach, C. (1978). Characteristics of staff burnout in mental health settings. *Hospital and Community Psychiatry, 29,* 233–237.

Pinsof, W. M. (1994). An integrative systems perspective on the therapeutic alliance: Theoretical, clinical, and research implications. In A. O. Horvath & L. S. Greenberg (Eds.), *The working alliance* (pp. 173–198). New York: John Wiley & Sons.

Pinsof, W. M., & Wynne, L. C. (2000). Toward progress research: Closing the gap between family therapy practice and research. *Journal of Marital and Family Therapy, 26,* 1–8.

Polo, P. M. (1993). The borderline case: A consideration from the point of view of Gestalt therapy. *Studies in Gestalt Therapy, 2,* 53–61.

Polster, E., & Polster, M. (1973). *Gestalt therapy integrated.* New York: Vintage.

Polster, M. (1987). *Every person's life is a novel.* New York: Norton.

Polster, M. E. (1992). *Eve's daughters.* San Francisco: Jossey-Bass.

Ponterotto, J., & Casas, M. (1991). *Handbook of racial/ethnic minority counseling research.* Springfield, IL: Charles C. Thomas.

Ponterotto, J., Casas, L., Suzuki, L., & Alexander, C. (Eds.). (1995). *Handbook of multicultural counseling.* Thousand Oaks, CA: Sage.

Ponterotto, J., & Sabnani, H. (1989). Classics in multicultural counseling: A systematic five-year content analysis. *Journal of Multicultural Counseling and Development, 17,* 23–37.

Poppen, W., Thompson, C., Cates, J., & Gang, M. (1976). Classroom discipline problems and reality therapy: Research support. *Elementary School Guidance and Counseling, 11*(2), 131–137.

Portnoy, D. (1999). Where humanistic and psychoanalytic psychotherapy converge. *Journal of Humanistic Psychology, 39,* 19–35.

Powers, R. L., & Griffith, J. (1987). *Understanding lifestyle: The psycho-clarity process.* Chicago, IL: The Americas Institute of Adlerian Studies.

Powers, W. (1973). *Behavior: The control of perception.* New York: Aldine.

Pramling, I., & Johansson, E. (1995). Existential questions in early childhood programs in Sweden: Teacher's conceptions and children's experience. *Child and Youth Care Forum, 24*(2), 125–146.

Pransky, G. S. (1998). *The renaissance of psychology.* New York: Sulzburger & Graham.

Pransky, G. S., Mills, R. C., Sedgeman, J. A., & Blevens, J. K. (1997). An emerging paradigm for brief treatment. In L. Vandecreek, S. Knapp, & T. L. Jackson (Eds.), *Innovations in clinical practice: A source book* (Vol. 15, pp. 401–420). Sarasota: Professional Resource Press.

Presbury, J. H., Echterling, L. G., & McKee, J. E. (2002). *Ideas and tools for brief counseling.* Upper SaddleRiver, NJ: Merrill/Prentice Hall.

Prochaska, J. O., & Norcross, J. C. (1994). *Systems of psychotherapy: A transtheoretical analysis* (3rd ed.). Pacific Grove, CA: Brooks/Cole.

Prochaska, J. O., & Norcross, J. C. (1999). *Systems of psychotherapy: A transtheoretical analysis* (4th ed.). Pacific Grove, CA: Brooks/Cole.

Prosnick, K. (2000). The relationship between reports of mystical experiences and gestalt resistance processes. *Gestalt Review, 4*(1), 42–46.

Prouty, G. (1998). Pretherapy and pre-symbolic experiencing: Evolutions in person-centered/experiential approaches to psychotic experience. In L. S. Greenberg & J. C. Watson (Eds.), *Handbook of experiential psychotherapy* (pp. 388–409), New York: Guilford.

Purkey, W. W., & Schmidt, J. J. (1987). *The inviting relationship: An expanded perspective for professional counseling.* Upper Saddle River, NJ: Prentice Hall.

Rabin, H. (1995). The liberating effect on the analyst of the paradigm shift in psychoanalysis. *Psychoanalytic Psychology, 12*(4), 467–483.

Ramey, L. (1998). The use of gestalt interventions in the treatment of the resistant alcohol-dependent client. *Journal of Mental Health Counseling, 20,* 202–216.

Rampage, C. (1998). Feminist couple therapy. In F. M. Dattilio (Ed.), *Case studies in couple and family therapy: Systemic and cognitive perspectives* (pp. 353–370). New York: Guilford.

Rand, M., & Fewster, G. (1997). Self, boundaries, and containment: Integrative body psychotherapy. In C. Caldwell (Ed.), *Getting in touch: The guide to new body-centered therapies* (pp. 71–88). Wheaton, IL: Theosophical Publishing House.

Rapaport, D., & Gill, M. M. (1959). The points of view and assumptions of metapsychology. *International Journal of Psychoanalysis, 40,* 153–162.

Rave, E. J., & Larsen, C. C. (1995). *Ethical decision making in therapy: Feminist perspectives.* New York: Guilford.

Reber, A. S. (1986). *Dictionary of psychology.* New York: Penguin.

Reed, T. L. (1995). *Lost days: Children from dysfunctional families in school.* Salt Lake City, UT: Northwest Publishing.

Reich, W. (1974). *Character analysis.* New York: Touchstone Books, Simon & Schuster, Inc.

Reiter, L. (1995). The client's affective impact on the therapist: Implications for therapist responsiveness. *Clinical Social Work Journal, 23*(1), 21–35.

Reker, G. T., & Chamberlain, K. (Eds.). (2000). *Exploring existential meaning: Optimizing human development across the life span.* Thousand Oaks, CA: Sage Publications.

Remer, P., Rostosky, S., & Wright, M. (2001). Counseling women from a feminist perspective. In E. R. Welfel & R. E. Ingersoll (Eds.), *Mental health desk reference* (pp. 341–347). New York: John Wiley & Sons.

Reynolds, D. K. (1976). *Morita psychotherapy.* Berkeley: University of California Press.

Reynolds, D. K. (1980). *The quiet therapies: Japanese pathways to personal growth.* Honolulu: University Press of Hawaii.

Reynolds, D. K. (1981a). Morita Psychotherapy. In R. J. Corsini (Ed.), *Handbook of innovative psychotherapies* (pp. 489–501). New York: John Wiley & Sons.

Reynolds, D. K. (1981b). Preface. *Psychiatric Quarterly, 53,* 201–202.

Reynolds, D. K. (1984a). *Constructive living*. Honolulu: University of Hawaii Press.

Reynolds, D. K. (1984b). *Playing ball on running water*. New York: Quill.

Reynolds, D. K. (1989). *Flowing bridges, quiet waters: Japanese psychotherapies, Morita and Naikan*. Albany: State University of New York Press.

Reynolds, D. K., & Kiefer, C. W. (1977). Cultural adaptability as an attribute of therapies: The case of Morita psychotherapy. *Culture, Medicine, and Psychiatry, 1*(4), 395–412.

Rhyne, J. (1970). The Gestalt art experience. In J. Fagan & I. L. Shepherd (Eds.), *Gestalt therapy now: Theory, techniques, applications* (pp. 274–284). Palo Alto, CA: Science and Behavior Books.

Richardson, B., & Wubbolding, R. (2001). Five interrelated challenges for using reality therapy with challenging students. *International Journal of Reality Therapy, 20*(2), 35–39.

Richardson, T. Q., & Molinaro, K. L. (1996). White counselor self-awareness: A prerequisite for developing multicultural competence. *Journal of Counseling and Development, 74*, 238–242.

Roberts, J. (1995). Exploring story styles. *The Family Journal: Counseling and Therapy for Couples and Families, 3*, 158–163.

Rock, I., & Palmer, S. (1990). *The legacy of Gestalt psychology*. Springfield, IL: Charles C. Thomas.

Roe, K., & Bowser, B. (1993). Health realization/community empowerment project. Evaluation of first year activities, submitted to East Bay Community Recovery Project.

Rogers, C. (1942). *Counseling and psychotherapy*. Boston: Houghton Mifflin.

Rogers, C. (1951). *Client centered therapy*. Boston: Houghton Mifflin.

Rogers, C. (1959). A theory of therapy, personality, and interpersonal relationships, as developed in the client centered framework. In S. Koch (Ed.), *Psychology: A study of a science* (Vol. 3, pp. 184–256). New York: McGraw Hill.

Rogers, C. (1961). *On becoming a person: A therapist's view of psychotherapy*. Boston: Houghton Mifflin.

Rogers, C. (Ed.). (1967). *The therapeutic relationship and its impact: A study of psychotherapy with schizophrenics*. Madison: University of Wisconsin Press.

Rogers, C. (1970). *Carl Rogers on encounter groups*. New York: Harper & Row.

Rogers, C. (1980). *A way of being*. Boston: Houghton Mifflin.

Rogers, C. (1986). Carl Rogers on the development of the person-centered approach. *Person-Centered Review, 1*(3), 257–259.

Rogers, C. (1987a). Inside the world of the Soviet professional. *Counseling and Values, 32*(1), 47–66.

Rogers, C. (1987b). Steps toward peace, 1948–1986: Tension reduction in theory and practice. *Counseling and Values, 32*(1), 12–16.

Rogers, C., & Dymond, R. (1954). *Psychotherapy and personality change*. Chicago: University of Chicago Press.

Rogers, C., & Sanford, R. (1987). Reflections on our South African experience. *Counseling and Values, 32*(1), 17–20.

Rogers, C. R. (1957). The necessary and sufficient conditions of therapeutic personality change. *Journal of Consulting Psychology, 21*, 95–103.

Rogers, C. R. (1961). *On becoming a person: A therapist's view of psychotherapy*. Boston: Houghton Mifflin.

Rogers, J. R. (2001). Theoretical grounding: The 'missing link' in suicide research. *Journal of Counseling and Development, 79*(1), 16–26.

Rogers, N. (2001). Person-centered expressive arts therapy. In J. A. Rubin (ed.), *Approaches to art therapy: Theory and technique* (2nd ed., pp. 163–177). Philadelphia: PA: Brunner-Rutledge.

Rolf, I. (1978). *Rolfing: The integration of human structures*. New York: Barnes and Noble Books.

Rosenberg, J., Rand, M., & Asay, D. (1985). *Body, self, and soul: Sustaining integration*. Atlanta, GA: Humanics.

Rosenblatt, A., Greenberg, J., Solomon, S., Pyszcznski, T., & Lyon, D. (1989). Evidence for terror management theory: I. The effects of mortality salience on reactions to those who violate or uphold cultural values. *Journal of Personality and Social Psychology, 57*, 681–690.

Rosenblatt, G. (1991). Interview with Laura Perls. *Gestalt Journal, 12*(2), 16–27.

Rosenbluth, M., & Yalom I. (1996). *Treating difficult personality disorders*. San Francisco, CA: Jossey-Bass.

Rosenfeld, E. (1978/1982). An oral history of Gestalt therapy part one: A conversation with Laura Perls. *The Gestalt Journal*. Highland, New York.

Rosenzweig, S. (1936). Some implicit common factors in diverse methods of psychotherapy. *American Journal of Orthopsychiarty, 6*, 412–415.

Rush, A. J., Beck, A. T., Kovacs, M., & Hollon, S. (1977). Comparative efficacy of cognitive therapy and pharmacotherapy in the treatment of depressed outpatients. *Cognitive Therapy and Research, 4,* 17–37.

Sabar, S. (2000). Bereavement, grief, and mourning: A gestalt perspective. *Gestalt Review, 4*(2), 152–159.

Saleebey, D. (Ed.). (1997). *The strengths perspective in social work practice* (2nd ed.). New York: Longman.

Salzberg, S. (1995). Loving kindness: *The revolutionary art of happiness.* Boston: Shambala.

Samler, J. (1960). Change in values: A goal in counseling. *Journal of Counseling Psychology, 7,* 32–39.

Sanderson, W. C., & Woody, S. (1995). *Manuals for empirically validated treatments.* Available: *http://www.apa.org/divisions/div12/est/manual60.html/*

Santos de Barona, M., & Dutton, M. A. (1997). Feminist perspectives on assessment. In J. Worell & N. G. Johnson (Eds.), *Shaping the future of feminist psychology: Education, research, and practice* (pp. 37–56). Washington, DC: American Psychological Association.

Sapp, M., Farrell, W., & Durand, H. (1995). Cognitive behavior therapy: Applications for African American middle-school at risk students. *Journal of Instructional Psychology, 22*(2), 169–177.

Sarbin, T. R. (1993). The narrative as the root metaphor for contextualism. In S. C. Hayes, L. J. Hayes, H. W. Reese, & T. R. Sarbin (Eds.), *Varieties of scientific contextualism* (pp. 51–65). Reno: Context Press.

Sarbin, T. R., & Kitsuse, J. I. (Eds.). (1994). *Constructing the social.* Thousand Oaks, CA: Sage.

Satir, V. (1983). *Conjoint family therapy* (3rd ed.). Palo Alto, CA: Science & Behavior Books.

Satir, V. M. (1983). *Conjoint family therapy* (Rev. ed.). Palo Alto: Science & Behavior Books.

Satir, V. M., & Bitter, J. R. (1991). The therapist and family therapy: Process model. In A. M. Horne & J. L. Passmore (Eds.), *Family counseling and therapy* (pp. 13–45). Itasca, IL: F. E. Peacock.

Sauber, R. S., L'Abate, L., Weeks, G. R., & Buchanan, W. L. (1993). *The dictionary of family psychology and family therapy.* Newbury Park, CA: Sage.

Schmidt, J. J. (2002). *Intentional helping: A philosophy for proficient caring relationships.* Upper Saddle River, NJ: Merrill/Prentice Hall.

Schmolling, P. (1984). Schizophrenia and the deletion of certainty: An existential case study. *Psychological Reports, 54,* 139–148.

Schulmeister, M. (2000). *Hakomi Institute of Europe's answers to the EAP's 15 questions about scientific validation of body-psychotherapy.* [Online]. Available: *http://www.eabp.org/scient_validity_hakomi.html*

Schulz, R., Greenley, J. R., & Brown, R. (1995). Organization, management, and client effects on staff burnout. *Journal of Health and Social Behavior, 36,* 333–345.

Schwartz, R. (1995). Internal family systems therapy. New York: Guilford.

Schwartz, T. (2000). The land mines of marriage: Intergenerational causes of marital conflict. *Gestalt Review, 4*(1), 47–62.

Sedgeman, J. A. (2001, March). *The principles underlying life experience: The beauty of simplicity.* Department of Community Medicine of the Robert C. Byrd Health Sciences Center, West Virginia University. Morgantown, WV: Sydney Banks Institute for Innate Health. Available: *http://www.hsc.wvu.edu/sbi/.*

Segal, L. (1991). Brief therapy: The MRI approach. In A. S. Gurman & D. P. Kniskern (Eds.), *Handbook of family therapy* (Vol. 2, pp. 171–199). New York: Brunner/Mazel.

Segal, M. (1997). *Points of influence: A guide to using personality theory at work.* San Francisco: Jossey-Bass.

Selekman, M. D. (1993). Solution-oriented brief therapy with difficult adolescents. In S. Friedman (Ed.), *The new language of change: Constructive collaboration in psychotherapy* (pp. 138–157). New York: Guilford.

Seligman, L. (1986). *Diagnosis and treatment planning and counseling.* New York: Human Sciences Press.

Seligman, L. (2001). *Systems, strategies, and skills of counseling and psychotherapy.* Upper Saddle River, NJ: Merrill/Prentice Hall.

Seltzer, L. (1986). *Paradoxical strategies in psychotherapy.* New York: John Wiley & Sons.

Serlin, I. A., & Shane, P. (1999). Laura Perls and Gestalt Therapy: Her life and values. In D. Moss (Ed.), *Humanistic and transpersonal psychology: A historical and biographical source book* (pp. 374–384). Westport, CT: Greenwood Press.

Sexton, T. L., & Whiston, S. C. (1994). The status of the counseling relationship: An empirical review, theoretical implications, and research directions. *Counseling Psychologist, 22,* 6–78.

Shane, P. (1999a). Fritz Perls and Paul Goodman: When Ahasuerus met Erasmus. In D. Moss (Ed.), *Humanistic and transpersonal psychology: A historical and biographical source book* (pp. 355–373). Westport, CT: Greenwood Press.

Shane, P. (1999b). Gestalt therapy: The once and future king. In D. Moss (Ed.), *Humanistic and transpersonal psychology: A historical and biographical source book* (pp. 49–65). Westport, CT: Greenwood Press.

Shannon, H. D., & Allen, T. W. (1998). The effectiveness of a REBT training program in increasing the performance of high school students in mathematics. *Journal of Rational-Emotive & Cognitive-Behavior Therapy, 16*(3), 197–209.

Shapiro, D. H., & Giber, D. (1984). Meditation and psychotherapeutic effects: Self-regulatory strategy and altered states of consciousness. In D. Shapiro & R. Walsh (Eds.), *Meditation: Classic and contemporary perspectives* (pp. 62–71). New York: Aldine Press.

Shapiro, S., Schwartz, G. E., & Bonner, G. (1998). Effects of mindfulness-based stress reduction on medical and pre-medical students. *Journal of Behavioral Medicine, 21,* 581–599.

Sharf, R. S. (2000). *Theories of psychotherapy and counseling: Concepts and cases* (3rd ed.). Pacific Grove, CA: Brooks/Cole.

Shaw, B. F. (1977). Comparison of cognitive therapy and behavior therapy in the treatment of depression. *Journal of Consulting and Clinical Psychology, 45,* 543–551.

Shea, G. (1973). The effects of reality therapy oriented group counseling with delinquent, behavior-disordered students. *Dissertation Abstracts International, 34,* 4889–4890.

Sheikh, J. I., & Yalom, I. (1996). *Treating the elderly.* San Francisco, CA: Jossey-Bass.

Shepherd, I. L. (1970). Limitations and cautions in the Gestalt approach. In J. Fagan & I. L. Shepherd (Eds.), *Gestalt therapy now: Theory techniques applications* (pp. 234–238.) Palo Alto, CA: Science and Behavior Books.

Shepherd, M. (1975). *Fritz.* New York: Saturday Review Press.

Sherman, R., & Dinkmeyer, D. (1987). *Systems of family therapy: An Adlerian integration.* New York: Brunner/Mazel.

Shoben, E. J., Jr. (1962). The counselor's theory as a personality trait. *American Personnel and Guidance Journal, 40,* 617–621.

Shreve, A. (1989). *Women together, women alone.* New York: Viking.

Shub, N. (2000). Gestalt therapy and self-esteem. *Gestalt Review, 4*(2), 111–123.

Shulman, B. H. (1951). Review of L. Way: Adler's place in psychology. *Individual Psychology Bulletin, 9,* 31–35.

Shulman, B. H. (1962). The meaning of people to the schizophrenic versus the manic-depressive. *Journal of Individual Psychology, 18,* 151–156.

Shulman, B. H. (1973). Confrontation techniques in Adlerian psychotherapy. *Contributions to Individual Psychology: Selected papers by Bernard H. Shulman, M.D.* (Originally published in 1971 in the *Journal of Individual Psychology, 27,* 167–175.)

Shulman, B. H., & Mosak, H. H. (1977). Birth order and ordinal position. *Journal of Individual Psychology, 33,* 114–121.

Shulman, B. H., & Mosak, H. H. (1988). *Manual for life style assessment.* Levittown, PA: Accelerated Development.

Sieber, C., & Lewis, R. E. (1999). Brief theories. In D. Capuzzi & D. R. Gross (Eds.), *Counseling and psychotherapy: Theories and interventions* (pp. 345–378). Upper Saddle River, NJ: Prentice Hall.

Siegel, D. (1999). *The developing mind: Toward a neurobiology of interpersonal experience.* New York: Guilford.

Skinner, B. F. (1969). *Contingencies of reinforcement: A theoretical analysis.* New York: Appleton Century-Crofts.

Sklare, G. B. (1997). *Brief counseling that works: A solution-focused approach for school counselors.* Thousand Oaks, CA: Corwin Press.

Skovholt, T. M. (2001). *The resilient practitioner: Burnout prevention and self-care strategies for counselors, therapists, teachers, and health professionals.* Needham Heights, MA: Allyn & Bacon.

Skowronski, J. J., & Lawrence, M. A. (2001). A comparative study of the implicit and explicit gender attitudes of children and college students. *Psychology of Women Quarterly, 25,* 155–165.

Smith, E. (1985). *The body in psychotherapy.* Jefferson, NC: McFarland & Company.

Smith, G. B., & Schwebel, A. I. (1995). Using a cognitive-behavioral family model in conjunction with systems and behavioral family therapy models. *American Journal of Family Therapy, 23,* 203–212.

Smith, M. L., & Glass, G. V. (1977). Meta-analysis of psychotherapy outcome studies. *American Psychologist, 32,* 752–760.

Solberg, E. E., & Halvorson, R. (2000). Effect of meditation on immune cells. *Stress Medicine, 16,* 185–191.

Solomon, S., Greenberg, J., & Pyszczynski, T. (1991). A terror management theory of social behavior: The psychological functions of self-esteem and world views. In L. Berkowitz (Ed.), *Advances in Experimental Social Psychology, 24,* 93–159.

Somerfield, M., Curbow, B., Wingard, J., & Baker, F. (1996). Coping with the physical and psychosocial sequelae of bone marrow transplantation among long-term survivors. *Journal of Behavioral Medicine, 19*(2), 163–184.

Staemmler, F. (1994). On layers and phases: A message from overseas. *Gestalt Journal, 17*(1), 5–31.

State of Ohio. (1984). *Counselor and Social Worker Law* (Chap. 4757, Rev. code). Columbus, OH: Author.

Steen, M. (1996). Essential structure and meaning of recovery from clinical depression for middle-aged adult women: A phenomenological study. *Issues in Mental Health Nursing, 17,* 73–92.

Stein, H. T., & Edwards, M. E. (1998). Classical Adlerian theory and practice. In P. Marcus & A. Rosenberg (Eds.), *Psychoanalytic versions of the human condition: Philosophies of life and their impact on practice* (pp. 64–93). New York: New York University Press.

Stephenson, W. (1953). *The study of behavior: Q-technique and its methodology.* Chicago: University of Chicago Press.

Stolorow, R., Brandshaft, B., & Atwood, G. (1987). *Psychoanalytic treatment: An intersubjective approach.* Hillsdale, NJ: The Analytic Press.

Strachey, J. (1934). The nature of therapeutic action in psychoanalysis. *International Journal of Psychoanalysis, 15,* 127–159.

Sturdivant, S. (1980). *Therapy with women: A feminist philosophy of treatment.* New York: Springer.

Sue, D. W., Arredondo, P., & McDavis, R. J. (1992). Multicultural competencies and standards: A pressing need. *Journal of Counseling and Development, 70,* 77–86.

Sue, D. W., Ivey, A., & Pedersen, P. (Eds.). (1996). *A theory of multicultural counseling and therapy.* Pacific Grove, CA: Brooks/Cole.

Sue, D., Sue, D., & Sue, S. (2000). *Understanding abnormal behavior* (6th ed.). New York: Houghton Mifflin.

Sue, D. W., & Sue, D. (1999). *Counseling the culturally different: Theory and practice* (3rd ed.). New York: John Wiley & Sons.

Sue, S. (1997). Community mental health services to minority groups: Some optimism, some pessimism. *American Psychologist, 32,* 616–624.

Sullivan, H. S. (1953). *The interpersonal theory of psychiatry.* New York: Norton.

Suzuki, D. T. (1970). *Zen mind, beginner's mind.* New York: Weatherhill.

Suzuki, T., & Suzuki, R. (1981). The effectiveness of inpatient Morita therapy. *Psychiatric Quarterly, 53,* 203–213.

Swanson, J. (1984). Gestalt counseling with an adult client [Videotape]. Corvallis: Oregon State University, Communications Media Productions.

Sweeney, T. J., & Witmer, J. M. (1991). Beyond social interest: Striving toward optimal health and wellness. *Individual Psychology, 47,* 527–540.

Szasz, T. (1987). Discussion by Thomas Szasz. In J. Zeig (Ed.), *The evolution of psychotherapy* (pp. 210–211). New York: Brunner/Mazel.

Tallman, K., & Bohart, A. C. (1999). The client as a common factor: Clients as self-healers. In M. A. Hubble, B. L. Duncan, & S. D. Miller (Eds.), *The heart and soul of change: What works in therapy* (pp. 91–131). Washington, DC: American Psychological Association.

Talmon, M. (1990). *Single-session therapy.* San Francisco: Jossey-Bass.

Taylor, E. (1999). An intellectual renaissance of humanistic psychology. *Journal of Humanistic Psychology, 39,* 7–26.

Terner, J., & Pew, W. L. (1978). *The courage to be imperfect: The life and work of Rudolf Dreikurs.* New York: Hawthorn.

Terry, A., Burden, C., & Pedersen, M. (1991). The helping relationship. In D. Capuzzi & D. Gross (Eds.), *Introduction to counseling: Perspectives for the 1990s* (pp. 44–68). Boston: Allyn & Bacon.

Teske, R. (1973). An analysis of status mobility patterns among middle-class Mexican Americans in Texas. *Dissertation Abstracts International, 42,* 7907a.

Thayer, L. (1987). An interview with Carl R. Rogers: Toward peaceful solutions to human conflict. Part I. *Michigan Journal of Counseling and Development, 18*(1), 58–63.

The Roster of the International Psychoanalytical Association. (1992–93). London: Broomhill's.

Thompson, C. L., & Rudolph, L. B. (2000). *Counseling children* (5th ed.). Belmont, CA: Brooks/Cole.

Thompson, P. (2000). Commentary on Leanne O'Shea's article "Sexuality: Old struggles and new challenges." *Gestalt Review 4*(1), 32–34.

Thompson, R. W. (1996). *Counseling techniques*. Washington DC: Accelerated Development, Taylor and Francis.

Tillett, R. (1991). Active and non-verbal therapeutic approaches. In J. Holmes (Ed.), *Textbook of psychotherapy in psychiatric practice*. Edinburgh: Churchill Livingstone.

Tillich, P. (1980). *The courage to be*. New Haven, CT: Yale University Press.

Tillich, P. (1987). *Paul Tillich: Theologian of the boundaries* (M. Taylor, Ed.). San Francisco, CA: Collins.

Tolman, D. L. (1991). Adolescent girls, women, and sexuality: Discerning dilemmas of desire. In C. Gilligan, A. Rogers, & D. Tolman (Eds.), *Women, girls, and psychotherapy: Reframing resistance* (pp. 55–70). New York: Haworth.

Torres-Rivera, E., Maples, M., & Thorn, A. (in press). *Who is teaching multicultural counseling in CACREP accredited institutions? Counselor Education and Supervision*.

Torres-Rivera, E., Phan, L. T., Maddux, C., Wilbur, M., & Garret, M. (2001). Process versus content: Integrating personal awareness and counseling skills to meet the multicultural challenge of the twenty-first century. *Counselor Education and Supervision, 41*(1), 28–40.

Trevino, J. G. (1996). World view and change in cross-culture. *The Counseling Psychologist, 24,* 198–215.

Trower, P., & Jones, J. (2001). How REBT can be less disturbing and remarkably more influential in Britain: A review of views of practitioners and researchers. *Journal of Rational-Emotive & Cognitive-Behavior Therapy, 19*(1), 21–30.

Truax, C. B., & Carkhuff, R. R. (1967). *Toward effective counseling and psychotherapy: Training and practice*. Chicago: Aldine.

Trungpa, C. (1983). Becoming a full human being. In J. Welwood (Ed.), *Awakening the heart: East/West approaches to psychotherapy and the healing relationship* (pp. 126–131). Boulder, CO: Shambala.

Turk, D. C., Meichenbaum, D., & Genest, M. (1983). *Pain and behavioral medicine: A cognitive-behavioral perspective*. New York: Guilford.

Typpo, M. H., & Hastings, J. M. (1984). *An elephant in the living room*. Minneapolis, MN: CompCare Publishers.

U. S. Bureau of the Census. (1993). *We, the first Americans*. Washington, DC: Government Printing Office.

U. S. Bureau of the Census. (1998). *Census Bureau Facts for Features*. CB-FF. 13. Washington, DC: Government Printing Office.

U. S. Bureau of the Census. (1999). *The population profile of the United States: 1999*. Washington, DC: Government Printing Office.

U. S. Bureau of the Census. (2000). *Educational attainment in the United States (Update)*. Washington, DC: Government Printing Office.

U. S. Bureau of the Census. (2001a). *Overview of race and hispanic origin*. Washington, DC: Government Printing Office.

U. S. Bureau of the Census. (2001b). *Update on Country's African American Population*. Washington, DC: Government Printing Office.

U. S. Bureau of the Census. (2001c). *The hispanic population*. Washington, DC: Government Printing Office.

Usher, C. H. (1989). Recognizing cultural bias in counseling theory and practice: The case of Rogers. *Journal of Multicultural Counseling and Development, 17,* 62–71.

Utter, J. (1993). *American Indians: Answers to today's questions*. Lake Ann, MI: National Woodlands Publishing Company.

Van der Kolk, B. A., McFarlane, A. C., & Weisaeth, L. (Eds.). (1996). *Traumatic stress: The effects of overwhelming experience on mind, body, and society*. New York: Guilford.

Van Kaam, A. (1966). *The art of existential counseling: A new perspective in psychotherapy*. Denville, NJ: Dimension Books.

VanDeurzen, E. (1998). *Paradox and passion in psychotherapy: An existential approach to therapy and counseling*. New York: John Wiley & Sons.

Vaughan, S. M., & Kinnier, R. T. (1996). Psychological effects of a life review intervention for persons with HIV disease. *Journal of Counseling and Development, 75,* 115–123.

Vernon, A. (1989a). *Thinking, feeling, behaving: An emotional education curriculum for children*. Champaign, IL: Research Press.

Vernon, A. (1989b). *Thinking, feeling, behaving: An emotional education curriculum for adolescents*. Champaign, IL: Research Press.

Vernon, A. (1998a). *The passport program: A journey through emotional, social, cognitive, and self-development (Grades 1–5)*. Champaign, IL: Research Press.

Vernon, A. (1998b). *The passport program: A journey through emotional, social, cognitive, and self-development (Grades 6–8)*. Champaign, IL: Research Press.

Vernon, A. (1998c). *The passport program: A journey through emotional, social, cognitive, and self-development (Grades 9–12)*. Champaign, IL: Research Press.

Vernon, A. (1999). Applications of rational-emotive behavior therapy with children and adolescents. In A. Vernon (Ed.), *Counseling children and adolescents* (2nd ed., pp. 140–157). Denver: Love.

Vernon, A. (in press). *What do you do after you say hello? Individual counseling interventions for children and adolescents*. Champaign, IL: Research Press.

Vontress, C. (1988). An existential approach to cross-cultural counseling. *Journal of Multicultural Counseling and Development, 16,* 73–83.

Vontress, C., Johnson, J., & Epp, L. (1999). *Cross-cultural counseling: A casebook*. Alexandria, VA: American Counseling Association.

Waldrop, D., Lightsey, O. R., Ethington, C. A., Woemmel, C. A., & Coke, A. L. (2001). Self-efficacy, optimism, health competence, and recovery from orthopedic surgery. *Journal of Counseling Psychology, 48*(2), 233–238.

Walen, S. R., DiGiuseppe, R., & Dryden, W. (1992). *A practitioner's guide to rational-emotive therapy* (2nd ed.). New York: Oxford University Press.

Walen, S. R., & Rader, M. W. (1991). Depression and RET: Perspectives from wounded healers. In M. E. Bernard (Ed.), *Using rational-emotive therapy effectively* (pp. 219–264). New York: Plenum.

Walker, L. (1994). *Abused women and survivor therapy: A practical guide for the psychotherapist*. Washington, DC: American Psychological Association.

Walker, L. E. (1990). A feminist therapist views the case. In D. W. Cantor (Ed.), *Women as therapists: A multitheoretical casebook* (pp. 78–95). New York: Springer.

Wallen, G. (1970). Gestalt therapy and Gestalt psychology. In J. Fagan & I. Shepherd (Eds.), *Gestalt therapy now: Theory, techniques, and applications* (pp. 116–117). Palo Alto: Science & Behavior Books.

Walsh, R. (1995). Asian psychotherapies. In R. J. Corsini (Ed.), Current psychotherapies (5th ed., pp. 387–398). Itasco, IL: Peacock.

Walsh, R. (1999). *Essential spirituality: The seven central practices to awaken heart and mind*. New York: John Wiley & Sons.

Walsh, R. (2000). Asian psychotherapies. In R. J. Corsini (Ed.), *Current psychotherapies* (6th ed., pp. 407–448). Itasca, IL: Peacock.

Walter, J. L., & Peller, J. E. (1992). *Becoming solution-focused in brief therapy*. New York: Brunner/Mazel.

Walter, J. L., & Peller, J. E. (2000). *Recreating brief therapy: Preferences and possibilities*. New York: Norton.

Walters, M., Carter, B., Papp, P., & Silverstein, P. (1988). *The invisible web: Gender patterns in family relationships*. New York: Guilford.

Walton, F. X. (1996a, March). Most memorable observation. Paper presented at UT Permian Basin Spring Counseling Workshop, Odessa, TX.

Walton, F. X. (1996b, March). An overview of a systematic approach to Adlerian family counseling. Paper presented at UT Permian Basin Spring Counseling Workshop, Odessa, TX.

Walton, F. X. (1996c, March). Questions for brief life style analysis. Paper presented at UT Permian Basin Spring Counseling Workshop, Odessa, TX.

Warah, A. (1993). Overactivity and boundary setting in anorexia nervosa: An existential perspective. *Journal of Adolescence, 16*(2), 93–100.

Warren, R. (1997). REBT and generalized anxiety disorder. In J. Yankura & W. Dryden (Eds.), *Using REBT with common psychological problems: A therapist's casebook* (pp. 6–43). New York: Springer Publishing Company.

Warwar, S., & Greenberg, L. S. (2000). Advances in theories and change of counseling. In S. Brown & R. W. Lent (Eds.), *Handbook of counseling psychology* (3rd ed., pp. 571–600). New York: John Wiley & Sons.

Watkins, C. E. (1982). A decade of research in support of Adlerian psychological theory. *Journal of Individual Psychology, 38,* 90–99.

Watkins, C. E. (1983). Some characteristics of research on Adlerian theory. *Journal of Individual Psychology, 39,* 99–110.

Watkins, C. E. (1992). Research activity with Adler's theory. *Journal of Individual Psychology, 48,* 107–108.

Watkins, C. E. (1993). Person centered theory and the contemporary practice of psychological testing. *Counseling Psychology Quarterly, 6*(1), 59–67.

Watson, G., Batchelor, S., & Claxton, G. (2000). *The psychology of awakening: Buddhism, science, and our day-to-day lives*. New Beach, ME: Samuel Weiser.

Watson, J. B. (1930). *Behaviorism* (2nd ed.). Chicago: University of Chicago Press.

Watson, N. (1984). The empirical status of Rogers's hypotheses of the necessary and sufficient conditions for effective psychotherapy. In R. F. Levant & J. M. Shlien (Eds.), *Client centered therapy and the person centered approach: New directions in theory, research, and practice* (pp. 17–40). New York: Praeger.

Watts, R. E. (2000). Adlerian counseling: A viable approach for contemporary practice. *TCA Journal, 28,* 11–23.

Way, L. (1962). *Adler's place in psychology.* New York: Collier Books.

Weeks, G., & L'Abate, L. (1982). *Paradoxical psychotherapy.* New York: Brunner/Mazel.

Wehrly, B. (1991). Preparing multicultural counselors. *Counseling and Human Development, 24,* 1–23.

Weinrach, S. G. (1988). Cognitive therapist: A dialogue with Aaron Beck. *Journal of Counseling and Development, 67,* 159–164.

Weinrach, S. G., & Thomas, K. R. (1998). Diversity-sensitive counseling today: A postmodern clash of values. *Journal of Counseling and Development, 76*(4), 115–122.

Weisman, A. D. (1993). *The vulnerable self: Confronting the ultimate questions.* New York: Plenum.

Weisz, J. R., Rothbaum, F. M., & Blackburn, T. C. (1984). Standing out and standing in: The psychology of control in America and Japan. *American Psychologist, 39,* 955–969.

West, M. (Ed.). (1987). *The psychology of meditation.* Oxford: Clarendon Press.

Wheeler, G. (1991). *Gestalt reconsidered: A new approach to contact and resistance.* New York: Gardner.

Whiston, S. C., & Sexton, T. L. (1993). An overview of psychotherapy outcome research: Implications for practice. *Professional Psychology: Research and Practice, 24,* 43–51.

White, M. (1989). *Selected papers.* Adelaide, Australia: Dulwich Centre Publications.

White, M. (1992). Deconstruction and therapy. In D. Epston & M. White (Eds.), *Experience, contradiction, narrative, and imagination: Selected papers of David Epston and Michael White, 1989–1991* (pp. 105–151). Adelaide, Australia: Dulwich Centre Publications.

White, M. (1995). *Re-authoring lives: Interviews and essays.* Adelaide, Australia: Dulwich Centre Publications.

White, M., & Epston, D. (1990). *Narrative means to therapeutic ends.* New York: Norton.

Wiener, N. (1948). *Cybernetics.* New York: John Wiley & Sons.

Wiener, N. (1950). *The human use of human beings: Cybernetics and society.* Boston: Houghton Mifflin.

Wilbur, K. (1977). *Spectrum of consciousness.* Boulder, CO: Shambala.

Wilber, K. (1986). The spectrum of psychopathology. In K. Wilber, J. Engler, & D. Brown (Eds.), *Transformations of consciousness* (pp. 65–159). Boston, MA: New Science Library.

Wilber, K. (1993). *The spectrum of consciousness* (2nd ed.). Wheaton, IL: Theosophical Publishing House.

Wilber, K. (1997). *In the eye of spirit: An integral vision for a world gone slightly mad.* Boston, MA: Shambhala.

Wilber, K. (2000). Integral psychology: *Consciousness, spirit, psychology, therapy.* Boston, MA: Shambhala.

Williamson, E. (1958). Value orientation in counseling. *Personnel and Guidance Journal, 36,* 520–528.

Willingham, W. K. (1986). Adlerian psychology: Background, current status, and future. *Texas Tech Journal of Education, 13,* 161–169.

Willis, R. J. (1994). *Transcendence in relationship: Existentialism and psychotherapy.* Norwood, NJ: Ablex.

Wilson, E. O. (1998). *Consilience: The unity of knowledge.* New York: Alfred A. Knopf.

Winnicott, D. W. (1958). *Collected papers.* New York: Basic Books.

Winslade, J. (2001, October). *Putting stories to work: narrative counseling in practice.* Workshop presented at Portland State University, Portland, OR.

Winslade, J., & Monk, G. (1999). *Narrative counseling in schools.* Thousand Oaks, CA: Corwin Press.

Witmer, J. M., & Sweeney, T. J. (1992). A holistic model for wellness and prevention over the life span. *Journal of Counseling and Development, 71,* 140–148.

Wolberg, L. (1977). *The technique of psychotherapy.* New York: Harcourt Brace Jovanovich.

Wolfe, W. B. (1930). Adler and our neurotic world. In A. Adler, *The pattern of life.* New York: Cosmopolitan Book Corp.

Wolfert, R., & Cook, C. A. (1999). Gestalt therapy in action. In D. Wiener (Ed.), *Beyond talk therapy: Using movement and expressive techniques in clinical practice* (pp. 3–28). Washington, DC: American Psychological Association.

Wolpe, J. (1958). *Psychotherapy by reciprocal inhibition.* Stanford: Stanford University Press.

Wong, P. T. (1997, June). *Charting the course of research on meaning seeking.* Paper presented at the meeting of the World Congress of Logotherapy, Dallas, TX.

Woody, S. R., & Sanderson, W. C. (1998). *Manuals for empirically supported treatments: 1998 update.* Available: *http://www.apa.org/divisions/div12/est/manual 60.html/*

Worden, M., & Worden, B. (1998). *The gender dance in couples therapy.* Pacific Grove, CA: Brooks/Cole.

Worell, J., & Johnson, D. (2001). Therapy with women: Feminist frameworks. In R. K. Unger (Ed.), *Handbook of the psychology of women and gender* (pp. 317–329). New York: John Wiley & Sons.

Worell, J., & Johnson, N. G. (Eds.). (1997). *Shaping the future of feminist psychology: Education, research, and practice.* Washington, DC: American Psychological Association.

Worell, J., & Remer, P. (1996). *Feminist perspectives in therapy: An empowerment model for women.* New York: John Wiley & Sons.

Worthen, V., & McNeill, B. W. (1996). A phenomenological investigation of "good" supervision events. *Journal of Counseling Psychology, 42,* 25–34.

Wrenn, C. G. (1962). The culturally encapsulated counselor. *Harvard Educational Review, 32,* 444–449.

Wrenn, C. G. (1985). Afterward: The culturally encapsulated counselor revisited. In P. B. Pedersen (Ed.), *Handbook of cross-cultural counseling and therapy* (pp. 110–126). Westport, CT: Greenwood.

Wubbolding, R. (1980). Teenage loneliness. In N. Glasser (Ed.), *What are you doing?* (pp. 120–129). New York: Harper & Row.

Wubbolding, R. (1981). Balancing the chart: Do it person and positive symptom person. *Journal of Reality Therapy, 1*(1), 4–7.

Wubbolding, R. (1984). Using paradox in reality therapy: Part I. *Journal of Reality Therapy, 4*(1), 3–9.

Wubbolding, R. (1985a). Characteristics of the inner picture album. *Journal of Reality Therapy, 5*(1), 28–30.

Wubbolding, R. (1985b). Counseling for results. *Not Out of Sight, 6,* 14–15.

Wubbolding, R. (1986). Professional ethics: Informed consent and professional disclosure in reality therapy. *Journal of Reality Therapy, 6*(1), 30–35.

Wubbolding, R. (1988). *Using reality therapy.* New York: Harper & Row.

Wubbolding, R. (1989). Radio station WDEP and other metaphors used in teaching reality therapy. *Journal of Reality Therapy, 8*(2), 74–79.

Wubbolding, R. (1990). Evaluation: The cornerstone in the practice of reality therapy. *Omar Psychological Series, 1*(2), 6–27.

Wubbolding, R. (1991). *Understanding reality therapy.* New York: HarperCollins.

Wubbolding, R. (1993). Reality therapy. In T. Kratochwill (Ed.), *Handbook of psychotherapy with children* (pp. 288–319). Boston: Allyn & Bacon.

Wubbolding, R. (1994). The early years of control theory: Forerunners Marcus Aurelius and Norbert Wiener. *Journal of Reality Therapy, 13*(2), 51–54.

Wubbolding, R. (1996). Working with suicidal clients. In B. Herlihy & J. Corey (Eds.), *ACA ethical standards casebook.* Alexandria, VA: American Association for Counseling and Development.

Wubbolding, R. (2000). *Reality therapy for the 21st century.* New York: Brunner-Routledge.

Wubbolding, R. (2002). *Reality therapy training manual* (12th revision). Cincinnati, OH: Center for Reality Therapy.

Wubbolding, R., & Brickell, J. (1999). *Counseling with reality therapy.* Bicester, England: Speechmark Publishing Limited.

Wubbolding, R., & Brickell, J. (2001). *A set of directions for putting and keeping yourself together.* Minneapolis: Educational Media Corporation.

Yalom, I. (1980). *Existential psychotherapy.* New York: Basic Books.

Yalom, I. (1988). *Existential psychotherapy.* New York: Basic Books.

Yalom, I. (1992). *When Nietzsche wept.* New York: Basic Books.

Yalom, I. (1995). *The theory and practice of group psychotherapy.* New York: Basic Books.

Yalom, I. (1999). *Momma and the meaning of life.* New York: Basic Books.

Yankura, J. (1997). REBT and panic disorder with agoraphobia. In J. Yankura & W. Dryden (Eds.), *Using REBT with common psychological problems: A therapist's casebook* (pp. 112–157). New York: Springer Publishing Company.

Yarish, P. (1986). Reality therapy and locus of control of juvenile offenders. *Journal of Reality Therapy, 6*(1), 3–10.

Yiu-kee, C., & Tang, C. S. (1995). Existential correlates of burnout among mental health professionals in Hong Kong. *Journal of Mental Health Counseling, 17,* 220–229.

Yontef, G. (1981). *Gestalt therapy: Past, present, and future.* Paper presented at the International Council of Psychologists Conference, London.

Yontef, G. (1993). *Awareness, dialogue, and process: Essays on Gestalt therapy.* Highland, NY: The Gestalt Journal Press.

Yontef, G. (1995). Gestalt therapy. In A. Gurman & S. Messer (Eds.), *Essential psychotherapies: Theories and practice*. New York: Guilford.

Yontef, G., & Simkin, J. (1989). Gestalt therapy. In R. Corsini & D. Wedding (Eds.), *Current psychotherapies* (4th ed., pp. 323–361). Itasca, IL: Peacock.

Yontif, G. (1998). Dialogic gestalt therapy. In L. S. Greenberg, J. C. Watson, & G. Lietaer (Eds.), *Handbook of experiential psychotherapy* (pp. 82–102). New York: Guilford.

Zeman, S. (1999). Person-centered care for the patient with mid- and late-stage dementia. *American Journal of Alzheimer's Disease, 14*(5), 308–310.

Zimmer, E., & Dunning, T. (1998). *Change agents. Village Voice, 43*(24), 76–82.

Zimmerman, J. L., & Dickerson, V. C. (1996). *If problems talked: Narrative therapy in action*. New York: Guilford.

Zinker, J. (1978). *Creative process in Gestalt therapy*. New York: Vintage.

Zinker, J. C., & Cardoso-Zinker, S. (2001). Process and silence: A phenomenology of couples therapy. *Gestalt Review, 5*(1), 11–23.

Name Index

Subject Index